# The Chief Executive

## FOURTH EDITION

LOUIS W. KOENIG

*New York University*

Harcourt Brace Jovanovich, Inc.

*New York   San Diego   Chicago   San Francisco   Atlanta*
*London   Sydney   Toronto*

*To Eleanor and Juliana*

ISBN: 0-15-506673-0

Library of Congress Catalog Card Number: 80-85140

Printed in the United States of America

# Preface

The contemporary presidency, which flourished until the mid-1970s, has since become a diminished office of declining power. This new edition of *The Chief Executive* is addressed to exploring and explaining that decline. The presidency has been adversely affected by the weakening of other institutions in the political system with which it interacts, especially by the diminution of the role of political parties and the diffusion of power in Congress wrought by recent reforms. Other deleterious trends are the negative impacts of television and public opinion polls on presidential functioning, the rise of interest groups that, intolerant of compromise, concentrate on particular policy issues, and the tendency of the reformed selection system to produce incumbents whose performance at winning elections is more adept than their governing. The presidency is also viewed in its new context of the "politics of scarcity": how can it best function in times of dwindling economic growth, energy shortages, American industrial decline, and high inflation? Simultaneously, demands by economic and social constituencies for enlarged programs and expenditures remain high. The presidency is seen as struggling with the dilemma of expectations and responsibilities that exceed its authority and its resources.

This is the fourth edition of a book that first appeared in 1964. Like its predecessors, this new version of *The Chief Executive* advocates an effective presidency of strength and compassion as a necessary force for human well-being in American society and in the world at large. But the abuses of Watergate and the episodes of misused power in the Indochina war require careful attention to the problem of keeping a presidency of strength within democratic bounds, of reconciling presidential power with democratic values and processes. The necessity of maintaining an equilibrium between the presidency and democracy is a central theme of this book.

This new edition has been revised to reflect the substantial body of new scholarship that has appeared for virtually every major aspect of the presidency, including the office's relations with Congress, with the bureaucracy, with the phenomenon of public opinion, and with foreign and military affairs. Chapter 13, "Political Personality," has been enlarged to encompass the findings of recent research, and the treatment of crisis management in Chapter 15 has been expanded with special attention to the hostage crisis in Iran. Presidential leadership, with its certain importance in the 1980s, has received increased analysis.

It is a pleasure to acknowledge my gratitude to Harry A. Bailey, Jr., of Temple University and Jack R. Van Der Slik of Trinity Christian College, who offered fruitful suggestions for improving this new edition over its predecessors. At Harcourt Brace Jovanovich the book has profited from the good offices of Joanne Daniels, who has overseen its development and progress, and from deft and cogent editing by Juliana Koenig. Special thanks are due Nancy Kirsh for her creativity in designing the book and Christine Pearson and Kenzi Sugihara for guiding it through all its stages. To my wife, Eleanor, I am again grateful for forbearance and encouragement.

*Louis W. Koenig*

iii

# Contents

Chapter Five

# Publics 93

Chapter Six

# Party Chief 120

Chapter Seven

# Legislative Leader 153

Chapter Eight

# Administrative Chief 184

Chapter Thirteen

# Political Personality 325

Chapter Fourteen

# Decision-Making 352

Chapter Fifteen

# Crisis 371

Chapter Sixteen

# The Presidency Compared 392

# Chapter One

# Perspectives on Presidential Power

Soon after becoming President, Jimmy Carter was conferring in his White House hideaway office with an aide when two mice scampered across the carpet. The General Services Administration (GSA), which cares for federal buildings, was summoned, and the President resumed his grapplings with the affairs of state.

But the mouse problem persisted. Days before the Latin American heads of government arrived for the signing of the Panama Canal treaties, one small gray creature crawled inside a White House wall and died. The Oval Office became scented with the odor of the deceased. The GSA was again summoned. The agency declared in its report to the President that it had killed all the mice inside the White House and that therefore the expired mouse must have come from outside the edifice. An "outside" mouse, GSA explained, was the responsibility of the Interior Department, which cares for the White House grounds.

The Interior Department respectfully, but firmly, demurred. Obviously, the mouse was now "inside" since it was embedded within a White House wall. "I can't even get a damned mouse out of my office," the President complained.[1] He summoned an official from each agency to sit before his desk to witness the odor. Soon the bureaucratic deadlock was broken and the Oval Office's normal atmosphere was restored. But the episode troubled an aide who had overseen its resolution and whose own grand notions of presidential power included the expectation that a presidential command, once given, was promptly and automatically obeyed. Ruefully he observed, "It took an interagency task force to get that mouse out of here."[2]

1

# The Diminished Presidency

Although other Presidents have known the housekeeping tribulations of Jimmy Carter, and worse, the mouse experience is acutely symbolic. Carter's tenure coincided with an interval of resistance, uncertainty, and decline in the presidency's strength and fortunes. The presidency of Carter was destined by forces well beyond his control to be considerably less than the presidencies of the Roosevelts, Johnson, and others of the twentieth century. The definite prospect is that Carter's successor, Ronald Reagan, and even his successor, will be afflicted by the same forces, no matter how substantial their political talents may be. Political scientist Clinton Rossiter's observation two decades ago that the presidency's responsibilities exceed its powers has extra validity today.

Carter and his successors of the near future must live with the heritage of Watergate and Vietnam, which serves to diminish the office's efficacy and impact. Both events seared in the nation's memory the presidency's capacity for wrongdoing and imprudence. The nation's fond recall of heroic presidential figures of the scale of Washington and Lincoln and a procession of lesser but revered successors is now jostled by a sorry memory of presidencies capable of wrongdoing and misjudgment. In the 1970s, when Watergate and Vietnam erupted, another force potent and independent of them—the reform spirit—ascended. Its hand was felt by two institutions with which the presidency interacts and on whose strength its own well-being depends—Congress and the political parties. Thanks to long-coming reforms that finally materialized, both Congress and the parties were changed from their historic form and, unfortunately, weakened as policy-producing institutions. So dependent is a presidency of strength on the presence of a strong Congress and effective parties, that its capacity for accomplishment is diminished if these other institutions are weakened, if their power is fractionalized, thanks to reform. If their ability to develop consensus, close ranks, and produce policies declines, the President suffers. Particularly in domestic affairs, producing public policies embodied in legislation is an act of partnership between the President, Congress, and the parties.

The major changes buffeting and debilitating both the Carter and Reagan presidencies in this present era of the diminished presidency include the following:

***The weakened party system***  A genuine, functioning two-party system is an historic foundation of the strong responsible presidency. The party was a prime weapon of Jefferson, Jackson, and the Roosevelts, among others—the instrument by which they mobilized great popular majorities to support their purposes. Citizens, whose individual power is slight, can count for much by uniting in party, and Presidents have not been slow in recognizing the opportunities presented both for policy accomplishment and for renewing their term of office.

But the major parties are rapidly declining. The partisan spirit is slackening; the body of independent voters, who now exceed those who identify with the Democratic party, by far the larger of the two major parties, continues to expand. Partisanship has been dampened by rising educational levels and a more sophisticated electorate, by the pervasiveness of television, which magnifies personality and underplays party and program, and by the reduced influence that reforms made by the parties themselves have accorded party professionals in the national party conventions. Worst of all, the proliferating primaries, also the offspring of reform, endlessly demonstrate the vulnerability of the party to the challenges of outsiders. Carter's nomination in 1976 and Reagan's in 1980 are showcases of this phenomenon.

*Congressional power*    Congress was long the least changing of national political institutions. But reflecting forces of reform afoot in the 1970s and the heritage of Watergate and Vietnam it is changing markedly in ways detrimental to an effective presidency. Theodore Roosevelt, contemplating his exceptional successes in the office, declared that a strong presidency required a strong Congress. In his day congressional power was centralized in the control of the legislature's party leaders and committee chairmen, and most spectacularly in "Uncle Joe" Cannon, the nonpareil Speaker of the House of Representatives. Today's Speaker, Thomas P. "Tip" O'Neill (D-Mass.), despite his exceptional political talents, is many notches below the power wielded by his distinguished predecessor of the 1960s, Sam Rayburn. The historic capacity of the Speaker and other party leaders of both congressional houses to assemble votes to support the President's policy projects, after ample legislative review, has gravely declined.

Thanks to the congressional reforms of the 1970s, power has flowed away from party leaders like the Speaker, from committee chairmen, another bastion of traditional leadership, to subcommittee chairmen, who are both more numerous and more anonymous, and therefore more capable of resisting the legislative party leadership and the President. Individual members of Congress, mindful of the heritage of Vietnam and Watergate, have far lower thresholds of suspicion and rejection of the President. Where once freshman legislators were deferential to congressional seniors and abstained for a decorous interval from entering debate, they now quickly join the fray and are their own leaders. Stuart Eizenstat, Carter's chief adviser for domestic affairs, after trudging through three years of dealing with Congress, declared, "Moses would have difficulty getting the Ten Commandments through [Congress] today." [3]

Congress's new assertiveness is also fed by its own expanding bureaucracy, professional and sophisticated, knowledgeable from previous experience in the executive branch, aggressive, and career-minded. Congress continues to apply to the President the checks honed during Vietnam and Watergate by limiting appropriations. It has incorporated in statute opportunities for legislative review and veto of executive actions, and its members enter into diplomatic negotiations, a turf traditionally reserved to the President and the executive branch. Congress has also limited more formally and sweepingly than ever before the President's power to use force in international affairs or to convey armaments to the nation's allies and friends.

*Remote bureaucracy*    The bureaucracy, so slow-footed in rescuing President Carter from the mice, thwarted his confident and oft-repeated promise in the 1976 elections to make it more efficient, less remote, and more sensitive to the everyday lives and needs of citizens. The changes eventually put into effect were fashioned less by the President than by the bureaucracy itself. They have had no discernible effect on its competence and responsiveness to the citizenry, a failure that is also limiting on presidential power.

*Special interests* Interest groups have attained a new plateau of efficient, self-interested assertion. Groups, hard-driving on one or several issues, provide delegates to the national conventions where they grind their special axes, nominate the President, and insert planks into national party platforms. With little provocation, they campaign against legislative candidates who displease them and on whose support the President depends. Political action committees (PACs), composed predominately of business organizations, well-financed, politically sophisticated, and deft in grassroots organization, are a growing force the President must reckon with. Facing this formidable reality, the Carter presidency increasingly included such groups in the task forces it created to develop its program proposals. The practice, however prudent politically, doubtless blunted the force and the coherence of the President's initiatives.

*The role of television* At best, the age of television is proving a mixed blessing for the presidency. Doubtless television has enhanced the office's position as the nation's supreme political symbol, but in other respects has clearly weakened it. When events take a downturn—when the Vietnam war drags on, when the Soviet Union launches a new thrust, the President is the readiest object on which to affix blame. He becomes a national scapegoat even though his powers for dealing with such eventualities are limited and shared with Congress.

After Watergate and Vietnam, television has sprouted with reporters who not only manifest the journalistic propensity for bad news over good news, but indulge in frequent moralizing over the policies and performance of Presidents and their administrations. Since presidential as well as other public policies seldom offer clear-cut moral choices, and since their implementation is easily hobbled by unpredictable, untoward events and by the frailties of the many human beings on whom that implementation depends, the President is easy prey for televised moralizing that reinforces the scapegoat function.

*The altered selection process* At the very moment when the nation's problems intensify and leadership is strained, the methods of choosing the President are altered to the point that incumbents who excel at winning elections are selected, but are no longer subject to tests of the older system of the candidates' capacity to govern. The proliferation of presidential primaries since the 1970s has turned the selection process into an extended popularity contest among a modest minority of voters who vote in the primaries. The older system, which required the candidates to pull together a network of support from congressional, state, and local party leaders, as well as to win in the primaries, was a revealing trial-run of the candidate's ability to perform a basic task of governing—to weave consensus from the many contradictory strands of the nation's politics.

In the clichés of his critics, Carter, the first President produced by the new selection process, was a nonleader, unskilled in the tasks of consensus-building. Carter initially campaigned for the presidency as an "outsider," untainted by Washington politics, a fresh moral and political force. Even as President, he continued to maintain that he never, or almost never, considered politics when he made government decisions.[4] This may be a path to sainthood but it does not lead to presidential power.

*Intractable problems*    Today's Presidents, Reagan and Carter, struggle with problems such as inflation and energy, dilemmas that faced their predecessors, Ford and Nixon, that defy solution and grievously afflict not limited sectors of the population but the entire citizenry. Carter's failure to cap inflation was a principal factor that drove him from the presidency. According to one poll, 58 percent of those voting for Reagan in 1980 cited inflation as "a determining issue."[5]

Just as Carter faced the exaggerated expectations of his supporters in 1976 of a better life, Reagan in 1981 faced similar expectations of even greater intensity. Republican chairman Bill Brock, amidst his party's jubilation over its sensational 1980 victories, offered a prudent caution that "we've got to act with some urgency to deal with the problems on which people voted," above all inflation. But Reagan was bedeviled by potent constraints. First were limitations of knowledge—no economist knew of a sure cure for inflation, and even the modest steps the new President might take toward taming the problem confronted formidable obstacles. Among other things, Reagan faced an upward wage spurt of 10 to 11 percent in 1981 and the statutory linkage of many federal benefits to the Consumer Price Index. Higher grain prices were predicted for 1981 as well as jumps in retail food prices of 10 to 15 percent. Events over which he could have little or no control could worsen the situation. Weather and blight could cripple harvests and push world-wide grain prices upward; the military adventures of other governments could prompt unexpected American military expenditures with inflationary consequences.

Let the President launch bold antiinflation measures—modifying farm price supports, halting the steady upward march of the minimum wage, diminishing the linkage of Social Security benefits and government pensions to the Consumer Price Index—and a rampage of aggrieved special interest groups would surely ensue. Concerns of aroused farmers, union leaders, business executives, and pensioners are felt more by individual Congressmen than the longings of the general citizenry to curb inflation.

And Reagan was under the gun to produce prompt results. Observed Senator Gary Hart (D-Colo.), "I give the Reagan administration about 18 to 24 months to prove it doesn't have any answers either."[6] Public opinion polls regularly monitor Reagan's progress, and congressional elections loom in 1982. If he falters retribution could be rough and swift. Nowadays presidential tenure is denoted by its brevity. The country has had six Presidents in the last eighteen years, and it has developed a voracious appetite for consuming its Chief Executives.

# Cycles of Presidential History

We have been looking at a snapshot taken at a moment in the life of an office almost two centuries old. A picture recorded at another time would have different lines and shadows, strengths and weaknesses. Like any long-enduring institution, the presidency's fortunes fluctuate. The talents of its incumbents differ; events smile and frown. In the American system, more than in the systems of other nations, the chief executive is unable to stabilize his political influence. Potent forces in American society and culture and in its politics cause fluctuations and discontinuities in the President's role. An overview of the many decades of foreign and domestic policy-making reveals rises and falls, ebb and flow in the President's influence and impact.

Partly the volatility of power results from the circumstance that it is shared between the executive and Congress, but the precise patterns of sharing are unclear and tentative, and even after nearly two centuries of constitutional practice, they remain largely unpredictable. Power also oscillates because of shifts in public mood that range to a degree seldom matched in other major nations. In foreign affairs, the American mood swings widely between high ideals and willingness to sustain great burdens, to absorption in domestic affairs and even to moods of disillusionment and resignation that set in when foreign policy fails to satisfy activist ideals, prompting withdrawal and isolation.

A similar fluctuation occurs in the domestic arena. Although enlarged executive power triumphed in Franklin Roosevelt's New Deal and Lyndon Johnson's Great Society, there are also interludes of counterpoint. Reaction sets in. The public becomes bored by the President's incessant demands on its attention. It prefers less presidential leadership and striving. After a siege of Kennedy-Johnson activism, society is more receptive to Nixon-Ford retrenchment. Expansions of domestic programs are now slowed, the remote Washington bureaucracy is discredited, and the cry is sounded to leave matters to the states or to private enterprise.

The American system has built-in regulators that assure impermanence in the President's power circumstances. For example, a psychology born of the separation of powers reinforces fluctuation. Congress as an offspring of separation of powers must, like the other branches, struggle to maintain its identity. For a time it can acquiesce to the President's initiatives, but sooner or later it must contest and reject them. Only by that course can its identity be retained; continued acquiescence erodes it. Similarly, the public mood, which the President must arouse if he is to accomplish memorable purposes, is controlled by a limited span of attention. The presidential summons to join in noble purpose can be sounded just so often in a society absorbed in private endeavor, whose rewards are showered on private achievement. Above all, the fortunes of the presidency at any moment depend on the incumbent, on his imagination, energy, values, and political skill. As skills fluctuate so do the sums of usable power.

An historical road-map of the presidency and its power, then, follows an erratic course of ascents and declines. President George Washington truly led the country, but his successor, John Adams, suffered decline. Thomas Jefferson, more a party leader than a chief executive, was a highly successful President, although too yielding to Congress. Under his weaker successors, the office waned. Andrew Jackson restored the presidency to its earlier vigor with his extraordinary popularity, but soon it again declined as its incumbents struggled with the insoluble problem of slavery, the nation's growing division, and stormy congressional deadlocks. In the Civil War, Lincoln applied a totality of power that has never since been equalled, converting the presidency into what Clinton Rossiter aptly called "a constitutional dictatorship."[7] Congress's inevitable reaction against this grand claim of power fell on Andrew Johnson. The presidency sustained a general decline for the remainder of the nineteenth century except for the incumbencies of Rutherford Hayes and Grover Cleveland.

The great restorer was Theodore Roosevelt, who with a dynamic political personality and an aggressive theory of presidential power that became known as the "stewardship theory," scored imposing initiatives in foreign and domestic affairs. A brief decline occurred under his successor, William Howard Taft, who interpreted power restrictively. Woodrow Wilson enlarged upon the Roosevelt model, thanks to the opportunities of the First World War. Harding, Coolidge, and Hoover all trimmed their presidential sails, but Franklin Roosevelt, faced with the Great Depression and the Second World War, embroidered elaborately on Theodore Roosevelt's stewardship theory. The Cold War and Johnson's gargantuan Great Society program comprised a long interval of sustained expansion. But reaction ultimately overtook the office when, in the incumbency of Richard Nixon it overreached itself in the criminality and constitutional subversion of Watergate and in the excessive costs it rolled up in a succession of presidencies in its lengthy, fruitless commitment to the Vietnam war. Although Ford, Carter, Reagan, and their successors reap the whirlwind and struggle with an office of diminished fortunes, history permits the confident prediction that the presidency will rise again.

# Theories of Presidential Power

The presidency's varied experience, its breadth and complexity, the diversity of its incumbents, have bred scholarly theories about how the office really functions. Since the presidency is a structure of many contours, it appears differently to different viewers, depending on their vantage points and perspectives.

## Presidential Power as Exaggeration and Myth

In a cogent essay, political scientist Thomas E. Cronin argues that notions of a "textbook presidency" permeated writing about the office in a long interval of its ascendance, 1940–66, receding in the maelstrom of Vietnam and Watergate, although its effects persist today. The textbook presidency takes flight from the extraordinary talent and admired works of Franklin Roosevelt. Its scholarship enshrines and institutionalizes his presidency for others to emulate.[8]

The textbook presidency creates a cult of the presidency that beholds the incumbent as benevolent, omnipotent, omniscient, and highly moral. It inflates presidential competence, expounds the necessity for strong central government, and a strong presidency to run it. Presidents themselves, not surprisingly, wholeheartedly support the textbook theory. "Only the President represents the national interest," proclaimed John F. Kennedy.[9] Jimmy Carter contended that "The President is the only person who can speak with a clear voice to the American people and set a standard of ethics and morality, excellence and greatness."[10]

The textbook presidency is also a recipe for citizen disillusionment. The promise of the office is overstated. Its actual accomplishments are far less than the open-ended promises of its lofty rhetoric. The long-standing approval of the power-maximizing President led to the gross abuses of Watergate. "Treated as exalted figures," writes Cronin, "Presidents began to believe and act that way."[11]

The intriguing thesis of the textbook presidency does not account for considerable writing in its glory period, the fifties and sixties, that emphasized its limitation to modest accomplishment in domestic affairs. James MacGregor Burns, for example, in *The Deadlock of Democracy,* emphasized that Franklin Roosevelt's last major domestic innovation was the Fair Labor Standards Act of 1938.[12] For the following six years, he suffered either defeat or deadlock in his domestic legislative initiatives. In 1950 a panel of the American Political Science Association, troubled by the snail's pace of the nation's political system, which left serious social problems to drift, looked longingly at the British party system, with its impressive ability to get laws passed. The panel advocated grafting its key features on to the lagging American party system, a root cause of the presidency's modest domestic accomplishments.[13]

## Presidential Power as Persuasion and Bargaining

In his classic study, *Presidential Power: The Politics of Leadership,* political scientist Richard E. Neustadt exposed realities of presidential power that long eluded writing on the presidency.[14] The President, Neustadt noted, cannot automatically evoke the support of others. Those he deals with—department heads, legislators, foreign leaders, among others—must respond to their own constituencies, obligations, and interests. Presidential decisions are not self-executing; the Chief Executive can discharge few of them directly. He must influence others to act in ways consistent with his purpose and interests. In actuality, the President has only a highly limited power to command and to employ only as a last resort. His most usable power is the power to persuade, or the ability to convince others that their interests are furthered by what he seeks to do.

Persuasion is often exercised through bargaining: the presidency contains manipulable resources such as jobs, contracts, conferrals of approval and support, to induce others to act. Bargaining has its own economy. An excelling President spends fewer resources and achieves greater results than less adroit incumbents. Above all, the President must avoid profligacy, or squandering quantities of resources on unimportant purposes like moving a minor law through Congress.

The President fares better in bargaining and persuading if he stands high in public prestige. Crucial is the public's perception of his job performance, the effect of his stewardship on the satisfactions and frustrations of their lives. The President can minimize frustrations if he avoids raising unfounded hopes and keeps citizen expectations in harmony with his office's realities. Popularity and public prestige ease the President's passage in the byways of power of the Washington community. But if public disapproval sets in, resistance builds from the community's denizens—members of Congress, bureaucrats, the press, governors, and diplomats.

Critiques of Neustadt contend that he overemphasizes bargaining and underemphasizes command. A broader view of command encompasses an internalized authoritative base by which shared norms, values, and expectations can induce the conduct the President seeks. Presidential and other human interactions are also governed by such elements of secondary relations as confidence, trust, and identification which render bargaining unnecessary.[15] British political journalist Henry Fairlie, in *The Kennedy Promise*, contends that Americans no longer are so confident that the strong leadership Neustadt prescribes is necessarily wholesome leadership; a power-maximizing President is not automatically a good President.[16] Other critics bridle at the President appearing as a lonely fighter against all others, especially when others are cast as "them."

## Presidential Power as Command

In his study, *The American Presidency*, political scientist Richard Pious contends that the key to understanding presidential power is the constitutional authority the Chief Executive exerts through rules of construction and interpretation of the Constitution's ambiguous language in acting to resolve crises and important policy issues.[17] The President's successful trodding of this path leads to the institutionalization of particular powers and their recurrent use. In so asserting his powers, the President often faces a crucial test in securing acquiescence from Congress and the courts. Big achievers like the Roosevelts expand the sum of usable powers, while rejections sustained by other Presidents strengthen the system of separation of powers.

So vital are the President's claims of constitutional authority to his office's functioning that Pious identifies the Chief Executive as essentially a practitioner of "prerogative government," from which three possible outcomes ensue. One, a "frontlash effect," signifies that the President has managed the crisis successfully. Congress and the courts acquiesce to his claims of authority, and the presidency of custom and precedent grows stronger. Second, in a "backlash effect," the crisis is also managed successfully, but the President's interpretation of his powers is challenged by the other branches. Party and popular support lessen, and his successors find their authority limited by statutes, court rulings, and public opinion. Finally, in the "overshoot and collapse effect" the President's claims of prerogative ignite a constitutional crisis. His legitimacy as a national leader is destroyed, and he may become caught up in the impeachment process. Andrew Johnson and Reconstruction, Richard Nixon and Watergate, are prime examples.[18]

By its nature, the command or constitutional power approach accords low importance to political factors in the President's fortunes such as elections, rallying public opinion, managing the party. Similarly, personality is downgraded, as are skills in persuasion, bargaining, and influence.

## Presidential Power as Prerogative

The political thinker most influential in the Founding Fathers' decisions establishing the presidency was the seventeenth-century British philosopher John Locke. His classic *Second Treatise of Government* (1690) sets forth doctrines of executive power and particularly of prerogative, which Presidents throughout the office's history have drawn upon to justify their claims of power.

Prerogative, Locke explained, is the exercise of power sanctioned by the law of self-preservation. Prerogative is a reserve power "to act according to discretion for the public good, without the prescription of law and sometimes against it." When emergencies overtake nations, Locke noted, and legislatures are too large, unwieldy, and slow to cope with them, the responsible executive must resort to exceptional power. Fortunately, this open-ended statement of power was subject to constraint. Although the executive initially acted on his own in finding an emergency, the question whether there really was one was subsequently determined by the community and the legislature to whom the executive reported his actions and whose approval he sought. The Founding Fathers did not specifically incorporate the idea of prerogative in their statement of presidential power, but the *Federalist* papers, in explaining and defending the Constitution, contended that it was "equal to any emergency."[19] Lincoln, coping with the eruption of the Civil War, Franklin Roosevelt aiding Britain despite restrictive neutrality laws after France was overrun in the Second World War, Truman seizing the steel mills in a labor-management dispute midway in the Korean war, support the *Federalist* contention.

In his much discussed study, *The Imperial Presidency*, historian Arthur M. Schlesinger, Jr., delineates how Lockean prerogative in the hands of activist Chief Executives vastly aggrandized presidential power and in some cases contributed to gross abuse. A steady aggrandizement of power, he argues, denotes American history, and it soars to far limits in the Indochina war and the Watergate affair.[20]

The most fertile ground of the imperial presidency is the President's war-making power. Notwithstanding that the Constitution associates the war-declaring power with Congress, the initiation of war has passed to the President, as the Korean and Indochina wars testify. Presidents even wage war without Congress's knowledge, as Nixon did in Cambodia. But the ultimate flight into the imperial yonder was taken by the Nixon presidency's resort to the criminality of Watergate, a lengthy list of indictable activities by members of the White House staff and the President himself. John Locke would have been flabbergasted by Nixon's statement to a television audience three years after leaving the presidency: "When the President does it, that means it is not illegal."[21]

But as the Nixon years also illustrate, the claim of power does not constitute actual power. The imperial presidency thesis excessively downgrades Congress and misstates the historical experience of the presidency. Time and again, Congress prevailed over Nixon. Congress ended his once secret war in Cambodia by cutting off its funds. His claims of massive powers to impound funds or abolish programs were rejected both by Congress and the courts. His modest program proposals were rejected by Congress more frequently than any other contemporary President. Ultimately, Nixon's certain impeachment by the House of Representatives drove him from the presidency. At other times in history, the presidency has known many chapters of failure, of rebuff of its initiatives by Congress, of its leadership by the public, of defeat in the courts. Its experience is far from being a smooth, ever-widening imperial highway. Rather, the office contains substantial weaknesses of power which the imperial thesis obscures.

# The Sun King Complex

Despite these reservations, the imperial presidency thesis aptly reminds us that presidential power is sometimes subject to excesses that violate constitutional and democratic norms, and they are most apt to transpire in upswings of the presidential cycle. Excesses are manifested in secret warmaking in Cambodia during most of Nixon's tenure, in initiating commitment to large-scale wars in distant lands simply by presidential fiat, as in the several wars conducted in Indochina. The power to declare war, given by the Constitution to Congress, was never exercised. Within the nation's borders excesses can also transpire on the scale of Watergate, itself an attack on democracy, with the burglarizing of the opposition party's headquarters, the wiretapping of journalists and civil servants, the attempted misuse of the Internal Revenue Service to harass political opponents, the attempted subversion of law enforcement agencies, and other acts in a lengthy skein of transgressions against civil liberties, and the Constitution's other basic institutions, Congress and the courts. Unfortunately, democratic liberties have been violated by other Presidents. Lincoln set aside normal governmental processes in the Civil War by suspending the writ of habeas corpus, shutting down newspapers, and jailing dissenters. At least several Presidents have used the income tax for political harassment. A most massive assault on civil liberties occurred during the Second World War when Franklin Roosevelt countenanced the uprooting of thousands of Japanese-Americans and Japanese aliens from the west coast·and removed them to inland internment camps encircled by barbed wire, police dogs, and armed guards.

The excessive presidency has a monarchic dimension. In his insightful study, *The Twilight of the Presidency*, George Reedy, a former aide to Lyndon Johnson, observed that "the life of the White House is the life of a court," its endeavor committed to a single purpose—"to serve the material needs and the desires of a single man."[22] To the sundry attendants of this regal enterprise, the President appears engrossed in problems of the most enormous consequence, and, that he might concentrate his efforts fully upon them, he is spared the distractions and vexations that buffet the average citizen. Upon the President is lavished every facility to ease the travail of daily living and to assist his encounters with the "great issues." If the President himself lags in donning monarchic trappings, others will put them on him. Kennedy's modesty and ready self-depreciation did not deter the press from creating a modern Camelot by likening the White House to the valorous Arthurian court.

Those inside the White House also contribute to the monarchic tendency.

The President is surrounded and served by the human appurtenances of the monarch—by clerks, aides, and courtiers, who do not speak unless spoken to first. Like kings of old, Presidents have abided not in one castle, but migrate regularly between several. Of all Presidents, the most blessed in this regard was Richard Nixon, who regularly peregrinated to Camp David in Maryland and to his respective private estates in Florida and California. In a Boeing 707 jet, "The Spirit of '76," Nixon journeyed to his estates, followed by a back-up plane and preceded by a Secret Service plane. When the presidential jet was en route, the Air Force regularly sent out sorties of fighter planes to assure the President's security from attack. One day a staff sergeant, seeing Lyndon Johnson, who was similarly favored with aircraft, start off toward the wrong helicopter, called, pointing, "Mr. President, *that* is your helicopter over there." The big Texan hugged the sergeant and explained, "Son, they are *all* my helicopters." [23]

Potentially, the most costly feature of the monarchic presidency is its tendency to wall off the incumbent Chief Executive from contact with reality. [24] Those faithful tools for comprehending reality—caution, introspection, and humility—are inundated by the distracting activity of ceremonies and heavy workloads and the automatic acquiescence of courtiers, whose numbers are constantly multiplied by the unrelenting growth of the White House staff. The President's insulation from reality is reinforced by the trappings of power, the endless attentions and comforts, and the inhibiting awe generated by the White House itself, where hallowed figures—Jefferson, Jackson, Lincoln—have dwelt. "The more a President sits surrounded only by his own views and those of his personal advisers," observed Senator Charles Mathias (R-Md.), "the more he lives in a house of mirrors in which all views and ideas tend to reflect and reinforce his own." [25] To a degree some contemporary Presidents have fought against their euphoric imprisonment. Johnson consulted a wide circle of acquaintances and authorities outside the White House, kept three television sets and three wire service teletypes running in the Oval Office, and each morning leafed avidly through newspapers and the *Congressional Record* to gauge his status according to external opinion.

# Democratic Ground Rules

In its many better hours during its lengthy experience of nearly two centuries, the presidency has pursued ideals and followed ground rules that support and even extend democratic government. Without that commitment, the presidency would long ago have fallen into place as another variant in a long line of dictatorships that has cursed humanity since earliest times. A number of ground rules can be identified whereby the historic presidency provides the best of two worlds by simultaneously exercising imposing powers while abiding by democratic constraints.

1. The power of the presidency must be wielded by constitutional means. The incumbent must observe the civil liberties incorporated in the Bill of Rights and understand and accept the processes of the other two great branches, Congress and the courts.

The constitutional presidency does not continuously subordinate its commitment to the fundamental law to other values—values, such as Nixon's open-ended commitment to "national security," to which he accorded expansive and ephemeral definition. As Egil Krogh, Jr., a White House aide noted, the use of "national security" as an all-purpose justification "served to block critical analysis." Eventually Krogh perceived that individual rights cannot be sacrificed "to the mere assertion of national security."[26]

2. The presidency must respect the capacity of the public to distinguish between good electoral candidates and bad, between wise men and fools. A presidency that becomes distrustful of public judgment and moves paternalistically to substitute its own has travelled well down the road to antidemocratic behavior. A springboard into malfeasance for the Nixon men was their judgment that the American public could not be counted on to reject George McGovern, who was perceived by the presidential entourage as a muddle-headed and dangerous candidate whose rejection at the polls they must assure by hook or crook.

3. The presidency must observe the rights of the opposition to criticize, to challenge, and possibly to overthrow its incumbency in a free election. To compile lists of enemies and to harass those "enemies" by subjecting their income tax returns to extra scrutiny and by other heavy-handed tactics is to negate the democratic politics of free debate, party competition, and open elections. This is not politics, but war.

4. The ethical behavior on which democracy is predicated extends to the President himself. At the very least, he ought to satisfy the obligations of good citizenship and comply with its elementals—pay his taxes and obey the laws.

5. Democracy and its public offices, including the presidency, require an ethical base in society. Appropriate ethical standards are less likely to govern the presidency if society itself is riddled with seamy practice. If the prevailing morality is that anything goes provided you can get away with it, if work is shoddy, if products are misrepresented, and if cheating is rampant, the President has little spur to set his ethical sights any higher than expediency dictates.

# The Need for an Effective Presidency

The United States and the world need a presidency that both performs with the degree of effectiveness required by the severity and complexity of today's problems and is simultaneously responsive to democratic constraints. Many of these problems have attained the magnitude of survival problems in which the very future of the human race or large portions of it is at stake: the threat of nuclear weapons technology; the persistence of war abroad; the remorseless growth of population, production and pollution and their endangering of the environment; grave unemployment and unchecked inflation; blighted cities and pervasive poverty and crime; excessive violations of civil rights and liberties; grossly inadequate provisions for health services, mass transit, education, and the care of the elderly—the list sweeps on. All afflict the human condition in the United States as well as abroad and will require decades of effort. Typically, the problems are seen individually, and less frequently in their interrelationships and cumulative character as an emerging world-wide crisis.[27]

It is natural and appropriate to look to the presidency to provide the quality of leadership that contemporary affairs require. Time and again, Presidents have performed creditably and often memorably in managing the nation's more severe trials and in advancing to important new stages in its development. The launching of the new government of 1789 was entrusted to the capable hands and impeccable character of the first President, Washington. In the Jefferson and Jackson eras, the republic became transformed into a more popular government. The successful emergence of the nation from the test of the Civil War was managed chiefly by the presidency.

The office also has led in the rigorous adjustments of the twentieth century. The presidency brought the nation out of its nineteenth-century isolation and onto the world stage, where it became a force for peace as well as the conductor of major wars. Some of these wars, especially the two World Wars, protected democracy. The presidency has diminished the crudities and oppressiveness of industry, provided indispensable succor to labor in its struggles to organize and defend itself, and helped the farmer through endless sequences of lean years. Presidents have championed racial justice against local repression and have protected natural resources against private exploitation.

But the presidency also knows failure, sometimes signified by the downward dips in the office's historical cycle. In this present era of the diminished presidency, the office is suffering a downturn as society's problems mount. All Presidents since Nixon have struggled to reform the welfare system, to cope with the energy crisis, to halt inflation, to reduce the unconscionable rates of unemployment. But all too often the results have been only defeat, deadlock, or minimal gain. After nearly a decade of explanation and exhortation, the country has no energy program worthy of the energy crisis. Urban problems have been patted and lamented over but persist little diminished. Similar negative assessments can be made of other items on the public agenda year after year. If these problems, and especially those with implications for human survival, are to be better managed, the diminished presidency must be supplanted by an effective presidency, with a leadership competence and a capacity for accomplishment comparable to the presidencies whose successes engendered rises in the office's cycle of historic experience.

To seek to replace the diminished presidency with an improved, more effective presidency, it is not necessary to invoke the spirit of the textbook presidency, nor to enlist under the banner of the imperial presidency. The effective presidency is the one originally conceived by the Founding Fathers. It therefore combines a generous conferral of power with its responsible exercise. The mythical textbook President is omnipotent and omniscient and extravagantly glorified. The historic effective President, as defined by the Founding Fathers and further delineated by experience, is a fallible individual, who can sometimes, but not always, cope with ponderous problems, but who for the sake of humanity's liberty and democracy's well-being must be checked and constrained, watched and challenged. Other sources in the political system may at times speak wisdom and truth better than the President, although day in and day out he is equipped with the special advantage of legions of staff and expert bureaucracies to inform his leadership. More likely, wisdom in public policy-making will emerge from his interactions with other components of the political system—Congress, party leaders, interest group spokesmen, and from soundings of public opinion.

Neither is the notion of an effective presidency an open invitation to establish an imperial presidency. The latter's incumbent is self-centered, self-aggrandizing, monopolistic of power, secretive, inhospitable to democracy. The effective President readily interacts with Congress, values the joint product of their labor, is attentive and elucidating to public opinion, and courts and values its support, without which, he realizes, he cannot govern long and well. A Franklin Roosevelt who in a series of radio addresses, his famous fireside chats, explains to the public his measures to fight the Great Depression and who in the Second World War painstakingly solicits support from a lagging public opinion and a doubting Congress for his plans to help the beleaguered allies, advancing and retreating according to his findings, can hardly be tabbed in this most basic behavior of his presidency as an imperial President. More accurately, he reflects the model of an effective President, dealing creatively and constructively with the nation's problems, while walking a democratic path of genuine interchange with Congress and the public.

# Practical Politics

The presence or absence of the effective presidency depends crucially upon how well a particular President fares in the political marketplace. Consequently, a quest for an active and effective presidency that performs in balanced accord with democratic constraints leads to the world of practical politics in which every President lives and functions.

Impressed by his own full and intimate knowledge of the limitations the Chief Executive toils under, Harry S Truman once observed, "The principal power that the President has is to bring people in and try to persuade them to do what they ought to do without persuasion. That's what I spend my time doing. That's what the powers of the President amount to."[28] Given the interdependence of its powers, the presidency is an intensive experience in practical politics. To lead, to win support, to achieve, the President must practice with skill and ardor the arts of political persuasion. Woodrow Wilson noted before taking up the presidency, "We have all been the disciples of Montesquieu, but we have also been practical politicians."[29] The President must woo party leaders, legislators, and chieftains of veto groups. He must bring the several parts of government, the private groups, and public opinion into harmonious effort to accomplish shared objectives.

To get his controversial measures enacted, whether in foreign or domestic affairs, the President, because of the unreliability of his own party, must often build a special coalition for his purpose from both major parties. Lyndon Johnson, this is to say, could not have secured civil rights legislation in 1964 and 1965 without Republican support. The coalitions keep forming and breaking up as their purpose is achieved. Moving on to new objectives, the President must develop a new combination of support. To make his way, the President must know when to spend and when to hoard his influence and how to build it. He must realize, as Richard Neustadt has suggested, that the essence of his persuasive task is to convince the legislators whose support he courts "that what the White House wants of them is what they ought to do for their sake and on their authority."[30] In playing the political game, the President occupies certain of the best vantage points in the political system. His power of publicity, his veto, his power over budget and expenditure, his power of appointment are means that exist nowhere else in the political structure. For all the limits upon his power, he is the major unifying force in a diffuse political system and pluralistic society. He, better than anyone else, can act affirmatively and flexibly.

But the President, if he shall write his name large on the pages of history, if he is to help save humanity from the perils to its survival, must do more than excel at practical politics, and dazzle at bargaining and persuading. Neustadt's model alone is not enough. Neither can this memorable leadership succeed solely by appeals to calculated self-interest. A sturdy measure of idealism must inspirit both leadership and the public. An excelling President must use political power to advance great ends. His shining hours occur in the Fourteen Points of Wilson, in the social purposes of Lincoln and the Roosevelts, and in the assertion of principle by Grover Cleveland against the test of events. He must rise to moments as Cleveland did when pressing the House Speaker to support an administration measure; Cleveland found him hesitant and fearful of the consequences to his future. "Mr. Speaker," Cleveland exclaimed, "what is your political future weighed in the balance against the fortunes of the country? Who are you and I compared with the welfare of the whole American people?"[31] The Speaker surrendered. But the President who, like Cleveland, chooses to enter the roaring furnace where political necessity and principle converge subjects himself to the burning anguish that reaches its highest intensity in the presidency itself. One day Cleveland invited a visitor, Dr. Wilton M. Smith, to listen to the draft of a speech. Cleveland, as he read on, worked up into a high pitch of emotion. He exclaimed, turning suddenly on his visitor,

> Doctor, I suppose at times you won't approve of many things I do, but I want you to know that I am trying to do what is right. . . . Sometimes the pressure is most overwhelming, and a President cannot always get at the exact truth; but I want you to know that I am trying to do what is right. *I am trying to do what is right.*[32]

Tears welled in the big President's eyes; he blew his nose hard and paced the room.

# Presidential Types

Without undue violence to history, it is possible to divide the Presidents the United States has had into three recurrent types with a view to assessing their suitability as models for the contemporary Chief Executive who is both effective and responsive to democratic constraints.

## The Literalist

The most numerous type is one that might be styled a "literalist" President. Madison, Buchanan, Taft, and, to a degree, Eisenhower are of this school. The mark of the literalist President, as his title suggests, is close obedience to the letter of the Constitution. If anything, he is apt to veer too far toward the democratic end of the spectrum and permit the undue sacrifice of power and initiative. Taft, who, with Buchanan, was the most literal of the Presidents, formulated the operative belief of the literalists:

> The true view of the Executive function is . . . that the President can exercise no power which cannot be fairly and reasonably traced to some specific grant of power or justly implied and included within such express grant as proper and necessary to its exercise. Such specific grant must be either in the Federal Constitution or in an act of Congress passed in pursuance thereof. There is no undefined residuum of power which he can exercise because it seems to him to be in the public interest.[33]

The Taft-like President tends also to live by the Whig assumption that the legislative power is popular and the executive monarchical. He is respectful, even deferential, to Congress. "My duty," James Buchanan was prone to say, "is to execute the laws . . . and not my individual opinions."[34] When Congress did nothing in the face of gathering rebellion, Buchanan too did nothing. The Taft-like President makes little use of his independent powers or prerogative (his powers, for example, as Commander-in-Chief and as implied in the executive power clause). He exerts political pressure sparingly. Symptomatic of his approach is British historian James Bryce's observation that the typical nineteenth-century President's communications to Congress were so perfunctory that "the expression of his wishes . . . in messages has not necessarily any more effect on Congress than an article in a prominent party newspaper."[35]

The literalist President has little taste for innovation in social policy. He is nostalgic for the past and urges it be used as a blueprint for the future. He feels, as Taft did, that the bane of government is "ill-digested legislation" and that "real progress in government must be by slow stages."[36] It is a view that Theodore Roosevelt found upheld in society by "most able lawyers who are past middle age" and "large numbers of well-meaning, respectable citizens."[37]

The presidency in the manner of Taft and Buchanan is, on its face, admirably responsive to democratic constraints, but inadequate for the necessities of the contemporary presidency faced with grave social and environmental problems at home and the dynamics of foreign affairs, with opportunities to provide good offices for building peace among nations, for disarmament and expanded trade, for gaining observance of human rights. The past, which the literalist presidency venerates, can be only a partial and imperfect guide to the present and future. It excessively limits the President's initiatives, which again and again have been a constructive force in times of crisis and change. Its neglect of politics abdicates action to passivity and, as the experience of many nineteenth-century Presidents proves, can thoroughly reduce the President from leader to clerk.

## The Effective President

At the opposite end of the spectrum from the literalist President is the effective President of initiative and action, typified by Washington, Jackson, Lincoln, Wilson, and the Roosevelts. He generally, although not exclusively, flourishes in times of crisis and change—during a war or a depression—and when political movements such as progressivism are at their crests. He interprets his powers with liberality; he is a precedent-maker and precedent-breaker to the point where the legality of his acts is questioned or disproved. His bible is the "stewardship theory" of Theodore Roosevelt, who felt that it was the President's "duty to do anything that the needs of the nation demand unless such action was forbidden by the Constitution or by the laws." "I acted for the public welfare," Roosevelt said. "I acted for the common well-being of all our people."[38] But the peril of this sometimes highly assertive presidency, as recent experience unfortunately illuminates, is its penchant for straying into illegality, its thrust beyond normal constraints, its excessive infringement of democratic values and processes. The march of its logic is toward excessive power, and the effort to keep it within acceptable democratic bounds imposes extra strains on the vigor and competence of surrogate institutions—Congress, the courts, the parties, interest groups, and organized opinion.

In his most fruitful moments, the effective President provides leadership, in Franklin Roosevelt's words, "alert and sensitive to change," which in the Jefferson-Jackson tradition means that the government must act positively in promoting a good life, and in the Wilson tradition means that the nation cannot shun or escape its obligations of world leadership. His orientation is less to the past than to the future, which he approaches with hope and plan. He is skillful politically and is concerned more with substance than with form. When necessary, he resorts to bold action, and has the gift of inspiring and rallying the people with messages that mix practicality and prophecy. In his view, the President as a person must dominate the presidency as an institution. He, a fleeting political figure, must bend, divert, and lead the cumbrous bureaucratic executive branch according to his purpose. But he must walk a tightrope in order not to slip into behavior that violates or jeopardizes democratic processes.

Between the effective and literalist Presidents is a middle ground that many Chief Executives have occupied; it unites elements of both extremes. This middle ground need not now detain us. The magnitude of problems and opportunities at home and abroad makes clear that only one of the three available presidential types is suitable for the future. For the United States to best cope with problems and capitalize on opportunities requires a presidency that is less cyclical and more continuously effective, as a major source of constructive accomplishment to deal positively with society's and the world's problems and to bring the greatest good to the greatest number of people. On the other hand, as the Watergate experience and the excesses of presidential war-making illuminate in clearest hieroglyphics that all may understand, the assertive presidency bears the risk of antidemocratic behavior. The risk must be managed and overcome by the enhancement of democratic safeguards capable of containing substantial presidential power within limits compatible with a free society. Most of the Framers of the Constitution—though not all—were confident that they had mastered the problem of the presidency of power coexisting harmoniously with human liberty. Since their time, the adequacy of their solution has sometimes come into question, especially after the Watergate tragedy. In the 1980s and beyond, a central problem of American politics and political science, if not *the* central problem, is the coupling of the presidency of power and effectiveness with the institutions and processes of democracy in ways that are enduring and safe for liberty. This book is addressed to that problem.

# Chapter Two

# Beginnings

**A** year before the Constitutional Convention of 1787, John Jay, in a letter to George Washington recounting the inadequacies of the existing government, moved boldly to the inevitable question: "Shall we have a king?"[1] It was indeed a question stirring in many influential minds, but few dared ask it openly. The propagandists of the Revolution had done their work too well in portraying that enterprise as a struggle against a tyrannical monarch, although their description of that monarch was much more appropriate for the earlier James I or Charles I than for the monarch of their day, the unfortunate, ineffective George III. The general revulsion from monarchy had produced in the states a prevailing pattern of the weak executive and in the Articles of Confederation almost no executive at all. But the weak executive was maintained at a high price. The event that drove Jay to his writing desk was Shays's Rebellion in Massachusetts, an upheaval exposing the impotence of government and foreshadowing for the young nation a desperate existence of anarchy, confiscation of property, possible military dictatorship, and foreign intervention.

Hard questions occupied responsible men's thoughts. How could the strong executive that circumstances required be best provided? Should there be a monarch, as Jay suggested? Or could some other form of strong executive be discovered or created, untainted with the tyranny that the country dreaded, yet endowed with sufficient authority? In the interlude before the Convention, men carried on the search, and at Philadelphia they struggled with it under the pressure of decision.

# The Governorship

## The Colonial Governor

The states, and before them the colonies, provided the major domestic experience with executive power. The colonial governor initially was a strong executive: commander-in-chief of the provincial forces and representative of the crown, embodying the several kingly prerogatives. He was the fountain of honor and privilege and thus created offices and filled them. With little exception he shared power with a council, usually of twelve members appointed by the crown at the governor's recommendation. The council functioned as the legislative upper house, advised and influenced the governor, and was his ally in local political struggles.[2]

As relations with the mother country deteriorated, the governorship passed under the increasing influence and direction of the assembly, the lower and more popular legislative house. Particularly in the French and Indian War, when the governor was constantly in need of money for the army, the assembly employed its control over supplies to pare down the governor's power. The American view of George III as the tyrant over Parliament spurred the hostility against his agent, the local governor.

The animus against executive power carried into the early state constitutions of the Revolutionary period. Power rushed to the legislature. The governor, or president as he was called in several states, was reduced almost to a cipher. His term was for one year, except in South Carolina where it was two and in Delaware where it was three. His reeligibility was strictly limited. He was chosen by, and was therefore the creature of, the legislature. The executive branch was deliberately disunified. The governor was saddled with a council chosen by the legislature, except in Pennsylvania. Most of the enumerated executive powers and functions were subject to council control. In Maryland the council was a "board" in which the executive had one vote "for the transacting of business." In Virginia Governor Edmund Randolph viewed himself as "a member of the executive."[3] The power that the legislature did not have by direct grant it could get by bold assertion against the other branches, which were endowed with little power to defend themselves. Thomas Jefferson observed of the Virginia as he might have of most state constitutions, "All the powers of government, legislative, executive and judiciary, result to the legislative body."[4]

The governor's drab plight was relieved only in Massachusetts, where he possessed the veto power (subject to overriding by two-thirds of the legislature) and was indefinitely reeligible, and in New York, where he could fairly be termed a strong executive.

## The New York Governor

The New York constitution was established late, in 1777, sometime after the creation of other state constitutions, and it profited from their imperfections. The folly of the weak chief executive characteristic of those constitutions was daily revealed in the urgencies of the Revolution, which demanded the summoning of effective executive power. New York's situation, exceedingly roughened by the onmarching British, made strong exec-

utive power imperative. The state convention that drafted the constitution
was literally chased up the state by the British army. It was a convention
on the run, which moved from Harlem to Kingsbridge and then successively to Philipse Manor, Fishkill, Poughkeepsie, and finally Kingston, as
the British pressed relentlessly northward.

The New York constitution rejected the ascendancy that the legislature
enjoyed in other state constitutions. In language instilled in the future federal Constitution "the supreme executive power and authority of the state"
was vested in the governor. The New York governor, in contrast to the
governors of other states, served a substantial term—three years—with no
limit upon his reeligibility. He was chosen not by the legislature, the prevailing pattern elsewhere, but by a constitutionally identified electorate, a
popular suffrage that for the time was generously defined. His electoral independence from the legislature was a giant step toward making the governor the strongest officer of his kind in the Confederation.

His further powers all foreshadowed the presidency. The governor was
commander-in-chief and admiral of the navy; he could convene the legislature on extraordinary occasions; and he could grant reprieves and pardons.
His duty was to inform the legislature of the condition of the state, recommend matters for their consideration, and take care that the laws were faithfully executed. He did not escape altogether the restraints commonly
imposed upon other governors. His power of appointment was shared with
a Council of Appointment of four senators elected by the assembly from
each of the four senatorial districts. The governor was president of the
council and possessed a casting vote. The governor shared his otherwise
strong veto power with a Council of Revision, consisting of the governor,
the chancellor, and the judges of the Supreme Court. They, or any three of
them, always including the governor, could veto legislative measures inconsistent with the spirit of the constitution or the public good. A two-thirds
vote in both houses could override the veto.[5]

But the offices a constitution creates cannot live on the written document
alone. They thrive upon skilled and vigorous incumbents. The New York
governorship, by rare good fortune, had as its first occupant a skillful and
courageous chief executive, George Clinton. Clinton's reign was rich and
memorable; Clinton used fully his store of power and became the dominant
political figure of his state. Particularly impressive to the federal Founding
Fathers was Clinton's ability, as a strong executive, to maintain public order. He put down the severe Doctors' Riots in New York City with the
militia and routed out the remnants of Shays's men who fled to New York
after springing their rebellion in Massachusetts.[6] The New York governorship's influence was further assured by the circumstance that a Founding
Father who was to be most influential in creating the presidency was a
principal draftsman of the New York constitution; Gouverneur Morris engaged in this double enterprise.

# The Philadelphia Convention

The Constitution-makers who gathered in Philadelphia in 1787, hailed by Thomas Jefferson as "an assembly of demi-gods," organized themselves by electing George Washington their "president" and Major William Jackson their secretary. Rules of procedure were adopted and precautions taken to keep the proceedings secret. In the weeks of lengthy, intense, and often disheartening deliberations, no single problem was more perplexing in building the new government than the office of President. The President must be endowed with impressive powers yet must not appear to the people, nor in fact be, another king and incipient tyrant. He must have sufficient but not excessive independence. He must be dependent but not, as state governors commonly were, the mere creature of the legislature.

The Convention began its hard grapple with specifics when it resolved itself on May 29 into a Committee of the Whole to consider several competing plans and proposals submitted by state delegations and individual members. Each plan dealt with the whole structure of a federal government, including the question of executive power.

The Virginia plan, which had been prepared chiefly by James Madison before the Convention assembled, called for a "national executive" to be chosen by the "National Legislature." The executive would be eligible only for a single term, and "besides a general authority to execute the National laws, [he] ought to enjoy the Executive rights vested in Congress by the Confederation." The Committee of the Whole at the Convention added certain features to the Virginia plan: The term of the executive would be seven years, he could make appointments "in cases not otherwise provided for," and he would be removable "on impeachment and conviction of malpractice, or neglect of duty." He could "negative" any legislative act unless overridden "by two third parts" of each branch of the legislature. With certain "members" of the judiciary, he could exercise the veto power. The Virginia plan was bold in conception. Instead of simply revising or altering the Articles, it aimed to enlarge them and proposed a national executive, legislature, and judiciary to do what was done, or should have been done, by the Continental Congress.[7]

The New Jersey plan, offered by William Paterson on June 15, was the response of the small states to the power of the large states that would have resulted from the Virginia plan. Whereas the Virginia plan undertook to replace the Articles with a document for a truly national government, the New Jersey plan merely revised them. It would endow the central government with powers to levy import duties and regulate foreign and domestic trade. The states were to collect taxes, but Congress could act if the states defaulted. The New Jersey plan called for a plural executive chosen by Congress, removable on the application of a majority of the state executives, ineligible for a second term, and empowered to direct all military operations though in no case to take command in the field.[8]

In addition to the rival plans of the large and small states, comprehensive plans of two Convention members dealt with the executive. One plan, by Alexander Hamilton, presented in a five-hour speech on June 18, was the most extreme proposal to be offered at the Convention for a strong executive and central government. Hamilton announced himself as "unfriendly" to both the Virginia and the New Jersey plans, terming the former, the stronger of the two, "pork still, with a little change of the sauce." The severity of the crisis required a central government of highest competence. "The general power whatever be its form if it preserves itself, must swallow up the State powers, otherwise it will be swallowed up by them." For the substance of the new government, Hamilton's probing gaze fell upon the British structure, "the best in the world"; he doubted "whether any thing short of it would do for America." Monarchy and Parliament he unreservedly admired. No good government could exist without a good executive, and no good executive could ever be established "on Republican principles." The hereditary monarch, endowed with great wealth, was above corruption from abroad and was "both sufficiently independent and sufficiently controlled, to answer the purpose of the institution at home."

The Hamilton plan called for a monarch and nobles, a single executive and a Senate for life or good behavior, and an inferior popular house. The states would have no powers except over local affairs. So extreme was the plan that it was supported by no other delegate and was not even discussed. Days later, on June 29, Hamilton left Philadelphia, despairing that the Convention would fail to recommend a strong central government and would "let slip the golden opportunity of rescuing the American empire from disunion, anarchy, and misery. No motley or feeble measure can answer the end or will finally receive the public support." The Virginia plan was "motley" and the New Jersey plan "feeble."[9]

Still another plan was advanced by Charles Pinckney of South Carolina, member of a congressional committee charged with recommending amendments to the Articles. His plan, most of it now lost, seems from its several surviving parts to have attempted to revise the Articles rather than supplant them. In drawing his executive, Pinckney relied heavily upon the New York constitution. The powers and duties of the executive and the contingencies of his death and removal all followed the New York arrangement. His election and term, however, did not. Pinckney's executive would be elected by Congress annually.[10]

## Decisions at Philadelphia

The Committee of the Whole debated the several plans with their conflicting conceptions. The issue of Virginia's proposed single executive versus New Jersey's plural executive quickly came to a head when James Wilson of Pennsylvania moved and Charles Pinckney seconded that the executive consist of one person. In the debate the principal argument made against the single executive was that it would constitute a standing invitation to the very kind of monarchy that the Revolution was intended to overcome. Edmund Randolph typified this opinion, according to Madison's *Journal*, when he "strongly opposed a unity in the Executive magistracy. He regarded it as the foetus of monarchy. We had, he said, no motive to be governed by the British Government as our prototype." Randolph also objected that a single magistrate could never evoke confidence and that the appointment would generally be in favor of some inhabitant near the "center of the Community," and the "remote parts" consequently "would not be on an equal footing." He preferred an executive department of three persons "drawn from different portions of the Country."[11]

James Wilson answered. Randolph, he contended, was less concerned with merit than with the popularity of the Convention's handiwork. Wilson, for his part, believed that the people well knew that "a single magistrate is not a King." All thirteen states, although agreeing upon almost nothing else in their constitutions, had established a single head as governor or president. "The idea of three heads," which promised neither "vigor" nor "tranquillity," "has taken place in none." Other Framers viewed the single executive not as an "absolute" monarch like the propagandized image of George III but as a kind of "limited" monarch, the most desirable of all executives. "A firm Executive," as John Dickinson of Delaware put it, "could only exist in a limited monarchy."[12] While the Convention analyzed the monarchy, stories circulated in the world outside that the Framers, in their love for that brand of executive, were bent upon importing a Hanoverian bishop to be king of the United States. Fortunately, the stories quickly subsided.[13]

A lengthy struggle centered upon two further questions, viewed as inseparable: the source of the executive's election and the length of his term. Three major types of election were advanced. James Wilson and Gouverneur Morris, friends of a strong executive, urged election, as Morris put it, "by the people at large, by the freeholders of the Country." When practical administrative difficulties were cited, Morris retorted that these had been overcome in New York and could be likewise in other states. The people, the doubters said, would be uninformed and misled by designing men. Morris preferred to be optimistic: "If the people should elect, they will never fail to prefer some man of distinguished character, or services; some man, if he might so speak, of continental reputation."[14] A second method was election by the legislature. That body's handling of the task, Morris contended, would be the work "of intrigue, of cabal, of faction." The final method, and the one ultimately adopted, was choice by electors. Advocates of an electoral system felt that it would best give effect to the dominant popular choice whose direct expression was barred for practical reasons. Many Fathers feared that citizens would blindly favor local candidates and would be ignorant of able men in other states.

Linked with method of choice were the questions of length of term and reeligibility. Elbridge Gerry of Massachusetts argued that the longer the term the less would the executive depend upon the legislature that chose him. Oliver Ellsworth of Connecticut likewise proposed a long term of six years. If elections were too frequent, the executive would not "be firm enough." (He said, "There must be duties which will make him unpopular for the moment.") Without a long term (seven years), Hugh Williamson of North Carolina argued, "The best men will not undertake the service and those of an inferior character will be liable to be corrupted."[15]

Proposals of six- or seven-year terms were predicated upon the assumption that the legislature would choose the President. A long term plus ineligibility for reelection, a common feature of such proposals, appeared the best means to safeguard executive independence of the legislature. Reeligibility would prompt the executive to court the legislature to win another term. The alternative of a shorter term and reeligibility came to the fore when selection by electors was ultimately settled upon.

The Fathers considered long and anxiously the question of annexing a council to the chief executive. A council would diminish the monarchical tendency and the danger of tyranny. Collective advice was deemed safer and more competent than the assorted individual advice that might befall the President. Various kinds of councils were proposed. The Pinckney plan vested in the executive "a Right to advise with the Heads of the different Departments as his Council." Ellsworth, rather fearful of personal government, would add to the council the President of the Senate and the Chief Justice. George Mason preferred a council representative of the chief sections of the country, the East, the Middle States, and the South. James Madison, a strong exponent of the council, proposed that it possess initiative to advise the President and to record its sentiments. But the floor discussion proved inconclusive, and ultimately the council idea was dropped.[16] The prospect that the venerated Washington would serve as first President drained much of the interest from the council proposal. Indeed many Fathers feared that a council of some power might harass the position of future President Washington.

In its final draft the Constitution not only failed to provide a council, it did not even call for the "cabinet" that appeared early in Washington's presidency. The Constitution merely specified that the Chief Executive could require the "opinions of the heads of his departments in writing." Hamilton, for one, considered even this provision redundant as the right "would result of itself from the office." Other critics were haunted to the very end by monarchical fears. George Mason, crying doom, warned that a presidency without a council was an "experiment" that even "the most despotic governments" had never undertaken. Benjamin Franklin, ordinarily optimistic, beheld a melancholy prospect, seeing only "caprice, the intrigues of favorites and mistresses, etc." in the absence of a council.[17]

The Fathers debated a score of issues in establishing the substantive powers of the executive. These were resolved with a tendency toward generosity to the executive, sparked by the prospect that Washington would become President. The veto power, remembered as an arbitrary instrument of the royal governors, was critically scrutinized. The Declaration of Independence's first indictment of George III was his refusal to "Assent to Laws, the most wholesome and necessary for the public good." But excesses by the state legislatures since Revolutionary days made the Fathers receptive to a strong veto power. The Virginia plan's coupling of the judiciary with the executive in the veto was dropped. The variant proposals for a Council of Revision met a like fate, and the President emerged as the solitary executive possessor of the veto power.

The appointing power was one of the knottier issues. James Wilson, constant friend of a strong presidency, opposed the eventual arrangement, a power shared between the President and the Senate. "There can be no good Executive," he argued, "without a responsible appointment of officers to execute." Responsibility was impaired by involving the Senate. Wilson's view was respected to a degree when the President was given an exclusive appointing power "in all cases not otherwise provided for."[18]

Treaty and war powers and the President's pay, removal, and disability also evoked considerable discussion. "What is the extent of the term 'disability' and who is to be the judge of it?" Dickinson asked, questions that the Framers were never able to resolve definitively. Debate waxed over the respective powers of Congress and the executive to "declare" and to "make" war.[19] When the dust of debate had settled, it did seem clear that the Convention did not want either to deny the President the power to respond to surprise attack or to give the President broad power to initiate hostilities. One motion on the subject shocked Gerry, who "never expected" to hear in a republic a proposal to empower the executive alone to declare war. Madison contended that the war power could not be safely entrusted to the President or the Senate. He was for "clogging" rather than "facilitating" war.[20]

## Drafting the Presidential Article

The work of the Committee of the Whole was supplemented by two drafting committees, the Committee of Detail and the Committee of Style. After discussion lasting some weeks, the Convention established the Committee of Detail—the members being Edward Rutledge (South Carolina), Randolph (Virginia), Nathaniel Gorham (Massachusetts), Ellsworth (Connecticut), and Wilson (Pennsylvania)—to reduce the delegates' ponderings to a systematic Constitution draft. The work of the Committee of Detail, a long stride toward the strong presidency, was aided by Convention-adopted resolutions providing for a single executive empowered to execute national laws, to veto national legislation, and to appoint to offices in cases not otherwise provided for. The executive was also made subject to impeachment. The Committee of Detail adapted these resolutions to its draft and, with an eye on the New York constitution, further elaborated the President's powers. The committee made it the President's duty to give information to the legislature, to recommend measures, to convene Congress into extraordinary session, and, in disagreement between the two houses on the subject, to adjourn them. The President would also receive ambassadors, grant pardons and reprieves, and act as Commander-in-Chief.[21]

The Convention debated intensively for five weeks, section by section, the draft of the Committee of Detail. On September 8 a Committee of Style headed by Gouverneur Morris was appointed to "revise the style and arrange the articles which had been agreed to by the house." This committee too was innovative. It installed the plan for choosing the President through electors and empowered him to make treaties, provided two-thirds of the Senators present concurred, and to nominate and, with the advice and consent of the Senate, appoint ambassadors, other public ministers and consuls, and justices of the Supreme Court. The President's term was put at four years with indefinite reeligibility. The Presidential Article II began with a sentence, attributed to Morris, of vast future significance: "The executive Power shall be vested in a President of the United States of America."

On September 13 the Committee of Style presented a draft of the Constitution to the Convention in the handwriting of Gouverneur Morris. Two days later the Constitution was adopted, and in another two days the Convention adjourned. The presidency, as it finally emerged, mirrored the ideal of a strong but responsible Chief Executive. The President would be a single, not a plural, executive, with no council but presumably heads of departments, although these were not specifically provided for. His election and identity were distinct and separate from Congress. His term of four years was longer than the state governors', and he was reeligible for an indefinite number of terms. His powers were generous and both specific and general. The opening language of Article II, "The executive Power shall be vested in a President," was clearly broader than the investiture of Article I, "All legislative Powers herein granted shall be vested in a Congress," or Article III, "The judicial Power shall extend to all cases, in Law and Equity, arising under this Constitution, the Laws of the United States, and Treaties."[22]

# Makers of the Presidency

In any listing of Founding Fathers who played a heroic part in creating a strong Chief Executive tempered by constraints, the name of James Wilson of Pennsylvania would take an honored place. Forty-five years of age at the time of the Convention, Wilson was a Scotsman by birth and education, tall, large-featured, and afflicted with nearsightedness, which with his glasses added a touch of sternness to his appearance. Endowed with a tough, perceptive mind, Wilson contributed more than anyone else to the concept of the strong but responsible presidency. He laid it persuasively before the Convention and was an instrumental member of the Committee of Detail that worked out the final revision. Wilson's success, although impressive, was not total. His chief defeat was the rejection of his proposal that the executive be chosen by the people.

Gouverneur Morris, chairman of the committee that wrote the final draft of the Constitution, is another hero. Draftsman of the New York constitution, member of the Continental Congress, and hardy *bon vivant*, he illuminated the Convention's deliberations with insights from the instructive New York experience. Eloquent, caustic, dynamic, and aggressive, Morris steadily championed the strong executive who would also be responsible and democratic. In Morris's eyes, the executive must be the advocate and defender of "the people, even of the lower classes," against legislative "tyranny," against "the great and the wealthy who, in the course of things, will compose the legislature."[23] Madison, too, stands among the heroes. He began conservatively on the question of executive power but gradually came around to Wilson's views.

The indispensable presence at the Convention was the presiding officer, the nation's future first Chief Executive, George Washington. Elected unanimously to his Convention post, his tall, heavy, ruddy presence, grave mien, his very embodiment of the young country's agony and triumph, marked him as the most conspicuous and the most influential delegate. Although he spoke but once, his commitment to strong central government was well known. "My wish is," he wrote to Madison, prior to Philadelphia, "that the convention may adopt no temporizing expedients, but probe the defects of the constitution to the bottom, and provide a radical cure, whether they are agreed to or not."[24] The prevailing assumption, candidly articulated in the Convention, was that he would become the first President. Pierce Butler of South Carolina expressed Washington's significance in the creation of the presidency when he wrote, "Entre nous, I do [not] believe they [the executive powers] would have been so great had not many members cast their eyes toward General Washington as President; and shaped their Ideas of the Powers to be given the President, by their opinions of his Virtue." [25]

But there were also prestigious voices that spoke of inherent dangers in the strong Chief Executive. Upon hearing of the necessity of secrecy, vigor, and dispatch in the discharge of public business, and the uniqueness of the executive in embodying those attributes, the perspicacious John Dickinson of Pennsylvania reminded his colleagues that, important as these qualities were, "that of responsibility is more so . . ." [26] Pierce Butler of South Carolina warned, "But why might not a Cataline or a Cromwell arise in this Country as well as in others?" [27] Benjamin Franklin, the Convention's worldly sage, illuminated a theme, widely embraced by his colleagues, that the transformation of executive power into tyranny, was, at bottom, the consequence of the evil lurking in human nature. Who, normally, would strive to possess the offices of government? Franklin's answer was knowing and confident: "the bold and violent, the men of strong passions and indefatigable activity in their selfish pursuits. These will thrust themselves into your Government and be your rulers." [28]

Observations like these spurred the Framers to search for means to forestall the abuses of that most dangerous combination, imperfect human nature coupled with substantial power.

## Structural Concepts

The making of the presidency adhered to two overarching structural concepts: the separation of powers and checks and balances. Mutually contradictory, even though directed toward the same ends, one posed division and independence, the other interaction and dependence.

The separation of powers was a basic principle in the works of several major political writers well known to the Framers. Although the writers differed in the ways these powers should be separated, they shared a common view of the nature and purpose of separated powers. John Locke's *Two Treatises of Government*, probably the most powerful philosophic influence at the Convention, Montesquieu's *Esprit des lois*, and William Blackstone's *Commentaries on the Laws of England* all viewed the concentration of power as an invitation to tyranny. Liberty was best preserved if power were distributed between several branches. Locke, for instance, divided governmental power between the legislative or lawmaking power, the executive or law-enforcing power, and the "federative" power of war and peace, leagues and alliances, and other foreign relations. Locke did not specify the judicial power but presumably intended to safeguard its independency by the Act of Settlement.

Although the Founding Fathers repeatedly and reverently invoked separation of powers, the doctrine fared unevenly at their hands. As political scientist Charles C. Thach has rightly observed, few governments exceed the functional overlapping of that created by the American Constitution. [29] Lawmaking is shared between the two-house Congress and the President, treaty-making and appointments between the President and the Senate, and so on. The Fathers did meticulously observe the doctrine in the sense of arranging a personal separation of powers in contrast to functional separation. The memberships of the three branches—executive, legislative, and judicial—were separated. An officer of one could not serve in another, except for the Vice President, who had minor duties in the Senate but a general identity with the executive.

Checks and balances, the second overarching doctrine for making the strong executive responsible and free of temptation to lapse into tyrannical ways, was also well articulated by influential writers. The theory of balanced government reached back to the Greeks and enjoyed vogue in the eighteenth century among English and continental writers. Montesquieu and Blackstone interpreted the English constitution as a complex of checks: the Lords against the Commons and both against the crown. Government was viewed not as a cooperative enterprise between its several parts but as an enduring conflict of opposite interests.

The leading American exponent of balanced government was John Adams, whose *Defence of the Constitutions of the United States of America Against the Attack of Mr. Turgot* was well known to the Founding Fathers. For liberty to be preserved and property safeguarded, Adams argued, government must be poised in an equilibrium. Governments, like the populations they govern, divide into three distinct entities: the one, the few, and the many; or the leader, the aristocracy of birth or property, and the mass of people. Each part is capable of abuse—of jealousy, encroachment, and folly. The wellspring of disequilibrium, in the words of Thucydides, is "thirst of power, from rapacious and ambitious passions." The art of constitution-making, as Adams perceived it, was the establishment of "a multitude of curious and ingenious inventions to balance in their turn, all those powers [legislative, executive, and judicial], to check the passions peculiar to them, and to control them from rushing into the exorbitancies to which they are most addicted." The stability and purposes of a government, in a word, were best achieved by a delicate balance between more or less equal powers vitalized by mutual jealousies.

The Founding Fathers were much preoccupied with the problem of balance. "It is [the] most difficult of all rightly to balance the Executive," Gouverneur Morris observed: "Make him too weak: the Legislature will usurp his power. Make him too strong: he will usurp on the Legislature." The leading analyst of balanced power was Madison, whose views are most fully stated in the *Federalist* paper Number 51. "The great security against a gradual concentration of the several powers in the same department," he wrote, "consists in giving to those who administer each department the necessary constitutional means and personal motives to resist encroachments of the others. Ambition must be made to counteract ambition."

# The Presidency Begins

The final phase of the creation of the presidency was Washington's nearly impeccable workmanship as the office's first incumbent. His strong and good hands imparted to the presidency a form and substance that have forever remained with it. In confronting his duties, Washington knew well that what he did possessed both present and future significance, that his every act was a potential precedent, and that the body of his conduct was creating an entire executive system.

On Inauguration Day, April 30, 1789, the joint inaugural committee of Congress arrived at the President-elect's temporary residence in New York to escort him to Federal Hall. Shortly after midday the general started out in a grand coach drawn by four horses, preceded by troops and the Senators of the joint committee and followed by his secretaries, the Representatives of the committee, Chancellor Robert Livingston, who would administer the oath, the heads of the federal departments, and a handful of eminent citizens. When the procession reached Federal Hall, Washington passed with simple dignity into the building and mounted the stairs to the Senate chamber, where members of the two houses of Congress, foreign diplomats, and other dignitaries had assembled. The general passed through an arched central door leading onto a small, half-enclosed portico overlooking Wall and Broad Streets. Cheers rolled up from the vast multitude below. Samuel Otis, Secretary of the Senate, lifted the Bible reposing on a red cushion on a small table. Washington placed his hand on the Bible, Livingston pronounced the oath, and Washington repeated it and kissed the Book. "It is done," Livingston declared, and, turning to the crowd, made a broad sweep with his hand and shouted, "Long live George Washington, President of the United States." The crowd roared back Livingston's words and "God bless our President"; church bells rang, the flag was run up in the cupola of Federal Hall, and guns were fired from the Battery and a Spanish sloop of war in the harbor. The presidency was now in being.[30]

# Presidential Strength: George Washington

In two terms of office Washington launched the presidency on a high note of success. Weathering times that were full of crisis, he left the republic stronger, more purposeful, and more confident than when he had begun his task. A string of measures, highly impressive by twentieth-century standards in their number and scope, steadily emerged from the Washington administration: a national currency was issued and the Bank of the United States was established to provide credit; manufacture and trade were fostered by tariffs and bounties; inventions were protected by patent and copyright laws; neutrality was preserved in the face of an enlarging European war; and the national security was enhanced by reorganization of the army and navy, the founding of West Point, and the building of fortifications in the East and West.

Washington exercised the powers of his office in a fashion that permitted vigorous and innovative administration, but he respected the necessities of legitimacy and responsibility. Midway in his term Washington wrote,

The powers of the Executive of the United States are more definite, and better understood perhaps than those of almost any other Country; and my aim has been and will continue to be, neither to stretch nor relax from them in any instance whatever, unless imperious circumstances should render the measure indispensable.[31]

Where authority was clearly his, Washington maintained his mastery. He truly dominated the executive branch. He was not long in office when he requested the heads of departments to provide "a full, precise and general *idea*" of the work entrusted to them.[32] With few exceptions he prescribed the duties of his department heads and kept abreast of daily detail. He read incoming and outgoing communications of the executive branch and passed upon important plans and actions that the departments submitted in writing. All loan and debt transactions were subject to his approval. Each use of the seal of the United States required his consent. No lighthouse keeper, customs collector, or captain of a cutter could be appointed without his consideration. So confident was he of his mastery that he brought into the leading posts of his administration two of the most gifted department heads the nation has ever known, Thomas Jefferson as Secretary of State and Alexander Hamilton as Secretary of the Treasury.

## Relations with Congress

Washington triumphed in an area where many of his successors have floundered: relationships with Congress. He converted his popularity into major laws without tarnishing his prestige in the inevitable struggle. In his deportment toward Congress he was the essence of constitutional propriety. He stayed officially aloof from most major struggles, leaving the heat and dust of battle to his subordinates, chiefly Hamilton.

Washington was careful to respect Congress. Following his Annual or State of the Union Address, the Senate and House prepared addresses in response. The great throng of lawmakers of both chambers, led by the Speaker and the bearer of the mace, symbol of congressional authority, gathered before the President. The Vice President and the Speaker spoke for their respective houses. The President, for his part, was also attentive to Congress with social and ceremonial gesture. Shortly before the inauguration, he visited the members of Congress, and his manner was agreeable. "He made us complaisant bows," Senator William Maclay of Pennsylvania noted, "one as he mounted and the other as he went away on horseback."[33] He regularly tendered dinners with a dozen and more guests from the Senate, the House, and his own administration.

The close work of researching and drafting legislative proposals and the chores of advocating them, rallying votes, and working out compromises were left to his lieutenant, Alexander Hamilton, Secretary of the Treasury and field leader of the Federalist party. Hamilton drafted the Great Reports, presenting with detail and justification the major legislation of the administration: public credit, the Bank, manufactures, and the like. Washington engaged in no public advocacy of these measures. He seems, however, to have been a behind-the-scenes influence when Jefferson and Hamilton arranged their famous compromise, the location of the future capital in Washington in exchange for federal assumption of state debts. The observant Senator Maclay confided to his diary, "The President of the United States has (in my opinion) had a great influence in this business. The game was played by him and his adherents . . . his name goes to wipe away blame and silence all murmuring." [34]

Washington was a resolute defender of the integrity of presidential power against all trespass, even when Congress was the offender. A most momentous challenge was the call by the Republican-controlled House of Representatives for the instructions and pertinent papers of John Jay's mission to negotiate the treaty bearing his name. The House's bold intrusion into an enterprise allotted by the Constitution to the President and Senate gripped the capital with tension. "Anxiety is on the tiptoe. . . . our galleries have been crowded," Representative Francis Preston of Virginia noted. Washington's response was strong and forthright. Foreign relations by their very nature, the President wrote, required secrecy; disclosure of the requested papers would be "impolitic" and "a dangerous precedent." The fundamental law did not require the House's assent to a treaty. "A just regard to the Constitution and to the duty of my Office . . . forbids a compliance with your request." The House opposition thundered and maneuvered, but all in vain, "What firmness does this great man display!" Senator William Plumer rejoiced. [35]

But another time, when the House of Representatives, investigating the failure of General St. Clair's expedition against northwest Indian tribes, requested from the executive "such persons, papers and records as may be necessary" to its inquiry, Washington readily acknowledged the propriety of the request. The House was rightfully conducting an "inquest" and, consequently, could make a general call for papers. But he also could anticipate that "there might be papers of so secret a nature, as that they ought not to be given up," and his executive colleagues agreed that such papers must be withheld "as would injure the public." [36] Concerning St. Clair, there were none, and Washington, complying fully with the House request, demonstrated that the strong President could also be accountable and responsible.

## Interpreting Presidential Power

Washington, the President of strength, was no slave to literal constitutional prescription but a resourceful innovator. The Constitution said little of how the President might secure advice in the daily business of decision- and policy-making. Washington exploited the freedom this silence permitted and instituted practices that Presidents since his time have followed. He founded the cabinet. In the autumn of 1791 he began bringing his department Secretaries—Jefferson, Hamilton, his Secretary of War Henry Knox, and his Attorney General Edmund Randolph—together for a joint consideration of policy. The cabinet meeting was a timesaver over individual consultation with the Secretaries and permitted the testing of the opinions of his counselors in the presence of their peers. The responsible Chief Executive, Washington believed, responded not merely to external constraints such as Congress and public opinion. He felt that responsibility could be nurtured by internal executive processes. The cabinet harmonized with these perceptions and with Washington's belief that advice should be competitive, that one individual's views should be checked against other sources. Repeatedly he ranged beyond the cabinet for counsel, to Congressman James Madison, for example, and Chief Justice John Jay, from whom he invited "ideas . . . not confined to matters judicial, but extended to all other topics which have occurred, or may occur to you, as fit subjects for general or private communications."[37] Washington also believed that advice should be broadly representative. He recruited his cabinet from the three principal sections of the country, the North, the South, and the Middle States. A close student of grass-roots opinion, he maintained correspondents in all the sections and instituted the grand tour, traveling the length and breadth of the republic to gather impressions firsthand.

But for Washington's presidency all was not serenity and assurance. His mind was often the battleground for conflicts that flared between the ideal of the strong presidency and the ideal of the responsible presidency. Often the line between them was blurred and therefore discoverable only by experience. Within the cabinet were redoubtable exponents of each kind of presidency—Hamilton articulated the energetic, assertive presidency and Jefferson the limited, accountable executive. One of their more dramatic clashes erupted when Washington unilaterally issued a proclamation of American neutrality in the Franco-British war. As justification, Hamilton argued that since foreign policy was by nature an executive function, the powers to declare war and approve treaties accorded the legislature in the Constitution were "exceptions out of the general 'executive power' vested in the President" and therefore were "to be construed strictly, and ought to be extended no futher than is essential to their execution." While Congress might declare war, the President was empowered to preserve peace prior to the declaration, as a concomitant of the "executive power" to do whatever the law of nations requires the United States to do in relations with other powers. Though executive action might "affect the exercise of the power of the legislature to declare war," that was insufficient reason, Hamilton argued, for the executive not to use his authority.

Disturbed by Hamilton's expansive interpretation of presidential power, Jefferson implored Madison to "select the most striking heresies and cut him to pieces in face of the public." A reluctant Madison denied that the power to make wars or treaties was inherently executive. Indeed, this "vicious" doctrine was patently borrowed from Britain, he claimed, and the fact that these were royal British prerogatives did not make them Presidential prerogatives. Only Congress could judge whether the United States must declare war, a judgment that could not be foreclosed by presidential proclamations of neutrality or by other executive actions creating "an antecedent state of things." As for Hamilton's suggestion of concurrent presidential and congressional authority, Madison cited an inherent absurdity: What if the President proclaimed neutrality and Congress declared war?[38] Although he went along with Hamilton, Washington quickly responded to the Madisonian interpretation when grand juries refused to indict offenders, since no neutrality law existed to violate. Accordingly, Washington was driven to recommend that Congress legislate, and, ever since, neutrality has remained the province of Congress.

As part of his conception of the strong presidency, Washington prized and jealously maintained the intrinsic dignity of the presidential office. He wanted, he said, to make the presidency "respectable." His natural taste for regal display was freely indulged.

But, more importantly, the presidency was sustained by the unfailing magnificence of Washington's character. Judgment, vision, skill in managing men, integrity, infinite patience, self-discipline—all were his marks. "His integrity was most pure," Thomas Jefferson observed, "his justice the most inflexible I have ever known. . . . He was indeed, in every sense of the words, a wise, a good and a great man. . . ."[39]

# Presidential Weakness: John Adams

But the presidency was not all strength, achievement, and glory; it also harbored weakness. Ironically, it was the leading American theoretician of checks and balances, the second President of the United States, who provided the earliest illustration of the weakness his ideas had helped create. John Adams was not long in the presidency when he demonstrated where the provision for the strong executive left off. He proved by his own experience the far depths of trouble in which the President can wallow as party chief, as legislative leader, and as general manager of the executive branch. For the first of these the Founding Fathers had made no provision; for the others, very little. The presidency was in several large particulars an unfinished office.

Adams the President was only the nominal leader of his Federalist party; its real leader was an outsider who held no public office at the time, the talented, driving, ubiquitous Alexander Hamilton. The contrast was exaggerated by a growing break between the two men. Thomas Jefferson, leader of the Anti-Federalists, noted that the Congressional Federalists were only "a little less hostile" to the President than to himself. The Jefferson men and disaffected legislative Federalists were unstinting in demonstrating the President's weakness as legislative leader. When relations with France crumbled and war threatened, Adams, anxious to maintain peace, recommended to Congress a defensive policy based upon expanded naval power. Hamilton, the covert influence, reputedly eager to drive the French out of North America, instructed his congressional followers to vote appropriations for an expanded army, which they did. Congress, in another defiance of presidential leadership, passed in succession the Alien and Sedition Acts, which empowered the President to deport undesirable aliens and made it a crime to criticize the federal government or its officials. Adams neither requested nor wanted either law.

But Adams drank his bitterest draught as chief administrator of the civil and military affairs of the executive branch. Yielding to Congress's enthusiasm for an army in an act designed to win the popular acclaim he so badly lacked, he drew George Washington out of retirement to command the provisional forces. This seemingly splendid triumph was suddenly jeopardized when Washington requested the appointment as his generals of the following in order of rank: Hamilton, Pinckney, and Knox. Adams disputed the order, holding that Knox rightfully should come first, followed by Pinckney and then Hamilton. Ironically, Washington, creator of the strong presidency, now became the agent of its degradation. In a forceful letter to Adams he insisted upon his listing; otherwise, he strongly implied, he would resign. The President, in all his political feebleness, could hardly afford the storm of Washington's resignation. The Commander-in-Chief yielded to his commanding general. Adams staggered on through a full agenda of woe. When upon his own initiative he nominated W. Vans Murray to be minister to the French Republic, his cabinet displayed unconcealed resentment at his failure to consult it. Other times the cabinet concentrated upon its major preoccupation of leaking secrets to Hamilton to assist his campaign against the President. Adams, the man of large talents and rich public experience, ultimately crowned his failure and abandoned his misery by sustaining defeat for reelection.

The Founding Fathers, the Washington-Adams experience reveals, had created a presidency of both strength and weakness. The first two presidencies were the beginning of a continuing dilemma in American history between the people's fear of executive power and their confidence in its necessity and capacity for good.

# Chapter Three

# Selection

The American presidency can be no better or stronger than the caliber of its incumbents. Being a highly personal office, it is foredoomed to an interlude of mediocrity if the Chief Executive who fills it can boast no more than middling talents. Being an intensely political office, it faces deadlock and futility, unless the processes of selecting its holders can screen out individuals lacking in the high order of political talent required to function successfully in a governmental system where power is much divided. In the modern era, the incumbent needs to be both a person of action and of thought, one who "can get things done" and one who is alert to new ideas, one who is adept at the practical politics of getting bills through Congress and one who can engage in dialogue with the universities and other incubators of thought, all to the end of producing policies of depth and sophistication, fit for times of complexity and change.

The processes of selection that will somehow produce this human paragon must make the widest possible search. If presidential hopefuls are heavily concentrated in the wealthy classes or dependent upon them for support, the recruiting base is obviously and practically too narrow, and it violates the democratic ideal of a widely available citizenry for office-holding. The selection outcome must be suffused with legitimacy. It cannot be if the victor's campaign is woven with deceit, if it exploits fears and prejudices, if it is a flood of words and images that say little about issues, or if it is a noncampaign of withdrawal and silence. Rational debate is the essence of democratic politics, to the point that political power, as it is normally exercised in the American system, is the power to persuade. Democracy requires elections that are free, honest, and serious.

Above all, selection must produce candidates who are democratic animals, who comprehend the bounds of constitutional government, who consort with a diversity of citizens, mighty and humble. If the process produces a candidate who deliberately and systematically violates democratic practice, it has committed a grievous lapse and unloosed a threat to democracy itself. Upon the electorate falls a heavy burden of assessing the democratic fitness of candidates, a task that is complicated by the media's capacity to exaggerate and mystify the qualities of presidential contenders.

There can be no effective President if the selection process fails to produce or reflect a social and political consensus that will sustain a constructive program for major public problems. Thus, the function of the selection process is not only to choose the incumbent but to build political union among disparate interests and sections. And ideally, to assure that the selection process will produce a Chief Executive who is democracy-oriented, the voter should be able to penetrate the smokescreen of the candidate's imagery and probe his earlier, formative years that produced his present political personality and provide the basis of predicting how he will perform in the presidency. Such a scrutiny would focus on the candidate as a child, a boy, and as a young man, and on his earlier campaigning and office-holding.

It is not altogether clear when the selection of a President actually begins. Often candidacies are launched two or even three years before the election itself. The long duration of the race and the lavish investment of effort and money it requires militate against the production of candidates who will treat the office with the modesty appropriate to democracy. Thus a dilemma is posed between the prodigious exertion that winning the office requires and the modesty of demeanor that becomes democracy. Still another dilemma hovers in the circumstance that no set of democratic standards can control the selection process from beginning to end. In a sense, the President selects himself; in a sense the party selects him; in a sense—and here the final decision lies—the people do the selecting themselves. To win the presidency, the aspirant must travel a long, hard, treacherous road abounding in bumps and quicksand and divisible into three distinct segments: the preconvention buildup, the national nominating convention, and the postconvention electoral campaign.

# The Preconvention Struggle

The preconvention phase is the longest, often the severest, part of the journey, and it may engage the candidate in fiercer struggles with his rival contenders for the nomination than his later race with the opposing nominee. Competition for the nomination, by contributing to voter choice, may or may not contribute to the bread-and-butter desideratum, party victory. According to a study, when harmony attends the nominating process for the party controlling the presidency, its chances of winning are good. But conflict leading to factional victory in the nomination renders the chances of the in-party poor. The opposite propositions hold for the out-party—less chance of capturing the presidency if the nomination is harmonious, and a better chance if factional strife flares.[1]

In this initial phase of the campaign struggles, the candidate surrounds himself with an entourage of helpers of assorted skills. The entourage has expanded from less than a handful in the nineteenth century to well-nigh a score for the serious modern candidate such as John Kennedy. His preconvention staff included his brother Robert, as general manager of operations, and Lawrence F. O'Brien, congenial, sagacious, and hard-working, as commander of the organizational base, a phalanx of young men who had done their political teething in the Senator's home state of Massachusetts. Kenneth O'Donnell, a taciturn former Harvard football captain and veteran of Kennedy's Massachusetts wars, was the candidate's link with the organization and transmitted Kennedy's reflections and directives to O'Brien. Theodore C. Sorensen was an "idea man" and star draftsman—"my intellectual blood bank," Kennedy called him.[2] Stephen Smith, a brother-in-law, discreet and business-trained, opened the Washington headquarters for the Kennedy staff and eventually became the general manager in charge of mobilizing scores of thousands of volunteers and employees. Pierre Salinger, a former California newspaperman, congressional investigator, and a big-cigar man, presided with joviality and shrewdness over press relations. Louis Harris, public opinion analyst and market research entrepreneur, was the candidate's personal polltaker. His findings were the basis of key campaign decisions. John Bailey, Connecticut Democratic chairman, coordinated the Northeastern bosses.

On the preconvention landscape are several other standard political types. Not the least important, of course, are the several species of opposing candidates: the serious contenders, the dark horses, and the favorite sons. For the 1976 race, Gerald Ford, promptly upon assuming the presidency, disclosed that he expected to run for the office in 1976, a move that insulated him from a lame-duck role in dealing with Congress and his party. And as early as 1973, Democratic candidates were afield: making speeches, issuing high-minded pronouncements, and courting support from influentials. The eventual winner, Jimmy Carter, was the darkest of dark horses. Notwithstanding his long, hyperactive candidacy, when he called a press conference in Philadelphia less than a year before the national Democratic convention nominated him, no one came.[3]

The landscape is also dotted with prestigious political figures who are not candidates but whose support is cherished and whose favor is courted: governors, Senators, Congressmen, party patriarchs, and labor, business, nationality, and racial leaders. In 1980 a sure sign of the grievous state of Edward Kennedy's candidacy and of Gerald Ford's wisdom in shunning the contest after brief flirtation was that precious few of these figures publicly declared their support.

Beyond Washington and into the American hinterland stretches the intricate continental tangle of party machinery, manned by a varied body of functionaries, known collectively as "organization politicians," the state and local party officialdom. Many a presidential aspirant has run aground from want of support from the organization politicians. A formidable obstacle to Wilson's 1912 candidacy was his cold rejection by the generality of organization politicians. "They have an impression of you," Wilson's manager,

William F. McCombs, wrote with frankness, "in a large degree that you are austere and dictatorial and that you will not have a due appreciation of what is to be done for you. . . . Another thing I hear much of, particularly throughout the East, is that you are unreliable."[4]

But contemporary seekers of the presidential nomination, particularly since the later 1960s, have become less dependent on state and local party organizations. Presidential aspirants base their quest for the nomination increasingly on television, public relations techniques, and personalized and public financing, and markedly less than their forebears on precinct work and traditional party fund-raising. Equally, at least a year or two before the first primary the contemporary candidate must mobilize a staff to plan the strategy of the campaign and a larger group of workers to do the advance preparations required to organize states for the approaching primary and caucus-convention contests.

Most crucial for contemporary candidates is early recognition by the media and positive mention in the news. Early in his first campaign, Carter's staff urged him to develop a list of important political columnists and editors and cultivate them by commenting favorably on their columns and by visiting them. Candidates can also inject themselves into the media by writing books and magazine articles, as John Kennedy did with his *Profiles in Courage*, Carter with his *Why Not the Best?*, and Reagan with his autobiography, *Where's the Rest of Me?*

# Preconvention Strategies

## Issues

Tours, visits, speeches, advertising, and television appearances—the chief preconvention activities—involve basic strategic and tactical choices. They can also lead the candidate onto some of the most treacherous terrain of his preconvention effort—taking a stand on issues. Worst of all is the unavoidable issue on which any position the candidate takes will alienate support he needs. Franklin Roosevelt in 1932 was bedeviled by a momentous question he could not avoid—his attitude toward United States membership in the League of Nations. William Randolph Hearst in his transcontinental newspaper chain attacked the candidate unmercifully as an "internationalist," quoting abundantly in front-page editorials Roosevelt's pro-League statements in his vice-presidential campaign of 1920.

In a carefully devised release Roosevelt acknowledged that in 1920 he had worked for American participation in the League. He said,

> But the League of Nations today is not the League conceived by Woodrow Wilson. . . . Too often through these years its major function has been not the broad overwhelming purpose of world peace, but rather a mere meeting place for the political discussion of strictly European political national difficulties. . . . Because of these facts, therefore, I do not favor American participation.[5]

Fortunately for Roosevelt, the statement accomplished its immediate purpose. Hearst ceased his attacks. But there were costs, which presumably the candidate and his managers had anticipated and weighed. The statement stretched to the uttermost the loyalty of the Wilsonians, a compact and powerful band of associates of the last Democratic President. Colonel Edward M. House, Wilson's former confidant, wrote to Farley that Roosevelt's position "created something akin to panic among the devoted Wilson followers." Intellectuals of the school of Walter Lippmann were sorely distressed. Roosevelt swabbed the disgruntled with a remedy that his secretary Louis Howe called "soothing syrup." One body of opinion Roosevelt could not allay was the cynics, a not uncommon breed among political professionals. Senator William E. Borah, eying Roosevelt's statement, muttered sarcastically, "Repent ye, for the kingdom of heaven is at hand."[6]

The candidate in the preconvention period is confronted with the possibility, and sometimes the necessity, of "deals" on issues and offices. The deals presumably will strengthen his chances for the nomination if, on balance, they gain more support than they lose. In the fall of 1895, with the future convention well in sight, Mark Hanna sat down with two great political dictators of the day, Senator Matt Quay of Pennsylvania and former Senator Tom ("Boss") Platt of New York. Both ruled their respective state machines absolutely and were grand masters of the arts of venality. Hanna met with the dark, cynical Quay and the scrawny, secretive Platt to bargain for the huge electoral votes of their respective states. With these William McKinley's nomination would be assured. The bosses' terms came high. Probably more than one cabinet seat was involved, and Platt wanted the Secretaryship of the Treasury for himself, in writing, please. Hanna rushed back to Ohio to report the terms of incipient victory to the candidate. He fortified McKinley first with a choice cigar. As Hanna spoke, McKinley listened in silence, pulled on his cigar, got up, and paced the floor. "There are some things in this world that come too high," he said at last. "If I cannot be President without promising to make Tom Platt Secretary of the Treasury, I will never be President." McKinley thus took a long stride toward sainthood.[7]

## Primaries

The candidate makes a major strategic decision in choosing among the many presidential primaries in which to make his race. In the 1980 elections, the 37 primaries that were held became the crucial battlegrounds in which about three-fourths of the delegates were chosen. Consequently, after a long, indifferent history, presidential primaries have acquired a new democratic dimension as a potential instrument of popular determination of the presidential nomination. With most delegates chosen by primaries for the first time in 1972, the tactic used by Hubert Humphrey in 1968 was precluded. Humphrey gained the support of key people, avoided the primaries, and won the nomination. In 1980 both nominees, Carter and Reagan, were swept into their nominations by overwhelming success in the primaries. It is no longer enough to gain the favor of party leaders and other would-be kingmakers. A possible exception to this seemingly democratic scenario is that if a succession of primaries produces a hodgepodge of winners, the kingmakers can roll up their sleeves and determine the outcome. Primaries sometimes stumble on the obstacle of low voter participation and expose the hollowness of their democratic pretensions. Although, typically, presidential primaries exceed other primaries in voter turnout, the turnout in the presidential election often exceeds by thirty points the rate for the primary. In 1980 the early primaries showed a marked rise in voter turnout, but turnout from middle primaries onward slacked off, sometimes drastically, with turnouts well under those of 1976.[8]

Viewed as a whole, the primaries are a jungle of complexity. Since the states determine their structure, they are characterized by a maze of varying detail. Some are mere expressions of preference for presidential candidates, "beauty contests," with no delegates actually being chosen. Others provide for state-wide delegate selection by congressional or state senatorial district, with or without proportional representation (under proportional representation, delegates are allotted according to the size of the popular vote received by each candidate).

The modern reform era has also witnessed adoption of the caucus system to choose delegates. It is a multitiered structure, functioning over several weeks or months, with mass participation at the initial level only. Delegates for succeeding levels are chosen by those at the preceding level. Typically, voter turnout rates are lower than for primaries, and caucus participants are drawn heavily from the ranks of local party leaders and activists.

Presidential contenders rightly complain of the inhuman strain upon their endurance caused by existing primaries and caucuses that force them to wage full-scale campaigns in a succession of states. Late in February 1972, for example, Edmund Muskie, then the front-running candidate, left Washington on a Thursday morning, spoke in Chicago that day and attended a reception, flew to Florida that night for a luncheon and two receptions on Friday, and then flew to New Hampshire that night. On Saturday, he conducted a television interview, a walking tour, appeared at dogsled races, and then flew to Hartford, Connecticut, for an evening speech.[9] For officeholders such as governors, primaries, with their weeks of intensive effort, mean neglect of official duties, and therefore discriminate in favor of unemployed politicians like Jimmy Carter in 1976 and Ronald Reagan in 1980, who can commit full time and energy to the effort.

Critiques of the 1980 primaries and caucuses emphasise that two early states, Iowa and New Hampshire, virtually determined the eventual nominees and the direction of the race. Political leaders in large states with later primaries—Michigan, Ohio, California—were irked by the disproportionate influence of smaller states with earlier primaries or caucuses. "George Bush beat Ronald Reagan 2 to 1 in Michigan," complained Governor William G. Milliken, who backed Bush in Michigan's May primary, "but that night the networks were saying it was all over for Bush because Reagan had so many delegates from earlier states."[10] Smaller states, like Iowa and New Hampshire, with early primaries and caucuses are not representative of the constituencies in either party. Neither state has any large cities nor any substantial minority population. In both 1976 and 1980 Carter did very well in the early primaries, not so well in the middle primaries, and toward the end, lost more often than he won. Even before the 1980 primaries concluded, states with later primaries drafted legislation to shift their primaries to an earlier date.[11]

The primary interlude is excessively long, three and a half months in 1980, or twice the length of the postnomination campaign. Primaries are also expensive, with shortages of funds a curse overtaking candidates and forcing them to drop out. Under some circumstances, primaries may not reliably indicate the candidate's likely performance in the postnomination campaign. In primaries with many contestants—the Democrats in 1972—a candidate such as McGovern, with a strong ideological position on issues (the Vietnam war, advocacy of school busing, relaxation of regulations on the use of marijuana, and clearly suggested approval of abortion) and favored with an efficient organization can outpace a centrist candidate such as Edmund Muskie, whose doughty occupancy of the middle ground caused him to appear bland on issues. But McGovern's strong ideological position in the postnomination campaign and the election worked badly when he was overwhelmed by another centrist opponent, Richard Nixon.

# The National Nominating Convention

The national nominating convention itself, the final arbiter, is as uniquely American as the hot dog and salt-water taffy. Everyone knows its spirit of carnival, the marching, shouting delegates, the distracted atmosphere, the frothy oratory, the grating brass bands, the milling about. As Congresswoman Barbara Jordan waited anxiously to deliver the keynote address to the 1976 Democratic convention, the party chairman Robert Strauss urged her not to be nervous. "Barbara," he said consolingly, "There'll be no one out in the hall listening to you. Forget them. Let them talk to each other. You're talking to millions of people on television." [12]

Like most citizens, H. L. Mencken, sage and cynic, viewed the nominating convention with mixed sentiments. "One sits through long sessions wishing heartily that all the delegates and alternates were in hell," he wrote, "—and then suddenly there comes a show so gaudy and hilarious, so melodramatic and obscene, so unimaginably exhilarating and preposterous that one lives a gorgeous year in an hour." [13]

## Convention Reform, 1972 and After

*The "left outs"*    Traditionally, the major parties choose delegates to their national convention by elaborate formulas that recognize the state and local organizations as the basic units of the party and that reward the performance of these organizations in past elections. In 1972, in the spirit of democracy, the national conventions, particularly the Democratic, applied "reforms" to delegate selection processes designed to make each delegation more representative of the diversity of a state's population. The Democratic party's reforms focused on improving the representation of several "left-out" population categories—blacks, women, and youth. A remarkable upsurge occurred in their presence in the party's 1972 national convention, with modest fluctuations in succeeding conventions, except for women who in 1980 increased their representation by 16 percent.

By singling out certain population groupings for studied treatment, the Democratic reforms necessarily slighted others. Among the heaviest losers at the hands of the reformers were white urban ethnics—Catholics most of all, but also Protestants and Jews. Organized labor, although favorably represented in numbers of delegates, exerted only a shadow of its usual influ-

## Representation of "Left-Out" Groups at the Democratic National Convention, 1968-80

| | Percentage of Delegates, 1968 | Percentage of Delegates, 1972 | Percentage of Delegates, 1976 | Percentage of Delegates, 1980 | Percentage of Population |
|---|---|---|---|---|---|
| Blacks | 6 | 14 | 11 | 14 | 11 |
| Women | 14 | 36 | 34 | 50 | 51 |
| Youth (30 years or under) | 2 | 23 | 15 | 11 | 30 |

Sources: Adapted from Denis G. Sullivan et al., *The Politics of Representation* (New York, 1974), p. 23; E. J. Dionne, Jr., "Minorities and Women Gain," *New York Times*, August 12, 1980; Democratic National Committee.

ence upon convention business. Accustomed to applying a decisive hand in selecting the presidential nominee, labor leaders had to swallow a candidate—George McGovern—to whom they were, and remained, largely hostile.[14] Prominent among the underrepresented were state and local party leaders, public officials, and big contributors. For all of the pretense of openness and fairness, the reform delegations in effect slighted the establishment figures who had for so long underrepresented them. Even more broadly, as Jeane Kirkpatrick notes, little attention was given in 1972 and since then to the representation of social classes. Although biological heterogeneity characterized both national conventions, social homogeneity was also the order of the day. Whether women, blacks, youth, or other categories of humanity found more traditionally at national conventions, the delegates bore the customary markings of elites: they were favored with more schooling, more income, and better jobs than most of their countrymen.[15] At the 1980 national conventions, the median income of Republican delegates was $47,000 a year, and of their Democratic counterparts $37,000 a year.[16]

*Amateurs and professionals*   In a second major recommendation, the McGovern Commission, the initial architect of the reforms, "urged" the replacement of winner-take-all primaries (primaries that award all delegates to the candidate who receives a plurality or better of the popular vote) by a method that allotted delegates proportionally according to the percentage of the popular vote received by each candidate in the primary.

McGovern's overwhelming defeat tarnished the allure of delegate selection reform, and in the Democratic party a protracted struggle commenced over how much the 1976 convention would modify the 1972 changes. In actuality, the struggle over delegate selection is a struggle for dominance between "professionals" and "amateurs"—between labor, party regulars, centrists, and old liberals, on the one hand, and insurgents, new liberals, leftists, and newer groups such as blacks, on the other.

To reconcile these camps, a commission led by Baltimore Councilwoman Barbara Mikulski simultaneously endorsed rules requiring "affirmative action plans" to encourage representation of "traditionally underrepresented groups" in the delegate selection process, and encouraged the selection of "public officials, party officials" as "at-large" delegates. The commission barred winner-take-all primaries, and required the use of proportional representation in allocating state delegates. To avoid an excess of frivolous candidacies a minimum cutoff of 15 percent of the vote was set for candidates running either in primaries and or in caucus-convention meetings, to qualify for delegates.[17]

A further effort to patch up differences between the professionals and the amateurs was made by a commission led by Morley Winograd, chairman of the Michigan Democratic party. A powerful new ingredient infused its labors when its pro-Carter members worked to ensure that rules prepared for 1980 would facilitate the President's renomination. The Carter forces and the party professionals united in pushing to raise the minimum cutoff of 15 percent to 20 percent. Ultimately a compromise arranged for the 1980 national convention allowed the state party to set the cutoff at no lower than 15 percent and no higher than 20 percent. The Democratic National Committee also adopted the Winograd commission's proposed rules for shortening the interval of delegate selection from six months to three months, for requiring states to set candidate-filing deadlines 30 to 90 days before the election, for increasing the size of state delegations by 10 percent to enlarge the representation of state party and elected officials, and for limiting participation in primaries to Democrats by barring cross-over primaries. Critics charged that these rule changes unduly favored the professionals over the amateurs and stifled potential challenges to Carter's renomination.

Subsequently, the amateurs gained concessions when the Democratic National Committee adopted rules requiring state delegations to the 1980 national convention to be equally divided between men and women and barring winner-take-all contests in single-delegate districts. (In some states, delegates are chosen by districts that usually correspond to congressional districts.) Consequently, all districts were required to select several delegates in 1980, divided proportionately among candidates whose support exceeded a state's minimum cut-off.[18]

The Republican party has made fewer and less sweeping changes in delegate selection. Recommendations of a Delegate and Organization Committee were adopted for the 1976 convention. These expanded the presence of "left-out groups" and reduced the inclusion of party leaders by eliminating them as *ex officio* delegates. Participation was enhanced by opening primaries and conventions to all citizens. The Republican party recommends, but does not require, that states adopt "affirmative-action plans" to expand the presence of minorities; winner-take-all primaries have not been abolished.

Clearly, the parties' rule changes and their tradition of allotting bonus votes for states which in the last election elected the party's candidates to national and state offices affect candidate strategies and prospects. In 1976, the smaller states gained under Republican rules, with greater advantage accruing to Reagan than to Ford. Meantime, Carter was disadvantaged by the Democrats' 1976 rules, which gave less weight to Southern states where he was strong, and more to the large industrial states of the Northeast and Midwest, where his rivals flourished. On the other hand, Carter's strong showing in the South in 1976 enabled it to achieve a greater gain of delegates than any other region for 1980.[19]

## The Convention at Work

The convention poses for the top contender and his managers two vitally important tasks, failure in either one of which might spell the difference between victory and defeat. The first is to keep the bloc of pledged or promised delegates "nailed fast" to prevent their straying "off the reservation" to another candidate. The second is to control the convention machinery to permit its manipulation for, rather than against, the candidate. In a contested convention these undertakings are a high-tension ordeal. Jim Farley wrote of the 1932 Democratic convention,

> The nervous strain during this period of suspense was very close to the limit of physical endurance. . . . I was working eighteen or nineteen hours a day, conversing with hundreds of people, constantly consulting with other leaders, receiving reports from every delegation, and meeting at least twice daily with several hundred newspapermen. I . . . slept a few hours just before dawn if the opportunity offered. . . . Hundreds of other men were caught in the same dizzy whirl and were trying to keep up the same maddening pace.[20]

To control the convention machinery, the candidate and his managers must concentrate upon several key parts. Much of their effort occurs before the convention begins and centers upon the national committee and the national chairman who decide when and where the convention is to be held and make the local arrangements. The national committee selects the temporary chairman of the convention, who delivers the keynote address. Since the tone and tendency of this oration shape the convention's initial and sometimes decisive mood, the selection of the temporary chairman may touch off a fierce struggle. His further power to hand down parliamentary rulings helpful to the candidate he favors adds zest to the combat.

Normally, an incumbent President seeking reelection can exert assured control over a convention. Nixon's direction of the 1972 Republican convention illuminates the phenomenon to the point that his White House aides induced conservative Republican delegates to swallow the bitter pill of omitting an antilabor plank. Nixon, courting the labor vote, could not bear a discordant sound on the subject, and there was none.[21]

But in 1980 Carter, although renominated, was in a far weaker position at the Democratic convention. His standing in the polls was abysmally low, and other Democratic office-seekers accepted his renomination but not without bitter grumbling. Edward Kennedy, his chief competitor, and his supporters prevailed in inserting into the platform proposals for a huge jobs program and for condemnation of high interest rates. Both planks repudiated Carter's ongoing policies. Carter's Republican opponent, Ronald Reagan, who in earlier candidacy had asked for a platform that would be "a banner of bold colors, no pastel shades," was also embarrassed in 1980 by the Republican platform's omission of the party's past endorsement of the equal rights amendment. In his acceptance address and other statements during the convention, Reagan emphasized his own commitment to fighting discrimination based on sex and to promoting equality of opportunity.

A race's outcome is often determined by "deals" arranged by the candidates' convention representatives. Franklin Roosevelt was eventually put across in 1932 by a bargain for the vice-presidency, which not a few times in the nation's history has determined the choice of the presidential nominee. A major rival for the presidential nomination, John Nance Garner of Texas, suddenly became the object of the Roosevelt camp's attention. Farley suggested to Garner's representative, Sam Rayburn, that if Texas threw its support to Roosevelt, Garner could have the vice-presidency. Rayburn answered crustily that he and his co-workers had come to Chicago to nominate Garner for President, although they did not want a stalemate. Eventually Garner made the decision. Fearful that an ugly convention deadlock might damage public confidence and cost the Democrats the election, Garner released his delegates and reluctantly exchanged his proud Speakership for the quietude of the vice-presidency. Texas and California, which were Garner delegations, went over to Roosevelt and the nomination was clinched.[22]

## The Convention Decides

The convention can also be viewed as a series of decisions, climbing, by phases, to the climax of the presidential nomination. The proceedings of the convention committees—credentials, rules, permanent organization, and platform or resolutions—are often the harbinger of things to come. The committees' reports to the whole convention often provide an early test of strength of the rival candidates. In the 1980 Democratic convention, Carter forces prevailed over the rival forces of Edward M. Kennedy when a rule was adopted early in the convention requiring delegates to vote on the first ballot for the presidential candidate they were elected to support. The showdown vote, assuring Carter of renomination, prompted Kennedy to terminate his candidacy.

The convention's balloting may simply be a routine ratification of the candidate's success constructed in the previous months of careful effort. The first-ballot nominations of Carter and Reagan in 1980 were no surprise. A succession of ballotings, which is not uncommon, reflects the continuing struggle for delegates and requires adroit maneuvers. It may seem that the prize of the nomination goes to the man with the best organization and the most compelling political personality. But actually nominees are weeded out in advance to some extent; not all able individuals are eligible in practice. One of America's favorite candidates has been the military hero. Of the thirty-nine men who have been elected President, thirteen have been military veterans. Both parties have thrice nominated former military men in the same year. The Republicans tapped no less than four Civil War generals; Theodore Roosevelt was the glamorous Rough Rider of the Spanish-American War; and Dwight Eisenhower achieved international military renown in World War II. John Kennedy's valor in that war was not forgotten, either. In this century governors have been the leading source of presidential candidates, eighteen of them having been nominated after 1900. The United States Senate, once a liability, is fast becoming a factory of presidential candidates. The chief Democratic contenders in 1972—McGovern, Muskie, Jackson, and Humphrey—were all Senators, and the Republican standard-bearer—Richard Nixon—was a former Senator. The Senator's importance has been enhanced in recent years by television and the dominance of foreign affairs, a subject that traditionally receives heavy attention in the Senate. The 1980 struggle between two former governors, Carter and Reagan, signaled a new ascendance of domestic problems.

The Mountain States did not provide a candidate until Barry Goldwater in 1964, nor did the South for more than a century until Lyndon Johnson's nomination in 1964. Of the sixty-five men nominated by the two parties since 1856, forty-one have come from either New York State or the Middle West. Population shifts favoring the South, Southwest, and Far West, will likely enhance the representation of those regions in future presidential nominations. The 1980 nominations of Carter and Reagan reflect these shifts. Religion, race, and sex have also been selective factors for the nomination. Kennedy's breakthrough in 1960 as the first Catholic to become President may, before many more elections come to pass, throw the gates open to all. Before this only a white Anglo-Saxon Protestant male was considered eligible. The increasing incidence of women candidates for offices at all levels of government enhances the likelihood of a woman being nominated for President or Vice President.

After the presidential nomination comes the usually anticlimactic selection of the Vice President. This decision is ordinarily governed by the tradition of "balancing the ticket" geographically. (Among the exceptions is the Truman-Barkley, Missouri-Kentucky, border state ticket of 1948.)

After Wilson's nomination in 1912, his manager, A. S. Burleson, telephoned to say that the convention was leaning toward Thomas R. Marshall of Indiana. "But, Burleson," Wilson remonstrated, "he is a very small caliber man." Burleson did not argue the point but noted that Marshall was from the Middle West and a doubtful state. His candidacy would ideally supplement Wilson's. "All right, go ahead," Wilson said, not too agreeably.[23] Wilson notwithstanding, the opinion of the presidential nominee is also weighty in choosing the Vice President. The degree to which the choice is specific varies.

Prior to his 1980 nomination, Ronald Reagan utilized a public opinion poll to determine which of various possible vice presidential nominees would most strengthen his ticket.[24] His pursuit of a "dream ticket," with Gerald Ford as his running mate, culminated in a package deal that reportedly called for dismembering the presidency, with Ford as Vice President in operational control of the executive branch, and Reagan as chairman of the board. Fortunately for the presidency, this sudden threat to its existence terminated when the deal collapsed and raced like a shooting star into oblivion.[25]

Although the presidential contest normally centers on the nominees of the two major parties, minor parties often advance presidential nominees, sometimes with marked effect. James B. Weaver, the Populist party nominee of 1892, Theodore Roosevelt as Bull Moose nominee in 1912, and George C. Wallace as nominee of the American party in 1968 were potent candidacies. Roosevelt, for instance, surpassed his Republican rival, Taft, in their three-way race with Wilson.

In 1980 John B. Anderson, Republican Congressman of Illinois, after scoring only limited success in the Republican primaries, announced his "independent candidacy" for President. Anderson's effort coincided with a feeble moment in the major parties' long history. Both parties were buffeted by steadily declining numbers of voters who identify with them. If Anderson's candidacy proved successful, not merely in the sense of winning, but by affecting the outcome for his rival candidates, the major parties would be given a further push down the slopes of decomposition, and candidates in future elections would be encouraged to imitate Anderson's course. Reagan's landslide victory deprived Anderson of this leverage, but Anderson's capture of a sizeable seven percent of the vote could make his type of candidacy consequential in future close elections.

# The Postconvention Campaign

### Strategy

Radio and television, wider press coverage, and a burgeoning transportation technology have made campaigning strenuous for the modern candidate and have driven him to enlarge his staff. The postconvention campaign, like other phases of the route to the presidency, requires a series of major strategic decisions. Strategy on one level is the selection of an array of voter entities, which when pieced together will provide an electoral majority. Kennedy's 1960 strategy focused upon nine large states (New York, Pennsylvania, California, Michigan, Texas, Illinois, Ohio, New Jersey, and Massachusetts) comprising 237 of the 269 electoral votes required to elect a President. These plus sixty more electoral votes added by Lyndon Johnson in the deep South or by several New England and Middle Western states would make victory certain. Indispensable to Nixon's narrow 1968 victory was a "Southern strategy" that produced a sufficient number of Southern electoral votes to bring success.[26] In 1976 Carter resolved to campaign widely to win a broad base of support: "I would rather have a six percent victory in all the states than a fifteen percent victory in fifteen states and lose the rest of them."[27]

A further phase of strategy is the welding of groups—national, racial, ideological, and economic—into a winning coalition. In both his 1968 and 1972 campaigns, Richard Nixon pursued a strategic vision of "a new American majority." In one of his most extended discourses on this subject, Nixon perceived a "new alignment" of political forces that "is already a new majority" that would endure "for generations to come." Strange bedfellows comprised the alignment—long-time Republicans committed to freedom and enterprise and wary of "centralized and domineering" government; the "new South," emancipated from "racist appeal" and one-party voting habits and moving rapidly in industrial development; the "black militant" who preferred black private enterprise to "handouts or welfare"; and the "new liberal" who valued participatory democracy with "more personal freedom and less government domination."[28] In 1972, Nixon further defined this "new American majority" to include at its core blue collar workers and Catholics, who, Nixon said, lived "in the rings around the cities, they're a new middle class."[29] He sounded themes alluring to workers and ethnics outside the central city, stressing the high note of patriotism and the work ethic. Nixon also pitched his appeal to many older Jews who had fled the cities for the suburbs and who were moving to the right of their usually liberal position on busing, scatter-site housing, and law and order.*

The candidate must also make several basic organizational choices. He can choose between relying heavily upon the regular party machinery or work largely outside it. In 1972, Nixon worked outside the party organization, utilizing the Committee for the Reelection of the President, headed by the President's campaign manager, John Mitchell, and his successor, former Minnesota Congressman Clark McGregor. Their top aides were drawn from the White House staff and such key presidential assistants as H. R. Haldeman, John Ehrlichman, and Charles W. Colson. Generally, the committee was disdainful of the regular party organization; nearly all the members were amateurs in politics and young men on-the-make, and the President's campaign resembled the style of California politics where candidates offer themselves as public figures rather than as party men, with their roles defined by such non-party types as public relations experts and tactical strategists.[30] The reelection committee recruited some three dozen "surrogates"—chiefly senators and governors—as stand-ins for the President, who did little campaigning himself. A finance committee raised untold quantities of money that would have left Mark Hanna aghast, using high pressure means that often strayed into extortion.

Be it also noted that the reelection committee, closely meshed with the

---

*For an evaluation of "the new American majority," see pp. 144–47.

White House staff, perpetrated the break-in at the national Democratic headquarters and acts of political espionage and sabotage. Not surprisingly, soon after becoming President, Gerald Ford made plain that he would not create a separate organization to conduct his electoral campaign in 1976.

Another strategic problem concerns the candidate's personal involvement in the campaign. How much of the campaign emphasis should be on issues and how much on personality? Eisenhower, national hero and international personage in 1952, was under less pressure to emphasize issues than the lesser known Kennedy in 1960, whose campaign stressed issues. In his 1972 reelection campaign, Nixon made a minimum of campaign appearances. "He doesn't have to campaign," said his chief of staff, H. R. Haldeman. "He doesn't have to establish his identity. He's been exposed for twenty-five years. Because of TV and his trip to China and the man on the moon, he's probably the best-known human being in the history of the world. For him to campaign would be counter-productive, superfluous." [31] To the extent that Nixon campaigned, he did so in discharging the duties and exploiting the resources of the presidency.

Should the candidate concentrate on mass appeal via radio, television, and big rallies? Or should he do the whistle-stop routine, as Harry Truman did in 1948, with folksy talks to hundreds of small audiences across the nation? For all of the magic of radio and television, candidates still heavily invest their time and treasure in going out to the voters. Although in 1960 the four television debates supplied the candidates with an audience of unsurpassed size, both Kennedy and Nixon traveled by rail and air to give brief talks in hundreds of communities and to shake thousands of hands. A powerful inducement for whistle-stopping is Truman's extraordinary success at it in 1948 in achieving a victory unpredicted by the public opinion polls or by any reputable politician save Truman himself.

Truman made his whistle-stop speeches from the back of a reconstructed Pullman car, the *Ferdinand Magellan*, purchased in 1942 for one dollar from the Association of American Railroads. According to the 1948 routine, the local high school band blared out "Hail to the Chief" upon Truman's arrival. Then came a gift for the President, his expression of thanks, his welcome to local Democratic leaders, and compliments to the citizenry for their new highway or factory. Hereupon Truman ripped into the Republicans and the Eightieth Congress with wild ridicule. His Republican listeners heard their party brethren referred to as "gluttons of privilege" and "bloodsuckers with offices in Wall Street." ("Ridicule is a wonderful weapon," Truman told his aides.) After his political talk, Truman asked the crowd, "Howja like to meet my family?" and he proceeded to introduce Mrs. Truman as "the boss" and his daughter Margaret as "my baby" and "the boss's boss." The family bit delighted the crowds. [32]

## Debates

In 1960 presidential campaigning took a new turn when the traditional political debate of congressional and local elections was adapted to the presidential canvass and the idiosyncracies of television. The resulting Kennedy-Nixon TV debates had sizeable impact upon the electoral outcome. When the debates began, Nixon appeared the likely electoral winner, with Kennedy rather well behind; when they ended, the contestants' positions were reversed. The debates helpfully provided the voters with a close-up of the candidates without their props of speechwriters and idea men. The candidates could be seen thinking and speaking under stress, a situation that casts a great shaft of light upon character.

But the debate system is not without flaws. The presidency has a limited need of forensic talent; the office is far more than a great debate. No President, fortunately, is expected to formulate in a matter of seconds answers to great questions of foreign policy. Debates, while revealing the candidates' personalities in sharp topographical relief, add little to public understanding of issues. Indeed a built-in drawback of TV debates may be overattention to personality and superficial examination of the issues.

In 1976, after a long hiatus, debates which had been consistently spurned by incumbent Presidents, were resumed, thanks to special circumstances. Neither nominee had ever faced a national electorate, and the incumbent President, Gerald Ford, was clearly the underdog. He had to debate to close the gap. Picking up momentum after the first debate, Ford, in the second encounter, committed an incredible gaffe when he declared that Eastern Europe was not under Soviet domination. A reporter who witnessed the debate recalled, "There was an audible intake of air. I kept thinking of the Alliance of Poles Hall in Cleveland, and how they might be throwing beer bottles at the screen by then."[33] Ford's gathering momentum now slowed, and its former speed was never regained. In 1980 Carter and Reagan met in a single debate, to the latter's profit. Reagan's campaign, which had become becalmed, was revived by his performance. The 1980 debate was consistent with the previous debates in working to the disadvantage of the presidential incumbent, whether Carter or Ford, or an incumbency's defender, as Vice President Nixon was of Eisenhower's presidency in 1960.

## New Technology, New Expertise

The selection of the contemporary President is assisted by a cluster of gadgetry contributed by science and technology. The computer has become a mighty sword of the presidential campaign. In 1972 for example, beginning in the New Hampshire primary, computers played a major part throughout Nixon's quest for reelection. In New Hampshire, the name of every registered Republican and every registered independent was fed into a computer by the Nixon organization. Everyone on the list was telephoned by a volunteer and was sent a letter typed and addressed by computer. The letter asked voters if they supported Nixon, and, if they answered that yes, a second computer letter asked if they would work in the President's behalf. Those who acquiesced received a further letter specifying how they could help, and just before primary day all those who answered yes to the first letter but did not volunteer to work received another letter reminding them to vote.[34]

In the postconvention campaign, computers carved census tracts into patterns; selected counties whose waverings in the past proved critical to their state's electoral vote; and had the names of their citizens sorted into categories labeled "independents," "gettable Democrats," and "don't knows," the information for which was obtained by massive telephone inquiries. The names, thus sorted, were stored in computers. Near the end of the campaign, in the nine largest states, eight million exhortative mailgrams were prepared and coded according to many variables (for example, county, age, income, Spanish-speaking, black, ethnic origin), while nine million letters were addressed to registered Republicans. Eventually seventeen million mailings ensued, then the mightiest direct mail effusion in American political history.

Is not the computer a boon to the ideal of an effective democratic presidency? In facilitating the dissemination of campaign material, in discovering the voter—independent or undecided—who might benefit from that material, the computer serves the higher vision. Clearly the quality of the material itself that the computer assists is crucial—well and good if it is reasoned and informed, but a disservice and even a danger if it falsifies and divides. As yet, computer services are unregulated by campaign laws, whether used for the compiling of mailing lists or for the identification of voters.

*Television*     During the 1950s and 1960s, outlays for television time rose at a galloping pace that finally slowed in 1972, when a new law forced broadcasters to charge their lowest rates for political advertising.[35] The lack of primary contests for the Republican presidential nomination also reduced spending, and, even more important, campaign strategists were impressed with research revealing that TV advertisements ranked low (twenty-fourth) among factors influencing undecided voters.[36]

By 1980, however, television was the most voracious consumer of campaign dollars, with the soaring costs of commercials well outpacing the rate of inflation. Richard G. Stearns, director of delegate selection for the Kennedy campaign observed, "It is impossible for a candidate to buy time at prevailing commercial rates with the amount of money we're allowed to raise and spend. Perhaps we're getting close to the point, given the cost of television, and if we're going to keep the constraints on the candidates that we have, that we're going to have to make free television time available."[37]

Television's news coverage of campaigns pays only scant attention to issues, concentrating instead on trivia that makes for flashy pictures—hecklers, motorcades, airport arrivals, balloons, rallies.[38] Television contains its own built-in biases on presidential candidates, preferring those who project cool attributes and a positive image, like John Kennedy, to the more voluble and emotional Hubert Humphrey.[39] Political scientists Thomas E. Patterson and Robert D. McClure contend that television, on which vast sums are spent, does not command results anywhere near commensurate with the candidate's expenditure. The public, they note, seldom evaluate candidates on the basis of looks and other surface phenomena emphasized by the image-makers, but on the basis of previous political performance that television does not communicate.[40]

At best, television is proving a mixed blessing in linking presidential selection processes to acceptable democratic standards. On the positive side, television can enable candidates who are little known to gain rapid recognition, as John Kennedy did in 1960, or to bring into the national political arena a serious latent issue, as Eugene McCarthy presented the Vietnam war in 1968. Since the presidency is a highly personal office, television, in its better moments, can be incredibly efficient in providing a national close-up of the candidate and his manner, which may be a key to his character and his thinking processes. But television also bears consequences inhospitable to democracy. It may overstress the candidate's appearance and style at the expense of personal substance and depth on issues. It injects new breeds of functionaries into presidential politics—advertising and marketing specialists and opinion manipulators—whose comprehension of, and commitment to, democratic ways may be frail.

*Opinion polls*   A major component of the modern presidential campaign is the public opinion poll conducted in the candidate's behalf, often by specialists in market research. From polls, the candidate learns how to reach voters better through television, radio, and the press, what issues to stress, what portions of his projected image to refurbish. Polls reveal candidate effectiveness in regard to issues and geographic areas and illuminate the impact of major campaign themes. Polls measure trends in the candidate's strength during the campaign, detecting surges and declines as they occur. Thanks to improved sample design and identification of likely voters, polls have steadily reduced their average error. A major hazard for polling error is the nonvoter, a formidable element in the primaries where turnouts of 10 to 25 percent are common. And polls can have a psychological dimension; if favorable, they buoy the confidence of workers, potential contributors, and voters. If starkly unfavorable, they fall like a palsied hand on the candidate's effort.[41] In 1964 the Goldwater organization cancelled a poll because it did not want to "pay for tidings of disaster,"[42] and Pat Caddell, McGovern's pollster, said that after bringing his results to the campaign's managers, he "felt like the recreation director on the Titanic."[43] By increasingly utilizing polls, candidates depend far less on local party leaders for grassroots information and can blithely bypass them.[44] Yet the shaky dependability of polls as predictors of electoral outcomes was glaringly revealed in 1980 when major polls unanimously anticipated a close election rather than a Reagan sweep.

*The professional campaign firm*   Altogether, the skills required to exploit the political uses of the computer, television, advertising, and the polls are represented in the professional firms that provide an emporium of services for the presidential candidate. Joseph Napolitan in Humphrey's 1968 campaign and David Garth in John Anderson's of 1980 are illustrative of this new breed. Managers, working with the candidate's staff, advise on campaign activities and themes by perceiving the election as a problem to be solved by research, planning, and management. Professionally managed campaigns have a look-alike quality that begins with demographic and survey research that becomes the foundation of formal planning. Advertising, particularly on television, direct mailings, and telephone banks are the professional's standard tools for communicating with the voters. The core of the professional's effort is research—demographic and past voting behavior studies, opinion polling, issue research, and research about the opposition. Just as soap is test-marketed, so are the candidate and the campaign.

The rise of the professionals is rooted in changes in the political environment, rampant growth of the primaries, and a highly mobile population. An estimated 20 percent of all Americans move each year, hobbling traditional precinct organization and impelling a massive shift from print to sight and sound communications. The vast majority of Americans obtain the bulk of their political information from television, and the first generation to grow up watching television has now entered the electorate.[45]

## The Money Problem

Where does the money come from to feed the voracious appetite of the campaign? From the 1950s onward, campaign spending has taken a quantum jump, thanks mainly to television and its exorbitant advertising costs, and the growing body of professionals who enlist in the campaign for robust fees. Nixon in 1972 spent six times his expenditure in 1960, and his opponent, George McGovern, spent three times as much as Nixon's earlier opponent, John Kennedy.[46] Until the 1976 election presidential campaign financing was virtually wide-open, permitting multi-million dollar contributions by individuals and unlimited spending.

*Financing Nixon's 1972 campaign*   For Nixon and his 1972 campaign, these had the makings of a cornucopia. As the postconvention campaign moved into high gear, the President's campaign treasurers took in an unprecedented $100,000 a day. The fund raiser without parallel who pressured business contributors heavy-handedly was Maurice H. Stans, former Secretary of Commerce and chairman of the Finance Committee to Relect the President. Hundred dollar bills—the standard remittance—inundated him to the point that he sometimes had as much as $350,000 to $700,000 in cash sconced in his safe at one time.

*Regulating campaign finance*   Notwithstanding the rampant wrongdoing of 1972, the early 1970s were a rare interval in American political history, when several reforms of campaign financing were instituted. The Federal Election Campaign Act of 1971, which became operative in April 1972 (Nixon's big money-raising was completed prior to that date) seeks to regulate the problem through publicity and disclosure. All political committees that anticipate receiving or spending more than $1,000 in any year for any federal candidate must register and submit periodic reports. The Act requires reporting of every expenditure and every contribution of $100 or more. Comprehensive disclosure is based on the assumption that in democracy voters have a right to know the sources of candidates' funds and that if questionable sources are publicly exposed, they will either cease or offend the voters to the candidate's detriment. The 1971 Act also limits media spending. A second reform, the Revenue Act of 1971, is designed to increase the number of small contributors. The Act provides that campaign contributors may claim a tax credit against a portion of their federal income tax, or a tax deduction for the full amount of contributions, up to specified limits. The 1971 law also allows taxpayers to designate $1 of their tax obligation to go to a fund to subsidize presidential campaigns.

*Post-Watergate regulation*   Following revelations of the gross fund-raising abuses of the Nixon campaign and his resignation from the presidency, Congress in 1974 amended the 1971 law. Contributions of individuals were henceforth limited to $1,000 and of committees of private individuals formed to elect a candidate, to $5,000 for each primary or election. Earlier limits on media spending were repealed and superseded by overall limits on primary and general election expenditures. Especially innovative was the provision for partial funding for presidential primaries. Matching funds up to $5.5 million were provided for any candidate successful in raising $5,000 in individual contributions of $250 or less in each of twenty states. In the preconvention stage, candidates can decline or accept public funding. In 1980 John Connally alone of the principal candidates chose to decline. Candidates accepting public funds in the preconvention stage were allowed to spend $17.7 million, a 35 percent increase over 1976 to reflect inflation. For the postconvention campaign, full public funding was provided. In 1980, each major party nominee was limited to $29.4 million, increased from $21.8 million in 1976 due to inflation.

The 1974 legislation created a full-time, bipartisan Federal Election Commission (FECA) of six members, with two each appointed by the President, the Speaker of the House, and the President pro tempore of the Senate. The Commission administers the federal election laws and their public finance provisions, and oversees the full disclosure requirements for campaign contributions and expenditures, resulting in voluminous, exacting reports, which prompted Richard B. Cheyney, Ford's chief of staff, to conclude that after dealing with FECA and its staff of lawyers and accountants, a candidate is "beter equipped to serve as director of the Office of Management and Budget than as President."[47]

Portions of the 1974 amendments ran afoul of the Supreme Court in *Buckley* v. *Valeo* (424 U.S. 1, 1976) which required presidential nomination and Senate approval of all members of the Federal Election Commission in order to comply with the constitutional doctrine of separation of powers. The court also ruled that limitations on the amount of expenditures by candidates and their families, by individuals making independent expenditures in behalf of a candidate, and overall limits on campaign expenditures violated the First Amendment's freedom of speech. However, if candidates accepted public financing, the court upheld limitations on overall expenditures as a condition of the grant. In 1976, amendments were adopted to the 1971 and 1974 laws, reflecting the court's decision.

Herbert Alexander, the leading authority on campaign finance, notes that the public campaign finance provisions were a key to Carter's success in 1976. The law handicapped better known candidates, attractive to wealthy contributors, who could have far outspent Carter. Likewise, without federal money, Carter could not have consolidated his early lead. In 1980, he enjoyed a diametrically opposite advantage, with more robust financial connections and an early lead in fund-raising over his Democratic rivals.[48]

Alexander also contends that FECA helped diminish the steady sharp increases in campaign spending, with total outlays in 1976 less than in 1972 for the postconvention campaign.[49] Advocates of the reforms assert that they drive out the traditional, influence-seeking fatcats and special interest groups and encourage the candidate to run an efficient organization and to muster creativity in fund-raising. Critics of the reforms believe that campaigns have become both overregulated and underfinanced—witness the decline of grass-roots activity and the virtual disappearance of such traditional campaign artifacts as buttons, banners, and bumperstickers.

In 1980, complaints of niggardly public financing intensified when rising campaign costs far outpaced the Consumer Price Index, to which public funding is geared. Television costs jumped upwards of 60 percent; airline charters soared, reflecting steep price increases in jet fuel; mailing costs rose 50 percent; and personnel costs followed with salaries of $40,000 to $50,000 as compared to $25,000 in 1976. Particular criticism was vented at the

$1,000 ceiling on individual contributions. Campaign managers advocated a rise to $1,500, but Congress did not respond. Other critics assailed the 1974 law as unduly curbing the candidate's ability to communicate with the public, by not adjusting sufficiently to the severe inflation of 1980 and the sharp increase in the number of primaries. Candidates chafe at the thickets of regulations and accounting controls. The 1974 act, contends Alexander, misses the point that "the purpose of campaigning is to reach the voter, not to keep a tidy set of books."[50]

# The Electoral College

The final stage of selecting the President—his actual election—was a very knotty, much debated issue at the Constitutional Convention. Eventually the electoral college method of choosing the President emerged as a compromise. In actuality, there are fifty electoral colleges, one in each state. The number of electors in a given state equals the number of its Senators and Representatives in Congress.

## Choosing the Electors

Each elector has one vote, and a majority of the whole number of electors appointed is required to choose the President. If no presidential candidate receives a majority, the Constitution directs the House of Representatives to complete the election of the President. The House is limited in choice to the three candidates receiving the greatest number of the electors' votes.

The Constitution authorizes each state to appoint its electors "in such manner as the legislature thereof may direct." In the first three presidential elections the electors were chosen chiefly by the state legislatures. Thereafter, popular choice gradually took hold. By 1824 electors were chosen by popular vote in all but six states, and in 1832 in all states but South Carolina, which clung to legislative election until 1864. Popular choice has been registered through two main systems—election of electors by districts and election of electors on a "general ticket." Each system spawned numerous variations. In the former method, the people would vote in districts relatively equal in population, each district choosing one elector. Districts often coincided with congressional districts. The district system was widely employed in the early days of the Constitution; indeed, according to Madison, most of the Founding Fathers strongly preferred it. In practice, electors were pledged to particular candidates. Whichever candidate's elector then carried a district was the official elector of that district. Since, in a given state, the elector of one candidate might triumph in one district, and the elector of a different candidate might win in another district, the total electoral vote of a state might be divided among several candidates. The division tended to follow the pattern of the congressional elections in the House districts.

In time a political party, having gained control of a state, would sniff an opportunity to avoid the division of its electoral strength by introducing the general ticket system, which applies an ancient principle of gamesmanship—"winner take all." The party carrying the state, by however small a popular plurality, wins all the state's electors and the minority party or parties get none. Since 1836 all states have used the general ticket system, except for a brief relapse in Michigan to the district system following the 1892 election.

Although the states determine the method of choosing their electors, the timetable of a presidential election is set by national law. On the first Tuesday after the first Monday in November, every fourth year, the qualified popular voters of the several states choose the presidential electors. On the first Monday after the second Wednesday in December the electors meet in their respective states to cast their votes for President. On January 6 the electoral votes are counted in the presence of the two houses of Congress and the results are announced by the presiding officer—the Vice President.

*The electors vote*    The Founding Fathers' expectation that the electors would exercise an element of free judgment in choosing the President was quickly crushed by the appearance of political parties, the Federalists and the Anti-Federalists, the latter soon becoming the Republican-Democratic party. George Washington's two presidential candidacies were untouched by electoral vote politics. Following his departure from the presidential scene, the electors took to party-line voting in choosing John Adams as President in 1796 over his chief rival, Thomas Jefferson. Thereafter, with rare individual exceptions, the electors have functioned as the automatons of their parties. Only rarely has an elector violated his pledge to vote for a particular presidential candidate, but none of these lapses has ever affected the outcome.

Custom, which dictates the electors' voting conduct, has been reinforced by legislation and court opinion. State statutes range from those calling for a party nomination of electors, which itself is a presumption of pledged electors, to the laws of two states prescribing that electors vote for the party nominees, regardless of personal preference. In *Ray* v. *Blair* (343 U.S. 214, 1952) the Supreme Court gave its blessing to these arrangements, upholding a state law empowering party organizations to fix the qualifications of candidates for nomination as electors. The state law, the Court said, simply converted custom into legal obligation.

*Popular vote*    The selection of electors has also been altered by revisions of the presidential ballot that confronts the popular voter in the polling booth. One is the requirement, first adopted in Nebraska in 1917, that electors be listed and voted for as a party group rather than individually. Another change brought the names of the presidential nominees on the ballot with those of the electors. The latest evolutionary step is the presidential short ballot, on which only the names of the presidential and vice-presidential nominees appear, an innovation speeded by the use of voting machines, which impose severer limitations of space than the paper ballot does. Each popular vote cast by the presidential short ballot counts for the elector whose name, although unknown to the voters, is on file with the state secretary of state.

Originally, under the Constitution, each elector cast two votes for President, one of which had to be for a candidate who was not an inhabitant of the elector's state. This provision, coupled with the necessity of an electoral vote majority for victory, barred even the largest state from choosing by itself a President from among its own inhabitants. The double feature virtually compelled the selection of a candidate of national reputation. The candidate receiving the second highest number of electoral votes became Vice President, a method that brought into the number-two post men of presidential caliber like John Adams and Thomas Jefferson. The double-voting system, for all of its seeming merit, was abandoned in 1804 with the adoption of the Twelfth Amendment. The double vote had crashed on the rocks in the election of 1800, when a deadlock developed between the Republican candidates, Jefferson and Aaron Burr. The election passed into the House of Representatives, where the rival Federalist party, which controlled the outcome, favored Burr but was pressured by Alexander Hamilton, its national chieftain, into backing Jefferson. Snatched from a disaster they wished never to encounter again, the Republicans championed the Twelfth Amendment, establishing separate electoral votes for the President and the Vice President.[51]

## Defects of the Electoral College

The existing electoral vote arrangements have long been the object of heavy criticism and dire warnings. The critics hold that the electoral system violates basic tenets of democracy and that its many mechanical flaws invite breakdown and the eruption of a presidential election into a nightmare of civil strife.[52]

The electoral college system has failed three times to elect a President: in 1800, 1824, and 1876. Three elections are also often indicted for flaunting the voice of the people, for electing Presidents who received fewer popular votes than their opponents. The suspected elections are John Quincy Adams' triumph over Jackson in 1824, Rutherford B. Hayes's over Samuel J. Tilden in 1876, and Benjamin Harrison's over Cleveland in 1888. Jackson's showing in 1824 is clouded by the fact that no popular votes were cast in six of the twenty-four states. In 1876 Tilden received some two hundred thousand more popular votes than Hayes. Since fraud and violence marked the popular voting in the South, North, and West, Tilden's popular margin is not unblemished. Harrison's victory by a popular minority over Cleveland cannot be gainsaid.

*General ticket system*    Of all the features of electoral college practice the general ticket system has raised the severest criticism. The general ticket, as political scientist Lucius Wilmerding demonstrates, puts the presidency on a federative rather than a national basis. It has taken "the choice of the President from the people of the nation at large and given it, in effect, to the people of the large states."[53] The principle of winner take all serves to disenfranchise a substantial minority of popular votes or even more outrageously transfers them to the use of the candidate against whom they were cast. Charles Evans Hughes in 1916, for instance, carried Minnesota by a popular plurality of only 359 but received all twelve of that state's electoral votes. A large part of those electoral votes were made possible by thousands of Minnesotans who voted against Hughes. On a national scale, John W. Davis received six million popular votes in 1924 that earned him no electoral votes at all—or in reality were transferred to the use of his rival, Calvin Coolidge—while two million others brought him 136 electoral votes.

The general ticket system's rough handling of minority popular votes extravagantly favors the large states. In 1980 the pluralities of the twelve largest states controlled 285 electoral votes. If these states should vote for a single candidate, he would be elected regardless of the strength of his opposition in those states and in the remaining thirty-eight states and the District of Columbia. The general ticket system, this is to say, enables the popular voter in the large states to participate in the choice of a larger number of electors than the voter of a small state. In 1964 a popular voter in New York shared in the choice of forty-three electors, and in Nevada only three. The candidate of the popular majority of the nation is far from certain to prevail in an electoral college where the representation of each state is not that of its people but of its plurality. The likelihood of minority Presidents will surely increase in our present era of close Presidential elections.

The general ticket system, with its winner-take-all principle that rewards the victor more lavishly than any other system, wreaks other distortions. It prods parties into seeking out their candidates in big states such as New York and Ohio, while ignoring the small states, whose citizens may be equally talented. The general ticket system also encouraged the historic one-party solid South. The Republican party, faced with a hopeless minority position, for years maintained no serious organization in Southern states. The general ticket system also causes party campaigning to be concentrated in doubtful states and in large states. New York, Ohio, and Illinois are regularly showered with relatively more campaign dollars and rhetorical fervor than states such as Maine, Nevada, or Georgia, which are safe or small. In 1960 Kennedy was hailed for his political wisdom in concentrating on the large industrial states, and McGovern pursued a similar strategy in 1972.

The general ticket system is also attacked for grossly inflating the bargaining power of pressure groups and minority parties in large doubtful states. A well-organized national, racial, religious, or economic group whose votes are concentrated upon a presidential candidate can more powerfully exact his commitment if the group is situated in a large state.

Defenders of the existing electoral system argue that its distortions serve the cause of social justice, that the system enables smaller masses of people to strike bargains that unshackle their oppressions. A more perfect system, presumably, would afford fewer liberating opportunities. Yet a standard that judges the quality of the electoral system in terms of whether the bargains struck are good or bad is of dubious merit. Wilmerding argues in *The Electoral College*,

> If the President is to be the man of the people, if all the people are to stand on the same footing, equal masses of people must be given equal votes, equal bargaining power. Their weight in the electoral count must be proportional to their numbers and not to the rightness or wrongness of their causes.[54]

The pretensions of distinguishing good groups from bad and of assigning greater electoral weight to the former than to the latter cannot be justified in democratic theory, nor can it long be asserted satisfactorily in practice.

## Alternatives to the Electoral College

Hardly a session of Congress passes when legislators, distressed by the flaws of the electoral college system, do not introduce proposals, embodied in drafts of constitutional amendments, to reform it. Although differing in detail, the proposals that perennially appear can be grouped into several broad categories:

*A national popular vote*    According to this proposal, the President would be chosen by the majority of the national popular vote. Electors and electoral votes would be tossed upon the political scrap heap.

The plan of national popular election offers powerful attractions. It is the only plan extant that assures against the election of a President receiving fewer popular votes than his opponent. Every voter, be he or she a New Yorker or a Nevadan, would have one vote of equal weight. Majoritarian democracy would be cleanly applied, in which 51 percent and above would rule. The several evils of the general ticket system would be banished at one fell swoop. The principle of presidential selection would be national rather than federative; minority votes of states would at least be counted; large states would be barred from consolidating their votes to the disadvantage of the small. The power of pressure groups and minor parties would be more nearly proportionate to their numbers. Political activity in safe states would rise and be meaningful.

The national popular vote carries several formidable defects. It would jeopardize our two-party system by encouraging minor parties, giving them a weight in the national popular vote that they lack in the electoral college system. It violates the federal principle by redistributing political power among the states: the proposal would shift power from the smaller states to the larger states; from states that are politically passive to states that are politically active.

Individual plans for popular elections introduced in Congress over the years have offered different provisions for the eventuality wherein no candidate wins a majority. Some would permit a plurality to elect; others would hold a run-off election limited to the two or three candidates polling the highest initial vote. Still others would throw the election into the House of Representatives, with each member having one vote.

*Proportional voting*    Under this plan, which has many variations, each candidate who polled a fraction of a state's popular votes would win the same fraction of its electoral votes. The candidate's national electoral vote would be the sum of his electoral votes in all fifty states. The President would continue to be chosen by electoral, not popular, votes. If no candidate received 40 percent of the entire electoral vote, the contest would be decided between the two highest candidates by the House and Senate jointly, with each member having one vote. The state legislatures would lose their present freedom to decide the methods of choosing electors and of voting.

The minority popular vote in each state would be accurately reflected in the electoral vote. The plan would abolish the evil of the one-party state and diminish the disproportionate influence of local pressure groups and the dread possibility that a candidate with a minority of the popular vote will win a majority of the electoral vote. The plan harmonizes with the federal structure by preserving the interests of the small states.

But proportional voting has heavy disadvantages. It would encourage the development of minor parties and would in time weaken or destroy the two-party system. The presidential constituency would cease to be primarily geographical and would become, instead, primarily mathematical or ideological. Groups rather than areas would be the focus of appeal. The geographical constituency encourages the candidate to be moderate in view and balanced in appeal to its diverse groups. To win an ideological constituency, the candidate must tend to extremes and subordinate himself to its special purposes. Proportional voting would increase rather than reduce the danger of electing minority Presidents. If, for example, proportional voting rather than the present electoral system had operated in the elections of 1880 and 1896, their outcomes would have been reversed. In 1880 James A. Garfield received more popular votes than Winfield Scott Hancock, and in 1896 McKinley more than Bryan. Proportional voting, however, would have converted Hancock and Bryan from losers into victors because of the way their popular votes were distributed among the states.

*The single-member district system*    Each state would be divided by the state legislature into districts equal to the number of Representatives the state is entitled to in Congress. Ideally, the districts would comprise contiguous and compact territory and, as nearly as possible, equal numbers of inhabitants. (Ideally, also, the electoral college districts would correspond with the districts of the House of Representatives.) Each district's voters would choose one elector. In addition, two electors would be chosen from the state at large. The candidate winning a majority of the electoral votes (some proposals require only 40 percent) would be deemed elected. If no candidate qualified, the House and Senate would jointly choose the President.

Like other proposals, the district system would take the method of electing the President out of the hands of the state legislatures and more nearly make the President the man of the people. It would end the power of large states, or their dominant party, to override the dominant party in the country at large. It would hamper minor parties and pressure groups in doubtful states from defeating, for their own ends, the will of the nation. Finally, it would force the parties to lift their eyes beyond the big states and into the country at large in their quest for candidates.

The district system has several forbidding weaknesses. It is vulnerable to the gerrymander. Its champions face the gerrymander evil by incorporating into their proposed constitutional amendment precise standards concerning population and territory by which districts would be made up. These the courts presumably would enforce. The districts still would not be equal in each state; large states would have districts with more populous constituencies than small states. Worst of all, the district plan would probably convert the present system, by which the American people engage in a national act focused upon national problems, into a series of petty campaigns in local districts. The district system would encourage minor parties by giving them a stronger opportunity to choose an elector in a district than the traditional system permits in a state. In a close election, a minor party might hold the balance in the national tally of electors.

*Keeping the electoral vote but dropping the electors*    In 1801 Jefferson wrote to Albert Gallatin of an "amendment which I know will be proposed, to wit, to have no electors, but let the people vote directly, and the ticket which has a plurality of the votes of any state to be considered as receiving the whole vote of the state." Presidents Johnson and Nixon both urged the step. The accompanying argument is undeniable. If the elector is faithful to the popular vote, he is useless; if he is not, he is dangerous.

*Altering the procedures of the House of Representatives*    The Twelfth Amendment specifies that if no candidate receives a majority of the electoral votes, the House of Representatives, voting by states, shall immediately choose the President by ballot "from the persons having the highest numbers not exceeding three on the list of those voted for as President." A majority of all the states is necessary for election. The present system of a single vote for each state is unjust in making one Representative from Alaska equal to thirty-four Representatives from New York.

Most proposals would have the Representatives vote by heads rather than by states, patently a fairer procedure. Still others would have the Senate and House sit jointly and vote by heads. Including the Senate would be a sop to the small states, who would lose strength if the House shifted from voting by the states as units to voting by heads. This method also preserves the advantage of the populous states in the electoral college and carries it into a possible multicandidate Presidential election in which no one candidate received a majority. The advantage, of course, would not have the solid impact of the general ticket system. Most state delegations in Congress would divide on party lines, although California with forty-three members in 1980 would still wield more power than Mississippi with five. A deadlock could be precluded by limiting the Congressional voting to the two leading candidates.

# Assessing the Changing Selection System

An overriding trend of the presidential selection process is democratization. Over time, more and more persons have shared in the process of choosing the President. The small circle of selectors who chose the Federalist party's nominees was replaced by the broader Congressional Caucus of Jefferson's Democratic-Republic party, and it in turn gave way to the still broader national nominating convention in Jackson's day. In the 1960s and 70s, the party and public officials who have traditionally dominated the convention yielded to methods that presumably enlarged the role of ordinary citizens in choosing convention delegates. The expansion of presidential primaries has speeded the trend of popular participation and control. The impact of reform is evident in the capture of presidential nominations by an "outsider" such as Jimmy Carter and in Ronald Reagan's near success in snatching the 1976 nomination from incumbent Gerald Ford, the latter strongly supported by Republican professional politicians.[55]

The reforms of the late 1960s and 70s, coupled with the potency of television, have moved power away from the professionals. The primaries, in their increasing number, enable the candidate to sweep into the nomination by enlisting bands of amateurs to work energetically for his cause, and to use television to maximize the impact of his personality, diminishing the necessity to court party figures. The test of building consensus by enlisting the support of party leaders dispersed in a federal system has markedly diminished. It has done so to the point that those who win elections are no longer sufficiently pretested for their capacity to govern. In a word, the selection system no longer performs with sufficient assurance its cardinal mission.

## The New Elites

Coupled with the reforms is the rise of political amateurs in both major parties committed to specific issues and often functioning in an antiestablishment vein, distressed by usual politics and its lackluster handling of national problems. Disdainful of compromise, the stock in trade of historic presidential politics and professional politicians, the zealous amateurs value candidates who are committed to "right" stands on issues, even though electoral success becomes unlikely. Jeane Kirkpatrick has noted that the broadened availability of higher education has helped produce the amateurs, with their independent political attitudes and alert interest in political issues. The reform rules of the Democratic party aid these newcomers to national conventions by placing a premium on verbal skills, self-confidence, ideological motivations inducing political participation, and possession of certain social—in contrast to political—characteristics, such as sex, race, and age. The amateurs comprise what Kirkpatrick calls a "new presidential elite," fighting for views divergent from those of party professionals and the general body of voters.[56]

Another rising elite are the news media. Where once party professionals discoursed with each other in choosing the party's nominee, the media now provide the link between candidates and between candidates and voters. Journalists have become the principal source of information about candidates' statements and activities. The media discover candidates, define their place in the race at any moment, and assess their prospects. The media expose a candidate's vulnerabilities and otherwise act as a public defender against whatever mischief the candidate springs on the unwary voter.

Still another elite are the array of communications specialists—the public relations experts, advertising careerists, media consultants, pollsters, direct-mail money raisers. Much of the effort of these high-priced specialists is manipulative—"selling" the candidate as a problem in market research, beguiling the voter with code words and themes. One would tremble for democracy's future were it not for political scientist V. O. Key's insight, which today is truer than when he expressed it nearly three decades ago, that "voters are not fools," and that they are "moved by concerns about central and relevant questions of public policy, government performance, and of executive personality."[57]

But voter turnout in presidential elections, unfortunately, has been declining since 1960. A ready rationalization is that lower turnout manifests voter satisfaction with public affairs. Evidence, alas, abounds to the contrary. Voters are troubled by the political system's unresponsiveness to their needs and are displeased with the caliber of political leaders. Confidence in the selection system cannot flourish when it is discovered, well into the 1980 selection process, that a majority of voters of both parties were dissatisfied with their prospective nominees, Carter and Reagan. But it must also be noted that voters in neither party focused on any other candidate, and the selection process gave ample opportunity for that candidate to emerge.

# ★ ★ ★  The Future Presidency  ★ ★ ★

In the interest of strengthening and democratizing the presidency, several innovations might advantageously be made in its selection procedures.

1. We ought, at the very least, to abolish the electoral college, which is a standing invitation to trouble. Even if we abolished the college, we could retain the electoral vote, which should automatically reflect the plurality of the popular vote.

2. We ought to review periodically the question of whether we might advantageously abandon both the electoral college and the electoral vote and substitute a plan for selecting the President on the basis of a national popular vote. A national popular vote is most in accord with democratic principle, and it would apply a standard of absolute fairness of "one American, one vote," which is badly violated by the present system. It would avoid the dread possibility, under the present electoral vote system, that the candidate winning a national popular majority will not prevail because he does not command a majority of the electoral votes. A serious drawback of the national popular vote plan is the possible necessity of a run-off election. But this is better in the bargain than the present danger that the popular vote winner will lose in the electoral college. There is, however, a formidable difficulty that to this writer makes prohibitive the adoption of the national vote system now. The system would encourage minor parties by affording them a recognition in the national popular vote that they do not have in the present electoral vote. The fact that their votes would count under the national popular vote plan would induce them to extend themselves nationally. Such a development would further weaken our already much too weak major parties.

    It could also weaken a sitting President, who, seeking reelection, might pander to them and the one or several issues to which they most likely would be devoted, either to still their opposition or to win their nomination.

3. When the House of Representatives is called upon to choose a President, it should vote by heads rather than by states. A vote by heads clearly

would better approximate the popular vote than the existing system. Best of all would be a combined Senate-House vote by heads, since Senators are chosen by the states at large and therefore reflect state-wide opinion.

4. Alternatively, modest repairs could be made in the electoral college system to overcome several defects while adopting advantageous features of the proposed national popular vote. A study, *The Reform of the Presidential Election System,* sponsored by the Twentieth Century Fund, would continue the present system of allocating electoral votes, while awarding an additional block of votes to the candidate with the highest national popular vote. In all, 102 of these "national" electoral votes would be available, with two allotted to each state plus the District of Columbia. This modification would both buttress federalism, important to many supporters of the Electoral College, while assuring that the candidate with the largest popular vote would become President. A raw nerve of potential trouble in the present system would henceforth be by-passed.

If no candidate received a majority of the electoral votes under these counting procedures, there would be a run-off election. This is viewed as preferable to present procedure which throws the election into the House of Representatives, whose composition may bear little relationship to voter preferences in the presidential contest.[58]

5. With primaries so numerous, it is time to adopt regional primaries to reduce the hectic travel and other punishing physical demands on the candidate. As Senator, Walter Mondale proposed six regional primary dates, each a month apart. Primary-holding states would be required to observe the assigned dates. Other proposals would have the sequence of the regions' primary elections chosen by lot or by ordered rotation, so that no one region would become dominant by perpetually being first.

Another approach would reduce the length of the primary season and better rationalize the process. Have, for example, four staggered once-a-month primary dates, starting in March and ending in June. States would be free to choose whether or not to have a primary, but any state holding one should choose one of the four established dates. A national primary has long been proposed, and in opinion polls the public has sometimes favored it. But a national primary would be enormously expensive, would probably require a run-off, and it would rule out larger roles in nominating politics to office-holders and party leaders.

6. The prime function of presidential selection is to choose incumbents who will excel in performing the duties of the office. The older system of presidential nomination, prevailing prior to the late 1960s, accorded the major role to professionals. To gain the nomination, the candidate had to weave together a majority of convention delegates and to do so, he wooed the party professionals, especially state and local leaders, throughout the country. His ability to persuade, bargain, cajole, entice this motley far-flung majority was deemed a fair test of his ability to serve as President, to master the office's formidable political arts.

Reform has gone too far; democracy has been misguidedly served at the expense of the presidency's effectiveness. As a corrective, a better balance might be restored between the amateurs and the professionals. The numbers of delegates chosen by primaries could be reduced while those chosen by professionals could be increased—the party leaders and their lieutenants and officeholders. If delegates were divided evenly between the two groups, two main objectives of the selection process might be fulfilled: an effective presidency would gain because candidates would again be subject to the test of persuading political professionals—a skill required for successful conduct of the office—and to further office-related tests of political management and consensus-building. Democracy would be served since the voter, thanks to a multitude of primaries, would continue to have a potent voice in choosing the nominee.

# Chapter Four

# Tenure

Tenure is power. Whether the presidency is a center of energy and direction or of weakness and futility depends in no small way upon the length and security of the Chief Executive's term of office, his eligibility for reelection, and the adequacy of arrangements available to bolster the office if his health—physical or mental—should falter. Tenure, therefore, depends partly upon the structuring of the office and partly upon the President's ability to escape the afflictions of biological frailty. If he does succumb to serious illness, the office, to function adequately, requires provision beforehand for a substitute President to take over with adequate preparation and authority.

But fixity of tenure can collide with the democratic imperatives of presidential power. With a term of defined duration that can be broken only with extreme difficulty, the President can embark on acts offensive to democratic norms and destroy public confidence but persist in office. Such was the case when Richard Nixon remained in office for months after Watergate, and other offenses were exposed that in a parliamentary system, where tenure is more readily interrupted, would have promptly resulted in his overthrow. While Nixon struggled with his crisis, across the Atlantic West German Chancellor Willy Brandt struggled with a lesser crisis and felt behooved to resign within days when an East German spy was discovered among his personal staff.

## The Founding Fathers Decide

The Founding Fathers, aware of the importance of tenure to the strong, but responsible, executive, debated the President's term and his reeligibility long and anxiously. The Fathers' anxiety about the President's term of office was reflected in their consideration at successive junctures of a term first of seven, then of six, and finally of four years. If Congress chose the President, as many favored, a long term without eligibility for reelection seemed best because a President otherwise might become a congressional yes-man in courting reelection. But once the electoral college system had been adopted, a shorter term with unlimited eligibility was agreed upon.

The Founding Fathers expected that George Washington would become the first President and would willingly serve the rest of his days. Their acceptance of the principle of indefinite eligibility ran counter to another American political principle deeply ingrained since Revolutionary times— that rotation in executive office is essential to liberty. The principle of unlimited eligibility for reelection was irreparably undermined by the man in whose behalf it had been established, George Washington himself. Washington announced upon completing his second presidential term that it was his personal wish not to serve another. By the Civil War, presidential observance had established the two-term principle in the core of American political doctrine.

## The Two-Term Tradition

Despite its formal observance, with only a single exception throughout presidential history, the two-term practice has occasionally been under siege. Although Franklin D. Roosevelt alone exceeded the two-term limitation, he was far from the first to try. In the decades between Lincoln and Franklin D. Roosevelt there was seldom a period when the third-term fever did not seize the Chief Executive. So menacing in fact did the third term boom of Ulysses S. Grant become in 1875 that the House of Representatives felt duty-driven to resolve, by a vote of 234 to 18, that departure from the two-term tradition would be "unwise, unpatriotic and fraught with peril to our free institutions." [1]

Theodore Roosevelt, like Grant before him and Calvin Coolidge later, took the pragmatic view that the two-term limitation applied only to a third consecutive term. He had sworn fealty to the two-term custom in the exuberance of his electoral victory of 1904, a pledge his foes gleefully recalled when he entered the presidential race of 1912. But Roosevelt was a supreme rationalizer and saw no contradiction between his words in 1904 and his actions in 1912. If he were to decline "a third cup of coffee," he explained, no one would suppose he meant never to take another cup. By his 1904 pledge, he said, "I meant, of course, a third consecutive term." [2]

Franklin D. Roosevelt's distinction in achieving reelection to a third and a fourth term was prevented from becoming more than a personal triumph by the Twenty-second Amendment. The amendment inscribes in the nation's fundamental law the prohibition, "No person shall be elected to the office of the President more than twice." For anyone like Ulysses S. Grant, who after two terms and an interlude of retirement strains to possess the office a third time, the amendment would provide a clear and unequivocal negative. For Presidents such as Theodore Roosevelt, Calvin Coolidge, and Lyndon Johnson, whose incumbencies stretched across a partial and a full term, the amendment continues in a fashion too clear to be misinterpreted: ". . . and no person who has held the office of President, or acted as President, for more than two years of a term to which some other person was elected President shall be elected to the office of the President more than once." Admirers of former President Eisenhower, the first casualty of the amendment, concluded after reading its text that he could well be restored as Chief Executive by electing him Vice President and then having the President elected with him step down in his favor. The Twenty-second Amendment is a mixture of political motivations, both partisan and personal. It was a posthumous revenge against Franklin Roosevelt for breaking the two-term tradition. It was also a desperate attempt to push back the rushing flood of executive authority. And to the career politician it was an assurance that the foremost prize of American politics would be available at regular intervals.

The amendment also instills certain weaknesses into the office of the presidency, however. It can gravely weaken the President's influence during the entire span of his second, and final, term. In 1957, the first year of Eisenhower's second term, the President was hampered by a noticeable weakening of his grip on Republican legislators and a softening of his hitherto staunch support from the press and business. Yet Eisenhower had been returned to power only a year earlier with a fresh and overwhelming mandate. Even worse is the amendment's potential mischief in a foreign affairs crisis. The nation could conceivably be deep in war, or on the brink of it, when the tenure of its Chief Executive was suddenly cut off. The amendment would require the nation to violate that wise old adage warning against changing horses in mid-stream. The electorate would be wrenched into choosing new leadership at a time when national unity was imperative; it would be deprived of a Chief Executive whose experience and knowledge of the ongoing crisis could not be duplicated. The crisis of war kept Franklin Roosevelt in office because the electorate concluded that the continuity of leadership and policy could not be safely shattered midway without peril. Had the Twenty-second Amendment then been in force, Roosevelt would automatically have been disbarred and new leadership imposed contrary to the electorate's judgment. The Twenty-second Amendment, whatever may be said in its favor, is antidemocratic in spirit, a frustration of the will of the people out of fear that the people might choose unwisely.[3]

# Resignation

The presidential tenure can be interrupted not only by restriction on reelection but by other means—resignation, for example, a means for which the Constitution provides. Only Richard Nixon has ever resigned, but Woodrow Wilson came close to committing that final act of voluntary separation. An admiring student of British governmental practice, which turns upon the Prime Minister's periodic resignation to seek a vote of public confidence for his party, Wilson twice as President contemplated resigning. If his rival in the 1916 presidential race, Charles Evans Hughes, had won, he proposed to resign to avoid a lame-duck presidency in the midst of world crisis. His plan was first to ask his Secretary of State, Robert Lansing, to resign so he could appoint President-elect Hughes as his successor. Thereupon President Wilson and Vice President Marshall would both resign, permitting Hughes's ascent to the presidency under the existing succession law.[4] Wilson's electoral victory rendered the novel plan unnecessary. In a later crisis, the fight for the Versailles peace treaty in 1919, Wilson briefly weighed the tactic of resigning and then immediately running again in a special presidential election permitted by the Succession Act of 1886 then in force. His election presumably would have expressed a national desire for membership in the League and sustained confidence in him. Wilson dropped this plan. The approaching elections of 1920 seemed to him to promise "a great and solemn" referendum on the treaty.[5]

In 1974, less than two years after his overwhelming reelection, Richard Nixon became the first President to resign from the office, a decision reached in the face of probable impeachment by the House and Senate. Resignation was a way of avoiding the disgrace implicit in a successful impeachment, and it preserved the pension rights and other perquisites of a former President that would have been lost in a completed impeachment. Further, resignation avoided an authoritative finding concerning Nixon's conduct by the constitutionally designated tribunal, the Senate. Resignation enabled Nixon to define his situation and judge his presidential incumbency himself, which he did in terms implying minimum culpability: He was resigning, he said, because "I no longer have a strong enough political base in Congress," and he acknowledged only that "if some of my judgments were wrong—and some were wrong—they were made in what I believed at the time to be in the best interests of the nation."

For Nixon, resignation was a painful and reluctant decision. "I have never been a quitter," he said, "and to leave is abhorrent, . . ." but he took the step after Barry Goldwater (R-Ariz.) disclosed that no more than fifteen votes against impeachment existed in the Senate, well short of the thirty-four necessary to escape conviction, and on the strong recommendations of his staff—including his chief of staff, General Alexander M. Haig, Jr.—and of Secretary of State Henry Kissinger that he step down in the national interest.[6] Nixon has written that he did so because "even if I had a chance in the Senate, the country simply could not afford six months with its President on trial."[7]

# Impeachment

According to Article II of the Constitution, the President can be "fired" via an impeachment process, for "treason, bribery, or other high crimes and misdemeanors."[8] Imitating existing state constitutions, the Founding Fathers empowered the House of Representatives to impeach the President, and the Senate, sitting as a law court with the Chief Justice of the United States presiding, to conduct the trial. A two-thirds vote of the Senators present is necessary for conviction. The penalties that the Constitution brings down upon the convicted President are removal from office, disqualification for "any office of honor, trust, or profit under the United States," and liability to "indictment, trial, judgment, and punishment, according to law."

## Impeaching Andrew Johnson

Although the introduction of impeachment resolutions is a favorite indulgence of members of Congress embittered by particular Presidents, Andrew Johnson enjoys distinction as the only President who has walked the impeachment gangplank to the point of a Senate vote. Far more importantly, he, and the presidency with him, came out of it alive. By a single vote Johnson missed conviction and the presidency was spared.

The Johnson case demonstrates the capacity of legislators to convert a solemn judicial function into what Gideon Welles, Johnson's Secretary of the Navy, termed "a deed of extreme partisanship."[9] The impeachment was built upon the creaky foundation of the Tenure of Office Act of 1867, which denied the President the right to remove civil officials, including members of his cabinet, without senatorial consent. Presidents had been removing cabinet Secretaries since the days of Washington. By the act of 1867 Congress was contravening precedent, stripping Johnson of control of his administration, and unconstitutionally violating his power to remove a member of the cabinet. Convinced that the Tenure Act was unconstitutional, Johnson requested and then ordered Secretary of War Edwin M. Stanton to resign and appointed General Lorenzo Thomas his successor. When Thomas appeared at the War Department, Stanton barricaded himself behind his office door.

Johnson himself was not without fault. Though principled and reverential toward the Constitution, he was barren of political skill. Incapable of seeing any merit in the opposition's position, he was disinclined to solve his problems by bargaining and compromise. Even when his most respected counsellors urged that he refrain from removing Stanton, for the sake of retaining a modicum of his party's support, Johnson was adamant. Nor was he deterred by events, by reports of whites committing atrocities against blacks in the South, reports that moved even moderate Republicans to concede the necessity of some military rule. Worst of all, Johnson himself was floundering in a state of acute political weakness: rejected at the polls, condemned by most of the Northern press, and loathed as an apostate by the Republicans, who controlled both congressional houses.[10]

On February 28, 1868, the House voted to impeach the President for "high crimes and misdemeanors." Eleven articles of impeachment were drawn, ten centering upon Stanton's removal. The remaining article, contrived from garbled newspaper accounts of the President's speeches, charged, among other things, that he used unseemly language and spoke in a loud voice. Johnson meanwhile expected to knock the props from under the impeachment proceedings by obtaining a ruling from the Supreme Court endorsing his views on the Tenure of Office law. But the Court, in a mood of "judicial restraint," declined to act.

The ensuing impeachment enterprise reeked with self-serving politics. If Johnson were convicted and deposed, the new President of the United States, owing to the vice-presidential vacancy and the line of succession in the applicable law of 1792, would be Ben Wade of Ohio, the vituperative President pro tempore of the Senate. When Wade's participation in the trial was objected to because of his not inconsiderable personal stake, the Senator replied with simple finality that he saw nothing wrong with serving as a judge. He would do impartial justice, he said, and was sworn. Chief Justice Salmon P. Chase, who presided, also wanted to be President, having for the office a craving that Lincoln once likened to insanity. By day Chase conducted the trial; by night he wrote letters building his claim to the next Democratic presidential nomination. That the trial would ooze with low politics was instantly apparent when after the President's counsel requested forty days to prepare their case, with its numerous intricacies of law and fact, they were permitted ten. The Chief Justice, empowered within narrowly defined limits to rule on points of law, heroically put political ambition aside and rose to the full height of his responsibilities. According to the Senate rules specially adopted for the trial, if one Senator objected to the Chief Justice's holding, the matter was voted by the entire body. The Chief Justice was overruled seventeen times, in most instances for the purpose of suppressing evidence favorable to the President.

President Johnson, for all of his reputation for wild epithet and the big blunder, was a model of decorum. His chief act of self-assertion lay in putting his case before the people in interviews with several friendly reporters. Said the President,

> Suppose Congress should pass a bill abolishing the veto power. . . . Suppose it should pass a dozen bills of this character—would the President be constitutionally bound to execute them as laws? Would it not be his duty, as in the present instance, to seek immediately judgment in the Supreme Court?[11]

The Radicals were desperate. The vote on Article XI, the first impeachment article to be disposed of, fell short of the two-thirds majority necessary for conviction. To revive their wilting plot, the Radicals maneuvered the Senate into an adjournment of ten days for the known, but carefully unacknowledged, purpose of lining up votes for Johnson's conviction. The adjournment occurred only after the Chief Justice's ruling against it was overridden. But the massive machinery of pressures and intrigue, unloosed upon Senators who were still on the fence or who conceivably might be lured or bullied into abandoning Johnson, failed. Johnson and the presidency were saved by a single vote. Senator Lyman Trumbull, who sided with the President, captured the significance of the lamentable episode in explaining his vote:

> Once set, the example of impeaching a President for what, when the excitement of the hour shall have subsided, will be regarded as insufficient cause, and no future President will be safe who happens to differ with the majority of the House and two-thirds of the Senate on any measure deemed by them important, particularly if of a political character.[12]

## Impeaching Richard Nixon

Richard Nixon is the only other President to be seriously threatened by impeachment. Like Johnson, Nixon faced a Congress dominated by the opposing party, and many legislators long resented his treatment of them;

but unlike Johnson, whose trial and its outcome centered on constitutional questions, the potential case against Nixon embraced his possible criminal conduct plus that of his subordinates, who in steady numbers were prosecuted, convicted, and jailed. Also at issue were a range of noncriminal acts, which suggested that the President had failed to carry out his constitutional duty to "take care" that the laws are faithfully executed.

Under prevailing political realities, the possible impeachment of Nixon derived primarily from what he himself did rather than from his subordinates' malfeasances. Although, normally, a chief executive in the private sector is, and should be, held responsible for his subordinates' conduct, and would be promptly ejected into the outer darkness for failings comparable to those of the Nixon men, the practical politics of impeachment, as well as the Constitutional grounds of that process, made clear that removal of the President must derive its force from his own specific acts. Not otherwise, it appeared, could a majority vote of the House be mustered, nor the more formidable two-thirds vote of the Senate.[13]

Eventually the House Judiciary Committee, which had jurisdiction over the matter, adopted three articles of impeachment, delineating many specific charges. Article I contended that Nixon engaged in a plan to obstruct investigations of the Watergate burglary and to cover up the facts of that undertaking. A second article accused Nixon of violating his oath to execute the laws and of broadly abusing presidential power in misusing the Internal Revenue Service to harass political opponents, imposing illegal wiretaps, in creating a "secret investigative unit" in the White House, and the like. A third article charged the President with conduct "subversive of constitutional government" in his refusal to comply with the Judiciary Committee's subpoenas for 147 tapes of his conversations and related documents.[14]

Almost simultaneously, the Supreme Court, in an 8-0 decision, rejected the President's contention that he had absolute power to withhold from the courts tapes of his conversations with assistants and ruled that he must provide quantities of tapes required in the criminal trials of his former subordinates.[15] Although the Court acknowledged that the President might validly invoke executive privilege because of national security, foreign policy, and other considerations, Nixon claimed none of those.[16] The unanimity and breadth of the decision spurred the impeachment drive in Congress.

Among the tapes the President was required to turn over to trial court Judge John Sirica were those of three discussions Nixon held on June 23, 1972, with his chief of staff, H. R. Haldeman, that disclosed, beyond doubt, that Nixon had attempted, but failed, to use the CIA to deflect an FBI investigation of the Watergate scandal. For more than two years Nixon claimed to be innocent of involvement in any cover-up, and the disparity between his previous statements and the newly revealed evidence swiftly eroded his remaining congressional and public support and made his impeachment inevitable. Its course was halted by his resignation.[17]

An unused process for more than a century, impeachment worked in 1974. A contemporary President, possessing power well beyond the design and imaginings of the Founding Fathers, had been forced from office. The Nixon experience is a reminder to future Presidents that, despite the heady temptations of their office to think otherwise, they are subject to the Constitution, as befits democracy. This includes their prescribed duty to see that the laws are faithfully executed. That duty is not faithfully executed when the President manipulates laws to favor friends, to violate the constitutional rights of private individuals, to punish political opponents, and to violate the criminal law.

From their skillful curbings of a presidential aberration, Congress and the courts gained new and needed prestige and a sense of accomplishment. Congress, and more particularly the House Judiciary Committee, functioned with a caution and deliberation that drained any possible validity from the contention of President Nixon's staunchest advocates that he had been "hounded from office."

But another perspective on the Nixon events and the impeachment process, with its adjunct, a virtually unbreakable four-year term, results in a less charitable appraisal of the presidential system. In a parliamentary system, Nixon, after only a few of his infractions, would have been swiftly ousted from office. But the cumbersome impeachment machinery and a fixed term of office enabled Nixon to dodge and parry for more than two years while the nation suffered and drifted.

# The President and Legal Processes

## Nixon and the Law

With the Constitution's language so sparse and experience so limited, important unanswered questions remain about impeachment and related legal processes. Some of these surfaced in the Nixon proceedings and were responded to by the courts, Congress, or the executive, while others were avoided and therefore left to another day.

*The special prosecutor*    The Watergate crimes were investigated and prosecuted by a Special Prosecutor who, under guidelines issued by Attorney General Elliott Richardson, was appointed by the Attorney General and functioned within the Department of Justice. To the Special Prosecutor, the Attorney General delegated full authority to investigate and prosecute allegations involving the President, his staff, and his appointees. The Special Prosecutor was empowered to conduct grand jury proceedings, to review all documentary evidence, to contest executive privilege, and to prosecute any individual. The Special Prosecutor could coordinate and direct all Justice Department personnel, and the Attorney General was not to interfere with his decisions and actions.[18]

The first of the Special Prosecutors, Archibald Cox, went to court to force the White House to turn over those tapes of presidential conversations he felt necessary for his investigation. At President Nixon's behest, Cox was fired; Richardson, refusing to comply with the President's directive, resigned; Deputy Attorney General William Ruckelshaus, also refusing, was fired. The upheaval became known as the "Saturday Night Massacre," but Cox's successor, Leon Jaworski, continued the Watergate prosecutions.

*Grand jury action*    Although the Constitution acknowledges that the President is liable to criminal indictment after his removal by impeachment, can a grand jury indict him without, or prior to, impeachment? Following the cover-up of the Watergate burglary, the federal grand jury investigating Watergate named President Nixon as an unindicted coconspirator. Special Prosecutor Jaworski dissuaded the jury from directly indicting the President, contending that the House Judiciary Committee was the proper forum for considering "matters of evidence relating to" a President.[19] Ultimately, the grand jury report and accompanying materials were turned over to the House Committee. In *Nixon* v. *United States*, the Supreme Court let the grand jury's action stand.[20] Although Jaworski believed that an incumbent President could be indicted for a heinous offense (such as murder), he had "grave doubts" that a sitting President was indictable for the offense of obstruction of justice, particularly when the House Judiciary Committee was then inquiring whether the President could be impeached on that very ground.[21]

***Subpoenaing the President***    Yes, the President can be subpoenaed, but can anyone subpoena him in any court, in any state, in any trial? A California superior court judge subpoenaed Nixon to appear as a witness at the trial of his former aide, John Ehrlichman. But Nixon rejected the subpoena, citing the contention of Thomas Jefferson that if the President were obliged to honor every subpoena, the courts could overwhelm the separation of powers principle and "keep him constantly trudging from North to South and East to West, and withdraw him entirely from his constitutional duties." That a state court was requesting his appearance enabled Nixon to cite traditional intergovernmental immunity.[22]

Must the President testify before the Watergate grand jury? When Special Prosecutor Jaworski requested that he do so, Nixon declined on grounds that it would be constitutionally improper, and Jaworski did not press the matter, nor did he accept the President's offer of written, or indirect, testimony.[23] Nixon drew on precedents set by Jefferson and Monroe. In the treason trial of Aaron Burr, President Jefferson was subpoenaed, and he responded by making evidence available to the federal trial court but did not testify personally. In 1818, Monroe was subpoenaed as a witness in a court martial but satisfied the request with written responses. Be it noted that, unlike Nixon, Jefferson and Monroe were not objects of criminal inquiry.

Must the President honor subpoenas calling for White House papers and tapes? For Nixon, the question arose in various contexts and partook of different outcomes. Special Prosecutor Jaworski requested sixty-four tapes needed as evidence for a pending Watergate cover-up trial, but the President refused to surrender them. Federal district judge Sirica ordered the President to turn over the tapes, rejecting his claim of executive privilege and his contention that since Jaworski was a subordinate in the executive branch he had no standing to sue his superior, the President, and that therefore the district court had no jurisdiction to enforce Jaworski's subpoena. The Supreme Court ruled unanimously that the President must provide potential evidence for the criminal trial for his former subordinates and rejected his contention that he had absolute authority to withhold the material.[24]

Nixon rejected the dictum of James K. Polk that in a House impeachment proceeding "all the archives and papers of the executive departments, public or private, would be subject to the inspection and control of a committee [of the House] . . ." After partly complying with requests by the House Judiciary Committee for tapes and documents as it considered impeachment, Nixon informed the Committee that he would not comply with two existing subpoenas nor with any future requests. Contending that he had already provided the committee with "a voluminous body of materials" that gave "the full story of Watergate," the President declared there would be "no end" to the requests "unless a line were drawn somewhere by someone. Since it is clear that the committee will not draw such a line, I have done so." Nixon cited "the principle of the separation of powers and of the executive as a coequal branch." Committee chairman Peter Rodino, Jr. warned that the President's action was "a very grave matter," implying that it could ultimately provide grounds for impeachment. Rodino wondered aloud whether the Watergate cover-up was not continuing full-sail even at the House stage of impeachment.[25]

*Pardoning Nixon*   After the President resigns or is successfully impeached, can his successor pardon him before he has been subject to possible indictment, trial, and judgment, to which Article I, Section 3 of the Constitution makes him liable? Yes, according to President Ford, who pardoned former President Nixon for all federal crimes that he "committed or may have committed or taken part in" while in office.[26] Ford's position is supported by long-standing English cases and by *ex parte Garland* (4 Wall. 333, 1867) in which the U.S. Supreme Court held that a pardon could be issued before conviction in a case involving a Confederate officer who was pardoned and reinstated as a member of the bar. The Nixon pardon, however, was a stark contradiction of the democratic ideal of equal justice. Other Watergate defendants underwent trial and punishment while the man with ultimate responsibility remained free, but as Jaworski has stated, the predominant consideration was that Nixon could never have received a fair trial—some 92 million watched the televised House Judiciary Committee proceedings. Newspapers everywhere reported in detail Nixon's complicity, and, when he resigned, press and airwaves were filled with inculpatory comments concerning his guilt.[27]

## Law Appointments

Beyond these more personal involvements, Presidents exercise a broad range of functions of utmost significance to legal processes. The President nominates appointees to the Supreme Court and lesser federal courts, and by the rulings of justices he has appointed, a President's influence is felt long after he leaves office. In 1979 alone, Carter nominated 137 federal judges, 113 of whom were assigned new judgships.[28] Reagan, to mollify women offended by his opposition to the Equal Rights Amendment, promised to appoint a woman to the Supreme Court.

Similarly, the President nominates the principal law officers of the executive branch—the Attorney General and other top Justice Department policy-makers—and through them determines the direction and emphasis of law enforcement in various policy fields; for example, what litigation is commenced, which cases appealed. Litigation promoting school desegregation was pursued more substantially in Johnson's presidency than in Nixon's; antitrust litigation was more voluminous under Theodore Roosevelt and Taft than under Coolidge and Harding.

## Interpreting and Enforcing the Law

Highly prominent among the President's varied interactions with legal processes is his role as interpreter of the law.[29] His executive orders and the rules and regulations of executive agencies constitute a huge volume of sub-legislation far exceeding the original congressional enactments that spawned them. At times the President's interpretations run afoul of the courts. For example, in carrying to far extremes his exercise of power to impound funds appropriated by Congress, President Nixon interpreted the Federal Water Pollution Control Act and its amendments of 1972 to permit him to allot only a fraction of the total funding Congress provided for federal aid to municipal sewers and sewage treatment works. After reviewing the act's legislative history, the Court concluded in *Train* v. *City of New York* (420 U.S. 35, 1974) that the President was duty-bound to allot the full sums, adding that it could not believe that Congress "scuttled the entire effort by providing the Executive with the seemingly limitless power to withhold funds from allotment and obligation."[30]

The President is the chief enforcer of the federal laws. Given their sheer volume and complexity, all laws cannot be enforced with equal attention and vigor, nor with uniform emphasis at all times. The President's personal values influence his choices. Enforcement of the environmental laws, for example, was less vigorous under Ford than under Carter, and the prospects were even worse under Reagan, with his disdain for governmental activism. Enforcement may also encounter circumstances requiring the President to employ force. When whiskey-making farmers shunned payment of federal taxes and shot tax collectors, President Washington activated a military force to combat the situation. An Act of February 28, 1795, utilized by Washington and interpreted decades later by the Court, made the President "the sole and exclusive judge" of the facts justifying the use of his powers under the Act.[31]

Domestic violence and insurrection and other obstructions of the enforcement of the laws may prompt the President to impose martial law. In *Luther* v. *Borden* (7 How. 62, 1849) the Court recognized that the government as a whole can treat an insurrection as a state of war. In the Prize cases of the Civil War (2 Bl. 635, 1863) the Court determined that the President, as Chief Executive and Commander-in-Chief, alone can impose martial law on a region in insurrection, setting aside the constitutional rights of its inhabitants. This sweeping doctrine was modified by the post–Civil War case, *Ex parte Milligan* (4 Wall. 2, 1866) holding that the courts must ultimately determine the necessity of imposing martial law.

Presidents have not hesitated to exercise some variant of Theodore Roosevelt's "stewardship theory," which claimed power for the Chief Executive to do in the people's behalf "anything that the needs of the Nation demanded unless such action was forbidden by the Constitution or by the laws."[32] This wide-open doctrine is encouraged by *in re Neagle* (135 U.S. 1, 1890) which recognized that the President's duty to "take care that the laws be faithfully executed" is not limited to enforcement of acts of Congress and treaties, but encompasses "the rights, duties, and obligations growing out of the Constitution itself, our international relations, and all the protection implied by the nature of the government under the Constitution." Asserted in many ways, "stewardship" has sometimes led to rebuff, as it did for Truman when, simply on his own authority, he seized the steel mills amidst a labor-management dispute.[33] But in the Indochina war, a challenge to Nixon, contesting his claim of autonomous power to wage war, was repulsed.[34]

# Disability

The President, as the Constitution anticipates and history demonstrates, may fall victim to crushing illness or to death. Eight Presidents (almost one out of five) have died in office, four by assassination. A sick President may be unable to discharge the duties of his office. According to Richard Hansen's computations, the cumulative periods of actual presidential disability add up to a full year in which the country was "without a President." Such periods unfortunately occurred during difficult times, when large issues demanded the Chief Executive's full vigor and skill. Until the Twenty-fifth Amendment was adopted in 1967, the problem of disability was treated by provisions in Article II, whose language was a quagmire of ambiguity.[35] Article II reads,

> In case of [the President's] inability to discharge the powers and duties of the said office, the same shall devolve on the Vice President, and the Congress may by law provide for the case of . . . inability, both of the President and Vice President, declaring what officer shall then act as President, and such officer shall act accordingly, until the disability be removed or a President shall be elected.

Neither here nor elsewhere in the original Constitution were the following questions answered: Who is authorized to say whether a President is unable to discharge the powers and duties of his office? If he is unable, does the office become vacant? To what does the Vice President succeed when the President is disabled—to the "powers and duties of the said office" or to the office itself? What is the election referred to—the next regular presidential election or a special election called by Congress?

## James A. Garfield

Twice in American experience Presidents have been incapacitated for extended periods. President Garfield lay stricken after July 2, 1881, when an assassin's bullet struck a vertebra of his spinal column and became deeply embedded in the muscles of his back. The White House was converted into a hospital, and fans in the President's sickroom blew cool breezes over ice to provide relief from the capital's broiling summer.[36] The President, a large, rugged man who faced his ordeal with unflagging heroism, rallied through most of July. In August he passed through cycles of decline and improvement. On September 6 he was transported by rail with maximum precautions to Elberon on the New Jersey coast, where it was hoped the sea air would by some miracle rally him. But his strength only dwindled, and in a few days he died.

During his entire illness, President Garfield committed only one official act. He signed an extradition paper, prepared in the State Department, after a physician read it aloud. He saw only Mrs. Garfield and his doctors and had no visitors except one day at Elberon, when members of his cabinet filed in for brief interviews. The Star Route frauds,* inherited from the previous Hayes administration, still bedeviled the Post Office Department, and the gush of illicit dollars from the United States Treasury into corrupt hands continued. The President's isolation brought to a standstill Secretary of State James G. Blaine's effort to modify the existing Clayton-Bulwer Treaty in the interest of the proposed Nicaraguan canal. (Blaine's ultimate purpose in this complex maneuver was to establish an isthmian canal under United States control.) A conference of American republics that the President had called was postponed.[37]

As the neglected problems accumulated, demands spiraled in the press, in Congress, and among the cabinet that Vice President Chester Arthur take over the duties of the incapacitated President. The cabinet, which was most distressed by the ravages of neglect, earnestly discussed the Vice President's possible assumption of presidential authority, a prospect that repelled them. Agitated meetings in the Secretaries' offices and homes quickly revealed disagreement on a thorny issue of constitutional interpretation. Four of the seven Secretaries believed that Arthur's exercise of presidential power would make him President for the remainder of the existing term and would immediately and permanently oust Garfield from the office. Legalistic interpretation was not the only bond joining those in the cabinet in opposition to the Vice President's assumption of presidential duties. Arthur, in their view, belonged to a low order of politicians—the "Stalwart" Republicans—who had wished Grant to be nominated for a third term and had fought Garfield with waspish oratory and savage deed ever since the onset of his presidency.

Chester Arthur, for his part, was facing the question of his assumption of the presidency with characteristic prudence. He stayed out of public view, dodged the press, and remained in New York as much as possible. The most painful element in Arthur's situation was the cold suspicion with which the President's friends beheld him.[38] But for all their revulsion toward Arthur, the cabinet in the later days of Garfield's illness again considered the question of the Vice President's succession. To the harried Secretaries the mounting pile of neglected problems left no choice. Postmaster General Thomas L. James was dispatched to New York to ascertain Arthur's views. The Vice President's answer was swift and categorical. Under no circumstances would he assume the responsibilities of the Presidency while Garfield was alive. The Vice President held to his point and public problems drifted. Not until his own formal investiture in the Presidency after Garfield's death did Arthur touch the power of the office.[39]

---

*These frauds occurred in the carriage of mails over roads marked by asterisks in the official records and popularly known as "star routes." The Post Office scandalously overpaid certain persons operating such lines, including the chairman of the Republican National Committee.

## Woodrow Wilson

The other occasion of extended presidential incapacity occurred during the second administration of Woodrow Wilson, at a time immeasurably more serious than Garfield's. During the ailing Wilson's taxing Western trip in September 1919 intended to rally the people behind the League of Nations, the President collapsed and was rushed back by train to Washington. Conflicting versions persist of the onset of the President's illness. One, by Mrs. Wilson and Rear Admiral Cary T. Grayson, the President's physician, contends that Wilson "collapsed" in the West, returned to Washington, and three days later suffered a stroke described by Mrs. Wilson as "paralyzing the left side of his body. An arm and one leg were useless."[40] A contrasting version by Joe Tumulty, the President's trusted secretary, holds that the stroke occurred in Colorado, during the Western journey. At 5 A.M. September 26 in Pueblo, where the presidential train had stopped, Tumulty was aroused by a knock on the door of his sleeping compartment. It was Dr. Grayson with word that the President was seriously ill. Tumulty rushed to the train's drawing room where the President, fully dressed, was seated in a chair. Tumulty stood transfixed by the spectacle. "His face was pale and wan," the secretary later described it. "One side of it had fallen, and his condition was indeed pitiful to behold. . . . His left arm and leg refused to function. I then realized that the President's whole left side was paralyzed."[41]

The White House was again transformed into a hospital. The President, who was not expected to live long, somehow clung to the edge of existence. Although his body was broken, his mind was clear. "Physically he was very weak," observed Grayson, "but mentally very alert."[42] Meanwhile, the nation was caught up in the cumbrous transition from warmaking to peacemaking. The peace treaty, with its controversial League of Nations provision, was before the Senate at midcourse, where it faced the hostility of the President's arch rival, Henry Cabot Lodge. On the autumn agenda were scheduled visits of European dignitaries with the President. Domestically, the economy was demobilizing to peacetime footing. In the din and lash of public business, the President lay crippled, his true condition known only to his wife, his physician, and the little ring of medical specialists who surrounded him and desperately administered their skills. The President, in their general opinion, was hopelessly beyond recovery. A year and a half of his term stretched ahead. What was to be done?

Dr. Francis X. Dercum, the eminent nerve authority, told Mrs. Wilson, "Madam, it is a grave situation, but I think you can solve it. Have everything come to you; weigh the importance of each matter, and see if it is possible by consultations with the respective heads of the Departments to solve them without the guidance of your husband. In this way you can save him a great deal. But always keep in mind that every time you take him a new anxiety or problem to excite him, you are turning a knife in an open wound. His nerves are crying out for rest, and any excitement is torture to him."[43] The *modus operandi* suggested by Dr. Dercum was quickly instituted for the remainder of Wilson's term. Officials coming to the White House took up with Mrs. Wilson business that hitherto they had discussed with the President.[44] In deciding what was important, Mrs. Wilson, of course, was making a vital kind of policy decision.

Even the trusted Tumulty, who had been accustomed to seeing the President whenever he chose, bent to the new procedure. Only Mrs. Wilson and Dr. Grayson saw the President. Somehow the public business limped forward. The hurdle of the State of the Union message, an annual and unalterable constitutional requirement, was managed when cabinet Secretaries, acting in accordance with the traditional procedure, submitted paragraphs reflecting their departmental concerns to the White House. There Tumulty received them and wove them together into a single document of reasonable coherence. It was read to Wilson and, with a few changes, the President approved it. On his better days, the President read state papers or listened as Mrs. Wilson read. He signed documents and in bursts of strength dictated notes for Senator Gilbert Hitchcock's guidance in the treaty fight.

But the President's dedicated helpers and his own valiant effort could not tame the mounting suspicion and unrest in the world outside. Secretary of State Robert Lansing believed that the President was not really writing the papers purporting to come from him. The Senate, collectively overcome by curiosity, appointed Hitchcock and Albert B. Fall, soon destined for exposure in the muck of Teapot Dome, as a committee to inquire into the condition of the President. After a visit with Wilson, they reported publicly that his mind was clear and that he was recovering. The baseless and misleading character of the latter finding appalled Mrs. Wilson. Nor did the Senators' reassurances deter several sensational newspapers from contending that the President was tightly secluded because he was insane, or that he was dead and his death was being kept secret.

The cabinet Secretary most concerned over the leaderless state of affairs was the head of the senior executive department, Secretary of State Robert Lansing. A responsible man of granitic integrity, he decided it was time to act. He arranged a private meeting with presidential secretary Tumulty in the cabinet room. As diplomatically as possible, Lansing said he wished to suggest that in view of Wilson's incapacity the Vice President be called in to act in lieu of the President. To reinforce his suggestion, he cited the disability provisions of the Constitution. Tumulty was outraged at this seeming invitation to mutiny, and candidly vented his displeasure. Who, he asked, could authoritatively determine the fact of the President's disability? Those having the best information of it, answered Lansing—Dr. Grayson and Tumulty himself. Dr. Grayson, when he learned of the proposal, helped Tumulty to kill it quickly. If "anyone outside the White House," Tumulty warned Lansing, attempted to certify that the President was unable to carry on his duties, the President's physician and secretary would jointly repudiate the notion.[45]

Tumulty's rebuff did not quiet Lansing's conscience, agonized by the drift of affairs. The Secretary of State tried another tactic. The cabinet, the President's chief body of counselors, had not met since the commencement of Wilson's illness. If the cabinet were to meet occasionally on its own initiative, Lansing reasoned, the country's confidence would be buoyed. He placed this new inspiration before his fellow Secretaries. Their response was favorable, and Lansing as senior Secretary began calling and holding meetings of his fellow department heads in his office. That Lansing took the venture seriously is attested by the fact that in the first four months of

Wilson's illness twenty-one cabinet meetings were called. When Wilson ultimately learned of them, he promptly wrote to Lansing pointing out that under established constitutional procedure only the President could convene the department heads into conference and no one but he and Congress were entitled to request their views, collectively or individually, on public questions. Wilson's letter blazed with implications that Lansing's resignation would not be unwelcome. It was quickly forthcoming.[46] Wilson remained an invalid for the rest of his life, and finished out his term with his activity highly curtailed.

## Dwight D. Eisenhower

The several illnesses of Dwight D. Eisenhower, although fortunately less severe than those of his predecessors, stirred national and world concern. In 1955 President Eisenhower sustained a coronary thrombosis, in 1956 an ileitis attack and operation, and in 1957 a mild stroke. In his first and most serious illness the President was totally removed from governmental affairs for only four days, after which he initialed papers. Sixteen weeks passed, however, before the President resumed his normal workload. Scarcely had he returned to full duty when the second illness crashed upon him. The combination of both illnesses left the President partially disabled for twenty-two weeks.

Eisenhower's first illness raised a question that was settled then and for his subsequent lesser illnesses. During the President's disability, full or partial, who should discharge his duties? Although the Constitution pointed to the Vice President, Richard M. Nixon, the smooth-working team of White House staff and department heads posed an alternative. So freely had Eisenhower delegated duties and authority to his aides since the outset of his administration that they could function almost autonomously in his absence forced by illness. The "team's" director was Sherman Adams, "the assistant to the President," widely viewed as the President's chief of staff. Another member of large importance was James Hagerty, the administration's chief public relations officer, the press secretary, who stood high in the President's esteem.[47]

Under the emerging formula Adams and the department heads handled the regular operations of the executive branch. Nixon took on certain established, more or less ceremonial capacities. He made public addresses and appearances and presided at meetings of the cabinet and the National Security Council, as he had done during past presidential absences. Press conferences with Hagerty were supplemented by occasional Nixon press conferences where a top official's comment was indispensable. Eisenhower's administrative machinery displayed an impressive capacity for self-direction, and thanks largely to Vice President Nixon's exemplary restraint there were no struggles for power.

Eisenhower's only incapacity of any duration, the heart attack, struck during a governmental lull. Congress was in recess, no international meetings or moves were afoot, public urgencies were few. In contrast, the third illness—the stroke—occurred during a critical period. The Russians had put their first Sputnik into orbit only a month before, and the prestige of America's military and technological might had become murkily suspect at home and abroad. A NATO meeting of heads of state was three weeks off, and the early signs of the acute 1958 economic recession were visible. But the gathering crisis was confined by the President's quick recovery.

# Handling Disability

### The Twenty-fifth Amendment

The nation's several encounters with presidential illness and its attendant constitutional and administrative problems stirred wide and thoughtful concern, which finally led to the passage of the Twenty-fifth Amendment in 1967. The amendment, often known as the Bayh amendment, after its chief congressional manager, Senator Birch Bayh of Indiana, was carried by an irresistible momentum following President Kennedy's assassination. Senator Kenneth Keating reflected the mood of Congress when he declared that "as distasteful as it is to entertain the thought, a matter of inches spelled the difference between the painless death of John F. Kennedy and the possibility of his permanent incapacity to exercise the duties of the highest office of the land."[48] An awareness swept through Congress that careful action could no longer be postponed to protect the nation from the peril of a headless government in the nuclear age. However, discussion and action were complicated by the multitude of proposals advanced and by the dispersal of attention over several key questions.

*What is disability?*   The Founding Fathers did not answer the question in the Constitution, nor does the Twenty-fifth Amendment undertake to define it. Disability encompasses literally dozens of conditions that defy exhaustive cataloguing. Ruth Silva, the leading authority on the subject, concludes that the Constitution contemplates "any *de facto* inability, whatever the cause or the duration, if it occurs at a time when the urgency of public business requires executive action."[49]

Disability is clearly not limited to physical illness but extends to mental illness as well and covers periods when the President is missing or captured in military operations. In an era of intercontinental missiles, when decisions on which national survival may turn must be taken in minutes, any definition of inability must be made carefully to include all contingencies. "The everpresent possibility of an attack on the United States was always hanging over us," Richard Nixon wrote of the brief period of Eisenhower's unavailability following his heart attack. "Would the President be well enough to make a decision? If not, who had the authority to push the button?" Or again, Eisenhower's ileitis seizure necessitated an operation at Walter Reed Hospital, where the President was under anesthesia for two hours. "The country," Eisenhower commented afterward to Nixon, "was without a Chief Executive, the armed forces without a Commander-in-Chief."[50]

*Who determines disability?*   The Twenty-fifth Amendment provides that the President determine his own disability but requires that he communicate his finding in writing to the President pro tempore of the Senate and the Speaker of the House.

But what if the President refuses to proclaim his disability or because of his physical and mental circumstances cannot? The amendment stipulates that the Vice President, acting in concert with a majority of the cabinet, or of such "other body" as Congress may by law provide, could advise the President pro tempore of the Senate and the Speaker that the President was disabled. The "other body" was described in Congressional debate as a commission of private citizens, doctors, or psychiatrists, who might be summoned to pass judgment upon the President's competence.

Most discussions of the disability problem agreed that the Vice President should not have to bear sole responsibility for finding the President disabled but that he should have help, preferably from the cabinet. The cabinet, the argument goes, thanks to its daily contacts with the President, would be best informed of his plight. The department Secretaries' deepest inclination would be to act loyally and fairly to the President, since their job security depends upon him.

The cabinet's critics hold that it would be too blinded by self-interested loyalty ever to certify the President's disability. The possibility of retaliation by the President, when he recovered sufficiently, would encourage cabinet inaction. Wilson dismissed Lansing, and Harry S. Truman once declared in post-presidential utterances that if his cabinet had ever declared him disabled while he was confined on the flat of his back, his first act upon rising would be to fire every culprit who had supported the finding.

The cabinet's limitations suggest the wisdom of the "other body," the alternative contained in the Twenty-fifth Amendment, whose members might include distinguished citizens and leading physicians and psychiatrists. Disability is most likely to be largely a medical question, for which authentic answers are best provided by qualified professionals. Disability is never only a medical question, however. It poses a tandem political question: Does the public interest at the time require the exercise of presidential power? Doctors have no inherent superiority over other citizens in assessing "public interest." Even in medical questions genuine professional differences as well as personal political preferences may hold sway in diagnostic judgment.

***To what does the Vice President succeed?***    If the President is disabled, does the Vice President assume the office's "powers and duties" or succeed to the office itself? Does he become Acting President, serving temporarily until the disabled President has recovered, or does he take over permanently for the remainder of the term? Vice Presidents Arthur and Marshall were deterred from taking over from their infirm Presidents by the wide opinion of their fellow public officials that a disabled President once pushed aside could never return. The Constitution, they reasoned, did not allow for two Presidents to exist simultaneously, one acting and the other ailing. The Twenty-fifth Amendment should settle the whole problem once and for all. It declares that when the President is disabled the Vice President shall assume "the powers and duties of the office as Acting President."

***Who determines when the disability ends?***    The amendment provides that the President shall decide. But what if the President wants to get back to work too soon, before he is sufficiently recovered from his disability? The amendment specifies that if the Vice President and a majority of the cabinet or of the "other body" did not agree that the President had re-covered, then Congress would resolve the issue. It could, by two-thirds vote of each house, decide that the President was still unable to discharge his duties, whereupon the Vice President would continue as Acting President.

While under congressional debate, the features of the Twenty-fifth Amendment permitting the Vice President and the "other body" to find the President disabled, as an alternative to a finding by the Vice President en-dorsed by the cabinet, were criticized. It was charged that such provisions would enable the Vice President to "shop around" for support of his view that the President was disabled. Senator Albert Gore warned that "this na-tion could undergo the potentially disastrous spectacle of competing claims to the power of the Presidency."[51] Senator Bayh contended that such a power scramble was unlikely, and the bulk of the testimony before his sub-committee stressed that the amendment's disability provisions would be in-voked only in the most extreme circumstances and that in the attending atmosphere of crisis executive officials and Congress could be expected to act responsibly. Witnesses paid no heed to the ghost of Andrew Johnson weeping at their folly. They were more impressed that in the nuclear age ambiguity was no longer tolerable and that it must be displaced with clearly defined rules and procedures. Committee witnesses, representatives of the legal profession, and citizen groups sounded a loud "amen" to Walter Lippmann's observation that the Twenty-fifth Amendment is "a great deal better than an endless search . . . for the absolutely perfect solution . . . which will never be found, and . . . is not necessary."[52]

# Succession

The Founding Fathers, who were geniuses at spotting thorny problems and passing them on to hapless posterity to wrestle with, applied their sure touch to presidential succession. The all-seeing Fathers anticipated the ca-lamitous day when a double vacancy might befall the nation—when both President and Vice President might be unavailable because of death, resig-nation, impeachment, or disability. The Fathers, accordingly, posed no so-lution, but simply empowered Congress to enact a law "declaring what officer shall then act as President." Congress has thrice passed such laws, the last in 1947, and each time its labors have provoked criticism and sent citizens scurrying for better remedies.

In its three laws, Congress vacillated between drawing upon its own lead-ers and the members of the cabinet in laying the lines of succession. Con-siderations of pure political science have seldom motivated Congress's actions. The first law of 1792 was not a solution rooted in Olympian wisdom but a narrow partisan act. The law's object was to prevent the succession of Secretary of State Thomas Jefferson. The conservative leaders of Congress, who abhorred Jefferson, simply by-passed him and voted one of themselves into the succession. If the presidency and the vice-presidency were vacant, the President pro tempore of the Senate, and after him the Speaker, would succeed. Neither officer was to become President upon the takeover, but only Acting President. If the double vacancy happened within the first two years and seven months of the presidential term, Congress was required to call a special election "forthwith."

In 1886 Congress passed a new law, the pendulum now swinging to the cabinet. In a future double vacancy the succession would run from the Secretary of State to the Secretary of the Interior in the order in which the departments were established. No Secretary could be wafted by fate and the act into the presidential chair if he could not satisfy the regular constitutional qualifications for the presidency. The 1792 act's special election feature was dropped.

During Harry Truman's first weeks in the presidency, into which he had been catapulted by Franklin Roosevelt's death, he perceived grievous limitations in the 1886 act. He incorporated his concern and recommendations for a new succession law in a special message to Congress on June 19, 1945. The 1886 act, placing the Secretary of State, an appointed and not an elected officer, next in line for the presidency in effect permitted Truman to name his own successor. "I do not believe that in a democracy," the President declared, "this power should rest with the Chief Executive." In the new legislation he proposed, Truman contended that after the President and Vice President in the succession line should come the Speaker of the House of Representatives, because he "is elected in his own district" and "is also elected to be the presiding officer of the House by a vote of all the representatives of all the people of the country." After the Speaker, in the Truman plan, would come the President pro tempore who is elected first by the people of his state and then by the whole Senate. Following the President pro tempore would be "the members of the Cabinet as provided now by law."[53]

Since Edward Stettinius, Jr., a career businessman, was Secretary of State at the time and Sam Rayburn, a career politician, the Speaker, the House of Representatives passed a bill reflecting Truman's views with vast cheers for Rayburn and a proud sense of doing something nice for one's own. When the bill reached the upper chamber, however, James F. Byrnes, a distinguished and popular former Senator and Congressman, had replaced Stettinius as Secretary of State. Congressional enthusiasm for the succession bill shriveled. It was nearly dead when the Republican triumph in the 1946 congressional elections suddenly revived it. The bill passed in 1947, and Truman dutifully signed it, thereby establishing not a Democratic but a Republican Speaker, Joe Martin, as his successor. After the Speaker, under the 1947 act, come the President pro tempore of the Senate, the Secretaries of State, the Treasury, and Defense, the Attorney General, the Postmaster General, and the Secretaries of the Interior, Agriculture, Commerce, and Labor. The Secretaries of Health and Human Services, Housing and Urban Development, Transportation, Energy, and Education also figure in the succession.

## The 1947 Act

Like bygone succession laws, the 1947 act stirred more reproach than praise. It trampled upon the separation of powers principle by bringing two legislative officers into the presidential line. Truman's estimable image of the Speakership as a popular "democratic" office is open to challenge. The Speaker's electorate is local rather than national, his district a patch of a few square miles on the face of a continental nation. His elevation to the Speakership reflects not simply the "popularity" Truman valued, but seniority, parliamentary skill, party fidelity, and finesse in personal politics. Even worse, Speakers as a lot compare unfavorably with Secretaries of State, the Treasury, or Defense as presidential timber. As executive officers the Secretaries would afford better continuity in succeeding to the presidency than an "outsider" like the Speaker. Ironically, the 1947 act revived the Ben Wade–Andrew Johnson "temptation" by creating for the Speaker and the President pro tempore a vested interest in the President's impeachment.

The 1947 act also stumbled upon the imperatives of the nuclear age. The act did not face up to the possibility that in a future nuclear war one tolerably aimed bomb could destroy Washington and with it the whole company of presidential successors. Earlier succession laws would have done no better.

The Twenty-fifth Amendment seeks to minimize the possibilities of a double vacancy occurring in the presidency and vice-presidency. The amendment requires the President in the event that the office of Vice President is vacant to nominate a Vice President who will take office upon confirmation by a majority vote of both houses of Congress. This feature of the Twenty-fifth Amendment attracted the greatest unanimity in the Bayh subcommittee hearings.

But history can be prankish with surprises, and the vice presidential provision of the amendment was invoked under grotesque, totally unanticipated circumstances. In 1973, Vice President Agnew suddenly resigned under an agreement with the Justice Department by which he admitted evasion of federal income taxes and bartered away his office to avoid imprisonment. The stage was therefore set for President Nixon, who had himself already moved under the shadow of impeachment, to fulfill the requirements of the Twenty-fifth Amendment and nominate a new Vice President. Initially, Nixon veered toward John B. Connally, an erstwhile Democrat who had become a Republican, but Democratic congressional leaders announced that they would oppose him. Nixon's ultimate selection, House Republican leader Gerald R. Ford, a popular figure on Capitol Hill, was instantly acclaimed.[54] Nevertheless, the episode itself is abhorrent to democratic standards. At a point when he was badly discredited and was soon to be driven from office, Nixon chose his own successor, thanks to the Twenty-fifth Amendment. The public had little, if any, voice in the selection of the new President. Even more, Ford chose his potential successor, Nelson Rockefeller, to fill the vice presidency, vacated by his own succession to the presidency. Again, the people's impact was minimal.

# Transition

The environment of the modern presidency makes imperative not only a rational method of succession but a smooth transition between the outgoing and the incoming Chief Executives. In an age when several foreign affairs crises can flame simultaneously around the globe, when weapons systems consume an average of seven years in passing from drawing board to operation, when the economy grows ever more intricate and sensitive, a snarl or lapse in public policy invites disaster.

Of modern Presidents, Hoover was the first to seek consultations and joint policy-making with the President-elect. Both Franklin Roosevelt and Truman, when running for reelection, permitted aides to supply the opposing candidates with vital information on foreign affairs. President Truman, mindful of his own sudden and unbriefed trajectory into the presidency, smoothed the transfer to the incoming Eisenhower administration, thus becoming the first outgoing Chief Executive to accept the responsibility squarely for orderly transition. President Eisenhower reciprocated by easing the Kennedy administration's advent in 1961.[55]

The Johnson-Nixon transfer of 1968–69 advanced the developing institutionalization of transition. Following his announcement on March 31, 1968, that he would not be a candidate for reelection, Johnson offered briefings by the CIA and the State and Defense Departments to all major candidates, and following their nominations, Johnson summoned Nixon and George Wallace to the White House for consultations. Throughout the campaign, Johnson briefed the candidates on his policies, including the bombing halt in Vietnam, and they in turn abstained from directly criticizing the war or in any way undercutting the President and negotiations for peace— a remarkable exercise of restraint, given the potential of the war issue for political gain.

In the 1972 elections, Nixon offered to brief his opponent, George McGovern, on the Vietnam war through his national security assistant, Henry Kissinger, which the Senator discounted, asserting that "I've frankly learned more about the realities of Vietnam from following the dispatches of good newspapermen than I have from official briefings in the White House." Throughout the campaign, McGovern maintained a distant and wary stance toward the Nixon administration. His approach to ending the conflict in Vietnam was poles apart from the administration's, and he did not mean to blur the difference by consorting with the White House.[56]

Days after his 1980 election, Ronald Reagan appointed a Transition Executive Committee, chaired by William J. Casey, his campaign director, with Edwin Meese III, his campaign chief of staff, as its director. Other committee members were Anne Armstrong and Senator Paul Laxalt of Nevada, who also played key roles in the campaign. Casey and Armstrong had held major posts in the Nixon and Ford administrations. President Carter appointed a transition group led by Jack Watson, White House chief of staff. Both sides issued statements brimming with expressions of cooperation and good will. The recipient of briefings from the Carter administration, Reagan hewed to transition etiquette in emphasizing that Carter was "still the President," and that he was "not going to intrude" in matters such as the hostage negotiations with Iran, then at a delicate stage.[57]

Generally, transitions are easier if the incumbent President is not a candidate for reelection. Transition is also facilitated if party turnover occurs at short intervals, since a party returning to power after a hiatus of only two presidential terms is still mindful of the complexities of policy problems and enjoys acquaintanceship among the higher echelons of the career service.

For all the surface appearance of cooperation and harmony, transitions are beset with tensions and cross-purposes of the outgoing and incoming Presidents. The outgoing President prizes continuity and order, the preservation of his policies, and the maturation of his half-begun projects in the next administration. The President-elect is cautious and aloof, watchful of involving his freedom and the mandate and prestige of his electoral victory in policies of the incumbent administration over which he has no control. The new President's personal philosophy may be radically at odds with the incumbent President's, as Eisenhower's laissez-faire preferences were miles removed from the welfare-state commitment of Truman. The new and old Presidents may differ in their view of presidential method: Harding's Whiggery was a long way from Wilson's dynamism. But the distance between Carter and Reagan was shorter, which eased their dealings.

★ ★ ★ **The Future Presidency** ★ ★ ★

Thoughtful concern and discussion regarding disability and succession is apt to wax well into the future. Viewing the President, as we do, under the cruel pressures of the nuclear age, what seems best on each of these scores for keeping the presidency continuously strong and responsive to democratic standards?

1. Although the Twenty-fifth Amendment is not flawless, it would probably be best to leave the subject of disability at rest and to anticipate, confidently and prayerfully, that its provisions could be applied in workable manner by responsible officials should the need arise.

2. There are several possible, although remote, contingencies of presidential tenure that never troubled us in quieter, bygone times. In the nuclear era, however, with its infinite perils and ever shrinking timetables, we should put our minds to them although the cloud they make on our political horizon is no larger than a human fist.

   (a) Suppose the presidential or vice-presidential candidate should die or become disabled prior to the popular election in November. The situation is not covered by law. Both major parties have empowered their national committees to fill the vacancy, and the Republican committee has the further option of summoning a new convention. We would be on firmer legal ground if the procedure were incorporated into law.

   (b) Suppose the presidential or vice-presidential candidate should die after the November popular election but before the electors met in their respective state capitals in December to cast their votes. Under present law the electors could vote for anyone they pleased. Both major parties, however, have authorized their national committees to fill the vacancy, and the likelihood is that the electors would vote for the new nominee. If the presidential nominee should die, the country would likely expect the vice-presidential nominee to fill the vacancy, and his place, in turn, to be filled by a new nominee. All this is a darkling plain, barren of precedent.

(c) Suppose that after the electors vote in their respective states and before January 6, when the electoral votes are opened, announced, and counted in Congress, the presidential candidate should die. The possibilities are grisly. The candidate's death would raise the question whether votes for a dead man could be counted. If they could and if he were the winner, the election would be thrown into the House of Representatives. Some authorities argue that Congress could reconvene the electoral college to permit the electors to change their votes. Still others hold that Congress could make the vice-presidential winner the President-elect. Probably the easiest way out would be to declare the dead candidate, if he was the winner, the President-elect, and, under the Twentieth Amendment, the Vice President–elect would become President on Inauguration Day, January 20.

(d) Suppose no presidential candidate receives a majority of the electoral votes, and the election is thrown into the House of Representatives, but before the House acts, one of the candidates eligible to be voted upon dies. No procedure exists for filling the vacancy. The Twentieth Amendment, however, empowers Congress to resolve the situation. Conceivably, Congress could permit the national committee of the party affected by the death to propose a replacement.

Fortunately, the law of probabilities runs strongly against the occurrence of these several nightmares. But on the theory that the governmental structure must never falter in our troubled day, these are fit subjects for study by Congress and interested citizens.

3. For reasons we have explored, the 1947 Succession Act is a mistake, and it ought to be repealed. To replace it, the act of 1886 might be restored with the line of succession proceeding through the cabinet, beginning with the Secretary of State. In addition, the line of succession might well be extended. Those now in the line pass most of their time in Washington, a circumstance that makes possible the extinction of the entire body of successors in a nuclear attack on the capital. Congress might well add to the succession persons distributed around the country. One possibility might be to include the governors ranked according to the population of their states in the last census.

4. The Twenty-fifth Amendment has been attacked as "a total howling political absurdity" that enables a President, under the murkiest suspicion of impeachable and criminal activity, to name his own successor.[58] Gerald Ford, the chief beneficiary of the amendment, whose appointment as Vice President, under its terms, permitted his ultimate ascendance to the presidency, concluded that it was "appropriate" to "take another look" at the constitutional provision through which his and Nelson Rockefeller's accession occurred.[59]

Defenders of the amendment contend that it facilitated the removal of Richard Nixon after he lost the confidence of Congress and the people. The amendment's chief author, Senator Birch Bayh (D-Ind.) and Congressman Peter Rodino (D-N.J.) who led the impeachment inquiry, contend that Nixon would never have resigned without the prospect of a Republican successor, which the amendment assured. "The 25th amendment works, and works well," Rodino has testified. Other defenders contend that the thorough Congressional scrutiny, to which both vice-presidential designates were subjected, furnished the public a far better conception of their qualifications than the provisions of the 1947 Succession Act, under which the Speaker of the House was automatically elevated.

The chief alternatives to the amendment are reliance on a congressionally provided line of succession similar to the Succession Act of 1947, and a proposal by Senator John Pastore (D-R.I.) for a special election of the President whenever an appointed Vice President becomes President, as Ford did, with more than one year remaining in the Presidential term. The Pastore proposal avoids the absurd circumstance of the discredited Nixon's selection of Ford. But critics of the special election proposal suggest that it too might become a nest of unwanted consequences. The election would be costly, involve delay and uncertainty, and it might polarize the country at a juncture when consensus would be imperative. Perhaps the better part of prudence would be to value the Twenty-fifth Amendment for what it is—an imperfect response to a tantalizing, unsolvable problem.

5. Supporters of an effective presidency and the democratic ideal of free electoral choice ought to work for the repeal of the Twenty-second Amendment. Even more, the electorate needs to do a better job in choosing Presidents who are democratically fit, as an easier alternative than the belated discovery of their defect after they are in office, with the anguish of impeachment or forced resignation as the only remedies.

# Chapter Five

# Publics

The hours when the American presidency has enjoyed its most brilliant effectiveness, when democracy and the strong executive seem in finest congruence, are those when the Chief Executive rallies public sentiment behind policies addressed to the common good. Theodore Roosevelt moving against the abuses of giant railroads, Woodrow Wilson advancing his New Freedom program of social justice, Franklin Roosevelt combating the Great Depression and reforming the economy were achievements of leadership that stirred the understanding and support of the generality of the people.[1] Ronald Reagan was tested in his ability to advocate policies alleviating inflation, energy, and other problems whose burdens fall heavily on the citizenry, and to convince the public of the plausibility of his measures.

## "Voice of the People"

The President's most profound and continuous relationship is with the American people, who not merely award the prize of election but are at once the source and affirmation of his policies. When the people are behind him, he can better withstand the lesser publics—the interest groups with their lobbyists, congressional spokesmen, and bureaucratic defenders—who often successfully oppose him. With fine flourish, Woodrow Wilson once hailed the President's capacity to incorporate the "Voice of the People":

His is the only national voice in affairs. Let him once win the admiration and confidence of the country, and no other single force can withstand him, no combination of forces will easily overpower him. His position takes the imagination of the country. . . . If he rightly interpret the national thought and boldly insist upon it, he is irresistible; and the country never feels the zest for action so much as when its President is of such insight and calibre.[2]

But the function celebrated by Wilson also has a repelling underside. The worst political disaster to befall a President is to lose the public's confidence and trust. Lyndon Johnson lost it in committing himself so wholeheartedly to the Vietnam war. When the mounting trouble of Watergate spurred Richard Nixon to dismiss Special Prosecutor Archibald Cox, and Attorney General Elliot Richardson resigned and Deputy Attorney General William Ruckelshaus was fired, a political firestorm burst upon the nation, Nixon's standing in the public's trust went up in flames, and with it his hold on the presidency.[3]

In the post-Watergate, post-Vietnam presidency, the Chief Executive has sometimes complained that a hard residue of distrust curtails and even cripples his ability to govern. Well into its term, for example, the Carter administration was depicted as "troubled by a gnawing fear that the country will not back it if it gets into a posture involving risks in foreign policy."[4] But according to a study of public opinion polls since Watergate, Presidents of the current era may sometimes exaggerate the less than prosperous fortunes of their office in public estimation. The presidency as an institution, after bottoming out in public esteem with Watergate and Nixon's resignation in 1974, has gained significantly since then, while Congress continues to decline. Frequently, public opinion polls do not adequately distinguish between confidence in particular presidential leadership and confidence in the office itself. The polls suggest that Carter's doubts are more traceable to his own performance than to the office he occupied, for the public's confidence in it and the country's future appears staunch.[5]

## Patterns of Presidential Leadership

The office of the presidency, with its wide-ranging functions and responsibilities, manifests the dynamics of leadership in many patterns. Leadership studies emphasize role and function, the tendency of leaders' characteristics to vary significantly, depending on their context. "Context" includes the situation to which leadership is addressed, whether, for example, the times are those of crisis or normalcy, with each calling for different leadership skills. "Situation" includes the "group" in whose behalf the leader functions. Its character and its needs shape, or even determine, the appropriateness of a leadership style. Drawing on political science and social science analyses of leadership, the following are among the more prominent patterns discernible in the President's leadership activities:

*Transactional, transformational*    In his study, *Leadership,* James MacGregor Burns distinguishes between these two types of leadership. In transactional leadership, the leader (President) and followers (public and groups) cultivate each other's support through exchanges of votes, jobs, subsidies, and promises embodied in platforms. Transactional leadership is "maintenance leadership" that keeps the political process oiled and the ship of state afloat. Pedestrian and bland, transactional leadership is denoted by minimal creativity, morality, and slender responsiveness to significant public problems.

In transformational leadership, the leader recognizes and responds seriously to basic needs and values and commits his talents to empowering his followers to attain their goals. The transforming leader (President) engages the full person of the follower (public and groups); each side stimulates and elevates the other to the point that followers are converted into leaders and leaders into moral agents. Leaders (Presidents) compete with other leaders, such as legislators and would-be Presidents, for followers' approval and act responsibly toward their commitments.[6] No President can escape the chores of transactional leadership—dispensing patronage and the porkbarrel of the executive branch, for example. The office thrusts upon the incumbent many opportunities for transformational leadership—the messages to Congress, election and reelection, the opportunities embodied in events, and the President's empowerment by Constitution and statute to deal with them. Some Presidents become bogged down in the tasks of transactional leadership, and others overextend themselves in transformational leadership, as Wilson did in his fight for the League of Nations. A President must find a balance between the two.

***Democratic elitism***    According to the theory of democratic elitism the President is one among a number of top-rank public and private elites who occupy the command posts of society in its economy and public offices. The presidency is attained primarily by the wealthy or those of upper-class backgrounds, and by those who hail from careers that have socialized them in elite values. The elite or "power presidency," comprising the President, his top advisers, and principal administrative lieutenants, is closely interlocked with and faithfully supportive of the private corporate power-structure. The consensus of these public and private circles establishes priorities and principles in the formation and execution of public policy.[7]

Leadership is subject to limited competition among elites, as two major parties supply candidates of elite backgrounds to contest for the presidency. To win elections, elites orient policies toward citizen desires, and the citizen, despite a normally low interest in politics, can through the vote and regularly held elections influence the conduct of the President and other officials. Elites, including Presidents, absorb democratic values and abide by the rules of the political game, such as observing civil liberties incorporated in the Bill of Rights, protective of democracy. With elections hanging over their heads, Presidents and other elites produce public policies that are moderately responsive to popular interests; the citizenry with its ignorance, prejudice, and lagging interest in politics is deemed best deterred from becoming too assertive and demanding, lest it push the presidential administration in imprudent directions.[8]

The elitist portrayal of the citizen as indifferent and satisfied is strikingly at odds with the presidency's recent experiences, particularly of the 60s and 70s when protest marches against the Vietnam war and rioting in the cities presented an opposite picture. The enactment of a great corpus of social legislation under presidential leadership (Roosevelt's New Deal and Johnson's Great Society program) discloses serious and not infrequent defeats for elites, who vigorously opposed these efforts. This suggests a lack of the degree of power that elite theory supposes. In contending that democracy's prime goals are stability and efficiency, elite theory leaves presidential leadership little opportunity to advance social justice and largely indifferent to utopian visions of what a good life for all might be.

*Political brokerage*    Although elites dominate the conduct of the social and the political orders, enabling the President and a relatively small number of decision-makers to control the government, leadership must be addressed to the basic task of winning and keeping voter support. Presidents project a verbal image of the good society and the means of constructing it. The President and his electoral challengers function in a two-party system predicated on a broadly encompassing ideological consensus, unlike a multiparty system which maximizes program and policy distinctions.

In constructing and maintaining consensus, Presidents, by making their platforms vague and ambiguous, encourage voters to be irrational. As they develop policies and programs, aware of the difficulty of inducing a majority of the public or Congress to support any single combination of public policies, Presidents tend to develop nonintegrated sets of policies, holding forth inducements for a wide array of potential supporters on the political scale. Consequently, presidential leadership is destined not to produce programs that are reasoned and logical and that respond connectedly to difficult public problems; instead leadership produces incremental gains and packages of disparate outcomes.[9]

The leadership of the broker President is predicated on, in Richard Neustadt's analysis, the power to persuade.[10] The President, surrounded by potent interest groups and the executive branch's bureaucracies with which they are allied, can seldom exercise leadership by issuing orders and commands. Rather, leadership consists of convincing the groups and the bureaus that it is in their interest to do what the President asks. To help these respondents see the light, the President holds forth inducements from the store of benefits and advantages his office provides, and he bargains to evoke the desired behavior and metes out punishments and rewards. If the President can awaken public opinion and enlist its support, he will diminish the formidable task of persuading and bargaining with the bureaus, the groups, and others. Leadership, Neustadt contends, includes a prudent husbanding of bargaining resources, of avoiding overspending and squandering a large investment on a small gain.

*Consensus leadership*    A common form of presidential leadership is rooted in the politics of consensus. According to Lyndon Johnson, one of its most thoroughgoing practitioners, there is for every national problem a national answer that reasonable men can construct through discussion and accommodation. The national answer is not simply what the majority wants. Majorities are transitory and ought not dominate the minority whose thought and action too might contribute valuably to consensus.

To produce consensus and action rather than disagreement and inaction, the President is at the center of the effort, possessing political means capable of invoking a fundamental unity of interest, purpose, and belief in all the nation. As a consensus leader, the President formulates goals having the broadest possible appeal and charts the route to them by offering the specifics of immediate action. The President tends to undertake what Johnson liked to call the "doable"—or that for which there are enough votes or support, a consensus. The President extends the scope of consensus by discovering and developing common denominators of agreement. Prior to the Education Act of 1965, bills providing general aid to education were steadily wrecked on the issue of public aid to church-supported schools. Through discussions with the National Education Association and the National Catholic Welfare Council, the Johnson administration developed a formula acceptable to both groups: to aid not schools as such but their children, whether in public or private schools, and especially in poor areas. With the two major education lobbies brought into a consensus, the administration incorporated the new-found formula into its education bill with an eye to securing maximum votes in Congress. The bill passed without major amendment and a political deadlock that had endured for decades was finally overcome.

The President who is a consensus leader uses his powers with restraint and prefers bipartisan support to partisan strife. For the legislative achievements of his presidency, including its remarkable record in the Eighty-ninth Congress, Johnson was careful to give credit to the minority Republican party and to praise Congress. The consensus President also seeks to broaden the base of his party by making it a party "which serves all our people." [11]

But the consensus approach, even in the hands of its most devoted presidential practitioners, carries certain weaknesses. When the hard business of constructing policy reaches the phase of choosing between competing interests, men divide, partisanship rises, and agreement is lost to conflict. Johnson was bedeviled by breakdowns or the sheer unavailability of consensus in the perversity of Ho Chi Minh in the Vietnam war, in the rioting in American cities, and in the unwillingness of Congress to flesh out his Great Society programs with substantial appropriations.

*Majoritarian president*    Instead of pursuing the consensus method, a President may act as a majoritarian leader who is prepared to take up, if necessary, the politics of combat. He puts himself at the head of a program behind which he rallies majority support and moves toward his goal by persuasion, manipulation, and conflict. His program is more definite and stable than the offerings of the consensus President, and his administration has more of an ideological coloring or emphasis. Andrew Jackson constructed a majority following and, among other things, engaged in a full struggle with the Second Bank of the United States, an agency of largely private economic power and regional rule.

The President who chooses the majoritarian path and the politics of combat uses different methods and resources than the consensus President and applies different values. The program or purpose of the majoritarian President takes precedence over the claims of his individual supporters. If a particular supporting group rejects portions of his program, he will hold to it and try to push it through, hoping that his remaining supporters still add up to a majority. He will take up causes in the full anticipation that in doing so the wrath of powerful groups will tumble down upon his head. Harry Truman pursued a strong response to the Soviet Union in the general deterioration of U.S.–U.S.S.R. relations following the Second World War, even though it meant the alienation of Henry A. Wallace and other influential New Dealers and the loss of a substantial heritage of political support left by his predecessor, Franklin Roosevelt. Truman offered a national health program even though he knew he would earn the unflagging opposition of the American Medical Association.

The majoritarian President who takes up the politics of combat tends to use certain resources of his office more than others. He is apt to "go to the people" to "educate" them on the issues, and, he hopes, to rally them to his side in the strife. He uses the veto power more, not simply to resist and reject, but as a dramatic weapon that serves well to identify him with his cause. His discourse carries a strong vocabulary, and he is prone to be mercilessly specific in identifying his enemies, as Truman did the Republican Eightieth Congress, which he labeled the "Do-Nothing Congress."

The majoritarian President is willing to lose battles in order eventually to win wars, even those where, in the final moment of victory, he may no longer be in office and another may bask in the success that rose from his efforts. He takes a broad view of success and is willing to sustain defeat as the price for changing, or setting into motion the forces that may change, the country's prevailing opinion. He appeals to emotion as much as to rationality and is apt to view presidential politics as not simply a continuing dialogue, seeking adjustments and accommodations, but as an enterprise analogous to a military campaign, with strategies and maneuvers, and fierce clashes with those of opposing interests.

*Social and political movements*    Normally, the presidency's leadership domain is confined to producing incremental change. Only when social or political movements materialize does substantial opportunity for effective change arise for presidential leadership. The black civil rights movement of the 1960s, the Populists' movement for free coinage of silver in the late nineteenth century, and the present day women's and environmental movements provide such opportunities. Social movements, to appear and flourish, depend on such delicately interlaced forces as mass unrest and excitement, attraction to intellectuals, the emergence of an indigenous leader who is both prophet and reformer (like Martin Luther King, Jr., in the black rights movement), the formation of local organizations, and the like.

As a movement develops, a President or presidential candidate may employ his leadership resources to co-opt the movement, as William Jennings Bryan, the Democratic presidential nominee of 1896 did the silver movement by also becoming the Populist nominee, and as John Kennedy and Lyndon Johnson did by thrusting themselves into positions of leadership in the black civil rights movement and annexing its demands and priorities to their own agenda of public leadership. The eventual institutionalization of the civil rights movement in new laws, programs, bureaucracies, and court decisions, comprised a far-ranging, highly innovative, accomplishing interlude for presidential leadership in public policy-making.[12]

# The President and Public Opinion

Given the realities of the political system in which he works, it is well that the President enjoys impressive resources for reaching the public and rallying public opinion. Because the national parties are weak organizations, they are unreliable and often pusillanimous as sources of help for presidential programs. The built-in conflict between the President and Congress assured by checks and balances, the ease with which Congress can rebuff him, leaves the President dependent upon his ability to summon broad public support as his most substantial means of bringing Congress around to an accommodation productive of policy and action.

## The President and the General Public

Drawing upon established research, the following propositions can be asserted about relationships between the President and the general public:

- The public perceives the presidency as an office of enormous importance. The President is by far the nation's best known official. According to one study, 98 percent of all adults knew who the President was, and the Vice President, alone of all other national officials, was a significant com-

### Awareness of Political Leaders on the Part of Adults and Children, 1969–70

| Office | Percentage Correct by Age | | |
| --- | --- | --- | --- |
| | Adult | 17 | 13 |
| President (Nixon) | 98 | 98 | 94 |
| Vice President (Agnew) | 87 | 79 | 60 |
| Secretary of State (Rogers) | 16 | 9 | 2 |
| Secretary of Defense (Laird) | 25 | 16 | 6 |
| Speaker of the House (McCormack) | 32 | 25 | 2 |
| Senate Majority Leader (Mansfield) | 23 | 14 | 4 |
| At Least One Senator from Own State | 57 | 44 | 16 |
| Both Senators from Own State | 31 | 18 | 6 |
| Congressman from Own District | 39 | 35 | 11 |

Source: Fred Greenstein, "What the President Means to Americans," in James Barber, ed., *Choosing the President* (Englewood Cliffs, N.J.: Prentice-Hall, 1974), p. 125. Copyright © 1974 by Prentice-Hall, Inc. Reprinted by permission.

petitor for public recognition.[13] As the single nationally elected official, the center of initiative and action in the country's political life, the figure in society covered most extensively by the media, the staunch historic symbol of coping with the nation's problems and crises of nearly two centuries, the President is unique in his claims upon the minds and sentiments of citizens.

• In the adult population trust in the presidency—prior to Watergate—was remarkably high. A 1966 study queried a national sample of adults about the kinds of occupations they respected most. The listed choices included a well-known doctor, clergyman, the head of a large corporation, a Supreme Court justice, a Senator and governor, and other public officials. The President was rated first by 52 percent of the sample.[14] The next most-respected occupations, the doctor and the clergyman, attracted little more than 10 percent of first-choice responses.

   Further studies disclose that in intervals of unrest or in the upheaval of a shattering event like Watergate, public confidence in the presidency and other political institutions can decline precipitously. Harris polls of 1966, 1971, and 1972 asked a national sample whether they had confidence in "the people in charge of running the executive branch," with choices consisting of a great deal of confidence, some confidence, and hardly any confidence. In 1966, 41 percent expressed a "great deal of confidence," but the total dropped to 23 percent in 1971, and rose slightly to 27 percent in 1972.[15] The period studied manifested unusual social unrest, to which these fluctuations of opinion can be reasonably and largely attributed. Nonetheless, the data must be used with reservation since the questions asked referred to the executive branch and not to the President exclusively.

• With remarkable consistency, the public, over time, and prior to Watergate, did not perceive the presidency as an office of extraordinary power nor did they want it to be. The public prefers collaboration between the presidency and Congress in policy-making. Like the Founding Fathers, the public believes that the most salutary arrangement of government is a balance of roles and responsibility between the branches.

   For example, a 1968 Harris poll asked a national sample whether they thought the President or Congress should have the principal responsibility in making foreign, economic, and racial policy. The dominant response felt that the President and Congress should play an equal role in all three policy areas. Sixty percent of the respondents were of this opinion for foreign policy, 58 percent for economic policy, and 63 percent for racial policy. The study also disclosed that substantially greater numbers preferred giving Congress, rather than the President, the principal policy-making role in all three policy fields.[16]

• Once the President has made a decision, he normally attracts public support. In one study, 56 percent of the respondents believed that the President merited support even if he made the wrong decision. In times of crisis, support is even higher, with two-thirds of the respondents believing the public should rally around him. Support, however, was not of the blind, unquestioning variety, a choice that only 24 percent approved.[17]

### Declines in Presidential Popularity

| | Percentage of Support upon Assuming Office | Percentage of Support at Beginning of Final Year of First Term |
|---|:---:|:---:|
| Truman | 87 | 36 |
| Eisenhower | 68 | 77 |
| Kennedy | 72 | — |
| Johnson | 79 | 80 |
| Nixon | 59 | 49 |
| Ford | 71 | 46 |
| Carter | 75 | 37 |

Sources: Data from 1945–71 are from George Gallup, *The Gallup Poll: Public Opinion 1935–1971* (New York: Random House, 1972). Data from 1972 on are from the monthly *Gallup Opinion Index*, except for Carter's final year, from ABC News-Harris Survey.

• A President's popularity is strongest at the beginning and in the earlier part of his first term, and declines thereafter. Gallup polls raising the question, "Do you approve or disapprove of the way the President is handling his job?" have covered all Presidents since Truman throughout their tenure. Four of the six Presidents covered had lower public approval ratings when they started the last year of their first term than when their tenure began. Eisenhower and Johnson are exceptions, with Eisenhower gaining 11 points at the start of his second term, probably because of his termination of the Korean war. Johnson gained a point in the final years of his first term over his support on assuming office, explainable by the circumstance that he became President only three months before the final year of Kennedy's uncompleted term. All Presidents, from Truman to Carter, left office with public approval ratings substantially lower than when their tenure began. Although a President's conduct may speed or diminish his decline, a decline, nevertheless, seems inevitable.

Underlying this finding is the honeymoon phenomenon, or the public's tendency to view approvingly the President's performance during his early months in office. The honeymoon period can be shrunk by events and by the President's own conduct—Ford's pardon of Nixon, for example, abruptly shattered the honeymoon. An accumulation of controversial decisions, of less intensity than the pardon, can also terminate the honeymoon, as well as the inevitable public realization that the President idealized in the campaign as decent and upright becomes tarnished as he grapples with the soiling business of compromise and with the emerging prospect that his accomplishments will fall well short of his campaign promises.

- Not surprisingly, a cataclysmic event like Watergate has a shattering effect on adult attitudes toward the presidency. A Survey Research Center study of 1972 disclosed that all major population subgroups except white Democrats felt greater trust in the presidency than in Congress or the Supreme Court. But in 1974, after Watergate, no subgroup rated it above the Supreme Court, and independents alone trusted it more than Congress. For virtually every principal subgroup, trust in the presidency declined by about 50 percent.[18]

  Available research is less clear about the longer term effects of Watergate. One study found that the number of people expressing "a great deal of confidence" in the executive branch—13 percent—did not change between 1974 and 1976, while those expressing a "fair amount of confidence" rose from 29 to 46 percent, and those expressing "not very much confidence" declined from 36 to 30 percent; those with no confidence at all dropped from 19 to 8 percent.[19] It is also notable that according to Harris surveys in 1973, during the worst days of Watergate, only 34 percent of the public had "hardly any confidence at all" in the executive branch, and a year later, with Watergate still at the forefront of national attention, the figure dropped to 18 percent.[20]

## The Presidency and Socialization

In the pre-Vietnam, pre-Watergate era, the adult public ordinarily took a favorable view of a President's performance, as data from Gallup polls suggest. Before the Watergate disaster engulfed him, Nixon attained a high of 68 percent, but as the scandal unfolded he plummeted to 23 percent, a low known only by Truman and Carter among contemporary Presidents.

A sizeable part of the President's ready popularity is attributable to processes of socialization. The President richly benefits from attitudes the public entertains about his office and its incumbents. Studies disclose that children know about the President at a very early age and that their knowledge is idealized. Already highly visible to the young child, the President is seen as benign, honest, exceptionally competent, better than most individuals, hard-working, and devoted to protecting all Americans. The young child's picture of the President is not democratic—a failing that may infiltrate adult perceptions—for the President is beheld as a boss who does more than anyone to make the laws, with Congress and others functioning as helpers. Generally, in early school grades, textbooks are uncritical of Presidents, identifying them with accomplishment and pride in the country's history and showing them as remote figures, untainted by flawed performance. As the child grows older, admiration for the President diminishes somewhat, but not until the seventh or eighth grades do children venture to make negative judgments about the presidency.[21]

In the adult world, the results of early socialization by family and school are reinforced by the regularly recurrent events of presidential elections and successions, and the tolerable effectiveness of the incumbents. A disruptive event such as the assassination of President Kennedy evoked many similar emotional reactions among primary and secondary school children and adults—sadness and mourning, shame and anger. Many college students displayed profound feelings of reassurance that the presidency's institutional feature of automatic succession by the Vice President had functioned effectively, and their impressions of Lyndon Johnson immediately became more favorable because of his assumption of the presidential role.[22]

Not surprisingly, the benevolent leader image burns brightest among the comfortably situated and weakest among those who fare less well in the distribution of society's benefits, such as blacks and the poor. In the Nixon era, public opinion analyst Louis Harris found that no more than 3 percent of all blacks expected significant assistance from the President; instead, according to the prevailing view among blacks, they must extract their own progress from a grudging white society.[23]

For both children and adults, the Watergate scandals were jarring and disruptive of the presidency's normal connections with socialization. Interviews with children disclosed that they perceived the morality of Watergate in simple terms, with the President appearing to have been bad, according to their criteria, and answerable to harsher standards than they applied to themselves. "He's the President," said a ten-year-old, "and is supposed to be protecting the people against crime, not making crime. He should be punished more."[24]

But according to a study of children of upper-income families made both during Watergate and two years after that event, the children's very negative assessments of the President in 1973 when Watergate occurred had become modified by 1975. But in the later study the attitudes remained negative and were decidedly not a return to the "benevolent leader" image. Clearly, extraordinary events like Watergate can tear away the protective insulation from politics provided children by their parents and teachers who screen out its negative aspects.[25]

# The President-Constituency Influence Process

In addition to the general public, the President deals with many lesser publics or constituencies whose demeanor toward him embraces a wide range of positive and negative behavior, from furious disdain to imperishable approval, dispositions that can shape his policies, their success and failure, his political future, and even his place in history. Constituencies express their feelings toward the President in diverse ways—with supportive and obstructive acts and sheer passivity, by giving and withholding benefits and penalties that are theirs to confer. The major constituencies that populate the President's world include political constituencies (the electorate, the parties, public officials at all levels of government, foreign leaders), administrative constituencies (department and agency heads, civil and military bureaucracies), economic constituencies (business and labor), social constituencies (racial, ethnic, sex, age identifications), and critic constituencies (professional critics: the press, clergy, intellectuals, political opponents).

The President and his constituencies are mutually dependent; each can do things that will help or hamper the other, and frequently their dealings have the appearance of a quid pro quo. Often their relationships are channeled by common processes, in which the following are major elements.

## Targets

The President and his constituencies serve as targets to each other, a focus of positive or negative behavior—of petition, influence and support, on the one hand, or attack, rejection, obstruction, on the other. The President is not a solitary target; his White House aides, department secretaries, and the executive bureaucracy are subsidiary targets that constituencies can aim at, to reach the President indirectly. Early in 1974, as gasoline shortages became severe, truckers and truck drivers, distressed by lowered speed limits and soaring gasoline prices, blockaded highways and articulated grievances to the Secretary of Transportation as steps toward influencing the President, who could not be reached or pressured directly but whose approval of major revisions of policy was necessary and eventually materialized.

Presidents choose targets from among their constituencies, as Nixon did in advancing his 1974 education proposals. He singled out several targets, soliciting support from some (affirmative targets), and attacking others (negative targets). His message to Congress was tailored to win approval from suburbanites with its high commendation of neighborhood schools where "parents know that the education of their children can most effectively be carried out." Among the targets the President attacked were inner city people, eager for genuine school integration, when he expressed support for antibusing legislation and disparaged "bureaucrats in Washington" who "cannot educate your children" and who must never be placed "in the role of master social planners." [26] A moderating influence on Ronald Reagan's conservative principles was his resolve to appeal to labor unions, minorities, and blue-collar Democrats.

In choosing his affirmative targets, or those whose support he seeks, the President calculates their readiness of response, the compatibility of their needs and aspirations with his own interests, and the likely costs and gains. The greater the costs of influencing the target, the less the President is apt to select it, and his choice is shaped by memories of past constituency performance, or the record of responsiveness to his attentions, and the kinds and amounts of political expenditure required.

## Construction of Social Reality

Each of the President's constituencies possesses its own construction of social reality—the beliefs, values, attitudes it holds that provide a frame of reference, a cognitive map for interpreting reality—that guides the exchange of information and influence.[27] Some constituencies depend upon the President, in whole or in part, for information and even for interpretation of reality. The degree of dependence differs sharply among subject matters—typically much less for domestic affairs that constituencies can observe readily and directly, and much more for foreign affairs that are more remote, whose surrounding secrecy curtails constituency scrutiny and therefore enlarges dependence on the President. What passes for "social reality" consists of great chunks of unreality, with the President selecting what he wants to tell and shaping his interpretations according to his interests, while the constituencies, for their part, are disposed to hear what they want to hear, a disposition that itself is a mighty censor of the President's selective interpretations.

But, as befits a democratic political system, the President is subject to constraints even in realms where he enjoys a nearly monopolistic sway over his constituencies' information. Hence, even in the Cuban missile crisis, a situation of acute constituency dependence on the President, Kennedy, as a source of information and interpretation, faced competition from Senators who had their own sources and enjoyed credibility with constituencies. The worst calamity the President can suffer in his role as reporter and interpreter of social reality is the onset of a "credibility gap": his constituencies' loss of confidence in his truthfulness and candor.

The President interprets reality in terms of a constituency's needs and entitlements, and articulates what redress social realities will tolerate and the commitment of his leadership might produce. The President can create demand, arousing among his constituencies a desire for products of his leadership. Toward the black community, for example, Kennedy and Johnson were creators of expectations, formulating goals of betterment and launching programs to obliterate injustices and long-suffered deprivations. In practicing the politics of expectations, Kennedy and Johnson, in addresses and statements, spoke glowingly of the power of their office, its possibilities in the pursuit of heroic goals, its shining historic accomplishments, all of which augured a ready actualization of black people's needs and their leaders' demands.

But, as sometimes happens in the presidency, Kennedy and Johnson, although providers of sizeable gains, raised expectations that exceeded the political system's capacity to deliver and that spurred black dwellers in the ghettos to overestimate the likely responses to their plight. To a degree, the consequent frustration and despair contributed to the rioting that was costly to themselves and their neighborhoods and aroused the hostilities of whites.

## Influence Modes

*Open and clandestine*    In their dealings and exchanges, the President and his constituencies employ several major modes of influence. His possible choices, for instance, include both "open" and "clandestine" modes. Open modes embrace threats and impositions of punishment and reward as well as the persuasive and dissuasive use of warnings. President Ford, in his initial package of proposals for Congress and the public to adopt to fight inflation and conserve energy, added the admonition, "Now if all of these steps fail to meet our current energy-saving goal I will not hesitate to ask for tougher measures." [28]

Clandestine modes utilize manipulation and concealed assertion for gaining compliant behavior from the target, sometimes without the target's awareness of the source and motive of control. The President employs cues to evoke predictable and what to him are desirable responses. Nixon could cry that the likely grounds offered for his impeachment would constitute a threat to the presidential office, a contention that could ignite support among many publics for a narrowing of the charges against him, quite apart from the merits of his case. The President can filter information to block the perception of possible alternative actions and to manipulate outcomes that are less than expected constituency gains. Initially, in offering his welfare reform proposals, Nixon projected gains for both the public and the welfare recipient. Later he altered his proposals, stressed "workfare" and took other steps that wrote off the welfare constituency, and appealed to such opposing constituencies as blue collar workers and white suburbanites, whose support Nixon valued as the 1970 elections approached.

In their evaluations of relevant constituency behavior, Presidents as a lot exhibit no clear preference for open or clandestine modes. Kennedy, for one, was suspicious and disparaging of "howlers," particularly in the domain of civil rights, where he felt that some of that genre exploited the issue for self-gain among minority and urban voters in lieu of undertaking the hard work of constructive action.[29]

*Hard and soft*    In their mutual dealings, Presidents and their constituencies also employ "hard" and "soft" modes of influence. Beleaguered by incessant revelations by the news media of Watergate wrongdoings, Nixon exclaimed, in a tense news conference, "I have never heard or seen such outrageous, vicious, distorted reporting in twenty-seven years of public life." Almost invariably, when he dealt with the media, Nixon resorted to the hard modes.

Fortunately, most Presidents are less combative than Nixon, and, ordinarily, constituencies shower a fiercer opprobrium on Presidents than Presidents do on them. Washington, Lincoln, and Jackson were mercilessly vilified, but the all-time record set by a target of sustained punishment is held by Lyndon Johnson, who was repeatedly termed a "murderer" and a full load of synonyms of that condemnation tumbled on him, unloosed even by members of his own party on the floor of the Senate, where presumably more than ordinary restraint prevailed. Even his announcement that he would not seek the presidency again did not diminish the attacks.

At least in their public conduct, Presidents are prone to employ soft modes of influence. Johnson assiduously courted dissidents of the Vietnam war, calling critical reporters into the Oval Office for long talks about the conflict, sugared with hints that his listener might soon be favored with an important exclusive. He sent forth aides for "good talk" with influential groups behind closed doors. He systematically presented his case to selected Congressmen at mealtimes and in a chain of White House receptions.[30] Playing over a broad range of soft modes, Johnson employed ample doses of cajolery, flattery, humor, and favors.

*Offensive and defensive*    The President and his constituencies employ "offensive" and "defensive" modes of influence toward one another. The first is exemplified by Lyndon Johnson's resolve to liberate the black constituency from enduring racial discrimination and to make the American black a first-class citizen. The resolve launched Johnson on a positive (offensive) civil rights program of legislation and administrative action, unmatched either before or since his presidency.

In resorting to defensive modes of influence, the Chief Executive enjoys a well-stocked armory of weapons and battle options. A favorite is the flanking movement and strategic retreat, in which Richard Nixon was well-practiced. Rather than engage in frontal combat with hostile constituencies, especially when he was vulnerable, Nixon chose to retreat to more tenable ground, while simultaneously proclaiming his action to be a spectacular advance. Pressed, for example, by critics of the Vietnam war and heavy U.S. defense spending, he began pulling troops out of Vietnam, pared the defense budget and the antiballistic missile program, and reduced American commitments abroad by proclaiming "the Nixon Doctrine." By these modest moves, he kept both doves and hawks tolerably quiet, and, at least for a season, accrued to himself credit for generosity and astute compromise. During the high moment of these maneuvers he appeared virtually as one who had originated the idea of peace in Vietnam and more harmonious relations with the Soviet Union.[31]

# Roles

In providing leadership and in otherwise dealing with his constituencies, whether the general public, the electorate, or more specialized components, the President acts through roles, or, in actuality, through a complex of roles that comprise his office. His roles, or patterns of behavior, derive from his major continuing tasks in party affairs, legislation, administration, and diplomacy, among others, which will be examined in subsequent chapters. Since roles tell the individual what he ought to do, the nature of role is crucial for the objective of achieving an effective presidency that is also compatible with a democratic political system. Roles can be structured in ways consistent with both purposes.[32]

A role, including presidential roles, possesses certain properties. It incorporates rights and obligations; role performance embraces their assertion and defense, including their expansion, modification, and surrender. Hence, early in the Watergate investigation, President Nixon cited executive privilege in the broadest imaginable terms as an inherent right of his office and forbade his White House aides and former aides from testifying before the Senate's Watergate investigating committee. The committee chairman, Sam J. Ervin, Jr. (D-N.C.), and others contended that the President had no power to withhold information and testimony relevant to a committed crime, such as the break-in at the national headquarters of the Democratic party, but an obligation to cooperate in the quest for wrongdoers and lawbreakers. Eventually, Nixon retreated somewhat from his absolute position.

Presidential roles have boundaries, or a range of behavior that conforms with the norms of constitutional democracy. But boundaries are also vague and are therefore subject to manipulation, a condition that strong Presidents are prone to exploit. Fortunately for democracy, and often, too, for the strong presidency, the Chief Executive is surrounded by boundary-watchers capable of restraining incumbent Presidents within limits of acceptable activity. The Courts provide surveillance of the President's conduct of his office and its accordance with the Constitution and statutes and can checkmate his transgressions. Congress pushes the President to and fro in its quest for acceptable boundaries, resorting to varied tactics that include investigations, overriding his veto, reviewing his appointments and treaties, and even impeachment. Boundaries are political as well as legal. Congress underfunded Johnson's many-faceted social programs, with the implicit rebuke that he was going too far too fast, after which it showered Nixon with more appropriations than he wanted, a remonstrance that he was falling well short of doing enough for the country's serious social problems.

Finally, role is a means of socialization, a regulator of an incumbent President's behavior. Thus the structuring of roles is a principal means of satisfying the requisites of democracy by prescribing specific behavior patterns for which the President is accountable. In roles, his tasks are allocated and defined, and they can be revised, if necessary, to bring the conduct they prescribe more into harmony with democratic ideals. And the constituencies are available to demand and enforce the President's observance of role norms that are also democratic. A constituency such as the courts can press for his deference to the civil liberties protections of the Constitution. Various constituencies can prevent or punish his overindulgence in deception and other acts of that genre that impair both democracy and the strong presidency. That largest of constituencies, the public at large, can inflict a most devastating penalty by withdrawing its confidence and trust. In ways obvious and subtle, in amounts large and small, the President can suffer the drain of real political power. These are penalties, coupled with democratic socialization, that can befall him for behavior that violates role norms.

# The Mass Media

## The Age of Television

Formulations of ideal democracy accord the communications media an heroic role as purveyors of information to citizens concerning public issues and events and the performance of those who govern. The media, which encompasses both television and print journalism, are also critics of officials and their work, and this function is indispensable in a democracy, since it serves to actualize a body of informed citizens and fosters the organization and expression of opposing opinions.

How well do the media perform these vital tasks in the context of the presidency? A study directed by Newton Minow, a former Federal Communications Commission chairman in the Kennedy administration, concluded that one component of the media, television, and the President's towering command of it, have altered the balance of political forces. Most people, it is clear, acquire their information about public affairs not from the press but from television, and deem it the most objective and believable of all the media.[33] Far more than any other national political figure, including leaders of Congress, the President dominates the television airways, and for him the medium can be a working tool of fabulous potential. Television enables the President to reach the people, not indirectly through a journalist, but through his own presence and statement.

As assessed by Fred Friendly, a former television producer and professor of journalism, the power television brings to presidential leadership is great: "No mighty king, no ambitious emperor, no pope, no prophet ever dreamt of such an awesome pulpit, so potent a magic wand."[34] John Kennedy, particularly, was a pathbreaker who deftly used television to concentrate attention on the presidency and, as political scientist Michael J. Robinson has suggested, "helped to make both network journalism and the presidency more powerful forces in American politics."[35] The President, thanks to his dominance of television, can determine the way issues are shaped and focus national attention on what he wants to accomplish.

For the post-Vietnam, post-Watergate President, television is also sometimes a witch's brew of handicaps and limitations. Television is by no means sheer advantage for the President, as it is often hailed to be. Though television enhances the President as the supreme symbol of the political system, it can also easily convert him into the object of blame for the nation's ills, although the degree of his responsibility is far less than the severity of his condemnation. Thanks largely to television, the Vietnam war became the President's war, although in actuality it was also Congress's war, supported annually for nearly a decade by generous legislative funding.

To public questions, including those in which the President might be interested, television applies an iron test: it prefers questions that are not too complicated to treat in one minute and fifteen seconds, and it is disinclined to take up questions that arise when no network camera is present. Television lives by visual drama and treats public questions in that context. In the 1960s and 70s, television told of school busing, but not of segregation, a less visible subject, and it emphasized confrontation and violence rather than reasoned discussion.[36] Presidents have had to bend to the imperatives of television. The full length expositions of issues permitted by radio are rarely tolerable in the Age of Television. Like other citizens, the President must encapsulate serious questions in order to enter that most prized domain, the evening news.

Television and the press are uneven, if not biased, in their treatment of Presidents and presidential candidates. They permitted John Kennedy to exhort that "we get the nation moving again," without pressing him to particularize how it would be done. But they insisted that Hubert Humphrey detail his precise divergence from Lyndon Johnson over the Vietnam war. Journalists of major news organizations of both television and the press favor the presidential candidate perceived as challenging the establishment—John Kennedy, Jimmy Carter, and John Anderson, for example, who create the kind of conflict that responds best to media needs. Established politicians such as Henry Jackson, Morris Udall, and Edmund Muskie are less newsworthy. But once the challengers are elected, the journalistic mood changes. Now elected, the once-favored contenders become part of the "establishment" and a ready target.[37]

The reporters of television and print journalism at the forefront of presentation and discussion of both national and presidential politics are a small elite who are unrepresentative, in background and viewpoint, of the great body of voters. David Broder of the Washington *Post* estimates that a "couple of dozen" political reporters employed by major news organizations covering national and presidential politics reside in the East, are between 30 and 45 years of age, well-paid, white, and likely to vote Democratic. They constitute, as Broder stated, "a narrow and rather peculiar slice of society."[38] A leading characteristic of this small but powerful circle is its lack of accountability to the public.

## Presidents and Press: A Constant Tension

One of the more confident predictions to be made about a presidency is that any incumbent will eventually come to dislike the press. Of contemporary Presidents only John Kennedy felt for the most part benignly toward the press, partly because of its excessively favorable treatment of his administration and his own earlier aspirations for a journalistic career. But even Kennedy suffered dark hours from the journalists and in one moment of pique cancelled the White House subscriptions to the New York *Herald Tribune*. At the far opposite extreme, Nixon perceived the press as heavily biased against his presidency, and he retaliated by means fair and foul, violating the press's constitutional freedoms.

Other recent Presidents have ranged over a broad middle ground in relations with the press. Eisenhower, confident and secure about his place in history, appeared untroubled by journalistic criticism. Lyndon Johnson, on the other hand, became obsessed with the press and its opinions and miscalculated his ability to influence reporters with unctuous praise and personal attention. Ultimately, this house of cards collapsed at great cost to Johnson. Near the close of his administration, he told a reporter, "Our most tragic error may have been our inability to establish a rapport and a confidence with the press and television. . . . I don't think the press has understood me."[39] Johnson attributed his failure partly to geography, "to where Mother was living when I was born"—to biases of Eastern reporters toward a Texan in the presidency, especially since the assassination of his predecessor had taken place in Texas. When Carter became President he pledged to conduct his administration with greater "openness" and to hold formal press conferences at least twice a month. An initial honeymoon period with the press was abruptly terminated by the Bert Lance affair and the forced departure of the Budget Director, who was a premier adviser and "close friend" to the President. At the White House, the press was perceived as having a major part in exposing Lance's earlier free-wheeling banking career. The Carter presidency assumed a wary stance toward reporters akin to a siege mentality. Although Carter and his aides complained about press coverage, they did not, like Nixon, threaten the press or transgress its freedom.[40]

A thread of inevitability runs through the steady chronicle of tension and trouble between the President and the press. An underlying conflict of interest produces this outcome: a President and his associates endeavor to convey a favorable image of what is happening in government, ideally an ever-flowing report of accomplishment and success. Spurred by professional training and commitment, and to seize readers' and viewers' attention, journalists purport to supply a full, true picture of presidential performance. An adversary relationship inevitably arises between beleaguered self-justifying Presidents and journalists who prefer to think of themselves as probing and powerless, confronting mighty officials who fend them off with remorseless deceit and intimidation.

Political scientists Michael Grossman and Francis Rourke caution that despite the pyrotechnics of conflict, an enduring substantial cooperation transpires between Presidents and the press based on a relationship of exchange.[41] Each side seeks a balance of trade favorable to itself, and each possesses the means to select items of information that will be defined as news. The President and his associates seek to confine the information disclosed to items favorable to themselves, and reporters aim to broaden the choice by encompassing both the favorable and unfavorable. In the exchange relationship, the President gains leverage from being the nation's principal newsmaker. For executive officials, secrecy is a potent weapon to conceal the administration's shortcomings, but the press's counterweapon is to broaden its network of contacts to reach the withheld information. The media provide the President a tie with public opinion, a relationship on which his power ultimately depends. It is here that recent Presidents have stumbled with disastrous consequences for which they must take full blame, however fiercely they fulminate against the press. Both Johnson and Nixon so conducted themselves that the public stopped believing and listening, and Carter was badly wounded as the image of incompetence continued to build. Presidents—not reporters—make their own worst press.

# The President's Media

## Communications Experts

Although the President is normally his own best publicity agent, he is assisted by a large and growing staff of communications experts. Presidents got along with a press secretary and a speech-writer or two earlier in this century, but it is possible for a present-day Chief Executive to become an enclave surrounded by communications specialists. Nixon's White House staff included more experts from the worlds of broadcasting, advertising, and public relations than any previous presidency. Carter maintained a resident image adviser, Gerald Rafshoon, an Atlanta advertising entrepreneur, who quickly acceded to the small circle of the President's closest senior advisers. Rafshoon's name soon became a verb in Washington parlance. To "Rafshoon" something was to politicize it for the image it creates. More modestly, Rafshoon contended that "My job is to help articulate and explain the central themes of Jimmy Carter's Presidency."[42]

The President's key helper for dealing with the news media is his press secretary, provider of advance texts and reports, daily briefings, and announcements of new policies and aspirations. In confronting reporters, he dodges questions, pleads ignorance, erupts in righteous anger, and stresses positive themes. He helps prepare the President for his news conferences and arranges presidential meetings with individual reports and writers. Ideally, he points out lapses to the President, goads him into better effort, and somehow maintains both the President's and the reporters' confidence.

President Johnson was known to employ the same secrecy in dealing with his own press secretaries as he did with reporters. He employed a series of press secretaries—Pierre Salinger, George Reedy, Bill Moyers, and George Christian—which in itself suggests that the function was handled uneasily. Because of his desire to preserve his options, to act only when he was politically ready to act, he was largely his own press secretary. The post of press secretary suffered something of a decline, owing to Johnson's working methods.[43]

Richard Nixon, whose relations with the press plunged to a nadir well below Johnson's, further demoted the press secretary in White House ranking. Ronald Ziegler, who endured in that post, sometimes miraculously, was subordinated to the White House general manager, initially H. R. Haldeman, and later General Alexander Haig. But Ziegler was also a part of Nixon's small inner circle and, after the Watergate scandal erupted, was one of a few who saw the President regularly. Nixon too was secretive toward his press secretary, and Ziegler often had to face the press handicapped by incomplete information.

Jimmy Carter's press secretary, Jody Powell, whose boyish down-home informality suggested a Tom Sawyer in the White House and who exuded the earnest integrity of Jimmy Stewart, was a full-fledged member of the White House inner circle. More than anyone he spoke for the President. Powell provided Carter with a daily news briefing and his across-the-board involvement in the President's affairs—standing, as he did, closer to Carter than any other press secretary had to his President since World War II—enabled Powell to function as adviser, image-manager, conciliator, and promoter of administration policies. Powell too is a Georgian and served as a volunteer in Carter's 1970 race for Governor, initially as his driver and later as press secretary. Although not a journalist, Powell's relations with reporters flourished; his cooperativeness and his disdain for pomposity and trivia nurtured their confidence.

With a staff of 46, Powell's post of press secretary markedly expanded since the days of the Roosevelts and Wilson. He oversaw a television studio, amphitheater, and the deploy of an armory of electronic gadgetry that sent the President's speeches around the world in seconds. The once dozen or so "regulars" among reporters covering the White House grew five fold. In Powell's stable were speechwriters, media liaison specialists, television experts, photographers, professional pollsters, travel advancemen, and in-house news synthesizers.[44]

## The News Conference

To reach their publics, most contemporary Presidents rely upon the news conference, an institution that harks back only to the administration of Woodrow Wilson. Soon after his inauguration, reporters gathered by general invitation in his office for a question-and-answer exchange on the administration's business. The reporters assembled with lofty expectations encouraged by Wilson's solemn invocation of "pitiless publicity" for public business in his pre-presidential writing on political science. The new practice of the press conference replaced the old arrangement by which Presidents had granted interviews only to selected reporters, a tactic permitting favoritism and penalization. In the news conference, reporters enjoy equal footing.

Unfortunately, the sessions under Wilson and his early successors fell far short of the initial optimism. Wilson's glacial reserve inhibited interchange. He was often irritated by the reporters' habit of speculating about the news and of persisting with questions before he was prepared to release information. He considered the reporters' cross-examining a reflection upon his honesty.

The advent of Franklin Roosevelt finally brought the little-tried institution into its own. Roosevelt set up two news conferences a week, canceled his predecessor's requirement of written questions, and with his facile charm turned the sessions into lively occasions on which he provided the public with a running account of what he was doing and what he proposed to do and why.[45] Eisenhower permitted the innovation of televising his news conferences and presenting them, with minor editing, to the public. With John Kennedy there was no editing; the televised presentation was made exactly as his encounters with the reporters occurred. Kennedy's news conferences were highly effective, his responses to questions revealing an almost photographic memory for detail and a gift for keeping abreast of policy development from incubation to implementation. His brisk assurance and his opening statements charged with newsworthy content lent zest and excitement to his administration.[46]

For Nixon, the news conference was both a useful arrangement and an object of neglect. Despite a pre-presidential background of pugnacious press relations, Nixon in his early months as President conducted highly effective news conferences. Employing a stand-up format, with only a microphone between himself and reporters instead of the usual podium or desk, Nixon was deft at analyzing ideas and issues and persuasive in presenting his program.[47] But he soon allowed the news conference to languish into disuse, a pattern that deepened as his tenure wore on. Thus, in 1971, he permitted *ad hoc* questioning by the White House press on only nine occasions, compared with an annual average of twenty-four to thirty-six by Presidents over the past quarter century. During the Watergate crisis his news conferences became even less frequent.

For both democracy and the Nixon presidency, his disuse of news conferences had serious costs: important issues and events came and went without public comment from the President—the India-Pakistan War, the release of Jimmy Hoffa from prison, increasing budget deficits, and the rising crime rate. Reticence deprived Nixon of a weapon that compels the bureaucracy to supply the President with reports and explanations of its lapses in policy making and implementation.[48]

In contrast, Gerald Ford, aspiring to an "open Presidency," a reversal of Nixon's seclusiveness, reverted to more frequent conferences, sometimes before a symbolic open door in the background, and selected his questioners from a balanced mix of men, women, blacks, young and old, old hands and new among White House reporters. He called those with journalistic specialties in for smaller conferences and held impromptu meetings. Instead of Nixon's bitterness toward the press, Ford radiated friendliness.[49]

Carter found the news conference useful for sending messages to other governments or to Congress, for teaching and preaching about problems on his agenda, for building confidence at home and abroad in his administration's integrity. Although precise about his principal message or theme, expressed in an opening statement, Carter sometimes fumbled secondary issues on which he could be mysteriously vague, to the consternation of listeners thirsting for meaning, such as the allies and congressional leaders.[50]

For all its slow start and erratic progress, the presidential news conference occupies a vital place in American political life. It is the only regular occasion on which the nation can view the Chief Executive in an active interchange with people outside his administration and without the props of speech writers and idea men. The sessions are also invaluable opportunities for the President to present his opinions and raise trial balloons. He can be sure that what he wants to say gets said by having it arranged beforehand for a reporter to ask a convenient question—a planted question—an old, productive device. The President can easily dodge and parry questions; no mere reporter can nail an incumbent of the awesome office to the wall. But despite its faults, the news conference merits jealous vigilance to assure its perpetuation.

## The Art of News Management

In the estimation of political analyst Arthur Krock, the Kennedy administration practiced the art of news management "boldly," "cynically," and "with the utmost subtlety and imagination." The reward of this effort, Krock contended, was a portrayal of the administration in the press with a radiant aura of approval that neither its achievement nor the country's circumstances warranted. In the Kennedy era, as in other eras, many critics voiced concern for the continued integrity of Thomas Jefferson's dictum that the people have a right to "full information of their affairs thro' the channel of the public papers."[51]

News management, which is a craft of many tricks, can cultivate the image of the President as infallible even in the face of flagrant error. If things go wrong, blame is placed upon others, usually his subordinates. A major tool of news management is the use of selective personal patronage, whereby those reporters who "behave," or write favorably of the administration, are granted privileges unavailable to their fellows. Thus Stewart Alsop and Charles Bartlett, coauthors of a widely noticed magazine article on the Cuban crisis, which could not have been undertaken without the unparalleled privilege of access to National Security Council proceedings, were candidly referred to by the President in a news conference as "old friends." Another plum was a 1962 year-end informal televised interview of the President by three cooperative reporters covering an extraordinary range of subjects and witnessed by a vast audience. A contrasting and less selective Kennedy tactic was the use of "social flattery," by which a succession of groups of editors and publishers were feted at the White House. Over several months, for example, the President had to luncheon eight editors from Florida, a throng of New Jersey publishers, and twenty-four publishers and news executives from the state of Washington. Kennedy reached reporters and editors on a large scale in occasional intimate, far-ranging background briefings. The press participants emerged, Krock observed, "in a state of protracted enchantment evoked by the President's charm and the awesome aura of his office." The mood carried over into the news columns and editorials.[52]

News management was not a creation of the Kennedy administration, however. It is an ancient and common practice of the presidency. Management assumes a variety of forms, from the complex to the simple little expedient Chester A. Arthur employed to present to his critics the appearance of being busy. Having a large reputation for indolence, Arthur maintained a "property basket" filled with official-looking documents that a secretary would carry into the President's office when he was with visitors to create the impression of industry.[53] The art of news management is constantly refined and updated. Compilations of Jimmy Carter's quotations were sent to two thousand editors and broadcasters.[54]

*Management by threat*   Harry Truman, whose dealings with the press were sometimes tempestuous, once said that he was "saving up four or five good hard punches on the nose" for reporters who, he felt, had been unfair.[55] More ominously, in the Nixon era news management evolved into many new forms, clearly directed toward presidential domination of the media. The fact that Nixon appeared on prime time television more than any other President, and during some intervals more than Eisenhower, Kennedy, and Johnson combined, did not allay his displeasure with the networks.[56] Through a variety of means, the Nixon administration moved to become the first in presidential experience to impose prior restraint of news reporting, an objective that violates the First Amendment and the civil libertarian base of American democracy.

In its several moves, the Nixon administration used the subpoena power to force reporters to turn over their raw notes. The administration opposed a shield bill before Congress that had been advanced by press and television representatives to protect the confidentiality of news sources. The director of the White House Office of Telecommunications Policy, Clay T. Whitehead, drafted and ardently promoted a broadcast license-renewal bill that would hold local television stations accountable for the balance and taste of all network news and entertainment programs they broadcast. In effect, local stations were to censor network programming. "Who else but [station] management," Whitehead asked, "can or should correct so-called professionals . . . who dispense elitist gossip in the guise of news analysis?" Concentrated efforts were directed at public broadcasting to purge it of commentators considered hostile to the President and to reorganize it by increasing the autonomy of stations by channeling larger shares of federal funds directly to them. The individual local public broadcasting stations were deemed more amenable to Nixon's purposes.[57]

Himself a close monitor of the media and their "biases," President Nixon was a fertile source of counterstrokes. He requested a White House aide to generate letters to *Newsweek* magazine detailing his "tremendous reception" in a visit to Mississippi and at a professional football game in Miami. Another time he directed his aide, Herbert G. Klein, to "have the *Chicago Tribune* hit Senator [Charles H.] Percy hard on his ties with the peace group." A log of the President's requests for the month between mid-September and mid-October 1969 reveals that he spurred complaints about coverage that were lodged with all three commercial television networks as well as with *Time, Newsweek, Life,* and with columnist Jack Anderson. Although nearly "double or triple" the total of the President's requests were made by others in the White House, an aide, in a comprehensive memorandum reviewing the media problem, concluded that this "shotgunning" was not really effective, that the administration could better "get the media" if it used harassment by the Internal Revenue Service and the Antitrust Division of the Justice Department.[58] But the President's principal avenging angel was Vice President Spiro Agnew, who regularly blasted network commentators.

### The People's Right to Know

The sorties of various Presidents into the fine, and sometimes dark, art of news management raise difficult but basic questions involving democratic values and practices. In deciding what to tell the nation, the President must strike a balance between the people's right to know what their government is doing and planning, the nation's safety and welfare (which may not always be served by disclosure), and his own political interests. Disclosures to the public might embarrass our relations with a friendly nation. But secrecy also may do nothing more than enable him to make gross errors in solitude. The opinion has been expressed, and Kennedy agreed with it, that less official secrecy and more publicity before the invasion of Cuba at the Bay of Pigs might have saved the nation from that debacle.[59] Clearly beyond the pale of tolerance in a democratic system is governmental intimidation of the news media and the imposition of censorship, including the media's self-censorship spurred by governmental pressure.

No neat formula for resolving the dilemma of secrecy versus disclosure can be constructed that would be meaningful or useful. The choices must be worked out in specific instances, with careful sensitivity for democratic necessities. Fortunately, the President has no monopoly of power or influence on this difficult terrain and can be buffeted toward a different course by those who raise their voices in criticism: legislators, group interest leaders, prestigious private individuals, and the press. In confronting the ways and wiles of the Chief Executive in managing the news, the press is not without defenses; it mustered sufficient strength to withstand the most concentrated onslaught yet launched, that of the Nixon presidency. Against lesser, more usual pressures, if the press is alert and professionally responsible it should be able to cope with the President's slickest manipulations. The media can, with ingenuity and enterprise, do their share of "managing" as well. They can, if they choose, put before the public an impression of the Chief Executive that it utterly contrary to reality. The newspapers converted the dour, colorless, futile Calvin Coolidge into a forceful, red-blooded, two-fisted, strong and silent "sage of Vermont," a man who never was. They can oppose and harass the President and overlook every shred of merit his administration possesses. Many of the most powerful press organs of Lincoln's day, for example, fought his administration without letup. "Mr. Lincoln deemed it more important to secure the [New York] *Herald*'s support than to obtain a victory in the field," explained Thurlow Weed, the administration's principal intermediary with the newspaper.[60]

# Public Opinion Polls

A major element in the working conditions of contemporary Presidents is the incessant taking of public opinion polls. Poll-taking flourishes to the point that it is a major industry, its findings read widely and avidly in the political community as barometers of the true health of a presidency at any given moment. Typically, polls are hailed as democracy-serving, as grand national town-meetings, with continuing dialogue between the presidential administration and the citizenry.[61] They provide a mirror of citizens' minds, of issues and attitudes that shape their perceptions of the political scene and the performance of office-holders. Not surprisingly, the White House and other executive agencies contract for private polling to make soundings of public reactions to policy trends. Polls enable the President to gauge his strength among specific portions of the population and in the country's different regions, which in bygone days were ascertained by the subjective moods and judgments of himself and his aides.

Polls have made steady advances in their methodological applications. They have reduced their margin of error. Between 1936–50 the Gallup poll's average error in its final pre-election survey, as published the day before the election, was 3.7 percentage points. The comparable figure for eight elections from 1954 to 1968 was 1.4 percentage points. Improvement is attributable to better sample design, better identification of likely voters, and improved measurement of shifts in voter preferences during the campaign.[62] 1980 was a bad year.

Although Presidents understandably cherish those moments when they are flourishing in the polls, they may overvalue that happy state of affairs to their subsequent political detriment. Nixon, for example, miscalculated the political potency of a Gallup poll, when after sending American forces into Cambodia and widening the Indochina war, 50 percent expressed approval "of the way President Nixon is handling the Cambodian situation"; 35 percent expressed disapproval, and 15 percent had no opinion.[63] Meanwhile a tidal wave of denunciation swept the country, with students, faculty, lawyers, doctors, architects, corporate executives and other elites protesting and demonstrating, lobbying Congress in droves to end the war, their efforts spotlighted by generous media coverage. Unlike Nixon, Congress was more impressed by the elite activists than the amorphous, largely passive "public opinion" of the polls, and it proceeded to limit the President's capacity to conduct the war.

In the post-Vietnam, post-Watergate presidency, with its confluence of intractable problems, such as inflation, energy, and the persisting distrust of governmental institutions, and with several incumbents lacking in skills of symbolic leadership, the presidency has been incessantly buffeted and hobbled by findings of the polls. Carter became locked in an incessant struggle to improve depressed poll scores that portrayed him as ineffectual. Doubtless Carter contributed to the problem, but its effect was exaggerated by the public's beliefs. For example, according to the polls, the public believed that the energy problem could be solved "by an effective President," a monstrous notion given the tortuous nature of energy politics and the problem's technical complexity.[64]

As Presidents of the post-Vietnam, post-Watergate era face problems that elude solution and frustrate the citizenry, a likely fate in an era of high inflation and unemployment and energy shortages, declining productivity, and other troubles, the polls will become an increasingly negative force against presidential leadership, weakening the Chief Executive's ability to win results in Congress and to retain support from the power centers of his party. Polls will inhibit creative leadership; their incessant readings allow small room for trial and error of innovative responses to public problems or to leadership thrusts that are momentarily unpopular.

# ★ ★ ★ The Future Presidency ★ ★ ★

The effective President has a gift of rallying public opinion, of bringing it to perceive the nation's problems and interest and the rightness of his measures. But public opinion, speaking through public and private leaders, through the communications media, and through the electorate, can also reach the President. Democracy requires this two-way flow of information and ideas, which makes the following questions crucial: How are the channels of communication and exchange to be kept in optimum working order? How, on the one hand, is the future President to be strong in his high task of educating and rallying the public? And how, on the other hand, is he to be subject, as befits democracy, to the competition of other political leaders, particularly on television, and to ideas and policy alternatives emanating from sources other than his own?

1. Toward such ends, the television roles of Congress and the opposition party might be expanded. Only the House permits televised coverage of its proceedings; the Senate should adopt a similar practice. The congressional houses should permit televised coverage, scheduled several or more times a year, in prime-time evening sessions, during which important issues would be discussed and voted on. Both here-and-now problems and likely longer-term questions could appear on the agenda.

2. The slender interest of the public in televised political programs might be enhanced by use of the debate format, like the 1960 Kennedy-Nixon, the 1976 Ford-Carter, and the 1980 Carter-Reagan "Great Debates" that drew huge audiences. The debate could deal with both present and future issues, with the participants chosen by the national party committees, whose interest would be to provide arresting personalities and accomplished debaters. The proposal would encourage the parties to develop positions on serious issues and to become more responsive to changes in public sentiment. If, as often happens, the President's party is divided on an issue, it could conceivably oppose his policies in these "national debates." Something of the imbalance between the President's domination of television relative to the opposition party could thus be redressed.

3. If the President wants to communicate effectively, he will need speech writers and other aides of whom at least some are not public relations professionals. The professional's attachment to the status quo and his tendency to subordinate policy to image mean that the President will need a representation of communications people of altogether different backgrounds—men like Samuel Rosenman, a lawyer of wide public experience who was a draftsman for Franklin Roosevelt; Malcolm Moos of the academic community, who served Eisenhower; or Theodore Sorensen, Kennedy's draftsman, whose background combined law and politics.

**4.** To promote the purposes of this chapter a variety of legal changes to ease the flow of information to the public are necessary. The Chief Justice Earl Warren Conference on Advocacy urged the establishment of a national journalists' privilege to exempt reporters from compulsion to reveal the sources of information gained in confidence, abolition of all governmental power to regulate program content on television and radio, creation of an independent agency to review national security documents to determine if the classification system is being abused, a requirement that the government pay costs for successful information suits, and that government be forced to justify the withholding of any portion of a document. The urgency of these proposals is spurred by the darkening clouds of uncertainty following Supreme Court rulings that journalists possess no right under the First Amendment to withhold confidential information from grand juries.[65]

# Chapter Six

# Party Chief

If there is an aspect of the presidency that is hobbled by uncertainty and frailty, it is the office's vague specifications for the role of party leader. The President is deprived of the advantage of strong party organization that the heads of government in parliamentary systems enjoy; the American national party organizations are strikingly weak, and their current trend is, alas, toward increasing weakness.

Parties are the best political invention yet struck by the human mind to stabilize political influence and to transpose promises into policy. For all of its handicaps, the historic two-party system has contributed crucially to the presidency's strength and effectiveness. Through his party, the President can mobilize majorities to transform his promises into legislated policies. Parties help meld differences springing from the nation's extraordinary social, economic, and regional diversity, a giant step toward policy. As party chief, the President can lead in building the consensus, in mobilizing help in the task from fellow party leaders in Congress and in the state and local governments.

## The Responsible Party Model

Nonetheless, even at their historic best, American parties have been well removed from "the responsible party" model of West European parties. In that model's workings, parties, through their platforms and candidates, present the voter with significant choices among competing offerings of policies and programs. European parties are committed to transposing, once their candidates have taken office, the promises of the campaign into enacted public policies. Officials, whether in the legislature or in the "government"—the Prime Minister and his cabinet—which is a committee of the legislature, are "disciplined" to act and vote in support of party commitments. Although they debate and wrangle in the privacy of the party caucus, they are, characteristically, united in public, including the all-important process of voting on measures in the legislature.

American parties, in contrast, are far less disciplined, far less cohesive. The President and the houses of Congress function through separate party organizations and therefore perform far less dependably and responsibly than European parties in transforming campaign platforms into governmental policies. However much Jimmy Carter inveighed against the tax system as a "disgrace" in his 1976 campaign, and notwithstanding his conscientious efforts as President, tax reform lay dormant on a far horizon. Congress, controlled by the President's own party, would not enact it. The loose American system allows problems to drift and tips the scales in favor of the status quo and of those who profit from its hard injustices.

# The Decline of the Parties

Always highly imperfect instruments, American parties in recent decades have steadily become weaker. Many forces feed into the parties' decline. The partisan feelings and identifications of Americans are diminishing. Both major parties, in terms of those identifying with them, are continuously becoming smaller. The rapid decomposition of the parties has weakened their traditional bases of support. The electorate is engaged in a grand reshuffling. Democrats can no longer rely on such great traditional constituencies as the white South and the Northern working class, while the Republicans are losing the Protestant upper middle-class in droves. Party decline is a consequence of the expanding accessibility of higher education whose constituency feels no need for parties as intermediaries in the voting decision. Today's electorate is more candidate-oriented, more issue-oriented, and therefore less party-oriented. Issue voting has increased because more citizens have issue positions by which to vote, and more citizens are guided by those issue positions when they vote. The parties, alas, while excelling as presenters of candidates, have long floundered as presenters of issues. All in all, an individuation of political life is transpiring. With little exception, group affiliation no longer indicates as reliably as it once did how a citizen will vote, given his or her region, religion, or class.

The largest and fastest growing constituency is the Independent voter. With something like 20 percent of eligible voters identifying with it, the Republican party qualifies more by tradition than by numbers as a major party. The Democratic party, once a majority presidential party, is no longer. Except for 1964, 1972, and 1980, elections since the Second World War have been close elections, with the outcome seesawing back and forth between the parties.[1]

Presidential elections are becoming less party contests and more personal contests. The age of television, in which candidates rather than parties are projected, and the flourishing primaries deflate traditional party power and inflate the potency of personality. In both his 1976 and 1980 races, Jimmy Carter cultivated his valued image as an "outsider," maintained by delimiting some distance between himself and his party organization, and Ronald Reagan in 1980 cultivated Democratic and independent voters.

The weakening, disaggrandizing trend of the parties is harmful both to presidential power and democracy. The presidency is handicapped in struggling with conundrums like inflation and energy by the diminished state of party organizations and their declining capacity to weave regional and local differences into the complex mosaic of a national consensus. Democracy is impaired when a President can largely bypass the regular party organization and work through a personal organization, as Richard Nixon did in fashioning his extraordinary victory in 1972. His personal organization, the Committee for the Reelection of the President (CREEP), committed corrupt and criminal acts that could hardly have transpired in an historically functioning national party structure whose largely autonomous congressional, state, and local organizations and leaders could have questioned and limited the Watergate malfeasances more readily than the controlled, acquiescent, personalized party of the President. Above all, parties are the chief instrument available for organizing and articulating the collective power of the many powerless against the relatively few who are individually or organizationally powerful.

Each major party has its own contagion of strength-draining maladies. The present-day Democratic party is rooted in the coalition contrived by Franklin Roosevelt in the 1930s and early 1940s that welded together the one-party Southern states, the "Solid South," which provided an agrarian foundation, and the large urban industrial states.[2] From the 1950s onward partisan disaggregation overtook the coalition, with major social groups rejecting its policy course, particularly its support for black civil rights. A long-building Democratic decline among Southern whites accelerated, and the numbers of blue collar workers identifying with the Democratic party diminished by 16 percent between 1940 and 1972. Comparable declines occurred among big city, working-class whites outside the South and among urban Catholics.[3] As working-class whites have moved up to middle-class status, their demands for equalitarian social change have diminished, and, consequently, so has their support of the Democrats. The Democrats' highest support levels are provided by blacks and Jews.[4]

The frailty of the Roosevelt coalition was well exposed in Carter's landslide defeat in 1980. Carter commanded little better than an even split among voters from union households, and his support among Jews, liberals, Roman Catholics, and low-income voters slid well below the percentages usually accorded Democrats. That bastion of the original Roosevelt coalition, the South, was overwhelmed by Reagan.

The wind-down of the Democratic party has not been paralleled by a surge of those who identify with the Republican party. Instead, the Republicans too are declining, a descent worse even than that of the Democrats. Increasingly assuming the image of the "new conservative party," predominately the party of upper middle-class white Protestants, the Republicans, as political scientist Everett C. Ladd, Jr. has stated, appear poorly equipped to articulate the frustrations of the new, emerging petit bourgeoisie, whether Southern whites, Catholics, Protestants, or blacks. Democrats are well ahead of Republicans in every age cohort and in all educational and income categories. Less than one-third of the business-professional stratum identifies with Republicans.[5]

In the 1980 elections, the Republican party made extraordinary gains, capturing the presidency, the Senate, picking up 33 House seats, plus comparable strides in gubernatorial and state legislative elections. But the upturn is unlikely to comprise a lasting massive influx of voters into the Republican fold or a new coalition to replace the old Roosevelt coalition. Rather it reflects momentary voter disaffection on economic issues and with Carter's performance, Republican building of more effective party apparatuses at state and local levels, the potency of conservative political action committees who concentrated on a hit list of progressive Democratic legislators, and the Democrats' failure to develop a capability for getting out the vote.

Despite their weakness in members, the Republicans have been remarkably adept at controlling the presidency. Between 1952 and 1980, they won five of eight presidential contests and came extraordinarily close in 1960 and 1976. The presidency is the place in the political system where the two-party system remains most operative. Everywhere else the party picture has been lopsided, with the Democrats holding sizeable edges in Congress, in governorships, and in state legislatures. The Republican landslide of 1980 redressed the balance—whether temporarily or enduringly remains to be determined in future elections. The shift is apt to be temporary if voters simply seek leaders and parties capable of providing relief from economic hardship. In their eager, unsatisfying quest, they have stumbled from Ford to Carter, and to Reagan. If leaders again fail, voters will again shift as they search for economic well-being in an era of high inflation. Why is the presidency so continuously a battleground of party competition? At the presidential level, far more than elsewhere in the political system, basic issues are raised, to which the electorate responds; and studies disclose impressive correlations between voters' issue orientations and candidate choice.

# The President and His Party

The lack of an effective national party institution forces the President into a heavy dependency upon his personal skills as party leader and makes the use of a personal organization tempting. His ability as a manipulator of party resources, such as funds and organization, and his exploitation of passing advantages produced by political events and circumstance are keys to his success as party leader. A few Presidents, notably endowed with party skills or favored by exceptional circumstances, have reaped impressive political harvests as party leaders. They have dominated the governmental machinery and scored glittering legislative victories. But because success in party leadership depends so heavily upon personal skill, the role has never stabilized. One President who excels as party leader has never been followed by another who even approximates his predecessor's accomplishment.

The party role was plastered onto the presidential office after the main structure was built. The Founding Fathers made no provision for parties in the Constitution, and their later emergence was attended with awkwardness. Although parties appeared in Washington's time, he abstained from functioning as party leader, deeming it incompatible with the nature of his office. For his successor, John Adams, the party was not an adjunct of the presidential office but an instrument that his political enemies employed against him. Under Jefferson, Jackson, and a sprinkling of their successors, party leadership flourished, but it has flourished even more in the states and localities, in the hands of governors, mayors, and local politicians.

## Tensions

The President's uneasy party role is aggravated by the continual tension between his responsibilities to his office and the claims of his party. His office, and therefore its duties and problems, presumably exceed any obligation the party can impose upon him. He is a politician who must also be a statesman. Yet the party often insistently violates this assumption. Senate Republicans, blithely heedless of President Eisenhower's struggle with great and manifold problems of state, required him to work in harness with their chosen leader, William F. Knowland, who opposed most of his foreign and much of his domestic policy. President Kennedy was expected, at the first electoral opportunity, to stump against Senator Everett Dirksen, Republican leader, who had provided indispensable support for the test ban treaty and a string of other important measures.

The tension between office and party is heightened by the party's and the President's almost frivolous disregard of their obligations to each other. He may by splendid electoral triumph plant the party standard in the White House and carry many a legislative party colleague on his coattails across the victory line only to see his proposals spurned, sometimes seriatim, by a Congress whose two houses his party controls. President Truman, despite his stunning electoral victory in 1948, which restored the Democrats to power in both Congressional houses, was able to obtain in the ensuing session the enactment of only several of a score of Fair Deal measures. President Kennedy, who summoned his fellow Democrats on Capitol Hill to rally behind an ambitious and popular program, did little better. He could well paraphrase for his own party role the memorable instruction of his inaugural address, "Ask not what your party can do for you; ask what you can do for your party."

President Eisenhower, just before his spectacular reelection victory in 1956, was questioned pointedly concerning the affinity of several old guard Republican Senators to his own Modern Republicanism. His perceptive response suggested several limits the President suffers as party chief. Eisenhower said,

> Now, let's remember there are no national parties in the United States. There are forty-eight state parties, then they are the ones that determine the people that belong to those parties. There is nothing I can do to say that [anyone] is not a Republican. The most I can say is that in many things they do not agree with me. . . . We have got to remember that these are state organizations, and there is nothing I can do to say so-and-so is a Republican and so-and-so is not a Republican.[6]

The President is an uncertain monarch of a loose and far-flung party empire of several satrapies and dependencies and a host of self-governing commonwealths. His sway is full over a few parts; over most it is little or nonexistent. He is a chief among chiefs. The local and state party organizations are beyond his control and are subject, at most, to his influence. The major parties function as viable national organizations only quadrennially, when their state and local parts more or less unite to win the presidency and its stakes of power. Thereafter the parts conduct themselves with jealously preserved autonomy. The state and local organizations command a solid corps of workers and followers, assert their own discipline, control the selection of senatorial and congressional candidates, and possess financial resources of their own. The Senate and House of Representatives maintain a quantity of party organizations: caucuses, steering committees, campaign committees, and policy committees. Senators and Congressmen render their principal allegiance not to the Chief Executive but to the state and local organizations to which they owe their nomination and election. Legislators of the President's party both help and hobble his program of legislation. The fact that a Long and a Cranston march under the Democratic banner and a Tower and a Percy under the Republican demonstrates how undependable the party label is as a guide to how legislators debate and vote. Nowhere in the vast party structure is there a constant and effective source of power that the President can confidently turn to for support. The national committee, where his strength is greatest and where the state and local organizations converge, is chiefly concerned with the choice and election of the presidential candidate.

## Necessity for Pragmatism

The unreliability of his party, the likelihood that numbers of its congressional members may oppose him, must lead any President to ponder privately just what good his party really is to him. Indeed, if he reads the texts of presidential history, he will discover that Presidents achieve many, if not most, of their important policies and programs, whether in domestic or foreign affairs, only with bipartisan support. The loyalty of his own party is never so dependable that it can assure a succession of program victories. This undependability makes it necessary for the President studiously to cultivate support in the opposition party. His own party's ambiguity of support promotes the President's necessary ambiguity as party leader. For his program's sake, he must not be so fiercely and devotedly the leader of his own party as to preclude his gaining support from the opposition.

The case for the President to treat his party role pragmatically and to conduct himself in a fashion that will pick up support beyond his party can be made in another way. The President is brought into office by a popular vote that is greater than his party vote. His electoral majority is a patchwork of voters from his own party, from the opposition party, and from the steadily growing body of independents. He may have large support from big groups such as organized labor and national and racial groups. His own party may have chosen him as its standard-bearer principally because of his presumed ability to attract broad support. Ironically, the Republican party denied Robert A. Taft its nomination because he was too much a Republican ("Mr. Republican," in fact), and therefore thought unable to lure Democratic and independent voters into his column. Without substantial outside support, he could not possibly have become a winner.

The President and Vice President are the only officers chosen by a national popular majority. In seeking to convert his promises to that majority into policy, the President is frustrated by the skillful arrangement of the governmental structure that permits what at most can be only limited majority rule. The system of checks and balances enables Congress, which is a series of disparate local majorities, to reject what the President, the voice of a national majority, proposes. The weakness of the parties assures that the principle of checks and balances, and therefore limited majority rule, will enjoy the full play the Founding Fathers intended. Congress's local constituencies, in contrast to the President's national constituency and Congress's internal organization of diffused power, tend to produce a legislature and an executive of dissimilar policy outlooks, even when the same party controls both branches. Except for Carter, contemporary Democratic Presidents have been more progressive than Democratic Congresses, and the single Republican President, Eisenhower, who, for a time, had a Republican Congress, was more "moderate," or "progressive," than his party's legislators. Reagan faced Republican legislators, some more conservative and others more progressive than himself.

The President is forced by checks and balances and party weakness to scramble for support by a variety of expedients. He must court approval in both congressional parties. He may endeavor as best he can to dominate portions of his own party by building alliances with state and local leaders and by discreetly influencing the choice of legislative candidates. He may rely heavily on his own personal organization to make his way in party affairs. He can move to change the popular base of his party by extending it to groups to whose interests his program is akin. Desperation is nowhere else so much the mother of invention as it is in the Chief Executive's party plight.

# The Presidential Nominee

Even in its most serviceable roles—selecting the presidential nominee and conducting the electoral campaign—the party's relation with its chosen candidate is uneasy and imperfect. The party provides no assurance that the platform he runs on accords with his wishes. His ability to make his preferences prevail depends upon a complex of factors—the power of his rivals, the nature of the issues, his own general political health. Franklin Roosevelt could confidently expect that the Democratic convention of 1936 would approve the platform prepared under his supervision. "I would like to have as short a platform as possible this year," he instructed his draftsmen, "and . . . I would like to have it based on the sentence of the Declaration of Independence, 'We hold these truths to be self-evident.' "[7] The convention approved the several parts of the Roosevelt-made platform with waves of ovations.

Grover Cleveland in 1888 had more difficulty. The tariff was the prickly issue of the day between progressives and conservatives, and the President's general political situation was not without weakness. Cleveland himself drafted the platform, carefully stating in moderate language the tariff question. For the sake of his own political necessities, Cleveland wished to provide the Republicans no opportunity to charge the Democratic party with free-trade principles. At the St. Louis convention, unfortunately for Cleveland, the low tariff men unshackled their bonds. They and Cleveland's emissaries of moderation were about evenly divided on the platform subcommittee on the tariff. The subcommittee met at dusk in a steaming room of the Southern Hotel and fought over the issue all night. The free-trade men, led by Henry Watterson, the Kentucky editor, ultimately prevailed.[8] In the ensuing election, tariff reform became the leading issue, and, although the election did not turn on the issue, Benjamin Harrison, staunch defender of the tariff, defeated Cleveland.

Many a presidential nominee views the available party organization as an enterprise of limited dependability and feels it the better part of wisdom to build a personal organization to conduct much of the postconvention campaign. John Kennedy relied upon an elaborate personal organization, consisting of his brothers, his brothers-in-law, a cadre of aides from his earliest political campaigns, and several members of the Harvard faculty, among others. In 1976, Carter waged his postconvention campaign with the team, essentially a coterie of Georgians, that won the nomination. The campaign was conducted from Atlanta, with the Democratic National Committee confined chiefly to fund raising and overseeing a lavish voter-registration drive. Despite copious uplifting talk of unity and enlarging the circle of participants, the Atlantans kept a tight rein. "We're not going to turn our campaign over to anybody in any state," proclaimed Hamilton Jordan, Carter's political major-domo.[9] Reagan's personal campaign organization in 1980 consisted of associates from his gubernatorial campaigns and recruits from the Nixon and Ford presidencies, well versed in party and campaign affairs.

## Working with the Congressional Party

The presidential nominee who becomes President works with something less than total ease and comfort with the other main branch of the national party organization, the congressional and senatorial campaign committees. The midterm congressional election is often a season for exposing divergences in the policy views of the President and legislators of his party. The lengths to which the malaise may go was suggested in a remarkable statement by Republican congressional campaign committee chairman Richard M. Simpson of Pennsylvania, in 1958. Republican candidates, Simpson counseled, should forget about Eisenhower's favors and supportive campaigning in the 1958 elections and "make known" to voters any "disagreement with the President's policies." Simpson, a conservative Republican, often opposed the President's Modern Republicanism.[10]

Despite the varying cordiality of the invitations he receives, the President has for many years now led the party in congressional elections. The results, like the invitations, are mixed. Woodrow Wilson began the practice by appealing for a Democratic Congress in 1918, with a disheartening result. His party lost control of both houses. Franklin Roosevelt launched his purge in 1938, for which the electorate slapped him hard. Not only did the purge fail, but the Democrats lost the incredible total of seventy seats in the

House and seven in the Senate. In the 1966 congressional elections Lyndon Johnson apparently concluded that he could help the Democratic cause most by staying away from the campaign trail and attending to his official duties. Many of his party's candidates for state and national office concurred in his judgment. The President and his policies at the time were sagging in popularity. In the South, Johnson was a symbol of desegregation, which many local politicians in both major parties were profitably exploiting. His coming as a campaigner would only spur their attacks upon desegregation as a local political issue. Elsewhere he symbolized an unwanted war, mounting prices, and the bane of neglected farmers. Many a congressional race seemed to turn on local issues and personality contests in which the President's influence was irrelevant. In the 1974 congressional elections, Gerald Ford toiled overtime with little appreciable effect, for Republican candidates, warning of the dangers of a "veto-proof" Democratic Congress; in 1978 Carter's effort and impact were equally slight.

On occasion the President undertakes a further function in congressional elections. His encouragement may be vital to inducing able citizens to become their party's nominees for legislative office. The national Republican chairman, Leonard Hall, concluded in 1956 that John Sherman Cooper, then ambassador to India, was urgently needed to run for the Senate in Kentucky. Cooper had triumphed in the Senate race in 1952, but in 1956 he was unwilling to sacrifice contentment in India for the travail of a Senate race. Eisenhower, who thought it inappropriate for the President to persuade anyone to run for office, was pressed to take on Cooper by both Hall and Presidential Assistant Sherman Adams, who had tried and failed. Cooper was brought to Eisenhower's office, and the President, who never did ask him to run, spoke eloquently of the opportunity for service in the Senate. Cooper capitulated, ran, and won.[11]

Contemporary Democratic Presidents experience the biennial or mini-national convention, a device Republicans have not yet adopted. In 1978, the Carter forces seemed to have that convention, held at Memphis, tolerably in hand, until Edward Kennedy, the President's pending rival in 1980, delivered a rafter-shaking speech championing emotionally appealing social programs, which Carter in an earlier appearance declared must be subordinated to halting inflation. By discrete use of political muscle, the Carter forces extracted a vote of confidence in the administration's policies, but an embarrassing 40 percent of the delegates opposed it, an ill-omen for Carter's rapport with his party's liberal wing.[12]

# Winning Renomination

The most important of a President's personal political objectives, needless to say, is securing renomination, and normally the party almost automatically grants this presidential wish. Even the high likelihood of defeat may not bar his renomination, as it did not for Hoover in 1932. Yet a few Presidents, such as Pierce, Buchanan, and Arthur, were denied renomination, and Benjamin Harrison achieved it only after a hard fight.

## Opposing the President

Truman waged a classic struggle for renomination in 1948, which he achieved in a steep uphill fight by a combination of pluck and luck. Before the convention, Truman's political stock was at rock bottom. The Republican congressional victory in 1946 foreshadowed a Republican presidential victory in 1948. Scandals had crashed upon the administration in waves. Henry A. Wallace had broken off from the Democratic party and announced his presidential candidacy. Labor and New Deal liberals were restive, and Southern Democrats stood at the brink of revolt. Truman's popularity in the opinion polls had fallen dismally. To hold back the avalanche, Truman, in January of 1948, used his State of the Union message to project a platform for his party. The message recapitulated a quantity of Fair Deal proposals with a request for an improbable tax cut thrown in. Truman's choice of theme sought to hold together the crumbling Roosevelt Democratic coalition and to forestall liberals and independents from drifting to Wallace. In June, Truman made a fiery whistle-stop tour through the Middle and Far West to show local Democratic leaders his strength with the crowds before the convention began.

But Truman's ability to be renominated depended not upon his own power and enterprise but upon the outcome of a caucus that gathered in Philadelphia, shortly before the convention, to arrange his overthrow. The caucus was called by Jacob M. Arvey, Chicago Democratic leader, James and Elliott Roosevelt, the late President's sons, and sixteen other party leaders. The active coalition against Truman was a cross section of the Democratic party and the old Roosevelt coalition.

The Philadelphia caucus saw inevitable electoral defeat unless a substitute candidate for Truman could be found. Their acquisitive gaze fell upon General Dwight D. Eisenhower, then on the crest of his popularity from his European military triumphs. But Eisenhower dashed the hopes of his would-be benefactors by issuing a statement a week before the convention, saying, "I will not at this time identify myself with any political party and could not accept nomination for any political office."

Truman was eventually renominated by default of the old coalition's failure to unite on an alternate candidate. The New York *Post* reflected the convention's mood when it wrote, "The Party might as well immediately concede the election to Dewey and save the wear and tear of campaigning." As the world knows, Truman went on to win in one of the most dramatic election upsets in the country's history.[13]

But Truman in 1952 and Johnson in 1968, confronted with formidable competitors for the nomination and an unhappy trend in the primaries, withdrew early in the struggle.

## Carter's Renomination

But not Jimmy Carter in 1980, whose popularity plummeted to depths unknown since public opinion polls had commenced their pulse-taking, and he was faced, at least at the outset, by an opponent presumed to be formidable, scion of a martyred political family, Edward M. Kennedy. A gnawing feeling persisted among the Carter circle that the administration had never really been accepted as legitimate by the Democratic party establishment and by the Washington political community. Kennedy's candidacy was perceived as a frontal assault on that legitimacy. As the nominating convention neared and Carter continued to wilt in the polls, far behind the Republican nominee, Ronald Reagan, murmurs of uprising were heard to deny Carter renomination. But the brewing revolt was less potent and less organized than the one against Truman, and it lacked a potential candidate as formidable as Eisenhower.

Carter exceeded all Presidents in his single-minded utilization of the resources of the presidency to secure renomination. Virtually no stone of the office's opportunities was left unturned, and the President's maneuvers were more akin to an old-school, mail-fisted Tammany boss than to the image of the decent, upright candidate so assiduously cultivated. Early on, and in anticipation of 1980, the Carter forces effected rule changes in delegate selection favorable to their candidate, and impairing the rise of competing candidates.

Carter instructed his cabinet officers to check the "dependability" of subordinates who were political appointees, making clear his expectation that all and sundry of that genre would be "actively engaged" in the campaign.[14] White House aides and others of the executive branch appeared in force to toil regularly in the primaries, with leave-taking from their regular duties made possible by suddenly arranged "vacations" and unpaid absence.

A Rose Garden strategy was unfurled, by which Carter asserted that the gravity of the hostage crisis in Iran and the Soviet invasion of Afghanistan required him to remain at his desk, the captain lashed to the wheel, so to speak, piloting the nation over its perilous course. Occasionally, just before a primary, Carter would step before the television cameras in the Oval Office to announce or assess some hopeful new development in Iran. It was all a callous manipulation, his opponents charged, to influence the voters. Particularly in early primaries the strategy worked, as the citizenry followed their accustomed course of rallying around the President in crisis and accorded Carter a string of primary triumphs. Meanwhile at the White House, Carter took generous leaves from his crisis duties to make quantities of telephone calls—sometimes twenty a day—to leaders and lesser citizens in primary states. He tirelessly entertained selected groups of businessmen, editors, politicians, and other local leaders at White House receptions and briefings timed to coincide with the state primary and caucus schedules.

Prior to the Florida Democratic caucus some three hundred Floridians were invited to Washington for high level briefings in foreign and domestic affairs, topped by a reception in the White House's East Room. Influential Florida Catholics were invited back to the White House reception for Pope John Paul II. Simultaneously Carter drenched Florida with federal money. Dade County, for example, was granted $19.9 million for housing projects, and additional grants were allotted to housing units for the elderly in cities throughout the state. The President's assistant for Hispanic affairs, Esteban Torres, was dispatched to Miami's "Little Havana" to promote tourism in the city's Cuban section.[15]

With such pointed ladling of federal largess, governors and mayors were wary not to offend the President. They were responsive to the Carterites' "endorsement strategy," initiated at a Washington dinner for over two hundred elected officials, including members of Congress, governors, mayors, and county officials. All were invited to provide endorsements, and the evening's speakers helped them understand why it was beneficial to do so. Invaluable groundwork had been laid by Jack Watson, presidential assistant for intergovernmental affairs, who had been cultivating the governors and mayors since the administration's outset. Endorsements by elected officials were welcomed by Carterites to offset the view that the President was a loser, hell-bent on dragging the Democratic party down to defeat. Only one governor dared endorse his rival, Edward Kennedy. Special punishment was meted out to Mayor Jane Byrne of Chicago, who, after initially endorsing Carter, reneged and endorsed Kennedy. To assist his fortunes in the crucial Illinois primary, Carter released $24.8 million in "discretionary" highway funds to the state. When his Secretary of Transportation journeyed to Chicago to proclaim the joyful news, the ceremony was held not in the office of the mayor, where by usual protocol it would be, but in the office of a "loyal" Congressman.[16]

Subsequently, Vice President Walter Mondale, in a fund-raising speech in the Chicago area did something national Democratic politicians, especially those seeking reelection, had not done in a decade. He ridiculed the mayor of Chicago, long the most powerful incumbency of party bosses, declaring he wanted to recognize "our dear friend." "Isn't she here?" he asked mockingly. "She assured me she'd be here." Later in riposte Mrs. Byrne confessed to having missed the occasion because "I was sleeping."[17]

# The Congressional Party

Once nominated and elected, or reelected, a President is concerned with getting his program through Congress, a venture in which the party leadership and rank and file are as likely to fail him as to help him. Few Congressmen view their loyalties to their own careers, constituents, and party organization as anything but superior in priority to their loyalty to their party's national standard-bearer and his program. Eisenhower's Senate leaders were successively Senator Taft, his chief rival for the presidential nomination, and Senator Knowland, who opposed him on a wide range of policy. Eisenhower steadily received more support from Democratic legislators than from Republicans. In Kennedy's time the House Democratic floor leader, and later Speaker, was John W. McCormack of Massachusetts, whose nephew contested with the President's brother Edward for the 1962 Democratic Massachusetts senatorial nomination. Mike Mansfield, Senate Democratic leader and long-time ally of President Johnson, broke with the administration on the wisdom of the Vietnam war policy and registered his dissent publicly, pointedly, and repeatedly. In no other governmental system in the world are such oddities of party life to be found.

The President's party equips him with remarkably few pressures he can apply to Congress, and these are highly imperfect at best. His most ancient pressure is, of course, patronage. Earlier Presidents were wholesale dispensers of offices, a part of their job that they dislike. In Lincoln's day job-seekers crammed the White House rooms, stairs, hallways, and even closets, prompting that noble spirit to cry out, "It is not the rebellion that is killing me, but the Pepperton post office."[18] The Civil Service Act of 1883, and its later extensions, protecting the tenure of designated employees, has gradually but sweepingly reduced the relative numbers of federal jobs tagged for patronage. A contemporary President's patronage appointments number a mere few thousand.

## Patronage

Patronage enables the President to strike at the legislator in his home district, to attract or alienate local groups upon whose support he depends. For the favor of his juicy patronage plums, the Chief Executive can exact a *quid pro quo*. Many a President, before handing out jobs, first checks the voting record of the interested Congressman on the administration's legislative program. The search may bring down the heavens upon the errant. When Samuel J. Randall, Democratic high tariff advocate, fought Grover Cleveland's grand enterprise to lower the tariff, retribution was swift and severe. Word went forth from Washington that no Randall man need expect any patronage. At Randall's political base in Pennsylvania, reaction was quick. Two key Randall organizations, the Randall Club of Pittsburgh and the Eleventh Ward Democratic Association of Philadelphia, hastened to repudiate their leader and endorse Cleveland's tariff position. When the state Democratic committee met to elect a chairman and adopt resolutions, Randall's candidate lost to a low tariff man and the committee voted a hearty endorsement of Cleveland's tariff stand.[19] Yet, as Presidents well know, many legislators whom they might strike at by withholding patronage are by no means defenseless. "It was a smart practice in government," Roosevelt's party chairman, Jim Farley, once said, "to avoid antagonizing the men who vote the appropriations."[20] He could add, too, legislators of large influence on other key congressional committees and those enjoying full sway over local party organizations.

The patronage weapon is not without flaw. Its worth rests upon the assumption that human gratitude is enduring, an assumption that sometimes falters in practice, especially in politics. Further, an appointment that recognizes a local political faction may antagonize competing factions. William Howard Taft, after a wealth of experience, concluded that every time he made a job appointment he created "nine enemies and one ingrate." Virtually anything the President does in the patronage field stirs bleats of disgruntlement.

## Preferments

In contemporary presidencies, far more important than the patronage of jobs is the patronage of expenditure and the untold variety of executive decisions, the granting of preferments, that can waft windfalls of largess into the laps of deliberately selected beneficiaries. In distributing funds for the Model Cities program, Lyndon Johnson allocated not on the basis of need but according to political criteria intended to reward the home towns of key congressional committee chairmen. Of the initial list of sixty-three cities, Cleveland and Los Angeles, scenes of severe racial outbreaks, received no grants at all while Smithville, Tennessee (population 2,300)—a community represented by Congressman Joe L. Evans, a Democrat and chairman of the House Housing and Urban Development Subcommittee on Independent Offices Appropriations—was favored. Ordinarily subtle, Johnson sometimes coupled his dispensations with naked threat. When Senator Frank Church (D-Idaho) tendered an article by Walter Lippmann to explain his opposition to the Vietnam war, an annoyed Johnson replied, "All right, the next time you need a dam for Idaho, you go ask Walter Lippmann."[21]

Preferments, dispensed administratively and often expeditiously, are grants of extraordinary treatment. They take many forms, such as the award of contracts for constructing public buildings, roads or parks, and, in the President's hands, can be used for party purposes. Preferments are incentives intended to evoke valued behavior by the recipient—donations to electoral campaigns or votes of the recipient's Congressman or Senators, who, pleased by the preference's economic windfall in their district or state, gladly support some presidentially championed measure. Or preferment may be the President's contribution toward strengthening the local party by sowing rewards that attract valued workers and leaders.[22]

## Policy Goals

The President also employs policy goals to woo the support of party colleagues at all governmental levels. The decline of patronage, the fading of traditional bosses and machines, leave the President and his party associates with fewer means of punishment and reward, and more dependent on the solidarity fostered by common policy goals. Studies disclose a high incidence of shared policy attitudes along party lines on the voting behavior of members of Congress. Non-Southern Democrats, for example, take the most internationalist position while their Southern colleagues are most isolationist. Republicans are positioned between the two groups, veering more to the isolationist than to the internationalist end of the scale. On social welfare issues, Democrats outside the South are more accepting and Republicans far less so, with Southern Democrats occupying a position in the middle, slightly closer to Republicans.[23] A President, functioning actively and prudently as party leader, can rally the predispositions of his congressional party colleagues on a breadth of policy issues.

## The Opposition Party

The party, when it does not control the presidency, may be expected, according to general political practice, to take on the democracy-serving function of responsible opposition. Difficulties afflict this expectation due to the low capacity of the congressional party organization to achieve party coherence. Soon after the 1956 election of Eisenhower, Senator Hubert Humphrey proposed that congressional Democrats adopt their own legislative program, consisting of sixteen points, including civil rights, as a responsible opposition alternative to the President's program. "If you have a platform," Democratic Mayor David Lawrence of Pittsburgh commented to reporters, "you ought to follow it up with a legislative program, not just throw it out after you are defeated in an election." Senate Democratic floor leader Lyndon Johnson and Speaker Sam Rayburn declared their opposition to Humphrey's step and suggested that Congress wait and act upon the Eisenhower legislative program. When later Rayburn and Johnson proved fairly congenial to the Eisenhower program, Truman, Stevenson, Humphrey, and other Democratic leaders moved to form a Democratic Advisory Committee (or Council, as it came to be called) to keep alive the spirit of creative opposition. But the Speaker and majority leader agreed only to "consult" the committee, holding that they must retain their independence of action for their congressional responsibilities. In such a tangled situation it is difficult if not impossible to find meaningful national party leadership. Stevenson was discredited because of his two defeats for the presidency, and Johnson's own party-mindedness, in light of his course, was a trifle obscure.[24]

Any incumbent President looks for support in the opposition's congressional party, an aspiration that constrains his stance toward that group. For his defense and foreign aid programs, Eisenhower appealed for help to Democratic congressional chieftains Rayburn and Johnson; at critical junctures in quests for civil rights legislation, Presidents Kennedy and Johnson sought much-needed aid from Senate Republican leader Everett Dirksen. Nixon's strongest congressional support came not from Republicans but from southern Democrats.

Like other Presidents, Nixon's demeanor in congressional elections toward opposition party members who helped him was conspicuously more benign than toward resolute foes. Consider the tender concern lavished on the reelection in 1972 of Senator James O. Eastland of Mississippi. As Senate Judiciary Committee chairman, Eastland had staunchly supported the administration's embattled Supreme Court nominees, Clement Haynsworth, Jr., and G. Harrold Carswell, and in the disputed and politically dangerous International Telephone and Telegraph Corporation case. When Vice President Agnew alighted in Mississippi, he announced that he could not associate himself with Eastland's Republican opponent, Gil Carmichael, and that the administration could do nothing to "help defeat someone who has been so helpful to us in the past." In a speech at the state capital, Agnew elaborately endorsed Mississippi's three Republican nominees for the House of Representatives but never mentioned Carmichael, who was conspicuously absent from the platform.[25]

# The Jeffersonian Success Model

The President's success in party affairs is a mixture of many things: his own personality, his public popularity, his skill at maneuvering, his intuitive sense. It is a game played not with rules but with a master's instinct for the shifting sources of power. Some Presidents revel in their role as party commander. Jefferson and Franklin Roosevelt, for example, enjoyed the game and usually played it with skill and finesse. John Quincy Adams and John Tyler, at the other extreme, were failures. And a President like Eisenhower accepted his party leadership reluctantly, holding that the White House should be above the party. It was as party leader that Lyndon Johnson accumulated considerably less success than he enjoyed in other branches of presidential endeavor. Eminent among Presidents as a legislative leader, as party leader he secured for himself a quantity of black marks in the books of political professionals. The experience of each of these men is, in different ways, instructive.

Of all the Presidents, Thomas Jefferson is unsurpassed in the authority he asserted as party leader and in the fealty he commanded from state and local party organizations. He held sway by means of a thoroughly formulated theory of party principles and functions and a sure grasp of the means of party action. For Jefferson, the party was preeminently the instrument of majority rule. The party joined the executive and Congress into a majoritarian unit. The President and his department Secretaries provided the legislative agenda; the party members in Congress transmuted it into law.

The presidential program was the party program, and fidelity to it in debate and vote was a principle to be jealously guarded and enforced. Jefferson wrote critically of his congressional party brethren,

> Our friends have not yet learned to draw well together, and there has been some danger of a small section of them, aided by the feds [the Federalist party], carrying a question against the larger section. They have seen however that this practice would end in enabling the feds to carry every thing as they please, by joining whichever section of Republicans they chose; and they will avoid this rock.[26]

Jefferson could not abide Republican legislators who acted independently of their party. He called them "wayward freaks, which now and then disturb the operations."[27]

Jefferson worked through and dominated the congressional party machinery. Caucuses of congressional Republicans were summoned at his direction, and sometimes reportedly he presided. Secretary of the Treasury Albert Gallatin devoted no little time and skill to laying before the caucus the President's messages and requests. Jefferson, Gallatin, and other cabinet Secretaries watched over the progress of administration measures in Congress at all stages until their enactment. Jefferson and his aides invented the "floor leader," a legislator in each house who efficiently shepherded the administration's fondest projects over the craggy terrain of votes, committee hearings and reports, and parliamentary maneuver.

At the outset of a legislative session John Randolph, House floor leader and Ways and Means Committee chairman until he fell from presidential grace, would dine with Jefferson to go over the administration's agenda. As the session proceeded, the Congressman was in almost daily touch with executive officials. Gallatin spoke of his "free communication of facts and opinions" to Randolph. Most of Gallatin's proposals were steered through the Ways and Means Committee and onto the House floor in the manner his fastidious tastes desired. Appropriations to purchase Florida, to establish a Mediterranean Fund, and to retire the debt moved steadily under Randolph's sure hand. As floor leader, he managed such major presidential projects as the repeal of the Judiciary Act, the reduction of civil expenditures, and the bringing of charges of impeachment against Supreme Court Justice Samuel Chase, a loud, violent Federalist who denounced Republicanism from the bench as a mash of anarchy, atheism, and the devil.

Jefferson viewed congressional elections as a grand opportunity to eliminate obstructors and import supporters. Although James A. Bayard, Federalist Congressman of Delaware, had by his vote finally ensured Jefferson's triumph over Aaron Burr in their struggle for the presidency, Bayard's subsequent leadership of the congressional opposition alienated the Chief Executive. The President, as he was wont to do, searched for a candidate to beat Bayard at the polls. "For God's sake, run for Congress against him," he implored Caesar A. Rodney of Delaware. Bayard's "long speeches and wicked workings at this session have added at least 30 days to its length, cost us 30,000 D. and filled the union with falsehoods and misrepresentations." Rodney ran and was elected. The President's occasional manipulations had their costs. Major lieutenants like Joseph Nicholson and Nathaniel Macon were sometimes bedeviled with rumors that he was maneuvering to throw them over. To such men he wrote what became known as his "tares" letters: "Some enemy, whom we know not, is sowing tares among us. Between you and myself nothing but opportunities of explanation can be necessary to defeat these endeavors. . . . I must therefore ask a conversation with you." [28]

Jefferson employed patronage to induce legislators to cooperate and to assure executive loyalty to his policies. When things went awry in the party organization, he was quick with redress. Randolph was dropped from his two high posts soon after he erred. He had managed and botched the prosecution of Justice Chase and had demurred at the President's seeming tenderness to the culprits of the Yazoo land fraud and at the President's request for a secret appropriation of two million dollars to purchase Florida if circumstances warranted. Randolph announced his dissents with merciless invective on the House floor. The affronted Jefferson dropped word to Senator William Plumer that "Mr. Randolph's late conduct is very astonishing and has given me much uneasiness." Jefferson and his followers moved to depose Randolph as floor leader and to substitute Barnabas Bidwell of Massachusetts. This plan was foiled when Bidwell was defeated for reelection. Administration business that normally went to the Ways and Means Committee was routed elsewhere as long as Randolph remained chairman. In a speech on the House floor Congressman Thomas Mann Randolph, Jefferson's son-in-law, savagely attacked John Randolph as a betrayer of secrets and an inciter of clamor. From his constituency in southern Virginia, the embattled Randolph complained that "every engine has been set to work to undo me in the estimation of my constituents, and not without effect." The local press maintained a steady, hostile chant, and two prestigious Virginia politicians, William B. Giles and Wilson Cary Nicholas, campaigned mightily against him. Another Jefferson son-in-law, John W. Eppes, took up residence in Randolph's district, contested his House seat, and eventually won it in 1813, when Jefferson was long retired.[29]

# Those Who Failed

If Jefferson achieved crowning success as party leader, John Quincy Adams and John Tyler floundered in the uttermost depths of failure. Adams won the disputed presidential election of 1824 in the House of Representatives and then only, his enemies said, by a corrupt bargain with Henry Clay. In return for Clay-controlled House votes to assure Adams' election, Adams promised the Kentuckian the post of Secretary of State. Andrew Jackson, one of the vanquished candidates, termed Clay "the Judas of the West."

## John Quincy Adams

Adams was endowed neither by personality nor by circumstance to be a party leader. Austere and principled, he faced a wretched political situation. His cabinet contained no one who had openly supported him for President. Although his party controlled the House, the opposition ruled the Senate. Key Senate committees like the Foreign Relations Committee constantly opposed him. Adams' perilous situation in the upper chamber came into sharp relief when he requested authority to dispatch a mission to the Panama Congress of Latin American states. The Foreign Relations Committee rejected his plan with a warning against entangling alliances, but somehow he managed to squeak through the Senate by a vote of twenty-four to twenty despite a punishing debate.

Randolph, who had returned to Congress in 1815, had a field day with the Panama Congress proposal. Charging that Clay had forged the invitations to the Congress, he resumed the attack upon the political partnership of the President and the Secretary of State. They were, he cried, "the coalition of Blifil and Black George . . . of the Puritan with the black leg." *
For Adams, the worst aspect of this rowdy day in the Senate was not Randolph's crudity but the fact that the President's own party permitted it. Not a single Republican Senator called Randolph to order, and Vice President John Calhoun, in the chair, permitted the breach of privilege. Adams, furious at Calhoun's laxity, made a slashing attack upon the Vice President, writing under the name "Patrick Henry," in the press. Calhoun, who used "Onslow" as his pen name, reciprocated fully. The two party giants, the President and Vice President, demonstrated their rich talents for controversy in several exchanges.[30]

Adams' personal encounters were never softened by the favors at his command as party chieftain. He conceivably could heal wounds by applying the salve of patronage. But his principles stood in the way, taking precedence over the claims of party, as General James Tallmadge, lieutenant governor of New York and Tammany chieftain, sadly learned. Tallmadge had backed Adams unstintingly in his narrow victory. In a savage fight the lieutenant governor had stopped a move by Martin Van Buren's New York machine to break up a joint session of the state legislature before the electors could be chosen. If Van Burean had succeeded, New York's electoral votes would have been wasted and Adams defeated. Van Buren and his ally, Governor De Witt Clinton, had their avenging knives poised. Tallmadge clearly needed to escape New York for a distant foreign mission if his political life was to be saved. Thurlow Weed, Tallmadge's emissary, laid the situation before the President. In a meeting that was "embarrassing and constrained," Adams quickly demonstrated his capacity to ignore political obligations. He could not appoint Tallmadge to any diplomatic post, he said, because another New Yorker, Rufus King, had just been named minister to Britain, and New York could not claim more than one overseas appoint-

---

*A reference to two conspiratorial characters in Fielding's *Tom Jones*.

ment. Weed sickened when he reflected that King had opposed Adams' election and Tallmadge had risked, perhaps given, his political life to assure it.[31]

## John Tyler

John Tyler, like Adams, is at the bottom of the league of party chieftains, although for different reasons. A sure-footed politician, he was the victim of the relentless ambition of the leader of the Whig party in Congress, again Henry Clay. The New York *Herald* wrote of Clay,

> He predominates over the Whig party with despotic sway. Old Hickory himself never lorded it over his followers with an authority more undisputed, or more supreme. With the exception of some two or three in the Senate and fifteen or twenty in the House, Mr. Clay's wish is the paramount law to the whole party.[32]

Clay coupled with his great power a fierce drive to become President. A towering obstacle was the incumbent President Tyler and his likely desire to be reelected.

Not without reason, Clay scornfully spoke of Tyler as "a President without a party." Tyler's Whig following in Congress was so small that it was called, half-derisively, "the Corporal's Guard." In the Senate, only William C. Rives supported Tyler in the heavy fighting. The President's party weakness extended to his cabinet, which he had inherited from his late predecessor, William Henry Harrison. All the cabinet Secretaries except Secretary of State Daniel Webster and Postmaster General Francis Granger were allied with Clay. Even of Webster and Granger, Tyler could not be certain. The President's chief sustenance in his political weakness was his personality—"approachable, courteous, always willing to do a kindly action"—and his unlimited courage.[33]

Without a party Tyler could not well put his chief measures through Congress; with a party Clay had Congress in his hand and the President largely at his mercy. Time and again Congress rebuffed the President and the President vetoed Congress. Clay, pursuing his American system, a series of measures to promote the nation's economic development, put through a bill creating a new bank of the United States. Tyler, whose states' rights disposition was offended, vetoed it, earning plaudits from Andrew Jackson. The Clay men drenched the President with invective. "The vocabulary of the language," a witness wrote, "seems to have been ransacked for words to express their angry denunciation."[34] A second bank bill passed, and Tyler vetoed it. At Clay's command, all his men in the cabinet resigned.

Tyler, bereft of party aid, saw many a favorite measure hacked to death in Congress. His proposed treaty with the German *Zollverein* was tabled in the Senate. His nominations to office habitually encountered rough handling in the same body. His fond project to annex Texas by treaty was lost, with every Whig but one voting against it. Eventually, almost miraculously, Tyler brought Texas into the Union by joint resolution.

Tyler's troubles lay not only in Congress. He was treated roughly in the organs of political communication, in the party press, and in the talk of the political professionals. Henry Clay was known to say that if it could have been foreseen at the Harrisburg convention, which created the Harrison-

Tyler ticket, that Harrison would die after a month as President and that Tyler would veto the Whig's bank bill, either the convention would have ignored Tyler or he would not have received a single electoral vote in the subsequent election. The Clay press reechoed its leader's hostility. The Richmond *Whig* called Tyler "the accident of the accident," "a vast nightmare over the Republic." And when a dread influenza epidemic overtook the country, the Whig press was quick to name it "the Tyler Grippe."[35]

# Varieties of Party Leadership

### Franklin Roosevelt as Party Renovator

Franklin Roosevelt, the most powerful of modern Presidents, was also the most assertive as party leader. Commanding unprecedented popular support, attested by his four-time election to the presidency, he dared to attempt drastic renovations of his party: to expand its voting base by extending its commitment to programs and to displace the Democratic congressional foes of the New Deal with those who promised to be its friends. Bold ventures almost inevitably involve a mixture of success and failure, and they did for Roosevelt.[36]

A rare President may intervene not only in the elections themselves but also in his party's primaries for congressional seats, seeking the nomination of candidates pledged to his support. Because of the grave hazards such an enterprise involves, most Chief Executives know all too well that the local voters resent the intrusions of outsiders. Franklin Roosevelt, however, mounted the heaviest presidential assault yet upon the inviolability of the local primary in his attempted 1938 purge of a handful of Democratic Senators and Congressmen. If it had succeeded, it would have brought about a major revision of the congressional Democratic party and the party's historic heterogeneity would have been displaced by loyalty to the New Deal program. The purge was sparked by the defeat of Roosevelt's Court-packing plan of 1937.* That defeat, the first major rebuff in five years of glittering victories, had rankled the President. Not a few Democrats who opposed the Court plan, he noted, had steadily voted against his New Deal measures. Roosevelt turned a receptive ear to his aides, Harold Ickes, Thomas G. Corcoran, and Harry Hopkins, who for months had talked of the desirability of a purge. On a hot June night he fired the opening salvo of the purge venture in a fireside chat. He declared,

> As the head of the Democratic party . . . charged with the responsibility of the definitely liberal declaration of principles set forth in the 1936 Democratic platform, I feel that I have every right to speak in those few instances where there

---

*Faced with a Supreme Court that repeatedly declared his New Deal legislation unconstitutional, Roosevelt sought to "pack" the Court with new members who presumably would be more favorable to his purposes. He proposed to add one new justice, up to a maximum of six, for every justice of the Court who, having passed the age of seventy and serving for ten years, failed to retire.

may be a clear issue between candidates for a Democratic nomination involving these principles, or involving a clear misuse of my own name.[37]

The purge took on more definite form in Roosevelt's zigzag trip across the nation. He proceeded to distinguish between those who were with and those who were against him. In Kentucky Roosevelt worked hard for Alben Barkley, his faithful Senate leader, embattled in a close race for his Senate seat with Governor Albert "Happy" Chandler, a strong campaigner with a potent machine. Roosevelt, upon reaching Kentucky, invited both Barkley and Chandler into his car for a drive to a huge political crowd at the Latonia racetrack. Roosevelt and Barkley were nettled when Chandler kept bowing to the right and left, acknowledging the great applause that presumably was directed chiefly to Roosevelt, and the President came roaring back with a speech heaping praise upon Barkley and dismissing Chandler as a young man who required many years to match Barkley's knowledge and experience. In a later statement Roosevelt hinted that Chandler had approached the White House with a deal in judicial appointments in an effort to clinch his Senate seat.[38]

The President was spurred on by the primary victory of Barkley and of another favorite, Senator Elmer Thomas of Oklahoma. He now concentrated his fire anew on eight Senators and three Congressmen as selected purge targets. Roosevelt personally carried the fight against his principal purgees. En route for a vacation at Warm Springs, he stopped at Gainesville, Georgia, to dedicate a public square named in his honor. Senator George introduced the President, who proceeded to ignore the Senator and beam approval upon Governor E. D. Rivers, who he hoped would run against George. When Rivers declined, Roosevelt recruited Lawrence S. Camp, United States District Attorney at Atlanta. In another Georgia visit, this time at Barnesville, and with Camp and George on the platform, Roosevelt referred to the Senator as "my old friend" and proceeded to demonstrate his inadequacy by New Deal standards. The President described his test:

> First, has the record of the candidate shown, while differing perhaps in details, a constant active fighting attitude in favor of the broad objectives of the party and of the Government as they are constituted today; and secondly, does the candidate really, in his heart, deep down in his heart, believe in these objectives?[39]

For all of Roosevelt's effort, the purge ended a wretched failure. Although certain of his favorites triumphed, every Senator and Congressman he marked for defeat won except Congressman O'Connor of New York, and O'Connor's loss was attributed by New York Democratic professionals not to the President's intervention but to O'Connor's own shortcomings—a poor campaign and a fat roster of enemies who joined together to take electoral revenge. In Georgia Roosevelt's candidate, Camp, ran a poor third; in Colorado Alva B. Adams was nominated without opposition; in Connecticut Augustine Lonergan prevailed in the Democratic state convention. "It's a bust," Jim Farley observed, as Roosevelt's political stock plummeted. In the face of Franklin Roosevelt's grisly and unforgettable failure, no President has ventured onto the purge trail since his day.

Yet despite Roosevelt's failure to transfer his own power and personal magnetism into victory against Congressmen who were entrenched in their local regions, he did shake his party at its roots and transform it through his own great political talent. The traditional Democratic party, on which he performed his drastic surgery, was a classical alliance of Northern city bosses and Southern and Western agrarians, held together by states' rights beliefs and federal patronage, and enlivened with intermittent bursts of progressivism. He replaced this old party order with a new Democratic coalition enduringly committed to positive government acting for national and group welfare. He had found the Democratic party a minority party. His graftings upon it of new group allegiances left it the instrument of the majority.

Roosevelt's vision of the new party was of one free from business domination and its debilitating effect upon political morality and public policy. He attracted into the party fold labor, farmers, racial and national groups, intellectuals, and women—all disadvantaged in the business culture. He brought in as well those businessmen who were restive under Wall Street and Eastern ascendance. Roosevelt established the new coalition by a lengthy, circuitous route. In staffing his administration after his 1932 victory, he drew talent not from the traditional Democratic organization but from the coalition. He brought Hugh Johnson, an independent, and Donald Richberg, a progressive, into NRA; Henry A. Wallace, a progressive, into agriculture; another progressive, Ickes, into public works; Hopkins, an independent, into relief administration; John Winant, a progressive, into social security; and Joseph P. Kennedy, a new entrepreneur, and James Landis, an independent, into securities regulation.

In Roosevelt's hands lawmaking was also an instrument of party reorganization. Major laws of his administration—the Social Security Act, the National Labor Relations Act, and the like—furnished the base of a new Democratic party, Northern and urban in orientation, attractive to city-centered groups, labor, Negroes, the new immigrants, women, and intellectuals. Policy and the unifying force of Roosevelt's personality, rather than pork barrel and patronage, cemented the new party. The breadth of his success was apparent as early as the 1934 congressional elections. The Democratic returns showed an upsurge of labor and Negro votes, and of Northern Democrats in Congress with an ebbing of the relative strength of the South. Of 69 Democrats in the Senate, only 24 were Southern; of 322 Representatives, the South had 108.

The next major stroke in the Democratic party's transformation was the infiltration of New Dealers, or coalitionists, into the party's councils and operations. New Deal emissaries Edward Roddan, Stanley High, and Leon Henderson took up stations in the national committee. In electoral contests the party's chief campaigners were the New Deal coalitionists: Roosevelt himself, of course, and Ickes, Wallace, and Hugh Johnson. Administration policy was readily manipulated to feed the political necessities of the coalition. When a WPA cutback in relief funds threatened the dismissal of many workers on October 1, Roosevelt instructed Secretary of the Treasury Henry Morgenthau, Jr., "You tell Corrington Gill that I don't give a goddam where he gets the money from but not one person is to be laid off on the first of October." [40]

The courted urban groups provided not only votes but money, organizing energy, and publicity. In 1936 organized labor created Labor's Nonpartisan League, whose wealth and manpower were consecrated to Roosevelt's candidacy. Spurred and indefatigably aided by Eleanor Roosevelt, he won the enduring loyalty of blacks to the New Deal. J. E. Spingarn, president of the National Association for the Advancement of Colored People, said of Roosevelt, "he has done more for the Negro than any Republican President since Lincoln."[41]

Roosevelt's experience showed that a powerful President can change the national image—and the reality behind the image—of his party. He succeeded by shrewd political finesse and also by promulgating a program with which many alienated groups could identify. And it was in defense of his new alliance, held together by a program—as well as in annoyance at the opposition—that he undertook the 1938 purge. The test of a party's success, he felt, was achievement of its program, and if a few entrenched party leaders had to go to achieve it, then this was a reasonable sacrifice. But he miscalculated local loyalties to long-time leaders and the refusal of local groups to think of the good of the party as a whole.

## Eisenhower as a Bipartisan

Most Presidents climb to their office by superior political skill and, upon arriving, eagerly take up their duties as party chief. But to a few Chief Executives, especially to hero-Presidents like Washington and Eisenhower, party activity is unwelcome, if not distasteful. Washington gladly delegated the partisan function to Alexander Hamilton, his Secretary of the Treasury, preferring to remain above the heat and dust of party battle himself. The new country, launched in perilous circumstances, required bipartisan unity in Washington's day. There was rather less compulsion for it in Eisenhower's. Nevertheless, during his two terms, Eisenhower resolutely, but not always successfully, shied away from partisan political duty. He immensely preferred nonpartisan and bipartisan politics to partisan. He could have been nominated for the presidency by either party, and, indeed, a concerted effort for his presidential services had been made by both parties. His most forceful lapses into partisanship occurred on the campaign trail, most notably his attacks upon the Truman administration in the 1952 electoral struggle. His foreign policy, which he largely entrusted to Secretary of State John Foster Dulles, was also hardly bipartisan.

Eisenhower's penchant for nonpartisan or bipartisan politics was a matter partly of temperament and partly of necessity. The strongest elements of his political faith were negative: return federal activities as far as possible to the states and to private responsibility, and balance the budget. His Modern Republicanism appeared to call for federal social measures, but these he chose not to push very hard. He eschewed partisan conflict, therefore, as something neither necessary nor relevant to his program, and avoided it if possible as activity that was troublesome and petty.

Eisenhower as President faced a Congress that had been dominated by the opposition party for a longer time and in greater numbers than any President since Zachary Taylor. Even in his first two years, when the Republicans controlled Congress, hard political reality necessitated cooperation with the Democrats. The Republicans' majority in the House was eleven, and in the Senate a mere one. Even more important was the inexperience of Republican legislators in cooperating with the Chief Executive. Not since 1931, nearly a quarter century before, had Republicans contolled the presidency and both houses of Congress simultaneously. Not a single Republican Senator of the Eighty-third Congress, which began on January 3, 1953, had ever served with a President of his own party. Of the 221 House Republicans, only 15 had ever experienced a Republican President. The Republican habit of opposition did not cease with Eisenhower's advent. Indeed, it is not impossible to argue that Republicans gave Eisenhower a harder time than they ever gave Kennedy and Johnson. Most Presidents would have agreed with Eisenhower, who decided, as he faced the congressional session of 1953, that the coming effort of the administration and of legislative Republicans should be devoted to redeeming the 1952 party platform and his own campaign pledges. Eisenhower's State of the Union message of February 2, 1953, diligently mirrored these party pronouncements. But in the early Eisenhower presidency, the Senate Republican leader was William F. Knowland of California, of whom Sherman Adams wrote, "It would have been difficult to find anybody more disposed to do battle with much of the President's program in Congress."[42]

On April 30, 1953, a historic explosion occurred when Eisenhower, meeting with congressional leaders, broke the news that despite severe cutting he could not balance the new budget as Robert A. Taft and others who were present had hoped. The President and Defense Department officials explained that part of the difficulty was that certain revisions were necessary in the nation's defense program. Suddenly Taft erupted, losing control of himself, pounding his fist on the cabinet table, and shouting at the stunned President seated opposite him. "With a program like this, we'll never elect a Republican Congress in 1954," Taft cried. "You're taking us down the same road Truman traveled. It's a repudiation of everything we promised in the campaign!" Taft went on excitedly, and when he stopped, tension gripped the room. Fortunately, several of those present commenced an aimless conversation until Eisenhower, flushed and upset, recovered himself to state in measured tones the necessities of global strategy.[43]

Republican legislators were the most relentless foes of Eisenhower's other initiatives. Not surprisingly, Eisenhower sometimes speculated privately with his aides whether he really belonged "in this kind of Republican party."[44] He mused over the desirability of forming a new political party, internationalist, welfare-oriented, but conservative in spending and economic regulation.

Out of such experience, Eisenhower, understandably, never wore his hat as party chieftain gladly. To the Republican faithful, he denied even that he was a politician. "Everybody knew I wasn't a politician—and I'm not yet," he told a group of Republican workers. He clung to his chosen nonpartisan demeanor, declaring at a news conference,

> I don't believe in bitter partisanship. I never believe that all wisdom is confined to one of the great parties, and I certainly have never in general terms criticized the other party, that is, to include its great membership. I believe there are good Americans in both parties, and I believe that the great mass of both parties is fundamentally and naturally sound.[45]

As the 1954 congressional elections neared, he cautioned his cabinet against an overly partisan approach, adding that he must take care himself to remain nonpartisan in using the national radio and television networks except on programs paid for by the party. And yet, as the 1954 elections came closer and the party pressures mounted, Eisenhower finally yielded and took off for ten thousand miles of travel and forty speeches. His spreading involvement never overcame his distaste for campaigning. "By golly, sometimes you sure get tired of all this clackety-clack," he remarked to Jim Hagerty, his press secretary, on election eve.[46]

Soon after the Democrats captured Congress in 1954, Eisenhower informed his cabinet he did not see how there could be any question of the need for the White House to work with the Democratic leadership. He held bipartisan meetings with the legislative leaders and, when major happenings were afoot, diligently kept both sets of party leaders informed. "Whenever he thought any one of us became too harsh," Sherman Adams wrote, "he would remind us that we were not going to get anywhere in Congress without Democratic votes."[47]

Each President, as party leader, is expected to assist the campaigns of Congressional candidates indiscriminately, including the campaigns of those whose election would injure his program more than their opponents' victories would. Roosevelt's attempt to flaunt this tradition had ended in failure. In the 1954 congressional elections President Eisenhower permitted himself to be photographed with a hundred or more Republican candidates, an imposing advantage in a local campaign. He also promised to make speeches delineating his program if he happened to be in the vicinity of a candidate who supported it and invited him to speak. Asked how he chose from among the Congressmen for bestowal of his photographic and rhetorical favors, he acknowledged that there was "a little bit of a check" on the legislators' voting record. In actuality, he was not known to withhold support in 1954 from any of the more recalcitrant legislators in his party who asked for it. For the President, loyalty to party generally transcended loyalty to program during campaigns.

So Eisenhower, whose temperament was bipartisan, or perhaps more accurately apolitical, was forced by circumstances into assuming a highly partisan role in election years and a bipartisan role in between in his relations with a Democratic Congress. Is it a political paradox that those Presidents who are less party-minded can be counted on to support the party most (but with least effect) and that those who are genuinely partisan—and strong—will defy the party when a few block the fulfillment of the party's promised program?

## Nixon and the New American Majority

Richard Nixon is one of a small handful of Presidents who strove to restructure his party by enlisting sufficient numbers of new adherents to transform it from a minority party into the majority party of future decades. As he advanced in his term of office, Nixon defined ever more clearly the constituencies to be melded into the new majority.

At its core were blue-collar workers, denizens of suburbia, a new middle class. Nixon perceived this constituency to cherish law and order, patriotism, and the work ethic. In the domestic furor over the Vietnam war, the members of this constituency were an absolute rock of support; Nixon's campaigning celebrated their values, and he entertained their leaders in the White House. With policy decisions, governmental favors, and concessions, Nixon courted union leaders and workers.[48]

Nixon's perception of the new majority possessed a religio-ethnic dimension. His aides spoke of a Catholic strategy; in major industrial states, Catholics were heavily represented among blue-collar workers and in the expanding suburban population, and their preferences on issues were strongly asserted in Nixon's discourse, which left his rival, George McGovern, securely identified with the "wrong" side. Accordingly, in traditionalist rhetoric, Nixon was perceived as rejecting abortion, marijuana, and amnesty for Vietnam deserters and draft dodgers.

The new majority also had definable geographic contours. Its favorite habitat was the burgeoning suburbs. The 1970 census indicated the gross population shifts in progress—declines in the cities and sharp increases in the suburban belts around the cities, resulting in two sharply contrasting worlds. Millions of white people were leaving the cities and moving to the suburbs, while black people and Spanish-speaking people replaced them. To suburbanites generally, Nixon's policy appeals to workers and ethnics seemed apt and welcome.

The new majority was also geographically delineated in Nixon's long-standing "Southern strategy," the essence of which incorporated his other appeals; here too were "white ethnics," living in scarred metropolitan areas and embittered by crime and busing. The South and Southwest were loci of the greatest population growth, according to the 1970 census, and their plethora of retirement homes and military and technological centers reinforced a conservative outlook on issues.[49]

To promote his Southern strategy, Nixon freely employed the resources of the presidency. He proposed that the original Voting Rights Act be revised to eliminate its "regional" provisions. His administration shifted school desegregation enforcement from HEW to the courts and with it any attendant voter resentments. His initial Supreme Court nominees, Haynsworth and Carswell, were Southerners, and their nominations were received warmly in the South. Nixon took on Harry S. Dent as a chief political aide. Dent had been chairman of South Carolina's Republican party and a former assistant to Senator Strom Thurmond (R-S.C.).[50]

It was not a "Republican" majority but an "American" majority, necessitating a presidential stance that would appeal to detachable non-Republicans. The campaign organization therefore became Nixonian rather than Republican. Not the National Committee, but a specially created Committee for the Reelection of the President (CREEP), administered by key presidential aides, ran the campaign. The Republican party played virtually no national role in the 1972 presidential elections. The President's handpicked national Republican chairman, an aggressive Kansas Senator, Robert Dole, was enchained in futility. An admirer of Nixon, Dole, despite repeated effort, was not even allowed by the White House staff to see the President. One day, after months of seeking an appointment, Dole received a telephone call from "an assistant President," as he characterized several staff members. "Hey, Bob, do you still want to see the President?" a youthful voice asked crisply. "When?" said Dole. "Tune in on Channel 9, he's coming on the tube in ten minutes."[51]

For the other Republican races of 1972, CREEP did almost nothing; it released precious little of its huge money hoard to other party candidates. Nixon himself campaigned minimally, less than any modern President since Franklin Roosevelt's fourth term candidacy during the Second World War.

---

**What a Majority Considered Most Dangerous or Harmful to the Country**

---

*1967*
*(the year before Nixon's initial successful Presidential candidacy)*

People who don't believe in God
Black militants
Student demonstrators
Prostitutes
Homosexuals

---

*1973*
*(after a year's exposure of the Watergate scandals)*

Political spies
Generals who conduct secret bombing raids
Politicians who engage in secret wiretapping
Businessmen who make illegal political contributions
Politicians who try to use the CIA, FBI,
   or Secret Service for political purposes
Politicians who try to restrict freedom

---

Sources: Interview with Louis Harris, *New York Times*, January 21, 1974; Louis Harris, *The Anguish of Change* (New York, 1973).

---

Meanwhile, professional Republicans were distressed by the President's newly conceived role as party leader, which he had redefined virtually to the point of its disappearance. One Republican Senator, frustrated by the President's seeming indifference to the fate of Republican candidates, exclaimed that 1972 was "the most selfish campaign in history,"[52] to which extra sting was added when Nixon's prodigious landslide victory was coupled with Republican losses in Congress and the states.

The new American majority—if there really is one—remains up for grabs. If Nixon claimed that he embodied it, by dint of his 1972 victory, so did the Democratic Congress created by the same election. And whatever grip Nixon had on it was weakened by the Watergate scandals, inflation, and the oil crisis. Whatever else it is, the new majority, or more accurately the electoral center, is, according to history, a phenomenon ephemeral in its perceptions and beliefs, as the following comparison suggests.

In every presidential election, the successful candidate must discover afresh "the new majority," or political center, in its most recently evolved, evanescent form and respond seriously to it.[53] As Louis Harris has suggested, the American people are pragmatic, and therefore shifting in the priorities they accord to issues, rather than ideological. Nixon's perception of "the new American majority" is founded on the opposite assumption. In fact, Harris's opinion analyses reveal, the foremost preoccupations of this majority in 1972 were not those that Nixon ascribed, but ending the war and establishing peace in Vietnam. Also, the stress on a new ideological majority has roots in the tendency of leaders who lack charismatic appeal, such as Nixon and Johnson, to read into their mandates, provided by massive outpourings of voters, deeper messages than are actually there.

But a counterview, encouraged by Ronald Reagan's 1980 monumental electoral victory, suggests that a profound voter shift was under way in Nixon's 1968 and 1972 elections, a trend that was interrupted by the nightmare of Watergate and by Carter's triumph in 1976. The trend resurfaced in 1980, to the point, some observers contend, of constituting a critical election: a massive shift of voters between the parties was stimulated by the cultural crisis of the 1960s, the economic crisis of the 1970s, and a renewed Soviet threat. In 1980, the white South, the West, the newly industrialized South and Southwest, waves of Catholic and Jewish voters, blue-collar workers and suburbanites shifted into a Republican party, until recently WASP in make-up, enabling it to command impressive new strength in congressional and state elections as well as in presidential elections. The awaiting question is whether this vast shift of voters will persist in the elections of 1982 and 1984. Such huge shifts in the past have endured over a long period of time.[54]

## Carter as Outsider

Carter in his 1976 campaign highlighted the theme that he was an outsider, fresh and unspoiled by any previous commingling with the tainting Washington political community, the hatchery of Watergate and disrupter of citizen confidence in the political system. By his apparent innocence of previous involvement in national party politics, Carter could more readily strike a posture of probity and offer psychological reassurance to a people who, after the trauma of Watergate, longed, above all, for a government and leaders worthy of their trust.

In many respects Carter indeed was an outsider. His previous significant office-holding was confined to a single term as governor of Georgia. He had had no tenure in Washington. But although he was an outsider to Congress and the upper echelons of the executive branch, he was no stranger to the politics of the national nominating convention. At the 1972 Democratic convention at Miami, he made two bold moves in behalf of a future national career. He nominated Senator Henry Jackson for the presidency, and he sought the vice-presidential nomination on the ticket headed by George McGovern. McGovernites deemed this striving ludicrous.[55]

After winning the 1976 nomination, Carter faced the dilemma of maintaining his profitable posture as outsider while running as the majority party's standard-bearer. How could he continue to flail the establishment when he was its newly anointed leader? It would be difficult, but not impossible. Although Carter's anti-Washington discourse diminished some degrees, it remained a major theme. To audiences he gibed at his opponent President Ford's long service in Washington, saying "Anything you don't like about Washington, I suggest you blame on him." To safeguard the purity of his anti-Washington image, precious few leading Democrats were invited to Carter's hearth at Plains. His press secretary, Jody Powell, articulated the problem: "It was hard to judge where the balance was between getting the support of Democratic organizations on the one hand and not appearing to be their captive on the other."[56]

After becoming President, Carter continued to belabor his profitable paradox and depict himself as a new leader who remained an outsider. With the Democratic party in control of both the executive and Congress, and in both houses by sizeable majorities, the test of remaining an outsider became even more severe. Yet, after more than a year in office, many members of Congress not only still perceived Carter as a genuine outsider, but outspokenly resented the attitudes and contrivances he used in dealings with the legislature to preserve that status.[57] Carter, for example, deliberately eschewed engaging in log-rolling and pork-barrel, two standard practices that enable a President and his legislative majority to get things done. To the astonishment and indignation of legislators, he launched a two-year fight over the funding of water projects, which to members of Congress are like manna from heaven. Legislators trade off benefits for their home areas (a dam for my district, a river-dredging project for yours), with constituents made happy by the stepped-up local economic activity. Sacrosanct and proceeding for decades without question, pork-barrel politics, as it was known, was suddenly challenged by Carter, without prior consultation with anyone in Congress.[58] Seldom had Presidents challenged the beneficence of water projects and never on the scale of Carter. Congress was stunned and angry.

Carter's own political characteristics drove a mighty wedge between the President and Democratic legislators. Frequently he shunned compromise, a fine art that holds politicians together and produces policy from conflict. A stubborn streak barred him from affirming this traditional working bond between the branches. Instead, in assessing his first term, he spoke pridefully of never ducking a problem because of its political consequences and of his sense of satisfaction in being able to withstand political pressure.[59] An introvert, he was little given to small talk and the comraderie and clubhouse socializing that can soften frictions between politicians.[60] His dealings with Congress suffered accordingly, diminishing his legislative accomplishments, but his outsider's role was reinforced.

In time, Carter alienated so many Democrats that his major victories in Congress resulted from Republican support and were attained despite sizeable Democratic defections.[61] His most fractious relations were with Senators George McGovern, Edward Kennedy, and others of the liberal wing of the Democratic party. Carter's approach to program and policy often seemed more akin to a Republican rather than a Democratic perspective. His State of the Union messages, where Presidents often herald leading policy innovations, were seldom the carriers of new programs. Rather they were typified by exhortations for better management of existing activities, a standard Republican theme. "It is not enough to have created a lot of government programs," Carter continued to declare well into his term in 1979, "Now we must make the good programs more effective, and improve or weed out those which are wasteful or unnecessary."[62] To which Nixon, Ford, and Reagan could subscribe a ready "Amen!"

By muffling social programs, Carter in effect transformed the meaning of traditional Democratic liberalism, established by Roosevelt's New Deal and Johnson's Great Society, into a commitment restricted to doing better what government was already doing. Carter also limited his partisan involvements by consciously avoiding the mobilization of a distinctly new liberal coalition. After being eight years out of office and sustaining a devastating defeat in 1972, most Democrats willingly followed his lead.[63]

# ★ ★ ★ The Future Presidency ★ ★ ★

At most, the President can be only a quasi-party leader. A variety of forces and pressures compel him to temper and contain his partisanship. He must at times give higher priority to his calling as leader of the nation, facing needs and goals greater than those of his party. He may face a Congress one or both of whose houses is dominated by the opposition party. The ability to appeal to the vast and ever-growing body of independent voters both during his quest for the presidency and after gaining it is an ever more crucial test of the Chief Executive. Thanks to weak party discipline, a President knows the difference between a "paper," or party, majority in Congress and a "working" majority. In many of his waking hours he is forced to be bipartisan or nonpartisan if he is to pick up needed legislative votes from the other party. Bipartisan leadership is exerted at a price. It rests upon consultation and compromise and necessarily reduces the forcefulness of policy and the President's program image.

Viewed another way, although the party system has enabled a national popular majority to choose a President, when he attempts to translate his electoral promises into policy he finds himself in a government that permits only limited majority rule because of separation of powers and checks and balances, among other things. Only a rare President, such as Jefferson or Franklin Roosevelt, succeeds in building enough strength as party leader to enable him to extend substantially the principle of majority rule. Despite the limiting realities of the party and the governmental structure, what can be done to help the strong President also be a strong party leader?

The President's party role is also highly relevant to a second proposition of this book; that is, that the strong Chief Executive should be confined within the boundaries of democratic practice. Parties are unsurpassed as the means by which the people, or organized masses of voters, can hold government—including Presidents—accountable to their will. Voters, acting through the party victorious at the polls, can throw out the presidential incumbent or bar the successor preferred by his party. At its best, the opposition party supplies the alternative candidate and therefore offers a choice for the voter, provides a different perspective on issues, and induces masses of people to vote. A crucial question emerges. If some Presidents measure up poorly as conformers to democratic standards, can parties be improved as regulators to produce candidates whose behavior, according to democratic norms, is more acceptable?

1. Within the past two decades, disparate forces have been effecting alterations of the parties to the point that, compared with their historic appearance, they have become scarcely recognizable. Television, primaries,

campaigning by jet aircraft, the increasingly augmented ranks of the independent voter, ticket-splitting, and such potent social forces as affluence, more widespread education, and enhanced population mobility have swiftly outmoded the traditional parties. Parties of yore consisted of baronies ensconced in state capitals, county courthouses, the cities, and, sometimes, in congressional incumbencies. Supported by interest groups, the barons' approval—or at least the avoidance of their veto—was requisite for winning the presidential nomination. After their designee took office, these groups enjoyed access to the President and dealt with him directly—not merely with his staff—to press demands and communicate dissatisfactions. All this was done from a vantage point of independent power and limited attachment to the President.

But now the older party fiefdoms are diminished and the power of the barons has been reduced. The barons have been replaced by candidate politics, campaign management firms, television, substantial public financing, and direct-mail drives, and the tasks of getting out the vote are handled by bands of dedicated volunteers. The supreme examples of the rout of the barons were provided by the 1972 Democratic convention, (from which they were largely excluded), by Nixon's personalized campaign, and again in 1976 by the triumph of Carter, the outsider.

What can be done to restore the parties to something of their former place as constraints—for the sake of democracy—on the President? Can these traditional institutions of mass democracy undergo revival and renewal? Conceivably, governors of the major states may become the future barons, raising money in the contemporary fashion and utilizing the latest managerial expertise and campaign technology. Mail drives, telephone campaigns, and zealous volunteers can flourish for the Governor as they do for the President. With these accouterments, the governors can again become arbiters and bargainers in the business of presidential selection, and the eventual Chief Executive will feel obligated to negotiate with these potentates for his own reelection or his party's continued retention of the office, for the progress of his programs in Congress, and for concordats on such matters of mutual concern as energy and inflation.[64]

Or, the parties may revive and serve as a constraint on the Chief Executive by better representing the disparate forces of society. The reforms preceding the 1972 Democratic convention were a significant, if clumsy, effort toward that end. Although the reforms were modified after the disastrous electoral defeat, the pressures of contemporary political forces, one can confidently predict, will compel parties in the future to better represent the less powerful—blacks and the Spanish-speaking, women and youth, people on welfare, consumers, the elderly, and others. As each underrepresented group becomes better organized, develops national leadership, and formulates specific programs and policies, it should become a force to be reckoned with at national conventions for both presidential nominations and platform making. Given their continuing power and role, the future President would feel that interchange with these groups was advisable after assuming office.

Historically and instinctively, the parties have reached out to aggrandize their ranks by developing new coalitions. A conceivable future Republican majority might comprise the white middle-class heartland coupled with an affluent but disaffected white working class. Or, on the other hand, a new liberal Democratic coalition is conceivable of the affluent and the intelligentsia, plus the least well-off members of society. Also possible is a "real" majority of middle Americans, or a reconstructed New Deal coalition based on common economic interest.

Yet at best any such coalitions are likely to be only temporary, evoked by a particular candidate and crumbling at his departure. Or the forging of new coalitions may, because of unfriendly present-day political currents, await a far future. The heritage of Watergate and Vietnam persists, hostile to government, parties, and politicians, and voters remain numb to the beckoning calls of possible new coalitions. The continued shocks of inflation and unemployment reinforce the disarray.[65]

2.  Both for the sake of a strong presidency enhanced by a more competent national party and for a Chief Executive who is subject to democratic safeguards through the party system, attention might be directed at improving the parties as forums for the discussion of issues and the review of policy. The Democratic party adopted a proposal for more frequent national conventions, including a "national issues convention" midway in the presidential term. The first "mini-convention" was held in Kansas City in 1974, and the second in Memphis in 1978.

In spirit and method, an issues convention might profitably imitate the annual conference or convention of British parties. A step in this direction was the Democrats' 1974 mini-convention which adopted a national party charter and a sweeping resolution detailing specific measures necessary for the nation's troubled economy. In 1978, the choice between budgetary restraint to check a booming inflation versus traditional Democratic commitment to social programs, including the enactment of national health legislation, was strenuously debated. In future years, the convention might more closely approximate the British model. Accordingly, participants would include delegates representing state and local party organizations, members of Congress, and the President and his department heads. Since the purpose of such a convention would not be to nominate candidates, which is the primary task of the regular quadrennial convention, attention could center on serious issues and vigorous debate. Ideally, the delegates could introduce resolutions embodying stands on issues, although their confinement to reasonable numbers might require regulation. The President and other party leaders would expound their policies, and, as in the annual conference of the British Labor party, an effort would be made to air every important issue. In effect, the President and other party leaders would be called on to explain and defend their policies to the general party membership.

Even if his administration won the likely approval of the convention, expressed through supportive resolutions, the President doubtless would be influenced by vigorous criticism or dissent. At its best, the issues convention can expose weaknesses in presidential policies and exert moral and psychological pressure for reform. But near unanimity of support for presidential policies could enormously strengthen the President in future quests for congressional support of his program. At its worst, the issues convention can be unattended and ignored by the President, or it can be furiously and inconclusively split over important issues.

In any event, it would be superior to that quadrennium of quietude following a national election, during which the President meets with no party assembly, which enables him and his White House staff all the more easily to ignore or hold at arm's length other party leaders and representatives.

3. Although television has weakened traditional party roles, it can also serve as a potent source for party renewal. A Twentieth Century Fund study has wisely proposed that the major parties be allotted greater shares of television time as a counterbalance to the inordinate amounts of time accorded the President.

First, the national committee of the opposition party should be empowered by law to claim time to respond to any presidential address broadcast during the ten months preceding a presidential election or within ninety days preceding a congressional election in non-presidential years. In addition, "national debates," held four times a year (but only twice in federal election years), should take place between spokespersons for the major parties. The debates should be scheduled in prime time and broadcast simultaneously by the networks.[66] This further spur to the parties' development as expositors of issues could rally both broader public and party support for presidential programs and policies and thereby promote the strong presidency. It could also diminish the undesirable withdrawal of the Chief Executive behind walls guarded by janissaries of the White House staff. As conduits of issues, the parties could force the President to explain and defend his policies before the court of public opinion. Thus, an invaluable link could be forged between the strong presidency and democratic processes.

# Chapter Seven

# Legislative Leader

In the tradition of great legislatures, Congress can be a potent instrument for keeping the strong President within democratic bounds. Congress can impose its positive will on the President and require him to do what he does not want to do. President Ford, for instance, reluctantly acquiesced to Congress's insistence that he cut off aid to Turkey, in certain contingencies, in the Cyprus war, despite two vetoes and his protest against the wisdom of the restriction.[1] Eager to assist a pro-American faction in the Angolan civil war, President Carter was blocked by the Clark amendment of 1976 to the Arms Export Act, prohibiting "any kind" of aid. Congress is master of the Grand Inquest, the legislative investigation into executive malfunction. To the grosser misdeeds of the President and executive officers, Congress can, if it chooses, apply the most drastic of remedies, impeachment and removal. Seldom can the President act for long without appropriations, which only Congress can provide and it can, within constitutional limits, set such conditions as it wishes. Presidents are often recruited from the houses of Congress, and some (though unfortunately not all) may bring to the executive branch democratic habits inculcated in the legislature: awareness of the legitimacy of the opposition and tolerance of its expression, habituation to the sharing of power, to compromise and accommodation, and regard for lesser power units.

The function on which Congress concentrates most of its energy and skill is legislation, which, by specific constitutional arrangement, is shared with the President. To some scholars, the combined elements of the President's

153

role appear so magnitudinous that they speak of him as "Chief Legislator," but the reality is less impressive than this grandiose title suggests.

No function of the President is more beset with uncertainty, is more vulnerable to breakdowns, and is more readily the victim of the will and whim of individuals whose outlooks and responsibilities tend to be different from his own than his duty to lead in legislation. Nowhere else in the presidential enterprise is there found a greater gap between what the Chief Executive wants to do, what he promises to the electorate in his contest for the office, and what he can do in bringing Congress to enact the laws that alone can give effect to his promises of policy and program in the previous campaign. In no other major nation is the program of a head of government more susceptible to rebuff in the legislature, to delay and crippling amendment, and to absolute, uncompromising rejection. The President runs an obstacle course on Capitol Hill that other heads of government would find strange and even incredible.

Even a President like Dwight Eisenhower, who generally viewed Congress with good will, was sometimes seized with sensations of futility.[2] In delineating his program at the outset of his term, he took pains to remind his cabinet and legislative leaders that the Republican platform of 1952 comprised "the minimum limits of achievement below which we must not fall." Eisenhower's dedication to the platform was received with open amusement by the legislative leaders. "To my astonishment," Eisenhower wrote, "I discovered that some of the men in the room could not seem to understand the seriousness with which I regarded our platform's provisions. . . . More than once I was to hear this view derided by 'practical politicians' who laughed off platforms as traps to catch voters."[3]

In his 1960 campaign John Kennedy spelled out a program by which alert and assertive leadership might move the country forward again. He put forth several hundred specific proposals, including parity for the farmer through a supply program, medical care for the aged under social security, full employment, equal rights for women, price stability, freer foreign trade, urban renewal, a new civil rights law, and the like. Most of Kennedy's campaign pledges required legislative fullfillment and therefore provided a ready foundation for his legislative program as President. But what came forth was a shrunken image of the earlier promises. Kennedy dropped permanent improvements in unemployment compensation and repeal of right-to-work laws, among other things; he trod softly on aid to education, oil depletion allowances, and medical care for the aged; and he postponed civil rights. There were no radical new ideas, no great transformations of policy like those implied in the rhetoric of the 1960 campaign. In the main his items were familiar holdovers from the Eisenhower era, items that might have been passed if Eisenhower had chosen to push them. Kennedy, in a sound appraisal of congressional realities, chose to set his sights low.

Richard Nixon, the first conservative President of contemporary Chief Executives, often found the torpor of Congress harmonious with his personal philosophy. In a presidency dedicated to holding the start of new social programs to a minimum, Nixon's purpose was seldom impaired by Congress. The Democratic Congresses of his two presidential terms yielded a meager harvest, chiefly mild environmental and consumer laws and revenue sharing. Welfare reform, which Nixon promoted in 1969 but soon lost his zeal for and half-heartedly reverted to in 1974, never evoked sufficient congressional enthusiasm to produce a new law. Nixon's most positive interlude, in 1971, when he advertised his legislative program as "a new American revolution," eventuated in barren results for two of its principal components, health insurance and welfare reform, and much of what he proposed never came to a vote that year.[4] Generally, Gerald Ford's and Ronald Reagan's conservative tilts were well served by the ineffectuality of Congress.

In legislative leadership, Jimmy Carter was more akin to his Republican than to his Democratic forebears. His approach to policy issues was more managerial than programmatic. His only major domestic proposal to journey through Congress unscathed was civil service reform legislation. It possessed the considerable advantage of costing little or nothing, and reforming the bureaucracy was a popular venture that both Democrats and Republicans rushed to acclaim.

# The Good Legislative Years

Congress, the historical record discloses, consistently follows the presidential lead chiefly in three types of situations. One is crisis, when the survival of the nation or its social system is at stake. In the gravity of the peril, national opinion demands action and the population looks to the President for initiative and brooks no denial. The crises of the two world wars and of the Great Depression created popular opinion that demanded nothing less than Congress's full support of presidential leadership.

The second situation in which presidential leadership is assured is found in national security and foreign affairs since the Second World War. In these, the President has enjoyed a high batting average of success. A Marshall Plan, a Truman Doctrine, a NATO, and wars in Korea and Vietnam (at least until its final months) were well supported, although the cement of union was provided not by presidential skill or legislative charity, but by the doings of the Russians, the Communist Chinese, the North Koreans, and the North Vietnamese.

The third situation of outstanding presidential success is produced by rare occurrences of political abnormality under circumstances highly favorable to the Chief Executive. Theodore Roosevelt in intervals during his two terms, Woodrow Wilson in 1913 and again in 1916, and Lyndon Johnson in 1965 and to a lesser degree in 1966, enjoyed this special status. All three were uncommonly skilled at manipulation in legislative encounters and basked in the sunlight of exceptionally favorable political circumstances. Roosevelt and Wilson thrived upon the nation's expanding progressive sentiment. Johnson reigned at an interval when the explosive urgency of urban problems no longer permitted Congress to sleep upon the President's program.

Both Wilson and Johnson were favored with towering working majorities in the houses of Congress. In the Senate, Wilson and his social program enjoyed the presence of progressives whose numbers comprised a majority in both parties. His Democratic majority in the House was large, and he was doubly blessed by the fact that 114 of 290 House Democrats had been elected for the first time. Eager to please, their future careers depending heavily upon executive patronage and the administration's general success, they were amenable to presidential direction.

In 1965, Johnson, too, reaped rich legislative harvests with the aid of a substantial corps of freshmen Democratic Congressmen. Coming into office in an era when Presidents enjoyed strong success in the Senate only to meet steady rebuff in the House, Johnson derived from the 1964 elections a crop of seventy-one freshmen Democratic Congressmen. Sixty-seven of these voted for the top items on his agenda—the education bill and Medicare— and the entire body of them supported the President more than 80 percent of the time on roll call votes. A precious by-product of the top-heavy Democratic supremacy was the corresponding increase of Democratic party ratios on House committees. The Ways and Means Committee, a graveyard of key measures in the Kennedy years, was altered when three Democratic vacancies were filled by staunch supporters of the President, and the committee proceeded to function in close harmony with the administration.[5] With such imposing political resources at his command and with shrewd strategy and relentless drive, Johnson in 1965 presided over more legislative innovations on the home front than any other President in any other single session of Congress in the twentieth century.

# Congress and the President: Basic Differences

Congress repeatedly checks and balances the President—whether to challenge his abuses of power or his proposals of constructive legislation— largely because it represents altogether contrasting constituencies. The President, chosen by the nation, is the natural instrument of majoritarian rule— is, as Max Lerner has written, "the greatest majority-weapon our democracy has thus far shaped."[6] It is, to be sure, a contrived majority, one normally more difficult to maintain than to create, an association of purposeful pressure groups and the great mass of little-organized citizenry, distributed across the several sections of the country, each with its distinctive social and cultural tradition and economic organization. Congress, in contrast, is the product of local constituencies: the Senate emerging from the substantial land mass of the states and the House, except for its members at large, from the smaller congressional districts. The validity of both the national and the local viewpoints found in the executive and legislative constituencies is affirmed by the federal principle of government incorporated in the Constitution.

Congress's relationship to the "national majority" differs in other respects from the President's. The totality of the two-house Congress is never the product of any conceivable national majority, since only one-third of the Senate is chosen in any given election. The President's national majority and the Senate's and House's local majorities have varying periods of legitimacy expressed in the terms of office allotted to the candidates they elect:

the Senators six years, the President four, the Congressmen two. The Senator or Congressman is identified with several kinds of majority: with the majority of his constituency, with the party majority in his house, and with the voting majority in his house. In carrying on the legislative process, the houses of Congress contain no continuing majority. A majority accumulates or emerges for limited purposes but never hardens into a durable entity. The legislative majority that passes a particular bill develops from a series of processes by which members are elected, the internal authority of the House and Senate are allocated, an agenda is selected, and procedures of debate and vote are followed. But once the bill is passed and others arise, new and almost invariably different majorities must be constructed. Congress is also the haven for the minority: the minority party, the maverick legislator. Congress speaks with many voices. The Chief Executive, with his concentration of authority and use of hierarchical organization, aims to speak with one. Congress represents the rich diversity of American life, the President its necessary unity.

Typically, the President wishes to move faster than Congress's glacial pace. When faced with an activist President who promotes comprehensive and controversial programs, Congress reacts with caution. Jimmy Carter quickly discovered how difficult it was to learn what Congress would do, and how often its leaders innocently misled him about when Congress would do it. Meeting with a congressional group to discuss the status of legislation he was promoting, Carter told his visitors pleasantly as they departed, "I always enjoy hearing from you." As he left the room, the President was heard to mutter, "I enjoy it, but I'm never sure it does any good." [7]

Despite their imposing differences, no one branch, executive or legislative, can claim inherent superiority in articulating the national or public interest. A Washington and a Wilson are shining beacons of public interest, but who can say that in the quest for the common good President Harding was superior to Senator George Norris, or President Coolidge to Senator Robert La Follette? During certain eras legislators sometimes speak with more initiative, force, and freedom on national issues than Presidents do. But distinguished legislators are more common than strong Congresses. In brutal truth, Congress is far more often weak in accomplishment than strong. However memorable a La Follette or a Norris may be, the houses of Congress are more than assemblages of individuals; they are also corporate bodies with a hearty preference for inaction and cautious leadership. Both the House and the Senate work with a body of procedures that have an awesome capacity either for preventing Congress from acting at all or for ensuring that it will act only after unconscionable delay.

Debate has sometimes flared among political scientists about the nature of the balance between the branches. In the Johnson era, with its huge Great Society program, when Congress seemed an open highway for the President to move through seemingly endless caravans of presidential proposals, political scientist Samuel Huntington was impressed that Congress's role was limited to vetoer or rubber stamp, and the choice posed an unhappy dilemma: "If Congress legislates, it subordinates itself to the President; if it refuses to legislate, it alienates itself from public opinion." But political scientist John R. Johannes, after examining a series of case studies, concluded that the President's position for initiating legislation was superior to Congress's because of the combined strength of powers and incentives, his place in the constitutional system, and his supportive resources—his staff and the executive bureaucracy, who enable him to lead in defining problems, issues, and solutions. Congress, however, excels at a review and oversight function, evaluating and revising the President's technical-political proposals, and reflecting the perspectives of a different, more segmented constituency to weigh the acceptability of the President's recommendations.[8]

Once a presidential proposal alights on Capitol Hill, and even after it is enacted, Congress plays a vital role in remolding the presidential handiwork through amendments and appropriations. Often Congress's contribution is underestimated because of the high visibility given the president's proposals and to his personal role. Political scientist Jack R. Van Der Slik in differentiating the roles of the branches, sees the President as preeminently a "policy promoter" and Congress as primarily a "policy adapter."[9]

# Congress and the President:
# An Imbalance?

The Founding Fathers, in providing for a strong President and a strong Congress, intended that a balance should persist between the branches, that neither would become unduly ascendant at the other's expense. As history unrolled, one branch, at some intervals, amassed superior power and impact at the expense of the other, followed by intervals when the pendulum of power swung back in favor of the other branch. The fluctuations of events foster the shift; public opinion soon wearies of whichever branch is dominant, and the diminished branch soon develops a mood of reassertion.

In important respects, the balance moved sharply in the President's favor from the Second World War until Watergate exploded in 1973, pushed both by events such as the Indochina war and self-serving presidential methods. For the better part of two presidential terms, Congress and Nixon struggled over priorities, and most of the victories fell to the President. The President applied the budget cleaver to domestic, and particularly to social, programs, while Congress preferred to decrease military expenditure.

## Power to the President: Nixon

The flow of undue power to the President was also induced by Nixon's methods. He moved his office away from its traditional accountability to Congress to a posture of autonomy and secrecy. In effect, Nixon asserted that the President alone determines what programs to cut and by how much, a contention made with the assurance derived from a landslide re-election victory, which he viewed as an overwhelming popular ratification of his definition of priorities. Nixon's posture toward Congress was the reverse of that of most contemporary Presidents, which also magnified his apparent power. Whereas his predecessors struggled to get laws passed and suffered many a congressional rebuff, his stance was negative: he aimed to scale down programs, phase them out, and, most of all, prevent them from starting—objectives that spurred him toward autonomy and negation.

In the magnification of his power, Nixon employed several major weapons:

*The veto*    On a scale unmatched by any previous President, Nixon applied the veto★ to a broad range of social programs. None seemed beyond his disapprobation—he vetoed appropriations for hospital construction, for aid to the handicapped, for education, health, and antipoverty measures, pollution control; the sums expunged were not merely millions, but billions of dollars. Nixon did not apply even the least shadow of a comparable scrutiny to military and space programs. Toward those programs he was the soul of liberality.

*Impoundment*    When his veto failed, Nixon's further recourse was impoundment, a historic process by which Presidents have withheld from programs funds Congress has appropriated. Prior to Nixon, Jefferson refused to purchase gunboats, Truman impounded appropriations for the Air Force, and other impoundments were applied to antimissile systems, flood control projects, and highways. Congress sometimes explicitly empowers the President to withhold funds, and, in impounding, Presidents frequently cite deficiencies in program design or operations and the need to make savings, justifications that normally delight Congress. Typically, past Presidents impounded funds only for a time, after which they became a matter of negotiation with Congress, and eventually most funds were released. But Nixon's procedure was quite different. He made perfectly clear that he would not release any impounded funds unless the courts forced him to do so.[10]

*Executive privilege*    Nixon also applied his style of expansive interpretation to the old doctrine of executive privilege. Again he stretched the elastic vagueness of the concept to an almost infinite dimension. The resistance he evoked moved toward precise definition of a practice that, as history suggests, is better left flexible and adaptive. Executive privilege was invoked by President Washington, who refused to supply the House with working papers developed in negotiations for the Jay Treaty. Succeeding Presidents applied the doctrine to preserve the confidentiality of information in foreign affairs and contended that the power to keep executive secrets was implied in the executive power clause. In support of executive privilege, Presidents have also cited the necessity of maintaining the confidentiality of advice from their staff and the loyalty of executive subordinates.

Later Presidents enlarged the doctrine of executive privilege, particularly Eisenhower, for whom the doctrine was a bulwark against Senator Joseph McCarthy's assaults on the executive branch, and Richard Nixon contrib-

---

★ According to the Constitution, the President can "veto" ("I forbid") legislation that Congress enacts. By a two-thirds vote of each house, Congress can override the veto, whereupon the legislation becomes law without the President's approval.

uted to the pattern of expansion with gusto, particularly as the Watergate crisis began building. At one juncture, he contended that not only members of the White House staff, but former members as well, are covered by the privilege, and acknowledged no time limit for their immunity. Attorney General Richard Kleindienst asserted that every employee and communication was covered, but, fortunately, the admininstration retreated from this interpretation that threatened to turn the executive branch into a walled city.[11] Various judicial rulings compelled Nixon to supply the federal district court of the District of Columbia with tapes of conversations held in his office and in which he participated that might bear on Watergate crimes.[12] The court holding was narrow and restrained and therefore left the executive privilege doctrine with its historic flexibility much intact.

*Appointments*   Presidential appointments that required the Senate's advice and consent were a major battleground in the interbranch struggle of the Nixon era. The most tumultuous conflict over appointments stemmed from Nixon's initial nominations to the Supreme Court. For the first time since 1894 a President suffered the rejection of two Court nominations by the Senate. In rebuffing Nixon's nominees, Clement Haynsworth, Jr., and G. Harrold Carswell, the Senate viewed itself as a defender of the Court and a variety of interest that felt aggrieved by the nominations. Nixon was perceived as using the nominations to serve his Southern strategy, and labor and civil rights groups protested that Judge Haynsworth had blemishes on his ethical record, that his labor and civil rights rulings as a federal judge disclosed hostility to those interests. After a free-swinging struggle, the Senate rejected the nomination.

Nixon retaliated by nominating a less qualified candidate, another Southerner and conservative, G. Harrold Carswell. Again controversy erupted and the nomination was rejected. All three Republican Senate leaders voted against Haynsworth and only one supported Carswell. Their combined opposition signified the extreme lengths to which Nixon had resorted in order to "rectify" the Court and its decisions, such as those on school desegregation, that he perceived as troubling his key constituencies, the South and the suburbs.[13] Nixon's tactics suggested that his overriding objective was to establish his own construction of the Constitution, at whatever cost to the Court. Thanks to the Senate, Nixon was forced to provide more professionally respectable nominations—Harry Blackmun, William Rehnquist, and Lewis Powell, whose competence was uncontested, and who shared some of the President's conservative preferences.

# Congress: Reclaiming Power

Ultimately Congress prevailed over Nixon, threatening his impeachment and forcing his resignation. Additionally, in response to the trauma of Watergate and the Indochina war, Congress took giant steps, of a magnitude and importance unique in its history, to reclaim power it had allowed to slide to the presidency and to forestall future abuses.

*Curbing war*   After forcing an end to American military involvement in Indochina, Congress enacted, over the President's veto, the War Powers Resolution of 1973, to bar longer-term wars without congressional approval.*

*Budget and impoundment*   Congress adopted the Budget and Impoundment Control Act of 1974, closely limiting the President's power to impound (not to spend) appropriations, reserving to Congress the ultimate word on whether the money will be spent.

For impoundments that merely defer or postpone spending, Congress can force the President to release the funds if either house passes a resolution calling for their expenditure. If the President seeks to terminate programs through impoundment or to cut total spending, congressional recision of its previous approval of the funds is necessary. Unless both houses pass a recision bill within forty-five days, the President must spend the money. If he refuses, Congress can go to court.[14]

The 1974 Act also establishes a new budget timetable and creates a Congressional Budget Office and budget committees in each house, enabling Congress to adopt overall spending and revenue goals and to adjust specific spending on functional categories such as defense, health, and income security within the confines of those goals. The new scheduling permits earlier congressional consideration than in the past, enhances opportunities for congressional initiatives, and more integrated review. Setting forth spending goals, the budget resolutions guide, but do not bind, Congress in acting on appropriations. After enacting its budget resolutions, Congress processes its regular appropriations bills through the Appropriations subcommittees and full committees of both houses, and then to floor and conference action.[15] The Congressional Budget Office, with a staff of several hundred, is of high professional calibre and wields a strong influence throughout the process.

These new procedures impart more order to a process that traditionally has been haphazard. Among outcomes clearly determined by Congress's expanded budget process are reductions in the defense budget for both fiscal 1976 and 1978, a slowing of the rate of growth of retirement benefits for federal employees in fiscal 1977, and the extensive reworking in 1980 of the fiscal 1981 budget.[16] The new procedures facilitate debate on macroeconomic issues and challenges by congressional committees to the President's dominance in initiating fiscal proposals.

*Policy analysis*   In 1972, Congress established its own Office of Technology Assessment, staffed with varieties of policy analysts, to provide the legislature with expertise in examining complex policy questions. The Office has explored policy options on a wide range of matters, such as energy, conservation, railroad safety, environmental contaminants, technology, and world trade. Congress has enlarged its own information base by expanding the roster of policy analysts and computer resources of the Congressional Research Service. Congressional committees also enjoy greater freedom to

---

*For more extended discussion of the War Powers Resolution, see p. 219.

contract out for assistance from groups and organizations with special expertise.

***Regulating presidential declarations of emergency***    In adopting the National Emergencies Act of 1976, Congress sheared much of the President's historic freedom to declare emergencies and simultaneously invoke sweeping powers. Spurred by Watergate and a congressional study that unearthed some 470 emergency statutes (in operation thanks to four separately declared emergencies by Presidents, reaching back to the 1930s) legislators moved to constrain the wideopen situation.

The 1976 Act rescinds all powers obtained by the President and others of the executive branch via previously declared emergencies. Future presidentially declared emergencies can be terminated by Congress by concurrent resolution, which is not subject to a presidential veto, or by presidential proclamation. In declaring a national emergency, the President must inform Congress of the provisions of law under which he acts. He and federal agencies must report to Congress all rules and regulations issued during an emergency, as well as expenditures, and at six month intervals Congress must consider whether or not the emergency should be terminated.[17]

The Act clearly enhances the President's accountability in a realm, where, historically, he has been a free-wheeling spirit—closing banks, seizing railroads, uprooting Japanese-Americans from the West coast during the Second World War without so much as a nod in advance to Congress. The 1976 act, of course, would do little to check the abuse of power when both the President and Congress yield civil liberties to momentary hysteria. President Ford, a critic of the act, implied that future Presidents might challenge congressional actions under its provisions.

## Carter and the New Congressional Assertiveness

Carter was the first Democratic President to serve in the new era of congressional assertion, governing with large congressional majorities. Has Congress in its new temper and with its freshly enlarged instrumentalities seriously constrained the President, possibly to the point of creating a new imbalance in favor of Capitol Hill?

After studying the legislative record of Carter's first year compared with that of other contemporary Presidents, political scientist Randall Ripley concluded that Carter did tolerably well, standing about midway between recent Presidents.[18] In his second and third years, Carter's performance measurably improved, again comparing favorably with contemporary Presidents. In more qualitative terms, Carter scored important legislative successes with the passage of the Panama Canal treaties, the creation of the Departments of Energy and Education, enactments of his reorganization proposals, and passage of his "windfall" profits tax on the oil industry.

On the other hand, Carter suffered defeats on major proposals addressed to problems uppermost on his administration's—and society's—agenda. He could not extract major energy legislation from Congress. His efforts to cap hospital costs, a volcano of inflation, were thwarted. His SALT II treaty faced a wobbly future well before the Soviet invasion of Afghanistan pushed it behind even the backburner. Clearly, Carter is well removed from such peaks of accomplishment as Roosevelt's in 1933–34 and Johnson's in 1964–65. And a complex of causes, wholly apart from Congress's new assertiveness, shaped the result. High among these surely were Carter's cherished image as outsider that ruffled congressional sensitivities; a long shakedown period for Carter and his staff before they became tolerably attuned to the meandering art of doing business with Congress; Carter's steep decline in public opinion polls; and the disinclination of Carter and his staff to push their legislative proposals vigorously enough to gain enactment.

# Inside Congress

## Born Again Congress

More important than Congress's expansion of power through statutory enactment are the changes in its attitudes, work habits, and structure in the post-Watergate era.

*Skepticism unlimited*   Congress displays a decided tilt toward independence, a firm intent to influence policy, domestic and foreign. A habit of skepticism has seized Congress; its members are no longer automatically willing to accept the President's word as revealed truth. At times, Congress, acting as a convocation of doubting Thomases, may go to extreme lengths, as it did, for example, when members expressed freely (and some, endlessly) their doubts over the validity of Carter's disclosure in 1978 that Cuban forces were present in Angola.

*The new generation*   Recent Congresses have experienced high turnover in membership in contrast to an historically more stable membership. When Carter was elected in 1976, only 23 Senators and 75 Representatives had been in office when John Kennedy became President. Carter's first Congress, the Ninety-fifth, contained 42 first-term Senators, and 150 Representatives in their first or second terms. A sizeable majority had never served with a Democratic President.

This new congressional generation is better educated, more confident, and less willing than its predecessors to observe a decorous reticence as backbenchers before achieving status and speaking out. Many owe their elections and therefore their allegiance to activist grassroots movements, such as the consumer, black civil rights, and environmental movements, rather than to county chairmen and other party leaders, a circumstance promoting early assertiveness, and a sense of owing little or nothing politically to the President.

The new legislators are interested in a broader range of issues than their predecessors, international—once shunned by all but a few legislators—as well as domestic. Many were elected because of their stands on issues, and while excelling at services to constituents, their best efforts are addressed to public problems and policies. "We're concerned about our districts," said one second-term Congressman, "but we're even more concerned about national problems."[19]

*535 Congresses*    Where Presidents like Eisenhower, Kennedy, and Johnson dealt with powerful committee chairmen, typically Southern barons when the Democrats controlled Congress, today's President must reckon with the entire 535 members of Congress ("There is not one Congress, but 535 Congresses," it has been said), who are disinclined to take direction from their legislative seniors and require individual attention. "Some of our younger members have never known what it's like to work with a Republican President," said Representative Robert Michel of Illinois, then Republican Whip, "We've got a lot of kids who are used to lobbing grenades." Instead of approaching simply the chairman of the Ways and Means committee to get a tax bill passed, former Representative Robert N. Giamo (D-Conn.) has explained, all 37 members of the committee must now be lobbied.

The power of committee chairmen has been diminished by procedural changes under the banner of the reform spirit that surged in Congress in the 70s, both before and after Watergate. Democrats require committee chairmen to stand for election by the party caucus at the beginning of each Congress. The autocratic, intransigent chairman, so often the bane of Truman, Eisenhower, and Kennedy, has learned a new obligatory lesson—indulgence of his fancies and impulses jeopardizes his job. Although seniority remains the key to power, the chairmen, in their new age of vulnerability, have lost much of the control they once exercised over their colleagues and the flow of legislation.

Republican chairmen have fewer fetters than their Democratic counterparts. In 1980, even as the fireworks of jubilation were bursting in the skies for the Republican capture of both the presidency and the Senate, two prospective committee chairmen were dissenting from the known positions of President-elect Reagan. Senator Bob Dole (R-Kans.), the pending Senate Finance Committee chairman, termed Reagan's proposal to cut taxes ten percent a year for three years "inflationary." Senator Strom Thurmond (R-S.C.), destined to become the Judiciary Committee's chairman, disavowed a plank of the Republican platform calling for appointment of judges who oppose abortion and favor traditional family values. Thurmond preferred to "consider the person as a whole," while Reagan declared it would be "cynical and callous" to turn his back on the platform.[20]

*Subcommittees rampant*    A major factor diminishing the power of committee chairmen and promotive of the general dispersal of congressional power is the exploding proliferation of subcommittees. Virtually every Senator in the later 1970s served either as chairman or ranking minority member of a subcommittee. Under altered rules of the House of Representatives, nearly half the Democrats and most Republicans hold positions of subcommittee leadership.

A "subcommittee bill of rights," adopted in 1973 by the House Democratic caucus, reduced the power of full committee chairmen and urged an enlarged autonomy for subcommittees. Nowadays, a President's program is sliced into parts that are considered by 100 highly autonomous units in the Senate, and, by one count, 137 units in the House. These many entities frame decisions and make policy with little coordination by external leadership.

For the President the changes wrought by reform produce a continuing dilemma. Either he and his helpers must invest prodigious effort to lobby his measures through the infinitely complicated committee maze, or he can pray that they will emerge in some tolerable form. Even if he succeeds at the committee stage, he can be rebuffed on the floor of the houses where far less inclination exists than in bygone times to accept committee and subcommittee decisions.[21]

*Staff expansion*   In the reform era of the 1970s, Congress rapidly developed its own bureaucracy, a keenly honed instrument for challenging the President. In 1980, the legislative branch had an estimated 38,000 employees, which, though dwarfed by the executive branch, is a precise and busy instrument for congressional probing. Both the committee staffs and legislators' personal staffs, as well as the historic General Accounting Office, created by the Budget and Accounting Act of 1921, have markedly expanded in numbers and competence. Branching out from its earlier, modestly defined role, emphasising accounting, the GAO has become a wide-ranging investigator and assessor of executive performance. Congress is also assisted by the highly professional Congressional Research Service, the Office of Technology Assessment, and the Congressional Budget Office. Carter was not long in office when he learned the potency of the economists of the Budget Office. Together they provided the research and analytical foundation for the main thrust to defeat his very first proposal, the $50 rebate plan of his energy program. The Senate maintains a computer center and the House an Information Systems. Congressional task forces and study groups have proliferated, and the expansion of congressional staffs is steadfastly supported by both conservative and liberal legislators.

Many congressional bureaucrats have previously served in the executive branch and are therefore schooled in its ways and wiles. The congressional bureaucracies exhibit the universal qualities of all robust bureaucracies—an appetite for self-aggrandizement, a proneness to make-work, jurisdictional pride. Above all, they enable Congress to deal confidently with complex issues and to make independent judgments, largely freed from an historic dependence on the executive branch for information and counsel.[22]

*Rules reform*   The era of reform has also entailed alterations of procedural rules in both houses, some with implications unfavorable to the President. For example, the House under its altered rules takes record votes on all important amendments to legislation. Previously, such votes were usually unrecorded, enabling the Congressman to respond easily and furtively to the demands of interest groups. Reform helps cure that and democracy gains, but the reform coin has another side. The new open procedure also enables interest groups to observe the vote of the legislator more closely than ever. Frequently their preferences are contrary to the President's positions. Meanwhile, how the legislator votes remains unknown to the bulk of his constituents, who, absorbed in their private lives, do not follow the voluminous daily grist of congressional business.

*Party influence*   The democratization of Congress through the dispersal of power weakens the power of party leaders like the House Speaker and the majority and minority leaders of both houses. Recorded voting and more open committee work make the legislator easy prey to formidable pressures to abandon party positions and to vote according to a standard of potential benefits to his district and according to the wishes of special interest groups whose support he values. The constituency and the groups—not the President—elect and reelect him.

The cumulative reforms reinforce Congress's historic function of naysaying, to reject the President's proposals without substituting positive measures of its own. Congress's most impressive performances in the past decade have been essentially negative—it rejected Supreme Court appointments, barred the construction of supersonic aircraft, stopped a rise in crude oil prices, and forestalled presidential initiatives in Vietnam, Cyprus, and Angola. Often neither democracy nor presidential power gain when Congress casts an absolute negative upon a presidential initiative and its efforts to provide substitute action become paralyzed.

# Congressional Majorities

Congress and the President, for all their built-in divergences, must somehow work together to secure enactment of beneficial legislation. "I am part of the legislative process," Eisenhower rightfully said in 1955.[23] Article II, section 3, of the Constitution is the launching ground for presidential leadership in legislation. The President is called upon to "give to the Congress information of the state of the Union, and recommend to their consideration such measures as he shall judge necessary and expedient." But what the President proposes Congress disposes, by approval, defeat, delay, or amendment. Congress, too, can initiate and the President dispose, by approval, or by veto that Congress, needing to muster a two-thirds vote of both its houses, can seldom override.

The President may have a paper majority of his party in Congress but no working majority. Dwight Eisenhower, brought into the presidency by the largest popular vote that had ever been cast and with his Republican party in control of both houses of Congress, quickly discovered the harsh realities of his new existence. A succession of hostile maneuvers were launched by his Republican colleagues on Capitol Hill, and all were directed at the White House. Not a few of the President's antagonists had been swept into office on his coattails, but neither sentiment nor gratitude dulled their purpose. Senator John Bricker of Ohio, a former Republican vice-presidential candidate, sponsored an amendment that would have emasculated the President's power to make executive agreements and convert the treaty power, already difficult in the constitutional arrangement, into the most cumbersome in the world. Senator Joseph McCarthy was in open war with the executive branch. Daniel A. Reed, the octogenarian chairman of the House Ways and Means Committee, fought for an income tax cut that threatened to throw the budget into gross imbalance and wreck the President's program set out in his State of the Union message.[24]

## The Conservative Coalition

The vagaries of congressional party loyalty compel the President, estimating his legislative prospects, to acknowledge a "conservative" coalition of Republicans and Southern Democrats who, voting together in Kennedy's first two years, comprised a majority in both chambers. This stark, imposing fact illuminated the necessity for the Kennedy administration to concentrate upon weaning away Republicans and Southerners from opposition to its bills. Notwithstanding the administration's acumen and zeal, the conservative coalition did heavy damage. In the Senate it defeated proposals for an urban affairs department and medical care for the aged. In the House it likewise killed the urban affairs cabinet post and the college aid bill. When the conservative coalition lost, as it often did, it was because the administration won over sufficient numbers of Republicans or Southern Democrats to support the rival "liberal" coalition. This coalition consists of a majority of voting Northern Democrats and minorities of Republicans and Southern Democrats, mostly from urban and suburban constituencies. Many of Kennedy's victories were owed to liberal and moderate Republican support. In the House, Republicans provided the margin of victory in the fight to enlarge the Rules Committee and the passage of the emergency feed grains, depressed areas, and minimum wage bills. Similar victories were won in the Senate. A *de facto* liberal coalition of Northern and Western Democrats and "liberal Republicans" provided the Kennedy administration with most of its successes.

In the Nixon era, the conservative coalition of Republicans and Southern Democrats thrived spectacularly; in 1971 it compiled the highest percentage of victories on votes taken in the House and Senate in more than a decade— 83 percent against a previous high of 73 percent in 1968. But, while for earlier Presidents this coalition was a bane, for Nixon it was a boon. Time and again, the coalition in both houses took positions agreeing with the President's. In the House, the coalition formed 29 times in 1971, for example, and won 24 of the votes on which it agreed with Nixon; in the Senate, the coalition-Nixon position appeared 21 times and won 17 votes.[25] In his other presidential years, Nixon's success was more modest. In 1973, for example, the victories of the conservative coalition fell to 61 percent. In the Senate, the President and the coalition coincided on 36 out of 43 votes. The Nixon-conservative coalition success rate in each house also underwent a comparable decline.[26] Conversely, Nixon was most embattled in his dealings with the liberal coalition.

When Carter became President, the conservative coalition flourished with new strength, appearing in 1977 in more than a quarter of all votes in the houses. Winning two-thirds of the time, it often frustrated the President's purposes. The 1978 congressional elections diminished the coalition's ranks, and it now materialized fewer times and gained fewer victories. Its political Waterloo was the Panama Canal treaties, while other major rebuffs were sustained on votes to revise the criminal code and on labor reform legislation, an object of intense grassroots lobbying.[27] Thanks to 1980's Republican landslide, the conservative coalition was redoubled in numbers and influence.

## President and Floor Leaders

The President conducts many of his legislative enterprises through the floor leaders of each house. Floor leaders, with their split role as party leader and the President's legislative leader, vary widely in interpreting their total responsibility. Robert Taft and William F. Knowland in the Eisenhower administration cherished their independence and the long mile between the White House and the Hill. Taft, of course, was Eisenhower's chief competitor for the 1952 Republican presidential nomination, and Knowland, when invited to switch California to Eisenhower to provide the general with a big victory, answered coldly, "We don't want any credit or any responsibility for *that* nomination." [28] In true congressional paradox, Eisenhower's best leader was Lyndon Johnson, the Democratic floor leader, whose entire distinguished service was spent under the Republican Eisenhower. Johnson consistently refused to turn Senate Democrats loose on Eisenhower at will but worked with the President with dispassionate professionalism, supporting or opposing as he believed he should. "We prod him," said Johnson of Eisenhower, "into doing everything we can get him to do, and when he does something good we give him a 21-gun salute." [29] Ford's dealings with the leaders were denoted by comraderie but it seldom yielded positive results.

Carter thrived in his personal relationship with Speaker Thomas P. ("Tip") O'Neill, a veteran of nearly a quarter-century in the House. Widely popular, a relentlessly loyal and partisan Democrat, O'Neill often committed his own prestige to enable the President to prevail. He also excelled at steering Carter and his administration past the boobytraps of congressional politics. With the more reserved Senate Majority Leader, Robert C. Byrd, Carter's relationship was more constrained. Where O'Neill helped drive Carter's controversial initial energy bill through the House, Byrd lifted not a finger to save the bill from gutting in committee.

# Working Tools of
# the Legislative Presidency

As the President seeks to exploit his constitutional powers, statutory processes such as budgeting, and political opportunities to assert leadership in the legislative process, what are his principal working tools? These are both diverse and substantial and their heavy-duty use maintains what political scientist Stephen Wayne has aptly termed "the Legislative Presidency." [30]

## Presidential Influence

Chief among the tools is the President's own influence in Congress. In an empirical study, political scientist George C. Edwards III identifies major components of that influence. These include the President's use of party to affect the votes of legislators who are members of his party, to exploit the incentive his party colleagues have of making him look good by not losing votes, and to capitalize on their personal and emotional commitments to their party. The President's electoral performance, particularly if his coat-tails influence congressional election outcomes, is a potential mobilizer of legislators' support. But studies reveal that the once flourishing coattails are declining with the general weakening of the parties. An analysis of the 1972 election, in which few House seats changed party control despite President Nixon's landslide reelection, attributed the result largely to the decline of parties and the increased electoral advantages of incumbents.[31]

The potentially more flourishing sources of presidential influence include the incumbent's prestige and popularity, and his skill at bargaining, threatening, timing, and extending amenities to legislators. Edwards concludes that congressional support for Presidents does not necessarily vary with the degree of presidential legislative skills. In fact, Kennedy, considered less skillful, received more support in the House from both Northern and Southern Democrats than did Johnson, considered more skillful, while Johnson attracted more support from Republicans.[32]

## The White House Staff

Members of the President's personal staff, or White House staff, are often key actors in interbranch relations. Franklin Roosevelt's special counsel, for example, Judge Samuel Rosenman, handled such legislative matters as message writing, legislative drafting, and making recommendations on legislation awaiting presidential action. Two youthful presidential assistants, Thomas G. Corcoran and Benjamin V. Cohen toiled on Capitol Hill promoting the President's program, seeking votes, and working out compromises to move their measures along. Truman and Eisenhower promoted the institutionalization of the White House staff in handling legislative functions, in the sense of more clearly differentiated duties and greater specialization and size.

Machinery has also developed to aid the President in the formulation of policy decisions. Since the 1930s, the Bureau of the Budget as part of the Executive Office of the President (reorganized in Nixon's day to become the Office of Management and Budget [OMB]) oversees a centralized clearance process for legislation. Department or agency requests for legislation must be reviewed by the OMB, which determines whether the request is in accord with the President's legislative program. Similarly, bills enacted by Congress are reviewed by OMB, in consultation with interested agencies, before they are recommended to the President for his approval or veto. Since the 1960s the White House staff has entered the process and subsequently, the Domestic Council of Nixon and Ford and the Domestic Policy Staff of Carter, creating a partnership of the President's personal and political appointees and the OMB's civil servants.

## Developing the Legislative Program

In developing their legislative programs, Kennedy and Johnson utilized task forces and advisory committees, whose members were drawn largely from outside the government. Johnson was impressed that the executive bureaucracy was wedded to the status quo, that in its processes "only the most powerful ideas can survive" and that the "cumbersome organization of government is simply not equipped to solve complex problems that cut across departmental jurisdictions."[33] The gleanings of outside advice were reshaped into proposals that became the foundation of his Great Society program's extraordinary array of legislation. Nixon's Domestic Council, led by John Ehrlichman, a principal White House aide, and organized hierarchically along subject-matter lines, provided an in-house mechanism for developing and analyzing policy proposals. Carter's domestic policy-making process, premised on the notion of a cabinet system, sought to improve the department and agency contributions, well linked, however, with the President's preferences. Carter's major legislative proposals, such as energy and welfare reform, were developed in interagency groups whose composition and target deadlines the President approved, and the Domestic Policy staff, headed by Stuart Eizenstat, provided administrative support.

## Congressional Liaison Office

Building upon beginnings by Roosevelt and Truman, Eisenhower established a congressional liaison office in the White House. In the Eisenhower and succeeding presidencies, the liaison aides function as policy advisers, conveyors of congressional views, participants in White House meetings where issues are thrashed out. The aides intercede on patronage questions and assist legislators on constituency matters. In the Kennedy and Johnson administrations, Lawrence F. O'Brien oversaw the liaison operation. He emphasized socializing, pep talks, and legislators' easy access to the President. He organized lobbying for the President's program on the Hill and performed favors and services for legislators—tickets for the small White House tour, cruises with the President down the Potomac—and he supervised the announcement of awards of government contracts. The style and impact of the liaison staffs depend critically on a given President's own stance toward Congress. Johnson and Ford mingled with the legislators most easily; Nixon was the most remote and Carter somewhat less so. The President's personality and inclination are a rock of Gibraltar that the staff can do little to move.

# Open and Closed Politics

## Instruments of Open Politics

The President advances his program in Congress by means which C. P. Snow, the British novelist and scientist, terms "open politics" and "closed politics," one visible and the other covert. In open politics the President sets forth his proposals for legislation, sends appointments and treaties to the Senate, brings Congress into extra session and puts an agenda before it, and makes public statements explaining and defending his legislative actions. His chief weapon in open politics is his messages—his State of the Union message rendered each January, followed since Woodrow Wilson's day by special messages that focus on single issues. These messages provide the record and delineate the scope of the administration's program.

Congress, too, invites messages, and therefore leadership, from the President. The Budget and Accounting Act of 1921 bids the President to submit an executive budget each January. This ponderous tome, equal in bulk to several metropolitan telephone directories, with its accompanying message is a detailed statement of policy objectives with means of achieving them for Congress's guidance. The Employment Act of 1946 calls for an Economic Report from the President that permits him to lay out policies fostering free competitive enterprise and maintaining employment, production, and purchasing power at maximum levels.

Theodore Roosevelt began the practice of supplementing his messages with actual drafts of bills. Although Roosevelt, mindful of the niceties of separation of powers, was a trifle sheepish and clandestine about it all, Wilson did it openly. Since then all Presidents, even Calvin Coolidge, despite his strict constitutionalism and tired blood, have drafted bills.

The Constitution endows the President with the veto, a most powerful weapon in the game of open politics. The veto's grave defect is that it is total and not partial. The President must accept or reject a bill as a whole; he cannot veto particular items and approve the rest. This permits Congress to engage with merry impunity in pork barrel legislation in appropriation bills and to attach riders like the one Senator Pat McCarran attached to the general appropriations bill for 1951, "That of this appropriation $100 million shall be used only for assistance to Spain." Nothing at the time was more alien to President Truman's foreign policy than to provide aid to Franco, the Spanish dictator. Early Presidents seldom used the veto and then chiefly to object on constitutional grounds. Andrew Jackson first employed the veto as a weapon of policy and of popular appeal in his war on the Second Bank of the United States. Franklin Roosevelt, who brandished the veto more than any predecessor, was known to say to his aides "Give me a bill that I can veto" to remind legislators that they had the President to reckon with. Harry Truman, taking his cue from Jackson, vetoed a string of measures of the Republican Eightieth Congress, peppering his sentences with vivid expletives like "dangerous," "clumsy," "arbitrary," "impossible," and "drastic," not so much for the legislators as for the public. Truman's vetoes were no small factor in his 1948 victory.[34] One of the busiest of vetoers, Nixon was also rejecting social programs. After a short-lived "honeymoon" with Congress, Ford too resorted frequently to the veto.

The President's enormous power to command the nation's attention endows him with a capacity no legislator enjoys. By skillfully leading the public, Presidents have brought Congress around to actions from which, left to its own instinct, it would refrain. Theodore Roosevelt was the first of the modern Presidents to rely heavily upon appeals to the public. Gifted and joyous in public combat, Roosevelt, blocked in Congress, went to the people. Woodrow Wilson perfected what Theodore Roosevelt had begun. "He is the spokesman of the Nation in everything," Wilson said, describing the President's special capacity. A spellbinder in times when oratory was admired, Wilson's lean, gripping prose and romantic moralism stirred his audience's better senses.[35]

Wilson and other successful practitioners of the popular appeal follow several rules. Wilson went to the public sparingly and only when the need was strong. The issue chosen must be important to the people and one about which their feelings can be instantly rallied. There must be careful preparation; when issues are sprung, they fare badly. As Wilson well knew, the venture carries the high risk that the people will respond only fleetingly or not at all. The appealing President is laying both his own political reputation and the prestige of his office on the line. Worst of all, the secluded executive session of a legislative committee and the artful parliamentary maneuver, where the controlling decisions on the President's program may be made, are not directly accessible to the legions of public opinion.[36]

## Playing Closed Politics

The President in his relations with Congress also engages in the processes of closed politics. Relatively unpublicized, unseen, and unofficial, closed politics employs the personal contact, the patronage lever, the choice viands of the pork barrel, and sundry other exertions of power and influence. The negotiation in the White House office or congressional cloakroom, the presidential phone call to the legislator deciding how to vote, the accommodations and compromises necessary to patch together a legislative majority for an administration bill, are the warp and woof of closed politics. The resort to closed politics is a constant reminder of the weakness of open politics. Because the Founding Fathers made so little provision for presidential leadership in legislation, the Chief Executive is driven to rely heavily upon the extraconstitutional resources of closed politics.

The President personally is, or should be, at the center of closed politics. There is no substitute for the force of his word and gesture. He therefore must explain and exhort to win backing for his program. His dealings and exertions cover the entire range from soft to hard sell. Lyndon Johnson brought to the presidency a high reputation and rich experience in the art of closed legislative politics, with service in both houses of Congress and a record as one of the most illustrious floor leaders in Senate history. He was master of two indispensable competences in closed politics. He was ingenious at discovering politically feasible compromises, and he commanded a relentless, overpowering persuasiveness at bringing those he confronted around to supporting them. His former occupancy of high Senate station provided him with an access to the centers of legislative power that Kennedy, whose Senate influence was considerably less, did not enjoy. Johnson as President seemed to range further and more insistently over legislative affairs than Kennedy ever did. "Kennedy came too late to many of his problems in Congress," said an official of both these presidential administrations, learned in the fauna of Capitol Hill. "He would hold back, let things develop, come in at the top of the crisis. Johnson likes to stay ahead and anticipate what will happen and how to meet it."[37]

In dealing and bargaining with legislators, the President operates from an array of vantage points. He can dole out various degrees of help in the next congressional elections. He manipulates the several executive beneficences like pork barrel and defense contracts. Not the least of the President's loaves and fishes is federal patronage, the art of bestowing offices upon legislators' protégés—with votes, it is hoped, the *quid pro quo*. Wilson sometimes disciplined legislators who persistently failed to support his policies by cutting off their patronage. "We not only ought to pay no attention to Senator Vardaman's recommendations for office," he wrote his Attorney

General, "but we ought studiously to avoid nominating men whom he picks out."[38]

If the President chooses to direct his available means of both closed and open politics upon a selected objective, he can gather an imposing arsenal. An impression of the administration's diverse weaponry is provided by Congressman Otto E. Passman, chairman of the House Appropriations Subcommittee, charged with responsibility for foreign aid. A skillful, doughty foe of foreign aid, Passman offered this picture of the Kennedy administration's legislative technique in its first foreign aid fight. The administration, Passman noted, relied heavily upon the testimony of Treasury Secretary Douglas Dillon, a Republican, "with his usual smile and personality." Passman continued,

> Then Democratic National Chairman Bailey sends wires to Democratic officials all over the country, trying to get them to put the pressure on Congress. . . . there were letters from Dillon and Rusk. . . . The program was talked up at a State Department briefing for editors. . . . There was the Ayub [President of Pakistan] pep-talk [urging foreign aid]. . . . The Citizens Committee for International Development was organized to exert more pressure. . . . McCormack [then House Democratic leader] sent letters to 2400 mayors across the United States including some in my own district. . . . Shriver [then Director of the Peace Corps and the President's brother-in-law] made a personal visit to every office on Capitol Hill. Although he came for the Peace Corps, foreign aid was mixed in. . . . The White House kept contacting business groups all over the country. . . . I jotted down some figures to show my thinking [i.e., of possible cuts in foreign aid spending]. A Republican subcommittee member leaked the figures to the President a few hours before the subcommittee was to act. . . . While I was presenting the subcommittee report in the full committee meeting, administration agents continued to place phone calls to committee members in the room. In the same meeting, letters from an Assistant Secretary of State to members of the committee, all calling for more funds, were actually slipped under the door.[39]

Yet for all the unstinting commitment of the President and his cohorts, Congressman Passman cut the foreign aid appropriation by 21 percent, or $896 million. After the deed was done, Passman observed simply, "This is a great day for the taxpayers." Kennedy and his aides were reported "stunned and angry."

# Approaches to Legislative Leadership

A Chief Executive can choose between several possible approaches in setting the tone, pace, and pressure level of his legislative leadership. No President, to be sure, limits himself to any one approach. Like baseball pitchers, he prefers to mix his delivery, and the choice of an approach, like a pitch, depends upon how the game stands at the moment. The sheer number and variety of approaches are themselves witness to presidential weakness in legislative leadership.

## Five Possibilities

*Fox versus lion*    All presidents engage in periods of the foxlike, or diplomatic, approach. The Constitution's endowment of Congress with vital powers of legislation and the President's consequent necessity of inducing its cooperation force him to be diplomatic in method. The President's personality and political ideology may bring him to prefer it. So also may special circumstances.

Gerald Ford, attaining the presidency after nearly nine years of executive-legislative estrangement commencing in the later years of Lyndon Johnson's tenure and culminating in the storm of Nixon's threatened impeachment, immediately accorded the highest priority to constructive relations with Congress. He had ample reasons to do so. The ever-deepening conflicts of his predecessors had been barren and unresponsive to domestic problems. Ford's prior tenure as House minority leader had schooled him in the give and take that could actualize his desire as President for "partnership" with Congress. Shortly before becoming President, Ford, recalling his legislative past, spoke confidently of working with a Democratic Congress—with all Democrats, "from Jo Waggonner," an ultra-conservative, "to Mo Udall," a liberal. In his initial address to Congress, Ford chose the diplomatic approach when he declared that his motto toward Congress would be "communication, conciliation, compromise and cooperation." Among the strengths that Ford commanded to further his motto were a staff he brought with him from Capitol Hill that was sensitive to congressional realities, a personal preference for "testing the waters" before proposing legislation, for negotiating with legislators rather than vetoing, and resolute faith that individuals of good will can sit together and solve difficult problems.[40]

In the foxlike approach the President fraternizes with legislators and plies them with blandishments. Franklin D. Roosevelt excelled at the art of congressional gratification, at giving out the easy first name, the warm handshake, the contagious smile, the intimate joke, the air of concern, the quasiconfidential interview, the picture snapped at the White House desk, the headline in the hometown newspaper.

One Saturday afternoon in blossom time in 1961, when Senator Harry F. Byrd's friends and neighbors gathered in his Virginia apple orchard to commemorate his birthday and eat fried chicken, there suddenly burst from the azure skies President Kennedy's whirring helicopter. The President had taken time from his heavy duties to come personally to honor the Senator. The attention did not deter Senator Byrd, one year later, and in the same apple orchard, from publicly criticizing Kennedy for requiring an excessive number of airplanes, yachts, and limousines to move about, and from proposing that he "set an example by getting along with a little less."[41]

The President who resorts to the direct, or lionlike, approach brandishes the veto power freely, turns on the pressures of patronage, pork barrel, and the ministrations of alert aides. He churns up public sentiment for his program to spur the legislators into support. The supreme example of the strong approach was Franklin Roosevelt in his first one hundred days, when in the depths of economic crisis Congress time and again put aside established procedures in the rush to do the President's bidding.

In fashioning his remarkable legislative successes in 1965, Lyndon Johnson, in many an interlude, moved about in his Congressional dealings as a menacing lion. Favored by extraordinary legislative majorities as a result of the 1964 elections, he acted quickly to reap a maximum yield on his wealth of political resources. He insisted that Congress begin work at once on two measures that had long eluded legislative action—education and medical care for the aged geared to the social security system. After impressive success with these, he pushed an avalanche of proposals upon Congress. In 1965 alone, in sixty-three separate documents, he requested a staggering variety of legislation and maintained a close personal watchfulness over its progress.

*Systematic versus buckshot*    President Eisenhower applied to legislative affairs the high degree of system apparent in other phases of his presidency. His legislative program was elaborately coordinated, setting forth the President's choices and priorities in every major area of federal action. The cycle began at midyear when the Bureau of the Budget (now the Office of Management and Budget) called upon the executive agencies to submit by September 15 a statement including *"all* items of legislation (other than appropriations) which the agency contemplates proposing during the ensuing twelve months." A month after the Bureau's call in 1953, Eisenhower, looking toward the coming State of the Union message, asked each cabinet Secretary for substantive ideas based upon a "thorough rethinking of the mission of your department and the . . . means to achieve it." The response was a vast outpouring of measures, many long advocated by the career service.

Sherman Adams, the President's chief assistant, and several aides spent two weeks with Bureau of the Budget help studying and sifting the proposals and checking with the President. Many complex and controversial measures of high policy and partisan significance—social security, taxation, agricultural assistance, and foreign aid—were tagged for presentation to the cabinet by the sponsoring department head. The White House staff previewed the presentations and gave advice. In November and December seven were presented to the full cabinet, with Eisenhower himself a leading participant, his questions and views sparking most of the changes made. In mid-December the President unveiled his program to Republican congressional leaders in a series of carefully staged eight-hour sessions at the White House. The Vice President, the Speaker, the majority leaders, whips, most of the cabinet, and several White House aides were also present. Congressional committee chairmen participated when their subjects were discussed. When legislative leaders expressed concern over some item, the President was apt to modify it. The principal purpose of the sessions, however, was to inform the legislators, not to secure their approval or commitment.[42]

In the three weeks between the leaders' meetings and the presentation of the President's messages in January, the several messages—the State of the Union address (put together by the White House largely from agency submissions), the Budget Report (written largely by the Bureau of the Budget), and the Economic Report (largely the work of the chairman of the Council of Economic Advisers)—were coordinated for consistency and coverage by the White House staff. Meanwhile, the departments concentrated on drafting special messages and detailed bills to follow promptly each proposal advanced in the more general messages. The State of the Union message of January 7, 1954, stated the President's program in general terms. Specifics were advanced in a series of seven special messages, delivered from January through March, on individual subjects such as social security, agriculture, Taft-Hartley, and foreign aid. An administration bill quickly followed each special message. Eisenhower's successors have continued his emphasis on system, each with his own variation.

President Truman was addicted to the buckshot method of presenting a legislative program. His message of September 6, 1945, "one of the most important of my administration," projecting the nation's conversion from war-making to peace-making, contained nothing less than twenty-one points of domestic legislation, ranging from agriculture to congressional salaries. Sixteen thousand words in all, the message was the longest since Theodore Roosevelt's marathon twenty thousand words in 1901.[43] Nor was this all. In subsequent weeks Truman sent up special messages with additional proposals. In his legislative presentation of 1962, President Kennedy followed a similar tactic by deluging Congress with requests for civil rights, special presidential authority to cut taxes and start public works to avert a recession, medical care for the aged, higher education, foreign aid, urban affairs, an international communications satellite, permanent unemployment compensation, and other things. Judged by its fruits, the buckshot approach is unimpressive. Only a few of Truman's and Kennedy's requests ever became law. Both sets of defeats were easily predictable beforehand.

Why, then, do Presidents resort to buckshot? In both the Truman and Kennedy instances, the Presidents were faced with approaching elections— the national elections of 1948 and the congressional elections of 1962. Both Presidents, firing a barrage of requests at Congress that were foredoomed to failure, aimed to exploit the Republican tendency to ride the brakes, to build a record for labeling it the "do-nothing" party in the electoral campaign. The buckshot approach is usually asserted in a cantankerous style. Truman blasphemed Congress, and Kennedy, who regularly employed a sober approach puffing congressional dignity, picked a fight on selected issues, particularly the creation of a department of urban affairs, which cast him in the hero's mold with masses of metropolitan voters. In the buckshot approach, the President invests noticeably less effort in working out compromises and patching together majorities.

Assessing his first year in office, Jimmy Carter acknowledged that he "asked for too much too soon"—the buckshot fever. Vice President Walter Mondale concurred, noting that "We found out in the first year that one must be careful not to overcrowd the institutions [of Congress] or try to solve too much too rapidly." Mondale's comment and Speaker Tip O'Neill's observation that "I told him [Carter] that we had too many balls in the air. We had too many balls in the air because we don't have time to do these things," suggest that Carter did not necessarily ask for too much.[44] Rather, he created a buckshot effect by the manner of making his requests: he asked for too many items all at once, without specifying his priorities. Subsequently, Carter mended his ways by applying priorities and by extending the timetable for dispatching his proposals to Congress.

***Involved versus aloof***    Far more than most Presidents, Woodrow Wilson was deeply involved personally in the legislative struggle. As a political scientist and an admirer of British public affairs, he had long been convinced that the President must be a kind of "prime minister, as much concerned with the guidance of legislation as with the just and orderly execution of law." Wilson oversaw the development of a body of legislation promoting economic and social justice, the "New Freedom." He believed that only the President could assure an integrated legislative program. Wilson, therefore, regularly planned it, shared in the toil and sweat of drafting bills, and oversaw their progress through Congress.

Preceding each congressional session, Wilson drew up lists of measures to be pushed, discussed them with the cabinet, and then conferred personally with House and Senate leaders or sent his "political ambassador," Postmaster General Albert S. Burleson, in his stead. Carter Glass, chief legislative sponsor of the Federal Reserve Act, has written that Wilson "dominated" the act's preparation. Congressman E. Y. Webb maintained that Wilson personally drafted the Clayton Act's famous clause that says "the labor of human beings is not a commodity or article of commerce," that he pressed legislative committees to report his bills out, watched the congressional calendars, and scrutinized amendments to forestall damaging changes. He also managed to keep in touch with conference committee deliberations, a traditional graveyard of progressive legislation.[45]

Wilson used his legislative influence selectively, pushing one measure at a time, but the key to his legislative approach was collaboration. The President, he said, in coming personally before Congress to promote his tariff legislation, should not be viewed as "a mere department of the Government hailing Congress from some isolated island of jealous power . . . he is a human being trying to cooperate with other human beings in a common service." Wilson put in a heavy schedule of hours on Capitol Hill. "Did you ever hear of a President occupying a room in the Capitol called 'the President's Room'? What would be thought of it," he asked the politically sophisticated Josephus Daniels, "if instead of asking Senators with whom I wished to consult to call at the White House, I should occupy that room for such conferences?" Daniels answered candidly that Senators would resent it. Wilson went ahead anyhow. When important bills were in the congressional crucible, Wilson would see a score of legislators in his Capitol Room. At the White House he saw even more and installed a special telephone to reach Senators quickly from his office. If Congress balked, he went to the people.[46]

Among contemporary Presidents, Johnson's interest in legislative relations covered the whole waterfront of executive concerns, large and small. "The President we have in the White House now," Representative Peter H. B. Frelinghuysen of New Jersey said, "follows with intense interest everything that affects his legislation. He apparently objects to any modification. He doesn't like a comma changed in anything he's proposed."[47]

In contrast to Wilson and Johnson, who were intensely involved, some Presidents have scrupulously held themselves aloof from the heat and dust of legislative combat. The progenitor of this approach was President Washington. The aloof style custom-fits the hero-President by removing him from the rough and tumble that might scratch the gilt of his flawless prestige. The aloof President addresses Congress in stately, general discourse and with a degree of deference. He avoids the specifics of issues, leaving them for Congress to determine, untutored by the Chief Executive.

A century and a half later another hero-President, Dwight D. Eisenhower, visualized his presidential service as a kind of unifying and moderating influence above the struggle. He was the good man above politics who eschewed conflict, reconciled differences, and healed divisions. He avoided involvement in political controversy and expressed frank distaste for partisan politics. "In the general derogatory sense," he declared in a press conference, "you can say that, of course, I do not like politics." [48] In legislative affairs Eisenhower took on the pleasant missions and left to his colleagues, principally Vice President Nixon and chief presidential assistant Sherman Adams, the tasks of conveying the harsh word and springing the fierce maneuver. Deeply respectful of the tripartite character of the government, Eisenhower was reluctant to assume executive leadership over a vast area that he viewed as legislative business.

*Bipartisan versus partisan*   A modern President chooses between a partisan and a bipartisan approach to legislation. In certain areas of affairs, bipartisanship is preferable, even imperative. In crisis, in much of foreign policy, and in major social legislation political realities require the modern President to employ bipartisanship to build his legislative majorities. In the depths of economic crisis Franklin Roosevelt conducted a nonpartisan administration, drawing large support from both parties. After 1936, with the crisis subsiding and with huge Democratic legislative majorities created by the elections, his administration took on a more partisan attitude.

President Eisenhower depended heavily upon bipartisan support throughout his two terms. His dependence was not less in his first two years, when the Republicans possessed a legislative majority, than in the following six years, when the Democrats controlled both houses. Eisenhower, writing to the House majority leader, Charles Halleck, early in 1954, said,

> Because of the thin Republican margins in both Houses, both you and Knowland obviously require Democratic support in almost every tough vote. This being so, we must by all means quickly show our readiness to cooperate in every decent way, and particularly in those areas where bipartisan action is vital to the national interest. [49]

Eisenhower's conciliatory pitch was well rewarded. From Democratic leaders Johnson and Rayburn he received, according to Adams, "more sympathy" than from the Republican Senate leader, William F. Knowland, who plagued the President with his one-track mind on the menace of Communist China, and Joe Martin, the House leader, whose support of the administration was spoken of in White House circles as "uninspired and lackadaisical." [50] Cooperation with the Democrats paid off at voting time. "Fifty-eight times," according to the *Congressional Quarterly Almanac* for 1953, the administration's worst legislative year, "Democrats saved the President . . . their votes providing the margin of victory when Republican defections or absences imperiled the happy glow." But Eisenhower paid a price for his collaboration. "This added more strain on his relationship with the right wing of his own party," Adams has written. [51] Though Gerald Ford shot flaming arrows of vituperation at the Democrats in the 1974 congressional elections, he sedulously maintained a bipartisan stance in Washington. He had to; the Democrats possessed overwhelming majorities in both congressional houses. Ronald Reagan lost little time in proclaiming his commitment to bipartisanship, particularly in foreign affairs.

Bipartisanship is attractive to the President whose party lacks or barely enjoys a majority in Congress. It may appeal to a President such as Johnson, whose party, thanks to the 1964 elections, gained overwhelming majorities in both houses. In putting through his record-breaking program of legislation in the Eighty-ninth Congress, he steadily courted Republican support and abstained from partisan conduct likely to offend Republicans. He consulted with the Republican opposition constantly before settling on his budget or announcing his domestic legislative program. He relied on Senator Dirksen almost as if the Republican leader were the Democratic leader in the Senate. In assessing the output of the Eighty-ninth Congress he was always careful to recognize the Republican contribution. "I think the Congress has done a good job," he said on one occasion. "I am not just talking about Democrats. I am talking about Congress generally."[52] Or again, "Most of the key measures have received some support from progressive and moderate Republicans, and all Republicans in some instances."[53]

Some Presidents have traffic with bipartisanship only from sheer political necessity. Otherwise, by instinct and preference they take the partisan road. Left to his own devices, Kennedy preferred a partisan approach to legislation. "Legislative leadership," he said, "is not possible without party leadership." Wilson's presidency was a telling application of this principle. In forwarding his New Freedom program, he acted true to his conceptions of the President as prime minister, party leader, and champion of a legislative program. Wilson advanced his legislative purposes through party means. He worked through Democratic legislative leaders and committee chairmen, cracked the patronage whip, and employed House and Senate caucuses in the English style. His tariff bill, for example, was taken up in the Democratic caucuses of each house at his insistence. The Senate occasion was termed "the first caucus of Democratic Senators that anyone can remember." Wilson triumphed in both forums. The House and Senate caucuses voted to support the tariff as a party measure. When the federal reserve bill was advancing, Wilson again resorted to caucus with happy result. The act was passed without any Democratic Senators opposing it; in the House only three Democrats dissented.

Wilson as legislative party leader traveled a rough road, given the divisiveness of parties and the localism of Congress. He had to cut through thickets of factional differences and convert the high-tariff Senator F. M. Simmons, the Finance Committee chairman, to espouse the administration's tariff reductions. The House Democratic caucus on the tariff teetered upon collapse when seven Ohio Congressmen threatened to revolt against free wool and the Louisiana delegation fought to break the sugar schedule. But the skillful majority leader, Oscar Underwood, held his ranks, and only thirteen Democrats refused, because of pledges to their constituencies, to abide by the caucus's decision endorsing the tariff reform bill.[54]

*Independent*   President-Congress relations may deteriorate into such a state of futility that one or both branches may seek its purposes not through the usual channels of cooperation, but by independent action. The President, for his part, despairing at legislative obstruction, resorts to his prerogative. Franklin Roosevelt, administering price controls in the Second World War, concluded that his efforts to hold the lid on inflation were imperiled by seven farm support provisions of the existing Emergency Price Control Act. In a message of September 7, 1942, he asked Congress to repeal the objectionable provisions by October 1. "In the event that the Congress shall fail to act, and act adequately," Roosevelt added, "I shall accept the responsibility, and I will act." How could the President legally carry out this threatened self-assertion? "The President has the powers, under the Constitution and under Congressional acts," said Roosevelt rather generally, "to take measures necessary to avert a disaster which would interfere with the winning of the war." Here in slightly different guise was the "stewardship theory" of Cousin Theodore.[55]

It is Abraham Lincoln who provides the most sweeping illustration of executive independence. At the outset of the Civil War he delayed calling Congress into session, judging presumably and altogether justifiably, in light of history, that the legislators might delay and obstruct while rebellion spread. Lincoln the Commander-in-Chief became for twelve crucial weeks the nation's lawmaker. The normal joint legislative-executive processes were suspended, and America had its first taste of dictatorship, fortunately a benevolent one.

Executive-legislative relations can also collapse into general debacle at Congress's instigation. In two of the worst crises the nation has known, Congress discarded every vestige of cooperation with the Chief Executive and pursued a bitter course of general sabotage. James Buchanan, who toiled hard and prayerfully to prevent the Civil War, and Andrew Johnson in the Reconstruction era were the victims of rampant congressional hostility. In Buchanan's case Congress denied the President nothing less than the essentials of governance. As the South continued to mobilize in spite of his entreaties, Buchanan requested more military funds. Congress responded by cutting his estimates to a fraction of their original amount and restricting the service of any additional volunteers who might be raised to the Utah territory. Even after Buchanan's message of January 8, 1861, declaring the existence of revolution and reminding Congress that it alone could muster troops, three weeks passed before a bill was introduced, only to be immediately withdrawn. Not until two months after South Carolina seceded and ten days after the Confederacy was formed was another, more modest, militia bill proposed. The House killed it with a resolution to postpone.[56]

# ★ ★ ★ The Future Presidency ★ ★ ★

"There is nothing more important for the future of popular government in America," historian Charles A. Beard once wrote, "than an overhauling of congressional methods and the establishment of better relations with the Executive." The problems to which Beard pointed have over the decades stirred thought in political and academic circles and have evoked a quantity of proposals for reform. The more extreme of these have urged that separation of powers and checks and balances be vigorously altered and that some variant of the British parliamentary system be adopted. The seeds of this alternative have always fallen on barren soil since it is alien to the entire American tradition. A historically assertive Congress would never bear the subordination of the legislature to the degree implied in the British system.

Any changes, if they are to occur, must be in accord with the spirit of an autonomous Congress endowed with considerable power.

We need a strong President and a strong Congress. The two are not incompatible but mutually reinforcing through their representation of valid constituencies—the President the nation, and the congressional houses the locality, state, and region. Both the national and local sectors of political society must be rallied behind major policy. Accordingly, neither Congress nor the President can have a monopoly of wisdom and an exclusive claim to the exercise of leadership. What we seek is effective cooperation between the two branches, with each a positive, constructive participant. We need to avoid both Lincoln's tendency toward exclusive leadership and the executive-legislative deadlocks of the past four decades.

A second essential contribution of Congress is to help keep the presidency on the path of constitutional decorum. Congress is a principal instrument, potentially the best of all governmental instruments, for holding the President accountable, for assuring that he functions as a responsible executive, within the law, and with sufficient conformity to the democratic ethos—its values and processes. As a lot, Chief Executives need to be coached and pushed by other political institutions to stay within constitutional parameters, and Congress is well qualified for the task, with members who are powerful and self-assertive and with resources and decision, to extend or withhold, on which the President depends.

On the other hand, as experience grows with congressional limitations on the presidency inspired by Watergate and the rush of internal congressional reforms of the 70s, an awaiting assessment for the 1980s must determine whether in some respects the swings in behalf of democracy have not proceeded too far, are too restrictive of presidential power, and warrant reconsideration.

1. Relations between the Congress and the President continue to be hobbled by excessive deadlock. Years after Carter depicted the energy shortages in graphically critical terms, the nation still lacks the enactment of legislation bearing anything approaching a comprehensive energy program. Carter's further rebuffs on top priority items like curbing soaring hospital costs and in seeking stand-by power to impose gasoline rationing, suggest the all too common prevalence of legislative-executive impasse. How can this persistent problem, with its high cost and hazard to the public, be diminished?

   For one thing, the President, the Senate, and the House could be simultaneously elected for a common term of four years. Historic data establish that we could rightfully expect that an election so administered would produce a President and two houses of Congress better attuned in party and political outlook than their present staggered elections permit. Under existing practice, the Senate, with its six-year term, is never wholly elected during a President's four-year term, and it is not until he is at his own midterm that even a majority—two-thirds—of the Senators who will serve during the President's tenure has been chosen. Also, the House's two-year term, and consequent election at the President's midterm, subjects his administration to a severe test of its popularity at an interval that is unfair, coming when his administration has barely started. Defeat in the election can be damaging to the President's prestige in both foreign and domestic politics. All too often, either his party loses control of the House or Senate, or its majority is reduced.

2. The reforms of Congress's structures and procedures, launched in the 60s and 70s to make the legislative process more democratic, are disclosing important side-effects in the 80s, which inhibit Congress's output of legislation and collaboration between the executive and legislative branches responsive to urgent public problems.

Both the procedural reforms and the mood of post-Watergate Congresses foster the new self-assertion of the individual member and profoundly diminish traditional institutional and leadership constraints. Many House members, commenting on the impact of the reforms, observe that they foment delays and make everyday legislative operations far more cumbersome and uncertain. By dispersing and curtailing power, reforms encourage the junior member as well as his seniors to speak up. The revised procedures of the House, traditionally a rules-bound and debate-controlled body, enable the individual member to delay consideration of major legislation by forcing consideration of numerous minor bills and amendments, time-consuming quorum calls and roll call votes, and other dilatory tactics. The member, consequently, can far more easily tie up floor action and refuse to support party positions, much less fearful than in bygone days of reprisal from party leaders.

In the Senate, for example, the filibuster has become a whole new art, wielded at times with extraordinary militancy. The filibusterer, in one of the newer wrinkles, can offer endless numbers of amendments to a bill, halting the Senate's major legislation in its tracks. Rules safeguarding debate, once exercised with due regard for the progress of the Senate's business, have become mighty howitzers in the hands of determined members.

What to do about these less welcome fruits of reform? Clearly Congress needs to reconsider its procedures and their aptness for maintaining the delicate balance between the freedom of the individual member and the necessity of getting its work done. Congressional procedures that serve less the ideal of free democratic discussion and more an easy opportunity to obstruct indefinitely the legislature's business should be reviewed and reconsidered. For example, procedural changes might reduce the time required for roll call votes. After cloture (Senate rules limiting debate of filibuster proportions) is imposed, instead of confining each member to an hour of debate, the present rule, let the minimum time be reduced to 30 minutes. Toward that limit, let the time be counted which is spent on quorum calls and roll call votes. Rule changes might also quell a major new Senate time-waster, the one-man filibuster, conducted by a reading of endless amendments to a bill.[57]

3. With Congress wallowing in fragmentation, speaking with 535 voices through 300 committees and subcommittees, manipulated by thousands of professional staff, an Elysian Field for monied, sophisticated special interests, is this finely splintered chaos beyond deliverance for constructive action?

A fruitful response of the Carter administration to Congress's fragmentation is the use of task forces. Organized under White House leadership, they both bring into their ranks and seek advice from interest groups and business leaders in formulating and revising legislation, with further inputs solicited from bureaus of the executive branch and from congressional committees and staffs. In later stages, after a consensus has been reached, the interest groups and other participants are enlisted to help lobby the bill through Congress, and, finally, regaled with a White House reception and letters of appreciation from the President. The task force effort was coupled with Carter's increased willingness to trade favors, appointments, and legislation for congressional votes.[58]

Admittedly, the task force approach rewards the powerful, privileged forces of society, and underrepresents the unorganized—the poor, the middle class, the consumer. Possibly the President, his White House staff, and sectors of the bureaucracy articulate the latter's interests occasionally. The nature of the issue also affects the utility of the task force device. It fares best with issues that stir little controversy and sail easily through Congress. But deeply divisive issues like energy and hospital cost-control cannot be rescued by mere gadgetry. On balance, task forces are a practical presidential response to the need to extract consensus from the gross diffusion of power in today's Congress.

# Chapter Eight

# Administrative Chief

**I**t is good for democracy but bad for an effective presidency—though by no means always for either—that the Chief Executive possesses a highly imperfect capacity to induce the vast officialdom of the executive branch to abide by his purposes and follow his directives. If there were any saving moments in the Watergate scandals, they occurred when two bureaus, the Internal Revenue Service and the FBI, beat back demands from White House associates of President Nixon that they approve or share in acts of wrongdoing.

But democracy is also enhanced when government through presidential leadership and administrative programs enables the private individual and group to utilize their freedoms more effectively, by overcoming illiteracy, for example, by raising levels of health care, by opening employment to racial minorities. More often than not the presidency is a force for good, and its capacity for positive accomplishment in forwarding programs responsive to society's problems is hobbled by administrative limitations.

## The Nonexecutive Chief

Unlike the typical business chief, the President finds no designation in his fundamental charter, the Constitution, as administrative chief, and neither do its collective provisions confer any equivalent authority. Indeed, political scientist Richard Rose contends that the President's title, "Chief Executive," is a misnomer. More accurately, the President can be described as a nonexecutive chief,[1] for the White House is far from being the command center of the executive branch. Although the President appoints the heads of the great operating departments and agencies, the principal resources on which they depend—their legal powers, the programs they administer, and their annual funding—are derived from acts of Congress. Programs and policies, to the extent that they are implemented, are carried out by tenured civil servants, who were on the job before the incumbent President arrived and will remain after he leaves.

Managing the executive branch is seldom an uppermost presidential priority. If the President does become engaged in the tasks of management, his objective is not to make the executive branch work for its sake but primarily for his sake. The President's foremost priorities are personal and political rather than administrative and managerial. Unlike civil servants, who are largely anonymous and sequestered from public view, the President is both highly visible and readily vulnerable. He is far more dependent upon his personal stakes in the political outcomes of the executive branch's performance than are the bureaucrats who share power without sharing risks. Typically, upon taking office, the President lacks knowledge of the intricate workings of the vast bureaucracy. Of the Presidents serving since the Second World War, only Eisenhower possessed prior high-level executive branch experience. Consequently, Presidents must devote a major share of their term to learning how the executive branch works, and why it so often fails to work.

## Powers and Functions

To make the situation more tantalizing, the President is given some powers to act administratively. These powers, however imperfect and incomplete, are sufficient for him to be perceived by the public as responsible for the conduct of the executive branch. The Constitution grants him the "executive power," language the Supreme Court has sometimes interpreted to include certain powers normally associated with an administrative chief. He is charged to see that the laws are "faithfully executed," which suggests a general administrative responsibility, but duty is not power. He also enjoys express powers such as the power to make appointments. Still other authority, to make a budget for the executive branch, for example, is conferred by act of Congress and by weight of custom. As well, he functions vis-à-vis the departments and agencies with a voluminous but imperfect communications system. Although avalanches of papers and reports constantly engulf him, the President lacks the most rudimentary administrative information. He has only a sparse and disjointed impression of the quality of performance by the departments and to what degree they are fulfilling his policies and purposes. Worst of all, he lacks any dependable system that will forewarn him of incipient malfunctions in the departments.[2]

The President supervises his immediate executive subordinates, the department secretaries, with an attitude ranging from the tolerance of Harding, who approved everything his Secretary of State, Charles Evans Hughes, did, to the definitiveness of Polk, who required his Secretaries, seated before his desk, to read their reports aloud before forwarding them to Congress. The President has only limited power to recruit, train, and promote the personnel of the executive branch. Most of his key appointments require the advice and consent of the Senate, and even more are subject to vagaries of senatorial courtesy. Since the first days of the republic he has shared general personnel powers with Congress, and since 1883, when the Civil Service Act (the Pendleton Act) became law, he surrendered his power to make tenured appointments in the executive branch.

His power to make removals, a subject on which the Constitution is silent, is likewise circumscribed by the civil service laws and by the courts. In *Myers* v. *United States* (272 U.S. 52, 1926) on President Wilson's removal of a postmaster, the Court seemed to find the President's removal authority unlimited. This sweeping ruling was trimmed back in *Humphrey's Executor* v. *United States* (295 U.S. 602, 1935). Humphrey, a Federal Trade Commissioner appointed by President Hoover, was removed by President Franklin Roosevelt not for causes cited in statute but, as Roosevelt candidly disclosed, because of policy differences between Humphrey and himself. The Court, finding for Humphrey, held that Congress can protect officials such as a Federal Trade Commissioner, who wield legislative or judicial power, against presidential removal. An "executive officer," however, or one "restricted to the performance of executive functions," the Court took pains to declare, could not be similarly protected. The distinction between an "executive officer" and one exercising "legislative or judicial power" remains blurred, although in *A. E. Morgan* v. *TVA* (115 Fed. [2d] 990, 1940) the Circuit Court of Appeals viewed a member of TVA's board of directors as an "executive officer."

The President delegates functions and authority, and by grace of the Budget and Accounting Act of 1921, develops an executive budget—his budget—covering federal income and outgo. He coordinates the several agencies of the executive branch or, as Harry Truman put it, he makes a "mesh" of things.[3] Almost continuously since the Reorganization Act of 1939, a consequence of the famous Brownlow Committee, he has had a limited power to reorganize executive agencies by redistributing functions and overhauling structures.

# Congress as Administrator

The executive branch has not one but two managers—the President and his rival, Congress. Nearly everything the President does Congress can do, sometimes with greater effect. The mission and structure of the departments are determined by act of Congress. Congress can give authority to subordinate officials to act independently of their department heads, prescribe specific and detailed administrative procedures, petrify the internal organization of an agency by statute, and require Senate confirmation for bureau chief appointments. Congress can establish independent regulatory commissions, like the Interstate Commerce Commission and the Federal Reserve Board, well removed from the President's direction and control. All executive agencies require annual appropriations that Congress provides as it chooses. The programs they administer Congress authorizes and amends. Congress can investigate departmental work in close detail, and its habit is not merely to query the leadership but to reach far down into the hierarchy.

Some Presidents, accepting the realities, give the congressional power centers a substantial part in the development of administrative decisions affecting program, budget, and personnel before consummating them and dispatching them to Capitol Hill. Lyndon Johnson was of this school. His appointment of a public commission, for example, to reconsider the entire foreign aid program served to diminish the rising outcry of congressional economizers. The Nixon era was characterized by running conflict between the President and Congress over domestic programs. Typically, the legislators championed the bureaus against the President's budget cuts and impoundments of funds, as well as the depredations of department secretaries, who, reflecting Nixon, interpreted program intent restrictively and even contrary to legislative mandates that had often been drafted by the bureaus in the first place.

# The Bureaucracy

Even more resistant to the President's quest for dominion over the executive branch is the giant bureaucracy itself, with its layers of specialists, its massive paper work and lumbering pace, its addiction to routine, its suspicion as a permanent power center committed to program and policy of a transitory, potentially disruptive presidential administration. The single most powerful figure in the great pyramid is the bureau chief, who in many subtle ways can frustrate the President's purposes when they diverge from his own. He cultivates ties with the pressure groups whose interests his organization serves and the congressional committees that provide him with money and authority. Congressional committees and subcommittees welcome his attentions since all are united in common purpose, protecting the integrity of the bureau's functions.

## Differences of Interest

Between the President and the massive departments are natural antagonisms of interest. The President wants to keep control, to receive early warning of items for his agenda before his options are foreclosed, to pick his issues and lift them out of normal channels, to obtain the bureaucracy's full support for his initiatives. The departments represent a wholly different bundle of purposes and needs. They cling to orderly routines, mountainous paper work, and time-consuming clearance procedures. They tend toward caution, and to the departments the President may represent a temporary intruder who threatens established policy.

The White House and the bureaucracy work by different norms. In assessing the bureaucracy, the White House is gratified when the bureaus provide teamwork in furthering its goals of interdepartmental coordination and follow-through in implementing the President's program. Typically, after fighting the battles to win legislation, the President prefers to leave its implementation to the bureaus. For Lyndon Johnson, the zest and the glory was moving the Great Society legislation through Congress; he had little taste for the laborious details and the low-yield political rewards of implementation. As for the bureaus, their natural dispositions are to advance and satisfy the goals of an incumbent presidency while simultaneously effecting departmental priorities and preserving the department's power and policy and program domain. If the White House will back an agency's requested budget increase or side with it in a jurisdictional dispute, well and good. But if the President or his staff is unsympathetic, the bureaus can well take matters in their own hands and circumvent the President by seeking help from legislators. The bureaus are encouraged by interested pressure groups and protected by congressional committees and subcommittees, or they can engage in open warfare with their bureaucratic competitors.[4] Time and again the Nixon staff discussed with acute distress cases where bureaucratic chieftains, without presidential authorization, went to Congress to plead for help in reversing higher level decisions, or attended meetings of interest groups around the country to win support for their activities. One day, President Kennedy said to a caller, "I agree with you, but I don't know if the government will.[5]

# President Versus Bureaucracy

Why do conflict and disgruntlement so often pervade President-bureaucracy interactions? Various forces regularly fuel the conflict. When the President and his White House helpers seek to impose his priorities on the bureaucracy, the President may, either consciously or unwittingly, be thrown into a combative role between two department secretaries who, with their bureaus, are competing for a presidential endorsement of their views as to what his administration's priorities should be. Generally, the presidency reflects short-term political changes, while the bureaucracy and Congress, relatively immune to their dynamics, are far less responsive. Occasionally the bureaucracy speaks for constituencies whose interests are largely ignored by the President, particularly if their memberships are small.[6]

## Perspectives and Values

To the departments, the President is overly "political;" to the President, the departments are distressingly "parochial." In interviews with Kennedy, Johnson, and Nixon staffs, Thomas Cronin found that the explanations they gave for their conflicts with the bureaucracy predominately emphasized roots in governmental size and complexity of public problems. The bureaucracies perceived White House aides as seeking to accomplish too much in too little time, as arrogant and insensitive, "breathing down the necks" of departmental chieftains, with the President impatient for results. To him the departments appear inert and obstructive, when actually they are struggling to forge a consensus on responses to complex problems.[7]

## Bureaucracy-White House Conflict

A sure road to conflict is the movement of the White House staff away from its usual advisory functions for the President toward outright involvement in a bureau's operations. Intervention brings the staff squarely onto the bureaus' territory and arouses their prickly defenses. Other troubles stem from the vagueness or even the absence of communications from the White House, leaving the bureaus confused as to presidential purpose and intent. Often White House directives are hazy, chiefly because the President and his aides have not yet decided and defined their policy objectives.

The incidence and intensity of conflict depend on several key variables. In a study of presidency-bureaucracy relationships in the Nixon administration, political scientists Joel Aberbach and Bert Rockman concluded that the worst conflicts occur between a forceful conservative Republican President and a federal bureaucracy, predominately Democratic in orientation. The study also found that the strongest opposition to the ideological bent of the Nixon administration came from younger and middle-aged Democrats in the bureaucracy, rather than from older Democrats of New Deal vintage. In the likelihood that social service programs attract administrators with more liberal beliefs, a conservative Republican President, to cope with the incipient conflict generated by bureaucratic resistance, must either sharply curtail the activity of administrators in those agencies, or politicize the agencies through replacement of top personnel, or, further, centralize decision-making in the White House.[8] Eventually Nixon pursued all these courses.

More ordinarily, conflict between the White House and the bureaucracy is modified by several norms. Most often a kind of natural partnership exists between the two domains. Members of the White House staff and the higher departmental echelons are joined by a comity nurtured by frequent personal association and a shared interest in the fruitful handling of a steady volume of business. Each needs the other's help to accomplish its objectives, and, other things being equal, each prefers the other's good will and harmony to conflict, with its risks and costs.

Political scientist Robert Sullivan cites the important distinction between high-level and lower-level bureaucracy concerning the problem of presidential influence and control. High-level bureaucracy is more susceptible to changes reflecting political and presidential values, such as the Vietnam war and poverty, while bureaucracy's lower levels are relatively isolated from the dynamics of the political and presidential systems. Direct presidential intervention in the lower-level bureaucracy is unattractive in that it risks resistance and brings disproportionately low pay-offs for the President's investment of valuable time and energy. White House staff assistants can intervene, but better still is the President, even as an indirect, remote influence. A politically deft President can create a "policy ethos" that will pervade decision-making at all bureaucratic levels. To do so, Sullivan notes, the President must be intellectually organized, strong-willed, and skilled at informing, energizing, and persuading the vast reaches of lower-level bureaucracy.[9]

# The Presidential Staff

## The White House Staff

To advance his purposes in the executive branch, the President can choose among several kinds of assistance—the White House staff or office, the cabinet, and the cluster of agencies composing the Executive Office of the President. The White House staff consists of approximately a score of senior assistants who bear such diverse titles as press secretary, special counsel to the President, appointments secretary, and special assistant for national security, or a miscellany of other affairs. There are many other staff members—the precise number in recent administrations is unknown. Some may be unlisted and unannounced publicly, and many are "loaned"—paid for by the departments, in which, technically, they continue to be employed, while toiling full-time in the White House. The staff is the President's "lengthened shadow." Staff members help prepare his messages, speeches, and correspondence; arrange his appointments; oversee the inflow and outflow of his communications; analyze and refine the problems confronting him; advance his purposes with legislators, departments, private groups, and party officialdom. Although many White House aides cherish their anonymity, they cannot escape importance. The White House staff is denoted by a steady accretion of influence over the decades, to the point that individual staff members, such as the assistant for national security affairs—a Kissinger or a Brzezinski—may equal or exceed the influence of their departmental counterparts, the Secretaries of State and Defense; the domestic policy adviser—an Eizenstat—enjoys almost similar ascendance over the domestic secretaries.

The White House staff has grown remorselessly despite solemn pledges to reduce it from a succession of Presidents. Carter's staff of about 500 was twice the size of Truman's of about 250. The staff's steady growth in both numbers and influence is spurred by presidential frustration over the bureaucracy's unresponsiveness, particularly its inability to provide initiatives for the urgent problems of his office. The staff's accretion is also attributable to heightened presidential interest in monitoring the departments and agencies to assure that his policies are implemented.[10] The White House staff has been expanded by the representation of interest groups within its rosters, by the assumption of responsibilities of coordinating programs shared by squabbling agencies, and by new proliferating functions such as public relations. Collectively, the staff tends to be more powerful than all other groups in the executive branch, including the cabinet and the National Security Council.

## The Cabinet

The cabinet, founded by Washington early in his presidency, has seldom been a source of advice upon which the President continuously relies. It exists by custom and functions by presidential initiative and is therefore largely what the Chief Executive chooses to make of it. "It lives," political scientist Richard F. Fenno has written, "in a state of institutional dependency to promote the effective exercise of the President's authority and to help implement his ultimate responsibilities."[11] Wilson, Franklin Roosevelt, and John Kennedy used it little. Quick and hard-driving, they chafed under extended group discussion. Truman, Eisenhower, and Carter resorted to it more but with uneven result. Johnson was more inclined than Kennedy to employ it, although often his purpose was not to secure counsel but to develop understanding and support in the cabinet "team" for a pending administration decision. Early on, Reagan announced his intention to restore "cabinet government," to make the cabinet the prime deliberative body of his administration.

Unlike the British Prime Minister, who, typically, brings into office a team of ministers or department heads who have long been associated in common legislative and party enterprises with houses of Parliament, many of the President's department Secretaries arrive with no acquaintance with each other and indeed little with the President himself. The two principal appointees of the Kennedy administration, Secretary of State Dean Rusk and Secretary of Defense Robert McNamara, were both strangers to the President until the moment he interviewed them for their respective jobs.[12] Historically, all sorts of considerations have governed the selection of department heads, including geography, to a degree: the Interior Secretary is ordinarily a Westerner, and the Secretary of Agriculture is hardly apt to hail from an Eastern metropolis but more likely from corn, wheat, or hog country. The Secretaries of Commerce and the Treasury will probably emerge from the business and financial worlds. A cabinet that includes strong political figures and personalities—a Charles Evans Hughes or a William Jennings Bryan—can be one of the most effective counterbalances to the strong President, with status and experience enabling them to question and resist presidential actions that they consider inappropriate. The strong Secretary is a potent safeguard against presidential abuse.

Political scientist Nelson Polsby observes that the President chooses between three major options in selecting his cabinet. First, he can find appointees with ties to client groups, with former political office-holders the main pool of such recruits. The norm of this type's performance is satisfying the clients. Second, the President can choose a cabinet of substantive specialists, with programmatic knowledge and experience. The norm for this type emphasizes the standards of the agency and the profession. And third, he may select a generalist executive from the law firms, the public relations firms, the universities, who is responsive to his own career and may respond to the President. His background relates to a variety of clients, and he is not closely committed to particular programs and policies. No modern President pursues a pure strategy of cabinet-building, but combines several types.[13]

## The Executive Office of the President

In addition to the White House Office and other units, the Executive Office of the President includes the National Security Council, patterned after the British Committee of Imperial Defence and created by the National Security Act of 1947. It advises the President on national security objectives and commitments and the integration of national security policy. The NSC's top-level membership includes the President, the Vice President, the Secretary of State, the Secretary of Defense, and the statutory advisers—the chairman of the Joint Chiefs of Staff and the director of the Central Intelligence Agency. The President can invite such other officials as he chooses to attend NSC sessions. In the Truman and Eisenhower administrations the NSC included a substructure of several working levels that was dropped by Kennedy. He found the NSC too large a group for developing policy on delicate national security problems. In planning strategy for the Vietnam war, Johnson dealt chiefly with a small group of advisers who lunched with him on Tuesdays. Johnson convened the full NSC primarily for "educational, ratification and ceremonial purposes."[14] Nixon, however, added to the NSC's committee structure in ways that expanded the influence of the assistant for national security affairs, Henry Kissinger.[15]

Under both Nixon and Ford, the NSC was subordinated to the virtuoso role of Kissinger. Although the NSC has settled into a limited role, its staff from Kennedy onward has steadily risen in numbers and influence. It too is the foundation of the steady ascendance of the national security adviser since that time. The staff's growth reflects the continuous frustration of Presidents with the seemingly slow responses and reluctant initiatives of the State Department bureaucracy. Carter's national security assistant, Zbigniew Brzezinski, likewise profited from the NSC's committee structure and staff. Ultimately both Kissinger and Brzezinski prevailed in competition with the Secretary of State for influence to the point that the Secretaries of State of both the Nixon and Carter administrations, William Rogers and Cyrus Vance, resigned.

The Office of Management and Budget (OMB), whose director may be involved in a wide range of presidential concerns, was created by the Budget and Accounting Act of 1921 and was known originally as the Bureau of the Budget. In the President's behalf the OMB prepares a single executive budget or consolidated financial program, clears and coordinates legislation for the President, monitors the implementation of presidential programs in the interests of economy and efficiency, and promotes management improvement in the executive branch.

In its lengthy history and shifting fortunes, the OMB and its predecessor have vacillated between several conceptions of its optimal operations. Its strength derives from the professional skills of its staff, and, particularly in its earlier decades, its ability to remind the President of the distinction between his political interests and his office's long-term interests. Led by bankers and accountants in the Eisenhower era, the Bureau's staff subsided largely to a tightly circumscribed role of budgetary technicians. During Johnson's cyclonic Great Society programs, the agency grappled with the complex problems of interdepartmental coordination and intergovernmental relations highlighting those programs.

In 1970, encouraged by long-building slippage in the agency's effectiveness and by the recommendations of outside studies, Nixon concluded that the agency should concentrate on the growing managerial demands of the presidency, and he changed its name from Bureau of the Budget to the Office of Management and Budget to reflect the new emphasis. By designating his confidant and long-time political ally Bert Lance as budget director, Carter brought the OMB into the center of his presidency. Lance's successor, James T. McIntyre, reverted to the OMB's professional role, but Carter's emphasis on budget-cutting in his fight against inflation assured McIntyre of a highly influential place.[16]

The Council of Economic Advisers, a child of the Employment Act of 1946, thinks, plans, and reports on the maintenance of economic prosperity. The three members of the Council are professional economists who advise the President on the entire range of leading economic issues, whether inflation, taxes, federal spending levels, unemployment, the dollar abroad. The Council must compete for influence in presidential economic policy-making with the Treasury Secretary, the OMB director, the Secretaries of Commerce and Labor, and the chairman of the Federal Reserve Board.

Carter's Domestic Policy Staff, by dint of his revamping, was the successor to the Nixon-created Domestic Council.[17] Headed by the President's assistant for domestic affairs and policy, Stuart Eizenstat, the staff explored the questions implicit in selected domestic issues, solicited agency inputs, mediated interagency conflicts, and asserted White House perspectives.[18]

## The Vice Presidency

The vice presidency, whose first incumbent, John Adams, termed it "the most insignificant office that ever the invention of man contrived or his imagination conceived,"[19] has, after dormancy through most of the nineteenth century, acquired occasional usefulness in the twentieth. A President prefers to work closely with associates whom he can discard easily, which he cannot do with the Vice President, whom he cannot fire. The Constitution also makes the Vice President the presiding officer of the Senate, a duty which, although light, makes difficult his assumption of large and fixed executive responsibilities. Vice Presidents of the past three decades have participated increasingly, although unevenly, in the President's administrative enterprises. Walter Mondale, exercising both a broader and deeper influence in the Carter presidency than has been the lot of any previous Vice President, ranged across the entire face of the presidency, in both foreign and domestic affairs.

The acute question facing the President is how best to harness the administrative resources of the executive branch to his democratically legitimate purposes—how can he transmute goal and plan into program and policy? How can he best awaken a sense of urgency in the bureaucracy and bestir its creativity? Presumably his best ally in these causes is the presidential staff, which after small and slow beginnings has, since the New Deal era—and especially since the Second World War and in the Nixon years—burgeoned into a substantial bureaucracy itself, occupying several buildings plus the east and west wings of the White House. Will the presidential bureaucracy succumb to supreme irony and itself assume the very qualities of the greater bureaucracy it is designed to combat?

On the other hand, the President himself is a bundle of frailties and inadequacies—of limited knowledge and imperfect information, of biases and blind spots, and, sometimes, unfortunately, of stunted ethical sensitivities, for which a well-functioning staff could be a corrective force. The President-staff relationship is therefore a problem of balance, of sufficient presidential dominion to advance his program and fulfill his electoral mandate, while simultaneously the staff retains a capacity to question the Chief Executive's thinking and worthiness of purpose, to put forward alternatives, to warn of pitfalls. Each President responds to these dilemmas and possibilities in his own way.

# Presidential Approaches to Administration

## Roosevelt as Unconventional Administrator

Franklin D. Roosevelt reigned as chief administrator by a highly unconventional system that gave the utmost play to his influence and enabled him to retain great power in his own hands. In pursuit of this supreme good he resorted to means that time and again violated the most sacred canons of efficient administration as taught with unflagging zeal in schools of business and public administration. For Roosevelt, organization blueprints were often scraps of paper, and the rules by which good executives, according to the texts, delegate authority were honored by their breach.

The textbooks warn that duplication must above all else be avoided in administration. Roosevelt went out of his way to indulge in it. He instituted the New Deal and its revolutionary changes, notwithstanding the bureaucracy he inherited from the previous Republican era. Roosevelt triumphed over the established bureaucracy with its elephantine pace and resistance to change partly by ignoring it. He established his own bureaucracy to administer much of the New Deal. The job of regulating stock exchanges was given not to the Treasury or Commerce Departments but to the newborn Securities and Exchange Commission. The Wagner Act, enhancing labor's opportunity to organize and engage in collective bargaining, was consigned not to the Labor Department but the National Labor Relations Board. The bold new Tennessee River Valley project fell not to the Interior Department but to a special Tennessee Valley Authority. Before the normal pathologies of bureaucracy could mature, the New Deal was a going operation.

Roosevelt as administrator drew freely from a large bag of tricks to get what he wanted done. He had little regard for the administrative niceties that are observed in most organizations. He was given, for example, to end-running his department heads and dealing directly with their subordinates. He applied a competitive theory of administration, which kept his administrators unsure, off balance, confused, and even exasperated. With ambition pitted against ambition, the power of decision remained more securely in his own hands. In Roosevelt's presidency, competition was also democracy-serving. Those of Roosevelt's staff who opposed the trend of policy or an incipient decision had every inducement to illuminate weaknesses—ethical flaws, transgressions of democratic values and electoral mandates, faulty assumptions, and misperceptions of events and situations. "There is something to be said," Roosevelt observed in behalf of his method of planned disorder, ". . . for having a little conflict between agencies. A little rivalry is stimulating, you know. It keeps everybody going to prove that he is a better fellow than the next man. It keeps them honest too." [20]

Roosevelt's devotion to the competitive principle and checks and balances led him often to prefer boards, commissions, and other variants of the plural executive to the single administrator. One of his more bizarre creations in the Second World War was the Office of Production Management, charged with administering much of the economy's mobilization. For this intricate and massive task, he resorted not to the leadership of a single administrator but to a biheaded authority consisting of William Knudsen of General Motors as Director General and Sidney Hillman of the CIO as Associate Director General. Although Knudsen's and Hillman's titles differed slightly, their authority, Roosevelt disclosed at a press conference, would be equal. But suppose, an incredulous reporter queried, Knudsen and Hillman disagreed, an altogether likely prospect given the conflicting premises of their respective worlds of management and labor. Might not the war effort be imperiled by dissension and impasse in OPM's biheadship? There would be no trouble whatever, Roosevelt answered confidently. If Knudsen and Hillman disagreed, he would simply lock them up in a room and not let them out until they could agree.[21]

Roosevelt, in the interest of competition, filled his administration with human opposites. His original Secretary of the Treasury, Will Woodin, was a conservative, respectable, trustworthy financier, and his first Director of the Budget, the economy-minded Lewis Douglas, viewed New Deal spending as "the end of Western civilization." Yet Roosevelt could also import a free-spender like Hopkins and legions of young lawyers schooled in the progressivism of Louis Brandeis and Felix Frankfurter. The philosophical pluralism of his administration enabled Roosevelt to play off not merely men against men but dogma against dogma. It was a kind of double insurance of Roosevelt's own retention of the power of decision.

The jewels in the crown of the formal organization, the department Secretaries, were individuals of initiative and drive, deep in their commitment to program. Roosevelt permitted them great scope. Their collective organization, the cabinet, however, he restricted to a modest role. He did not value the cabinet as a source of collective wisdom, and its meetings were apt to be hollow affairs. The President began typically by engaging in a monologue of pleasantries, recounting stories and joshing selected Secretaries. He would then throw out a problem, usually one that he had been considering just prior to the meeting. Discussion rambled and was inconclusive. Roosevelt's next move was to turn to the Secretary of State and say, "Well, Cordell, what's on your mind today?" The same query continued around the table in order of the Secretaries' precedence. They responded usually with items of minor importance, preferring to take up larger matters privately with the President just before or after the meeting. Large matters, the Secretaries feared, might be excessively mauled or leaked to the Hill or to the gossip columnists.[22]

Roosevelt steadily employed a free-roving assistant who shepherded the President's fondest projects over the assorted hurdles in the executive branch and outside. The assistant, acting for the President ("This is the White House calling"), made short shrift of departmental hierarchy and red tape in expediting action. He was a major tool by which the President might prevail against the vast, sluggish executive branch. Among these general assistants were Raymond Moley, Rexford Tugwell, Thomas Corcoran, and Harry Hopkins. In the Second World War Hopkins was Roosevelt's number-one trouble-shooter. Known as "Generalissimo of the Needle Brigade," he prodded industry to speed war production, harassed laggard military administrators, and oversaw the distribution of supplies to the fighting fronts. Hopkins was Roosevelt's personal liaison with the war overseas. In conferences with Churchill and Stalin and military chieftains he did the legwork on which Roosevelt's central decisions were founded.

The Roosevelt method is the surest yet invented for maximizing the President's personal influence and for asserting his sway over the executive branch. It spurred the flow of information and ideas into his possession and magnified his impact on policy. It released the energies of men from confining bureaucratic routine. In the main, Roosevelt's competitive administration operated within the bounds of the New Deal's purposes, which were humane (democratic), and they saved many administrators, though not all, from becoming merely self-seeking in their striving. For the contemporary presidency, however, the Roosevelt method has limited relevance. The new costliness of error in foreign affairs and the sheer scale of today's federal government make the Rooseveltian system of haphazard consultation, by which some departments may be left out, unthinkable. The internecine strife which marked the system is also barred by the necessity that the national executive appear before the world with the face of unity. Roosevelt enjoyed a luxury his successors are doomed never to know. He could create much of his own bureaucracy, first in the New Deal and then in the war. His successors must work with an inherited bureaucracy.

## Eisenhower's Staff System

At a far opposite extreme from Franklin Roosevelt's highly personal managerial method was Dwight D. Eisenhower's preference for institutionalizing presidential relationships in the executive branch. The Eisenhower method was a product of his military experience and several long-entertained convictions concerning White House practice. "For years I had been in frequent contact in the executive office of the White House," Eisenhower has written, "and I had certain ideas about the system, or lack of system, under which it operated. With my training in problems involving organization it was inconceivable to me that the work of the White House could not be better systemized than had been the case in the years I observed it." [23]

Eisenhower's key tactic was to delegate duties, tasks, and initiatives to subordinates. After their study and formulation of decision, he, as Chief Executive, might ultimately accept or reject. "The marks of a good executive," he advised his department heads, "are courage in delegating work to subordinates and his own skill in coordinating and directing their effort." Eisenhower's subsequent illnesses speeded his inclination to delegate. [24]

The vehicle of his delegations was the staff system. At its apex was the assistant to the President, Sherman Adams, a former Congressman, governor of New Hampshire, and early organizer of Eisenhower's presidential candidacy. Eisenhower, Adams has written, "simply expected me to manage a staff that would boil down, simplify and expedite the urgent business that had to be brought to his personal attention and to keep as much work of secondary importance as possible off his desk." Any issue, no matter how complex, Eisenhower believed, could be reduced to some bare essence. "If a proposition can't be stated in one page," he declared, "it isn't worth saying." Impatient with the torrential paper work of the presidency and not one who took to reading gladly, Eisenhower insisted that his subordinates digest lengthy, involved documents into one-page summaries, "which," said Adams, "was sometimes next to impossible to do."[25]

Except in the singular case of Secretary of State John Foster Dulles, cabinet Secretaries approached the President through Adams. Policy proposals were made in writing, the fruit of staff study and recommendation. Adams' task was to see that every expert in the executive branch who could contribute to a proposal had his opportunity to do so.

Eisenhower kept the system on its toes by his own close knowledge of governmental detail mastered in a long military career and a capacity to put sharp, piercing questions that could reduce premises and argument to a shambles. He could not bear flawed performance, a sentiment conveyed at times by fierce outbursts of the presidential temper. Both Eisenhower's queries and Adams' zealously pursued mission to see that no relevant opinion, fact, or option eluded the President were democracy-serving. Both fostered competition among the departments and representation of their functional viewpoints; both permitted questions to be raised concerning the values, morality, and practicality of pending decisions. Eisenhower, his questions often revealed, was acutely aware of the nature of democratic administration, of sensitivity to and regard for the opposition, and the need for policy to extend beyond responsiveness merely to a narrow, privileged economic class. But there was also danger: that the emphasis on order and system, on paperwork and routine, could create busyness without accomplishment and dampen zeal for innovation and risk, qualities that sometimes produce policies and programs leading to major democratic gains.

The staff secretary, who presided over a system installed under Eisenhower's supervision, kept records on hundreds of papers, many of high import and secrecy, dealing with national security and domestic affairs. Within minutes, Adams, thanks to the staff secretariat, could track down the location and status of reports, memoranda, and letters that had come into the White House or gone out for clearances in the far reaches of the executive branch. He could tell who had prepared a given document, the concurrences received and objections encountered, who was dragging his feet, and other essential facts of paper-work life.

The ancient institution of the cabinet also felt Eisenhower's reforming hand. Shocked that the department Secretaries, the government's principal executives, should gather without any preconception of the business to be considered, Eisenhower created the post of cabinet secretary. This new official arranged an agenda for cabinet meetings, circulated it beforehand among the members, oversaw the preparation of "cabinet papers" presenting proposals for the President's action, and recorded the results of cabinet discussion. Keenly aware of the gap between presidential decision and departmental reliability in carrying it out, Eisenhower had his cabinet secretary meet after a session of the cabinet with "cabinet assistants," a group of assistant secretaries and departmental executive assistants with responsibilities for implementation. Every several months a cabinet meeting was converted into "Judgment Day" on the "Action Status Report," in which each department head revealed how much (or little) he had honored his obligations to take actions called for by the President's decisions in cabinet.

In adapting the military staff system to the presidency, Eisenhower viewed his cabinet Secretaries essentially as theater commanders. Like field generals, the Secretaries were invested with broad initiative and responsibility for their allotted sectors of operation. For their assertions, the President, most of the time, provided political defense. When a score of Middle Western Republican Congressmen, with elections in prospect, grew restive over Agriculture Secretary Benson's hard line on farm price supports and suggested it would help politically if he would resign, Eisenhower, controlling his fury, answered at a press conference that "for any group of Congressmen, either informally or formally, to raise a question concerning my appointment to the Cabinet would not seem to be in order."[26] If dispersal of executive power, to a degree, befits democracy, Eisenhower's concept of the initiating, responsible department head warrants imitation by future Presidents.

One of the more complex and important elements of Eisenhower's institutionalized Presidency was the National Security Council. Eisenhower, who utilized the NSC heavily, often met with it two or more times a month, with an agenda of intelligence reports, policies to be innovated or revised, and reports on progress in fulfilling established policies.

The attraction of the Eisenhower system is the assurance it promises that the President will have the benefit of coordinated counsel in an age when major problems require the expertise of several or more departments. Adams' operation strove systematically to include every relevant department. The omission of skill and information, given the world's dangers, could be severely costly. At its best, it maintained a kind of competition and system of administrative checks and balances that provided parameters for Eisenhower's administrators and staff that were conducive to ethical and democratic behavior. At its worst, it could, engrossed in its managerial procedures, ignore or downgrade rising social problems like civil rights, health, and education, and postpone serious responses to another day and another Presidency. Meanwhile the problems worsened at public expense.

## Nixonian Centralism

Determined to be an "activist President," oriented toward intervention in the departments, Richard Nixon was confirmed in his resolve by his perception of the bureaus as hostile, comprised largely of Democrats recruited by previous Presidents of that party. The bureaus were proponents of "the welfare state" that he was resolved to prune back and reform, and therefore a source of potential obstruction.[27] In deploying his staff, Nixon, like other Presidents, gave vent to his needs and preferences. Essentially, the staff helped assure his privacy, his removal from the unwelcome demands of administration, and his transaction of business with a tiny circle of associates with whom he felt at ease.

Nixon adapted and embellished on the formal staff systems he had observed as Vice President in the Eisenhower years. His Sherman Adams, or chief of staff, was Harry Robbins (Bob) Haldeman, who, before becoming encoiled in the Watergate scandal, was called, like Adams, "the second most powerful man in Washington." An executive of the J. Walter Thompson advertising agency where he promoted Seven-Up and Black Flag insecticide, with periodic leaves for service in Nixon's earlier campaigns, Haldeman was injected by the 1968 electoral victory into his post as "Special Assistant to the President," to which he brought little familiarity with democratic practice and the power centers of national politics. A Janus-like guardian of Nixon's door, Haldeman determined whom the President saw, as well as what he read. With the air of a Marine Corps drill sergeant and a manner that bespoke his conviction that "every President needs his s.o.b., and I'm Nixon's," Haldeman steadily rebuffed Senators and Cabinet secretaries without ceremony or ado.[28]

A second top position on the Nixon staff was the assistant for domestic affairs, initially John Ehrlichman, who too was a veteran of Nixon's early campaigns.[29] A former land-use lawyer in Seattle, Ehrlichman watched over transitory "project" groups recruited from the departments and agencies and the White House staff to develop proposals on matters like welfare reform, manpower training, and pollution control. Ehrlichman's office also helped draft the necessary legislation and scrutinized the expected costs of programs against their benefits. Ehrlichman's power was enlarged by his role as chief executive officer of the Domestic Council and by his working relationship with the President. As well, he profited from the opportunity to pick and choose among the ideas that reached his desk for presentation to the President, and from his control over follow-up. In his heyday, Ehrlichman commanded more influence over domestic policy than any cabinet Secretary.[30]

For foreign policy and national security affairs, the instrument of Nixonian centralism was the assistant for national security, Henry Kissinger. Although such predecessors as McGeorge Bundy and Walt W. Rostow wielded great power, Kissinger, in the hospitable clime of centralism, exceeded them and institutionalized his office to unprecedented degree. As Nixon's chief adviser on foreign policy, Kissinger, more than Ehrlichman or Haldeman, became the formulator, negotiator, and implementer of presidential decision.

For the rest, the White House staff was studded with young men, in their twenties and thirties, some of whom gained notoriety in the Watergate scandals. Typically, they emerged from comfortable, even wealthy, families and from business—especially advertising—backgrounds. In impeccable Brooks Brothers attire, with an enamelled flag in their lapels, articulate and socially poised, they were orthodox in their view of the world, ambitious, intelligent but not thoughtful, and bereft of any controlling ethic except to do what their bosses wanted. Typically, they were unhampered by democratic socialization—by awareness of democratic values and processes or of American history and philosophy, which nourish such appreciation.[31]

In addition to the "advertising crowd," Nixon's staff contained several "tough political handymen," including, at various times, Murray Chotiner, Harry S. Dent, and Charles W. Colson. Seasoned and aggressive, they reported to Haldeman, who gave them wide latitude but kept track of their activities and transmitted special assignments in the President's behalf. These no-holds-barred political sophisticates were expected to overcome the lack of political savoir faire of the advertising men, and, as one staff man said, to "do the dirty work when it is necessary."[32]

To a degree that no President had attempted before, Nixon aimed to control, even dominate, the departments and agencies. Dissenting department heads and bureau chiefs like Interior Secretary Walter J. Hickel and Education Commissioner James E. Allen, Jr., were banished summarily into the outer darkness. Following his smashing 1972 electoral victory,

Nixon moved to tame the department that most inherently contradicted his Horatio Alger precepts of individual self-reliance, the Department of Health, Education and Welfare (HEW). In 1973, he appointed as the new Secretary Caspar W. Weinberger, who in earlier service as Director of the Office of Management and Budget demonstrated such flair at program reduction that he became known among the disgruntled as "Cap the Knife." In HEW, Weinberger quickly demonstrated the potency of the President's appointment of a hostile Secretary by drastically cutting HEW's budget and by employing the discretionary rule-making power of his office as a blunderbuss against social programs.[33] In HEW, as in other departments, Nixonian lieutenants were installed at secondary and tertiary levels, where they maintained surveillance on the top command and intervened down the line to stamp out incipient heresies.

Nixon regulated the bureaucracy by threat of reorganization—no other President has unloosed a heavier barrage of departmental reorganizations. Through them, Nixon moved to reduce or abolish agencies that were ill-suited to his administration's philosophy. The poverty program and its agency, the Office of Economic Opportunity (OEO), were favorite objects of attack. Functions and administrative units were detached and assigned elsewhere or lost in consolidation. Entire programs and even OEO itself were headed for liquidation, catastrophes that were slowed as clientele groups appealed successfully to the courts. The loose-strung HEW underwent a consolidation of grants and the delegation of functions and authority to state and local governments.[34]

In the Executive Office of the President, Nixon effected reorganizations that extended his reach into the departments. He transformed the Bureau of the Budget into the Office of Management and Budget, thereby increasing that agency's supervisory and management powers, and thereby, indirectly, the White House's power over the departments. He established a Domestic Council in the Executive Office, directed it to devise new programs, and endowed it with supervisory powers designed to foster greater conformity in the agencies to his policies and wishes. For a time, Nixon designated as counselors to the President four of his cabinet Secretaries and charged them with overseeing broad domains—the economy, community development, and human and natural resources—while retaining their Secretary functions. The effect was to centralize power further in the Presidency, with the counselors reporting directly to the Chief Executive and supervising clusters of activity in several or more departments and agencies. By executive fiat, Nixon had embarked on a potentially far-reaching reorganization, but, facing outcries following the Watergate disclosures, which contended that the presidency had fallen into deep trouble because it had become excessively centralized, Nixon dropped the counselor structure.

Convinced that personnel changes, to be really effective, must reach below the most senior level, Nixon called for relaxation of civil service rules that protected tenure and seniority. Potentially, this would be a mighty scythe in presidential hands with which to mow down recalcitrant civil servants, whose most humane fate might be reassignment to other duties. Most audacious of all was Nixon's proposed transformation of seven cabinet departments—HEW, Labor, HUD, Agriculture, Interior, and Transportation—into four departments for natural resources, community development, human resources, and economic affairs. The plan would have left the remaining departments intact. These and other proposals that Congress rejected were weakened by the President's own political enfeeblement following the Watergate disclosures.[35] Nonetheless, the plan contained the promise of developing more coherent domestic policies usually precluded by the present diffused departmental structures and their consequently fragmented programs. It was also alluring because it seemed to promise cost reduction and more efficient operation.[36] Smaller agencies that had functioned as independent fiefdoms, would, under the Nixon plan, have passed under a larger command powerful enough to evoke allegiance to broad departmental goals. But on the other side of the coin lurks a formidable danger: in large organizations, such as Nixon contemplated, top leadership can more easily starve and suppress particular programs that fall into disfavor.

Many of Nixon's efforts at centralism by reorganization are of a piece with what students of political science and public administration have long been urging. Others are the climax of trends that commenced under Eisenhower and persisted with Kennedy and Johnson. In theory, democracy, to be fulfilled, requires the election of political officers, such as the President, who run on platforms containing program pledges and who are faithfully supported by the tenured bureaucracy. At least to some degree, the President must be able to direct and control the bureaucracy if he is to accomplish the goals promised in his election campaign and on which the voters expressed approval. Historically, the presidency is replete with incumbents' complaints of the bureaucracy's ability to resist and frustrate the Chief Executive. A succession of Presidents have endeavored to make the bureaucracy more responsive, and Nixon's performance illuminates the dangers lurking in that objective.

Against the centralized presidency that Nixon and other Presidents have dreamed of and striven for, several objections must be raised. His plans would consolidate power not merely in the President's hands but in the grasp of an elitist corps, the White House staff and the Executive Office of the President, the members of which are appointed with little public scrutiny and who function in a veiled domain removed from review by Congress and beyond the normal vision of the press. Hardly a picture of robust democracy. Moreover, the men in the White House and Executive Office, as Nixon's centralism illuminates, may possess extraordinary similarity of social background, previous employment, and outlook—a concentration of attributes that hardly accords with the variety of American society. In contrast, the untidy departments, with their breadth of functions and wide recruitment of personnel, offer diversity, valuable, if not indispensable, for democracy. Department leaders are subject to scrutiny by Congress and the news media, and the lesser departmental echelons include a polyglot of program advocates and professionals, skilled politicians, transplanted academicians, pressure group axe-grinders, and innovators—a mélange surely not found in the White House, but which articulates, better than the narrowly based White House staff, the interests and aspirations of much of society.

## Carter: The Outsider as Manager

A major reliance of Jimmy Carter for establishing his credentials as "outsider" was the image, sedulously cultivated in the 1976 campaign, of the experienced public manager who, having realigned and scrubbed a once wasteful, scraggly government in Georgia, meant to apply the same redeeming treatment to the "bureaucratic mess" in Washington. An engineer by training and a self-made millionaire businessman, Carter offered the electorate not new domestic programs or claimed mastery of the intricacies of foreign affairs. Instead, he was committed to apply to the costly, faltering federal government his dedication and talent for effecting order and economy.

In his campaign and after becoming President, Carter persisted in depreciating the federal bureaucracy. In talks to groups visiting the White House, the President dwelt upon "the horrible federal bureaucracy" and made much ado about a chart depicting how an average of nineteen months was required to fire a substandard employee. Even after he was well into his administration and had effected important management changes, Carter vowed to audiences of his 1980 campaign to weed out "duds" and "maligners," conveying the unmistakable message that bureaucrats must either work harder or be discharged.[37]

Soon after taking office in 1977, Carter moved idealistically to decentralize power to the departments individually and to the cabinet collectively, at the expense of the White House staff still tinged with the scandal of Watergate, while retaining final decision-making authority in the Oval Office.

Carter was reportedly influenced by political scientist Stephen Hess's study, *Organizing the Presidency*, which contends that a President errs if he strives to establish himself as general manager of the executive branch.[38] Rather, he should function as the administration's chief political officer, since his foremost tasks are political decisions arising in different contexts— preparing the budget, developing a legislative program, choosing national security strategies. Department heads, Hess argues, should perform the principal tasks of administration, each in his own jurisdiction. The cabinet would take on a new vitality, providing the President opportunity to set the overall direction and tone of the government. The cabinet experience would enable the department secretaries to become primary spokesmen for the administration, and it would provide a focal point for White House staff operations. An approximation of Hess's plan was applied with marked success by President Eisenhower. For Jimmy Carter, unfortunately, the results were less gratifying.

Quickly he was confronted with a multitude of semiautonomous bureaucratic fiefdoms, competing and quarrelling fiercely among themselves and speaking self-interestedly in a cacophony of voices to the public. Carter soon discovered that making policy in such turmoil is like trying to negotiate a new constitution with today's proud, individualistic provinces of Canada.[39] A major factor in the contrasting experiences of Eisenhower and Carter is the bureaucracy's enormous growth in function and expenditure. Noting how Carter had to deal with many more power centers than those of the 1960s, Joseph Califano, a principal White House aide in the Johnson years and former HEW Secretary in the Carter administration, concluded: "Interest groups and Congress now get into the act very early. They've become more sophisticated."[40]

In prior administrations, subcabinet posts have sometimes been reserved for appointees with management skills. A similar allocation failed to materialize in the Carter administration, despite the emphasis in the 1976 campaign on management improvement. The posts of deputy secretary, under secretary, and assistant secretary were not conferred upon those with managerial experience or expertise. Instead they were filled in answer to a new kind of patronage—representation of the groups, blocs, and movements that form the new nonparty basis of electoral coalitions. Women, blacks, Hispanics were allotted posts by a roughly calculated quota system, together with leaders drawn from the environmental and consumer movements, and even from the peace movement of the Vietnam war. Characteristically, these appointees were zealots about policy and policy-making, with little appetite and fewer credentials for the tasks of management.[41]

Presumably, Carter as reformist manager needed help, and it came most logically from the White House staff and the Executive Office of the President. Early on, he tightened those structures to further his managerial and policy-making tasks. What was termed a new "policy staff management system" in domestic policy was instituted when a Domestic Policy Staff was structured to function in ways emulating the policy-development staff of the National Security Council (NSC). The Domestic Policy Staff adopted the NSC's "Presidential Review Memorandum System" (PRM) as a means of studying problems and developing policy solutions.[42] The PRM process drew upon the policy research and recommendations of the departments and agencies, and enabled the President to approve the composition, objectives, and deadlines of interagency groups, whose basic task was to formulate options for the President in "priority areas." The Domestic Policy Staff coordinated the groups.

But gadgetry like the PRMs had limited utility for Carter. A far more formidable testing awaited his selection of personnel to occupy the key posts of his White House and Executive Office staffs. Appealing to voters as one who has not been defiled by experience and contact with the abysmal Washington establishment, Carter could hardly load his staff with old hands from that repudiated source. Instead, he filled his key White House posts with the staff of his Georgia governorship. Thoroughly innocent in the ways of the national capital, they too qualified as outsiders.

The general lack of experienced Washingtonians committed the Carter administration to two years and more of costly on-the-job training. Top leaders in the executive branch suffered a diminished capacity to anticipate problems, to set priorities, to develop strategies and programs on a broad scale in order to coordinate agencies, and, generally, to get things done.[43] These lapses contributed mightily to a public perception of the administration as ineffectual, which cost Carter dearly in the public opinion polls.

As Carter's presidency unfolded, the meaning and dimensions of his emphasis on "management" became more clear. He laid out few new programs; his favorite exhortation was the improved management of government's existing commitments. He resorted to innovative managerial gadgetry such as zero-base budgeting (ZBB)* but its consequences for improved management seemed infinitesimal, with little impact evident on the size or character of the federal budget. The 1979 budget, the first prepared completely under ZBB, was a virtual carbon copy of the preceding budget. Carter's managerial aspirations ran afoul of budgeting's political realities, with 75 percent of its expenditures uncontrollable or beyond the President's

---

*Under zero-base budgeting, the department or agency must justify not only new expenditures, it must also rejustify each year all current expenditures.

reach and only 25 percent, at most, touchable by the budgetary process. Carter quickly displayed awareness of the political handwriting on the budgetary wall that to cut that segment of expenditure would offend constituencies whose votes had elected him.[44]

A milestone achievement whose discussion reaches back to the era of Franklin Roosevelt replaced the Civil Service Commission with two new organizations: the Office of Personnel Management and the Merit Systems Protection Board. Potentially important was the creation of a Senior Executive Service for about 9,000 upper-level civil servants. The Service provides agency managers with greater flexibility in reassigning executive personnel and opportunity to build their own "management teams." Annual pay increases for service executives are based on "productivity," and special bonuses are awarded to highly productive performers.

In contrast to Carter's lofty promises, the modest accomplishment of the reorganization venture is explicable in terms of several historical truths, which his experience reaffirmed. Agency reorganization is a political hotbed of jealousies and jurisdictional conflicts. Congressional committees presented a towering resistance: the Government Operations Committee in both houses and the authorizing committees habitually take umbrage at seeing "their" agencies dismantled or reshaped. Time and again the threat of a veto materializing from an aroused committee or its incensed chairman stopped a reorganization proposal dead in its tracks.

As his term wore on, with his position in the public opinion polls dropping to abysmal lows and with the 1980 elections looming, Carter undertook a review and restructuring of his administration at its top levels to salvage his floundering presidency. In a series of extraordinary conferences at Camp David in 1979 with selected aides, governors, and phalanxes of distinguished citizens, Carter launched an unprecedented reshuffling of his administration. Discordant cabinet secretaries were ejected and replaced with others perceived with a good potential for teamplay.[45]

Like Carter, Reagan commenced his presidency dedicated to bringing back "cabinet government." Reagan proposed to do most of his policy-making with an inner circle of cabinet members, coordinated by a top-level counselor of cabinet rank, Edwin Meese III. Reagan expected the department Secretaries to counsel on policy issues from the standpoint of the President's perspectives and interests. But this is a mental leap that few Secretaries can take. The Secretary is primarily a partisan for his department, and if he falters in promoting its interests, woe betide him. His department's bureaus and clients will soon write him off as a weakling, and advance their purposes by other means. Reagan's best prospects for bringing his cabinet theory to fruitful result requires his cultivation of his secretaries' understanding that they cannot count on the President's lobbying support unless they, in turn, put their shoulders to the wheels of the administration's direction and priorities.

# Presidential Staffing: Trends and Problems

In the nearly half century since Franklin Roosevelt revolutionized presidential staffing, the outline of its patterns and trends are clearly visible. Much of the staffing as it has developed has followed the familiar guideposts of bureaucratization: what begins as personal staffs—for national security, press relations, congressional affairs, for example—becomes institutionalized. Jurisdictions, once blurred and overlapping, become clarified and delineated. Tasks once handled by generalists are committed to specialists. Senior advisers and assistants require buttressing by a cadre of junior assistants. Where once the President saw all or most of his small family of assistants personally and daily, he later sees only a select few. Formalization, routinization, records, files, meetings—the standard paraphernalia of bureaucracy—have overtaken the presidency and implanted a presidential bureaucracy. The bureaucracy develops its own interests, dissimilar to the President's, and its jurisdictions and procedures reduce his impact. Also important has been the continuously ascending influence of the presidential staff at the expense of the Chief Executive's most traditional helpers, the department secretaries and the cabinet. Presidents have tried valiantly to reduce the numbers and influence of the White House staff, but their efforts have been no more availing than King Canute commanding the incoming tide to recede.

In presidential staffing, the trends are also the problems, threatening and elusive, and among the principal of these are the following:

*Problem 1*  The President can, to large degree, withdraw from the real world and its jangle of quarrels and pressures, into his own self-made euphoric enclosure. He can see fewer visitors and only those of his staff who can be depended on to apply an adulatory gloss to all his works.[46] Nixon provides the most extreme example of withdrawal, and Johnson saw fewer people and tolerated less criticism as the Vietnam war deteriorated.

In presidential practice, several antidotes are available for these threatening symptoms. The best medicine is to choose as President in the first place a personality less inclined to withdrawal, a Gerald Ford, for example, a model of openness and accessibility, both to his own staff, the cabinet, and to visitors from outside the government. Many more aides regularly saw Ford than Nixon, and decision-making was far more broadly based. "Ford sees everyone in sight," observed a Nixon holdover. Ford also revived the organs of collective advice, the cabinet and the National Security Council, which Nixon had largely let lapse. Exposure to collegial interaction and counsel reduces presidential isolation.

*Problem 2*  Crucial to the White House operation is the President's attitude toward his staff. His demeanor may reduce them to groveling sycophants or elevate them as conduits of candor, wisdom, reasoned discussion. Since the presidency is a heady place, its incumbent succumbs easily to arrogance and his readiest victims are his immediate staff. Nixon and Johnson again were prime offenders, both lacking in personal security, infected by the plague of arrogance, creating an intellectually stultifying atmosphere at times in their immediate circle. Reports are common of Johnson bullying and humiliating his staff and demanding total commitment of time and loyalty. Those who challenged his Vietnam policy lost their access or were let go. An aide who brought disquieting information to Nixon suffered unnerving consequences: "For three solid months I did not receive a speech assignment from the President, or a phone call, or a memo, or a nod in the hall as he was passing by."[47]

Here too the faults of presidential personality seem to suffocate all possible solutions. Something is gained if such a President has staff with the status conferred by previous political experience and officeholding, who have a place to go if they are ejected from the White House, such as a resumed career in the law or journalism. Aides with ties to interest groups, collective forums—the cabinet, staff working groups, task forces of insiders and outsiders—may serve as props and pressures to lure the President away from arrogance and into the rational conduct his office requires.

*Problem 3*    The reverse side of presidential arrogance is staff obsequiousness, the staff that fawns on the President, blinks away harsh realities and reports only good news. Even a President whose personality is relatively even-keeled may have trouble inducing his staff to speak with candor. Robert Kennedy noted that the office has "an almost cowering effect on men."[48] A Nixon aide acknowledged, "During the time I served in the White House, I rarely questioned a presidential order. Infrequently did I question the President's judgment. I had one rule—to get done that which the President wanted done."[49]

Fortunate is the President who has on his staff a Louis Howe, a shrewd soldier in the service of Franklin Roosevelt's political fortunes for nearly a quarter century, who could bring the optimistic Roosevelt to see occasionally the darker side of issues, and was his only aide whose candor stretched to the point where, confronted by a presidential note, he could snort, "Tell the President to go to hell." A likely route to a role of plain-speaking to the President is for the adviser or assistant to gain sufficient status in the President's eyes (as Howe did with Roosevelt and Kissinger with Nixon) to awaken presidential tolerance. Also important is the assistant's skill and sensitivity in perceiving the personal realities of the President. Nixon, for example, was given to issuing "not appealable" orders, a favorite phrase, but Kissinger and others who grew to know him discerned that the expression denoted uncertainty. For astute assistants, it was a signal to accelerate rather than slow down appeals.[50]

*Problem 4*    Power has gravitated excessively from the departments and the cabinet to the presidential staff. Repeatedly the departments have been undercut, their access to the President reduced, and even their operating responsibilities taken over by White House aides. The expertise and information resources of the departments are squandered and their greater objectivity is superseded by White House aides living and breathing the subjectivity of the President's personal and political interests.

Both Ford and Carter sought surcease from the problem, with Ford the more successful. He retrieved the cabinet from its fate of abject neglect under Nixon by establishing monthly cabinet meetings. He encouraged individual cabinet members to meet with him privately and used cabinet meetings seriously to review issues cutting across departmental lines. But the road remained rocky, with the President firing one member; another resigned on principle, while still another, Earl Butz, had to resign after embarrassing the administration by privately telling racist and ethnic jokes that were later publicly revealed.

Again, presidential attitude is the key. The cabinet member's most unwelcome plight is lack of access to the President. "Nobody ever screens out a cabinet member," observed Richard Cheyney, Ford's chief of staff.[51] The best leverage for capturing the President's attention is exercised by department heads whose missions most impinge on the President's own priorities and concerns—chiefly State, Defense, an economic department such as Treasury, and Justice with its preoccupation with law enforcement. These Secretaries have better opportunities for close, productive ties; others may gain temporary importance when problems of crisis proportions emerge. Many cabinet members have been victims of neglect because of the President's constant and sometimes excessive preoccupation with foreign affairs. But the intrusion of economic problems like inflation, unemployment, and energy may force the President into more involving relationships with more department leaders.

# ★ ★ ★ The Future Presidency ★ ★ ★

The activist President, intent upon extracting as much mileage as possible from his resources as general manager, must plainly commit great quantities of his own personal energy and talent fully to the task. The presidency is no place for semiretirement. The President does best with a small cadre of assistants, with flexible assignments and responsibilities of both action-forcing and program-building nature. Yet he must be watchful that his immediate staff does not, intentionally or no, exercise its enlarging authority for its own purposes rather than his, and, even worse, for antidemocratic activity of the Watergate genre. The competitive principle of advice and action has been successfully used by activist Presidents since the days of Washington. It is the surest means yet devised for extending their influence and control and for inducing behavior consonant with democracy.

But no contemporary President can live by personal assistants alone. He must make large use of the presidency's institutions such as the Office of Management and Budget, the NSC, the CEA. Given the enormity of his problems and the dangers of the times he can no longer reign with the informal splendor of a Franklin Roosevelt of the 1930s. The institutionalized presidency is the best available guarantee that the multiple specializations a major problem requires will be addressed to that problem. With an independent power base and more security of tenure than the personal staff, and with superior professional knowledge and analytical skill, the institutions are better able to warn the President of impending decisions that will produce faulty policy, or are not well honed to democratic and ethical criteria.

In the Nixon era, the personal staff, the White House office, came under increasing attack on grounds of efficiency and democracy, and in Carter's time for its inadequate workmanship in developing policy. The staff is excessively powerful, removed from even the minimum accountability required by democratic standards. Secretive, aloof from Congressional inquiry, distant from the electoral process, and frequently beset by presidential cronyism, the staff functions with an autonomy that flaunts the pretensions of democratic governent. And, as experience discloses, the staff can lapse into corruption, criminality, and gross errors of policy. It can misinform and mislead the President and as Watergate reveals, can seriously—if not irreparably—cripple his administration. For the sake of democracy and efficiency, what safeguards are in order to ward off the disaster of a misguided, overweening White House staff?

1.  The President must strike a balance between an "open door" and "closed door" stance toward his staff. If he employs a chief of staff, an Adams, a Haldeman, or a Jordan, he should restrict such types to facilitative administration—to monitoring, but not unduly diminishing, the flow of visitors and paperwork, while simultaneously according direct access to other staff who represent diverse approaches to policy issues. Above all, the President must not become overcommitted to the chief-of-staff concept. If he does, he will see too few people and hear an insufficient variety of interests and viewpoints. He should remain directly accessible to department heads, key bureau chiefs, the heads of his institutional staffs, and such central figures of his personal staff as his special counsel, appointments secretary, and policy aides, as well as a diversity of legislators, party figures, and interest group representatives. The inability of Secretary of State Cyrus Vance, in the final weeks of his tenure, to see President Carter clearly violates this standard.

2.  The President can function with better regard for democracy and efficiency if he builds links with a wide gamut of interest and opinion in American life. He must be in touch with not only the corporations and labor unions but with the professions, the city and state governments, minorities, youth and the elderly, with those on welfare, and with other disadvantaged groups. In a word, presidential decision-making should reflect the pluralism of society in order to foster the representative and participating phases of democracy and rational efficiency.

    In many ways, President Johnson sought to advance this concept by perceiving presidential administration as a consensus process and by setting priorities and fashioning key policies through consultation with multiple sectors of opinion. In Johnson's view, legitimate sources of counsel were not limited to the White House staff or government in general, but extended to the business executive, the labor leader, the universities, to spokesmen for minority groups, and of course to Congress.

    The President-group relationship can also be structured and regularized by extending processes flourishing in recent presidencies. The task force device lends itself well to pluralism in presidential counsel. It can be used to study and report on a full range of presidential subjects, and its membership can constitute a representative cross-section of concerned interests, both among groups and in Congress. Consultation could occur at more or less regularized intervals, in the sense that recent Presidents, or their representatives, have met with the Business Council, a body of corporation leaders, or the annual civil rights conference that flourished in the Kennedy-Johnson era, the conferences on nutrition of the early Nixon years, and Ford's summit meetings on the economy, and the task force of Carter's principal economic aides and congressional leaders who received the federal budget in the twin storms of inflation and recession in 1980. Admittedly, meetings, particularly those with private groups, become manipulated and desultory, but whatever their faults, they will expose the President and the presidency to a variety of opinion, as befits democracy, and spare the office from intolerable insulation and overresponsiveness to narrow, usually well-heeled interests.

3. Key White House staff members such as a chief of staff and top assistants for national security and domestic affairs ought, if they engage in operations, to be subject to at least a minimum of democratic control external to the presidency itself. Since they exercise enormous power over national policy, their appointments warrant Senate confirmation. The Senate's review of their qualifications might stress several ingredients highly germane to democracy and efficiency. Above all, the quality of democratic socialization of the prospective appointees should be probed: how well they comprehend democratic values and processes as evidenced by their past behavior. A distressing aspect of the Watergate investigations was the obtuseness of a lengthy parade of presidential assistants to the nature and imperatives of democratic deportment. If conspicuous gaps appear in the democratic socialization of any nominees, they should be rejected, since their inadequacy is then self-evident. Likewise, the known offenses of Ehrlichman and Haldeman in Nixon's pre-presidential political campaigns should have been assessed in a Senate review, and should have disqualified them for White House service.

Many of the Carter staff provide a case history of the unfortunate truth that those who are skilled in winning elections are not necessarily competent in the art of governing. The high cost of their on-the-job training, the repeated stumbling of slow learners, produce a needless burden for the President and the country.

Senate confirmation would constitute a pressure on the Chief Executive to nominate individuals with a more rounded sophistication in politics and more skill in governing than merely that derived from service in campaigns as advance men. Broader political and governmental experience is apt to produce a better understanding of democratic processes and the demands of office-holding than a life history lacking that exposure.

4. To avoid possible future lapses of the presidential staff into the antidemocratic excesses of Watergate, it might be salutary to establish a permanent commission on democratic government. The commission has several analogues, including the commission on civil rights, created by the first modern civil rights legislation in 1957, charged with pointing out flaws in civil rights administration and ways to improvement, and the British Royal Commission of Inquiry, composed of distinguished

persons, who study major issues and draft authoritative reports that lead to legislation and administrative action.

A commission on democratic government would constitute a permanent inquiry into trends and developments affecting the health and prospects of democracy. The presidency and the White House staff would be included in its ambit. The commission would be empowered to conduct studies, take testimony, and make public reports that would stress both positive and negative features of current developments.

Ideally, the commission, in the manner of its British prototype, should be composed of citizens who have gained eminence in a profession or calling, including previous public service, and who are not currently engaged in nor envision a further political career. Father Theodore Hesburgh, president of Notre Dame, former chairman of the civil rights commission, typifies a suitable member. One third of the proposed commission might be appointed by the President, one-third by the Speaker of the House, and one-third by the president pro tempore of the Senate, as the two Hoover Commissions were, with a substantial tenure of at least six years. The prestige of the members and the importance of their business would command attention from the news media, and the desire to avoid its criticism would induce the President and his staff to shun even a shred of the transgressions against democracy committed in the Watergate era.

# Chapter Nine

# Chief Diplomat

I make American foreign policy," said Harry S Truman, discoursing on his office one day to a visiting body of Jewish War Veterans.[1] Truman's candid dictum finds support in the pronouncement of another Chief Executive, Thomas Jefferson, who once termed the conduct of foreign affairs "executive altogether."[2] But from no less venerable authority than James Madison comes an opposite view, that Congress determines foreign policy, by dint of its power to declare war, with the President limited to instrumental powers and circumscribed discretion.[3]

According to history, both Truman and Madison are correct; at different times both formulations of presidential power have prevailed. Frequently, the President is decidedly ascendant, initiating war and other foreign policy undertakings, with Congress largely passive and acquiescent. The interval between the Second World War and the later stages of the prolonged Indochina war was an era of presidential dominance, with Congress a lesser participant. But as the nation tired of that long-dragging war and the Watergate scandals exploded, a tainted presidency passed into a diminished, more circumscribed role, accompanied by a public mood tinged with neo-isolationism, with both public and Congress wary of foreign commitments, especially those potentially engaging the armed forces.

# Cycles of Ascendance

Ascendance in foreign policy-making has often shifted between Congress and the President. The Spanish-American War was a congressional war, promoted by legislators and reluctantly acquiesced in by a peace-minded President, William McKinley. Theodore Roosevelt and Woodrow Wilson were sterling activists, although the Senate rebuffed Wilson seeking his crowning achievement, American membership in the League of Nations. Between the two world wars, Congress dominated foreign policy-making, reflecting a public mood weary of international entanglements and seeking respite in isolationism. In the Second World War, in the Korean war, and in the early and middle periods of the Vietnam war, the presidency thrived, while in Vietnam's later stages, Congress resurged, and it has continued to do so in the era following the conclusion of the war.

Clearly a cycle or rhythm is present in foreign policy-making, fluctuating between presidential and congressional ascendance. Each branch has a large capacity for self-assertion. At particular moments—soon after the Second World War, for example, when the Cold War flourished—the President is more powerful in foreign affairs than any other executive in the world. Simultaneously, his competitor, Congress, is more powerful than any other modern legislative body. The cycle's dynamic springs from the circumstance that power is shared between the executive and Congress, but the precise patterns of sharing are tentative and unclear, and after nearly two centuries of constitutional practice they remain puzzling and largely unpredictable. Also contributing to the erratic swings of power are shifts in public mood from high ideals and willingness to sustain heavy burdens, to disillusionment and resignation, occurring when foreign policy falters, and the country resorts to withdrawal and isolation.

# The Two Presidencies

## The Autonomous Presidency

In the march of historic experience, two presidencies are visible in foreign affairs. Although both have parallel powers and functions, they are radically opposite in nature. One especially apparent in moments of high presidential ascendance possesses a maximum autonomy, in which the President in relative privacy can make decisions that choose between war and peace, that commit treasure and lives, and that may determine the nation's foremost priorities for years to come. The President may take these decisions in secrecy and freedom, beyond the reach and even the knowledge of Congress and the people. Or, if Congress or the people are related to the decision, they can act only marginally. They have no real choice but to ratify what the President has done or will do. It is this presidency that has grown by leaps and bounds in the nuclear age. It is this presidency in which the largest decisions in foreign affairs repose, an invitation to coin the maxim that the larger the issue the more freedom the President has to act upon it. This is the presidency that allowed Truman to order the use of the atomic bomb against Japan and to make his choice risking only the private criticism of a limited circle of counselors. This is the presidency that can act on an instant's notice, that could respond to the outbreak in Korea in 1950, that could launch an indirect invasion of Cuba in 1961, and that could send an ever-increasing force to Vietnam.

Without doubt the worst assaults upon democratic norms were the secret B-52 bomber raids in Cambodia, commencing in 1969, which were not disclosed publicly until 1973 when a congressional investigation uncovered them. While more than three thousand raids were flown in 1969 and 1970, White House and State Department spokesmen declared repeatedly that American policy respected Cambodian neutrality.[4] To preserve the secrecy of the raids, the Defense Department sent falsified reports to the Senate Armed Services Committee.[5] Even more, when the press disclosed in 1969 that the raids were occurring, at least seventeen wiretaps were imposed on civil servants and journalists, many directly authorized by President Nixon and concurred in by his national security assistant, Henry Kissinger. These acts were, at least in part, but the culmination of long-building trends of secrecy and deviousness of the presidencies of the 1960s.

## The Interacting, Dependent Presidency

The other presidency in foreign affairs is marked by its interaction with and dependence upon Congress and upon public opinion. Instead of operating with autonomy, its method and emphasis are cooperation and accommodation. It fits the democratic image of the powerful, responsible executive whose decisions are open to external view and debate. This presidency is especially evident when the Chief Executive requires congressional support to carry out a foreign policy the President proclaims, such as appropriations or new laws, to administer a foreign aid law that he has proposed. It is also evident in intervals of congressional ascendance. Undertakings like the Monroe Doctrine, which aimed to bar European intervention in the Western Hemisphere, and the Marshall Plan, by which the United States swiftly repaired the destruction of the Second World War and restored the economies of Western Europe, are products of presidential-congressional cooperation. But an assertive Congress can withhold support and enact restrictions upon the President's freedom to act, curbing his ability to engage the forces in combat, to render economic and military aid to friendly nations, to conduct covert intelligence. This congressional stance is particularly vivid in the post-Vietnam, post-Watergate era.

To a remarkable degree, each presidency can, action for action, discover constitutional powers and institutional resources that are counterparts of the other's. The independent presidency employs the executive agreement to commit the United States in its relations with others, freely uses special agents or personnel to carry forward the President's missions and purposes, and utilizes the Commander-in-Chief power to conduct the enterprise that might well be called presidential war-making. The "dependent," or cooperative, presidency has legal powers and institutional resources that include the treaty power, which involves Senate participation, and the executive agreement when money or other congressional support is required for its effectiveness; the appointment of ambassadors, ministers, and other officers of foreign affairs with the advice and consent of the senate; and the concrete provision of the Constitution by which war is declared by Congress. To understand the nature of the two presidencies in foreign affairs, we must look more closely at their several kinds of resources.

# Constitutional Limitations

### The Treaty Power

The Constitution, in Article II, section 2, provides that the President "shall have power, by and with the advice and consent of the Senate, to make treaties, provided two-thirds of the Senators present concur." Significantly, this language associates the President with the Senate throughout the course of treaty-making. President Washington, interpreting the Constitution literally, understandably felt obligated to secure the advice of the Senate on certain questions arising in the course of treaty negotiations with the Southern Indian tribes. But the Senate chose to respond churlishly, resolving to consider the questions privately, without the Chief Executive present. Washington, incensed by this treatment, withdrew, according to Senator William Maclay, "with sullen dignity."[6] This little set-to finished Washington, and for that matter all future Presidents, on consultations with the full Senate. Not, however, with individual Senators. Although the Executive negotiates treaties, he has deemed it wise on occasion to involve key Senators in the enterprise. Senators Tom Connally and Arthur Vandenberg were members of the United States delegation to San Francisco to construct the United Nations Charter. Negotiations of the 1963 test ban treaty were conducted in the presence of a panel of Senators. Some historians blame Wilson's League of Nations defeat on his failure to include Senators in the United States delegation to the Paris peace conference.

In practice, the Senate can approve or reject a treaty outright or impose conditions or reservations that may or may not be acceptable to the President. The two treaties committing the United States to turn over the Panama Canal to Panama each contained reservations President Carter felt compelled to accept to make the treaties viable. The Senate approved the initial treaty only after the President acquiesced to a reservation offered by Senator Dennis De Concini (D-Ariz.), asserting the right of the United States to send troops into Panama to keep the canal open. Similarly, the second treaty required a reservation disavowing any United States intention of interfering in Panama's internal affairs. Stated in cautious phrases, the reservation was designed simultaneously to soothe angry Panamanians and not offend nationalistic Senators whose votes were necessary for the treaty's passage.[7]

The constitutional requirement that two-thirds of the Senate give its advice and consent reduces the President when the outcome is doubtful (as it was for the Panama Canal treaties) to a posture of grubbing for votes and of ready vulnerability to the idiosyncrasies of individual Senators, such as De Concini's reservation. Carter was forced to remind wavering Senators urgently that his ability to conduct foreign affairs hung in the balance, a plea that gained victory by only one vote and robbed his success of much of its political impact. The two-thirds vote establishes for the President the unavoidable and sometimes difficult test of winning support from the opposition party. Wilson's failure to attract sufficient Republican backing wrecked United States membership in the League of Nations. Franklin Roosevelt, anxious to avoid the Wilsonian disaster in his quest for a United Nations organization, took elaborate precautions to win both Republican and Democratic cooperation.

## Executive Agreements

The President may choose to disregard the treaty procedure and resort to "executive agreements." These entail no senatorial review, and may stem from several types of independent presidential authority—the executive power clause or his power as Commander-in-Chief—and from statute or treaty. Executive agreements are not mentioned specifically in the Constitution. The exchange of United States destroyers for British bases in the Second World War was founded upon the Commander-in-Chief power and executive power clauses and a statute permitting the transfer of "obsolescent" military materiel. Presidents have used executive agreements for nearly every conceivable diplomatic subject: fishing rights, boundary disputes, the annexation of territory, and so on. In *United States* v. *Curtiss-Wright Corp.* (299 U.S. 304, 1936) the Supreme Court seemed to contemplate an almost limitless variety of matters for executive agreements. Yet what the President can do in law he may be unable to do in politics. Most executive agreements depend for their effectiveness upon support from Congress, which can assert itself, if it chooses. Hence, when the United States and the Soviet Union reached agreement in 1972 on a sweeping trade package, an impressive by-product of détente, the diplomatic enterprise depended upon congressional approval for granting credits and tariff concessions. Immediately, no less than seventy-six Senators served notice that they would block passage of the accords if the U.S.S.R. did not lift its oppressive exit fees on Jews and others seeking to emigrate.[8]

Repeatedly, modern Congresses have moved to limit the President's power to make executive agreements. A 1950 statute requires publication of "all international agreements other than treaties to which the United States is a party," and the Case Act of 1972 requires transmittal of all executive agreements to Congress and provides for submission of secret agreements to the Senate Foreign Affairs Committee and the House International Relations Committee, which supposedly keep them confidential.

Reflecting the post-Vietnam, post-Watergate revulsion against executive power and the spirit of assertiveness burgeoning on Capitol Hill, legislation was introduced in 1975 to limit presidential authority to enter into agreements by giving Congress sixty days to reject them before they became effective. By throwing himself unstintingly into the fight, President Ford staved off this potential disrupter of executive management of foreign affairs. The legislation, as Ford contended, would paralyze the President's negotiating ability, instill uncertainty into the foreign offices of other nations, risk the undoing of sensitive compromises during the sixty-day waiting period, and above all, it would violate the President's historic constitutional powers.[9]

## Diplomatic Appointments

The President, the Constitution says, "shall nominate, and by and with the advice and consent of the Senate, shall appoint ambassadors, other public ministers and consuls. . . ." Ordinarily, the Senate raises no objections to the President's nominees for diplomatic posts, but trouble is by no means unknown, and President Eisenhower drew a full draught of it early in his term when he nominated Charles E. Bohlen as ambassador to the Soviet Union. A leading expert on the U.S.S.R., Bohlen numbered among his experiences service as Franklin Roosevelt's Russian language interpreter and adviser on Russian affairs at the Yalta conference.

Bohlen's presence there made him a renegade in the eyes of many Republican Senators, who felt that excessive concessions had been made to the Soviet Union. His prospects did not improve when he testified to the Senate Foreign Relations Committee that he saw nothing wrong with the Yalta agreements. Senators Joseph McCarthy and Pat McCarran questioned Bohlen's loyalty, compelling Eisenhower to come out strongly for Bohlen in a press conference. Senator Robert A. Taft, the Republican leader, backed up the President, and the Bohlen nomination finally prevailed. Mopping his brow, Taft got word to Eisenhower that he did not want to carry any more Bohlens through the Senate.[10]

## Diplomatic Recognition

The Constitution empowers the President to receive the diplomatic representatives of other nations. The power to receive or exchange ambassadors enables the President to recognize new governments without consulting Congress. Congress, however, can pass resolutions expressing its wishes and intent, as well as providing or withholding appropriations. Normally, the President alone grants or terminates diplomatic recognition. Building on Nixon's initiative of establishing limited relationships with Communist China, short of formal recognition, Carter recognized the People's Republic of China (Communist China) "as the sole legal government of China." Simultaneously, he terminated diplomatic relations and a mutual defense treaty with Taiwan, the Nationalist government of China and acknowledged that "there is but one China and Taiwan is part of China."[11]

# Presidential War-making

Although the Constitution vests in Congress the power to declare war, the United States has declared war in only five of its eleven major conflicts with other countries. In each of the five instances, Congress declared war only in response to the President's acts or recommendations.[12] The five declared wars were the War of 1812, the Mexican War, the Spanish-American War, and the two world wars. A declaration of war was neither made by Congress nor requested by the President in the naval war with France (1798–1800), the first Barbary War (1801–05), the second Barbary War (1815), the Mexican-American clashes (1914–17), and the Korean and Vietnam conflicts. Presidents, evidently, have tended to apply to the fullest limits the view of Alexander Hamilton that the Constitution intends "that it is the peculiar and exclusive province of Congress, when the nation is at peace, to change that state into a state of war"; but "when a foreign nation declares or openly and avowedly makes war upon the United States, they are then by the very fact already at war and any declaration on the part of Congress is nugatory; it is at least unnecessary."[13]

The President claims authority for involvement in violence or potential violence as Commander-in-Chief, as custodian of the executive power, and, on certain occasions since the Second World War, under Article XLIII of the United Nations Charter. Sometimes Congress prods the President to exercise his initiative. Within a period of two weeks in 1962, for instance, the House of Representatives adopted resolutions expressing determination to use all means, including force, to defend United States rights in Berlin, about which a crisis was stirring, although the wall had gone up some months before; a similar resolution was adopted for the Cuban missile crisis.

President Eisenhower introduced a novel variation to presidential war-making when in 1955 he initiated and Congress approved a resolution authorizing the President "to employ the Armed Forces of the United States as he deems necessary for the specific purpose of securing and protecting Formosa and the Pescadores against armed attack." Communist China had been engaging in some menacing activity directed at those off-shore areas. In his request, Eisenhower was careful to say that "the authority for some of the actions which might be required would be inherent in the authority of the Commander-in-Chief."[14] He believed that by associating Congress with his effort, his declaration of his readiness to fight for Formosa would have greater impact on Peking. Furthermore, Eisenhower did not want to repeat what he considered Truman's mistake in sending forces into Korea without consulting Congress. When, eventually, the Korean conflict became politically unpopular, President Truman took the brunt. Eisenhower invited Congress to share any similar liability in a drawn-out Formosan struggle. The technique of the Formosa resolution was renewed in the 1956 Middle Eastern crisis. Eisenhower again brought Congress to authorize the President to resist "overt armed aggression" by "any nation controlled by international Communism" in the "general area" of the Middle East.[15]

## The Indochina War

A similar resolution, which subsequently became the subject of bitter controversy, was adopted in 1964 following a reported attack on two United States destroyers by North Vietnamese PT boats in the Gulf of Tonkin. The resolution, which Congress passed with only two dissenting votes, was couched in sweeping language. It authorized the President to take "all necessary measures" to "repel any armed attack" against United States forces and "to prevent further aggression." As the Vietnam war escalated, critics, including members of the Senate Foreign Relations Committee, contended that the President had exceeded the intent of the resolution, that he used the resolution to dispatch ground forces to Vietnam and to order bombing attacks upon North Vietnam, including territory close to the border of Communist China—actions that were uncontemplated when the resolution was passed. The response to a minor incident was used to undergird a major war. Nor was friction diminished when many legislators subsequently became convinced that the incident in the Tonkin Gulf had not been fully reported by the President and the executive branch, that American and South Vietnamese provocations had instigated the Communist attack.[16] Eventually, as division over the protracted war mounted, Congress repealed the resolution.

The phenomenon of independent presidential war-making continued to blossom as the Indochina war waxed on. Beginning in 1969, secret American air raids were conducted over Cambodia. In 1970, Nixon dispatched U.S. ground forces into neutral Cambodia to destroy supply centers and staging areas for North Vietnam's operations in South Vietnam. In 1972, the President ordered, again on his own, the mining of North Vietnamese ports to forestall the flow of arms to South Vietnam, a decision that risked incidents involving Russian and Chinese supply vessels in the harbors and confrontations with those powers.[17]

When, in 1973, North Vietnam dallied in concluding a truce, the President ordered carpet-bombing of Hanoi and Haiphong, again without consulting Congress. But eventually North Vietnam returned to the negotiating table and a truce was concluded. The truce and its terms were wholly the enterprise of the President and his aides, without significant consultation of Congress. Subsequently, American forces withdrew from Vietnam, and North Vietnam, casting its commitments under the truce to the winds, overran all of South Vietnam.

The claimed authority for conducting and terminating the Indochina war was the President's power as Commander-in-Chief, his investiture with the executive power and, as is therefore implied, with the military power ordinarily possessed by heads of government. Historic practice was also cited— Jefferson sending naval frigates to fight the Tripolitan pirates, McKinley dispatching troops to China to subdue the Boxer Rebellion, Roosevelt ordering the Navy to fire "on sight" at Axis naval craft, Kennedy throwing a naval blockade around Cuba.

But as a practical matter, so lengthy and costly a war as the Indochina conflict could not have been waged by the President alone, no matter how expansive were his claims to independent power. Over its long years, the war could not be sustained without positive acts of congressional cooperation, and, throughout the war, these were amply forthcoming. The Senate approved the SEATO treaty, providing commitment and structure for American military support of the Southeast Asian region. Congress overwhelmingly approved the Tonkin resolution, a step for which, despite any possible executive legerdemain, it must shoulder responsibility. Most important of all, the engines of war required vast and repeated infusions of money, which only Congress could and did supply. Over the drawn-out course of the war, and until its final stages, Congress provided funding unstintingly and without reservation. In a war whose duration traversed five presidencies, Congress attached no serious qualification to its own cooperation until the late date of 1973, when it specified that its appropriations were not to support American ground combat in Laos. Thanks to its appropriations power, Congress could review annually its commitment to the Indochina war, and its decision was almost invariably a reaffirmation.

## The War Powers Resolution of 1973

Congress's most significant challenge to presidential authority is the War Powers Resolution, passed in 1973 during Nixon's political enfeeblement from Watergate. As its sponsor, Senator Jacob K. Javits (R-N.Y.), pointed out, the act is a towering reminder of congressional rejection of the little-inhibited exercise of presidential power represented by the Indochina war.[18] Under the Resolution, the President can undertake emergency military action in the absence of a declaration of war, but within forty-eight hours after committing the armed forces to combat abroad he must report the event to Congress in writing. The President "in every possible instance" shall consult with Congress before introducing armed forces into combat, or into situations where their involvement in hostilities is likely. The combat action must end in sixty days, unless Congress authorizes the commitment. But this deadline could be extended for thirty days if the President certified the extension's necessity for the forces' safe withdrawal. Most important, at any time within the sixty-day or ninety-day period, Congress could order an immediate removal of the forces by adopting a concurrent resolution, which is not subject to presidential veto.

Is this law to be hailed as a useful containment of presidential power? Certainly it well reminds the Chief Executive of the congressional presence as a sharer in decisions of war, and it is a constructive effort to adapt Congress's war-declaring power, fashioned in the eighteenth century, to the swift tempo of today's affairs. For delicate international security emergencies of the future, however, it provides cumbersome procedures that could become snarled in congressional delays and deadlock between the houses. Decision-making will become less assured and American intentions less clear. Since foreign affairs crises often arise from obscure communications and misreadings of intent, the new law could add immeasurably to these maladies.

The War Powers Resolution bears seeds of future constitutional crisis. Passed in an hour when an incumbent President was drained of political effectuality, the law is unlikely to be accepted with equanimity in future, more normal presidencies. The law's constitutionality is dubious, and it is unclear that the courts could effectively intervene to decide the controversies it might engender, which would then be left to wrangling between the branches, most likely in time of crisis. Precisely how Congress, as a practical matter, could reverse presidential commitment of the armed forces strains one's imagination. Worst of all, despite the appearance of limiting the President, the law may actually enlarge the Executive's war-making capacity to extremes that even the most bellicose Presidents would never dream of. For the War Powers Resolution can be read as a blank-check empowerment of the Chief Executive to fight anywhere, for whatever cause, subject only to a sixty- to ninety-day time-limit, indefinitely renewable. With ample cause, after making this reflection, Senator Thomas F. Eagleton (D-Mo.) exclaimed to his Senate colleagues, "How short can memories be? My God, we just got out of a nightmare."[19]

## Presidential War-making Since Vietnam

The first major testing of the Resolution transpired in 1975 when Cambodian Communists seized the American container ship, *Mayagüez*, and at President Ford's direction American forces, by ground and air attacks, retrieved the vessel and its crew. Subsequently, legislators criticized the President's handling of the consultations required by the War Powers Resolution, and congressional leaders complained that instead of being consulted they were merely informed of a presidential decision already taken. But a widely expressed congressional approval of his actions enabled Ford to treat the War Powers Resolution lightly.[20]

The post-Vietnam 70s were marked by insistent Soviet expansion in Africa. Pouring in armaments and advisers, the Soviet, aided by large-scale infusions of Cuban troops, sided with a Marxist faction in Angola's civil strife, while President Ford urgently appealed for funds to assist a pro-American faction. Simultaneously, he insisted that American troops would never be sent. But the Senate, professedly bent on "avoiding another Vietnam," rejected the President's request. For a time, the Ford administration assisted favored factions in Angola with military supplies from available funds.[21] Deftly waging guerilla warfare, the factions prolonged the struggle, and President Carter, determined to continue arms aid but with existing appropriations rapidly depleting, was stopped by legislation—a 1976 amendment to the Arms Export Act, sponsored by Senator Dick Clark (D-Ia.), prohibiting "any kind" of assistance to promote military operations in Angola. Although Carter complained that restrictions like the Clark amendment impaired his direction of foreign policy, he heeded advisers opposing a confrontation with Congress.[22]

Zaire became a further African testing ground when forces from Angola, including Cuban soldiery, invaded its borders. Long a loyal supporter of American policy in central Africa, Zaire pleaded for American military equipment. But Carter assumed a stance of aloof reserve. At most, he provided modest amounts of equipment, spare parts, and medical supplies, but no weapons or ammunition. Zaire's crisis, Carter declared, was an African problem best solved by Africans.

Fortunately for Zaire, more substantial help arrived from Belgium, which airlifted arms, and France transported both weapons and Moroccan combat forces to the Zairian province of Shaba where fighting raged. Scrupulously informing congressional leaders of the crisis and his moves, Carter emphasized that he would provide "only aid already authorized by Congress."[23] Zaire President Mobutu bitterly condemned Carter for having "capitulated" to the Russian-Cuban axis.

Evidently the Carter administration feared that deeper involvement would inflame Congress and public opinion. Fortunately, the assistance rendered by America's allies prevailed. Casting aside his reserve, Carter now declared that the episode of Zaire compelled him to reflect on "the ability of our government to help countries whose security is threatened."[24]

# Cooperation with Congress:
# The Post-Vietnam Presidency

When the President needs money or new authority—and for an abundance of his policies he needs one or the other, as Carter's African experiences reveal—he must forsake the independent presidency and enter into the cooperative phase of his office. Some eras, such as the initial years following the Second World War, are marked by extraordinary outputs of cooperative policy-making: Senate approval of the United Nations Charter; aid to Greece and Turkey; aid to the developing countries via Truman's Point Four program; presidential negotiation and Senate approbation of regional security treaties such as NATO; and the Marshall Plan, a vast enterprise to rebuild the nations of Europe from the destruction of the Second World War. A miracle of achievement, the Marshall Plan flourished thanks largely to sustained collaboration between the presidency and Congress.

The post-Vietnam presidency provides no cluster of major foreign policy innovations founded on interbranch cooperation comparable to the post–World War II era. Successful collaboration is confined to sporadic ventures like the Panama Canal treaties, and the continuation of long-standing activities, such as foreign aid, the military budget, the information program. In fact, powerful forces at work in the post-Vietnam presidency hobble cooperation between the branches and promote conflict. The post-Vietnam presidency is characterized by the markedly increased assertiveness and enlarged influence of Congress on foreign policy. A confluence of forces and practices nurtures this trend:

- Opposition to the Vietnam war taught legislators a lesson they are pleased to repeat in the postwar era—that foreign policy initiatives, and above all opposition to the presidential administration, once deemed politically unprofitable, are sure-fire magnets for media attention and popular recognition.

- Congress took a giant stride toward perpetuating its expanded involvement in foreign affairs by establishing its own foreign affairs bureaucracy. As the Vietnam war encountered rising criticism, Congress developed its own counter–State Department, a mini-army of young, aggressive, Washington-experienced experts intent upon making their imprint on foreign policy.

- In the Vietnam and Watergate eras, Congress forged an arsenal of weapons highly serviceable in the new age. Congress can easily and punitively limit or prohibit United States aid to other countries. As the 80s began, restrictions were imposed on twenty-six nations, including Afghanistan, for which aid was banned until its government apologized for the killing there of the American ambassador in 1978.

- Congress has access to intelligence information it could never obtain before Watergate. Intelligence agencies are required by the Hughes-Ryan amendment to report to eight congressional committees, of some two hundred members, enabling legislators to obtain sensitive information, and, when it serves their purposes, to leak it out. Where once the executive branch routinely withheld information from legislators because it was classified, accommodation now prevails.

• A strong upsurge in congressional travel abroad has occurred—in 1978, 293 legislators made a total of 505 trips abroad—and some legislators have developed a taste for negotiating directly with foreign leaders. Congressman George Hansen (R-Ida.), in a 1979 visit to Teheran, interviewed the American hostages and their captors, a sortie in freelance diplomacy distressful to the Carter administration. Carter yielded to the new order when he publicly declared support for the efforts of three Senators who visited Cambodia in 1979 to expedite aid to refugees facing imminent starvation.

• The Nelson-Bingham Act empowers Congress to invoke a legislative veto of arms sales and requires the President to report to Congress all sales exceeding $7 million, after which Congress has thirty days to veto the sale by concurrent resolution. Although no veto has yet occurred, its impending possibility has induced the President to abandon projects such as an arms sale to Somalia because of congressional opposition, and the provisions of some transactions have been altered.[25]

The new congressional assertiveness evoked complaints from the first two Presidents who lived with it. Gerald Ford declared that "Congress has put its oar in where it doesn't belong" and "encroached on the day-to-day operations of foreign policy," and Jimmy Carter complained that congressional restrictions on foreign aid precluded aid to countries seeking to escape Soviet domination. For example, congressional limitations on aid to Uganda were intended to frustrate its former dictator Idi Amin, but, following his overthrow, they handcuffed American ability to help establish a stable government there.

The expanding congressional assertiveness diminishes the President's flexibility of operations in foreign affairs, and impairs his capacity to respond swiftly to international crisis. It impedes his ability to conclude secret agreements and to launch covert operations whose deployment is sometimes necessary to safeguard the national interest. Allied diplomats in Washington chafed under the new order; Peter Jay, the British ambassador, remarked to Frank Church (D-Ida.), "Senator, do you think it's time for all of us to establish our embassies up on the Hill instead of going indirectly through the State Department?"[26]

# The Secretary of State

Given the high moment of foreign policy to their administrations' success, many Presidents have become, as the cliché goes, "their own Secretaries of State." The Roosevelts, Woodrow Wilson, and John Kennedy are rightly remembered as such. A President who is his own Secretary of State closely involves himself in major problems, sets high policy, intrudes upon routine, and engages heavily in diplomatic negotiation. He is both general commander and front-line soldier. But an activist President by no means requires a passive Secretary of State. The dynamic Theodore Roosevelt successively retained two eminent Secretaries, John Hay and Elihu Root, whose distinction increased with their tenure.

At another extreme are the Presidents who delegate freely to their Secretaries of State, as Harding did to Charles Evans Hughes and Eisenhower to John Foster Dulles. But this pattern presents difficulties for both the ideals of the strong President and democratic norms. Dulles enjoyed an unparalleled authority as policy formulator, negotiator, and chief spokesman in foreign affairs. Indeed Dulles's sweeping power brought Senator J. W. Fulbright to protest that "Secretary Dulles seemed at times to be exercising those 'delicate, plenary, and exclusive powers' which are supposed to be vested in the President." [27] Eisenhower himself contended that Dulles never made a major decision without presidential knowledge and approval. In the judgment of Sherman Adams, "Far from relieving Eisenhower of the burden of foreign problems, this unique partnership required him to spend more time in consultation with Dulles than he did with other department heads." [28] As Nixon's Secretary of State, Henry Kissinger roamed the world with an equally sweeping gift of authority from the President, matched the prodigious travels of Dulles, and brilliantly patched together an accord that halted the Middle East war of 1973, its provisions evidently harmonizing with the wishes of Nixon, who was distracted by pressures for his impeachment. Early in the Ford presidency, Kissinger continued his peripatetic global ways, with key missions to the Middle East, India, and the Soviet Union. In the Carter administration, Cyrus Vance as Secretary of State maintained a tight grip on his foreign policy role by functioning steadily as a premier negotiator. But the roof fell in on his strategy of patient diplomacy when the Soviet Union invaded Afghanistan. He quickly lost status at the White House, and when the abortive mission to rescue the American hostages in Iran was launched against his earnest warnings, he resigned.

The tension between the strong President and democratic needs can be most intense when the Secretary of State is a major political figure. The least promising appointee is one who believes the higher office should have been his. Lincoln's Secretary of State, William H. Seward, had expected to win the 1860 Republican nomination and regarded the victorious Lincoln as an upstart. Ability was now serving mediocrity. Seward in his rationalizations began thinking of the President as monarch and the Secretary of State as Prime Minister, and the train of these quaint ideas led to a memorandum entitled "Thoughts for the President's Consideration," probably the most extraordinary document ever presented to a Chief Executive by a subordinate. "We are at the end of a month's administration," it read, "and yet without a policy, domestic or foreign." Further delay will "bring scandal on the administration and danger upon the country." Seward generously offered to take on the great task of policy-building himself. Lincoln's reply, fortunately, was an unsparing squelch. "If this must be done," he said, "I must do it." [29]

Later Presidents who have brought in erstwhile political rivals as Secretaries of State have fared no better. Wilson chose for his Secretary the perennial Democratic presidential nominee, William Jennings Bryan. His stubborn pacifism and neutrality eventually collided with Wilson's drift toward involvement and its risk of war, and the nation was rocked by the Secretary's resignation.[30] Harry S. Truman appointed as his Secretary of State James F. Byrnes, his rival for the 1944 vice-presidential nomination, the route to the presidency upon Roosevelt's death. Truman indeed had nominated Byrnes for the vice presidency. After the convention made its choice, Truman wrote that "Byrnes, undoubtedly, was deeply disappointed and hurt. I thought that my calling on him at this time might help balance things up."[31] Again, the relationship did not work. A latter-day exception to this dreary pattern is Edmund Muskie, former presidential candidate, eminent figure in the Senate and the Democratic party, who quickly erased whatever political loss Carter sustained by Cyrus Vance's startling resignation.

# The President's Staff

Power for the President reflects, among other things, the quality and usefulness of his staff. Upon them he depends for the funneling of information and problems to himself and the communication and interpretation of his directives to those sectors of the huge, sprawling executive branch that administer the diplomatic, economic, military, scientific, intelligence, and psychological phases of foreign policy. Whether the executive agencies are alert and effective, whether they can perceive his own interests and necessities, instead of representing merely their own preferences, may have much to do with how well or ill the President fares in foreign policy.

### The White House Staff and the National Security Council

All recent Presidents have regularly used the White House staff to maximize their own involvement in foreign affairs. Kennedy relied heavily upon his national security assistant, McGeorge Bundy, and a small band of aides to monitor foreign policy and national security problems and the progress of decisions throughout the executive branch. President Johnson continued to employ Bundy as national security assistant at a level of influence equal to that under President Kennedy. In the Washington community, Bundy, in both presidential administrations, was widely regarded as the virtual equal of Secretary of State Dean Rusk and Secretary of Defense Robert McNamara. However, unlike the Secretaries, who were subject to the constant scrutiny of legislative committees, Bundy conducted his duties in well-protected privacy. His status as presidential assistant made him privileged against congressional inquiry while allowing him to function as a leading adviser on policy. After Bundy's departure for a private career, his title and most of his function passed to his former deputy, Walt W. Rostow, who too became a leading influence in foreign policy-making.

With Henry Kissinger's incumbency in the Nixon administration, the post of national security assistant came into fullest flower. Like his predecessors, Kissinger helped to create policy, but unlike them, he conducted crucial international negotiations to carry it out.[32] On policy, Kissinger and

Nixon seemed in fullest accord. Prior to the administration, both had published articles on the Vietnam war and other international questions, and their views were extraordinarily similar. In the subsequent administration, the general harmony persisted, with the more informed Kissinger improving on Nixon's instincts and judgments.[33] Kissinger was assisted by a large staff, some fifty-four "substantive officers," compared with Rostow's twelve. In addition, Kissinger was chairman of a half dozen interagency committees covering the entire range of foreign policy, and manager of "working groups" that prepared staff studies for top-level policy-making.[34] Eventually the power that accrued to Kissinger enabled him to assert an impact on foreign policy that plainly exceeded that of the Secretary of State, and a leading member of the Senate Foreign Relations Committee, Senator Stuart Symington (D-Mo.), was moved to exclaim that the national security assistant had become "Secretary of State in everything but title."[35]

Symington's assessment was symptomatic of the lack of congruence of Kissinger's position with democratic norms. In a presidential administration notable for its undervaluing of democracy, Kissinger was a consistent part of the pattern. The heroes of his academic studies were not American democratic politicians, but Castlereagh, Metternich, and Bismarck, autonomous master diplomats, intellectually and politically superior, who ran the worlds of their day with maneuver, threat, secrecy, and surprise. They played their diplomatic power game remote from public scrutiny, legislative interrogation, and even from their heads of state. Kissinger's own deportment reflected his admired prototypes. Sometimes he operated free of Nixon's oversight and pitilessly excluded the State Department from serious participation in his policy-making ventures. The few State Department officials who were recruited to Kissinger's staff were abjured not to disclose their activities to the department. In their meetings with Chou En-lai and Brezhnev, Kissinger and Nixon used Chinese and Russian interpreters rather than a State Department interpreter who might inform the Secretary of State of matters in progress.[36] Kissinger was also distant from Congress, declining to testify publicly and limiting himself to private appearances on Capitol Hill. Doubtless Kissinger's sharpest departure from democratic deportment was his acquiescence to wiretaps imposed on members of his staff who were regarded as possible sources of information leaks.

While claims of the effective presidency to confidentiality for the national security assistant are necessary and tolerable, Kissinger's extension of his post into operations—negotiating an armistice, reviewing the military budget—makes the claim challengeable, at least for operations. Clearly too much foreign policy is removed from public discussion if these operations are included, a contention encouraged by the clear evidence of recent American experience that no one has a monopoly of wisdom in foreign affairs. The plain lesson of the Vietnam war is that it is salutary and necessary to challenge assumptions and question policy. For all of its successes, which easily place him in the front rank of American diplomats, Kissinger's performance was not without blemishes—the slights to Japan in the lack of forewarning of the coming American rapprochement with Communist China, the flagging attention to Western Europe, the stumblings of international economic policies, the dubious "tilt" that favored Pakistan in its futile 1971 war with India. Later, when he became Secretary of State in the Nixon and Ford administrations, Kissinger became more accessible to Congress, the press, and other sectors of the political system, and more prey to their pressures and criticisms.

Carter, too, imported an Ivy League specialist in international affairs, Zbigniew Brzezinski.[37] As national security adviser, Brzezinski was executive officer of the National Security Council through which virtually all critical foreign policy and national security policy was initiated, reviewed, and articulated. With a staff of seventy-two and a budget of $3.5 million in 1979, Brzezinski directed a miniature bureaucracy capable of moving faster than its competitor, the State Department. Like his predecessors, Brzezinski provided the President a daily briefing on the foreign affairs–national security scene and otherwise enjoyed ready access to his chief. Brzezinski chaired review committees and task forces of the National Security Council, and, with his staff, provided analytical research and acted as liaison to the departments and agencies. The Brzezinski office shared in drafting the Presidential Review Memorandum (PRM), which laid out an issue and the available options. No foreign policy matter reached Carter without being filtered through Brzezinski and the NSC system.[38] His hard-line approach to the Soviet Union provided Carter an alternative to the patient negotiating style of Secretary of State Cyrus Vance. Eventually Brzezinski prevailed, thanks considerably to the Soviet invasion of Afghanistan.[39]

Other institutions that the President may turn to include the Central Intelligence Agency, the cabinet, the National Security Council, and the Joint Chiefs of Staff. The cabinet originated in the diplomatic crisis of 1793, when it charted United States neutrality in the Franco-British war. The cabinet's role has been erratic. It reached the height of its influence in fashioning the Monroe Doctrine; in the two world wars its activity was slight. The fortunes of the National Security Council, which has largely displaced the cabinet in foreign affairs, have also wavered. Truman and Eisenhower regularly resorted to the NSC, but Kennedy used it infrequently, preferring instead meetings with administrators individually, and in small groups. Johnson and Nixon turned more to the NSC, particularly during critical decisions concerning Vietnam and the Middle East. Ford, faced with Turkey's invasion of Cyprus, instability in the Middle East, and other international perils and opportunities in his early presidency, frequently resorted to the NSC. Potentially, the NSC is democracy-serving, since several agencies with diverse functions and perspectives participate jointly, permitting different views to be advanced and debated in the Chief Executive's presence.[40] But in the Nixon-reorganized NSC, consequences ensued that were inimical to democracy. Power gravitated excessively to the assistant for national security affairs, Kissinger. The committee structure, which Kissinger headed, facilitated his access to the various departmental power centers, and his own elite staff, expanded by recruits from the State Department, helped push the Secretary of State, William Rogers, to the outer perimeters of the NSC system, while Kissinger occupied its center.[41] The cumulative changes of the NSC, according to one critic, tilted the decision machinery in favor of the military and were responsible "for some of the most serious misjudgments" of recent presidencies.

For much of his presidency, Carter abided by his commitment of the 1976 campaign to allot the State and Defense Departments a larger part in the policy process than they garnered in the heyday of Kissinger's phenomenal ascendance. The earlier committee structure was somewhat diminished and NSC operations revolved around two groups, the Policy Review Committee and the Special Coordinating Committee. The first handled specific issues like the Panama Canal treaties, and the second continuing issues like the strategic arms talks. Both Vance and his successor, Edmund Muskie, were activist Secretaries of State. Like Carter, Reagan entered the presidency resolved to reduce the role of the national security assistant and enlarge that of the Secretary of State. The assistant, Reagan declared, "should not be a rival of the Secretary of State," but the President's "liaison to the Secretary," as the President and the Secretary deal with policy.[42]

The ideal of democratic policy-making based upon the interaction of administrators, with perspectives drawn from differentiated bureaucratic functions, is also advanced by the common practice of modern Presidents who throw together *ad hoc* groups to provide counsel in diplomatic crises. To weigh the American response when Israel invaded Egypt in 1956, Eisenhower summoned to the White House Secretary of State Dulles, chairman of the Joint Chiefs of Staff Admiral Arthur Radford, Secretary of Defense Wilson, CIA Director Allen Dulles, and Sherman Adams.[43]

## The Central Intelligence Agency

Created by the National Security Act of 1947, with Truman's firm approval, the CIA has had a mercurial career. Housed in architecturally sterile headquarters, above whose entrance are chiseled the words, "The Truth Shall Make You Free," the CIA enjoyed its strongest influence, in playing its advisory role to the President and the NSC, in the Truman and Eisenhower eras of the 1950s and early 1960s. In pursuing its standard duties of gathering raw intelligence, interpreting its meanings, and in estimating the likely consequences of policy moves by the United States or other nations, the CIA churned into top policy-making circles a steady flow of intelligence analyses and projections on a wide range of subjects. More than anything else, what the President wants determines what the CIA does. Under Kennedy, who preferred to deal with selected individuals rather than institutions, and even more so under Johnson, the CIA suffered a declining influence. Strikingly, Johnson, who was preoccupied with Vietnam and who refers extensively in his memoirs[44] to memoranda and reports that influenced his thinking, makes no allusion to any CIA study. In the Nixon era, the NSC system, expanded under Kissinger's impress, produced no marked enhancement of the CIA's role. Ironically, the Pentagon Papers released by Daniel Ellsberg make the CIA look good in its studies and forecasts on Vietnam. Alas, they commanded little readership in top policy circles.[45]

In the Ford presidency, the CIA stirred national attention and criticism when its long-standing clandestine and disruptive activities against adversaries burst into prominence with revelations of its role during the Nixon years in the overthrow of the Allende government in Chile. In an $8 million campaign (from 1970 to 1973) against the Marxist leader, the CIA, among other things, helped finance strikes and demonstrations to "destabilize" Allende's government. Eventually, the government fell and Allende was murdered—how much the government's collapse was due to the CIA and how much to its own errors remains problematical. A considerable body of informed opinion holds that the Allende regime would have toppled by itself and that the CIA's intervention was superfluous and foolish.[46]

For the CIA to engage in subversion of foreign governments seems a blatant contradiction of the democratic pretensions of the American political system. How, in ethics and conscience, can such a system practice abroad what it professes to abhor at home? President Ford justified the CIA's activity in the name of that ready cover-all, "national security," a concept whose easy abuse had been demonstrated in the Watergate malfeasances by the Nixon presidency. Furthermore, Ford contended, "I am reliably informed that Communist nations spend vastly more money than we do for the same kind of purposes."[47]

## Reforming the C.I.A.

Jimmy Carter, who promised in his 1976 campaign to become something of a new broom to sweep the CIA clean, made it a target of an early reorganization. Carter vested in the Director of Central Intelligence, his Annapolis classmate, Admiral Stansfield Turner, unprecedented authority over the entire national intelligence budget, including intelligence agencies of the Defense Department, evidently on the theory that to centralize authority also centralizes responsibility.[48]

To bolster accountability, Carter empowered the Attorney General to oversee intelligence agencies' compliance with American laws, and required presidential approval of counterintelligence operations directed at a suspected foreign agent. Committees of the National Security Council, headed by the President's national security adviser Brzezinski, set intelligence priorities, authorized covert operations, and helped prepare the annual intelligence budget.

Carter's reining in of the CIA was buffeted by strong countertrends stirred by revolution in Iran, the Soviet's overrunning of Afghanistan, and his own conclusion, after experience in the presidency, that the cumulative presidential and congressional restrictions were excessive. Carter urged that disclosures of covert operations be limited to the two intelligence committees of Congress where security would presumably be tighter and called for relaxation of other restrictions to facilitate small-scale covert operations abroad.[49]

## The State Department

For counsel and action the President turns also to the Department of State, home of a vast assemblage of specialists, and to the United States Foreign Service, a distinguished career organization. Many activist Presidents have become disenchanted with the State Department and the Foreign Service, however. Woodrow Wilson and Franklin Roosevelt, for example, held them in low esteem. Forewarned by Adlai Stevenson that he would find the State Department a "tremendous institutional inertial force," John Kennedy soon spoke of the department as "a bowl of jelly" and complained bitterly, "They never have any ideas over there: never come up with anything new."[50] Presidents and their aides regard the State Department's staff work as lacking in quality, as unduly devoted to established policy at the expense of alternatives, as bereft of thorough and broad analysis and prone to reflect pained reluctance in carrying out presidential decisions. To department officials, the President is a temporary intruder whose idiosyncratic interests and work habits are both resented and somehow coped with. When asked by John Kennedy what was wrong with "that goddamned department of yours," career ambassador Charles Bohlen replied, "You are."[51]

## Special Agents

Presidents enjoy almost limitless freedom to employ special agents on high missions abroad if for any reason they prefer not to use the regular ambassadors. Unlike ambassadors and ministers, special agents are appointed solely by the President, without referral to the Senate; they are not mentioned specifically in the Constitution, although their employ is implied by the treaty power and the all-purpose "executive power" clause. George Washington dispatched John Jay to England to negotiate the treaty bearing his name; Thomas Jefferson sent James Monroe to the court of Napoleon to help Robert Livingston arrange the Louisiana Purchase; and Lyndon Johnson had Attorney General Robert F. Kennedy go to Indonesia to induce Indonesian President Sukarno not to fulfill his threat to crush the new country of Malaysia.

Special agents command the President's confidence and trust, which is not always the case with ambassadors. Special agents know better than anyone else the latest intentions and objectives of their Chief Executives. They radiate prestige because they come directly from the White House, and at their approach the gates of foreign ministries open wide. But special agents are at best a mixed blessing. They often lack relevant diplomatic training or experience—Harry Hopkins, who was Franklin Roosevelt's chief liaison with foreign affairs and the Second World War overseas, was a former social worker and administrator of domestic New Deal programs. Special agents undercut the resident ambassador, whether intentionally or not. During the blooming of American-Soviet détente, Kissinger conducted close-to-the-vest diplomacy in Moscow in which the American ambassador, Jacob D. Beam, did not participate. Pictures in the Soviet press showed Leonid Brezhnev, the Communist party leader, Andrei Gromyko, the Foreign Minister, and Anatoly Dobrynin, the Soviet ambassador to Washington, together with Kissinger accompanied by two White House aides. Ambassador Beam was conspicuously absent. At the time, American and other diplomats commented that Soviet officials would surely note the omission and that it would hurt the embassy's prospects for gaining regular and easy access to Soviet leaders once the special agent departed. "When Kissinger is here, we're left out in the cold," said a middle-level American diplomat, "and when he's gone, we're still out in the cold."[52]

# Foreign Leaders

For the President, power in foreign affairs lies in the ability to persuade foreign leaders, whether friend or foe or neutral, to back or accept his policies. His chief policy objectives—stepping up or winding down the Vietnam war, building constructive relations with the Soviet Union and China, recasting the alliances with Western Europe and Japan in recognition of their new strength and autonomy—have usually led him to pursue these contacts diligently with meetings and correspondence.

The Johnson era witnessed a steady trek by heads of other governments to the White House. To the President these occasions are valuable not so much for the specific agreements they produce, which are few, but for several intangibles. The meetings may clear away suspicions, cement personal relations, and lead to broad understanding of positions.

The many personal letters that Kennedy dispatched to a wide circle of foreign leaders were no mere puffs of good will, but dealt with major problems. At the height of the 1962 Cuban crisis, the Kennedy-Khrushchev exchanges opened up an understanding that averted general war. An essential feature of the arrangement was the secrecy both countries maintained about the exchange. Personal communication permitted greater privacy and was less susceptible to leaks than regular channels, and, unlike formal diplomatic notes, custom does not require its publication. The Soviet news media did not mention the exchange at all. The White House kept secret the number of letters involved, the content of most of them, and the channels used. Top-level communication was also nicely attuned to Khrushchev's preference for personal diplomacy and to that of his Foreign Minister, Andrei Gromyko, who functioned as a technician rather than a policy-maker. Nevertheless, the Kennedy-Khrushchev notes were not a substitute for normal diplomatic endeavor, but a supplement, resorted to when the diplomats were unable to agree or when the problem exceeded the bounds of the forum in which they were negotiating.

## Domestic Politics

A President's relationship with world leaders may be buffeted by the vagaries of American domestic politics. With American domestic opinion clamorous against the Vietnam war, Israeli leaders grew accustomed to Johnson's and Nixon's habit of linking that war, in expositions of its rationale and validity, to the cause of Israel in Middle East crises. The comparison presumably would discomfort some critics of the Vietnam war who nevertheless favored strong support for Israel. For Nixon's speech, opposing "precipitate withdrawal" of American troops from Vietnam as a possible trigger of violence in the Middle East, Israeli Premier Golda Meir offered praise, since it "encourages and strengthens freedom-loving small nations the world over."[53]

But the President can also become a terribly disruptive force to the political fortunes of foreign leaders, as Nixon was to Premier Eisaku Sato of Japan. While Japanese exports were pouring into the United States, the American economy, in the early 1970s, was lurching along with heavy unemployment and no foreseeable recovery. Nixon pressed Sato to curb textile exports and believed he had the Premier's promise to do so. Japanese businessmen resisted, and only after concerted American pressure were exports slowed, with Nixon meanwhile feeling that Sato had broken his word.[54] Then came Nixon's surprise announcement that he would visit Peking, a step taken without any advance consultation with Japan, a key American ally. Sato (who learned of the venture from television) and his government felt slighted, if not humiliated, and assessed Nixon's conduct as revenge for the textile embroglio. America's sudden new China policy sent shock waves through Japan, and opposition leaders and even key figures in Sato's own party assailed him for ineptitude. Soon Sato was departing as premier, a development that could be attributed, as much as anything, to his jagged relations with Nixon.[55]

The President may also strike hefty blows to help the domestic political fortunes of foreign leaders in moments of extra peril. In the 1978 French elections, Carter, visiting France, made two conspicuous moves in behalf of the embattled President Valéry Giscard d'Estaing. First, Carter cautioned publicly the Socialist leader, François Mitterand, against renewing the Socialist political alliance with the Communist party. Mitterand's efforts to patch up the broken alliance were thrown into immediate turmoil.[56] Giscard was further buoyed when Carter failed to visit the City Hall of Paris and Mayor Jacques Chirac, head of the neo-Gaullists, whose party participated in the Government coalition, but who was laboring mightily to propel himself into the national limelight, alongside his wary ally, Giscard. Carter's Parisian maneuvers enabled Giscard to score points with his constituents.

## Summit Conferences

The President as chief diplomat often engages in diplomatic ventures himself, notably the summit conference. From Franklin D. Roosevelt onward, the summit, a rare experience prior to the Second World War, has become standard presidential fare: Roosevelt at Yalta, Truman at Potsdam, Eisenhower at Paris, Kennedy at Vienna, Johnson at Glassboro, Nixon at Moscow and Peking, Ford at Vladivostok, and Carter at Vienna.

Presidents sometimes display no great enthusiasm for summitry. Truman did not go to Potsdam gladly, holding that the State, War, and Navy Departments should negotiate with their foreign counterparts instead. Kennedy early in his administration pointedly expressed appreciation for the quiet, normal diplomatic channels. Johnson, soon after taking office, proclaimed his readiness to meet with any world leader, including Premier Nikita Khrushchev, should such a meeting contribute to his loftiest goal, achieving "peace and prosperity." But in actuality, Johnson, with the exception of the conference with Kosygin at Glassboro, did not indulge in meetings of the kind implied by his statement.Reagan recalled a "happier time when there was a tradition that the President of the United States never left our shores, but I don't say that you could do that today."

Pressures for summit meetings beat most insistently upon the President in time of great crisis. Indeed, an almost invariable Soviet tactic in such moments, especially during the peak of the Cold War, was to propose a meeting of chief executives. Khrushchev did so in the 1962 Cuban crisis and at several junctures when Berlin issues were at their crest. For the Soviets, the move was a fruitful propaganda stroke and a brake on the momentum of the President's moves. Most Presidents have found that summits work best when dealing with questions well prepared at lower diplomatic levels. Sometimes they unfreeze disagreements that regular diplomacy cannot resolve. Kennedy, meeting Khrushchev in Vienna, was eager to size up the Soviet leader. Even more, Kennedy said afterwards, "The direct give and take was of immeasurable value in making clear and precise what we consider vital." But the sizing up of Khrushchev was also a grim experience, as Kennedy made clear in reporting to the nation. The U.S.-

U.S.S.R. quarrel over Laos, then at high flame, was "not materially reduced," and his hopes for a nuclear test ban agreement had received "a
serious blow." With the thawing of the Cold War, the stiffness of summitry
diminished and the possibilities of constructive results became enhanced.
Johnson's meeting with Kosygin at Glassboro was valuable in underscoring
the interest of both powers in avoiding situations threatening nuclear war,
in permitting first-hand exchanges of view, and in establishing a potentially
useful personal acquaintance.

For Nixon, the summit conference was the forum for the most acclaimed
achievements of his presidency. The visit to Communist China, after a
quarter-century void of suspended official relations between the countries,
was in essence an Event, a televised extravaganza, commanding an audience
of the magnitude that witnessed the first landing on the moon. Peking's
Great Hall and north China's Great Wall were stages for the presidential
television drama in which the long-dedicated anti-Communist, Nixon, was
undertaking what no presidential predecessor dared to do, making "the
long march" to China as a prelude to expanded future relations. For Nixon,
the Peking summit also commanded rewards at home—heightened validity
to his claimed role as the great peacemaker despite the then little-abated
Vietnam war, and the exhilaration of widespread public approval.[57]

Where Nixon and the Chinese leaders could speak in general platitudes
of high-minded goals about which there could be little disagreement,
Nixon's successors have had to grapple with more specific issues stemming
from the divergent interests of China and the United States. Carter, for
example, meeting with Teng Hsiao-ping, China's senior deputy Prime Minister, encountered sharply contrasting views on Soviet intentions and on the
wisdom of concluding a new strategic arms limitation agreement (SALT
II). At every opportunity, Teng berated the Soviet drive for "hegemony,"
its threat as "a hotbed of war," and he complained that the United States
was "in strategic retreat." Teng openly summoned the United States "to
place curbs on the Soviet bear."

Carter and his aides, whose perceptions of the Soviet Union, at least at
the time, were far more benign, toiled to explain the American attitude of
the necessity of detente with the Soviet and the indispensability of a new
arms agreement.[58]

# Alliances

Alliances can trigger presidential war. The conflicts in Korea and Vietnam
evoked United States involvement in response to alliances and understandings, and, as the war in Indochina stumbled on, a web of agreements
evolved that was fashioned by presidential deputies functioning with high
autonomy and secrecy. In 1972 the Senate Foreign Relations Committee
spotlighted a hitherto secret American commitment to provide up to $100
million a year to support a Thai "irregular army" of 10,000 men in Laos,
using American equipment and ammunition and flying American helicopter
gunships. Indignant legislators cited the 1971 Defense Procurement Act,
which prohibited the use of defense funds for forces of a third country,

such as Thailand, fighting in support of Laos or Cambodia. By dint of some tortuous semantical hair-splitting, the executive branch contended that the act was inapplicable to the Thai volunteers, thus rounding out a common scenario of the Indochina war, that of congressional prohibition and executive circumvention.[59]

Keeping an alliance intact may sometimes become a major presidential preoccupation. Gerald Ford had scarcely assumed the presidency when war erupted in Cyprus and two long-standing allies of the United States entered a passage of tense relations as Turkey invaded the island and Greece mobilized its forces. Greece, to express displeasure with an initial American preference for Turkey, withdrew from NATO. Ford and his aides had the arduous task of restraining Turkey's spreading military dominion over Cyprus, of dispelling Greece's ill-feeling toward the United States, and of curbing congressional opinion that Turkey be punished for its aggression.

## NATO

NATO, today's most intricate alliance, reaches back to the Second World War. When NATO, a defensive alliance of fifteen Western Nations, was forming, Truman promised "the support which the situation requires": he backed the bipartisan Vandenberg resolution endorsing the United States' association with NATO, featured the treaty in his 1949 inaugural address, urged upon Congress a vast program of military aid to the NATO countries, and assured its passage by announcing the first atomic explosion in the Soviet Union. Presidents have led in NATO's sharper turns of direction, too. Truman pushed West Germany's rearmament and inclusion in the western European defense system. Eisenhower promoted the European Defense Community treaty to merge the armed forces of six western European nations into a "hard and dependable core" for NATO. Kennedy advocated a NATO missile fleet of surface ships manned by crews of mixed nationality. Johnson led in the adjustment of NATO following De Gaulle's assault upon its military structure in requiring the removal from France of all military units or bases not under complete French control.

In pursuing his proudly proclaimed policy of detente, Nixon in effect modified the inherited NATO system by solidifying relations with the Soviet Union, to the point of at least a quasi-alliance. A consequent malaise developed in the ranks of the NATO allies, not so much because of the substance·of the agreements made with the Russians as the methods of the Nixon presidency in concluding them. NATO leaders bemoaned the "deceptions" involved and the callous disregard, if not contempt, for the allies. When a Western European diplomat asked American officials, including the Secretary of State, "Will you talk about things (in Moscow) that concern all of us," the response was negative. NATO representatives knew nothing of a U.S.–U.S.S.R. statement of principles until it was released in Moscow during the 1972 summit. Even worse, the statement contained provisions that contradicted portions of a NATO draft, in which the United States had joined, of a comparable declaration by the alliance. The latter, for example, called for freer movement between East and West, a resolve that was dropped in the Soviet-American text. "You abandoned in Moscow what you were urging us here to support," said a NATO official to a presidential representative.[60]

## Disruptive Forces

Alliances are also ensnarled by the domestic politics of member nations, differences in their leaders' styles, and their conflicting perceptions of self-interest in formulating their respective foreign policies. Reacting to the Soviet invasion of Afghanistan, Carter imposed several punitive sanctions, including a boycott of the 1980 Summer Olympics to be held in Moscow. The President was affronted when West Germany, which, of the NATO allies, lay most immediately in the Soviet path, did not join readily in the boycott, in general took a diffident stance toward the Soviet aggression, and seemed to waver on an earlier agreement to permit the positioning of advanced nuclear weapons on her soil. German Chancellor Helmut Schmidt, facing an approaching national election, was assailed by opponents from every side. Some urged a harder, and others a sofer, anti-Soviet line; all portrayed him as a disloyal ally. Days before the 1980 Venice conference of the heads of governments of Western industrial states, Carter joined the attack in a sharply worded letter to Schmidt. Whether or not Carter intended the letter primarily for Schmidt or primarily to enhance competition with his 1980 election opponent, Ronald Reagan, for voters preferring a hard-line toward the Soviet Union, is an open question.[61] Nonetheless, in the Carter White House, Schmidt continued to be suspected of harboring ambition to push his country to a position somewhere between the superpowers, affording for himself a role of innovative leadership.[62]

# Presidential Competence
# in Foreign Affairs

The contemporary President personally performs many of the most important functions in foreign affairs, despite the huge numbers of experts in the executive branch and skilled White House assistants. How well he discharges these tasks does much to determine the level of his administration's foreign policy attainments.

For analytical convenience, the President's competence can be weighed according to a rubric of two major influences upon the quality of his activity—his perceptions and his working skills.

## Perceptions

At best, Presidents take office with only limited experience in foreign affairs. Of contemporary Presidents, Eisenhower possessed the most voluminous, high-level international background, thanks to his responsibilities as Allied commanding general in the Second World War. More typically, the backgrounds of contemporary Presidents are tilted to domestic affairs, or to nonexecutive affiliations with foreign affairs, such as office-holding in the Senate.

Since the presidency is an intensive short-term work experience, its incumbents grasp at fragments of their limited backgrounds for any prudent, pragmatic concepts that might help to guide their passage through the presidency's stranger byways. At first, Truman saw Stalin as essentially "another politician," and Soviet relations could be understood "if you understand Jackson county," Truman's home county in Missouri where he once was chief administrator.[63] Events and the far more complex realities of the presidential office and relations with the Soviet Union soon shattered these perceptions. How much effect the trauma of that transformation had on the onset of the Cold War remains problematic.

In his first major foreign policy address, and in a mood of exhilarating optimism, Carter proclaimed that "We are now free of that inordinate fear of Communism"; "We hope to persuade the Soviet Union that one country cannot impose its own social system upon another, either through direct military intervention or through the use of a client state's military force."[64] Unfortunately, Soviet-Cuban adventurism in Africa soon jarred these benign perceptions, and the Soviet invasion of Afghanistan utterly shattered them. Carter was now thrown into the depths of disillusion. "This action of the Soviets," he declared, "has made a more dramatic change in my own opinion of what the Soviet's ultimate goals are than anything they've done in the previous time I've been in office." Spurred by the force of his disillusionment, Carter launched a series of punitive countermoves. Western allies felt that he overreacted, and other critics attacked his statements as a confession of naiveté.[65]

## Skills

The President's tasks and involvements in foreign affairs can be stated in terms of skills. Skill in negotiation is high among them, since Presidents often take on important diplomatic negotiations. In their long association, Kissinger was impressed that Nixon, better than any other leader of the day, understood the dynamics of negotiation: that discussion seldom produces results by itself; only a balance of incentives and penalties can nurture gains.[66] To Kissinger, Nixon also excelled at grasping overall relationships, of seeing problems not simply in their individuality but in their relevance to the entire international checkerboad of interests and situations.[67]

Is it a fair test of a President that his foreign policies be coherent? A recurrent criticism of Carter's foreign policy-making was its frequent incoherence. The prestigious International Institute for Strategic Studies contended that the Carter presidency presented "a complicated and at times inconsistent picture to the world," that it "often lacks centralized means of translating differences of opinion into coherent policy." In 1978, when this opinion was expressed, the administration seemed to vacillate: supporting the Shah of Iran, yet cultivating his potential successors; dispatching a naval task force to the Persian Gulf, but becalming it after it journeyed halfway there.[68] In 1979 Carter announced first that the presence of Soviet troops in Cuba was intolerable, and subsequently that the troops posed no threat and were no cause to delay Senate approval of the arms treaty (SALT II). A Soviet aide likened Carter's contradictory pronouncements to *solyanka*, a thick Russian soup of many ingredients.[69]

But a price of coherence may be the personalism that denoted the foreign policy-making of Nixon and Kissinger. Whatever essences those two minds gyrated in tight, imperious secrecy served as policy. Their method was scornful of democratic principles, of the role of the elected Congress and of public opinion. Their pretensions of coherence were often disguised by guile, verbal dexterity, theatrics fawned over by the press, and grand *ex post facto* conceptualizations. Carter's foreign policy-making in contrast, could be excused for at least some of its rough edges by its far stronger links to democracy than the Nixon-Kissinger virtuosity allowed. Congress was a far stronger participant in the time of Carter; the State Department and other foreign affairs bureaucracy, instead of being largely shut out, were major participants.

Above all, Carter pursued a far wider range of foreign policies than his predecessors, from championing human rights to imposing sanctions against the Soviet Union. If his course sometimes seemed erratic, it was because he was manager of a range of contradictory purposes in foreign affairs—from helping other states wage defensive warfare to providing food to starving Cambodians In a foreign policy of such scale, incoherence is unavoidable, for the task is one of managing contradictions: policies must be traded off; not every good is reconcilable. And in the post-Vietnam, post-Watergate era Carter struggled with a national mood where blind trust was no longer reposed in the President and deference had vanished, where a new congressional culture hesitated not a moment to challenge the President. Carter and his aides did not have the luxury of a Kissinger-type adulation and the passivity it evoked on Capitol Hill. The Carter era, as Thomas Hughes, a principal State Department official in the Nixon years, noted, was a time of "maximum democracy and minimum Machiavelli."[70]

# The United Nations

In setting his foreign policy, the modern President must reckon, of course, with the United Nations. Kennedy, striving to alter the tone of U.S.–U.S.S.R. relations, found the UN General Assembly a useful forum in which to urge that in the future the two nations compete in "leadership and responsibility" instead of competing in a search for better methods of destruction.[71] In Kennedy's 1962 confrontation with the U.S.S.R. over Cuba, the UN served its classic functions as a forum in which the American complaint could be ventilated and world opinion courted, and where machinery could be found for negotiation and conciliation. But for the President the UN may also be a hazard. Kennedy, in the agony of a Berlin crisis, was urged by certain of his counselors to lay the problem before the UN General Assembly. Charge Khrushchev, they said, with threatening the peace over Berlin and call for economic sanctions if he fails to accept the UN verdict. Kennedy quickly spurned this advice, pointing out that a UN verdict might favor Khrushchev and that the neutralist nations might be persuaded to accept his suggestions for a free city.

For the President faced with situations where military forces must be utilized, the United Nations will often provide a better alternative than the direct engagement of American power. Bringing to bear the UN's international policing apparatus has entailed less expense, misunderstanding, and abuse than the direct involvements that Presidents have chosen to make in Korea and Vietnam. UN policing in the Congo and Cyprus, and the insertion of a UN buffer force beween Israeli and Egyptian troops in 1973 plainly displayed the attractions of international action. UN procedures are also valuable as a face-saving or cooling-off device, as the *Pueblo* crisis of 1968 demonstrates. President, Johnson, faced with a grave affront to the United States, was able, by resorting to the UN, to provide a semblance of action rather than undertake a more direct and dangerous response.

Confronted with a burgeoning international food crisis in 1974 the Ford presidency, in proposing remedial measures, urged the utilization of the UN and its related organizations. For example, as a means of improving nutrition through food of higher quality Ford recommended the establishment of a "global nutrition surveillance system" by the World Health Organization, the Food and Agriculture Organization, and the United Nations Children's Fund.[72] For Carter, the United Nations was a valued source of diplomatic initiatives in the delicate negotiation with Iran to release the hostages seized in Teheran.

But except for an occasional speech by the President or the Secretary of State at the United Nations, which provides a useful forum, the world body has largely been neglected and shunned by contemporary Presidents, who look askance at the frequently hostile vetoes of the Security Council and the unfavorable votes emanating from the General Assembly.

# ★ ★ ★ The Future Presidency ★ ★ ★

The post-Vietnam, post-Watergate presidency has witnessed an era of greater sharing of power between the executive and legislative branches. Congress has abandoned its earlier deference to the President, its passive approbation of the stewardship of an imposing Secretary of State like Henry Kissinger. Congress is more demanding, more questioning, more rejecting. Democracy is in fresh bloom on Capitol Hill. Yet at several points in this chapter the question is raised or implied whether sometimes Congress goes too far, whether its appropriations power is sometimes used to limit the executive too closely, even shackling his ability to counter the latest twists and turns of Soviet, Cuban, and other powers' assertion. An awaiting task is to arrange a more prudent balance between the branches, simultaneously holding the presidency to the democratic path while enabling it to act with sufficient effectiveness in an age of huge Soviet rearmament, energy shortages, international terrorism, and the dollar fluctuating mercurially on the international exchanges.

1. Can functions be divided between Congress and the President in ways satisfying to the needs of power as well as to the needs of democracy? For example, should not the President be the sole conductor of foreign policy, its single implementer? If so, then Congress would leave to the President and his executive associates the function of diplomatic negotiation, and, more generally, day-to-day tactical decisions. These require

adjustment to changing circumstance; the unpredictable is always around the corner in foreign affairs. Both branches would deal with goals, and Congress would scrutinize and assess the consequences of diplomacy.

2. The treaty power should be revised by constitutional amendment to replace the required two-thirds approval of the Senate with one of simple majority. The present high majority required imposes upon the President the necessity to secure bipartisan support, in which lurks the peril of easy defeat, of which the League of Nations fight is the classic example. The present requirement, as the Panama Canal treaties make clear, can subject the treaty process to a snail-like pace while the huge senatorial majority is painstakingly compiled, and makes the President vulnerable to the idiosyncratic notions of individual Senators of what a proper foreign policy should be, a standing invitation to drop a monkey-wrench into sensitive proceedings.

3. In this era of congressional assertiveness, the time may be at hand for the President to include key legislators in deliberations of the National Security Council whenever the agenda includes items likely to require congressional support—new laws, appropriations, additional administrative structures. Discussion with legislators, such as the chairmen and possibly the ranking members of the foreign affairs, armed services, and appropriations committees of both houses, would impart to presidential decision-making a keener sense of legislative realities and the opportunity to incorporate congressional viewpoints, which could ease the measures' later progress on Capitol Hill. Admittedly, there would be a danger of leaks useful to the political interests of the legislators. A likely byproduct is that the National Security Council, which is sometimes largely unused by Presidents, would be taken more seriously.

4. Future presidencies would do well to follow a striking tendency of the Carter presidency: to develop foreign policy through a process of administrative pluralism. Carter alone of recent Presidents tolerated a triad of power centers, each with its own perspectives and interests: a Secretary of State, Secretary of Defense, and a national security adviser, each a major force. Carter's principal finance officers, the Secretary of the Treasury and the Director of the Office of Management and Budget, were also at the center of foreign policy-making, and other departments and agencies as well played important roles. Carter also tolerated the often clashing perspectives and preferences of his associates: the Secretary of State's partiality to détente and patient negotiation, fostered by both Vance and Muskie, and national security adviser Brzezinski's advocacy of a harder line. Pluralism permits advancement of opposing views, and vigorous debate of frankly stated options.

To be sure, administrative pluralism has its price. When bureaucratic haggling goes public, it can embarrass the President. As his decisions vacillate between factions, the President risks appearing weak, of being perceived as not in charge. But pluralism rather than the Nixon-Kissinger monism is appropriate for the post-Vietnam, post-Watergate milieu. In times of diminished deference to the presidency, when policy is increasingly questioned, and the electorate hardened and sophisticated by harsh recent experience, administrative pluralism is both logical and viable.

# Chapter Ten

# Commander-in-Chief

A democracy, like any other state, must be capable of defending itself and assuring its survival. If a democracy is powerful, like the United States, it is also expected to defend other less powerful states, some of them democracies and others embarrassingly not. Equally paradoxical is the chief agency of defense, the military, in structure and organization antithetical to democracy, stressing obedience to authority, hierarchy and command. Its central enterprise—war—with its concomitants, death and destruction, is the negation of democracy, whose actualization requires life and peace.

As the constitutionally designated Commander-in-Chief, the President is the focus of the unresolved dilemmas of democracy and force as the maker of decisions that can be costly, hazardous, and, in the nuclear age, horrendous. Since the Second World War, military matters have been a top priority for all Presidents. The most formidable criticisms of the presidency have centered upon its military power, viewed as expansive and encroaching, to the point that those accouterments of democracy, legislative oversight and electoral review by informed public opinion, are evaded and frustrated. Not only are Presidents perceived as abusing power; their active role as Commander-in-Chief has entrapped them in prolonged wars that, for all of America's military power, they have been unable to win, and, worse, little able to extricate themselves from. Caught and flailing in military quicksands, Presidents have paid a high political price. Truman, bogged down in the Korean war, abstained in 1952 from running for reelection, wisely declining to test a war-weary electorate. The chief presidential casualty of the protracted Vietnam war was Lyndon Johnson, who refrained from seeking reelection, in the face of tumultuous country-wide protest and dissent, much of which stemmed from his continued waging of the Vietnam war.

On the other hand, war and lesser trouble can be a boon to the President's political fortunes. With the 1980 elections looming and his popularity sagging, Jimmy Carter's lowly standing in the polls was suddenly reversed when the Soviet Union invaded Afghanistan, and the President warned that if the Russians made further encroachments in the Persian Gulf region, the United States would "fight." As they are wont to do in moments of perceived danger, Americans rallied around the President, and Carter's popularity climbed.

# Limitations on Presidential Power

As active Commanders-in-Chief, contemporary Presidents have given off contradictory images of themselves and their office. Time and again, they appear to wield arbitrary power—commencing an invasion of Cuba, enlarging the war in Vietnam, conducting a secret war in Cambodia, without even a gesture of consultation with Congress, which the Constitution empowers to declare war. But a glance at history and the participants in national security policy-making reveals that there are also limitations upon the President's military power, and its exercise can be affected by potent regulators. Events, like the seizure of American hostages by Iranian revolutionaries, may produce situations where, as a practical matter, military power is unavailing. No military action could promptly extricate the American hostages from the Teheran embassy unharmed.

Despite his designation as Commander-in-Chief, the President enjoys no monopoly of direction over American military power but shares it with others who may withhold what he needs, challenge or even veto what he does, or commit acts that leave him no choice but to respond within channels that they, rather than he, establish. Congress has a substantial military power. It can provide or withhold appropriations, reduce the numbers of American forces abroad, and bar specified kinds of military action. The professional military, some steps removed from an image of absolute obedience, may resist, delay, and amend. The courts may upset what the President does in their duty to protect the rights and liberties guaranteed by the Constitution. And in wartime the electorate may weigh the quality of his military stewardship and decide whether to keep him in office or fire him. Power that is shared and balanced, as the Framers wisely perceived, is more apt to be used prudently than if it is concentrated or monopolized.

# The Defense Department

The President's main reliance and help in his duty as Commander-in-Chief is the Defense Department, which shelters most of the military endeavor. In the Kennedy-Johnson era, power was centralized in the department, as never before or since, during Robert McNamara's assertive tenure as Secretary. A systems-analysis staff attached to his office utilized techniques of cost effectiveness and strategic analysis in reviewing the military's proposals. Often what eventually emerged from the thoroughgoing top-level review were decisions so different from the original proposals that they materialized into a series of independent weapons programs and strategic studies geared to both conventional and nuclear war.[1]

Clothed in trappings of quantification, McNamara could speak on complex national security matters with confidence and authority, and his Presidents, impressed and grateful, showered encomiums upon him. Unfortunately, the Vietnam war exposed latent weaknesses of the Secretary's approach. During his visits to Saigon, those who viewed the war as a hopeless quagmire were troubled by McNamara's imperturbable certitude and facilely summoned statistics.[2] McNamara's system stumbled when it was addressed to the less measurable aspects of national security policy. It underestimated the tenacity of North Vietnam and the psychological drain of corruption and dependence of the United States upon South Vietnam's will to fight. Assumptions underlying McNamara's tidy analyses endured too long without serious questioning, and guerrilla warfare in the Asian jungle possessed nuances that escaped the tabulators and chart-makers in remote Washington.

Every President revises to some degree his predecessor's structuring of Defense Department operations. Variation imparts a sense of fresh policymaking and identity to his administration, and it may be forced by new realities and by the trend of his own work habits. In the Nixon era, the initial Secretary of Defense, Melvin R. Laird, launched changes, perpetuated by his successors, embodying clear departures from the McNamara system. Roles were now reversed. The Joint Chiefs of Staff and the service departments were restored to something of their pre-McNamara influence. Laird and Nixon preferred to seek out military counsel in decision-making and allotted to the Joint Chiefs full opportunities for advocacy in both the Defense Department and the National Security Council. Nixon's reorganization of the latter facilitated the Joint Chiefs' access.[3]

Practical politics also undergirded the Laird-Nixon pattern. The hazardous task of extricating the United States from the Vietnam war, through graduated troop reductions, required at least the acquiescence of the Joint Chiefs; their dissent would have enormously complicated, even jeopardized, that difficult maneuver. But Nixon's restructuring of the NSC also promoted the principle of civilian direction. The reorganized National Security Council in effect substituted rigorous civilian institutional procedures at the President's level for McNamara's Defense Department-centered civilian systems analysis. By altering the budget system to require early submission of tentative budget plans to the President, Jimmy Carter allowed himself nine additional months to consider the military budget.

## The Joint Chiefs of Staff

With the Joint Chiefs of Staff, his principal military advisers, the President's relations are frequently attended by tension and conflict. Truman, reluctant to depend on the military as primary policy advisers, was forced with the outbreak of the Korean war to adopt a stance of closer dependence.

As an impeccable military hero, Eisenhower could indulge his preference to hold the military at arm's length and his wish to avoid the likely charge of his political opponents that, because of his background, he would allow the military excessive influence. But as his administration proceeded, he was faced with a series of international crises in Indochina, over the Chinese offshore islands and the Suez, and in Hungary and Berlin, which, in their cumulative effect, brought the JCS chairman, Admiral Arthur W. Radford, into a position of uppermost influence in foreign policy councils second only to Secretary of State John Foster Dulles. Kennedy, who felt that Eisenhower was sometimes too severe with his generals, especially on budgetary questions, initially accorded the JCS freer access to his policy councils. Unfortunately, the new relationship fell flat on its face in the Bay of Pigs disaster. The Joint Chiefs' chairman, General Lyman Lemnitzer, was shifted to Europe as commander of United States forces and was replaced by General Maxwell Taylor, whose return from retirement into private life reflected badly upon the military.

Nixon, who according to Chief of Naval Operations, Admiral Elmo R. Zumwalt, Jr., had excellent grasp of military details, held the Chiefs at arm's length. "It was in no sense a working session," wrote Zumwalt of their meetings with Nixon, "at which the military went back and forth with the Commander-in-Chief. Rather, it was a ceremony, a ritual even, at which Mr. Nixon listened to things he already knew and made responses he and Kissinger [the President's national security assistant] had contrived beforehand."[4]

Carter significantly altered the nature of the Chiefs by appointing officers who were managers and technicians, unlike the combat veterans, the prestigious and aggressive warriors of World War II, who manned the Chiefs in the 1950s and 60s. Air Force General David C. Jones, the Carter-appointed chairman of the Joint Chiefs, was a military professional whose high reputation came from his skill as administrator and bureaucratic manager rather than from the battlefield. Carter's other appointments to the Chiefs were of similar genre. Among his fellow military, Jones was criticized for not fighting sufficiently for the B-1 bomber, a proposed weapons system that Carter rejected, and of being too pliant to the President's budget-cutting.[5]

Nonetheless, the Chiefs did enjoy moments of successful assertion. Early in his administration, taking a benign view of the world, Carter called for the withdrawal of American troops from South Korea. After prickly maneuver, the Chiefs induced the President to qualify his decision with three conditions: to effect the withdrawal in a manner not destabilizing to the delicate situation in Korea; to pledge to uphold American defense obligations to South Korea; and to affirm American intent to remain a Pacific power. As his administration wore on and his view of Asian realities hardened, Carter shelved his plan to reduce American forces.[6]

## President-Military Interactions

The President's fluctuating dealings with the military reflect a malaise that springs at least partly from several kinds of acute dependence. First, it is difficult for the Chief Executive to find alternative sources of military advice. He can summon retired military, as Kennedy did General Maxwell

Taylor, but their access to operational information is limited. The President's chief civilian deputy, the Secretary of Defense, depends upon data and evaluations supplied by the military. As national security assistant to Ford and Nixon, Kissinger found the military invariably suspicious of any formulation of military doctrine that subsequently might interfere with their procurement decisions. A presidential directive of 1969, inquiring into the rationale of naval programs, was never answered satisfactorily during his eight years of tenure. Kissinger noted: "The response was always short of being insubordinate but also short of being useful."[7]

Military chieftains gain leverage in the executive branch from the influence they enjoy with congressional leaders. Legislation empowers the military to inform congressional committees of their reservations and differences respecting presidential policy, if asked, and presidential proposals to reorganize military structures and programs stand little chance of moving through Congress without military assent. If he fears right-wing attack, the President will act all the more guardedly toward the military, aware of their strength in that constituency. Above all, the President is acutely dependent on the military to implement his decisions. The military's penchant for standard procedures may cause his orders to be distorted through simplification, and the JCS is apt to defer to field commanders and not oversee closely their compliance with presidential direction.[8]

But the President, fortunately, can fight back against these threatened limitations on his power to gain the information and advice he needs and support for implementing his decisions. He can launch reorganizations to secure coordinated advice rather than separate advice from the services, and he can enlarge the NSC system to augment the variety of views on military problems. He can install an independent military counselor in the White House, as Kennedy did General Maxwell Taylor and as Nixon did General Andrew Goodpaster. The assistant for national security affairs is a civilian adviser in the White House, aided by an expert staff, and is a source of additional information, advice, and options. As a free-roving presidential assistant, he can press for compliance with the Chief Executive's decisions. Other officers and bureaus of the executive branch provide the President alternative information and advice—scientists who counsel on weapons systems; the Office of Management and Budget, which provides professional scrutiny of the military budget; and ad hoc groups, commissions, and individuals, who can report on military questions.

# The President and the Generals

As Commander-in-Chief the President appoints and removes his field generals. In wartime the responsibility is especially important because of the consequences of the President's choice for the nation's survival and his own political future. Lyndon Johnson's grip on the presidency was loosened by the inability of his generals to win a decisive victory in Vietnam, despite prodigious escalations of American military commitment. For Richard Nixon, a most perilous shoal to be circumnavigated was the withdrawal of

American troops without sustaining defeat or serious loss, disasters that might inflame domestic opinion, but from which he was spared by the skill of his generals.

## Truman Fires MacArthur

Truman experienced a confrontation intended to keep a field general within the bounds of constitutional government. General Douglas MacArthur, commander of the United Nations forces in Korea, had built a military career of rare distinction: peerless hero of the Pacific theater in the Second World War, successful viceroy of postwar Japan, and a widely mentioned potential Republican presidential nominee. His handsome, erect presence and majestic eloquence were marks of an imperious figure.

Truman's difficulties began when the general, midway in the Korean war, visited Chiang Kai-shek at Formosa. After their meeting, Chiang declared, "The foundation for Sino-American military cooperation has been laid." [9] Since these words were both obscure and potentially expansive and the administration was anxious to keep Formosa neutralized, Truman dispatched Averell Harriman to review with MacArthur the entire Far Eastern political situation. Harriman's apparent success was shattered when MacArthur released a statement to the commander of the Veterans of Foreign Wars urging a more dynamic United States–Formosa partnership. The President himself now went forth to see MacArthur in a hastily cleared-out Quonset hut on Wake Island. According to information released to a subsequent senatorial investigation, the whole Eastern policy was broadly and congenially discussed. The part of Truman's visit that the public saw seemed entirely happy. The President pinned the Distinguished Service Medal on the general and presented a five-pound box of candied plums to Mrs. MacArthur. The general reciprocated by declaring, through the President's press secretary, "No commander in the history of war has had more complete and admirable support from the agencies in Washington than I have during the Korean operation." [10]

MacArthur pressed the war forward, routed the North Koreans, and received approval from the United Nations General Assembly to pursue the fleeing foe across the thirty-eighth parallel, the division between the two Koreas. Hereupon Communist China entered the war. The struggle proceeded to seesaw between MacArthur's forces and the enlarged enemy. On March 17, 1951, in a public statement issued from his United Nations headquarters, MacArthur lamented the "abnormal military inhibitions" upon his command and pointed to the necessity for "vital decisions—yet to be made." These presumably were to incorporate his proposals to the Joint Chiefs for broadened military action against Communist China: a blockade, air bombardment, and ultimately invasion. MacArthur's public statement was issued simultaneously with efforts of the President and the State Department to end the Korean conflict by reopening diplomatic negotiations. [11]

MacArthur made other public statements, not the least of which was a reply to Joseph W. Martin, the House minority leader, who had asked the general for his views on the use of Chinese Nationalist troops. MacArthur indeed believed they should be employed, and added, in words implying that it was necessary to vastly expand the Korean conflict, "Here we fight

Europe's war with arms while the diplomats there still fight it with words. . . . if we lose the war to Communism in Asia the fall of Europe is inevitable." Congressman Martin read MacArthur's letter on the House floor.[12]

Anxiety flowed like wine in foreign capitals. President Truman now concluded that decisive action was unavoidable if presidential authority, civil supremacy, and established policy were to be preserved. He wrote to a friend, "I reached a decision yesterday morning after much consideration and consultation on the Commanding General in the Pacific. It will undoubtedly create a great furor but under the circumstances I could do nothing else and still be President of the United States." On April 11 the President announced MacArthur's removal from his command.[13]

Truman explained his decision in an address to the nation. MacArthur, returning to the United States, addressed Congress and advanced his policy tenets with superb oratorical skill. Several legislators moved to impeach Truman, and the Senate Armed Services and Foreign Relations Committees commenced a joint investigation. The top military unqualifiedly supported the President.

Presidential power was eventually vindicated by Truman, and civil supremacy maintained over the professional military, a cardinal arrangement of the democratic state. Truman in his self-assertion faced grave political risks: the possibility that the successor of the deposed MacArthur would compile a less favorable military record, that public opinion would feel affronted, and that legislators would exploit the situation for personal political gain. But Truman clung to duty and brushed aside political expediency and the temptation not to act. The military rallied around him, the public understood, and ultimately the Chief Executive, as Commander-in-Chief, was reaffirmed; but he trod no certain, primrose path.

# Sources of Authority

The President, functioning as he does in a democratic state, requires legal authority to pursue his military purposes. The quest sends him to the Constitution to contemplate how much authority its lean language really provides, or to enactments like the War Powers Resolution of 1973.* And in what he does he must reckon with the courts, guardians of the fundamental law and private right against governmental, and therefore presidential, encroachment.

## The Lincolnian Pattern

Presidents in the nation's major wars have invoked two contrasting patterns of legal justification for their acts. One, the Lincolnian, asserts an expansive view of the President's independent authority based on the Commander-in-Chief clause in Article II, section 2, of the Constitution and on the duty "to take care that the laws be faithfully executed" expressed in section 3. In the

---

*The President's constitutional and statutory authority is discussed in Chapter 9, pp. 211–22.

twelve weeks between the outbreak at Fort Sumter and the convening of Congress in special session on July 4, 1861, Lincoln employed these two clauses to sanction measures whose magnitude suggests dictatorship.

In the twelve-week interval, Lincoln added 23,000 men to the Regular Army and 18,000 to the Navy, called 40,000 volunteers for three years' service; summoned the state militias into a ninety-day volunteer force; paid $2 million from the Treasury's unappropriated funds for purposes unauthorized by Congress; closed the Post Office to "treasonable correspondence"; imposed a blockade on Southern ports; suspended the writ of habeas corpus, which protects the citizen against arbitrary arrest, in certain parts of the country; and caused the arrest and military detention of persons "who were represented to him" as engaging in or contemplating "treasonable practices." He later instituted a militia draft when voluntary recruiting broke down and extended the suspension of the habeas corpus privilege to a nation-wide basis for persons "guilty of any disloyal practice." His first Emancipation Proclamation freed the slaves in states in rebellion against the United States and pledged "the Executive Government of the United States, including the military and naval authority thereof," to protect the freedom conferred. Lincoln invited Congress to "ratify" his enlargement of the armed forces, which it did, and it sanctioned his handling of the writ of habeas corpus. Altogether, Lincoln's actions, as Edward S. Corwin has written, "assert for the President, for the first time in our history, an initiative of indefinite scope and legislative in effect in meeting the domestic aspects of a war emergency."[14]

## The Joint President-Congress Pattern

The world war presidencies of Woodrow Wilson and Franklin Roosevelt afford a contrasting pattern. The spreading character of war, its encroachment upon the economy, the involvement of growing numbers of people, and the resort to propaganda necessitated presidential approaches to Congress both for legal authority and political support, and the process fostered an executive-legislative partnership in war leadership. In both world wars statutes were passed delegating broad powers to the Chief Executive. Selective service laws in both wars enabled the President to administer a vast manpower draft. The Lever Act of 1917 empowered the Executive to license the mining, importation, manufacture, storage, and distribution of necessities; it authorized the seizure of factories, pipelines, mines, and the like; and it fixed the prices of wheat, coal, and other basic commodities. In the Second World War the Lend Lease Act permitted the President and his deputies to transfer "defense articles," meaning anything from bacon to battleships, to the "government of any country whose defense the President judged vital to the defense of the United States," on any terms he "deems satisfactory."

By gift of legislation, Roosevelt managed much of the domestic economy in the Second World War. Through deputies, he allocated "materials," fixed prices, controlled rents, settled labor disputes, and seized strikebound plants. Like Wilson, Roosevelt as Commander-in-Chief created "executive agencies," such as the Office of Price Administration and the National War Labor Board, to administer delegated legislative power.

The President needs not only laws from Congress but a variety of other cooperative deeds to assure effective military policy and administration. By grace of the Constitution, with its mechanisms of checks and balances, the Chief Executive shares a wide range of military powers with Congress. Congress raises the armed forces, provides for their regulation, and investigates the military enterprise; the Senate gives its advice and consent to military nominations; Congress passes laws governing military organization, appropriates vast funds for equipment and materiel, and declares war. Its powers, Presidents would gladly testify, enable it to act forcefully in military affairs. The results are not always positive and cooperative. Checks and balances, bolstered by rivalries between the armed services, sometimes bring the President and Congress into incipient or actual conflict.

In 1962 President Kennedy faced a gathering crisis that threatened to become a head-on clash not simply over the merits of a military artifact, but between Congress's and the President's respective military powers. The subject of controversy was the RS-70 bomber, then in its final stages of development. Air Force leaders strongly backed the RS-70, stressing the necessity of a manned bomber program to avoid excessive reliance upon missiles. Substantial Soviet bomber advances were cited. Army and Navy leaders, and President Kennedy, like President Eisenhower earlier, opposed the RS-70, holding that great numbers of long-range missiles would be available before the new bomber could be produced in sufficient quantity. When the Kennedy administration requested $180 million in 1962 to continue the RS-70 development program, the House Armed Services Committee lavishly authorized $491 million. The committee's bill "directed" that the funds it authorized be spent. The choice of this particular word signified the beginning of a possible massive constitutional confrontation between Congress and the President for dominion over military policy. The House committee based its wording "direct" upon Article I, section 8, of the Constitution, which vests in Congress the responsibility for raising and maintaining the military forces.

President Kennedy refrained from picking up the gauntlet of the constitutional issue thrown down by the House Committee and its chairman, the powerful Congressman Carl Vinson of Georgia. Instead he took the "Swamp Fox of Georgia," as Vinson was otherwise known, for a stroll one sunny March afternoon in the White House rose garden. The President and the Congressman fortunately arranged an honorable, peace-making compromise by which the administration agreed to spend more than was originally budgeted for the RS-70 if a new review and technological developments warranted an increase.[15]

Presidents must also reckon with a favorite preoccupation of Congress in the military realm—investigation. Truman's Senate Committee to Investigate the Defense Program was a model of searching, but constructive, criticism that produced fruitful change in the administration of the Second World War. Success as a wartime investigator established Truman's chief claim upon his subsequent vice presidential nomination. A contrasting view of the investigatory power is provided by a great cross Lincoln had to bear in the Civil War, the Joint Committee on the Conduct of the War, which, in a typically unflattering estimate of the administration, wrote, "Folly, folly, folly reigns supreme. The President is a weak man." Lincoln reciprocated in his judgment of the committee. He said,

I have never faltered in my faith of being ultimately able to suppress this rebellion and of reuniting this divided country; but this improvised vigilant committee . . . is a marplot, and its greatest purpose seems to be to hamper my action and obstruct the military operations.[16]

# The Courts

As Commander-in-Chief the President also faces tensions with the remaining governmental branch concerned with military affairs—the federal courts—with its high duty in a democratic state to protect the Constitution and the laws against encroachment. The most perplexing and consequential issues between the Executive and the courts may arise during actual war, when the President feels driven to curtail, or even to suppress, key liberties sanctioned in the Bill of Rights. To further the progress of war, to safeguard what he cites as the nation's imperiled safety, the President has set aside political and economic liberties that in peacetime are inviolable.

### The Civil War and Civil Liberties

The Civil War, fought within the nation's borders and jeopardizing its capital, was resented and resisted in many sectors of the North sympathetic to the Confederacy, to the point that President Lincoln promulgated several orders and proclamations restricting individual liberty. The most important of these was his suspension of the constitutional privilege of the writ of habeas corpus. Lincoln's first habeas corpus proclamation, issued in the war's early weeks, was triggered by events in Maryland. Underground resistance and open defiance were rampant in that state. Federal troops were attacked by mobs in Baltimore, communications to the capital were severed, and the mayor and police chief were unabashedly pro-Confederate and anti-Lincoln. Bridges were destroyed to hamper the passage of Union troops, and newspapers hostile to the administration fanned disunion sentiment. The state legislature was soon to convene, and a formidable bloc of its members aimed to have the state secede from the Union.

Union generals moved to nip the growing conspiracy by arresting the mayor of Baltimore, the chief of police, and several police commissioners. Even more sensational was the arrest of members of the Maryland legislature. To forestall the passage of an act of secession, Union General Nathaniel P. Banks barred the legislature from meeting and arrested nine of its members and the chief clerk of the senate. Still other Marylanders were arrested, including one John Merryman "charged with various acts of treason." Merryman was languishing in Fort McHenry when the Chief Justice of the United States, Roger B. Taney, on circuit duty, ordered "the body of John Merryman [produced] and . . . the day and cause of [his] capture and detention" made known. A head-on clash between the President and the Court, between the war and the Constitution, was in the making. Taney, to the administration's great relief, confined himself to declaring that the power to suspend the writ, which should be exercised only with "extreme caution," belonged to Congress, and not to the President (17 Fed.

Cas. 144). Taney's opinion, nevertheless, put the administration under the cloud of the likelihood of a hostile Supreme Court decision, an event the Attorney General, Edward Bates, said would "do more to paralyze the Executive . . . than the worst defeat our armies have yet sustained."[17]

The administration's position was strengthened when Congress, after much struggle, passed the Habeas Corpus Act of 1863, affirming the President's power to suspend the writ. Despite several procedural devices incorporated to placate the courts, the act left to the Executive the setting of policy concerning arrests and imprisonments. Prisoners were tried, as before, by military tribunal and punished or released under authority of the War Department. Arrests continued apace. Clement L. Vallandigham, fiery Copperhead, after his arrest, trial, and sentencing by a military commission, appealed to the United States Supreme Court to lift his case into civil court. But the Supreme Court ruled that it had no jursidiction, since a military commission was not a "court," to which the federal judiciary was limited under existing law (*Ex parte Vallandigham*, 68 U.S. 243, 1864).

Although Vallandigham never lived to see it, his legal position was ultimately vindicated in the celebrated case of *Ex parte Milligan* (4 Wallace 2, 1866). Milligan too was a Copperhead, tried by a military commission for "treasonable" speeches. Condemned to hang, he invoked the habeas corpus writ. But the war was now over, and the Court was prepared to act boldly. It ruled that Indiana, where Milligan resided and spoke, was not part of the "theater of war" and that the civil courts there were "open" and therefore available to conduct his trial. Under such a combination of circumstances, the writ could not be constitutionally suspended. The *Milligan* case, needless to say, has become the source of permanent consternation to the friends of presidential power and of hope to the friends of civil liberties. In *Milligan*, the interests of the latter clearly were paramount.

## The Second World War

Despite the potential restrictiveness of the *Milligan* doctrine, the Court proved tolerant of presidential power in the two world wars. In *Ex parte Quirin* (317 U.S. 1, 1942) the Court broadly construed the Commander-in-Chief's capacity as executor of the Articles of War, enacted by Congress to further the United States' obligations under the laws of war, a branch of international law. The Articles of War provide for their enforcement through courts-martial and military commissions. *Ex parte Quirin* concerned eight saboteurs, seven Germans and one American, who were trained in a Berlin espionage school and deposited on Long Island and the Florida coast by German submarines in 1942. They doffed their German military uniforms for civilian attire, and with their tools of sabotage set out for New York City, Jacksonville, and other points to practice their art on American war industries. Arrested by the FBI before they could get down to work, they were turned over to the provost marshal of the District of Columbia. As Commander-in-Chief, President Franklin D. Roosevelt appointed a military commission to try the would-be saboteurs for violating the laws of war by not wearing fixed emblems revealing their combatant status. Midway in the trial the defendants petitioned the United States Supreme Court and the District Court for the District of Columbia for leave to bring habeas corpus proceedings.

The defendants argued that the offense charged against them was not known to the laws of the United States and was not one "arising in the land and naval forces," as described by the Fifth Amendment of the Constitution. Nor was the military tribunal that was trying them, they said, constituted in keeping with the Articles of War. The Court struck down the latter contention by declining to distinguish between the powers of the President as Commander-in-Chief and of Congress to create a military commission. The Court rejected the other arguments, holding that cases involving enemy personnel had never been deemed to fall under the constitutional guarantees of the Fifth and Sixth Amendments. The Court also cited the long-standing practice represented by an act of 1806 that imposed the death penalty on alien spies "according to the law and usage of nations, by sentence of general court martial." The saboteurs, accordingly, were tried and sentenced by military commission.

The most extreme application of the Commander-in-Chief's power to designate the theater of military operations was President Roosevelt's executive order of February 19, 1942, directed at the presumed danger of Japanese sabotage on the West Coast. In the high excitement over the Japanese bombing of Pearl Harbor, Roosevelt was pressed by the military, Congress, West Coast groups, and the newspapers to remove persons of Japanese ancestry from that area farther into the mainland. By Executive Order No. 9066 Roosevelt empowered the Secretary of War to establish "military areas" from which "any or all persons" might be excluded to prevent espionage and sabotage, and he designated military commanders to police these areas. The Secretary of War was directed to provide food, shelter, and transportation for persons evacuated. Soon the three westernmost states and a part of Arizona were declared "military areas 1 and 2" by Lieutenant General J. L. DeWitt. In a brief resolution of March 21, 1942, Congress endorsed the presidential action by making it a misdemeanor "to knowingly enter, remain in, or leave prescribed military areas" of the Secretary of War or of the commanding officer. A War Relocation Authority was established to care for persons cleared out of the military areas. In all, some 112,000 persons were removed from the West Coast, of whom the vast majority— 70,000—were United States citizens. Both the transplanted United States citizens and the aliens were eventually placed in ten "relocation centers" in California, Arizona, Idaho, Utah, Colorado, Wyoming, and Arkansas.

The relocation enterprise was challenged several times, but never effectively. In *Hirabayashi* v. *United States* (320 U.S. 81, 1943) the Court, by the drastic surgery of legal technicalities, reduced the issue to the right of the West Coast commander to subject citizens of Japanese ancestry to a special curfew order. The Court stressed the nation's plight and the state of the war in reaching its decision. Japan was achieving striking victories in 1943, the West Coast lay exposed, defense plants were heavily concentrated there, and, in the eyes of the Court, the ethnic affiliation of Japanese-Americans with the enemy posed a danger unknown from those of other ancestry. The Court deemed relocation within the powers of the President and Congress "acting in cooperation." In *Korematsu* v. *United States* (323 U.S. 214, 1944) a United States citizen, a Japanese-American, was convicted in district court for remaining in his California home. The Supreme Court again severely narrowed its decision and reasserted the reasoning of earlier relocation cases, though Japan was now in full retreat throughout the Pacific.

The most general abrogation of civil liberties in the Second World War occurred in the territory of Hawaii. Soon after the Japanese bombed Pearl Harbor, Governor J. B. Poindexter of Hawaii invoked section 67 of the Hawaiian Organic Act of April 30, 1900, proclaimed martial law throughout the territory, and turned over to the commanding general of the Hawaiian Department the exercise of all normal gubernatorial powers "during the present emergency and until the danger of invasion is removed." President Roosevelt approved Poindexter's decision, and a regime of martial law commenced that remained in force until October 24, 1944, when a presidential proclamation terminated it. Habeas corpus was suspended and the civil courts were supplanted by military tribunals in which civilians were tried for crimes by summary procedures.

The Hawaiian arrangement was challenged in 1943, when District Judge Delbert E. Metzger issued a writ of habeas corpus in behalf of two naturalized Germans interned by the Army. The Hawaiian commander, Lieutenant General Robert C. Richardson, countered by forbidding writs of habeas corpus, including those of Judge Metzger. The issue was soon settled administratively.

Eventually, the Court, in *Duncan* v. *Kahanamoku, Sheriff* (327 U.S. 304, 1946) cited section 5 of the Hawaiian Organic Act, which declares that the Constitution of the United States has "the same effect within said Territory as elsewhere in the United States." The war was now well past, and the Court declared that the suspension of normal judicial processes had been unlawful. The Organic Act of 1900, it found, did not authorize the supplanting of civil courts by military tribunals.

In addition to seizing persons, the President as Commander-in-Chief has also seized property. Six months before Pearl Harbor, while the nation was still officially at peace, President Roosevelt, citing his earlier proclamation of an "unlimited national emergency," seized the strikebound North American Aviation plant at Inglewood, California. Roosevelt's claim of authority was sweeping and somewhat imprecise: "the duty constitutionally and inherently resting upon the President to exert his civil and military as well as his moral authority to keep the defense efforts of the United States a going concern," and "to obtain supplies for which Congress has appropriated money, and which it has directed the President to obtain." Both before and after the United States became a belligerent, Roosevelt seized other aircraft plants, shipyards, and a railroad.

## Korea and Indochina

In the Korean conflict, President Truman brought the Supreme Court down upon his head when he ordered the seizure of most of the nation's steel mills in the face of a threatened strike, citing "the authority vested in me by the Constitution and laws of the United States." The President ignored the Taft-Hartley Act, which established special procedures for national labor emergencies but did not give him the power of seizure. The Supreme Court, in *Youngstown Sheet and Tube Co.* v. *Sawyer* (343 U.S. 579, 1952), ordered the President and his executive colleagues to say out of the steel mills, holding that in seizing them he had seized legislative power. Only Congress could have ordered the mills seized; the President lacked power to seize them without its authorization. Like the *Milligan* case, this hastily improvised opinion throws a lasting shadow of doubt over the President's independent seizure power.

Labor too has felt the pressure of the Commander-in-Chief's power. In the Second World War the President by executive order created a War Manpower Commission to manage the mobilization of manpower for employment in the war production industries. Later Roosevelt added to the commission's province the administration of the Selective Service System. The WMC was not long in issuing a "work or fight" order requiring all workers designated as "nondeferable," or those engaged in "nonessential" enterprise, to choose between induction into the armed services and transfer to war production jobs. Draft requirements were simultaneously lowered, and the nation's workers faced a categorical choice: work in a war plant or be drafted into the armed forces.

Conceivably, the courts might declare that the hosilities in which the President has engaged the armed forces are unconstitutional. In the concluding weeks of American air bombing of Cambodia, a federal district judge ruled that the bombing must stop because it was "unauthorized and unlawful." But the ruling was overturned by the Court of Appeals, and the Supreme Court declined to review the case. In effect, the high court acquiesced to the appellate court's view that the legality of the Cambodian action was a political question not reviewable by the courts.[18]

# Communist War-making

What the President does as Commander-in-Chief, how he uses his power, is not the simple choice of a self-willed Chief Executive. Not the least of the novelties the President has had to cope with are the several species of warfare that the communist powers choose to wage and with which the United States has had little, if any, experience. These are the techniques of guerrilla warfare, infiltration, and takeover waged by communist operatives. Contemporary Presidents have faced large-scale "police action," or undeclared war, in Korea, civil war in Greece, guerrilla war in Indochina, insurrection in the Canal Zone, a communist revolution in Cuba, and communist infiltration and takeover in other lands. In 1979, for the first time since the Second World War, the Soviet Union dispatched its own forces into combat by invading neighboring Afghanistan.

A favorite Soviet tactic is war by proxy, by which it supplies arms and encouragement to other peoples and nations, such as North Vietnam, Cuba and sundry Arab states, who bear the burden of fighting. According to a 1972 report by the Stockholm International Peace Research Institute, the Soviet Union, apart from its contributions to the Vietnam war, had become the largest supplier of weapons to Third World peoples.[19] The recipients of Soviet assistance, particularly if they are communist states or forces, often prove their deserts by unstinting dedication to the battlefield. Cubans have fought in Angola, Zaire, Ethiopia, and Yemen, among other places. The unflagging North Vietnamese outdo even the Prussians in warlike tenacity. Since 1945, they have fought to impose their will on the people of South Vietnam and neighboring Laos and Cambodia as well.

In response, Presidents have committed American forces to combat, as in Korea and Indochina, and to watch over a change of government in the Dominican Republic. The President oversees vast programs of military and economic aid to nations around the globe, particularly on the communist periphery. He engages in a range of other acts of fluctuating subtlety and success through the CIA. And he can launch bold indirect counterthrusts at the U.S.S.R.'s promotions of war by proxy. Thus in 1979, when Carter faced strong infusions of Soviet arms, the presence of Cuban advisers in Marxist-ruled South Yemen (whose forces penetrated Yemen), and the knowledge that both countries border Saudi Arabia (an ally and premier petroleum supplier of the United States), he chose to respond with military countermeasures. The President speeded delivery of fighter planes, armored personnel carriers, and tanks to Yemen. American military advisers were also committed to help train the Yemen military; to further emphasize his concern, Carter dispatched a carrier task force to the Arabian sea.[20] In succeeding months the situation fluctuated between incipient explosion and uneasy quietude.

## Invasion of Afghanistan

In his surprise and shock at the Soviet invasion of Afghanistan, Carter invoked a range of measures. Warning that he would use force to protect America's vital petroleum supplies in the Persian Gulf, he proposed the creation of a rapid deployment force, higher military spending, diminished constraints on intelligence activities, aid to Pakistan, American presence and access to military facilities adjacent to the Indian Ocean, and revived draft registration in peacetime. In independent actions, he suspended grain deliveries and the sale of high technology to the Soviet Union, curtailed Soviet fishing privileges in American waters, and rallied a boycott of the 1980 Summer Olympics in Moscow. The CIA launched covert missions to supply light infantry weapons to Afghan insurgents, and Egypt, recipient of bountiful American military aid, provided additional weapons and training. Doubtless the Afghans' own doughty resistance was more effective than Carter's combined measures, but no totality of effort could dislodge the Soviets.

The invasion of Afghanistan brought into sharper focus the extraordinary build-up of Soviet military strength since the Cuban missile crisis of 1962, which presumably emboldened it to undertake the Afghan adventure. A CIA report estimated that Soviet military spending in 1979 was fifty percent higher than American spending, and in presenting his 1980 budget, Defense Secretary Harold Brown emphasised the "uneasy balance" of military power between the United States and the Soviet Union.[21] Despite Carter's response of stepped-up budgetary commitments, military officials predicted that at least a decade would be required to redress imbalances between the countries.[22]

## Civil War in Central America

Civil war, followed by takeover by a Marxist regime, has become a recurrent tableau in Third World countries. In Nicaragua, the Carter presidency was caught off guard by the rapidly failing dictatorship of Anastasio Somoza

Debayle, fatally threatened by Sandanista guerrillas with firm ties to Cuba. The administration sought vainly to enlist intervention by members of the Organization of American States (OAS) to halt the fighting in Nicaragua and to obtain agreement on a centrist, broadly based transitional government. But the long identification of the United States with the exploitative Somoza regime left the OAS countries unenthusiastic for the venture, and the Sandanists stormed to power.[23]

When, subsequently, civil upheaval overthrew El Salvador's dictator, President Carlos Humberto Romero, the Carter administration strove mightily to prop up a succeeding moderate regime, with grants for economic development, housing, "Food for Peace," public works, and community development. Accomplishment was meagre. Assailed by both Marxist and rightist forces, the new government barely clung to existence. Although in Salvador as in Nicaragua, Carter moved to promote democratic, nonviolent solutions, he was hampered by a legacy of resented United States interventions in Central America and its frequent support of dictatorial regimes.[24]

# Alliances

In another major response to the division between the western and communist worlds, the contemporary President is heavily engaged as a builder and custodian of alliances, a responsibility his forebears never had to face. He and his deputies have constructed bilateral alliances with nations around the world, committing money, technicians, armaments, and even American soldiers. He has played a leading role in the founding of such multilateral alliances as NATO, and ANZUS.* He buoys up the alliances when their inspiration lags in seasons of communist quiet and enheartens them when disaster threatens. He is apt to view alliances at times as a step toward a world community, a vehicle for advancing objectives urgent for all humankind. He and his fellow chief executives are restrained and goaded in the common task by the pressures of their inescapable domestic political necessities. The promise and frustration alliances hold for American Chief Executives are illustrated by several encounters John Kennedy experienced with allies.

## Weapons Policies

Kennedy included among his objectives the adoption by the United States and its allies of efficient and economical American-built weapons systems. He also worked mightily to forestall individual European nations from building their own nuclear weapons, but proposed that their development and use be integrated into the NATO alliance. Kennedy, whose keen sense of political realism extended to the international plane, took up his task conscious that "you can't possibly carry out any policy without causing major frictions."

*Australia, New Zealand, and the United States.

Kennedy and his principles were severely tested in his confrontation with British Prime Minister Macmillan at their meeting in the Bahamas in December 1962. The subject of discussion was Skybolt, a nuclear-tipped missile with a thousand-mile range, launched from high-speed bombers. In a conference with President Eisenhower at Camp David in 1959, Macmillan had arranged for the purchase of one hundred Skybolts at a relatively low price for delivery in 1964. The United States Air Force's candidate for the top weapons vehicle of the next generation, Skybolt was being developed in competition with Polaris and Minuteman. Relying upon Skybolt, the British abandoned their own Blue Streak, a land-based missile, in 1960. The Kennedy administration, faced with climbing weapons costs, decided to abandon Skybolt and concentrate upon other weapons systems. The land-based Minuteman, tests proved, could reach any Skybolt target from underground launching silos in the United States. The administration felt that Minuteman plus Polaris, a submarine-launched missile, would satisfy both American and allied needs for long-range weapons. Abandoning Skybolt would slow the big weapons drain on the United States budget, and, if the British could be induced to accept Polaris, Kennedy could advance another valued objective—the vesting of nuclear weapons not in individual nations but in the trust of alliances to which the United States belonged.

At Nassau, Kennedy gave Macmillan the tidings that Skybolt would be no more and proposed instead that Britain adopt Polaris within a framework of NATO control. Macmillan apparently had little forewarning of the proposal, the President and his aides having just emerged from the engrossing Cuban missile crisis. The Skybolt cancellation was a hard blow to the Royal Air Force and its manned bomber. It was bad budget news for Macmillan because Skybolt, coupled with existing British bombers, was the cheapest possible way of maintaining an independent British deterrent. The cancellation also had implications for British domestic politics. Several days before venturing to Nassau, Macmillan had been a supplicant at the court of Charles de Gaulle, seeking entry to the European Common Market. The Prime Minister suffered the political ignominy of rebuff. At Nassau, with Kennedy's sudden confrontation, he was threatened with a second major political defeat. His party's fortunes were already badly in eclipse at home and an election was impending. Looming political disaster brought Macmillan to drop his accustomed Edwardian gentility and roar back at his presidential antagonist. But Kennedy held fast and offered Polaris to the British at the lowest possible price, with the proviso that although missiles would operate under NATO, they would pass under British command in "supreme national" emergency. Macmillan ultimately acquiesced, enabling Kennedy to improve his budgetary position and advance his purpose of internationalizing nuclear weapons.[25]

## Rapprochement with the Soviet and China

Major events and shifts in American objectives can jolt even the sturdiest alliances. For both Asian and European allies, Nixon's initiations of rapprochement with the Soviet Union and Communist China evoked nightmares of uncertainty concerning future American resolve to live up to the traditional military commitments of its alliances. The distress was exacerbated by the minimum forewarning given to allies and the modesty of subsequent assurances.

In both East and West, allies reacted with defiance and distress. In South Korea, President Park Chung Hee declared that his country would not accept any big-power decision on the fate of Korea made without the consent and participation of his government.[26] In western Europe, improved U.S.–U.S.S.R. relations were beheld as a prelude to the withdrawal of some American forces from the continent while the heavy build-up of Soviet strength continued, steps that could lead to an overwhelming preponderance of Soviet power at the threshold of Central Europe.[27] As for China, its interest in the tri-part relation was to retain and enhance its American option as a depressing force on the Soviet military machine sitting at its borders.[28]

The Carter Presidency's confident optimism about U.S.–U.S.S.R. relations provoked persistent uneasiness among Western European allies. Carter's initial foreign policies were perceived as dangerously naive: his pledge to reduce American forces in South Korea, his out-of-hand rejection of any military support for Yugoslavia after Tito's death, his decision to halt development of the B-1 bomber, his reductions of the Navy's construction program, and deferment of a decision on producing the neutron bomb, drove European NATO commanders, mindful of the vast Soviet military build-up, to deep despair. "They are stronger, comparatively, than they ever were," a West German general lamented, "Is this the time to give up the neutron bomb, to abandon a new long-range bomber?"[29]

But later, when Carter was roughly awakened by the seizure of American hostages in Teheran and by the Soviet invasion of Afghanistan, West Europeans were again troubled, this time by the dour state of the President's new assumptions. After having assumed the best in Moscow's intentions, Carter now assumed the worst: the Afghan venture was a premeditated strategic step toward domination of the oil fields and sea lanes of the Middle East—a plot to strangle the fuel supplies of the industrial West, clearly, he said, the most ominous crisis since World War II. But West Europeans, in contrast, attributed less disturbing motives to the Soviets, such as fear of the spread of Islamic chaos from Iran into Afghanistan and on across their borders to inflame their own huge Islamic community. Impressed with the shortage of resources available for NATO's defense of Western Europe, the allies were loath to heed Carter's call for assistance if the United States should confront the Soviet in the Persian Gulf. These under-supported forces were coveted for European defense.[30]

# Nuclear Weaponry

The President bears the awesome responsibility to our allies, to his own people, indeed to all humankind, of deciding when, if ever, to use the vast arsenal of American nuclear weaponry. Under law only he, the Commander-in-Chief, can give the order. He has done so on but one occasion—near the end of the Second World War, when Truman ordered atomic bombs to be dropped on Hiroshima and Nagasaki in 1945. Later Presidents have threatened to use nuclear weapons. In 1953 President Eisenhower threatened Communist China with nuclear attack unless it supported a truce in Korea.[31] In his 1962 confrontation with the Soviets over their emplacement of offensive missiles in Cuba, President Kennedy put the Strategic Air Command and Air Force missile crews on maximum alert. In the 1973 Middle East War, with signs that Soviet forces might intervene to rescue entrapped Egyptian army units, Secretary of Defense James R. Schlesinger instructed the chairman of the Joint Chiefs of Staff, Admiral Thomas H. Moorer, to put U.S. armed forces on general stand-by alert, including the Strategic Air Command and the North American Air Defense Command, custodians of nuclear arms. Although Schlesinger acted without talking directly with the President, the Secretary asserted that Nixon was "in complete command at all times," and later approved "a whole series of decisions" adopted by the National Security Council.[32] This example of a remote President who merely ratifies the deliberations of subordinates is dangerous and distressing. Without the President in active command, communications can more easily become confusing in the leaderless negotiations of coequal department secretaries, and the dreaded risks of accidental war increase. And subordinates, unconstrained by the responsibility that is vested in the President alone, are more prey to temptations to overreach themselves. More typically and rightly, Presidents are active participants as major decisions develop that can potentially affect the use of nuclear weapons.

## Internal Executive-Branch Controls

In facing their responsibilities for nuclear weapons, Chief Executives, typically, have been absorbed in two concerns. One is keeping the ultimate decision in their own hands. "I don't want some young Colonel to decide when to drop an atomic bomb," President Truman was known to say. The other is the avoidance of the dread possibility of an "accidental" nuclear war. Both problems thrust the President well into a complex of mechanisms and procedures regulating the release of nuclear weapons.[33]

The complex begins at the Ballistic Missile Early Warning System (BMEWS) in Thule, Greenland, where radar screens are poised to pick up Soviet missiles, if they are ever launched against the United States. Infrared satellites can detect missile exhaust, and radar on the Massachusetts coast can pick up Soviet submarine-launched rockets. Intelligence from these sources is simultaneously flashed to the North American Air Defense Command (NORAD) at Cheyenne Mountain, Colorado, for interpretation; to the Strategic Air Command (SAC) control post near Omaha, Nebraska; to the Joint War Room of the Joint Chiefs of Staff in the Pentagon; and to the President. Several kinds of radio systems, telephones, teletypes, and television link these points. Multiple routings, frequencies, and circuits; alternate locations; verifications by senders and recipients that the messages actually come from their presumed source; procedures to challenge and counter-challenge the verifications; hundreds of men to pass the word to the button-pushers, who also number in the hundreds: all conribute to the vast effort to find safety.

The policy-makers, generals, psychologists, sociologists, and physicists charged with tightening the safety factor must deal with several types of possible human failure. Elaborate testing and "redundancy" procedures help thwart the kind of situation that arose in 1958 when a berserk sergeant threatened to fire a pistol at a nuclear bomb, but was fortunately talked out of it by a supervisor. In 1980, several false nuclear alarms provoked by malfunctioning computers were opportunely detected. Suppose the President of the United States "goes ape," as the military say? Or suppose he singlehandedly decides to reverse national policy and launch a preventive war? The President too is subject to checks. Even he cannot simply pick up his telephone and order "go," nor does he know the one signal for a nuclear strike—the "go code." In an emergency he would receive intelligence via the "gold phone circuit" that connects him with the offices, action stations, and homes of the Secretary of Defense, the Joint Chiefs of Staff, the SAC commander, and others, all of whom could assist in his decision. An agenda with key questions concerning the probable emergency has been prepared, which could be administered quickly and in code. Time is a slight safety factor. In the existing state of weapons systems, the President has a possible thirty minutes after the report of ground-launched enemy ICBM's and fifteen minutes for submarine-launched rockets to consult and await further information before unleashing a full, irrevocable "go."

Chief Executives have been concerned with several types of safety and control. Kennedy arranged the "hot line" to Moscow to deal with breakdowns and miscalculations of the kind featured in the novel *Fail-Safe*.[34] The Kennedy administration also instituted a new lock system for the nation's huge and far-flung nuclear weapons arsenal. Kennedy consummated the 1963 test ban treaty with the Soviet Union, and Johnson promoted the treaty prohibiting states from placing nuclear arms or other weapons of mass destruction in orbit around the earth or installing those weapons on the moon or on other celestial bodies.[35] In 1968 Johnson could hail the adoption of a treaty to prevent the spread of nuclear weapons by barring the five nuclear powers from transferring nuclear weapons to nations that do not have them.

## Arms Limitations Agreements

The 1972 Nixon-Brezhnev arms accords limited each side's defensive missile systems, with a commitment not to build nationwide antimissile defenses. In addition, an interim five-year agreement concerning offensive systems froze land-based and submarine-based intercontinental missiles at existing levels. Although a solid advance, the accords were nevertheless flawed by gaping loopholes that were quickly exploited. A further Nixon-Brezhnev agreement, reached during their Washington 1973 summit, called for immediate and "urgent consultations" if relations between their countries, or between one of them and another country, "appear to involve the risk of nuclear conflict." Thereupon the two superpowers shall "make every effort to avert this risk."[36] In 1974 at Vladivostok, Ford and Brezhnev reached a tentative agreement to limit the number of all offensive strategic nuclear weapons and delivery vehicles through 1985. The agreement left wide latitude for quantitative and technological expansions.

Neither the 1972 or later agreements contained provision for on-site inspection to check violations, but American officals were confident that other means of verification would suffice. According to an "open sky" provision of the 1972 agreements, neither side would "use deliberate concealment measures which impede verification" of compliance through the employment by both the United States and the Soviet Union of reconnaissance satellites.[37] But by 1974, Defense Department officials suspected that the Soviet was camouflaging some weapons programs and concealing its deployment of strategic missiles. Pentagon officials cited the placement of canvas covers over construction ways at a shipyard near Murmansk where nuclear-powered missile-carrying submarines are constructed. As well, the Soviet Union, according to these officials, was employing countermeasures to thwart American electronic methods.[38] Electronic intelligence surveillance is important for monitoring Soviet missile programs during their development phases, while photographic intelligence through reconnaissance satellites keeps watch of missiles once they are deployed.

*Salt II*    Until the Afghan crisis exploded, Carter was dedicated to pushing the Strategic Arms Limitation Treaty (SALT II) negotiations with the Soviet Union to fruition in the Senate. "I've only got one life to live and one opportunity to serve in the highest elected office in our land," he said, "I will never have a chance so momentous to contribute to world peace as to negotiate and to see ratified this SALT treaty."[39] An oversize document exceeding one-hundred pages, the treaty, which Carter submitted to the Senate, would run until 1985 and would limit both heavy bombers and ballistic missiles; a three-year protocol would restrict the deployment of cruise missiles. (A ballistic missile is a long-range missile that flies to its target at high speed and high elevation, above the atmosphere. A cruise missile is a winged missile that can fly toward its target at lower speed and altitude than a ballistic missile.) The treaty also imposes limited controls on the modernization of existing arms and constrains the deployment of new systems.[40]

As evidence of the Soviet Union's prodigious arms expansion grew, the Senate's enthusiasm for the treaty waned. The Senate was further affronted by the series of aggressive Soviet ventures in Africa and Asia. The Soviet invasion of Afghanistan made defeat of the treaty a certainty. Carter's several retaliations included a request that Senate Majority Leader Robert C. Byrd (D-W.Va.) "delay consideration of the SALT II treaty on the Senate floor." Carter simultaneously emphasized that the treaty was still in the national interest.[41] In pre-inaugural statements, Reagan declared that SALT II must be renegotiated and that those negotiations must be linked to Soviet "policies of aggression around the world."

*Curtailing the spread of nuclear weapons*    Carter diligently pursued initiatives to curtail the spread and danger of nuclear weapons. In an early action, he urged that all nuclear testing be halted "instantly and completely."[42] Subsequently, he announced that the United States would not use plutonium to fuel nuclear reactors to produce electricity, and he championed legislation empowering the President to penalize countries violating agreements designed to prevent the spread of nuclear weapons. West Germany spurned his urgings that it not sell Brazil equipment capable of producing atomic weapons. But Carter induced the Soviet Union to join in a pact that would bar earth satellites from carrying radioactive material in order to avert possible contamination during reentry into the atmosphere.

# Weapons Systems

Among the more nerve-racking presidential responsibilities is deciding whether or not to develop new weapons and to choose between competing proposals advanced by the individual military services. The arms race is a contest in human inventiveness and technological know-how to produce weapons of high destructive potential and a capacity to elude conceivable defenses. Presidents labor on a treadmill of uncertainty, of high risk, and under formidable pressure. No matter how the President chooses, he will displease some branch of the military, our allies, and professional military critics, a growing community of private specialists.

For Carter, who had to decide the fate of more major weapons systems than other Presidents, 1977 was a watershed year. Three momentous decisions faced him: should he order development of the long-range cruise missile as the nuclear wonder-weapon of the 1980s, build or abandon the B-1 manned bomber, and continue or postpone production of the MX mobile missile?

## B-1 Bomber Decision

In his 1976 campaign, Carter criticized the prevailing high spending levels for weapons systems, and he particularly singled out the long-researched B-1 bomber as an example of military profligacy. Air Force leaders were convinced that the B-1 could penetrate the ever more formidable Soviet air defenses or approach Russian targets to the point where short-range attack missiles could be used effectively. The Ford administration's departing Air Force Secretary, Thomas C. Reed, said "it would be irresponsible not to initiate B-1 production" given the "expansion" of Soviet strategic forces.[43] But critics of the B-1 contended that it would be unable to break through sophisticated Soviet air defenses in the 80s.

At midyear 1977, Carter announced his decision to halt production of the B-1 bomber. Explanations of the President's decision emphasized that with the B-1s costing $102 million each, many billions of dollars could be saved and the immediate defense budget materially reduced. The President was also seen as favoring a trend away from the development of increasingly sophisticated and hideously expensive military technology, America's strong suit in competition with the Soviet.[44]

But the principal factor in his decision, Carter disclosed, was an odd-shaped little weapon, relatively inexpensive ($750,000 per unit), launched from air, ground, or sea, with nuclear warheads—the cruise missile. With a range of twelve hundred miles, the cruise missile could be launched from B-52 bombers hovering outside the Soviet Union. Low flying and pilotless, the cruise missile was credited with high accuracy and unrivalled ability to penetrate Soviet air defenses. "It's cheap. It's accurate. It's powerful. It's the weapon of the 80s," a Congressman rejoiced.[45]

Carter's further 1977 decision was to postpone production of the MX mobile missile designed for deployment on railroad cars in the American Southwest, each missile bearing ten independently targeted nuclear warheads.

## Redeciding

Carter's trio of decisions aroused a strident outcry. Critics asserted that the decisions, considered together, constituted an unacceptable risk in an interval when the Soviet Union was progressing swiftly in nuclear weaponry. Air Force strategists warned that before the cruise missiles could be deployed, the Soviets would surely develop a barrier defense with airborne warning and control aircraft and thousands of interceptors. John Taylor, editor of "Jane's All the World's Aircraft," concluded, in doomsday tones, that "1977 might be recorded as the year in which the seeds of defeat for the Western powers were sown." [46]

Given the volatility of the world of weapons systems, presidential decision is apt to look, with passing time, not better, but worse. By 1979 the blush of earlier optimism had faded for the cruise missile. The once modest expenditure, which made the weapon so attractive to Carter, had soared to $10 million per missile. Reports abounded of new Soviet efficiency to deter the missile, including an advanced "look down" radar that detects low flying planes and cruise missiles. But from his place on the treadmill of weapons systems, the President could extract a few grains of comfort. To substitute for the confidence seemingly misplaced on the cruise missile, the Air Force proposed to modify a medium-range bomber, the FB-111, into a new strategic weapon for the 80s. Already highly capable of penetrating enemy airspace, it could, with further development, execute missions of six thousand miles, bearing short-range attack missiles with nuclear warheads.[47] Of one thing the President can be certain: his salvation is only temporary—to be enjoyed until his present weapon, on which hopes are pinned, is blunted by the next new counterweapon.

# ★ ★ ★ The Future Presidency ★ ★ ★

The Commander-in-Chief must be both strong and restrained, qualities that are vital to the well-being of democracy and presidential power. Like any other form of government, democracy must maintain and reconcile to its processes a military establishment. A major means to that end is civilian control over the military, and the effective assertion of that principle depends centrally upon the President, who as Commander-in-Chief is a civilian officer to whom the military are subordinate. In an era of huge military budgets and devastating weapons, the presidency's effectiveness as the vehicle of civilian control becomes crucial. How can the President, in the best sense, function both as a strong and a democratic Commander-in-Chief?

1. The most costly decisions that escalated the American commitment to the Vietnam war were made in an interlude when power in the Pentagon was concentrated in the Secretary of Defense, and military advice from the Joint Chiefs of Staff was "unified" in the hands of the Chairman. The quality of the advice rising to the President suffered from the tendency to compromise among the services to produce a common position,

or to engage in log-rolling in which recommendations of all the services are endorsed.

Better military advice might be forthcoming if the Chairman of the Joint Chiefs of Staff is separated from the service chiefs (Army, Navy, Air). Thereupon the President and the Secretary of Defense would invite the separate views of each service chief and the JCS Chairman, and even, when useful, the views of field commanders, such as those for Europe and Asia and the head of the Strategic Air Command. Under this structure of multiple sources of advice, the President and the Secretary of Defense would be apprised of different viewpoints rather than simply a negotiated compromise. Instead of being engrossed in developing the compromise, the JCS Chairman could formulate a military judgment separate from the perspective of the services—with a military overview supplied by the Chairman and the opinions of the operators provided by the service chiefs. A report prepared for the Carter administration by Richard C. Steadman, on reorganization within the Pentagon, supports this view.[48]

In making his decisions as Commander-in-Chief, the President, under this arrangement, is more apt to obtain proposals that are imaginative and innovative and is more likely to be aware of the diversity of military opinions rather than to become lulled by the misbelief that the views of his advisers are unified.[49] Also, the President would be freed of the awkwardness of having to develop a new position that in effect overrules all the military. Clearly, a further vital ingredient is the President himself. Unless he is receptive to structural diversity, a system such as that sketched will not work. Nixon was not attuned to multiple advocacy, nor was Johnson through most of his encounter with the Vietnam war, but Truman and Eisenhower were, and likewise Carter.

2. Decision-making concerning the military budget and the invocation of military force ought to flow, after initial preparation, to points outside the Defense Department, into broader arenas where participants are drawn from other departments and agencies as well as from the White House office. Nixon moved in that direction in his restructuring of the National Security Council. Consequently, one NSC group became a forum in which military, diplomatic, and intelligence evaluations of possible use of force could be brought together systematically. Another NSC committee reviewed the Defense budget, its size and major programs, and the participants included Defense, State, the Arms Control and Disarmament Agency, the Council of Economic Advisers, and the Office of Management and Budget.[50] In the Nixon years, these and other NSC committees were chaired by the powerful assistant for national security affairs, Henry Kissinger, which suggests that the net change was minimal, that centralized power had moved from the Defense Secretary to a new locus, the national security assistant. Such unwanted concentration could easily be dissipated by future Presidents simply by designating a different official as chairman of each of the NSC committees and thereby enhancing the possibility of varied advice emerging from the NSC structure.

3. President Carter, more than any of his predecessors since the Second World War, was faced with the prodigious growth of Soviet military strength and the relative decline of American power over the past dec-

ade. A study by the Congressional Research Service in 1976 concluded that "the quantitative balance continues to shift toward the Soviet Union," and that American qualitative superiority "in certain respects, is slowly slipping away." [51]

Altogether, this might be a sufficiently crucial juncture for the United States to reevaluate its defense policies: to review what its appropriate military missions are, how much of its gross national product to commit to defense; and to spotlight weakness in the intricate military fabric: possible deficiencies of naval power, the readiness and mobility of the forces, their recruitment and training, the military base structure, and so on. Traditionally, these and other components of defense are subject to budgetary trade-offs and obscure discourse by military specialists, bewildering to the general public.

It is now opportune for a comprehensive review of military policy, possibly by a commission composed of about twenty knowledgeable and prestigious persons, appointed by the President. Thomas S. Gates, a Defense Secretary in the Eisenhower Administration suggests that the commission include former President Ford, the chairmen and ranking minority members of the House and Senate Armed Services and Defense Appropriations Committees, the present Secretaries of State, Treasury, Defense, and the Chairman of the Joint Chiefs of Staff plus distinguished private individuals. [52] Former President Carter could also join the group. The commission's findings and recommendations could provide a coherent, integrated statement of defense needs, against which future budgets and other military decisions could be evaluated.

4. The limitation of the arms race through international agreement ought to remain a large preoccupation of the President. Only an effective Chief Executive can press the case upon Congress and the people that an upward spiraling arms race is a threat to the nation's security. The individual services and the congressional committees to which they are allied can be expected to provide resistance that only the Chief Executive can overcome. He is best situated to keep alive useful proposals that at first are rejected and to assure that new possibilities are considered. The Commander-in-Chief does not simply conduct war or stay prepared for the threat of it. He has a further mission upon which the nation's and the world's future depends—the Commander-in-Chief also keeps the peace.

# Chapter Eleven

# The Economy

In his economic duties the Chief Executive is caught in a power gap. He functions in the one major nation of the world whose economic order and tradition are founded on private enterprise. He presides over a pluralistic economy in which private enterprise makes the key decisions of what and how much to produce, when and at what price, and how profits shall be used. The extent of private decision is evidenced by the gap that may exist between what the President tries to do and what he accomplishes. The President can toil, plan, and hope for prosperity, but there may be only depression. He can thunder against the trusts, but big enterprise may grow apace. He can come into office pledged to get the country "moving again," but for all his exertion the economy may only lag.

## Economic Policy Agencies

The several administrative and policy-formulating agencies of the executive branch dealing with the economy differ widely in their responsiveness to the President. The Office of Management and Budget and the Council of Economic Advisers are *his* agencies and behave accordingly. As developer and overseer of the budget, the OMB services the President's most powerful economic weapon, the federal budget, the most massive source of expenditure in the nation's economy. Typically, the Council of Economic Advisers, its chairman, and two other members, are professional economists, aided by a staff of nearly forty. The great operating departments—Treasury, Commerce, Labor, and Agriculture—are part of the President's cabinet family and partners to large and intimate decisions of the administration. An array of independent regulatory commissions—the Federal Reserve Board, the Securities and Exchange Commission, the Interstate Commerce Commission, and the like—make basic decisions in vital economic areas such as banking and credit, the sale of securities, the conduct of the stock exchanges, transportation, and communications. The independent commissions are carefully removed from the President's line of command. He has influence but lacks authority over them.

## Limitations of Power

The limitations of his economic powers enthrone the President on the jagged prongs of a predicament. His authority over the economy does not equal his responsibility for its condition. Legally and administratively, he has important but severely limited means to influence its health and growth. As Martin Van Buren, Herbert Hoover, and Jimmy Carter would gladly have testified on the election nights of 1840, 1932, and 1980, the voters hold the Chief Executive responsible for the plight of their jobs and their pocketbooks above all else.

Yet for all the limitations the President suffers in his authority, he has more impact upon the economy than any single source or possible combination of private power. The substantial authority and influence he possesses make him the head of the economic administration of the country. He applies quantities of laws promoting, regulating, and planning economic affairs. The Employment Act of 1946, a grand codification of his responsibilities, broadly charges him to lay before Congress each January an economic report on levels and trends of production, employment, and purchasing power, and to recommend ways to stimulate them. He is sometimes empowered to administer controls of prices, wages, and rents, which in the Nixon years were applied with widely varying and suddenly altering degrees of intensity, with each shift determined solely by the President. He collects taxes to provide roads, airports, research, and other services vital to industry. Thanks to its military needs, the executive branch, which the President manages, is the nation's largest purchaser. The aircraft and shipping industries would indeed be in a perilous state and railroads that were once great and Chrysler as an automobile manufacturer would vanish altogether if the United States government were not their best customer or guarantor. Through loans and guarantees administered by executive agencies, the President reduces or erases the risk to private enterprise. If the energy crisis of the 80s is to be diminished and the devastation it wreaks on the economy is to be constrained, the President is best situated to mount a coherent attack on the problem.

In effectuating the confinement of the strong President within the norms of democratic accountability, the economy plays a vital part. It embraces the most powerful of the domestic constituencies, to which, to attract their valued approval and support, he must justify programs and policies and plead for cooperative private economic decisions, on which his own policies critically depend. Labor and business leaders play fluctuating roles in presidential nominations and provide wherewithal for political campaigns, a basis for future demands on the President for concessions on program and policy. Pluralist democracy requires the flourishing of a variety of private economic enterprises and labor organizations and depends upon the existence of multiple power centers that assert initiatives and checks toward other centers, including the presidency. In turn, the Chief Executive can weaken or strengthen economic pluralism by formulating policies that assist the concentration of private economic power or that resist it and foster increases of power units.

# The President as Friend of Business

Living as they do in an economic world where decisions of private industry have much to do with economic health, Presidents as a lot assume that harmony and confidence between government and business are profitable to both. This benign assumption burns weakest in economic depression and brightest in war, when the nation's survival depends upon coordinated public and private economic effort. Presidents, for all their good intentions, differ widely in their individual dispositions toward business. Calvin Coolidge's worshipful dictum "The business of America is business" bespeaks his administration's total dedication to helping business. Jimmy Carter was the first full-fledged businessman to become President, and his personal core values were those idealized by business—hard work, thrift, self-reliance. Of contemporary Presidents, Richard Nixon aligned himself most squarely on the side of business and property. As President he preferred the company of self-made millionaires and cherished the comforts of their luxurious estates. In his lengthy congressional career, Gerald Ford developed his closest friendships with several of Washington's most powerful corporate lobbyists, including those for the Ford Motor Company, Procter and Gamble, and U.S. Steel. The day before Nixon resigned a presidential transition meeting between representatives of the outgoing and incoming Presidents took place at the Georgetown home of William G. White, vice president and top Washington representative of U.S. Steel, and Ford's old and trusted friend.[1] Ronald Reagan's close friends include five prominent Southern California businessmen, all self-made millionaires.

No President can be said to be antibusiness. Franklin D. Roosevelt, who waged fierce struggles to reform the worst business malpractices and said harsh things about "economic royalists" and "unscrupulous money-changers," accepted the basic structure and premises of the business community. "I am certain," his Secretary of Labor, Frances Perkins, well observed, "that he had no dream of great changes in the economic or political patterns of our life."[2] Roosevelt limited his rejection of private enterprise to TVA and several sister projects in the belief that popular and business power needs could not be adequately supplied by private means. He apparently never wished government to take over the railroads, the coal mines, or any other basic industry. He considered government ownership both clumsy and unnecessary.

Democratic Presidents have also learned that social reform encounters less opposition from the business community if the reform is made profitable for business. Shrewdly, Johnson contracted out management of Job

Corps Centers, a major component of his War on Poverty, to corporations. Carter founded his urban policy on loans and tax incentives for business.

The President's relations with the components of the business community may differ widely at any one time. The community is not a monolith but a sprawling, continental—indeed intercontinental—pluralism whose members' interests differ markedly by region (Wall Street and the East versus the West), by size (big, intermediate, and small business), and by function (manufacture, wholesale, and retail). A single industry may contain both "liberal" enterprises that are public-minded and public-relations conscious and "conservative" enterprises whose self-interest blinds them to national necessity and who habitually fight governmental regulation in Congress and the courts. Presidents are wily enough to exploit business differences. The easiest and most commonly employed tactic is to pursue policies toward the business community that appeal to the many and offend the few. In launching his famous antitrust suit against the Northern Securities Company, a giant consolidation of the James J. Hill, J. P. Morgan, and E. H. Harriman railways, which embraced nothing less than the Northern Pacific, the Great Northern, and the Chicago, Burlington, and Quincy systems, Theodore Roosevelt scored a ten-strike in the esteem of the majority of the business world. They hailed Roosevelt's crusade joyfully because the Northern Securities Company was the outcome of a massive struggle between Morgan and Harriman on which most businessmen blamed the panic of 1901.

By word and deed the business community bestows its approval or disfavor upon the Presidents. The United States Steel Corporation abstained from raising its prices in the eight presidential years of Dwight Eisenhower but boosted them twice during the three years of John Kennedy. The New Deal's cleansing and chastising of business created a lasting embitterment. No President has been more widely hated in the upper economic stratum than Franklin Roosevelt was. Visitors to J. P. Morgan in New Deal days were forewarned against mentioning the Roosevelt name lest it launch the mighty financier into apoplectic rage.[3]

# Winning Business Confidence

If democracy is denoted by communication exchange and mutual confidence, Presidents respond to those norms by their attentions to the sometimes hard task of securing business approval, aware that their own powers can be used more effectively if business's resistance is minimized. At the very least, Presidents desire to rouse business confidence in their administrations, for which they apply a variety of old and proven nostrums. A standard remedy is the appointment of businessmen to responsible administration posts. Even Presidents like the Roosevelts, with large reputations for ferocity toward business, carefully provided "balance" in their administrations by including prestigious businessmen in them. Franklin Roosevelt counted heavily upon Jesse H. Jones, chairman of the Reconstruction Finance Corporation, to maintain an image of respectability in the eyes of the business community. A wealthy, monumental Texan who had built a fortune in the grand manner in banking, real estate, and newspapers, Jones was a paragon of success by business standards. The price of his services came high, but Roosevelt cheerfully paid it. "Whenever we did anything of importance, that was on the borderline of our authority," Jones said once in explaining the ground rules at RFC, "I would try at first opportunity to tell the President about it, but after the fact. He was always interested, and he never criticized." Roosevelt, in turn, never failed to appreciate the usefulness of Jones's gilt-edged prestige with business and Congress. "Your conservatism is a good thing for us in this Administration," the President would reassure the great Texan.[4] In the Kennedy and Johnson, as well as in the Nixon, Ford, and Carter years, the Treasury and Commerce posts were reserved for appointees who stood high in the confidence and regard of the business community.

## Interlocking Public and Private Policy-makers

Time and again, presidencies provide ready evidence that the Chief Executive, his leading advisers, and principal administrators, are well interlocked with the private corporate structure. Analyses by sociologists C. Wright Mills[5] and Irving Louis Horowitz[6] provide a conceptualization of the "power presidency," based on a mutuality of interest of these public and private sectors. The essential role of government and the presidency is to assure the well-being of the great corporate structure. To this desideratum all else is subordinated. Officers move easily between the public and private sectors in furthering their careers, communicate readily on economic matters of mutual concern, and are also occupied, according to Horowitz, in "manufacturing and manipulating political formulas." As it happened, leading members of Carter's original cabinet and his other major advisers all had the shared experience of some previous affiliation with the International Business Machines Corporation. Secretary of Defense Harold Brown was an IBM director and chairman of its audit committee. Patricia Harris, then Secretary of Housing and Urban Development, was also an IBM director and advised the company on executive compensation. Attorney General Griffin Bell and Charles Kirbo, a prime Carter adviser, were both members of a leading Atlanta law firm which represents IBM interests in Georgia. Secretary of the Treasury W. Michael Blumenthal, a former head of the Bendix Corporation, was, by grace of that experience, a reassuring figure to the business world.[7]

## Means of Cultivating Confidence

In cultivating business confidence, Presidents work hard at tilling an image of fiscal responsibility. When national circumstances force the budget into imbalance, Presidents, with the aid of wizard-technicians of the fiscal arts, resort to elaborate hocus-pocus to maintain at least the window-dressing of fiscal respectability. For example, in his early presidential years Franklin Roosevelt could face the nation with a balanced budget by the simple expedient of putting his costly recovery programs into a separate account. Invariably he included among his counselors those whose lives represented an unbroken consecration to conventional fiscal policy. Lewis Douglas, Director of the Budget, chanted the virtues of the balanced budget and a Hoover-like program of subsistence relief, with wages, hours, and prices shaped by natural economic forces. When Douglas eventually departed, Henry Morgenthau, Jr., as Secretary of the Treasury, made temperate public spending his special cause.

Jimmy Carter, faced with seemingly contradictory pledges—on the one hand, to balance the budget, and, on the other, of increasing defense spending by 3 percent, after inflation, for 1981—resolved his dilemma simply by reducing defense spending by that percentage in fiscal 1980. The amount established for 1981 came out to a 3 percent increase after all,[8] and the budget's balance, at least at this juncture, was preserved. Budgeting can often be a wonderland of magic and miracles.

A President may keep business confidence at high flame by fraternizing with leading businessmen conspicuously more than with any other species of citizenry. The guests most frequently invited to President Eisenhower's stag dinners, social functions with incidental discussions of the administration's purposes, were businessmen. In his hours on the golf course Eisenhower's favorite companions were George E. Allen, a puckish corporation director; William E. Robinson, president of Coca-Cola; and Clifford G. Roberts, a New York banker. A President and his aides may seek to rally the business community behind their cause by wooing it with speeches. During his first year in office Kennedy waged a campaign of proportions unequaled in presidential history to induce industry's cooperation in his efforts to maintain stable prices, without which he could not hope to secure labor's vital support in paring down its wage and fringe demands. Business could swallow the bitter price medicine more easily if it were sweetened with evidences of the administration's general concern for its interests. Administration officials plied business with sympathetic speeches and promised a balanced budget, better depreciation allowances, and other policies that business cherished.

Much of the President's economic policy may advance both the President's and business's purposes. The income tax, established by constitutional amendment in 1913, is not merely an enormous producer of revenue but a reflector of an administration's underlying economic philosophy and a means of slowing or quickening general economic activity. Presidents Harding, Coolidge, and Hoover were more or less the spokesmen for the view of their Secretary of the Treasury, Andrew Mellon, that "the prosperity of the middle and lower classes depended upon the good fortunes and light taxes of the rich." Taxes that were too high, Mellon believed, would prevent the rich from saving and would make them reluctant to invest. If they failed to save and invest, the economy would ultimately falter.

The most pervasive of all taxes—the tariff—can also advance or obstruct a broad sweep of the President's economic policies. Harding and Coolidge, employing discretionary authority under the Fordney-McCumber Act, raised rates and fostered the concentration of domestic economic power.

But discretionary presidential authority to adjust rates may also promote trade, as demonstrated by the Trade Expansion Act of 1962, which authorizes the President to cut tariffs in general as much as 50 percent and to eliminate tariffs on certain goods. But mounting trade deficits and grave weakening of the dollar abroad moved Nixon to devalue the dollar and request from Congress new authority to raise, as well as lower, trade barriers to gain a "fairer shake" for American products in world trade.

Appropriate to his premier orientation to business's interests and approval, Nixon was the first contemporary President to have a top-ranking, wide-ranging White House assistant—Peter M. Flanigan—to nurture those objectives. An investment banker, Flanigan became a pro-business surrogate of the consumer affairs program, promoted the administration's oil policy, supervised the White House's relations with the regulatory agencies, and drew plans to revitalize the nation's near-moribund merchant marine.

Flanigan's skill at achieving results pleasing to business in the torpid federal bureaucracy was acclaimed from every side. "He's the guy who people in our industry turn to," said a steel executive. "And we wouldn't turn to him unless he came through." A Commerce Department official observed that at top echelons "the business community pays no attention to this department; if you have a policy problem, you go see Peter Flanigan—and he is available." But to critics, he was a fixer. A Democratic Congressman noted that "Flanigan is a manipulator of the first order. He's a master of the compromise that works out best for vested interests." A bureaucratic critic added, "It's very subtle, very discreet. You create an atmosphere, a relationship, a sense of debts, a series of understandings. There are political pay-offs all the time. But nothing is written down. Things don't have to be said. Most things are left unsaid and there are just 'understandings.' Anyone who looks for specific deals is just naive."[9] The incipient conflict between these assessments and the ethical standards of democratic government came to a head in the International Telephone and Telegraph (ITT) affair, in which a developing antitrust action against the company was settled on a basis highly favorable to ITT. In reluctant testimony to a congressional investigation, Flanigan declined to discuss his contacts with that huge conglomerate. Flanigan's reticence was a negation of democratic norms, and his functions aligned the presidency with dominant economic power at the expense of small and weaker economic units, the consumer, the worker. To function by democratic criteria, the President must be responsive to all of the economy, not merely to the dominant segment.

# Caretaker of the Economy

A paramount preoccupation of any President is the economy's good health. One of the surer auguries of his reelection is a thriving economy; if it falters, so do his electoral chances. Since the Kennedy-Johnson era, each President, in his idiosyncratic way, has practiced the "new economics," by which government acts as manager of prosperity in addition to playing savior in the depths of a depression or recession. The President's involvements have paralleled both the economy's growth, its increasing complexity and sensitivity, and the enlarging competence of professional economists, whose skills Presidents enlist. Today's Presidents perform several politically obligatory responsibilities concerning the economy, for which policies must be provided.

## Sectors of Responsibility

*Inflation*   Contemporary Presidents behold inflation as the most horrendous spectre of economic trouble. Despite their policy-activity and solemn pronouncements, they have played a losing game as inflation has soared from single-digit to double-digit proportions. Simultaneously, with only brief exception in the Nixon years, Presidents have shunned the most obvious and drastic of remedies, wage and price controls. Instead, all Presidents since Kennedy have utilized price and wage "guidelines" applicable to labor-management wage negotiations and to industry's price policies. Guidelines provide a formula for determining whether particular wage or price increases are inflationary. The incoming Reagan administration, however, was committed to revoking existing guidelines.

Characteristically, guidelines succumb to several hazards. Over time, business fares markedly better than labor on the inflation merry-go-round. In the Kennedy-Johnson years, although industry was held more closely to account for its prices, its profit levels (67 percent) far outdistanced wage gains (21 percent). In the Carter years, prices raced far beyond wages, pushed by many factors, including walloping increases in prices for OPEC (Organization of Petroleum Exporting Countries) oil. Guidelines lack an enforcement apparatus, making violation easy.

For further assaults upon inflation Presidents draw selectively from a kit of economic nostrums. Major Carter prescriptions included increased interest rates by the Federal Reserve Board, tightened consumer credit, reduced federal spending, and a balanced budget. These accumulated body blows to inflation can so slow the economy that a recession sets in. This is another kettle of unwanted trouble, productive of a further horrendous spectre—mass unemployment—that looms its fearsome worst as an election approaches, as it did for Carter in 1980.

In the inflation- and recession-ridden decades since the Second World War, a President in his struggles with economic policy is driven to determine a cutoff point when he judges that the political costs of fighting inflation become too high as reductions of economic demand push unemployment upward. According to economists' estimates in 1979, the cost of knocking a percentage point off the basic inflation rate by cutting aggregate demand was $250 billion and the loss of five million jobs over a five year period, an exorbitant price for a tiny cut in the inflation rate.[10] The nadir of presidential effectiveness in fighting inflation was reached by Jimmy Carter in 1979, when it attained an annual compounded rate of 18.5 percent, intersecting with a plunging 19 percent rate of public support for the President in the polls. This desperate scenario contributed to a burgeoning image of the Carter presidency as incompetent and galvanized Carter's rivals for the 1980 Democratic nomination. Although Carter blamed rising oil prices for the disaster, energy accounted for less than 3 percent of the jump in the cost of living. Far more potent causes were a spreading inflation psychology that pushed prices upward and inadequate government influence on wages and prices. Further, resounding governmental deficits stimulated the economy away from dreaded recession and its politically intolerable unemployment levels, into higher inflation.

***Budget and taxation***   Both Kennedy and Johnson freely employed tax and spending policies to restrain a business boom or to halt the plunge toward a recession. Initially, with the economy proceeding at a reasonably satisfying tempo, Nixon eschewed this tampering; but suddenly the dynamics of economic forces erupted as unemployment jumped to unexpected levels and inflation soared. In a demonstration of how Presidents examine economic problems through a political microscope, Nixon pondered how badly Republican congressional candidates with economic preferences similar to his had fared in the 1970 elections, and, as his own electoral test of 1972 approached, he suddenly shifted economic gears. Whereas earlier he had denounced his Democratic predecessors as spendthrifts rolling up endless deficits, his new budget for fiscal 1972 projected a huge deficit. Having determined that, at least at this juncture, fighting unemployment was more important than fighting inflation, Nixon ruefully announced, "I am now a Keynesian." [11]

In 1980, with inflation running amuck and a presidential election at hand, Carter's initial budget for fiscal 1981 was of a distinctly middle-of-the-road genre, as befits an election appeal. It offered a bow to conservatives by reducing the deficit and increasing military outlays and a thoughtful nod to liberals by abstaining from major cuts in social programs. Nonetheless, the budget unmistakably implied that controlling inflation remained the administration's top priority, and it reflected the assumption that it is easier for government to stimulate a lagging economy, even belatedly, than to slow down inflation by using the stimulus of a tax cut too soon. Carter's economic strategy for the 1980 election seemed aimed more at preempting conservative Republican issues than at averting criticism from his Democratic rival, Edward M. Kennedy. [12]

But several months later, Carter changed his budgetary tune. In strong discourse, he publicly flailed the budget adopted in House-Senate conference as a budget that "severely restrains" programs "for jobs, for cities, for training, for education—those very things that would prevent recession from getting out of hand—and we cannot afford to slash those too deeply and add money to a budget for defense, for instance, which is more than we actually need." [13] Another administration spokesman cited a shortage of about $750 million in funds needed for income security programs—unemployment insurance, food stamps, and Social Security benefits. In such fields as education and training, including federally funded jobs in local government for the long-term unemployed, the congressional shortfall from the White House's stated expectations was $1.1 billion. [14]

Erupting anger at Carter's statement transformed Capitol Hill into a political Mt. St. Helens. Legislators were offended by Carter's flagrant turnaround from a statement made several days earlier aboard the aircraft carrier *Nimitz*, when he expressed support for a military pay increase that would add $700 million to the military budget. Senator Ernest F. Hollings (D-S.C.), chairman of the Senate Budget Committee, was unsparing as he and other Democratic congressional leaders recoiled from the President's statement. Carter, cried Hollings, was a "hypocrite," guilty of "outrageous, deplorable conduct."

Hollings offered his own explanation of the President's behavior: "He doesn't want a balanced budget; he wants a campaign budget." In his earlier position on the budget, Carter alienated many liberal Congressmen by demanding a balanced budget and increased military spending. His new stand offended moderate and conservative members with his appeal for reductions in military spending and for increases in social programs. As the 1980 election grew closer, the President's altered position seemed an effort to win back the traditional Democratic coalition of urban, labor, and minority groups.[15]

**Recession**   Here is an economic time bomb capable of destroying the political health and reelection chances of an incumbent President. The onset of a recession in 1975 helped topple Ford in 1976, and Nixon was nudged out by Kennedy in 1960, thanks to a recession that had commenced in the Eisenhower administration, with Nixon its Vice President.

In 1980, Carter faced the worst of possible economic worlds with both inflation and recession, accompanied by rising unemployment. Layoffs piled up, soon reaching a quarter million auto workers. Further dolorous trends developed in steel, tires, housing construction, and elsewhere. In the time-honored custom of Presidents, Carter depicted the recession in hopeful, consoling terms, acknowledging an economic slowdown, but maintaining that "any recession will be mild and short." Thanks to the Congressional Budget Office (CBO), a presidential prognosis is subject to second-guessing, and the CBO forecasted a far more severe recession. "The Administration has to put an optimistic hue on its forecasts," a CBO economist said, "because it is political. We can afford to be more objective."[16]

On Carter, the 1980 recession tumbled endless agonizing decisions, stemming from his high resolve to check expanding unemployment without aggravating inflation. His administration was besieged to relax its drive for a balanced budget, and the Federal Reserve was pressed to loosen its restrictive money and credit policies. Businessmen widely feared that Carter might become too rigid, shunning tax cuts until the recession got out of hand. The banking and investment community dreaded that the inflation fight might be abandoned too soon, with chaotic consequences for interest rates and the bond and stock markets.[17]

Congress, mindful of the 1980 elections, successfully pressured the administration to subsidize additional housing construction and to cut mortgage interest costs, a boon to builders saddled with unsold homes. Earlier, Carter opposed implementing the subsidy program; now, with a deepening recession, he urged its expansion. In recession, consistency walketh behind.

**Energy**   Every President since Nixon has struggled with the economy's abject dependence on Middle East oil and the extortionate prices set by the OPEC countries, causing erosion of the dollar and stupefying inflation. All Presidents propose plans for coping with the energy crisis—Carter offered several in a single presidential term. Even after numerous presidential television addresses and statements on the energy problem, the public (57 percent), as late as 1979, did not believe the President's contention that shortages existed.[18] Nor have Presidents been any more successful in moving a substantial energy program through Congress. With distrust of government pervasive, with oil companies piling up unprecedented profits, and with presidential popularity at low ebb, prospects for establishing public policies of any real consequence remained sparse.

Carter was the first President to become engrossed with energy, and he described it as a problem of crisis proportions; but his recommendations, at most, were pallid. He exhorted Americans to practice conservation, a prudent, inexpensive thrust. But conservation does not provide an immediate dramatic response, and it lacks political appeal. This failing pushed Carter to urge the development of synthetic fuels, with huge public outlays and much fanfare, while blinking away the likely ravaging of vast acreages of agricultural lands and the production of carcinogenic and other pollutants of air and water. Although studies have urged greater reliance on solar energy, underscored by the near-disaster of nuclear power on Three Mile Island, the Energy Department called for cuts in solar spending and rises in outlays for nuclear and fossil fuels.[19] The presidency has amply demonstrated its proclivity for favoring established utilities and corporate interests that prefer programs entailing vast public outlays. The presidency is unlikely to be in the vanguard of change if future energy realities require emphasis on conservation or solar power and their realization through smaller economic enterprises, in contrast to the traditional large corporations.

***Environment***    Jimmy Carter is the first contemporary President to be identified with the environmental movement. Inaction and obstruction by his predecessors, Ford and Nixon, were anathema to conservationists. Environmental organizations provided invaluable support in Carter's 1976 primary campaigns and looked confidently to his presidency for enhancement of their programs.

Carter's initial environmental message to Congress proposed no new major programs but promised vigorous enforcement of existing laws. An overriding theme was the necessity to protect public health through environmental health, especially by diminishing the presence of carcinogens and other dangerous substances in air and drinking water. He proposed an integrated pest control program to reduce dependence on pesticides threatening to human health and wildlife. Carter also urged sizeable economic penalties for air and water polluters "to make pollution unprofitable as well as illegal." He called for strict exhaust fume limitations for automobiles and encouraged recycling and other waste reduction. Maintaining environmental standards, he argued, was compatible with developing energy resources, and protecting the environment was a national interest parallel to a sound economy.[20]

But the President's evolving energy policies shattered whatever reassurance his initial message provided environmentalists. His program to reduce oil imports by crash development of synthetic fuels and his attempt to establish an Energy Mobilization Board to demolish obstacles to developing energy resources alarmed environmentalists as potential desecrations of the environment. In a second message to Congress, Carter preached the necessity of "trade-offs" between energy needs and the need to protect the environment. With a dash of reassurance for environmentalists, Carter appointed Gus Speth, of the environmental movement, chairman of the Council on Environmental Quality.[21]

Environmentalists were further jolted when regulations of the Environmental Protection Agency (EPA) were increasingly subjected to White House review, under a presidential order that called for scrutiny of the costs of all regulations and alternative studies to make government rules more cost efficient and less burdensome. There was an explosion when a memorandum by Charles L. Schultze, chairman of the Council of Economic Advisers (CEA) and inflation adviser Alfred E. Kahn declared that EPA's pending water clean-up rules were "prohibitively expensive" and that the entire program should be reexamined to relate costs to benefits. EPA officials grumbled that White House review "amounts to giving industry one more shot at weakening the regulations." [22]

*Regulatory reform*    Carter perpetuated Gerald Ford's ardent advocacy of deregulation and regulatory reform. With various Congressmen, Carter supported the progress of legislation that would establish regulatory reform along the lengthy legislative journey to enactment. The legislation undertakes to make government regulations more sensitive to the costs of compliance incurred by business, to provide better planning and administration, and to reduce delay—government's worst irritant of the regulated. Existing regulations must also be reviewed periodically.

Carter's effort to apply this reform scheme to the independent regulatory agencies unleashed a torrent of congressional protest. Similarly controversial was his establishment of the Regulatory Analysis Review Group (RARG) in the White House. RARG was a cadre of representatives of the principal economic and regulatory agencies, led by CEA's Charles Schultze, whose philosophy was that "Effective regulation requires economic analysis and attention to costs." Henceforth agencies were required to provide more detailed justification, or "regulatory analyses," for their rules. [23]

*Rescuing American business*    The presidency has long provided aid to business, and the relationship has stretched to new dimensions in the contemporary economic upheavals ignited by the energy crisis, by OPEC's exorbitant pricing, by soaring inflation, and by the lagging capacity and will of American corporate giants to adapt to changing circumstances. The Carter presidency is the first to be thrust into a new responsibility for fashioning "industrial policy," which looms as a top economic issue of the 1980s.

In 1978, the Carter administration wet its toes in this policy domain when it pledged to guarantee up to $550 million in private loans for steel plant modernization and simultaneously provided the industry protection from imports with a trigger-price mechanism designed to prevent imported steel from being sold below cost. (Japan and West European countries commonly provide government support for private businesses engaged in export—ought not American government do so as well?)

As rescuer of beleaguered private enterprise, Carter plunged into deeper waters when he chose to help the financially disintegrating Chrysler Corporation with $1.5 billion in federal loan guarantees. Helping Chrysler entailed many choices. Initially the auto manufacturer, whose sales had sunk disastrously, sought $1 billion in outright cash; but the Carter administration insisted on loans from private sources, which the government would guarantee, plus "substantial contributions or concessions from all those who have an interest in Chrysler's future"—defined as "management, employees, stockholders, creditors, suppliers, other business associates and governmental units." [24] The administration supplemented Chrysler's desperate lobbying effort to move the loan guarantee plan through Congress. Some seven hundred Chrysler dealers and legions of the United Automobile Workers Union descended on Capitol Hill. "I had twenty dealers in my office last week. They're hunting in packs," cried Les Aspin (D-Wis.), who had no Chrysler plant in his district.[25]

Meanwhile, the Carter presidency as well as private study groups, wrestled with possible formulations of "industrial policy" both for Chrysler and for other ailing American industries in the 1980s. Stuart Eizenstat, Carter's chief domestic policy adviser, sounded the rallying cry: "We must strengthen the basic industries in our country—modernize them, increase their productivity and their competitiveness in world markets; we cannot let them deteriorate one by one." Conceivably, resulting policies might provide aid to the automobile industry as a whole, embracing import protection, relief from compliance with clean air and safety regulations, and tax advantages. Other industries with outstretched hands might include steel, electronics, and data processing.[26]

# Making Economic Policy

The President's economic decisions reflect a potpourri of forces, combining the rational and the irrational, information and ignorance, knowledge and ideological bias—the stuff of politics.

## Incentives to Act

The President is responsive to various incentives to act, to embark on decision and policy. Typically he acts when the tide of economic forces passes into the realm of politics, when these forces are perceived as providing significant profit or threatening loss to the President and his political future. His vulnerabilities increase as elections near, especially if great and valued constituencies, such as automobile workers and segments of the middle class, are endangered or offended. Massive unemployment in the automobile industry or the threatened bankruptcy of Chrysler are events whose disastrous consequences no President can passively tolerate. Incentives to act emerge from many different sources and circumstances. Thus campaign promises of tax reform and better protection of the environment, key Carter planks in 1976, cannot be brushed aside in the subsequent presidential administration. Alert, articulate groups wait to inform the world of the President's performance or non-performance, particularly the latter. The favor and support of these sensitive monitors must be maintained, be they business, organized labor, the elderly, environmental groups, and their favorable assessment of his economic policies and its consequences carefully nourished. The next election is soon at hand.

## The President as Economist

Economic policies mirror the President's personal idiosyncrasies: his own economic values, his political operating style, his approach to decision-management, his perception of the course of conduct necessary to make his office politically "livable." Carter, for example, was perceived by economists as pursuing a highly erratic course in economic policy. He had a habit of reacting to events rather than anticipating them, of striving to satisfy diverse constituencies, of holding policy to modest levels, of making policy commitments tentative and adjustable, and of being, literally, all things to all people. His persistent low standing in public opinion polls, the thinness of his support among economic groups make these stances toward policy understandable.

Largely for these reasons, the record of Carter's economic policies is constantly zigzagging and lacking in coherence. In his 1976 campaign he endorsed standby wage and price control authority; as President he opposed it. Early on, he proposed stimulative spending increases and tax cuts, including a $50 per person rebate. Soon he abandoned the rebate. A year later he asked for sizeable tax relief, only again to delay and drastically reduce it because of inflationary pressures. "Each time a policy was developed, the policy was too weak for the problems that appeared," observed Barry Bosworth, Carter's former director of the Council on Wage and Price Stability.[27]

## Administrative Participants

What the President does in economic policy also depends upon the cavernous world of department secretaries, bureaus, and expertise in the executive branch, a network of agencies that include the Council of Economic Advisers, the Treasury, Federal Reserve, and a host of other departments and agencies with stakes in economic policy—Commerce, Labor, and Agriculture, the Securities and Exchange Commission, among them. Allied with the bureaus and career bureau chiefs are businesses and labor unions and their practiced lobbyists, all accustomed to dealing with each other over many years. Presidential economic policy is often a kind of peace treaty resulting from the agencies' competing strivings, differing functional perspectives, clashes of interest, and varying skills in conflict politics.

The more relevant that economic policy is to the President's political well-being, the more likely it is that the circle of advisers closest to him personally and politically will dominate policy-making. The influence of advisers more distant from that circle will be correspondingly downgraded. For example, Carter's new economic policy, devised for his 1980 campaign, a patently crucial political moment for the President, was dominated by an inner circle consisting of Vice President Walter Mondale, Stuart Eizenstat, the domestic affairs adviser, James McIntyre, the Budget Director, Charles Schultze, chairman of the Council of Economic Advisers, and G. William Miller, Secretary of the Treasury. More removed and reportedly resentful of their modest influence were Commerce Secretary Philip Klutznick, Labor Secretary Ray Marshall, and anti-inflation counselor Alfred Kahn. That Miller was somewhere on the edges of the inner circle was suggested when Schultze took over the presentation of the new policy to the press.[28]

## The Congressional Role

Economic policy is also a substantial domain of Congress, thanks to its constitutional power to regulate commerce, to tax, to provide for agriculture, to establish the currency and credit and to carry out other enumerated powers. This often leaves the President in the position of simply proposing policy while Congress disposes of what he provides. Though Carter had the first word on tax reform, Congress had the word that counted most—the last. The degree to which the President can impose his will on bureaucratic and congressional processes depends on his political skill in bargaining and exerting influence, and in using his office's most unique resource—his visibility. His best chance for dominating an economic issue rests on his skills in publicizing it, and he has means for bringing it into the limelight that no one else has.

Above all, the President as policy-maker is affected by the state of economic knowledge. According to Sir John Hicks, Oxford University's Nobel prize-winning economist, "Economic knowledge, though not negligible, is so extremely imperfect, there are very few economic facts which we know with precision. . . . There are few economic 'laws' which can be regarded as at all firmly based." [29] The limitations of economic knowledge both circumscribe the domain of professional economists in policy-making and enlarge the domain of the President's personal and political judgments, and, of course, his vexations with uncertainty.

# Labor Leaders and the President

The second member of the great economic tandem, labor, like other groups, attracted significant attention from the President of the United States only after it attained major political strength. Samuel Gompers, president of the American Federation of Labor, was not given the privilege of visits with Presidents until the late nineteenth century, and even then the occasions are few and brief. Gompers first extracted sustained presidential interest from Theodore Roosevelt. Roosevelt invited the labor leader to the White House socially, consulted him on a wide range of subjects, and meted out honorific recognitions. Upon receiving the Nobel prize, for example, the President set up an industrial peace foundation and named Gompers to its board of directors.

### Franklin Roosevelt and Labor

Of all Presidents, Franklin Roosevelt maintained the most extensive relations with labor leaders. With labor he employed the same technique he applied to other private organizations. Viewing the nation's politics as essentially group politics, Franklin Roosevelt was wont to approach groups whose support he cherished through their leaders. Roosevelt's dealings with labor leaders ran the gamut from intimacy to mortal enmity. Dan Tobin of the Teamsters' Union was such an exalted favorite that Roosevelt made his "labor speech" of the 1944 campaign at a Teamsters' dinner, after rejecting entreaties of a dozen other unions for his presence.

Roosevelt's most intimate and profitable rapport was with Sidney Hillman, president of the Amalgamated Clothing Workers and vice president of the CIO. Hillman's sensitivity and appreciation of social workers, intellectuals, and others outside the labor movement set him apart from rougher-hewn colleagues. He served in responsible government posts in the New Deal and the Second World War, on NRA's Labor Advisory Board, on the National Defense Advisory Council, and as Associate Director of the Office of Production Management. To Roosevelt, Hillman was one of "the longest-headed individuals I have ever met." A constant visitor at the White House, Hillman enjoyed the rare privilege of a right-of-way by telephone to the Chief Executive. By the mid-1930s, a CIO official could plausibly assert that "a whisper from Sidney Hillman of the Amalgamated is louder than the loudest shout of almost anyone in the national Cabinet." And CIO president John L. Lewis, even when he was beholding the CIO vice president with a critical eye, declared, "Sidney Hillman was after all the driving force behind many of the measures attributed to the New Deal. If it had not been for him there would probably have been no Fair Labor Standards Act." [30] Probably Hillman's thorniest assignment in the mid-1930s was smoothing the troubled waters that kept churning up between his superior, John L. Lewis, and Franklin D. Roosevelt. Hillman's busy diplomacy was made doubly difficult by Lewis' resentment of his aide's privileged closeness to Roosevelt. The ordeal ended when Lewis finally broke with Roosevelt in 1940.

The Hillman-Roosevelt nexus, although resting upon a sturdy underpinning of personal regard, was mutually advantageous. For Hillman, an unrivaled access to the White House meant speedy advancement in his labor career. For Roosevelt, Hillman was a constant friend in the court of labor who could cushion the blows of unwelcome policy decisions such as the administration's proposed labor draft in the Second World War. In the New Deal and the early war years, Hillman was a kind of auxiliary Secretary of Labor at the White House's beck and call on myriad problems. Indeed, Roosevelt seems to have seriously considered making Hillman his Labor Secretary at several junctures, but was dissuaded by Mrs. Roosevelt, who did not like having her old friend, Secretary Frances Perkins, the only woman in the cabinet, superseded. [31]

With John L. Lewis, the leonine, bushy-browed master of ornate rhetoric, Franklin Roosevelt's relations were unceasingly tempestuous. Lewis, like Roosevelt, loved power and position; when they met, giants clashed. A stickler for the amenities for himself and his office, Roosevelt was offended by Lewis' spiny arrogance. The President, who had a large talent for noncommittal generalities, would be brought up short when Lewis would stop him in mid-sentence to ask, "Well, will it be yes or no?" Roosevelt was also distressed by Lewis' occasional crudity in exploiting his White House access. Soon after Section 7a of the National Industrial Recovery Act (a provision designed to encourage union organization) went into effect, for example, Lewis' United Mine Workers organizers raced through the coal fields shouting, "The President wants you to join the Union." This unseemly and wholly unauthorized use of the presidential office put Roosevelt squarely on the spot. Politically, he could not disavow the organizers' activity but could only writhe in private anguish. By 1936 Lewis was referring to Roosevelt as "my man." Roosevelt conveyed his own estimate of the labor leader in an interview with Max Lerner. "You know, Max," said the President, "this is really a great country. The framework of democracy is so strong and so elastic that it can get along and absorb both a Huey Long and a John L. Lewis." Lewis, when he heard the remark, growled, "The statement is incomplete. It should also include 'and Franklin Delano Roosevelt.' "[32]

In 1940 the fragile Roosevelt-Lewis connection was snapped by the coming of the war and Roosevelt's third-term candidacy. During a White House visit in January 1940, according to Frances Perkins (whose report of the interview was corroborated by Philip Murray, a later CIO president, and denied by Lewis), the United Mine Workers chief made a startling proposal. He suggested to the President that he, Lewis, should run for Vice President of the United States on the third-term ticket. A strong labor man, Lewis argued, would ensure full labor support plus the support of all the liberals who, he added pointedly, would be a little troubled by the constitutional irregularity of a third term.[33]

The rebuff of Lewis' vice-presidential aspirations launched a train of bizarre events that widened the chasm between himself and the President from miles to oceans. After weeks of intensive wooing by the camp of Wendell Willkie, the Republican presidential candidate, Lewis abandoned Roosevelt. "He is not an aristocrat," Lewis said, endorsing Willkie in a labor-oriented statement, "He has the common touch. He was born to the friar and not to the purple. He has worked with his hands, and has known the pangs of hunger." In a radio address Lewis urged the workers of America to vote against Roosevelt. In a flourish that left his fellow labor leaders gasping with disbelief, Lewis declared he would consider Roosevelt's reelection a vote of no confidence in himself and would thereupon resign from his CIO presidency. The labor rank and file, forced to choose between Roosevelt, beloved as their President, and Lewis, their adulated leader, chose Roosevelt at the polls. Honoring his threat, Lewis resigned from the CIO leadership.[34]

## Contemporary Presidents and Labor

Although George Meany labored mightily to keep Richard Nixon out of the White House, the AFL-CIO leader, a doughty pragmatist beneath his gruff exterior, scrupulously preserved his White House connection, developed in the previous Democratic administrations. Access to the White House has long been a dynamic element in Meany's own power in the labor movement. And he gratifyingly found in Nixon a sharer of valued sentiments. As long-standing anti-Communists, both were united on the Vietnam war, and both were antipathetic to long-haired war protesters. Meany was further propelled into Nixon's embrace by the necessity of softening the President for future ample wage settlements that would have adverse inflationary effects and by his growing view that the Democratic party was disintegrating, with "extremists" taking over, ejecting good labor men from their accustomed places of influence, and causing union workers to look outside the party for acceptable candidates.[35]

Nixon was responsive, at least in symbolic ways. He quickly let it be known that Meany, and Meany alone, was the only true voice of labor. Even more, Nixon accorded what Democratic Presidents had never granted, a celebration of Labor Day 1970 at the White House for labor leaders and their wives, and a fiesta on the White House lawn for scores of lesser lights among the guests. Thereafter, the Nixon-Meany relation went downhill. Many of the President's emerging policies sparked Meany's opposition. He and the AFL-CIO lobbied the Senate against the Supreme Court nominations of Clement Haynsworth and G. Harrold Carswell, grumbling that the President went shopping for his Court choices on a dark night with Senator Strom Thurmond of South Carolina as his guide. For Meany, Nixon's price and wage controls were "Robin Hood in reverse," robbing the "poor to give to the rich." [36]

Consistent with the recent presidential pattern, Gerald Ford's relations with organized labor began on a high note, even though in his quarter century in Congress Ford's average of "right" votes on the AFL-CIO scorecard was a wretched .148. An early White House visitor, Meany counseled the President on how best to combat inflation and unemployment, and organized labor played a premier part in Ford's 1974 summit conference on the economy. Meany and other union leaders welcomed Ford's early announced aversion to wage and price controls and endeavored to nudge the President a step or two away from his selection of inflation as the nation's top economic problem. Union leaders stressed the need to check growing unemployment by stimulating economic activity. They were critical of the President's antiinflation policies—such as monetary restraints, high interest rates, and federal budget cutting of social programs beneficial to labor. The leaders contended that Ford's policies would worsen the developing recession and expand the intolerably high jobless rate. Ford responded by promising to make more funds available for public service employment.[37]

The affability reigning between Ford and Meany was reinforced by the President's selection of Nelson Rockefeller for the vice presidency; Rockefeller was also Meany's number-one choice. As Governor of New York, Rockefeller had exceeded the pharaohs of Egypt in his lavish public building programs, and among the prime beneficiaries were the construction unions, including the plumbers from whose ranks Meany had sprung to leadership of the AFL-CIO.

The conservatism of Jimmy Carter's economic outlook Meany likened to that of Grover Cleveland and Calvin Coolidge. Carter's relations with labor were often ambivalent and tense. Meany's successor, Lane Kirkland, termed the President's economic policies "destructive" and "backward." But notwithstanding such outbursts, Carter–AFL-CIO relationships ordinarily were mutually supportive. Labor provided generous backing for such major controversial planks in Carter's legislative programs as the new strategic arms limitation treaty, his energy program, and his national health insurance plan.

Above all, the AFL-CIO entered a "national accord" with Carter, supportive of his antiinflation policy, agreeing to hold wage and other demands within the government's guidelines.[38] Subsequently, word leaked out of a series of unannounced concessions made by the administration to help win union acquiescence, including an agreement not to use sanctions against offenders. Pressed by booming inflation, Kirkland was soon informing labor leaders of their "legal duty" to ignore the wage guidelines, in labor's eyes wretchedly unrealistic. But even in its worst moments of disenchantment with Carter, the leadership of organized labor remained steadfast in supporting his 1980 presidential candidacy, beholding his Republican rival as a dread alternative. Union members and their families did not, however.

An estimated 44 percent voted for Reagan, an outcome attributed to fears about inflation and unemployment and resentment at American humiliation in the hostage crisis in Iran.[39]

# How Presidents Are Useful to Labor

Twentieth-century Presidents, particularly those of Democratic vintage, perform various functions to further labor's interests. Since 1933 all Presidents, Republican and Democratic alike, have promoted new legislation beneficial to labor. The removal of obstacles to the effective exertion of labor's economic power, the increase of labor's legal rights, and the enlargement of the government's welfare services are areas of legislation that vitally interest labor. Since labor legislation ordinarily is not passed without a long and impassioned struggle, a President proposing it sets the agenda not merely of his own administration, but often of future administrations. In 1905 Theodore Roosevelt proposed that Congress "regulate" the "procedure" for granting labor injunctions. Not until twenty-seven years after his initiative, in the Norris–La Guardia Act of 1932, did Congress finally do it.

## Franklin Roosevelt, Reluctant Hero

Although most of the laws promoting labor's fundamental interests were enacted in Franklin Roosevelt's administration, and he of all Presidents is the most revered in the labor community, the truth of the matter is that Roosevelt was not an eager champion of labor's causes, but a reluctant hero. In the enactment of each of the three basic labor laws of his administration—Section 7a of the National Industrial Recovery Act, the Wagner Act of 1935, and the Fair Labor Standards Act of 1938—his participation was cautious and halfhearted. Section 7a was included in the National Industrial Recovery Act not because Roosevelt rushed to put it in, but because John L. Lewis insisted on it. Roosevelt's principal involvement in the NIRA's preparation was to order the industrialists and labor leaders who drafted individual bills to "get into a room and weave it all together." In the ensuing congressional phase of the NIRA, Lewis was fearful that 7a, blessed with little presidential support, might be dropped, so he entered into an intrigue with a labor-minded White House assistant. Lewis would write to the President, and the compliant assistant, who drafted Franklin Roosevelt's reply, would slip in a dash of exhortation for 7a. The tampering, according to Lewis, passed unnoticed. With the letter in hand, the labor leader spread the word among fence-sitting legislators that Roosevelt really wanted 7a.[40]

Roosevelt's commitment to the Wagner, or national labor relations, bill, which enhanced labor's right to organize and obliged employers to engage in collective bargaining, was also mild. In 1934, indeed, a presidential decision had sidetracked the Wagner bill. Senator Robert Wagner was encouraged to reintroduce his measure the following year, not by the President, but by the labor movement. Franklin Roosevelt, to Wagner's dismay, despite expressions of mild approval the year before, now took a hands-off attitude. Even in the bill's late stages, Secretary of Commerce Daniel Roper was predicting a presidential veto. After the bill had passed the House, and just before the Senate's final action, Roosevelt convened a White House conference where Senator Wagner and Donald R. Richberg, the administration's labor adviser who opposed the bill, debated its merits at the President's invitation. Midway in the discussion, Roosevelt, whose position still was unknown, finally made clear that he wanted the bill. On the fair labor standards bill of 1938, Roosevelt likewise engaged in belated, feet-dragging decision. It was not the President or his administration, but Sidney Hillman, the CIO vice president, who rallied the labor bloc of legislators and worked out the minimum wage of twenty-five cents an hour in a hard-wrought compromise with the Southern Democrats. Roosevelt, ever skeptical of the bill's chances, gave help only when its success was assured and political prudence required that he quickly identify himself with it.[41]

Why was Roosevelt so chronically reserved and reluctant? For one thing, born into comfortable gentility, he had no firsthand understanding of labor problems. Instinctively and intellectually he sympathized with labor's objectives, but he had little grasp of its needs and feelings. On setting the priorities of his administration, he gave labor's objectives a secondary place. In the depression years of 1934 and 1935 and in the recession of 1938 his primary interest was economic recovery. Time and again he seems to have been impressed by the argument that production might climb faster in the depression-bound economy if labor decisions could be postponed until business was on its feet again. Labor's most drastic weapon, the strike, sometimes annoyed him, especially when it obstructed his own political and economic purposes. In the main, he envisioned himself not as labor's champion but as a balancer and adjuster between labor and management in which he approached both sides with a good measure of judicious detachment.

In the post–Franklin D. Roosevelt era the fate and substance of labor legislation have varied strikingly between the Republican Eisenhower and Nixon presidencies and the Democratic presidencies of Harry Truman, John Kennedy, and Lyndon Johnson. Eisenhower's personal preference for state rather than federal action and his apparent lack of philosophical sympathy with labor's aims wrought results considerably below labor's aspirations. Kennedy, in contrast, stressed national action in labor matters, pushed through legislation for depressed areas, which Eisenhower had vetoed, and the $1.25 minimum wage, which Eisenhower had resisted. Kennedy also won liberalizing amendments to the Social Security Act that increased minimum benefits and lowered the eligibility age. He won legislation extending unemployment compensation for up to thirteen weeks and giving special benefits to the children of the unemployed.

## Nixon's Labor Strategy

Despite the frequent acrimony of their relations and labor's revulsion at Nixon's wage-price policies, Nixon and the AFL-CIO were united on various legislative enterprises that produced greater employment and fatter paychecks. Labor was an unfaltering friend of the full-blown national security budget. In the President's determined but unavailing fight for the SST, the unions, which had much at stake, led the intensive lobbying on

Capitol Hill. Their efforts were equally unstinting for another bread-and-butter program, the Rail Passenger Service Act of 1970, which created a semipublic corporation to operate a nationwide railway passenger system.[42] Nixon's social policies synchronized with the fears and predilections of the blue-collar worker. The President's deploring pronouncements on crime, on welfare recipients and the work ethic, on long-haired youth and antiwar demonstrations, articulated the workers' deeper resentments. With perfect ideological ease, Nixon could indulge in the gesture of entertaining hardhats in the White House and donning a hard hat himself to affirm the bonds between them.

But while Nixon played artfully on the harp of labor's fears, he pursued economic policies that devastated the workingman's bread-and-butter interests. Following his 1972 reelection, he abruptly terminated price controls, a move that unleashed record-breaking inflation, while wages increased only modestly. His tight credit and monetary policies fostered steadily climbing unemployment and sharply curtailed new housing construction and the tempo of other industries vital to labor. While Nixon fraternized with hardhats, he simultaneously cut their jobs from under them.

## Labor's Expectations

Since the days of Franklin D. Roosevelt, labor has expected Presidents, particularly Democratic Presidents, to resist legislation hostile to its interests. The noisiest and most politically profitable instance of presidential jousting in labor's behalf was Harry S. Truman's veto of the Taft-Hartley bill of 1947. An omnibus measure that was passed in the wake of a large upsurge in strikes, Taft-Hartley aimed to equalize employer-employee responsibilities by regulating union organization and practices. After polling the Democratic National Committee and the state Democratic chairmen and vice chairmen for advice, Truman delivered a fiery veto that was overridden by the Republican-controlled Congress. For Truman, the defeat was merely the beginning of a long, implacable, politically rewarding crusade. In the 1948 presidential campaign and after, he lost no opportunity to identify the legislation with Republican conservatism, though a majority of the Democrats in both houses had voted for it. Taft-Hartley, which remains on the books, has become a political dead letter.

The President may bring labor into his official family by appointing as his Secretary of Labor a figure from the organized labor movement. Woodrow Wilson inaugurated the practice when he made William B. Wilson of the United Mine Workers his Secretary of Labor in 1913. The precedent was renewed not by his Democratic successors Roosevelt and Truman but by the Republican Eisenhower, who named Martin Durkin, president of the plumbers' union, Secretary of Labor. Likewise, Nixon appointed Peter J. Brennan, president of the Building and Construction Trades Council of Greater New York, as Secretary of Labor. Kennedy's first Secretary of Labor, Arthur Goldberg, general counsel to the United Steel Workers' Union, did not, like Durkin and Brennan, hail from the workers' ranks, but from labor's growing professional wing. In appointing a nonlabor man as Labor Secretary, a contemporary President will make a selection that is inoffensive to the labor movement.

Since the 1930s the great bulk of leaders of organized labor have made a clear and absolute choice in presidential politics by casting their lot with Democratic candidates and opposing the Republicans. The single aberration was the presidential election of 1972, in which Meany and most labor chieftains tacitly supported the Republican nominee, Richard Nixon.

When a Republican occupies the White House, labor constitutes a major opposition force second only to the Democratic party. If the Democratic party is divided and dominated by moderates and conservatives, as it was in Eisenhower's first term, organized labor "plays a role of *the* major loyal opposition within American politics," as James Tracy Crown has put it.[43] In the Nixon era, on the supreme bread-and-butter issue of wage and price policies, George Meany and the AFL-CIO ranked foremost among the administration's critics. No one attacked the President with more barbed vehemence than Meany. "This fight between Meany and the President," an AFL-CIO official observed, "should stiffen the back of Congress. Now the Democrats on the Hill will have to take sides."[44] Nonetheless, the strongest institutional supporter in American society of the Vietnam war was the AFL-CIO. When Nixon launched his controversial 1970 incursion into Cambodia, one of the earliest voices raised in his support, above the cacophony of criticism, was George Meany's.

From Franklin D. Roosevelt onward until George McGovern's nomination in 1972, labor has played a central part in selecting Democratic candidates for the presidency. Indeed, no Democratic candidate during that time was named without its approval. There was truth in Kennedy's jest when he acknowledged in a speech to the 1961 AFL-CIO convention that he was "one whose work and continuity of employment has depended in part upon the union movement."

Labor has displayed an almost equal interest in the selection of Democratic vice presidential candidates. In the fateful selection of Harry S. Truman for the vice presidency in 1944, labor had at least as great a part as the incumbent President, Franklin Roosevelt. The latter's frail health, a fact well known to the labor leaders, lent urgency to their task. Roosevelt himself contributed only confusion by recommending no less than four candidates for the vice presidency. Robert E. Hannegan, Franklin Roosevelt's representative embarking for the Chicago convention, beseeched his chief for instructions on the vice presidential question. Before making a final selection, Roosevelt was heard to say Hannegan and his aides must first "clear it with Sidney" (Sidney Hillman), the CIO vice president. The union leaders, after rejecting James M. Byrnes and expressing indifference toward Henry Wallace, the incumbent Vice President, settled upon Truman. "Clear it with Sidney" quickly took its place in the national lexicon and raised a drumfire of conservative indignation. Cried columnist Westbrook Pegler, "How came this nontoiling sedentary conspirator who never held American office or worked in the Democratic organization to give orders to the Democrats of the United States!"[45]

Also since Franklin Roosevelt's day, Democratic presidential campaigns have counted heavily upon labor's contributions of funds and legwork. "The election of John F. Kennedy is Labor's number one job," proclaimed George Meany in 1960.[46] Union halls across the nation were turned into Kennedy campaign centers, and union registration drives in the cities were indispensable to his success. Franklin D. Roosevelt cemented labor and the Democratic presidency into close bond in the embittered election of 1936, when he courted the aid of AFL and CIO leaders. They responded lavishly in the conviction that for labor's fortunes and future everything turned on Roosevelt's reelection.

Sidney Hillman made it plain that labor expected something of a *quid pro quo* in a telegram to Franklin Roosevelt after his union pledged its financial backing. "Labor anticipates your support," Hillman wired bluntly, "for decent labor legislation . . . the guarantee of the right to organize and the enactment of minimum labor standards." Roosevelt in a letter to "Dear Sidney" expressed gratitude and blithely ignored the suggestion of a bargain, saying merely that Amalgamated's action had given him "new strength and courage." Following the electoral victory, when Lewis began growling that Roosevelt had better start reciprocating, the labor leader expressed impatience with those who were shocked by his temerity in demanding a dividend on labor's investment. "Is anyone fool enough to believe, for one instant," asked Lewis, "that we gave this money to Roosevelt because we were spellbound by his voice?" [47]

The Lewis-Hillman technique of direct financial contributions was banned by law in 1943 and again by the Taft-Hartley Act in 1947, which also prohibits direct union expenditures for candidates for public office. But union members can help by giving financially through "voluntary" committees, and unions can contribute in potent nonfinancial ways, such as conducting registration drives and getting out the vote.

# Labor-Management Disputes

Twentieth-century Presidents have regularly become entangled in labor-management disputes over union recognition, collective bargaining, and bread-and-butter issues of wages, hours, and general working conditions. The President's participation ranges from leadership in labor-management negotiations—personally or through deputies—to the seizure of struck properties and the use of the military to maintain law and order. In his earliest interventions in labor-management disputes, the President used military force under acts of Congress of 1792, 1795, and 1807 to enforce national laws in local disorders and to guard the states against domestic violence as guaranteed in Article IV, section 4, of the Constitution. In the 1877 railroad strike that affected ten states, Rutherford B. Hayes furnished state authorities with arms from national arsenals and, as Commander-in-Chief, transferred troops from remote posts to the scenes of trouble. In the Pullman strike of 1894, President Cleveland, against Governor Altgeld's strenuous protests, dispatched troops to Chicago to protect United States property and "to remove obstructions to the United States mails." The Supreme Court upheld Cleveland in *In re Debs* (158 U.S. 564).

Theodore Roosevelt reversed the presidency's promanagement tendencies in resolving the anthracite coal strike in 1902, the largest work stoppage up to that time. The severity of approaching winter, the popularity of the miners' cause, and the anthracite industry's membership in a close-knit trust drew Roosevelt actively into the crisis. He ordered his commissioner of labor to investigate the strike and make recommendations, which furnished the basis of a compromise solution that Roosevelt proposed to the operators and miners. When the operators rejected it, Secretary of War Elihu Root rushed to New York to confer with J. P. Morgan, and together they drafted an agreement to submit the dispute to an arbitration commission. The imperious Morgan pressed the agreement upon George Baer, president of the Reading Railroad Company and the operators' chief negotiator. Morgan's achievement approaches the awesome, for Baer had sprouted a bad case of self-righteous intransigence. "The rights and interests of the laboring man," he maintained, "will be protected and cared for not by the labor agitators, but by the Christian men to whom God in his infinite wisdom has given the control of the property interests of the country, and upon the successful management of which so much depends." [48]

Acting on the Root-Morgan agreement, Roosevelt appointed an arbitration commission. To assure that the award would not go too decidedly against the miners, Roosevelt took pains to include a cleric and a union official, the latter filling the place designated for an "eminent sociologist." The commission's findings were made and accepted by both sides, and the strike ended. It remains a landmark of presidential innovation in labor policy. For the first time in a labor dispute, representatives of both capital and labor were called to the White House, where presidential influence induced a negotiated settlement. For the first time, both sides promised to accept the decision of a presidentially appointed arbitration board. If the board had failed, Roosevelt, in an equally innovative step, was prepared to "put in" the army to "dispossess the operators and run the mines as a receiver."

## The Modern Presidency

Franklin D. Roosevelt clung to his preference for keeping out of specific labor-management disputes even in the most ruinous confrontation of his time, the sit-down strikes of 1936. In the Second World War strikes were few, thanks largely to Roosevelt's and Truman's insistence that labor-management disputes must not hamper war production. When strikes erupted in vital war industries, both Presidents seized and operated the struck industries. In the Truman era of postwar reconversion, with labor meaning to hold its wartime gains, strikes soared. A corporation-wide General Motors strike, national steel and railroad stoppages, the CIO Electrical Workers strikes against General Electric, General Motors, and Westinghouse, and several coal strikes hobbled the economy and blanketed the nation's cities with "dim-outs" and "brown-outs." The embattled Truman resorted to fact-finding boards, and his principal assistant, John R. Steelman, was not for nothing plucked from the directorship of the U.S. Conciliation Service. Much of Steelman's time was devoted to White House conferences with the disputants in key labor-management impasses.

Dwight Eisenhower and John Kennedy both avoided Truman's personal involvement in labor-management disputes. Truman's successors have benefited from increasing labor-management stability and by labor's marked shift in tactical emphasis from the strike to the bargaining table. In contrast to Truman, Eisenhower and Kennedy had no Steelmans, but kept labor-management issues largely locked up in the Labor Department. Under pressure of the Vietnam war, Lyndon Johnson moved strongly and personally to avert strikes in vital industries. Though Johnson's interventions were fruitful, the reserved stances of Eisenhower and Kennedy seem preferable. The President's personal intervention in labor-management disputes has certain drawbacks. The knowledge that the President is available through ultimate appeal may prompt the parties, particularly labor, to treat less seriously the earlier stages of negotiations. The President, in intervening, also takes substantial risks. If the parties do not agree, after his best efforts, his prestige and influence suffer damage, which can wilt his effectiveness in other interventions. He cannot intervene too much, or his efforts shrink in value. He can intervene successfully only if he can exert sufficient pressures, and these in turn depend upon the presence of a genuine national danger if a work stoppage occurs in the industry involved.

In the Nixon-Ford era, the principal regulator of labor-management disputes was the high-inflation, high-unemployment economy, which undermined labor's capacity to bargain and strike. "What's the point of striking," asked a union leader early in the Ford presidency, "if you lose a month's pay to get more money that isn't worth anything when you get it?"[49]

## Carter and the Coal Strike

In 1978, both the presidency and Jimmy Carter were tested by a lengthy midwinter coal strike of 160 thousand miners in a twelve-state area of the East and Midwest, which quickly halved the nation's coal production. Initially, despite burgeoning industry layoffs, Carter maintained a low profile. Doubtless he considered that his intervention might fail to produce a union-management agreement, with the union members a highly volatile force, possessors of a staunch reputation for defying Presidents and judges, and failure would tarnish the President's prestige.

Intervention would encourage other unions to push their disputes into the White House to win heftier concessions, and the president would feel compelled to endorse a settlement that might far exceed the administration's antiinflation guidelines. Meanwhile, as Carter deliberated, factories, schools, and stores shut down and unemployment spread. Sporadic violence erupted in the Appalachian coal country.

Carter persisted in choosing not to act like his presidential predecessors and invoke the Taft-Hartley Act or seize the coal mines. Instead, he pressed industry to meet union demands despite their spiral far beyond the wage guidelines. Among other things, Carter's governmental negotiators broadly implied that the steel companies, which commonly owned the coal mines, could expect little help from the administration in reducing low-priced Japanese steel imports if they failed to compromise with the United Mine Workers Union. Later Carter threatened to chastise the industry managers on national television. Ultimately, industry yielded, but why it did is not altogether clear—whether because of the President's threats and the skilled, salty jawboning of his chief negotiator, Robert S. Strauss, or whether, simply, the steel companies were running out of coal for themselves. One industry representative explained, "We weren't negotiating with the UMW any longer. We were negotiating with the government."[50]

But the miners rejected the pact, and Carter was driven to invoke a temporary Taft-Hartley injunction, which they widely defied, and violence spread. A new contract was hastily drawn, sweetened with juicy concessions to the miners. Mercifully they ratified it.

Why did the miners relent and spare Carter from further embarrassing exposure of the inadequacy of his power? Coal mined in western states, thanks to Taft-Hartley, was diminishing the effects of the strike. Predictions of massive layoffs did not materialize. Miners were hurting economically from their long layoff, and if food stamps were cut off, a step the Carter administration was contemplating, the pinch would be acute. Nature also helped when the weather turned warmer, reducing the consumption of coal. Psychologically, the miners could be well satisfied with their display of power; not the least of their accomplishments was their ample and highly visible flouting of presidential authority.

# ★ ★ ★ The Future Presidency ★ ★ ★

Both democracy and the objective of a strong but safe presidency are advanced if business and labor serve as constraints on the Chief Executive, as constituencies whose understanding and support must be solicited and whose veto can block presidential excesses. But he in turn merits, and needs, strong powers over them to assert public interest against their narrower, selfish interests and to protect those of weaker economic power—the poor, the unorganized worker, the consumer, the local community, the middle class.

1. The ability of the strong presidency to function simultaneously as a democracy-serving presidency has depended, historically, upon the Chief Executive's capacity to use his powers to improve the distribution of economic benefits by assisting the less powerful groups in the economy in their struggle for more power. Thus Franklin Roosevelt used and enhanced presidential powers over the economy by speeding the growth of the organized labor movement, with a consequent improvement in the distribution of income.

    For later Presidents, unions do not offer similar democracy-serving opportunities. Structural changes in the economy, the shift in the national job pattern toward more white-collar workers, and the absence of the organizing spirit of the 1930s and 1940s all contribute to making union memberships static or declining. Unions have become an elitist component of the economy, with less than a fourth of the work force unionized. Their doors are opened only a crack to racial minorities, and the incomes and hourly wages of union workers are far above those of nonunion workers.[51] The impaired utility of organized labor to the President as an avenue to the economic betterment of the general body of citizens may require the President to rely more heavily upon racial and national groups and to direct his appeal more pointedly to consumer interest.

2. As long as the vital processes of collective bargaining are adequately safeguarded, the President might be given increased, although carefully limited, authority to intervene in disputes that might create a national emergency. The President might be provided more possibilities of action

than he now enjoys under the Taft-Hartley and Railway Labor Acts. If the President's alternatives are increased, both labor and management will be uncertain that he will intervene at all, and if he does, what he will do. Presidential intervention will be taken less for granted than it is now. If presidential authority were used sparingly, it would hold to a minimum strikes that are deemed emergency-creating, and genuine collective bargaining would be best preserved.

3. The President will gain strength and will function in accord with democratic means if he regards his economic policies as enterprises in consensus building. He and his aides can use the conference method more widely to spread information and to help form opinion as, for example, among industry and union leaders and consumer representatives on issues of price and wage stability. Power can be more safely entrusted to the President if the full diversity of interested groups are consulted and participate in policy development. Since business and organized labor have ample records of placing self-interest above the public good, the President needs to forge communication ties with groups that can provide critical assessments of axe-grindings by the economic giants. The likely articulators of concepts approximating the public good include Common Cause, the Ralph Nader organization, and various environmental and consumer groups. Since, generally, these groups express middle-class perspectives and values, the President ought to extend his consultations to the lower classes and to others inadequately represented by established groups—to the poor and the unorganized worker. The future President must devise means to make their voices heard in the framing of national economic policies, which have so much effect, often for the worse, upon their lives.

4. In the 80s, debate will intensify on the desirability of employing presidential power to promote "industrial policy," or assisting major industries like automobiles and steel to survive and grow, as foreign competitors become increasingly formidable. Opinion in the Carter administration differed. In one view, "It's a way to make the free enterprise system work better. It's not socialism." But other opinion contended that the effort "would be a disaster," that industrial policy would prolong "a history of *ad hoc*, reactive responses" by government, and that industrial policy would be little more than "the push and pull of people with political power." [52]

# Chapter Twelve

# Social Justice

**P**residents face a struggle that they can neither direct nor control—a struggle that goes on in our society, as in any other society, between those who have wealth and power and are loath to share them and those who do not have wealth and power and seek to get them. The advantaged want to hold to their privileged position and the disadvantaged to improve their condition. A dynamic democracy makes no lasting arbitration between the contestants, and their conflict is an enduring feature of politics. The President, as the principal elective officer of American democratic society, has made no enduring and unqualified commitment to either the advantaged or the disadvantaged. Particular Chief Executives have been heavily committed to one of the sides; others have remained largely indifferent or have been distracted by other problems. Nineteenth-century Presidents were uneven and chiefly negative in their attention to social justice; in the twentieth century unevenness still prevails, but positive actions have become far more numerous and more forceful. Yet if one thing is clear, it is that the President can effect no lasting accommodation that will bring the struggle for wealth and power to a close. Its endurance and the likelihood that it will move on to new phases and intensities provide some of the more formidable facts of the President's political life.

Social justice and its policies are addressed to sensitive problems whose complexity is aggravated by a political system of dispersed power. So dependent is the President upon sources in society and the political system, each highly autonomous and self-assertive, that what he loftily promises in electoral campaigns, he cannot accomplish through the resources of the

presidency. Nor can social problems be resolved merely by sweeping legislation. A President dared declare war on poverty, with congressional sanction and support, but poverty remains a national blight.

Many factors contribute to presidential frustration. Because the individual human being comprises almost infinitely varied combinations of needs,
talents, perceptions, and lacks even the most elementary self-sufficiency,
because he or she is vulnerable to disease, accident, and age, to prejudice
and embitterment, to the free-wheeling self-interest of exploiters, the task
of responding to the problems that the individual creates or is a victim of
poses great risk of error and inadequacy and eludes neat, systematically
calculated solutions. In dealing with social problems and social justice, the
President is one among many participants. Most of the time he shares
power with Congressmen mindful of the imminent test of reelection, bureaucrats with iron-clad tenure, and delivery systems with a high probabil-
ity of faulty performance. Contemporary Presidents are well aware that
lapses in social policy and implementation are distinctly less well tolerated
than inadequacies of military equipment and space gadgetry. Any contemporary President suffers the added pressure of responding to social problems with reduced reaction times and decision time-frames. In the age of
television and a better educated citizenry, the President conducts social policy under the blare and glare of relentless criticism by interest-group leaders
and militants who can skillfully generate and escalate dissatisfactions and
force the President's priorities, timing, and decision.[1]

Social justice has a dimension beyond social rights and social welfare. It
includes the civil liberties of the individual and their protection against encroachments by government. In this sense government is conceived of not
simply as the promoter of social justice but as the perpetrator of social or
individual injustice. Government and the individual are linked in a basic
tension that Lincoln expressed in his message to Congress about the newborn Civil War on July 4, 1861: "Must a government of necessity be too
*strong* for the liberties of its own people, or too *weak* to maintain its own
existence?" In the deepest sense, Lincoln was expressing a fundamental
problem of democratic society—finding the proper balance between the individual's liberty to live life as he or she will and government's authority to
protect and enhance the welfare of its people.

# The Historical Context

Except for an occasional landmark development, like Andrew Jackson's
emergence as a rallying point for the rights and welfare of the common man
and Lincoln's Emancipation Proclamation, which commenced a lengthy,
erratic reversal of injustices suffered by a massive class, the nineteenth century was not an era of notable advance for social justice. As the century
wore on, the country was engrossed in its own development. Wealth dominated commonwealth, the ethics of business was the ethics of politics, and
the President, most of the time, was little more than a titular leader.

## The Roosevelts and Wilson

If the history of social justice possesses turning points, one indeed is the ascent of Theodore Roosevelt to the presidency. The talents and instincts of that extraordinary man and the climactic momentum of forces that had gathered great speed in the final decades of the nineteenth century combined to produce an epoch of presidential social achievement. The forces were many and diverse. The two great groups most injured by big industrialism—agriculture and labor—were well astir. The first President to wage large-scale war upon economic abuse, Roosevelt viewed his office as a "bully pulpit." Endowed with moral fervor and oratorical gifts, he awakened Congress and the people to the urgency of reform. The curbing of railroad rate discriminations, the pure food and meat inspection laws, the brassy warfare upon the trusts, and the federal employers' liability act typify his trail-blazing achievements. Certain of his proposals were so far-reaching that they were not adopted until the distant day of the New Deal.

Theodore Roosevelt was spurred by his own large capacity for social initiative and moral fervor and the play of forces about him. Progressive sentiment was at a crest. If social reform tends to come when economic power becomes too concentrated too fast, when disparities between wealth and poverty become too glaring, the times indeed were right. Huge corporate profits and the lack of graduated income or inheritance taxes had created at the economy's apex a set of fabulously wealthy people.

Woodrow Wilson could hardly have gained his New Freedom's social and economic reforms without the thunderous schooling of the Democratic party in progressivism by William Jennings Bryan in his three races for the presidency. Wilson also prospered from the progressive's infiltration of Middle Western Republicanism. With good working majorities in both houses of Congress, Wilson swept through a bulging social program. But the closer the United States drew to involvement in the First World War, the more strenuously Wilson campaigned to ease tensions between government and business. He cut back his antitrust prosecutions as a first step and petted the business community with soothing deeds and honeyed words of confidence. War or threat of it smothers the ardor for reform.

Franklin Roosevelt, more than any other Democratic President, identified his party with social and economic reform and with the desires of major disadvantaged groups, such as labor and blacks, to better their position. The New Deal, like the "deals" of other reforming Presidents, implied that in the game of life a beneficent superintending government can deal out a better playing hand to the great mass than can the unregulated market place of society. In the breadth and number of its innovations, the New Deal stands at the head of the list. Relief for the jobless, insurance against unemployment, pensions for the aged, help for labor to organize, aid to the farmer, protection for blacks against discrimination in employment, regulation of securities and the stock exchanges, the Tennessee Valley Authority—the list is lengthy. The depths of the Great Depression provided Roosevelt with a magnificent opportunity to act. Social justice, paradoxically, advances most in times of misery.

## The Great Society and Beyond

Lyndon Johnson's Great Society program would have made William Jennings Bryan, the Roosevelts, and other stalwarts of social justice beam with pride as he succeeded in putting on the statute books measures long struggled for in American political life and as he took on new goals that earlier Presidents would never have dared to entertain. The Great Society program aimed to erase poverty and the inequities that afflict the underprivileged. Johnson sought to make blacks equal partners with whites in American society. In its further dimensions, the Great Society program offered something to everybody, privileged and underprivileged, by waging intensive drives against disease, crime, and ugliness. The beautification of the nation through the development of national park areas, the elimination of billboards and junkyards from highways, the reduction of pollution in air and water, and the encouragement of the arts and humanities promised a better life for all and testified to a basic working principle of the Great Society that maintained that social justice is indeed for everyone. In the same vein, Johnson took up causes beneficial to the consumer—and everyone is a consumer—by promoting higher safety standards in automobile production, the control of pesticides, truth in lending, and the like. A host of evils that Americans have endured beyond memory were marked for extinction in the Great Society. But the drain of the Vietnam war and modest appropriations relegated the Great Society program more to the realm of promise than to here-and-now fulfillment.

In contrast to the full plate of social policy initiatives of the Johnson era, Nixon offered consolidation and digestion of his predecessor's fare, and prescriptions for reform of faltering administrative machinery: a revamped welfare system to provide a guaranteed income to poor families, an overhauled poverty program, a revenue-sharing plan devolving many social programs to the states, cost-of-living adjustments in Social Security, elimination of the military draft, and a quantity of lesser reorganizations and reforms.[2] To hold down social expenditures, Nixon freely vetoed appropriations and impounded funds. But when elections neared, whether presidential or congressional, Nixon invariably displayed more tolerance of social measures. With his own election test awaiting in 1972, and with unemployment at unacceptable levels, Nixon proclaimed a "new American Revolution," whose components included his newly proposed national health program, environmental and antipollution measures, enhanced consumer protection, and more vigorous advocacy of his welfare reform and revenue-sharing. Typically, after an election, Nixon's ardor for social policy evaporated, and he reverted to his tactics of curtailment. The chief exception, subsequent to his massive 1972 victory, was his national health insurance program, which, despite some national governmental participation, depended chiefly upon private financing and management. Significantly, Nixon did not advance his program until Senator Edward Kennedy (D-Mass.) offered a more ambitious plan.

Despite a conservative voting record in Congress, Ford as President proved receptive to social policies. He supported the Housing Act of 1974, the first omnibus housing and community development legislation to be enacted since 1968.[3] Ford also backed long-term mass transit legislation, but it became stuck in the House Rules Committee in 1974, and the President's efforts to pry it loose were less than strenuous.[4] After opposing, in his later congressional days, the Equal Rights Amendment, which proposed to ban sex discrimination based on governmental action, Ford as President rallied behind the amendment and approved legislation prohibitng corporations from denying credit to women on the basis of sex.[5] Ford also urged the passage of a national health insurance plan, as congressional committees and leaders vied over rival proposals.[6] In these and other gestures in behalf of social betterment, Ford acted without the manipulative bravado of the Roosevelts or the moral fervor of Wilson. His contribution was uniformly low-key.

## Carter and the "New Realities"

The Carter presidency was marked by a paucity of new social programs. Its continuous theme was the necessity of better management of existing ones.[7] Carter endeavored to improve the performance of ongoing programs through reorganization, particularly by applying the principle of centralizing responsibilities scattered among several agencies—by designating, for example, the Equal Employment Opportunity Commission as the chief agency to combat job discrimination. Although centralization has no clearly proven superiority over the dispersal of functions, Carter was its steadfast disciple.

The heaviest hand to fall on social programs was not the President's, but inflation. When inflation jumped to an annual rate of 18.2 percent in February 1979, forty-three Senators joined in a cry for a balanced budget, and after eight days of joint congressional-administration negotiations, coupled with Carter's own call for balancing the 1981 budget, cuts of $16 billion were imposed on his original 1981 budget. Programs whose reductions were most severe included those providing public service jobs, antirecession aid for cities, food stamps, community action, student loan assistance. "The days of the 50s, 60s and mid-70s are over for the country and the federal government," said Representative Robert N. Giamo (D-Conn.), chairman of the House Budget Committee. Once a staunch supporter of social programs, Giano in 1980 termed those programs "shopworn and ineffective," adding that "We're being told to cut spending by liberal economists, people who would have cut out their tongues if they had said that 15 years ago."[8] Carter's chief adviser on domestic policy, Stuart E. Eizenstat, pointed to "new realities" which required both the President and the Democratic party to reshape its "historic mission" of helping the poor, the unemployed, and minority groups.[9]

Among the dissenters from Carter's perceptions of the "new realities" was his chief rival for the 1980 Democratic nomination, Senator Edward Kennedy, who urged that the party and governmental policy persist in their traditional social commitments. Nor were economists fully agreed that reductions in social programs were necessary to stem inflation. Economist Lester C. Thurow of the Massachusetts Institute of Technology contended that inflation could not be traced to simple excess demand for goods and services, including that generated by social programs. A balanced federal budget, he added, would do little to reduce inflation, since it is caused primarily by a cost-push momentum built into the economy resulting from cost-of-living escalators in wage and price contracts, from rises in oil, food,

Social Security tax, and minimum wage increases, and from inflationary expectations—the belief that prices will rise generates wage and price demands. Rather than slow the rate of inflation, reductions of social expenditures slow the rate of economic growth and galvanize the forces of recession.[10]

In the milieu of constraint Carter applied to social policy, his few important initiatives were characterized by several patterns. Toward constituencies who could be counted on, such as blacks, whose support in his 1976 election was massive and indispensable, he was resolutely abstemious. Human rights policy, for example, was pursued abroad, but not at home, and not among blacks and other minorities for whom a considerable unfinished rights agenda remained. Carter was more responsive to other constituencies in his social innovations, but only in terms free of large-scale costs threatening his goals of balancing the budget and slowing inflation. He kept a campaign promise to the National Education Association, which had taken the rare step of endorsing his 1976 candidacy, by creating a Department of Education, chiefly by lopping off a branch of the over-large Department of Health, Education and Welfare.

To environmentalists, whose zealous campaigning was vital to his 1976 primary victories, Carter was responsive, although within the confines of his objective of slowing inflation. His principal environmental moves were devoid of huge, immediate outlays. His most spectacular initiative was the removal of nearly 100 million acres of Alaska's federal lands, one of the finest remaining natural scenic and wildlife areas in the United States, from private mineral or oil development. Any initial costs of this most far-reaching environmental initiative of any President were modest at most.

Otherwise on environmental questions, Carter subordinated his initiatives to inflation. Consequently, the application of costly new federal environmental curbs on strip mining were postponed.[11] Environmental regulations were scrutinized for their costs to the economy and industry, and they were widely modified as inflationary pressures worsened. Environmentalists bemoaned the threat of these curtailments to clean air and water standards, and health safeguards.[12]

Carter had little choice but to respond to what was the most grandiose promise of his 1976 campaign, welfare reform. He then pledged "a complete overhaul" of the welfare system which he characterized as "an insult to those who pay the bill and those who honestly need help." His initial reform plan consolidated several individual welfare programs, such as food stamps, Aid to Families with Dependent Children, and Supplementary Security Income (SSI) for the aged, blind, disabled, and other assisted categories. Carter also proposed a two-track welfare system, one for unemployed but able-bodied persons who would be trained for and offered a job which they had to accept or be ineligible for further benefits, while the other was devoted to unemployables who would receive a standard payment "adequate to meet the necessities of life."[13]

Like other presidential plans for welfare reform, Carter's quickly became bogged down in Congress. With its likely high cost a major obstacle, Carter and congressional leaders agreed on a much scaled-down version and a procedure of step by step changes rather than wholesale restructuring. Carter's plan passed the House, the first to do so in nine years of presidential effort for welfare change, but competing plans blocked it in the Senate.[14]

Carter's other principal initiative was a national health plan that placed as much emphasis on curbing soaring medical costs as on assuring health care for all citizens. The core of the plan was insurance coverage for "catastrophically" high medical bills after the family had paid several thousand dollars or after exhausting private coverage. The poor and disabled would receive full coverage, while others would pay a part of the premiums as well as a part of their medical expenses, which health economists contended would help keep costs down. Edward Kennedy and other Senators opposed the Carter plan as too limited, fearing that its emphasis on catastrophic insurance would reduce pressure for a more comprehensive program.[15]

Carter's other principal health initiative was for legislation granting the President standby authority to make hospital cost controls mandatory if hospitals failed voluntarily to hold down their skyrocketing prices. Hospital costs had been rising twice as fast as the overall cost of living. Abounding with exceptions, Carter's plan was modest, covering only 57 percent of the nation's hospitals. Powerful pressure groups—hospital organizations, the American Medical Association, and business groups—mounted a heavy, sophisticated campaign against Carter's proposal, and it was easily killed in the House of Representatives. Instead, the House created a study commission on hospital costs and allotted some further funds to state cost control programs. Press secretary Jody Powell termed the House's efforts "a joke."[16]

Carter's urban program was a grab bag of public works, employer tax credits, guaranteed loans to develop "distressed areas," fiscal assistance to financially imperiled cities, assistance for neighborhood renewal, mass transit, consumer cooperatives, and education in low income areas.[17] The emphasis on aid to business and neighborhoods reflected the spirit of the times, critical and rejecting of remote, government-operated programs. Doubtless history's judgment will be that Carter, despite the conservative mood of the times, the antigovernment spirit, oppressive inflation, and an unreceptive Congress, did exceptionally well in keeping the flame of social compassion burning as much as he did—in his welfare, urban, and health initiatives, which went well beyond the tolerances of viable politics.

# The President as Social Critic

Social reform depends upon more than a set of special circumstances; it also requires the vital ingredient of the man—the President. Without his talent and involvement, circumstances, however favorable, will be wasted. If circumstances are not advantageous, we may well wonder whether a President endowed with conviction and creative gifts can bring off major achievement in the face of limited opportunity. Those Presidents who have wrought the greatest social achievements—the two Roosevelts and Woodrow Wilson— were all endowed with certain personal qualities. However much they differed otherwise, each possessed a strong sense of right, a confident faith in man's capacity for progress, and an aristocratic heritage of *noblesse oblige*. Wilson, the Calvinist, *knew* what was right and faced public questions with bristling faith in his predestined ability to find righteous solutions with

God's help. "Talking to Wilson," Clemenceau once remarked, "is like talking to Jesus Christ."[18] Theodore Roosevelt, morally, was rather different. He had a strict sense of personal morality that he followed impeccably in private life and held others to in public life. In pursuing public or political ends, however, Theodore Roosevelt often forgot his moral code in choosing means. Gifford Pinchot once told Roosevelt that he had to be either a great politician or a great moral teacher; he couldn't be both. But as historian John M. Blum has pointed out, Theodore Roosevelt had to be, and he was, both.[19]

The Roosevelts and Wilson were all, in their way, aristocrats—Wilson by dint of his Calvinistic faith; the Roosevelts by birth and fortune. They were men apart from the usual run of aristocrats who evidence no particular sense of responsibility for others. The Roosevelts each bore a hard vein of benevolent paternalism; Theodore Roosevelt often articulated his conviction that superior station meant superior responsibilities to the less fortunate and to the state. Wilson was inspired by the ideal of service as man's highest endeavor. By grace of their aristocratic condition, all three Presidents enjoyed detachment from the existing economic order. Neither their material sustenance nor their moral tenets depended upon it. They were free to be its critics. Franklin Roosevelt's limited experience in business—he dabbled briefly in law and insurance—his lack of understanding of the importance of making a profit, Frances Perkins, his Secretary of Labor, deemed all to the good. "It gave him freedom to think," she was convinced, "in fields in which common people need their leaders to think."[20]

All three Presidents were cosmopolitan, endowed with a sturdy intelligence and curiosity to seek out new and provocative ideas. They were not rigid and inflexible in their sympathies and associations, as aristocrats tend to be, but were eager to know the world about them and excelled as assimilators of ideas. They represented, in a word, the aristocratic tradition at its best. No modern President has brought to the office a more enterprising or cosmopolitan intelligence than did Theodore Roosevelt. At the age of forty-three, when he assumed the presidency, his far-ranging interests had established him as a naturalist, a discoverer of rivers, and a prolific author. Scientists, labor leaders, corporation executives, and religious chieftains numbered among his friends, and for them, as indeed for anyone of distinction, the welcome mat was always out. The White House calling lists in Theodore Roosevelt's day read like an occupational encyclopedia.

Woodrow Wilson began his gubernatorial candidacy as a spokesman of Democratic conservatism, which was the viewpoint of his sponsor, boss James Smith, Jr. Quickly learning the issues that were agitating the people, Wilson displayed his capacity for assimilation by cutting loose from the Smith machine and supporting the reforms that progressives of both parties had been pressing for a decade.

Franklin D. Roosevelt was also a great assimilator. "He was easy of access to many types of mind," Frances Perkins noted. The roots of his social philosophy, nourished by many sources, reached far back into his life. "One who is trying to discover the economic origins of New Deal," Rexford G. Tugwell has written, "cannot ignore the Harvard class of 1903."[21] There Franklin Roosevelt took in W. Z. Ripley's strictures on corporate finance and the lectures of O. M. W. Sprague, a future New Deal adviser, on the merits of central banking and credit control as devices for economic stability. Certainly one of his foremost teachers in the elements of social justice was Eleanor Roosevelt. Observant and reportorial, especially after his illness, Mrs. Roosevelt excelled at bringing to her husband persons expert and stimulating in social subjects. Among Mrs. Roosevelt's importations were Rose Schneiderman and Maude Schwartz of the Women's Trade Union League, who subtly tutored Roosevelt in the mission of trade unionism. He habitually preferred to assimilate background from conversations rather than from books. "I doubt," acknowledged Frances Perkins, "that he had ever read any of the standard works on trade unionism." It was during his Albany days that Roosevelt, with the encouragement and guidance of his counsel, Samuel I. Rosenman, founded his brain trust of Raymond Moley, Tugwell, Adolf Berle, and other Columbia professors. In gubernatorial seminars with his university friends, Roosevelt, as Tugwell put it, was brought "to grapple with the complex realities of industrial life, and to move beyond his oversimple reactions which were insufficient as guides to policy."[22]

Wilson and the Roosevelts all had a faith in man's capacity for progress and in government's ability to help achieve it. All had a vision of presidential leadership that was positive and assertive. They discovered what the people wanted or needed and rallied them with great gifts of oratory. Social justice requires in large degree the passage of legislation, and all three possessed a dynamic philosophy of the presidential role as legislative leader and a sturdy knack of success. Indeed, they exploited the full legal and political potentialities of the presidential keyboard. "I believe in a strong executive," Theodore Roosevelt exclaimed, "I believe in power."[23] To this Wilson and Franklin Roosevelt would add a firm amen.

# The Limitations of Politics

The President's political necessities take priority over ventures in social justice. No matter how lofty the cause or how intense the Chief Executive's dedication, he obeys a higher law of political survival. He must win the next election and carry on his coattails his fellow party candidates on national and local tickets. One day Franklin Roosevelt, pressed by the impatient idealism of several youthful aides, discoursed on the realities of the political world in which he and they worked. Roosevelt began,

> You know, the first thing a President has to do in order to put through good legislation? He has to get elected! If I were now back on the porch at Hyde Park as a private citizen, there is very little I could do about any of the things that I have worked on. So don't throw away votes by rushing the gun—unless there is some good sound reason. You have to get the votes first—then you can do the good work.[24]

The subordination of ideology to politics means that even those Presidents whose achievements of social justice are monumental often make their way by a course that is bafflingly erratic. Their social undertakings evolve not according to master plan but piecemeal, with quick and not too costly visible results preferred. The President's course is full of half-steps, forward and backward, covered with smoke clouds of obfuscation.

Like any other political leader, the President can at most push his ideas only a little beyond the tolerance of his constituents. As Tugwell has written, he must balance "the risk of alienating support against his conviction about what must be done and his desire to put it into practice."[25] Franklin Roosevelt thus had to find a broad base of support and gain the specific consent of powerful groups he had to work with: labor, national and racial groups, and the like. He had to impress upon them that no matter what happened, he cherished their interests at heart. Yet he also had to carry a congressional majority. He could not alienate articulate groups such as business, the press, the lobbyists, or vote-rich groups like the several immigrant bodies and the Catholic Church. Or, more precisely, he could not alienate enough of them at once to bring real trouble.

No President of the United States has been or is ever likely to be a social zealot. The political system which selects him for the great office precludes it. To win election, he must cast the net of his promises wide; the more he can offer to more people of diverse economic interests, geographic sections, and national and racial groups, the more likely he is to triumph. The balancing effect of promise upon promise keeps the President from extremes. Indeed, the political system sifts so finely that it has invariably produced Presidents who are "safe" not merely in public utterance but in personal conviction. Franklin Roosevelt was altogether accurate in speaking of himself as "a little left of center," despite his opponents' fierce characterizations of him as a "socialist" and a "Bolshevik." Theodore Roosevelt likewise was a safe man. He is well described by George E. Mowry as an orthodox heretic, a respectable agitator, an intellectual Philistine, and a conservative revolutionist.[26] "At times I feel an almost Greek horror of extremes," Theodore Roosevelt once said. He abhorred "the dull, purblind folly of the very rich men, their greed and arrogance." At the other extreme, he possessed an almost morbid fear of socialists and social violence. To Theodore Roosevelt, the Populist William Jennings Bryan and the Socialist Eugene Debs were the monstrous American replicas of Marat and Robespierre.[27] His own high and solemn function, as Roosevelt saw it, was to bring balance between the greedy rich and the violent poor.

Likewise, social justice politics imposes constraints on Presidents whose preferences carry them to the opposite side of the ideological street from the Roosevelts. Richard Nixon heartily subscribed to the ideal that all Americans should work hard like Horatio Alger heroes and make their way in an economic market place asserted to be as pristine and free as in the days of Adam Smith. But the President was constrained from indulging his preferences by a variety of regulators. For considerable time he was inhibited by his likely opponents in the 1972 elections. They and their public policy preferences determined his stand on social issues as much, if not more, than his convictions. Two potential Democratic rivals, Senators Edmund Muskie and Henry Jackson, became proponents of successful environmental legislation. To forestall their taking over this rising social issue, Nixon moved to identify himself with it. When Muskie proposed a single independent agency to administer environmental policies, Nixon countered by recommending a close variant, and when Muskie proposed to enhance the federal role in checking water pollution, Nixon men worked to enlarge the role of the states.[28]

Against another potential rival, Senator Edward Kennedy, who championed national health insurance, Nixon countered with a competing plan. His eventual 1972 opponent, Senator George McGovern, stressed the problem of hunger, and Nixon depicted his welfare reform proposals as its eradicator.

Among other regulators of Nixon's parsimonious ideals was the budget. Despite the President's fervid prayers for reduced outlays, the budget contained many items that, as inexorably as the tides, required steadily increasing expenditures—already legislated increases in Social Security benefits, caseload and unit cost increases under Medicare and Medicaid, and expanded outlays for pollution control and housing. Although Nixon sometimes sounded like Scrooge, he often followed the path of political practicality suggested by Daniel P. Moynihan, to "talk conservative and act liberal." Thus for fiscal 1974, Nixon's budget called for federal outlays of more than $21.7 billion for health purposes, the largest amount ever expended, nearly twice as much as the expenditure for fiscal 1969, when Nixon assumed office. His call for more state, local, and private action did not reduce national outlays; they were increased.

Congress too was a regulator. While Nixon tirelessly recommended curtailment of social policies, Congress increased his budgets substantially each year. The bureaucracy, wise in the ways of resisting Presidents, was another obstacle. Faithful to his commitment to abolish the Office of Economic Opportunity, Nixon appointed an administrator dedicated to that resolve—without the required confirmation by the Senate—to liquidate the agency. Instead, thanks to legal actions brought to OEO clienteles and employees, the incumbency of the administrator was declared illegal.[29] An undeterred Nixon continued the battle, and the warfare rolled on.

# The President Keeps the Balance

In working for social justice, the President must strike a balance between that element least interested in its promotion—usually business—and those elements most devoted—once known as "progressives" and now as "liberals." He must shun extremists on both sides.

Despite the caution and balance of Presidents, their administrations tend to show a predominant concern either for the advantaged or for the disadvantaged. Since the Civil War Republican Presidents have been largely disposed to favor business and Democratic Presidents labor and blacks. The Republican party of Coolidge is the party of business; the Democratic party of Franklin Roosevelt is the party of the disadvantaged groups. Roosevelt remains enshrined in business's embittered memory. He and his two Democratic successors—Harry Truman and John Kennedy—were involved in severe altercations with business. Kennedy's outcry upon discovering the steel price rise of 1962, "My father always told me that all [steel] businessmen were sons of bitches," is memorable not only for its unbridled candor but as a display of viscera not uncommon among Democratic Presidents. Equally, it is unlikely that portraits of Richard Nixon, foe of school busing and stern commentator on welfare programs, will adorn the walls of the urban poor.

## Tensions of Reform

The President who aspires to do things for the disadvantaged ordinarily is regarded with suspicion and even with disapproval by the progressives or liberals whose reform convictions are more advanced than his. Tension regularly prevailed between Wilson and the advanced reformers. To them he loomed as a slippery rhetorician whose heart belonged to small businessmen and manufacturers. Advanced progressives gagged over his devotion to states' rights and his simple faith that regulated competition could solve the big business evil and bring to pass a fairer distribution of wealth. Inevitably, Wilson was compared to his disadvantage with such urban-Democratic reform mayors as Tom L. Johnson of Cleveland, an apostle of Henry George, and John Purroy Mitchel of New York City, who cleansed city hall of corrupting business influence, combated urban squalor with enlightened social services, and brought mass transportation under public ownership. Franklin Roosevelt, in his day, was widely regarded by progressives as a chameleon who spurned progressivism in 1934 and embraced it in 1935. Roosevelt, who cherished acceptance by the progressives, courted their favor with mixed success. John Kennedy, in his turn, experienced a frequent questioning of his social course by a major political organization to the left of him, the Americans for Democratic Action. Lyndon Johnson, in the eyes of his social critics, readily escalated the war in Vietnam instead of escalating the war on the urban front.

The reform President also views uneasily the rare elements of the extremists who achieve major political strength. Franklin Roosevelt's adoption of a program of old age assistance was encouraged by the rise of the Townsend movement, named for Francis Everett Townsend, an unemployed physician who, looking out his bathroom window while shaving one morning, saw in an alley below, cluttered with rubbish barrels and garbage cans, "three haggard, very old women, stooped with great age, bending over the barrels, clawing into the contents." Angered by this indignity to his generation, Townsend launched a plan for old age pensions calling for two hundred dollars a month for everyone over sixty, a sum that in those deflated days seemed outrageous. Eventually other economic lures were embroidered onto the movement. By 1935 its membership and impact had mounted so that Raymond Moley was calling it "easily the outstanding political sensation as this year ends," and Edwin Witte was writing, "The battle against the Townsend Plan has been lost, I think, in pretty nearly every state west of the Mississippi, and the entire Middle Western area is likewise badly infected."[30] With the Townsend fever burning high, Franklin Roosevelt, moving with a decisiveness he never showed for unemployment compensation, directed that an old age insurance plan be incorporated into the social security bill.

# Reform as Legislation

When the President's reform proposals require legislation, they must traverse a labyrinthian course filled with obstructions and quicksands. They must run the gauntlet of committee hearings and floor debates, parliamentary motions and conference committees, where a reversal at any time may be fatal. A common ordeal for Theodore Roosevelt was the predisposed negativism of both houses. In the Senate the "Big Four" Republican leaders, all intractable conservatives, ruled with a firm hand and a granitic hostility to change. In the House a tyrannical Speaker, "Uncle Joe" Cannon, held sway. Cannon controlled committee appointments and rules of procedure and acted as a crusty, unsleeping, self-appointed watchdog over the federal treasury. He greeted every proposal of social reform with the cry, "This country is a hell of a success." Cannon and the Big Four stacked the key committees with members whose conservative instincts, they knew, would prompt them to nip Theodore Roosevelt's measures in the bud.

## Supportive Legislators

By uncommon good fortune, a President may discover a legislator whose prestige, committee assignments, parliamentary skill, and ideological convictions all harmonize with executive necessities. By these criteria, Senator George Norris's service in the cause of Franklin Roosevelt's fond dream of a Tennessee Valley Authority was almost idyllic. Prestigious progressive and chairman of the Senate Agriculture Committee, Norris for years had pushed for public power development in the Tennessee region. In 1933 Franklin Roosevelt and Norris drove through the shabby, eroded countryside along the Tennessee River in the President's open touring car, happily devising plans for a millennium of cheap electric power, flood control, soil conservation, afforestation, diversified industry, retirement of marginal farm land, and general developmental planning. Norris hailed Roosevelt's message to Congress broadly delineating the bold new idea of TVA as "the most wonderful and far-reaching humanitarian document that has ever come from the White House."[31]

Time and again, Speaker Tip O'Neill (D-Mass.) was benefactor to Jimmy Carter and his reform measures. To expedite Carter's welfare reform plan, O'Neill created a special subcommittee to handle the legislation and avoid the long delay of normal procedures.[32]

## The Appropriation Process

One of the more formidable hazards a social measure must survive is the appropriation process, hostilely manipulated by the foes of reform. But in the Nixon era, appropriations were a busy battleground between a Democratic Congress, more generously disposed toward social programs, and a presidential administration that beheld them with a colder eye. A standard scenario ensued: Congress appropriated sums substantially beyond administration budgetary requests. Thus Nixon, during a peak of tolerance toward social programs, approved a $5.15 billion education appropriation that was $375 million above his original request. Although Nixon budgets provided for higher overall outlays, Congress pressed to raise them even higher. In his 1970 veto of the education appropriation, Nixon noted that his budget provided for a 28 percent increase in education spending and doubled spending for HUD's urban programs above the previous year. In all, Congress appropriated $453 million more than the President requested for education and $541 million more than his request for HUD. In part, the Nixon-Congress battles over appropriations were battles over national priorities. Typically, the Democratic Congress cut the President's military, foreign aid, and space requests, and added to domestic programs, especially health, education, manpower training, and pollution control. Ford's experiences with Democratic Congresses also followed this pattern. But faced with double-digit inflation and an approaching election, Carter and a Democratic Congress together cut $15 billion from social programs in the 1981 budget.

## Coalitions

Social legislation in the contemporary era faces a hostile coalition that reaches back to the Franklin Roosevelt administration. In the Eisenhower administration Southern Democrats and conservative Republicans repeatedly played a decisive part in defeating or modifying social legislation for civil rights and medical care for the aged. The same coalition flourished in Kennedy's time. (As defined by the *Congressional Quarterly Weekly Report*, the coalition exists in a house when a majority of the voting Southern Democrats and a majority of the voting Republicans oppose the position of a majority of the Northern Democrats.) In what Kennedy styled as his "Big Five" programs of 1961—medical care for the aged, aid to education, aid for housing, a higher minimum wage, and aid to depressed areas—the only item on which the coalition did not operate in the House of Representatives was housing. The coalition's single absolute victory was on federal aid to education; the medical care bill, bottled in committee, did not come to a vote. In the Senate the coalition appeared in the voting on four bills: depressed areas, minimum wage, housing, and school aid. On none of these was the coalition victorious. Despite the coalition's eclipsed influence, Kennedy was consistently wary. He withheld civil rights legislation until late in his term, anxious not to alienate Southern Democrats either simply on civil rights or on other social proposals.

For the cause of social justice, the real significance of the 1964 election was that it smashed the conservative coalition. Johnson responded swiftly by moving onto the statute books the three major measures long blocked by the coalition: civil rights, education, and Medicare. When the 1966 congressional elections restored the conservative coalition to dominance in the House, Johnson responded to the change in political atmosphere by scaling down his requests for new social legislation. Kennedy's successes against the conservative coalition and Johnson's achievments after 1966 were vitally assisted by an offsetting bipartisan liberal coalition. Most of Kennedy's victories where opposition was strong were indebted to liberal Democratic and Republican support. The Nixon period was marked by general primacy of the conservative coalition in Congress—in 1971 it prevailed in 83 percent of the votes on which it appeared, compared with a previous high of 73 percent in 1968—and its positions on social questions were frequently compatible with the President's. They disagreed on only two votes.

When Nixon undertook positive initiatives in social policy rather different coalitions appeared than the customary straight-line liberal and conservative. Since Nixon typically provided morsels for both sides in his initiatives, the resulting coalitions were a hybrid of each. To liberals, for example, he tossed the bone of raising the stipend of the guaranteed income called for by his welfare reform plan from $1600 to $2400, and to conservatives who feared that the plan would enormously inflate welfare rolls, he stiffened the "workfare" provisions, in effect requiring most able-bodied welfare recipients to work and the antifraud regulations to deal with that arch-villain of welfare critics, the welfare cheater. (Actually, those on welfare seldom conform to this stereotype. Most welfare recipients are white, somewhat fewer are black, and most are working mothers. Other major categories of recipients include the blind, the disabled, and the elderly.) Nevertheless, welfare reform, after passing the House, fell becalmed in the Senate. Liberal Senators grumbled that the plan's benefit payments were too low and its requirement that welfare recipients work, if possible, too harsh, while conservatives lamented that the total plan was too costly. Nixon and his helpers endeavored to pick up additional support from both camps, to attract, by further concessions tacked on the legislation, more liberals and conservatives to the Nixon welfare banner. But these efforts failed.[33]

Behind the hybridized congressional coalitions on the welfare issue was a motley array of seemingly incompatible interest groups, which once again proved that ageless truism that politics makes strange bedfellows. The potential pattern was delineated in Nixon's own rhetoric when he said, in behalf of his plan, "Let us be generous to those who can't work, without increasing the burden of those who do work," a double-think formulation, palatable to both liberals and conservatives. Working together for Nixon's welfare reform plan were such improbable allies, for example, as the National Association of Manufacturers and the National Welfare Rights Organization. Though their views on what the legislation should contain were highly divergent, they were united in resolve to overcome the congressional inactivity that had becalmed the legislation previously.[34]

# The Executive Branch

The executive branch, with its abundance of talent, data, and organizations, provides the President with vital resources of social reform. His success in social enterprises depends in no small way upon his skill in exploiting these resources, particularly his cache of human talent. Within the executive branch are various specialists whose common effort is required to transmute the President's reform agenda into reality.

## Advisers

Presidents resort to solitary advisers and to whole teams of them like Franklin Roosevelt's Brain Trust. John Kennedy, Carter, and Reagan, preparing for the presidency, recruited task forces to study and report on foreign and domestic problems. Lyndon Johnson, faced with the urgency of urban problems, appointed in 1967 several commissions to develop recommendations in specific areas of federal concern. One commission, headed by the industrialist Edgar Kaiser, was assigned to prepare a plan to lower the cost of housing for the poor through less expensive and more efficient methods of construction and financing. Another commission, led by former Senator Paul Douglas, examined local zoning laws and building codes to see how they might be altered to speed construction of low-cost housing. Both Johnson and Nixon used task forces, composed largely of distinguished private citizens with relevant expertise, to develop proposals for a wide range of social matters. Ford, confronting demands for a new federal energy policy in light of worsening shortages, was supplied a massive tome by the Federal Energy Administration, a 762-page report, backed by 30 volumes, that the FEA contended, "will form the basis for energy policy decisions for years to come." [35]

Presidential advisers hail from all sorts of nooks and crannies of the executive branch and of society at large. Andrew Jackson's principal counselor in his war upon the Bank of the United States was Amos Kendall, fourth auditor of the Treasury. The President's adviser may be a general counselor whose attention to a social justice project is but one of a host of assignments. Edward House, whose main beat was foreign policy, worked mightily in the service of Woodrow Wilson to bring about the Federal Reserve System. House harried the nation's professors of economics for the cream of their theory and data and conferred with bankers of varying viewpoints on the issue. Or again, the President's chief adviser may be, as plain logic suggests, the cabinet Secretary whose department bears most closely upon the social reform at stake. Frances Perkins, Franklin Roosevelt's Secretary of Labor, for example, made the social security program her special cause. A social worker and New York Industrial Commissioner during Roosevelt's governorship, Perkins, before accepting appointment to the national cabinet, had laid out a program, including unemployment and old age assistance, that she would insist upon if she came to Washington. Franklin Roosevelt promptly invited her to come along.

## Experts

Since projects of social justice are founded upon the conceptualizations and data of social science's several branches, experts and technicians play leading roles in presidential ventures. The chief expert toiling for the creation of the Social Security Act in 1935 was Edwin E. Witte, executive director of the Cabinet Committee on Economic Security. With this lordly bureaucratic title, Witte oversaw numerous outside experts, a technical board of government experts, an advisory council, and a national conference. Prior to these responsibilities, Witte had served as secretary to progressive Congressman John M. Nelson, statistician and secretary to the Wisconsin Industrial Commission, and chief of the Wisconsin Legislative Reference

Library. In the last capacity he drafted pioneering social legislation for which Wisconsin is distinguished. He taught at the state's university, served as acting director of the Wisconsin unemployment compensation law and studied social insurance methods in Europe.[36]

To launch his new Washington job, Witte made a month's grand tour of the American social security world, conferring with knowledgeable Washington officialdom, professors, mayors, state legislators, business executives, and social workers. "Very contradictory advice was given me by the people consulted," he noted, "but I still regard these conferences as having been distinctly worthwhile, as they served to rapidly acquaint me with the widely varying views entertained within the Administration circle and the difficulties to be overcome."[37] At the behest of Raymond Moley, then a leading presidential adviser, Witte prepared a lengthy statement on the problems of economic security for inclusion in Franklin Roosevelt's scheduled speech at Green Bay, Wisconsin. Although only two of Witte's sentences were eventually used, their effect was electric. The stock market dropped five points. Appalled high Treasury Department officials sprang forth to demand that social security be soft-pedaled at once.

Witte's most trying task was to find and hire social security experts willing to subordinate their professional predilections to the necessities of the executive committee and the President. Working under severe time limitations set down by Roosevelt, Witte had to badger the specialists into putting aside their accustomed standards of perfection so their reports would be finished on schedule. Witte had to shepherd the executive committee's report, which emerged from the specialists' reports, through agonizing rounds of negotiations. Several committee members refused to sign the report without having every word in it and the accompanying draft legislation scrutinized by subordinates in whom they had absolute confidence. Witte's worst hours were spent in the Treasury where two groups opposed social security, one conservative, bent upon holding down expenditures and avoiding any stir that might alarm business, the other liberal, which felt that given the deep economic morass in which the country was wallowing the proposals had little value. Witte's ordeal was topped off with four days of testimony on the technical phases of social security before the House Ways and Means Committee and three days before the Senate Finance Committee. His experience illuminates a common fate of presidential experts. Their talents are useful at both ends of Pennsylvania Avenue.

## Promoters

Social justice measures, taking the form of legislation, have touched off the most violent battles that Congress has witnessed. Among the most inflamed of these scenes was the Franklin Roosevelt administration's public utility bill, with its "death sentence" provision, designed to outlaw some of the grosser abuses of the holding companies of gas and electric utilities. To guide his cherished legislation through the pending strife, the President turned to a lieutenant with proven talent for the rough and tumble of legislative politics, Thomas G. Corcoran, a youthful, cherub-faced protégé of Felix Frankfurter and former law clerk of Oliver Wendell Holmes.[38]

Nominally a counsel of the Reconstruction Finance Corporation, Corcoran, with his partner in several New Deal enterprises, Benjamin V.

Cohen, the counsel of the Power Policy Committee, had drafted the utilities bill they were now promoting. To touch off his campaign, Corcoran prepared a presidential letter of fitting exhortation to accompany the bill to Capitol Hill. He provided full-time, all-around assistance to the bill's sponsors, Senator Burton K. Wheeler of Montana and Congressman Sam Rayburn of Texas. Corcoran and Cohen coached the sponsors and a parade of government witnesses on the bill's many intricacies. For Senators and Congressmen friendly to the bill, they ghostwrote letters addressed to legislative colleagues and influential constituents, entreating their support. Corcoran negotiated compromises on hostile amendments and frantically lobbied in cloakrooms and hallways, lining up votes. The juggernaut of influence that the utilities were wheeling through Congress lifted his effort to a high and steady pitch.

The President's youthful promoter was faring tolerably well until an explosion of ominous publicity was touched off by Congressman Ralph O. Brewster of Maine. At the height of battle, Brewster rose in the House to declare,

> During the consideration of the "death sentence" clause in the Holding Company bill, Thomas G. Corcoran, Esquire . . . came to me in the lobby of the Capitol and stated to me with what he termed "brutal frankness" that, if I should vote against the death sentence for public utility companies he would find it necessary to stop construction on the Passamaquoddy dam in my district.*

Promptly after Brewster's disclosure, Corcoran was faced with two inquiries. One, a cryptic request from Franklin Roosevelt, read "Please send me as promptly as possible a complete statement of all your dealings on governmental matters" with Congressman Brewster.[39] The second was a House committee investigation of the incident. Corcoran passed both tests with flying colors. In putting his case before the House committee, he had the advantage of a witness, a fellow official of the executive branch, while Brewster was handicapped by having no corroborator. Meantime the utility bill was passed.

## Administrators

A victory won in social legislation can be lost in the selection of the administrative agency to carry it out. Since the President initiates the selection of the agency's leadership, he is sometimes the perpetrator of defeat. In reality, he may yield to conservative pressures. To the newly established Federal Reserve Board, Wilson appointed an array of leading bankers and businessmen, a stroke that put the progressive community into a state of shock. "Why, it looks as if Mr. Vanderlip [president of the National City Bank of New York] has selected them," sputtered one dazed progressive. When Wilson, in a similar tactic, loaded the Interstate Commerce Commission with devoted friends of American railroads, Senator Robert La Follette exclaimed, "What an inspiring spectacle to the millions who voted for Wilson as a true Progressive."

---

*The dam was a huge work relief project established primarily to develop public power. "Quoddy," situated across from Campobello, Franklin Roosevelt's summer home, was a pet enterprise of the President.

The cabinet of Franklin Roosevelt was, in its majority sentiment, at least middle-of-the-road and even conservative toward social questions. The state of the cabinet partly reflects the mixed sentiment of the body politic itself regarding social reform and partly the unsettled attitude of the President. Roosevelt's original Budget director, Lewis Douglas, and his Secretary of State, Cordell Hull, were devoted to sound money, fiscal orthodoxy, and tariff reduction. Old-line progressivism was embodied in Harold Ickes, a Bull Mooser, and the preferability of government-business collaboration in Raymond Moley on the right and Rexford Tugwell, Assistant Secretary of Agriculture, on the left. These and other philosophical schools scored successes, although the predominant image that emerged was of social reform. It was part of Franklin Roosevelt's administrative genius that he encouraged his diverse administrators to ride and expand their own programs vigorously and never think of sparing him. "Thus a very energetic set of people were stimulated by their leader to develop programs of reform and action," Frances Perkins noted.[40]

# How Presidents Resist Social Programs

Richard Nixon, exponent of the work ethic and of parsimony and prudence in social expenditure, wielded a variety of executive swords to effectuate his beliefs. Particularly after his 1972 landslide reelection, Nixon moved to implement his ascetic philosophy—for the poor, that is, not for himself, the wealthy, or others with a taste and the wherewithal for luxurious living. "We are going to shuck off," he declared, ". . . and trim down those programs that have proved simply to be failures." Precisely what rational tests or measurements were to be applied to warrant a program's condemnation remained unclear. Head Start, a preschool compensatory education program designed to help slum children to overcome environmental disadvantages, was marked for extinction when a White House aide announced that "Head Start is clearly a failure. It is nothing but a babysitting service for welfare mothers."[41] A possible opposite judgment that Head Start was remarkable in achieving much in little time and at little cost was dismissed out of hand.

Reform and reorganization in the name of efficiency and economy became the order of the day for many social programs, a disguise behind which lurked drastic cut-backs and outright scuttling. Nixon's most sustained "reorganization" assault was on the Office of Economic Opportunity (OEO), nerve-center of Johnson's "war on poverty." From the premise that "when programs are ineffectively administered, those hurt most . . . are the poor," the President moved to detach two key OEO programs and assign them elsewhere, relegating Head Start to HEW and the Job Corps to the Labor Department. Both quickly shrank into mere shadows of their former selves. The other major reorganization device was revenue sharing, foundation of Nixon's New Federalism, which funneled federal funds to the states and localities and was aimed at building an expanded role for them in social programs, with a corresponding reduction of federal activity. The change from federal to state and local control, as Vernon E. Jordan, Jr., executive director of the National Urban League, noted, meant hardship for minority citizens whose needs, historically, have evoked far more response from national than from state and local governments. Black people, said Jordan, could not "rely on some magical mixture of local good will along with a heavy dose of individual initiative." In the national government, time and again, key social programs were handed over to conservative administrators, to whom they were anathema. HEW was entrusted to Caspar Weinberger, a conservative Californian, and, to head OEO and the poverty program, Nixon designated Howard Phillips, a founder of Young Americans for Freedom, a conservative student organization. Phillips' highest duty, in his own and Nixon's eyes, was to dismantle the agency.[42]

Finally, when Congress appropriated more funds than the President requested, which it often did, Nixon employed the veto, with uncommon latitude. He vetoed appropriations for entire social program departments—HEW, Labor, and HUD—and even for such popular, long-standing social measures as the Hill-Burton program for construction and modernization of hospitals and other medical facilities. Nixon's other favorite weapon was the impoundment of funds, also brandished on a scale hitherto unknown to Presidents. Thus Nixon cut $6 billion from pollution funds for the states; $400 million in a given year was withheld from the food stamp program. Big city mayors complained that cutbacks in urban programs were "placing an added burden on already beleaguered cities."[43]

Yet it is also impressive that the President time and again was checkmated or routed into retreat by other components of the democratic political system. His impoundment of funds withered after repeated court findings that they were illegal. Howard Phillips was deposed from OEO, again by court action, because his appointment, without Senate approval, was illegal. Some Nixon social vetoes were overridden and, characteristically, the President retreated from broadly stated and firmly asserted positions when opposing political forces gathered in strength.

# The Politics of Scarcity

Jimmy Carter, the first President unconnected with Watergate, was also the first contemporary President to face issues of social policy in a context of economic scarcity. When the Roosevelts, Wilson, Johnson, and other Presidents launched major social programs, they labored in an era of actual or anticipated economic growth, affording a residue of wealth that government could allot to the less advantaged. Abundance was taken for granted. Carter's situation was wholly different. For years productivity had been slackening, and economic growth, during much of his tenure, ground to a halt. Oil shortages and the clear perception of petroleum as a finite resource, the failure of a substitute fuel to emerge, and huge prices inflicted devastating dislocations on the economy. Foreign dominance of the American automobile market, long the preserve of American auto manufacturers, record interest rates, the dollar diminishing internationally, created a whirlwind of forces that suddenly made large-scale spending on innovative social policy politically unacceptable.

Instead, the country became caught up in survival politics, as it struggled with energy crises and its progeny, double-digit inflation. Social policy was also besmirched by clichés derogatory of the efficiency of governmental bureaucracy. Carter enlisted as a Don Quioxte tilting remorselessly during his electoral campaign and throughout his Presidency with bureaucratic incompetence. Government was unworkable and undependable, bureaucracy insensitive and profligate. "It's not our moment," observed Congressman Stephen J. Solarz (D-N.Y.), "The entire liberal agenda has really been turned around. Instead of fighting to expand programs, now we are just fighting to hang on and to avoid cut-backs." [44]

## Cost Constraints

All of Carter's major attempts at social initiatives were severely constrained by considerations of costs, with Congress at times applying the paring knife more drastically than the President. To speed the cutting processes for the fiscal 1980 budget, Carter imposed interagency zero-based budgeting (IZBB) requiring agencies to rank their programs against those of other agencies. In effect the agencies were cast into a pit to claw among themselves for the shrinking resources of an austerity budget. [45]

The brunt of cuts fell upon health care, education, school lunch programs, and public assistance. Carter's fiscal 1981 budget was characterized by the fifteen black members of Congress as "an unmitigated disaster for the poor, the unemployed and minorities." [46] Political movements flourishing in the 60s and 70s with program starts, now fell upon lean years.

The environment, for example, seemed destined to take a back seat in the 80s to inflation and energy after striking achievements in the Carter presidency's initial years. By 1979, environmentalists quavered at Carter's energy policies—his pressures, for example, on the Environmental Protection Agency (EPA) to increase unleaded gas supplies by relaxing regulations of two pollution-causing gasoline additives, lead and MMT which extend gasoline supplies but cause smog. Carter's huge plans for synthetic fuels distressed environmentalists who warned that the contemplated use of coal-based fuel would upset the environment by releasing nearly twice the carbon dioxide than coal, oil, or natural gas do when burned directly. Even less did environmentalists welcome Carter's proposed Energy Mobilization Board, charged with putting energy projects on a fast track, perceived as a potential monster bypassing and wrecking the environmental laws. [47]

In his occasional expressions of reassurance, Carter declared, "We will protect the environment. But if the nation needs to build a pipeline or refinery, we will build them." Environmentalists were not pacified; many were gnawed by a sense of betrayal. "It takes more than a few vague words," said David Swick of the Clean Water Action Project, "to mollify us about the enormous amounts of damage that could be done by his energy program." [48]

## Attacks on Social Programs

While groups supportive of social programs suffer declining influence, other groups implacably hostile to those programs are enjoying a muscular resurgence in the age of scarcity. "Political Action Committees" (PACs), chiefly corporate action committees, are growing phenomenally—from 89 in 1974 to 566 in 1978, according to the Federal Election Commission. PACs solicit contributions from corporate executives, employees, and stockholders and dispense the funds to political groups—to lobby Congress, for example, and to finance Congressional campaigns, "the use of money," according to a critic, "to effect and determine political results."[49]

In the Carter years, a favorite target of the PACs was the Federal Trade Commission (FTC), a principal consumer-oriented agency established in 1914. The agency encountered a vast storm of trouble when legislation was introduced providing for a legislative veto by merely one congressional house of any FTC rule. A vision was stirred of interest groups, offended by the FTC, endlessly beating at Congress's door, imploring a veto. The legislation imposed further manacles on the agency, but when all seemed lost, FTC's most likely rescuer—the President—saved it, and the clouds lifted until another day.[50]

Despite the pieties bandied about in the age of scarcity of the need for governmental efficiency, PACs and other interest groups watch hawk-eyed over programs, including social programs, lest they lose some vested advantage on which they fatten. Thus although experimentation sometimes discloses methods less costly and more efficient for conducting particular programs, they often remain unimplemented. For example, it was found that cash housing allowances often worked better than costly, cumbersome subsidy programs, but White House officials shunned resorting to allowances because the commercial and professional interests profiting off the subsidy programs would rush to block such a move.[51]

## Untested Assumptions

Practitioners of the politics of scarcity employ heavy exaggeration in their discourse and freely flaunt untested assumptions. Time and again, emotion and ideology reign over reason and fact-based analysis. Bureaucracy and big government have suddenly become all-purpose scapegoats. Henry Ford II, himself a major victim in the new era of scarcity, blamed big government for nothing less than unemployment, inflation, and declining productivity. Although it abounds with faults, excessive belittlement of government and its social and regulatory policies opens the gates to those of superior wealth and power to exploit with new freedom the less favorably situated, including the general body of citizens.

Some of the more specific assumptions surfacing in the age of scarcity are proving vulnerable to challenge. A favorite target of antigovernment groups, federal clean air and water programs have, according to one study, a slight inflationary impact at most: an average of three-tenths of a percentage point a year, a figure that does not reflect cost-savings in health and other benefits.[52] Similarly, a Brookings study challenged criticism of the federal public service jobs program, established by the Comprehensive Employment and Training Act (CETA), often assailed for its fraud and inefficiencies. While the Brookings study did not assess these criticisms, it found that CETA was effective in satisfying two of its main goals—to provide public services and to help disadvantaged workers prepare for regular, permanent jobs.[53]

In an era when social programs are sitting targets for hostile interest groups, when Presidents are wavering or indifferent, are willing defenders anywhere to be found? Social programs' staunchest friends are the career bureaucracies in which they have become institutionalized. To the bureaus the programs are the staple of survival, the opportunity to apply professional skills and theories, and to find career fulfillment. The bureaus are indeed alert guardians of their program turf. When Carter's Council of Economic Advisers moved to dismantle environmental regulations in the name of fighting inflation and making the regulatory process more efficient, the counterattack was mounted by the chief bureaucratic defender of the environment, the Environmental Protection Agency. Rushing to EPA's aid were powerful allies outside the executive branch, a covey of proenvironment interest groups, and a highly supportive Senate Environmental Pollution Subcommittee, whose chairman, Senator Edmund S. Muskie (D-Me.), declared that White House intervention in environmental regulations raised constitutional issues of separation of powers between the legislative and executive branches. Hereupon Carter hastened to proclaim that "We are certainly not going to abrogate or to cancel the enforcement of air and water pollution standards," and hailed his administration's "excellent record of enforcement." [54]

# Civil Rights

## Early Efforts

Of all social justice fields, civil rights for blacks has evoked the most various and sometimes the most enterprising executive responses. It has also been frequently ignored by Presidents.

Despite the beacon light of Lincoln's Emancipation Proclamation, Presidents have dealt gingerly with black civil rights until Theodore Roosevelt became the first President to act assertively, at least by the standards of his day. He was attentive to Booker T. Washington, the eminent black educator, and in his administration he appointed William Crum as customs collector in Charleston and Minnie Cox as postmistress in Indianola, Alabama, both blacks. Although Roosevelt's moves seemingly championed the black cause, they were not unalloyed. His eye was fixed upon the 1904 presidential nomination and his considerable rival, Mark Hanna. The latter's awesome strength of past presidential nominating conventions was founded importantly upon unswerving Southern delegations of "lily-white" Republicans. To counterweigh Hanna, Roosevelt had to enlist the "black and tan" Republicans, and for this high enterprise Booker T. Washington was his staff and reed.

Roosevelt's good progress was suddenly jeopardized by the Brownsville affair, when black soldiers, angered at their treatment by the local folk of Brownsville, Texas, made a shooting sortie into the town, killing a citizen. Efforts to lay responsibility for the slaying failed; the soldiers would not talk. Roosevelt, the Commander-in-Chief, conscious of his duty to maintain discipline, meted out punishment by discharging "without honor" every man of three black companies. Republican politicians, mindful of the traditional black vote for their party, grew fearful, and Roosevelt redoubled his attentions.

Although Woodrow Wilson appealed openly for black support in the 1912 elections, once in office he and his principal administrators quickly exhibited the predominant Southern background of his presidency. Civil service workers were rigidly segregated in offices, shops, restrooms, and lunchrooms. Black political appointees, including those with civil service status, were widely dismissed. Herbert Hoover, despite his Quaker roots, evidenced little interest in the black's plight. He made, said W. E. B. Du Bois, "fewer first-class appointments of Negroes to office than any President since Andrew Jackson."[55] Franklin Roosevelt accomplished the awesome feat of transferring the blacks' traditional loyalty to the Republican party, which had been cemented by Lincoln, from that party to the Democrats. The New Deal was, by contrast to the barren Democratic past, rich in its dispensations to blacks. The National Industrial Recovery Act set a single standard for black and white wage earners in the South. Relief funds, housing projects in the wake of slum clearance, rural resettlement, land-utilization schemes providing parks, picnic grounds, and beaches for blacks, and growing federal attention to education and health were a great boon to that race, which suffered more than any other part of the population in the depression. Harry Truman created a Commission on Civil Rights whose distinguished report, *To Secure These Rights*, charted a wide ground for future action. He accepted the 1948 presidential nomination with a fiery speech, broadcasting his future call of Congress into special session to act on civil rights. Truman tarnished his promising record by never mentioning civil rights again in his ensuing campaign until a wind-up speech in New York's Harlem. Otherwise Truman moved to establish a permanent Fair Employment Practices Commission, fought the Senate filibuster by prodding Democratic leaders to bring about an amendment of the Senate rules, attacked racial discrimination, and backed the United Nations' Declaration of Human Rights.

Black civil rights first assumed crisis proportions, in the Presidential view, in the 1957 Little Rock school episode of the Eisenhower era. The several Supreme Court rulings of 1954 striking down segregated public schools as a violation of the Fourteenth Amendment's requirement of equal protection of the laws were followed by widespread resistance by state and local government to the point where activity in the South toward integration came almost to a halt. President Eisenhower made little effort through federal policy to support the Supreme Court holdings, leaving the question of compliance to voluntary action and local lawsuits. He intervened personally only after Governor Orval Faubus of Arkansas defied a federal court order and employed the National Guard to prevent black school children from attending the Little Rock Central High School. In addition, after withdrawing the guard, the governor failed to prevent a mob from blocking the black children's entry to the school. Eisenhower, stung by the governor's defiance, federalized the Arkansas National Guard and called out Regular Army units to enforce the court order and protect the black children. Eisenhower, nevertheless, refused to declare that he personally favored elimination of segregation from public schools, holding that policy on the question was the province of the Supreme Court and not the President. He sometimes remarked that race relations could not be effectively regulated by law but depended upon voluntary action.

# John Kennedy and Civil Rights

John Kennedy, in contrast, became the first Chief Executive to place himself at the head of the black civil rights movement. He publicly asserted his support of the Supreme Court's rulings in the school segregation cases; enforced the enrollment of James Meredith at the University of Mississippi and of Vivian Malone and James Hood at the University of Alabama; quelled the raging strife in Birmingham, Albany, Jackson, and other cities, North and South; and quietly encouraged or at least failed to discourage the 1963 march on Washington. Kennedy was faced with social revolution and had to act. That it was congenial to his own nature to act made his stand more consistent and more forceful. In meeting the civil rights issue, whether in its more subdued stage earlier in his administration or in its later critical phase, Kennedy and his aides wielded, with skill and enterprise, a variety of executive tools.

*Litigation*    The 1957 Civil Rights Act authorizes the Justice Department to sue in federal courts or to seek injunctive relief where the right to vote is denied or threatened. Kennedy's Justice Department stepped up the tempo of school segregation cases and forged a major innovation by casting itself as plaintiff in the Prince Edward County, Virginia, case. When the city of Albany, Georgia, sought an injunction banning further black protest demonstrations in that city, the Justice Department filed a friend-of-the-court brief in opposition.

*The presidential constabulary*    The United States Code authorizes the President to suppress domestic violence stemming from unlawful assembly or a state's inability or unwillingness to protect a constitutional right. To keep order, the President is assisted by a tripartite constabulary: the Regular Army, the federalized National Guard, and the United States marshals. Thus James Meredith's presence and safety at the University of Mississippi depended, at least in its early season, upon units of the Regular Army and the federalized Mississippi National Guard. The busiest unit of the President's constabulary was the United States marshals, called upon to protect variously the freedom riders and demonstrators in Albany, Georgia. When a mob took over the bus station in Montgomery, Alabama, six hundred marshals moved in to fill the law enforcement vacuum.

*The government contract*    Presidents since Franklin Roosevelt have employed the government contract as a weapon to clear pathways for civil rights advances. The one hundred largest defense contractors and their subcontractors employ approximately ten million persons. Countless other workers are employed under federal contracts or aid. From Franklin Roosevelt onward, interdepartmental committees composed of the departments contracting most heavily have existed to overcome job discrimination by private employers performing government contracts. Congress's disinclination to establish a fair employment practices commission has made reliance upon the interdepartmental committees all the heavier. Through the committees, Presidents have insisted upon antidiscrimination provisos in government contracts, heeding their implied duty as executors of the

Constitution, with its affirmation of equal rights, to see that federal money is not tainted with racial prejudice.

*The civil service*     The United States government, as the nation's largest employer, has its own house to put in order. Legal authority to do so is abundant. The 1883 Civil Service Act established merit as the primary test for federal employment, and from 1940 onward various statutes prohibit discrimination "on account of race, creed, or color." The President's official oath and responsibility as chief administrator impart further authority. The Kennedy administration's personnel policies put new stress upon the appointment and upgrading of qualified blacks. Complaint procedures concerning discrimination were liberalized and the Committee on Equal Employment Opportunity investigated agency compliance.

*Administrative regulation*     The freedom riders' visitations in Southern territory spurred the Kennedy administration to petition the Interstate Commerce Commission to desegregate facilities in terminals providing interstate bus travel. After months of delay and insistent Justice Department pressure, the desegregation order was issued. The administration lacked power to move similarly upon airports under the Civil Aeronautics Act. To foster desegregation in various Southern airport facilities, the Justice Department relied upon court action and private persuasion.

*Federal funds*     The expenditure of federal funds is a presidential weapon of vast potency in behalf of civil rights. Few aspects of American life are untouched by the incessant outpouring of federal money. In his 1960 campaign Kennedy flayed the Eisenhower administration for not blotting out racial discrimination in federally supported housing, holding it could be achieved merely by "a stroke of the pen." After long delay and much pressure by racial groups, the President finally issued an executive order on November 21, 1962, barring discrimination in the sale or rental of housing financed through federal assistance, but the executive order's seeming breadth was badly sheared by administrative interpretation.

*Public appeals*     In the major civil rights crises, Kennedy as a regular tactic made radio and television addresses, pleading and lecturing to the nation, stressing the moral aspects and local responsibilities. In the University of Alabama episode of 1963, Governor George C. Wallace stood in the doorway of a university building to prevent the registration of two black students, Vivian Malone and James Hood. Kennedy's public expressions included an appeal to Wallace to stay away from the university campus. The governor's plan, the President said in a published telegram, was "the only announced threat to orderly compliance with the law." The students eventually embarked upon their studies with the help of the National Guard. In his television address on the Alabama episode, Kennedy termed the rising tide of black discontent "a moral crisis," which "faces us all in every city of the North as well as the South." The problem of the black's place in American life, the President declared, "must be solved in the homes of every American across the country."[56] Kennedy's public appeals were also put to specific local communities and their key citizens.

*Private persuasion*   To head off brewing civil rights crises or to steady them at a low boiling point, President Kennedy, Attorney General Robert Kennedy, and their aides counted heavily upon the arts of private persuasion. President Kennedy met at the White House with whole delegations of Southern businessmen, theater owners, and newspaper editors to present the case for voluntary desegregation and warn of the danger that black extremists might gain power should the moderates fail. Cabinet Secretaries sometimes joined the effort. Secretary of Commerce Luther Hodges, a North Carolinian, wrote letters of encouragement to fellow Southerners; the Attorney General telephoned friendly and unfriendly local officials, encouraging, persuading, or scolding, as required. The Justice Department in private, unpublicized talks helped some Southern communities desegregate their schools without incident. That department also quieted several violent intervals in Birmingham by negotiating agreements between the contending groups; as tensions mounted in Jackson, Mississippi, in June 1963, a peace-building meeting took place in the local Masonic Lodge between John Doar, Assistant Attorney General for Civil Rights, and black representatives. In its discussions with white Southern leaders, the administration stiffened its language with appeals to party loyalty and used higher and lower forms of political inducement. The administration also engaged in dialogue with black civil rights leaders, including an intensive discussion in New York at the peak of the 1963 crisis when Robert Kennedy reviewed with the leaders both what they were seeking and what the administration could do.

## Lyndon Johnson and Civil Rights

Lyndon Johnson, hailed by NAACP head Roy Wilkins as one who gave "the greatest impetus to civil rights in the history of our country," also employed the substantial armory of his executive powers to advance civil rights, including public appeals, the manipulation of federal funds, and litigation. He broke precedent by bringing distinguished black citizens onto the Supreme Court and into the cabinet by his appointments of Thurgood Marshall as a justice and of Robert Weaver as Secretary of Housing and Urban Development. Johnson also appointed Carl Rowan as director of the United States Information Agency. It was in the Johnson era that civil rights legislation pressed by Kennedy before his death became law in 1964, followed by the Voting Rights Act of 1965, which largely demolished discrimination in voting and prompted a rapid expansion of black voters. In 1966 Johnson labored to bring Congress to enact open housing legislation, the first civil rights bill to affect the North. But the slipping popularity of the civil rights movement and widespread white Northern hostility assured the legislation's defeat. The more conservative make-up of Congress following the 1966 elections imperiled any major legislation. Johnson, nevertheless, managed to steer through Congress the modest Civil Rights Act of 1967, making it a federal crime for anyone to interfere with another's civil rights. And finally, in 1968, following the assassination of Dr. King, President Johnson secured passage of the long-awaited open housing bill. The several civil rights laws more or less close the chapter of the Kennedy-Johnson struggle for legal freedom and equality for blacks.

## The Diminution of the Black Rights Movement

Nixon was the first contemporary President to be elected without significant black voter support. He also courted and drew heavy backing from such constituencies as white suburbanites, trade union hard-hats, and the South, all largely antipathetic to white-black equality. Although political incentive was presumably lacking for Nixon to respond to the black community, he had to govern as well as win elections, and that necessity, and the continued critical proportions of black social and economic problems forced Nixon, like all other contemporary Presidents, to put black needs on his agenda.

The centerpiece of Nixon's most positive assertions in behalf of black people was the "Philadelphia Plan," consisting of minority hiring guidelines for various skilled construction crafts working on federally assisted projects in Philadelphia. Potentially, the plan could diminish the long-standing imperviousness of white trade unions to black memberships, the ticket of admission to skilled jobs.[57]

Nixon's severest hammer blow on black rights fell upon school segregation. Making ingeniously narrow interpretations of his duties according to existing court decisions, the President announced his opposition to "any compulsory busing of pupils beyond normal geographic school zones for the purpose of achieving racial balance." When subsequently a unanimous Supreme Court ruled that school busing could be ordered to end "all vestiges of state-imposed segregation," Nixon restated his opposition to busing and ordered its use restricted "to the minimum required by law." In actuality, Nixon was responding to the preferences of his suburban constituency and the necessities of his Southern strategy. He was handsomely rewarded by both sectors with a floodtide of votes in 1972.[58] Promptly upon becoming President, Gerald Ford moved to dispel the atmosphere of manipulative hostility that marked his predecessor's stance toward the black community. But any initial optimism was suddenly chilled by Ford's responses to the 1974 school busing crisis in Boston. Following a court order, black and white students were bused to achieve racial balance. Violence erupted and a lengthy crisis commenced. State police assisted Boston's police, and when Massachusetts Governor Francis W. Sargent requested the President to send federal troops into Boston, Ford declined, holding that the step should be taken only "as a last resort," and not until the Governor had used "the full resources of the state."[59] In commenting on the Boston situation, Ford urged citizens "to respect the law" but added that busing for integration was "not the best solution to quality education in Boston." Mayor Kevin White, beset by turmoil, cried that the President's remarks "fanned the flames of resistance."[60]

Like Nixon, Ford was aligning the presidency on the side of Northern resistance to school integration. Their posture reflected the region's political realities. Local school boards were either timid or intransigent in refusing to obey the law in the Supreme Court's historic 1954 decision in *Brown* v. *The Board of Education of Topeka* (347 U.S. 483, 1954). Housing patterns also contributed to school segregation by leaving black children trapped in inferior schools in urban centers and white children concentrated in the superior schools of the suburbs.

Another contributing factor was bureaucratic timidity and indifference at the national level, in the chief federal enforcement agency, the Office of

Civil Rights of HEW. The agency, according to a study by the Center for National Policy Review, failed to enforce the law against discrimination and, consequently, permitted federal aid money to flow freely to segregated schools. HEW investigations shunned the major Northern metropolitan areas and concentrated on smaller school districts where legal issues were less complicated and court challenges easier to win.[61]

In the Nixon-Ford era, bureaucratic foot-dragging in other sectors of civil rights slowed accomplishment. The U.S. Commission on Civil Rights, a watchdog of federal performance, found that executive agencies were lax in enforcing fair housing standards and freely permitted local officials to use zoning regulations, building codes, and highway construction to keep out or remove poor and minority group families from suburban areas.[62] The Commission also found that key federal regulatory agencies were failing to carry out their responsibilities under law to eliminate employment discrimination in the industries they regulate.[63] While in the 1960s presidential leadership challenged bureaucratic lethargy, in the 1970s a becalmed presidency merely reinforced it.

Poor presidential performance was somewhat counterbalanced by the sharp rise in black office-holding in the 1970s, a harvest from seed sown in the Kennedy-Johnson years. The 1974 elections produced black lieutenant governors in California and Colorado, the highest state offices ever attained by blacks.[64] Blacks were elected mayor in such major cities as Los Angeles, Detroit, Atlanta, Cincinnati, Dayton, and Raleigh. Most black mayors have been elected in cities composed predominately of blacks and other minorities, and the most dramatic gains were concentrated in the South.

Despite Jimmy Carter's warm professions of brotherhood with blacks and their overwhelming support of his presidential candidacies, his stance toward black rights issues was so constrained that Vernon E. Jordan of the National Urban League complained of the administration's "insensitivity," its disinclination to "fight hard enough." [65] Carter's principal legislative venture was the proposal of the Fair Housing Act of 1980, hailed as the most important civil rights legislation in a decade, enabling the Department of Housing and Urban Development to file housing discrimination complaints before an administrative law judge appointed by the Justice Department. The judge was empowered to settle complaints and impose fines.[66]

Carter's other major legislative effort centered on a large-scale program on youth unemployment, whose incidence among blacks is severe. In his efforts at executive branch reorganization, Carter overhauled the long-faltering Equal Employment Opportunity Commission, into which all employment discrimination functions were concentrated. A revision of EEOC's enforcement strategies led to markedly improved performance.[67]

# Consequences of Power

After more than a decade since the civil rights movement peaked in the 1960s, have black political gains been paralleled by black economic progress? Data from the federal Bureau of the Census and the Bureau of Labor Statistics show that unemployment for blacks in the 70s was consistently twice as high as that for whites, and black teenage unemployment was about three times that of whites. Such figures are contested by both optimists and pessimists, the latter contending that if black job seekers who became discouraged looking for work and quit were included, the black unemployment figure would double. Optimists emphasize that in the mid-70s, unemployment for married black men was only infinitesimally higher than the white figure. In the later 70s, median black family income was only about 60 percent of white family median income. Thirty percent of all black families earned $15,000 or more compared with 2 percent a decade earlier.

## Economic

A RAND study, commissioned by the National Science Foundation, found that by the later 70s, the wage gap between white workers and black workers had narrowed substantially, and between black and white women, the gap had almost disappeared. Black men's salaries were three-fourths those of white men. The major causal factor of black gains, the study said, was increased and improved education, making blacks more competitive in the job market. The study deemed government-mandated affirmative action programs "a relatively minor contributor to rising relative wages of blacks." [68]

At the spectrum's other extreme, the poverty rate for blacks is more than three times that for whites, a figure disputed by some economists who perceive a brighter picture for blacks based on illicit or unreported income and in-kind benefits such as food stamps, medical care, and housing subsidies. The Congressional Budget office asserts that if these benefits are counted, the poverty rate for black families is reduced by half.[69]

## Social

Although blacks have made great strides in education, on which their gains in jobs and income are based, various studies and tests disclose that the quality of blacks' education lags far behind that of whites. Thanks to Medicaid and Medicare, many blacks gained their first access to decent health care. By the later 70s, infant mortality rates for blacks diminished by half, while remaining well above that of whites. Black life expectancy gained three years but lagged six years behind white figures. In education and health, blacks have benefited from the huge outlays of Great Society programs. For example, black children received between one-third and one-half of all federal money allocated to elementary and secondary education.[70]

One of the starker emerging realities is the presence of two great black classes: one of middle-class blacks and the other of poor blacks. The former became upwardly mobile thanks to their natural gifts, education, and utilization of opportunities generated by the civil rights movement. Poor blacks are mired in poverty, inhabiting bleak urban ghettos and their milieu of crime, drugs, dilapidated housing, fatherless homes, poor schooling, and unemployment. Poor blacks remain even more powerless, following the flight of middle-class blacks from the ghetto with their talents and leadership skills.[71] Sociologist William Julius Wilson notes that government programs do not deal effectively with the structural barriers confronting the black poor who are shut out of corporate and government employment because of deficient training and education.[72]

Both black poor and white poor are subject to the political vicissitudes of transfer payment programs, to cuts in appropriations, benefit-reducing "reforms," rising demand springing from unexpectedly high levels of inflation and unemployment that strain funding levels. For example, in a belt-tightening mood in 1979, Congress reduced child nutrition programs for 1980 by $150 million, including cuts in the supplemental feeding program for infants, children, and pregnant women in low-income families.[73] Likewise, the food stamp program, provider of the bread of life for countless poor, verged on running out of funds in 1979, thanks to suddenly worsening unemployment and rapidly rising food prices. Congress spurned Carter's request to remove its ceilings on the program, and grudgingly raised its existing cap.[74]

# Other Social Groups

## Hispanics

In contrast to the substantial imprint on the presidency made by blacks is the modest effect achieved by Hispanics. The nation's fastest-growing minority, Hispanics, in contrast to blacks, are conspicuously absent from top-level positions in presidential administrations, although they occupy top posts in state and local government. Carter, for whom 81 percent of Hispanics voted in 1976, appointed none to his administration's first ranks despite strong pressure from the Hispanic community. Eventually, after their repeated protest, he named Esteban J. E. Torres to be his special assistant for Hispanic affairs.

Why have Hispanics fared so indifferently in the Presidency's politics? The lack of a visible, identifiable leadership keeps the Hispanic community out of focus. Hispanics are several groups rather than one—Mexicans, Cubans, Puerto Ricans, and other Central and South Americans whose common experience is limited to variants of the Spanish language and culture. Consequently, Hispanics lack the cohesiveness of blacks. Their poor access to appointments to the national administration is traceable to the rivalries of Puerto Ricans and Mexican Americans whose disputes often lost positions by default. Hispanics have not been able to muster a national political movement, and black civil rights largely preempted the terrain of legislation and court battles, leaving little opportunity for major gains to other groups. Hispanics must concentrate on the executive branch, a rambling, convoluted domain whose trails of power are obscure and complex.

In his presidency's later years, Carter appointed Hispanics to positions of assistant secretary or higher and to some ambassadorships. Joseph Aragón, the first Hispanic to have an office in the White House's West Wing, a Carter appointee, hailed his chief as "the first President to really make for us dramatic advances in terms of participation in government."[75]

## Women

Women's movements have risen frequently in American history and their paths have sometimes crossed the President's. A women's rights movement, organized in 1848, was at the forefront of the early antislavery struggle. In their interactions with the presidency, women's movements have fought their political battles on two main terrains: adding amendments to the Constitution and securing recognition of their goals in the national party platforms. Women's most protracted struggle was for the adoption of a woman's suffrage amendment, which began in 1869 and was not consummated until 1920 when the amendment was finally adopted. The many Presidents during that interval were either standoffish or outright hostile. President Wilson, in whose term success transpired, had once opposed the amendment, but now hailed its adoption in his administration as "one of the greatest honors of my life." [76]

The principal political focus of the contemporary women's movement is the adoption of the proposed equal rights amendment (ERA) designed primarily to eliminate discrimination against women. Documentation abounds that women are discriminated against in equal payment for the same jobs men hold and in selection for high level employment, and an abundance of laws at every level of government sanction discrimination based on sex. State abortion laws restrict a woman's right to decide whether or not she will have a child. Repeatedly introduced in Congress since 1923, the amendment finally emerged from Congress in 1972, and persists in its long journey seeking ratification by the states. It became an issue in the 1980 presidential election when the Republicans abandoned their long-standing practice of endorsing the amendment and promoted a constitutional amendment banning abortion. In contrast, the Democratic platform placed a "high priority" on ratification of ERA, upheld the right to choose abortions, and opposed any amendment interfering with that right.

Half the delegates to the 1980 Democratic convention were women, a mighty factor in their successes with the party platform. Their Republican figure was only 29 percent. In a major battle at the Democratic convention, a coalition of women's groups vanquished the Carter forces in insisting that the party withhold financing and campaign assistance from candidates who do not support ERA. The Carter forces contended that the tactic would help Republican candidates and that such a litmus test for support was undemocratic.

Easily the most accessible of contemporary Presidents to women's groups, Jimmy Carter also experienced several abrasive encounters in their shared political life. Margaret "Midge" Costanza, a presidential assistant and an early supporter of his 1976 race, took a strong stand in favor of abortion that clashed with Carter's policies. Her outspokenness on other issues brought conflicts with senior White House aides, after which her role was downgraded and she was moved to a basement office. After being barred by the President's public relations adviser from appearing on a television talkshow, she resigned.[77] Especially tumultous was Carter's angry exchange with former Congresswoman Bella Abzug, who cochaired his National Advisory Committee on Women. During a White House meeting and before a sizable audience, Abzug attempted to lecture the President on the committee's duties and its role in serving the needs of its constituents. Carter was even more incensed by a critical press release distributed prior to the meeting that attacked the impact of his economic policies on women. Within minutes after the meeting ended, Carter ousted Abzug.[78]

The women's movement too has special handicaps. Its political centerpiece, ERA, is opposed more by women than by men, and potent women's groups are arrayed on both sides of the issue. The high success of women's efforts at the 1980 Democratic Convention owed much to a newly formed National Coalition for Women's Rights, an *ad hoc* group of individuals and organizations including women who are party leaders, office-holders at various governmental levels, and presidents and executive directors of women's organizations. The coalition principle, joining great numbers of women in common purpose, is a proven key to winning the President's attention and support.

# ★ ★ ★ An Overview ★ ★ ★

Social justice brings the President, Congress, the parties, and the nation to grips with urgent and difficult choices in public affairs. It is a continuous testing of the capacity of individuals and institutions to adjust to change. It provokes struggle between those, on the one hand, whose self-interest weds them to the status quo or fills them with nostalgia for the past, and those, on the other hand, who are disadvantaged in present society or are troubled in conscience by the severe inequities dealt by economic and social forces to their fellow human beings. The exponents of social justice are not only alive in conscience; they believe progress is possible and look confidently to the future.

To compound the difficulties, social justice is itself wrapped at times in obscurity, its substance and meaning anything but clear. When does government welfare stray into paternalism; when does public authority unjustifiably intrude upon private initiative and private right? Since social justice is a human enterprise, those it involves can err. It is dispensed by no omniscient, infallible source, and the individuals, groups, and sections of the nation associated with it have no monopoly of wisdom and rectitude. A Theodore Roosevelt fights splendidly for conservation of natural resources but acts with questionable judgment and severity against the black regiments in the Brownsville episode. Franklin Roosevelt champions the New Deal, a vast mission of mercy for the downtrodden, but countenances the uprooting of Japanese-Americans in the Second World War, one of the most flagrant mass injustices in the nation's history. The South, although a locus of racial injustice, produces for the United States Senate a Lister Hill and a Claude Pepper, whose political toil played no little part in identifying the New Deal with the blacks' cause. In one of those strange ironies of history, it is the South or Southwest that produced the President who moved to the most advanced ground on black civil rights, Lyndon Johnson. The East is a stronghold of traditional business resistance to social change; yet it also produced three Presidents—the Roosevelts and Kennedy—who perceived the character of social change most acutely and acted on what they saw. The Middle West can look askance at "do-good" internationalism, but it still produced Bryan and La Follette, whose influence upon the presidency's commitment to social reform was enormous.

The strong presidency of the future will need to be seriously involved in furthering social justice. The ambitions and resentments of disadvantaged peoples at home and abroad have long passed the point where presidential attention to social justice can be a part-time concern, or predominantly the pursuit of one major political party rather than the other.

Above all, the presidency needs improvement in its resources and techniques for decision and planning. If anything, the office is over-involved in patching and piecing policy together for coping with flare-ups. It is too little engaged in long-range planning. Social-planning and decision-making must be better linked to the pluralist structure of society, with its many reference points—the cities and states, corporations and unions, professional groups and universities, minority groups, and age components. All are affected but are not linked to governmental decision structures in ways that produce the most rational outcomes. All could provide feedback on the consequences and worth of existing policies, matters concerning which remote Washington bureaucracies are prone to be deaf and dumb or to misperceive in fantasies of optimism. Lyndon Johnson well perceived that decisions about goals and programs best derive from interaction and consensus, involving governmental decision-makers with the full range of constituencies. The policy-planning task forces of Johnson and Carter, and sometimes of Nixon, at least initiated the inclusion of arrays of reference groups.

Social-planning—in the sense of selected and established goals, the measurement of distance and difficulties from the present to their future fulfillment, their periodic modification in light of experience with incremental actions—can be advanced through building on Johnson's consensus practices, on Nixon's Domestic Council, on Carter's Domestic Policy Staff, and by developing a multiyear budget. A fully developed policy-planning staff could formulate common premises on which planning could be based. The staff could assess problems and trends and channel its findings to the President, who in turn could place them before Congress with recommendations of goals. In the dual political arenas of the presidency and Congress, competing goals and values could be assessed, conflicting interests resolved, and a necessary base of political support established. The nation can no longer afford, as Michael Reagan has suggested, to cross bridges as it comes to them.[79]

# Chapter Thirteen

# Political Personality

To win and keep office, to maximize exploitation of its opportunities and its resources, the President functions as a political personality. "Personality" is useful as an integrative concept, a kind of union of his needs, values, and traits or style in the context of his office.[1] Far more than most offices, the presidency is plastic and responsive to variations in the political personalities of its incumbents, a circumstance that mirrors the commonplace observation that what the presidency is at any moment in history depends supremely upon who is occupying the office. Lesser offices can be regulated, institutionalized, and bureaucratized, but the presidency has eluded the rigidity and servitude of impersonality.

Like other human beings, the President is apt to have certain needs that find gratification in political endeavor. As a political personality, the President may have needs that earlier office-holding has responded to and that find even more fulfillment in the larger dimensions of the post of Chief Executive. The needs a President seeks to satisfy in his office can be inferred from conduct, and they sometimes are articulated. For example, an examination of Theodore Roosevelt's political career from its state and local beginnings to the presidential and post-presidential phases reveals a hunger for popularity and a dread that the public might reject him. Almost invariably, he was convinced that he would lose the election for which he was campaigning. Between elections, he was certain that his support was shrinking, and even in political triumph, he remained pessimistic. After important successes in the New York legislature, he wrote, "I realize very thoroughly the absolutely ephemeral nature of the hold I have upon the people."[2]

Roosevelt used public office with enormous imagination and success to win and maintain popularity. He was blessed with a powerful personal magnetism and was astute in projecting it by exploiting the resources and opportunities of office-holding. Time and again, his specific conduct reflects his need. His craving for popularity drove him to a kind of perpetual political exhibitionism. One evidence of this phenomenon was his love of costumes. For years he struck his favorite photographic pose in his Rough Rider uniform and in his cowboy clothes, complete with pistol and rifle. Attired in a favorite cowboy suit, "I feel able to face anything," he once claimed. As New York police commissioner, he made headlines, checking up on his underlings by prowling about the streets at night in evening clothes.

The President is driven by the need to maintain his self-esteem. Woodrow Wilson, one of the more hard-driven of Presidents in this need, was goaded by Calvinistic upbringing and faith to prove to himself regularly that he was an adequate and virtuous human being. He struggled with this aspect of his ego on the ample proving grounds of the presidency. The opportunities for assertion in the presidency helped compensate for the damaged self-esteem of his youth sustained from an exacting father. Yet the adult Woodrow Wilson's brittle self-esteem also crippled his capacity to react objectively to the issues of his administration, a failing that reached disastrous proportions in the League of Nations fight. He needed to dominate others, such as his formidable antagonist in the League of Nations struggle, Henry Cabot Lodge, and to achieve his political objectives in order to bolster his self-esteem. Another criterion of his continuous self-evaluation was provided by his religion that stressed "good works"—the League—for which he strove and fought even to the point of his own physical collapse.[3] For Wilson, the League of Nations represented a value to which he committed his energies and his reputation unstintingly.

The reconcilability of the strong President with the requisites of democracy depends crucially upon the personality of the incumbent, upon how well his values, character, and style harmonize with democratic ways. The other two branches of government, the judiciary and the legislature, possess more built-in procedures than the executive that protect democracy, and their functions more readily synchronize with it than executive power, which bears many undemocratic or even antidemocratic elements. The executive branch is disposed to action and is judged by its capacity for positive achievement, which can make it impatient with opposition and callous in regard to civil liberties. The executive functions according to hierarchy and command and is predicated upon compliant and obedient subordinates.

Yet, like any society, democracy also needs authority; otherwise it would fall into chaos. The ideal is a strong presidency, effective and constructive in contributing to the good life, while obeisant to democratic processes. The realization of this happy conjunction depends heavily upon the personality of the incumbent, and most particularly upon his values.

# The Personal System

Presidents, like their fellow humankind, have what political scientists Fred Greenstein and Michael Lerner call a "personal system." Its multiple ingredients include: (1) psychophysical and psychosocial attributes such as age, temperamental qualities—energy level, excitability—as well as educational attainment, previous occupation, and income; (2) the idea system encompassing the content and patterning of ideas, the level and kinds of information, the broader conceptions of humanity, nature, and the cosmos; (3) the personality structure embracing character traits, core values, moral standards, anxieties, conflicts, and other elements that produce a pattern of psychodynamic dispositions; (4) modes of adaptation and behavioral striving as personality is manifested in action, with the individual coming to grips with the demands and opportunities of the external world.[4]

Psychologists and sociologists offer contrasting conceptions of the personal system. Psychologists emphasize "mirage" theories, holding that the individual's unconscious motives and defenses shape personality. Sociologists champion "sponge" theories, contending that the individual's values, goals, and behavior simply reflect the social structure. One's only distinctly personal behavior consists of those modes of response and reaction deemed unique or idiosyncratic (Andrew Jackson's use of contrived anger, for example, to manage problems and situations of his Presidency).

## Personal System and the Presidency

The personal system of the President is manifested in the organization of which he is a part, the presidency. He is subject to its pressures, demands, and needs, to its norms and responsibilities, to struggling with the contradictions and conflicts of his duties. He adapts to the pressures of his roles by conforming to their norms or by subtly by-passing or openly violating them. His adaptations occur at both an ideational level embracing his role conceptions, and at the behavioral level, the patterns of his actual role performance.

To resolve conflicting demands and to utilize and create situations and opportunities, the President develops role definitions. His conception of role is shaped by his basic values, the paramount goals he envisions for himself and his incumbency, and his conception of self—his ego identity. Crucial in his conduct in office are his ways of handling its stressful aspects, directed by his impulses, anxieties, and modes of defense. The President's personal role-definition combines both intrapersonal and structural-environmental contexts.[5]

An office or organization such as the presidency also exists in the context of a sociocultural system. That system includes ecological characteristics such as physical properties, technology, bureaucracies. Its resources produce environments of affluence and scarcity and roles, some allowing broad discretion for presidential performance while others are scrutinized by Congress and the electoral opposition. The presidency's sociocultural system includes structural properties, the arrangement of positions, the bases of recruitment, and the communication of ideas, information, and feelings. Finally, the sociocultural system includes a social process or means for coordinating its members' activities, normative requirements, means of punishment and reward, incentives, cliques, emotional climate, and the qualities of mind the President values, whether bland or stimulating.

In summary, a personal system—the President's—interacts with the organization of which he is a part—the presidency. From the perspectives of democracy and presidential power, important issues are at stake: To what extent does the office require personality characteristics that harmonize with democracy? To what extent, also, can the President evade these characteristics, and what consequences befall the office and the political system if harmony does not materialize?

# Values

Values, as social psychologist Gordon W. Allport has suggested, are usually social in nature and are objects of common regard by socialized individuals.[6] From one perspective, a democratically functioning presidency depends vitally on its observance of values that impose restraint on the President: Does he accord a high place in his value system to due process and the array of civil liberties catalogued in the Bill of Rights? Can he tolerate disagreement and diversity, differences in taste and character? Is he cautious and controlled in confronting international incidents inviting violent response? Is he mindful of the imperative of legality in democracy, determined in large degree by his relations with the courts and Congress? But values in reference to democracy also have a positive function. Basic values such as power, well-being, wealth, enlightenment, brotherhood are, if advanced by presidential effort, democracy-enhancing. If the President promotes popular sharing in these and similar values, he provides a sure sign of a vigorous democratic polity.

## Personality and Values

Personality is said to be like a steering wheel in the learning and acceptance of values.[7] The content and direction of a President's values depend on his psychological make-up. According to psychological tests, high self-esteem promotes commitment to democratic values, while low self-esteem increases susceptibility to extreme political views. The latter induces fear and suspicion; the outside world is perceived as in disarray, as bewildering and threatening. A lack of faith in oneself prompts lack of faith in others. Anxiety and hostility and a rejection of democratic values are the natural outgrowth of low self-esteem.[8] Values may silence the President in controversy or send him roaring into the front line of combat. They may bring him eagerly to shoulder a task as altogether worthy of his administration or cause him to turn it aside.

Values have enormous variety, and in any contemporary presidency an ample catalogue of democracy-related values finds representation in the Chief Executive's statements and actions. Values have an inherent vagueness and require definition that is prompted by their application in specific situations. How and when the President defines values is determined both by his own choices and the opportunities, pressures, and necessities of his office. Doubtless spurred by the vote-getting necessities of his 1976 campaign, Jimmy Carter was often perceived as a modern-day Populist, committed to bettering the lot of the poor, of minorities who suffered discrimination, to obliterating the inequities of the tax system, and to rescuing the cities and the environment with positive, ameliorative programs.

Once in office, Carter was confronted by the rising costs of government programs, spiraling inflation, a spreading Proposition Thirteen fever demanding restraint in public expenditure. Carter's initiatives in social policy promptly became muted, and he displayed commitment to a set of values little mentioned in his campaign, yet highly resonant with the realities of office-holding. These were, it turned out, the staple values of old-fashioned self-reliance that gladdened the hearts of Horatio Alger and Calvin Coolidge. Carter's central values were competition and religion, toughness and morality, determination and discipline. Carter preached and practiced the work ethic and was regarded by Washington's veteran President-watchers as the hardest working President since Franklin Roosevelt. In Carter's eyes, the work ethic was appropriate not only for himself but for his fellow countrymen too. He was intolerant of those who seem lazy and fail to make maximum use of their abilities. As governor and presidential candidate, he readily espoused a conservative welfare position: offer job training to all welfare recipients able to work, cut off the welfare payments of any employable who will not take a job.[9]

In public leadership and choice of program, as well as in the internal workings of his administration, the President's values do much to set its tone, direction, and levels of aspiration. In the eyes of a disillusioned former speech writer, Jimmy Carter's values were sadly misapropros for a dynamic, creative administration essential for enhancing a democratic society. According to the speech writer, James Fallows, "By choosing stability, harmony and order as his internal goals, by offering few rewards for ingenuity and few penalties for dullness or failure, Jimmy Carter created an administration in which (so it seemed to me) people were more concerned with holding their jobs than with using them." By Fallows's description, Carter's yearnings for stability and order resulted in a kind of feudal system in the White House, its jurisdictions set and hierarchies constant, with each individual effectively discouraged from seeking departures from assigned tasks. Orderly performance and team play took clear precedence over competence and creativity.[10]

A President, as political scientist Erwin Hargrove has suggested, can have a healthy personality and still stray into costly decisions because of deficiencies in his values. British journalist Henry Fairlie's study discloses that John Kennedy and his associates prized such values as drive, vitality, activism, and tough-minded realism. Inactivity was discounted, including the slow, studied cultivation of possibilities in the foreign and domestic crises denoting the Kennedy presidency. In the Cuban missile crisis, he precluded diplomatic and nonmilitary responses at the outset, considered only a narrow set of military options, and came perilously close to ordering an air strike. Presidential values are derived from the culture, and Kennedy's tough rhetoric and veneration of activism mirrored American society's prevailing Cold

War values of the day—the high regard for militant activism and obsession with the nation's mission in the world, which led Kennedy, the presidency, and the country into the morass of the Vietnam war.[11]

## Ranking Values

As a concept, democracy is characterized by complexity and vagueness and is not in its fullness readily comprehended by Presidents. In their multi-dimensional office, Presidents perform many functions, some supportive of democracy, others antithetical, and each worthy and justifiable. Although Presidents sort out their values in a kind of hierarchy, no set structure of values is duplicated from one presidency to the next. Each President composes his own priority list of values, with varying consequences for democracy. Gerald Ford, impressed with the absolute necessity of slowing inflation in 1974, resolved to cut the federal budget; but he quickly made clear that the sector of expenditure most protected against reduction was national defense. Everything else was more vulnerable. "A strong defense," he declared, "is the surest way to peace," a strong requirement of democracy.[12] In the value scheme that President Grant applied to his decisions, education ranked high and religion low in his estimation. Education, he felt, was a boon to the republic and general well-being and merited unstinting emphasis in public policy. "We are a republic," he declared, "whereof one man is as good as another before the law. . . . Hence the education of the masses becomes the first necessity for the preservation of our institutions." Grant's conviction led him to propose a constitutional amendment requiring each state to "establish and forever maintain free public schools" for all children irrespective of "sex, color, birthplace, or religion." Toward churches, however, Grant displayed a hostility as ardent as his devotion to education. He seldom let pass an opportunity to strike at churches or put them in their place. Impressed, for example, that one billion dollars worth of church property was tax free, Grant contended in a message to Congress that "so vast a sum . . . will not be looked upon acquiescently by those who have to pay the taxes." In an extraordinary step for a President, he bluntly proposed that church property be taxed.[13]

Characteristically, Presidents give democracy a back seat to survival values. Abraham Lincoln acknowledged that he knowingly violated provisions of the Constitution in order to assure the nation's survival. Survival, not the Constitution, was the fundamental law. In the absence of the critical national plight that Lincoln grappled with, Presidents have attached the highest value to preserving the Constitution and the integrity of their office. As Andrew Johnson's troubles boiled up furiously in Congress—to reduce the President to a figurehead, Congress had virtually deprived him of control of the army and denied him the right to remove all civil officials, including cabinet members, without consent of the Senate—he perceived his duty to be one of upholding his office and the Constitution. The means he must use for this highest of purposes, he reasoned, must also be constitutional. For all the severe unconstitutional treatment he sustained from Congress, he held himself closely to the path of legality and rejected the counsel of well-intentioned friends that he employ the Army to reorganize the legislators plus an array of less drastic, but clearly unconstitutional acts. Nor would he, to save his own job, submit to the congressional radicals, who, to destroy him, were bent upon running a steamroller over the Constitution. If the Constitution went down, he would go down with it.[14]

The jeopardy of a superior survival value may bring a President to act when a lesser value cannot. President Eisenhower long maintained the detachment of himself and his office from a most dynamic issue of his time—civil rights. When asked whether he endorsed the epochal ruling of the Supreme Court in *Brown* v. *Board of Education of Topeka* (347 U.S. 483, 1954), which held that separate schools for blacks, although equal in quality to white schools, violated the Constitution, or whether he merely accepted it, as the Republican platform did, he replied, "I think it makes no difference whether or not I endorse it. . . . The Constitution is as the Supreme Court interprets it. . . ."[15] In other expressions on civil rights, Eisenhower similarly abstained from committing himself on presidential power. He observed several times that laws could not change morality or that "laws could not change men's hearts." In a news conference he declared, "I can't imagine any set of circumstances that would ever induce me to send federal troops . . . into any area to enforce the orders of a federal court, because I believe that the common sense of America will never require it . . . I would never believe that it would be a wise thing to do."[16] These several utterances constituted in a sense Eisenhower's own private dissent from the Supreme Court's decision.

Eisenhower's expressions of presidential self-abnegation spurred Governor Orval Faubus of Arkansas to order his state troops to defy the Supreme Court's desegregation decision by blocking the entry of black children to the Little Rock high school. Faubus' defiance was, in the constitutional sense, a challenge to presidential power and to federal authority. Quite possibly it was also founded upon a misapprehension of Eisenhower's value system. Eisenhower hesitated, then negotiated with Faubus, but in vain, and finally asserted federal authority by issuing a statement warning that he would "use the full power of the United States, including whatever force may be necessary." The Arkansas National Guard was federalized, and troops from U.S. 101st Airborne Division were ordered to Little Rock to join in patrolling the high school. For Eisenhower, to see a cherished lesser value pushed aside by the dictates of the higher value of constitutional and presidential authority created a bitter choice. Sending the paratroopers into Little Rock, his assistant Sherman Adams observed, was the performance by the President of "a Constitutional duty which was the most repugnant to him of all his acts in his eight years at the White House."[17]

The President may attach a higher value to a role or function in which he is skilled or experienced and a lesser value to sectors of his office with which he is little familiar. Eisenhower, for example, was more intellectually at home and more committed by personal taste to meetings of the National Security Council than to meetings of the Republican National Committee. The higher value he attached to foreign affairs, in which he was deeply experienced, was also reflected in his greater receptivity to decisions in that sphere in contrast to the more restricted record of his presidency in domestic affairs, with which previously he had little encounter.

## Morality and Power

The arrangement of a President's hierarchy of values is determined substantially by his attitudes toward morality and power. His emphasis of one over the other will produce a strikingly different roster of values than if his choice were reversed. He may stress morality and neglect power. Andrew Johnson, conceiving of what he thought was right, pursued it with little attention to power—to the winning of allies in Congress and the parties, to the construction of compromises that might assure that at least part of what he deemed right would prevail while lesser parts might be sacrificed. Johnson's predecessor, Lincoln, viewed morality and power as complementary. He rose to the heights of moral splendor in his Gettysburg and second inaugural addresses and yet perceived that what he proposed to achieve required a bold, resourceful assertion of all available—and sometimes unavailable—power of the Constitution. For most Presidents, as well as for other leaders, choices between power and morality are shaped by the inner dynamics of personality and are productive of mixed, rather than consistent, responses. Theodore Roosevelt, for example, loved life and politics and enjoyed many shining hours of moral leadership. But under stress he was driven by insecurity into aggression. Flourishing spiritual health is not a common attribute of Presidents and other political leaders.[18]

Some Presidents, Gerald Ford, for example, believe that morality is best advanced through example and practice, and they discount the capacity of legislation and executive rule-making to promote that value. When asked, at the outset of his Presidency—with the wrongdoings of Watergate in stark view—whether he planned to establish a Code of Ethics for the Executive Branch, the new President replied, "The code of ethics that will be followed will be the example that I set."[19] Likewise, Ford declined to speak out for campaign reform legislation, impressed by the superior means "of sacred scriptures to guide us on the path of personal right living and exemplary official conduct."[20]

In matters of importance or controversy, most Presidents take pains to clothe their actions in rectitude. They prefer to act or prefer to appear to act, not upon grounds of expediency, as they may seem to, but upon grounds of what is "right." Wilson liked to visualize his work as a kind of "service," an ennobling moral framework in which he fitted a remarkable variety of deeds. Andrew Johnson, faced with a decision whether to approve or veto the Freedmen's Bureau bill, which created an agency to relieve white and Negro suffering in the postwar South, was buffeted by ponderous forces, some eager to punish the South, others aiming to heal the wounds of war quickly and restore the Union. If he withheld his veto, he was promised, Senators and Representatives from his own state of Tennessee would be admitted to Congress and he could enjoy their voting support, which he badly needed. Leading members of his cabinet, Edwin M. Stanton, James Harlan, and James Speed urged him not to veto. But Johnson was unyielding to bribes or intimidation. "He could do no wrong," he told the cabinet, "to assure right."[21]

Sometimes the values Presidents articulate may be quite different from the values expressed in their actions—what they say versus what they do. In his 1968 campaign, Richard Nixon proclaimed his commitment to "an open administration—open to ideas from the people, and open in its communication with the people—an administration of open doors, open eyes and open minds."[22] Again, in outlining his plans for his second term, he declared, "we are going to have an open administration, contact with the press, and so forth."[23] Even the most benign observer would be hard pressed to find any resemblance between these professions and the actual performance of the Nixon presidency, which all but eliminated the news conference and was typified by long periods of the Chief Executive's withdrawal, during which he made no public comment on major issues. Nixon associated not with a wide and representative circle of "the people," but with a narrow cluster of the economically well-to-do, some with tainted reputations. One of the more gigantic chasms between actions and words opened up when revelations of the Watergate wrongdoings were appalling the nation. Nixon at that time unabashedly pledged his administration to "halt the erosion of moral fiber in American life and the denial of individual accountability for individual action."[24]

As Nixon's presidency also demonstrated, good values can be invoked as a cover for the pursuit of values that are bad or dubious. Nixon linked his advocacy of a work requirement for welfare recipients on grounds of the "Puritan ethic," and he vetoed legislation for day-care centers, contending that such establishments would erode family life and therefore undermine basic support of American "moral and religious principles." No word came from the President's lips recognizing the needs of the poor or society's obligations to them. Time and again he affirmed his belief in hard work, competitive personal effort, a spare life style, and patriotism—a belief that other politicians have championed, but which in his advocacy seemed divisive and antiquated.[25]

# Goals

The President acts not only in response to values. He also chooses goals for himself and his administration. His commitment to goals tells much of the maturity and sophistication of his presidency, the level of its commitment to democracy, and of the degree of his involvement in the tasks of the nation and the opportunities of his office. In choosing goals, he sets the tone and character of his administration, the level of its striving, and the missions to which his aides and supporters may subscribe their energy, skill, and loyalty.

## Uses of Goals

Goals come in assorted shapes and sizes. Some, on their face, are well attuned to democracy. Lyndon Johnson considered that the common mark of great political leaders, which he aspired to be, was their talent at achieving reconciliation. Similarly hospitable to democracy was his conviction that power and success must be used to benefit others.[26] Goals may be finely precise or general to the point of vagueness. Presidents may establish goals in several or more of the multiple roles of their office. Some goals that a President chooses to support have the attraction of guaranteeing almost universal approbation and support. Only a rare and contrary-minded member of society could reject the ringing commitment some Presidents have offered to "a better life for all" or—and sometimes almost in the same breath—to reduce taxes. Presidential roles permit the selection of goals that create an instantaneous impression of absolute high-mindedness. Time and again the President as administrative chief has proclaimed his devotion to the administrative reform of the executive branch for the sake of efficiency and economy, a goal that carries an unfailing aura of moral nobility and excites well-nigh universal support, at least so long as it stands as a broadly stated proposition.

The President may sometimes manipulate goals in one area of national interest to deflect attention from public tensions and animosities raging in another area. James Buchanan so related himself to domestic and foreign affairs. Beset by the crashing tempest of "bleeding" Kansas where the winds of Northern and Southern sectionalism converged, he chose, in composing his second annual message to Congress in December 1858, to turn the nation's attention to foreign affairs. Buchanan posed a series of goals for foreign policy worthy of the nation's united effort for years to come. He aimed to enable the United States to "attract to itself much of the trade and travel of all nations passing between Europe and Asia" and to become thereby the wealthiest nation on the globe. He proposed a string of measures that would make large claims upon the nation's resources of men and money: the purchase of Cuba to assure the United States' dominance in the Caribbean; the increase of the navy to enlarge and protect transportation routes through Panama, Nicaragua, and Mexico; the conclusion of commercial treaties with China, Japan, and other countries of the Far East; the revision of the tariff to increase revenues; the construction of a Pacific railroad. How much better, Buchanan left little doubt, for the nation to pursue these acts of self-aggrandizement than to dissipate its strength in internal strife.[27]

The President entertains personal goals, the more common of which are his reelection, a vote of confidence in a congressional election, and the prevailing of his choice of a successor. He may aim to provide the deeds and words for the use of future historians in inscribing an admiring account of the wonders of his administration. His several goals, whether in foreign affairs, social justice, or whatever, may well reflect his underlying philosophy of life, which in actuality is his supreme personal goal. "What is your philosophy?" a young man once asked Franklin Roosevelt. "Philosophy?" Roosevelt answered. "Philsophy? I am a Christian and a Democrat—that's all." Church and party implied for Roosevelt a series of commitments: respect for fellow man, nature, and freedom, or what was the very essence of his New Deal and wartime administrations. Asked the same question, Truman was equally apt but less elegant: "Never kick a fresh turd on a hot day."[28]

## Understanding Carter

The personal goals of some Presidents may be the key to their personality and to understanding the nature and direction of their administrations. "The central idea of the Carter administration," wrote his former speechwriter James Fallows, "is Jimmy Carter himself, his own mixture of traits, since the only thing that finally gives coherence to the items of his creed is that he happens to believe them all. . . . I came to think that Carter believes fifty things, but no one thing. He holds explicit thorough positions on every issue under the sun, but he has no large view of the relations between them, no line indicating which goals . . . will take precedence over which. . . ."[29]

In her thoughtful, thoroughly researched biography of Jimmy Carter, political scientist Betty Glad contends that both he and the grab bag quality of his policy positions might be best understood through an expansionistic, narcissistic personality model developed by psychiatrist Karen Horney. According to Horney, such individuals manifest highly idealized images of themselves "with which they identify and which they love." In living out these images, the individual displays exceptional buoyancy and resilience and abundant self-confidence, coupled, usually, with captivating charm. The expansionistic, narcissistic personality radiates the air of the "man of destiny, the prophet, the great giver. . . ." He conveys a sense of mastery through his conviction that there is nothing he cannot do, and he gives the impression to himself and others that he "loves" people.[30] His efforts are directed at winning high position or accomplishing great things, not to satisfy any real interest of belief or policy but to establish himself as the center of attention.[31]

Betty Glad found that Carter's self-presentation emphasized the perfectionist features of the idealized self delineated by Horney. Carter, Glad notes, projected a somewhat grandiose self, exaggerating past accomplishments and minimizing present inadequacies. Time and again, Carter was inhospitable to external questioning. When civil rights leader Vernon Jordan criticized the administration for being insensitive to the needs of the poor, Carter warned him privately that "erroneous or demagogic statements" would remove "the last hope of the poor."[32]

Carter's self-centeredness, Glad notes, was often evident in his speeches, with exaggerated recollections of his boyhood and of the attention he attracted of the powerful, such as Admiral Hyman Rickover. When nominating Senator Henry Jackson for President in 1972, he presented himself as much as his candidate. Speechwriter Fallows was impressed that Carter's speeches took fire when he talked about what most inspired him—"not what he proposed to *do*, but what he *was*."[33]

Carter's claims for himself tended toward the grandiose—the ability, for example, to love individuals he met on assembly lines, his pledge never to tell a lie, his lack of awe of the presidency, and his iron-clad certainty that he would become President. His charm opened doors to his political advance. His ability to rivet attention and energy on his chosen personal goals, his easy flexibility in selecting strategies, and his freedom from such internal constraints as personal loyalties and political commitments, fueled his progress.

Carter's preoccupation with personal goals had major consequences for his presidency. He emphasized public relations techniques, directing the spotlight to his own person and political well-being rather than to his policies and programs. The policy profile of his administration is far different from the integrated corpus of policies denoting Wilson's New Freedom or Johnson's Great Society. The policy substance of the Carter era consisted of a shopping list of promises made on the campaign trail and in his presidency's reactions to events, regulated by his personal political interests. True to the expansionistic, narcissistic model, the major debate of the Carter years focused on his personal goals and qualities: whether he learned while in office, whether he was tough enough for the job, how well he handled the latest crisis, particularly its consequences for his popularity and political future.

Nonetheless, some large chunks of evidence threaten the viability of this thesis. Carter was not so bland and uncommitted to policy as the analysis suggests. His goal to keep the nation at peace was maintained despite repeated Soviet-Cuban adventurism in Africa and the urgings of top-rank advisers to intervene. He boldly took on formidable policy problems such as tax and welfare reform, consumer protection, and national health insurance, and although he did not succeed, "no President had worked harder in trying to achieve them," a veteran Washington journalist noted.[34] By prodigious effort he pushed through the Panama Canal treaties that four predecessors tried unsuccessfully to do, and he brought off the hardest part of normalizing relations with China on terms Congress accepted. Frequently, Carter showed a receptivity to criticism and willingness to acknowledge mistakes. Admitting that his administration's relations with Congress were poorly conducted, in private meetings with legislators he was a patient, attentive listener, and invariably ended his sessions by saying, "I've learned a lot."

Unlike the expansionistic model, Carter was not volatile in loyalty to his associates. He clung to his budget director, Bert Lance, until the end, in the face of the evidence. In shaking up his administration in 1979, he dismissed cabinet secretaries, but did not touch his Georgia group of the White House staff to whom many of his administration's troubles were attributed.

It is also easy to exaggerate, as perhaps Fallows does, the differences between Carter and other Presidents concerning their policy goals. In the eyes of one veteran politician, the core of difference between Carter and program-minded Presidents like Franklin Roosevelt and Lyndon Johnson stems from their working methods rather than from deep-running forces of personality. Roosevelt and Johnson, according to the veteran politician, had no grand design for the New Deal and the Great Society. Instead, "They were masters at sending up those bills. And they overlapped. They weren't neat and comprehensive, which is what Carter wants." Carter, the analysis continued, was the engineer who sought comprehensive solutions, a perfectionist who wanted "to read all the papers in all the departments, and then make all the changes," who treated campaign promises as sacred covenants while many a predecessor made light of them. "A President," the analysis concluded, "must learn to concentrate on a few basic things, and that has been a real problem for Carter." The President was likened to a diner at a smorgasbord who could not resist eating everything. He could seldom concentrate on one or several policies but was overwhelmed by eagerness to do many things.[35]

The critique of Carter as an expansionistic, narcissistic personality presumes a chasm between personal goals and policy goals that does not exist. Carter took on such high-risk issues as energy, the Panama Canal, the Camp David negotiations between Israel and Egypt, and curtailing the water projects so dear to the hearts of Congressmen.[36] All entailed potentially costly, personal political risks for the President that his predecessors had shunned or barely touched. Underlying these ventures were goals of peace and efficiency which seemed to direct Carter's conduct as much as any other forces. Probably no single master-key can unlock a President's personality; many keys are necessary.

## Varieties of Goals

Goals, like values, are not coins of common worth but exist in relationship to each other. There are the greater and the lesser. The greatest is a presidential administration's central purpose, vision, or grand design. Terms like the "New Deal" or the "New Freedom" conjure up a vision of the central purposes of Franklin Roosevelt and Woodrow Wilson. A President's foreign and domestic politics may join harmoniously in support of his grand design. President Kennedy well discerned the central purpose in the administrations of several of his Democratic forebears when he declared in Ann Arbor, Michigan, in October 1960 that "because it fitted in exactly with what they were trying to do here in the United States, the Fourteen Points were the international counterpart of the New Freedom; the Four Freedoms of Franklin Roosevelt were directly tied to the aspirations of the New Deal; and the Marshall Plan, NATO, the Truman Doctrine, and Point Four were directly tied to the kind of America that President Truman was trying to build." [37]

Below the generalized grand design may stretch a great array of lesser goals that both individually and collectively may constitute the distinguishing mark of the presidential administration. Some may be vaguely and others precisely defined. Grover Cleveland, choosing to embark on the settlement of the long simmering dispute between Britain and Venezuela over the latter's boundary with British Guiana, confided to a friend that his aim was to bring, at one sharp stroke, the whole matter into his own control, push Britain into arbitration, and put Congress in a position where it could not interfere. "My action, you see," the President said, "has been in the interests of peace—permanent peace."

Goals set the level of aspiration of an administration. John Kennedy contended, altogether plausibly, that goals should be inspiring, no matter how great the difficulties and delays in their realization. Goal-setting reflects the President's instinct for the future, his understanding of the past, and his mastery of the present. It must capture the nation's needs and yearnings, perceive the potential of its resources, and grasp the directions in which the world is moving. "The President's got to set the sights," [38] Truman once said.

However the President, if the record of his administration is to be impressive, must be able to formulate solid, possible goals. Wilson had a special knack for selecting as his political goals projects that were ripe for realization and excelled at carrying them out with shrewd political maneuver. The goal-setting President must think in terms of trends, of locating his administration and its times in the stream of events; he must be capable of developmental thinking, of conjuring up pictures of the future, of perceiving alternatives to achieve his goals, and of choosing wisely between them. He must also excel in configurative thinking, visualizing each available power, tool, and project as part of the total process and keeping them in balance. [39]

# Style

The President develops in the eyes of those who view his conduct over time the appearance, or impression, of a "style." The raw material, or input, of style embraces the President's gestures and flairs, his communicative acts oral and written, his enthusiasms, prejudices, and interests. Style, as an output, is a cumulative, more or less representative impression inferred from all of these elements of conduct.

Style as the product of gesture, speech, mood, and manner may tell much or little of the President's controlling impulses, attitudes, and approach to duty and decision. The cliché that appearances are misleading has special point in estimates of Presidents. Senator Robert M. La Follette, a shrewd judge of men, witnessing the passing of the presidency from Chester Arthur to Grover Cleveland, was moved to compare the new President with the old. La Follette noted, "The contrast with Arthur, who was a fine handsome figure, was very striking. Cleveland's coarse face, his heavy inert body, his great shapeless hands, confirmed in my mind the attacks made upon him during the campaign." Before many days of the new President, however, La Follette revised his initial estimate and came "to admire the courage and conscientiousness of his character."[40]

A President can deliberately alter elements of his style over time. In 1976 Jimmy Carter campaigned on a platform of honesty and trust, emphasizing his stance as outsider, a future Chief Executive innocent of the wiles and nefarious ways of Washington. In his 1980 quest for the presidency, the pose of innocence was tossed overboard. To win renomination and reelection in 1980, Carter showed himself not as the decent, moral, upright candidate of 1976, but as just another politician, single-mindedly devoted to winning the election and ruthlessly employing his office's resources toward that end. States with primaries approaching were suffused with federal money; influential citizens were wooed at White House gatherings; snide assaults were made on the character of his opponent, Edward Kennedy. Carter's presidential style was more cynical aldermanic than democratic or imperial.[41]

Style also springs from the vast, diverse realm of temperament. Cleveland was at times impulsive, as in sending in troops in the Pullman strike without awaiting a request from Governor Altgeld of Illinois; Wilson was at times compulsive, rigid in dealings with others, which led to his disastrous confrontation with Senator Henry Cabot Lodge in his fight for United States membership in the League of Nations. A President's temperament, as it is manifested in private, may be wholly different from its public display. James Buchanan was known to the nation and the world as an exemplar of the quiet, flexible negotiator and compromiser. His private demeanor, according to testimony of aides, was altogether different from his public reputation. Attorney General Jeremiah S. Black voiced the general opinion of his cabinet colleagues when he said of Buchanan, "He is a stubborn old gentleman—very fond of having his own way. . . ." John B. Floyd, Buchanan's Secretary of War, who also knew Andrew Jackson well, observed, "Mr. Buchanan was different from General Jackson; . . . General Jackson could be *coaxed* from his purpose, but . . . Mr. B. could neither be coaxed nor driven."[42]

## Stylistic Traits

A President's private stylistic traits can serve to evoke the confidence and loyalty of his associates and to extend his influence in the executive branch. Franklin Roosevelt provided a model of such artistry. "It was part of his conception of his role," his Undersecretary of Agriculture and intimate counselor, Rexford G. Tugwell has written, "that he should never show exhaustion, boredom, or irritation." His patience, grasp of detail, his composure as emergencies fell upon him, his timing, evasiveness, and humor, his reserve, his occasional severity, his sense of office and history numbered among the rewarding stylistic administrative traits by which he held sway in the executive branch.[43]

Another style, by no means uncommon among Presidents, is that of the compromiser. "I am a compromiser and a manipulator," Lyndon Johnson said. His critics spoke of him, less flatteringly, as a "wheeler-dealer" type. The Chief Executive, in Johnson's view, dispenses the good things of life to every class and group. His perceptions of the nature of power moved him more to the backstage than to frontstage in the political drama. "In every town," he said, "there's some guy on top of the hill in a big white house who can get things done. I want to get that man on my side."[44] Johnson, then, was prone to think and act not in terms of "the people" but to carry the play to the legislative committee, the leaders of the big interest groups, and other power centers whose favor or decision could provide what he believed the country needed. The manipulator-compromiser style carried a built-in cautionary device. By the very nature of the style, nothing is ever final; everything is susceptible to accommodation and adjustment. Or, at least, the President will exercise his "options" to perpetuate as long as he can his freedom to act in a given situation. Johnson adhered to an elaborate course to avoid booby traps. He consulted beyond his staff with departmental officers, private counselors, key legislators, random visitors, and labor and business leaders. The extended procedure often created delays, reversals of decisions, the impression of tentativeness, of lack of conviction and confidence.

Some expressions of style may be little more than minor excrescences of personality; others may be purposefully indulged in to facilitate the presidential task. Franklin Roosevelt and Andrew Jackson were masters of delay, a pose they found highly valuable in politics. Thanks to delay, tumultuous political forces had more time to settle or grow distinct; the President could better weigh factors and consequences before choosing his course. Jackson also, to a degree rare among Presidents, employed the terrible rage as a standard administrative weapon. Time and again, he would break up meetings and conferences with rousing demonstrations that were shrewdly calculated and rendered so convincingly that visitors retreated in utter confusion, forgetting what they had come for. Jackson steadily preferred this volcanic method to time-consuming and perhaps inconclusive argument. Martin Van Buren, Jackson's discerning associate, perceived that the President's view of his general political strength was also an element in shaping his conduct. "The conciliation of individuals," Van Buren said of Jackson, "formed the smallest, perhaps too small a part of his policy. His strength lay with the masses, and he knew it."[45]

Presidents have stylistic traits that may become the mark of their reign and an element of their memorability in history. Benjamin Harrison is accurately remembered as frigid and intellectual. President Grant's administration was handicapped by an abysmal lack of political facility. Grant had launched his administration on a high note in an inaugural address that the New York *Tribune* hailed as "the utterance of a man of the best intentions profoundly desirous to govern wisely and justly. . . ." But the *Tribune* also sensed from the address what was to become the underlying cause of the egregious failure of the future Grant administration. Grant, the *Tribune* noted, was "profoundly ignorant of the means by which good government is secured." In a day when waves of corruption beat upon his administration, a bold statement from the President conveying his own high purpose and moral rigor would have served himself and the country well, but Grant, who was endowed with an inarticulateness that amounted to a kind of verbal lockjaw, responded feebly.[46]

Lyndon Johnson's reign was marked by a patriarchal concept of politics, which controlled his style. This concept holds that politics and its storm and stress are the preserve of the President, and from them the private citizen is spared. Except when the election campaigns of 1964 and 1966 were in progress, Johnson in public discourse tended toward a pose of serenity that exhorted good men to do good deeds, dispensed praise, and gave scant acknowledgment to problems. Doubt, defeat, and strife are repressed from view in a haze of serenity, according to the patriarchal theory. Policy must appear to evolve smoothly: It does not shift suddenly.[47] If the roof falls in, it is the sunlight that is seen. Enemies may be acknowledged, but they are not scolded. Under the patriarchal concept of the presidency, which is utterly alien to the norms of democratic politics, the people are not privy to the President's current concerns and feelings. The concept worked both favorably and adversely in the Johnson era. In the upheaval of John Kennedy's assassination, Johnson gratified and reassured the nation by a masterful display of composure while he quickly and privately restored to normal working order the presidential machinery. The patriarchal concept served him less well in the lengthy, tortuous, shifting war in Vietnam, with whose pressures he struggled largely in private. His course did little to promote the understanding and support of the nation.

Presidents appear divided into two schools on the question of choice of external stylistic traits. One school tends toward the model of George Washington, fitting their conduct to the intrinsic dignity of the office. In modern day, Franklin Roosevelt and Dwight Eisenhower wrapped themselves in the mantle of dignity in public appearance. Eisenhower's manly candor inspired confidence. John Kennedy veered to this school, although he tempered his proper decorum with an apposite sense of humor. At the other extreme is the warm, little-inhibited manner of Andrew Johnson, Harry Truman, or Lyndon Johnson on his better behavior. President Truman, soon after taking office, conveyed the flavor of his style in a visit to the Pemiscot County Fair at Carhuthersville, Missouri. The new President mingled with the crowd on a "Harry" basis and discussed local problems with farmers wearing overalls. When a doddering American Legion locomotive came by, he ran into the street to toot its whistle. He played piano for the Methodist Church ladies, winking broadly as he said, "When I played this, Stalin signed the Potsdam Agreement."[48]

# High-Democracy and Low-Democracy Presidential Types

A principal objective of the Framers of the Constitution was the avoidance of tyrants who would overwhelm the carefully constructed system of balanced powers. Fortunately, the many incumbents of the presidency have numbered no tyrants in the classic sense. No presidential personality has matched the type that has sometimes attracted wide interest among social scientists, the authoritarian personality,[49] although occasionally particular behavior has. The behavior of Presidents swings across a sufficiently wide arc of variation, in its proximity to and distance from democratic norms, that it becomes desirable, for the sake of democracy's safety, to distinguish those aspects of presidential personality and behavior that are more akin to democracy (high-democracy type) from those that are distinctly less so (low-democracy type). The strong presidency and the enhancement of presidential power enlarges both tendencies. The identification of those aspects of personality and behavior that are less beneficial to democracy, or even antidemocratic, focuses attention on strengthening safeguards, on deploying staff aides in ways that minimize negative behaviors, of probing, in presidential selection, for personality characteristics inimical to democracy. Such characteristics, if serious enough, might be spotlighted, and party leaders and the public forewarned, to the point that they might halt the incipient, but clearly inappropriate, candidate.

## Low-Democracy Type

Personality and its expression in behavior that suggests these types contain two main elements. One is content—the substance of what a President does, his programs, policies, and actions. The second is process, or how he acts. As well, the types reflect the innermost forces of personality. According to political scientist Harold Lasswell, what is here called the low-democracy type is subject to the "social anxiety hypothesis": personality failure is often a failure of basic character formation, and defective character is a function of interpersonal situations in which a low estimate of self develops. From such low estimates come defensive reactions that imperil the potentialities of the person to enter into fully congenial and creative relations with others. Social anxiety engenders acute concern for the deference responses of others. As stated by psychiatrist Harry Stack Sullivan, a democratic character develops only in those who esteem themselves enough to esteem others.[50]

The low-democracy type, in attitudes and behavior, is apt to be engrossed in "externalization and ego defense." By externalization, he copes with his inner psychological problems by treating outside objects and events as if they were the inner difficulties.[51] The more Lyndon Johnson's popularity slipped, noted his biographer Doris Kearns, the greater became his need for evidence that he was not at fault. His selected scapegoat was variously the press, liberals, intellectuals, and the Kennedys. Johnson's ensuing feeling of martyrdom brought a temporary rise in self-esteem.[52] The low-democracy type is intensely power-oriented, demands power and other values for the self, and sacrifices others for the convenience of his power. He invests substantial energies toward maintaining an inner equilibrium, toward defending the self against the often conflicting demands of impulses and conscience.[53]

## High-Democracy Type

The high-democracy type, according to Lasswell, maintains an "open ego," or an orientation toward other persons inviting the formation of genuine relationships, including "friendship." The democratic attitude toward other persons is warm rather than frigid, inclusive and expanding rather than exclusive and constricting. The democratic type shares power rather than appropriating it for himself, and he subordinates power to respect for the dignity of the human personality. This type identifies with humanity as a whole and with all subordinate groups whose demands harmonize with the larger loyalty. The high-democracy type is denoted by high self-esteem, is psychologically well-integrated, and his unconscious energies are not at war with other elements of his personality. This fortunate state of affairs is productive of faith in people and promotive of the trust and tolerance that induces the personal restraint necessary for democracy and buttresses commitment to democratic procedures.[54] The democratic character incorporates many values rather than a few. If the President should concentrate his effort on a single value, his ties to other values will be jeopardized to democracy's disadvantage. The democratic personality is flexible and adaptive, tolerant of ambiguity and differences, relatively free of anxiety, open- rather than close-minded, and able to control and accept inner impulses.

The high-democracy type, employing methods appropriate to democracy, promotes policies productive of a social equilibrium, enabling democracy to be maintained and enhanced. Democracy requires the curbing of human destructiveness and, therefore, a cool deliberate mien toward conflict situations at home and abroad. The high-democracy type strives to construct a network of congenial and creative interpersonal relations.[55]

No President completely fulfills either type; instead, his personality and behavior manifest both. However, he may tend markedly toward one rather than the other during particular intervals of his incumbency, or his overall performance may do so. These types suggest a continuous dynamic in which the President is engaged. Their representative elements are listed on page 343.

## Nixon and Democratic Types

In the personality and behavior of any particular President both types are represented, just as they are in any individual. Presidential roles also foster the dual pattern, with some, such as that of Commander-in-Chief, calling for low-democracy modes of behavior, while others, such as that of protecting civil liberties, virtually compel high-democracy behavior.

Studies of Richard Nixon, for example, reveal interlacings of these types and the presence of regulators within his personality whose successes or failures had much to do with whether specific behavior tended toward either extreme.[56] According to historian Bruce Mazlish, Nixon exalted strength,

| The High-Democracy Type | The Low-Democracy Type |
|---|---|
| 1. Acts in ways that advance or enlarge the civil rights of individuals and groups. Observes the civil liberties provisions of the Bill of Rights. | 1. Is inactive or regressive concerning civil rights. Is indifferent to civil liberties or readily violates them to advance a cited higher value such as national security or law and order, whose scope he interprets expansively. |
| 2. Develops and supports economic and social programs and policies responsive to the needs of many groups, not just the very powerful. Responds to the ideal of being President of all the people. | 2. Is overresponsive to the needs and concerns of the economically powerful and indifferent or manipulative toward those with little. |
| 3. Is accessible to a wide variety of individuals and groups. Does not identify too emphatically with any one class or group. | 3. Is accessible to only a limited variety of groups, like the economically powerful. Is excessively remote from other classes and groups. |
| 4. In political campaigns, discusses important issues meaningfully and constructively. | 4. Stresses in political campaigns citizen fears and irrationalities. A force for divisiveness rather than integration. |
| 5. Encourages subordinates and associates to communicate with him in candor. Does not suppress or penalize criticism or dissent but respects it and profits from it, within bounds of basic loyalty, in order to comprehend the reality of the world in which he functions. | 5. Is manipulative and secretive both toward subordinates in the executive branch and toward the public. Displays low tolerance of criticism and discredits opponents rather than confronting their contentions responsively. |
| 6. Manifests a sturdy socialization in democratic values and processes. | 6. Displays weak socialization in democratic values and practices, concerning which he is ignorant or indifferent. Shows little regard for the Bill of Rights. |
| 7. Responds to public problems opportunely and constructively for the common good. | 7. Allows problems to drift; assures their neglect by pursuing outmoded assumptions. Is unresponsive to resulting human hardship. |
| 8. Is reasonably respectful of the rights and of the roles of other branches. | 8. Encroaches on the other branches of government; derogates their role; acts to promote self-aggrandizement. |
| 9. Acts with restraint and prudence in war-threatening situations. Seeks support of Congress and public opinion for his actions. Places great value on peace. | 9. Resorts readily to presidential war, launched merely by his own decision; minimizes or excludes congressional participation; conducts war with secrecy and deception. |

dreaded passivity, and projected unacceptable impulses on others; he was wracked by uncertainty concerning his courage, especially in crisis. Haunted by his father's "failure," he harbored potent aggressive impulses and felt driven to avoid failure himself and redeem his parent. He identified his personal interest with the national interest; his crises were his country-men's crises. His environment was divided into stark absolutes—"I think we can win the struggle against slavery and for freedom throughout the world"—a world of all good and all bad, slavery and freedom, aggressor and peace-lover. Ominous for the stability of democratic processes was Nixon's preoccupation with "testing" himself through crisis, even periodi-cally creating them to prove himself. In justifying his 1970 invasion of Cam-bodia, he contended that "our" character was being tested, and we must not be found wanting.[57]

But in the Nixon make-up elements propitious for democracy were also present. Nixon had an "obsession" (his own word) with peace. In keeping with the Freudian pattern, one parent, his mother, a dedicated Quaker, was devoted to peace, in contrast to his irascible, pugnacious father. To Nixon, it was the peaceful mother who seemed strong and the competitive father "weak," because of his lack of success. Nixon appears to have identified with his mother's peaceful soul as much as with his father's pugnacity, which encouraged the conclusion that the President was endowed with strong, genuine dedication to international peace. Simultaneously, his mother's influence rankled his conscience concerning his aggressiveness.[58] Accordingly, much of the time, Nixon was engaged in self-management, to resist the "temptation" to strike at his enemies. In Watergate and related episodes, his self-control failed and wrecked his presidency.

# What Kind of Strong President Is Most Compatible with Democracy?

A response to this question is aided by psychobiographical studies and es-pecially by political scientist James David Barber's formulation of presiden-tial types in his study, *The Presidential Character*.[59] Barber asserts that presidential personality is determined essentially by character, world view, and style, and their combination in a dynamic package. "Character" is "the way the President orients himself toward life," in a broad sense. Character is developed chiefly in childhood, manifested in the individual's stance to-ward parents and siblings, and school peers. "World view" consists of "his primary politically relevant beliefs," such as those about social trends, hu-man nature, and the central moral conflicts of the day. These basic philo-sophical and ideological beliefs shape behavior. "Style" is his "habitual way of performing his political roles," specified as rhetoric, personal relations, and homework, or the tasks of the office. Style is the creative adaptation of the individual's needs and resources to the opportunities presented by the situations he encounters. Of these elements, the major emphasis is on char-acter.

## Barber's Presidential Categories

Barber contends that a President's basic stance toward the office partakes of any one of four types or categories. His classification in these types depends on how active he is and whether or not he gives the impression that he enjoys his political life. Four basic character patterns emerge: (1) The *active-positive* combines a high volume and fast tempo of activity with enjoyment of them. This President displays strong self-esteem and distinct success in relating to the environment. He cherishes productiveness as a value, is supple in adapting his style, stresses well-defined personal goals and rational self-mastery. (2) The *active-negative* manifests intense effort from which he derives low emotional reward. A compulsive quality permeates his effort, as though work were an escape from anxiety. This President is ambitious, aggressive toward the environment, and struggles persistently to contain his intense feelings. His self-image is vague and discontinuous, and he perceives politics as a struggle to gain and maintain power. (3) The *passive-positive* is receptive, compliant, and other-directed; an individual of low self-esteem, whose dependence and fragility of character make disappointment in politics highly likely. (4) The *passive-negative* type is especially oriented toward dutiful service as compensation for low self-esteem. This type tends to shun the conflict and uncertainty of politics, assisted by his tendency to stress vague principles, prohibitions, and procedural limitations. How various Presidents fare in Barber's application of his categories is reported in the following figure.

---

### Barber's Typology of Modern Presidents

| | *Affect Toward the Presidency* | |
| | *Positive* | *Negative* |
| --- | --- | --- |
| *Active* | Franklin Roosevelt | Woodrow Wilson |
| | Harry Truman | Herbert Hoover |
| | John Kennedy | Lyndon Johnson |
| | Jimmy Carter | Richard Nixon |
| *Passive* | William Howard Taft | Calvin Coolidge |
| | Warren Harding | Dwight Eisenhower |
| | Ronald Reagan | |

Sources: Adapted from James David Barber, *The Presidential Character* (Englewood Cliffs, N.J.: Prentice-Hall, 1977); and the *New York Times* Sept. 8, 1980.

In predicting a passive-positive classification for Ronald Reagan, Barber is impressed with Reagan's exuding optimism, good-guy charm, and leisurely-paced activity even in the heat of a presidential race. A danger of this type, Barber warns, is that he will cave in to pressure since he hates a scrap. Seeking affection and approval from politics, he clings to friends and associates as he drifts toward a disaster. Crucial is his selection of staff for his administration, because with his mind-set, they have the potential to do him in.

The most intriguing of Barber's types is the active-negative, with each President allotted to it offering an episode of tempestuous drama—Wilson and the League of Nations struggle, Hoover and the Great Depression, Johnson and the Vietnam war, Nixon and Watergate. Wilson readily fits the category in his pre-presidential career. As president of Princeton and Governor of New Jersey, he became locked in fierce struggles that were resolved only when he moved on to another position. Nixon is not so accommodating in his pre-presidential career and through most of his tenure as President, displaying extraordinary adaptiveness in dealings with Communist nations and reversing ardent anti-Communist positions of his earlier career. Nonetheless, he became locksd into a position on Watergate leading to his loss of office, a far severer penalty than any incurred by Wilson. Barber deals with the Wilson-Nixon discrepancies by noting that Wilson felt personally threatened by defeat on issues on which he took a moral stand, while Nixon felt threatened chiefly by "threats to his independence." In effect, Nixon becomes a subcategory of the active-negativs type.

In a critique of Barber, Alexander George argues that other Presidents of the active-negative category, Hoover and Johnson, do not match up with Wilson any better than Nixon since they too differ significantly from Wilson and from each other concerning motives and goals and their ability to shape their motives to attain those goals. Performance in the presidency is subject to many constraints, George notes, and those afflicting one President may not fall upon another. Thus Hoover's trouble is traceable to a restrictive world view, a malady that surely did not trouble Wilson, whose world view was the ultimate in expansiveness.[60]

Of Barber's types, only the first two—the active-positive and the active-negative—seriously respond to the needs of the strong presidency. With their obdurate passivity, ths last two fall well short of its requisites. Which of the first two is better responsive to democracy? The qualities of the active-positive President appear highly compatible with democracy, its sturdy self-esteem, adaptiveness, harmony with the environment, and healthy enjoyment of politics. The active-negative type, denoted by low self-esteem, aggressiveness, and vulnerability to conflict highly costly to presidential effectiveness and the political system, easily becomes threatening to democracy.

Clearly, the active-positive type better synchronizes with the ideal of the strong-democratic President than the active-negative. Yet the active-positive Presidents do not posssss an altogether clear path to fulfilling democratic criteria. They too encounter stumbling blocks. Some have made presidential war, with large doses of secrecy and deceit. Of contemporary active-positive Presidents, three—Roosevelt, Truman, and Kennedy—have waged war. Kennedy, and in some moments Roosevelt, supplied motifs to the strong presidency that are dissonant with the democratic spirit. The expansive rhetoric of Kennedy's addresses bears an exalted view of "the burden and the glory" of the presidency, sounding themes of popular sacrifice, with overtones a shade alien to the democratic conception of the high validity of the individual's own life and aspirations.[61]

# Views of the Presidency

What the President does and how he behaves depend much upon his own view of the presidency. His view is not an unsegmented monolith but a mosaic of many pieces of different sizes and hues. He brings into office predispositions consisting of beliefs, opinions, and attitudes that shape his subsequent behavior as he addresses himself to the presidential office, its powers and opportunities, the problems and situations arising in his course of duty. Typically, he summons a mix of attitudes in beholding a given situation, which he employs in "object appraisal," as he sizes up significant aspects of his office and the world around it in terms of their relevance to his opinions, motives, interests, and values.

President Eisenhower began his incumbency with the uncontrovertible proposition that the American people should not look to the Chief Executive to solve all their problems. This general view was supported by a more specific philosophy according to which President Eisenhower, by personal preference, chose to eliminate large sectors of problems from the purview and therefore the action of his presidency. His expressed fear of "the menace of bankrupting waste inherent in a centralized bureaucracy . . ." lent force to his ambition to return various federal functions to the states or to private activity. For example, his views on electric power development, the "partnership" principle, as it was known, called for a larger role for state and local government and for privately owned utilities than was known in previous presidential administrations. Or again, when pressures developed in his administration for substantial national programs to improve schools, hospitals, and other welfare services, Eisenhower stressed the responsibilities of local governments and citizens, declaring, "Here we rely not primarily upon government grant or political panacea but upon our own wisdom and industry to bring us the good and comforting things of life."[62]

A view of the presidency includes a view of legal authority, especially the basic law of the Constitution, and of relationships with the two other branches—the legislature and the judiciary. Presidents' views of Congress, their great political competitor, range from Lincoln's, which regarded the legislature as a nuisance to be avoided if at all possible, to Buchanan's, which was deferential almost to the point of abjectness. Andrew Johnson, on the brink of launching his Reconstruction policy, took an expansive legal view of his office and, as events proved, a disastrously simplistic view of its politics. Johnson reasoned that if Lincoln inaugurated the war by deeming that the states were in rebellion and, in effect, declared war, then his successor in the presidency had the corresponding power to say when the states were no longer in rebellion and when each was fit to return to its place in the Union. As Lincoln had, Johnson relied on the Commander-in-Chief power, his duty to take care that laws are faithfully executed, his oath of office, and the constitutional guarantee of a republican form of government to each state.[63] The boldness of this legal doctrine, Johnson's rugged tenacity, and his utter lack of political sense provided the ingredients for a struggle that came to threaten, as none ever had, the presidency's very existence.

Above all, the President's view of his office depends upon his view of politics. To achieve policy, to use the enormous potentialities of his office, he must act by political means. The Presidents who have extracted major successes from the office—Jefferson, Jackson, Wilson, and the Roosevelts—all were eminent presidential politicians. Politics have been notably eschewed by some Presidents, a Washington or an Eisenhower, whose extraordinary ability to symbolize the nation's intrinsic unity was little tarnished by personal political involvement. Some Presidents notably prefer certain forms of political activity to others. John Kennedy loved the arts of political management but was wary of taking his programs to the public in a nationally televised appeal. Lyndon Johnson displayed a prowess in many branches of politics that compared with the ablest political figures of any age. Yet in this strength there also lay weakness. He was so adept at politics that his mastery of that suspect art became legendary and hampered his ability, as President, to command national popular confidence. If there be a first commandment in presidential politics, it must be this: Let the President excel at politics, but let him not be obvious about it.

# Assessing Eisenhower

Something of the hazards of assessing presidential personality and performance is illustrated by the shifting evaluations of Dwight D. Eisenhower. Both during his presidency and in its aftermath, it was fashionable among journalists and scholars to discount Eisenhower's presidential performance as that of an aging hero who reigned more than he ruled, who consigned the day's principal problems of civil rights, health, and housing to neglect and drift, who permitted his extraordinary popularity to waste without producing milestones of accomplishment in program and policy, who was a minimalist leaving the burdens of office to subordinates, and who abhorred and shunned politics.

Barber classifies Eisenhower as a passive-negative President, impressed with his proclivity to inaction, his distaste for politics and conflict, his protective retreats to principle, ritual, and virtue. Although a passive-negative like Eisenhower inspires confidence and trust and calms the turbulent waters (inherited from Truman in Eisenhower's case) by persistent reasonableness and moderation, his presidency leaves few definable marks on history. The passive-negative President fails to commit his impressive personal gifts and seize the opportunities of office to provide initiating, energizing leadership.[64] When, for example, Secretary of Defense Charles E. Wilson troubled him excessively with details, Eisenhower exploded, "Look here, Charlie, I want *you* to run Defense. We *both* can't run it, and I *won't* run it. I was elected to worry about a lot of things other than the day-to-day operations of a department."[65]

Since these judgments were rendered, the assessment of Eisenhower as a political personality has been undergoing considerable study and revision. In allotting him to a passive-negative classification, Barber acknowledged that "his case presents certain difficulties." [66] Several influences have contributed momentum to revising estimates of Eisenhower. As the only President elected to two terms, subsequent to the Twenty-Second Amendment, it is self-evident that he must have done something right. He apparently gave the people what they wanted: peace and security in foreign affairs and prosperity and economic gains at home. His achievement contrasts with the performance of his successors, each of whom shared in committing the country to a decade of costly war. Close study of Eisenhower's performance discloses that he waged peace with utmost skill and vigor, avoiding the entrapments of events and turning aside counselors advocating force. As peace-keeper, Eisenhower provides a copybook performance for future Presidents. [67]

## Concepts of the Presidency

In contrast to the activist, conflict-prone strong Presidents who succeeded him, Eisenhower offered a wholly different view of the presidency, emphasizing its dignity and the virtue of constraint, shunning the rough-and-tumble of the office's politics. Impressed that presidential power had been growing excessively at Congress's expense, Eisenhower strove to restore a better balance between the branches. Similarly, his sense of place for the office caused him to decline to take initiatives in the nation's debates over issues. [68]

An early warning that Eisenhower was considerably more than an old hero of high-minded ineffectuality was sounded by Richard Nixon, following his tenure as Eisenhower's Vice President. Wrote Nixon: "He was a far more complex and devious man than most people realized, and in the best sense of those words. Not shackled to a one-track mind, he always applied two, three, or four lines of reasoning to a single problem, and he usually preferred the indirect approach where it would serve him better than the direct attack on a problem. His mind was quick and facile." [69]

## Eisenhower as Activist

A revised view perceives Eisenhower as a President who formulated definite views about his office and how it should be conducted, as well as explicit convictions about the preferable nature of governmental policies and priorities. Eisenhower was extraordinarily successful in imposing his views on his administration. The activism, which so decisively influences Barber's classification of Presidents, was in Eisenhower's case far more subtle but of no less impact than the most active Presidents. As Fred Greenstein suggests, Eisenhower fullfils every reasonable criterion of activism: voluminous activity and hard work, commitment to employing his office to shape policy, and productive of success. [70]

Since Eisenhower practiced a covert style of leadership, much of his activity was unknown to the public. Countless callers and appointments, a large private correspondence outside the White House's mainstream, reveal a President far busier than he was depicted in the press. Eisenhower's considerable efforts at party leadership were concealed largely because of his public commitment to a bipartisan approach to a Democratic-controlled Congress, and his conception of his office as representative of all the people.

Early evaluations of Eisenhower were misled by his practice of delegating authority freely to his Secretary of State, John Foster Dulles, and other cabinet officials and to his chief of staff, Sherman Adams. Eisenhower believed that in large organizations effective leadership requires extensive delegations of authority. Alert to Dulles's and Adams's deficiencies and strengths, Eisenhower kept his aides under close surveillance while pursuing other accesses to information and opinion through his cabinet, meetings with legislative leaders, and his "stag dinners" with distinguished citizens of different callings. Of Eisenhower's technique of delegating authority, his White House aide Stephen Hess has written that it was "artfully constructed . . . an elaborate maze of buffer zones. Eisenhower gave himself considerable freedom of action by giving his subordinates considerable lattitude to act." [71]

As practitioner of presidential leadership, Eisenhower placed greater value on preserving his prestige with the public than in cultivating the professional reputation, emphasized by Richard Neustadt, in the community of politicians. Eisenhower preferred to work through intermediaries and often turned to his own advantage his supposed lack of political skill. Even the fractured prose that so often surfaced in his news conferences was sometimes motivated. When his press secretary urgently reminded him that the State Department was anxious that he not discuss a topic at a news conference, he replied, "Don't worry, Jim, I'll just confuse them." [72]

The high order of Eisenhower's policy successes is evident in his transformation of the two principal promises of his 1952 campaign into actual accomplishment. He ended the Korean war and he reduced the budget, including the military budget. Eisenhower imposed his own definite conceptions of military strategy, consisting of nuclear deterrence, the enhancement of nuclear technology, and reduced dependence on conventional forces. Much of his purpose was achieved through the National Security Council, which he restructured by broadening its membership and by increasing its layers of participants and activities. Although critics decried the excessive stylization of the revised NSC, Eisenhower deftly used it to build consensus and as a forum to announce and coordinate decisions. Most impressive of all, Eisenhower imposed his views on the military and restrained Congress from coming to their rescue. Eisenhower reemerges as a skilled practitioner of closed politics, dominating and manipulating a set of powerful political and military appointees.[73] His reassessment makes clear that the activism valued by Barber takes many subtle forms.

## ★ ★ ★ An Overview ★ ★ ★

The President as a political personality, we have seen, combines in that concept the man, his needs, and the office. He may have personal needs that find satisfaction in political office-holding and, above all, in the presidency. The President is a broker in values that shape his decisions and policies. He chooses between values, gives higher priority to some than others, and may over time shift his support of them. He may formulate and subscribe to goals that set the achievement levels of his administration. Above all, as a political personality, he can be seen as possessing a bundle of traits, which both separately and in combination constitute that elusive, mysterious element called "style."

The relation of the President, or the man, to the office is dynamic to the extent that an incumbent may come into office not particularly admired, as was the case with Lincoln and Truman, and develop and display a combination of values and traits that arouses widespread public approval and even admiration. A reverse tendency may also take place. Lyndon Johnson, confident, assertive and self-reliant, gratified the nation with the skill of his take-over in the turmoil of the Kennedy assassination. But these very qualities seemed to weaken his popular standing in the context of the Vietnam war.

On occasion it has appeared that how the President does things is more important than what he does. A President who does less may be better appreciated than one who does more. An underachiever who is blessed with a collection of traits or style that delights the public and even the historians may fare better in the public opinion of his day or in his country's annals than the overachiever whose major sin may be that he does not possess a comparably pleasing style.

The President lives in a culture in which the profession of politician has uncertain status. The values of his society emphasize private endeavor and private success. Politics is tainted as a calling less worthy than most private pursuits. To succeed in the presidency in the largest sense, the incumbent must be a master politician. But society and the culture are reluctant that he be so. Not the least restraint upon the strong President is the distaste society is apt to have for the strong politician.

# Chapter Fourteen

# Decision-Making

**D**ecision-making is an area where the strong presidency depends most upon the strong President—upon the caliber of the incumbent, his talents, prudence, and resolution. His choices point up the issues of the presidency, give substance to its policies and effect to its purposes. Decision-making is a continuous process of the President's existence. His choices tend to be difficult, and the end-products often have great consequences. "There are no easy matters that will come to you as President," Eisenhower counseled the incoming President Kennedy. "If they are easy, they will be settled at a lower level." [1]

## The Process of Decision-Making

### Varieties of Decision

Actually, the President makes all kinds of decisions: routine or programed decisions (which focus upon tasks rather than problems); adaptive decisions (the adjustment of existing policy to new circumstances); and innovative decisions (major departures from established policy). Some Chief Executives may choose to devote themselves to one kind at the expense of the others.

Jimmy Carter thrived on decision-making perceived as a sequence of defined steps directed at problem-solving. His absorption in the details, the nuts and bolts of a decision, left little time or inclination for considering its political dimensions. "Carter's an engineering officer, a protégé of Admiral Rickover," explained former Energy Secretary James Schlesinger, "Rickover has to know how every single engine or pump works. Carter is that way. He looks upon government as machinery to be improved, to be lubricated." Consequently, when Carter spoke of reform—welfare reform, tax reform—his decisions were not sweepingly innovative in concept or design, but stressed renovation of existing programs, in the sense of patching and filling, to make them work better.[2] Career bureaucrats were dazzled by Carter's grasp of the intricacies of arms control, farm-price supports, and the costs of inspecting faulty dams. His staff marvelled at how closely he read memoranda, returning them with acute handwritten comments. But while Carter poured over details, he seemed oblivious to the larger tasks of political and public leadership that accompany decision-making at the presidential level.

Decisions are the building blocks of policy. Henry Kissinger describes policy as an accumulation of nuances, an orchestration of individual moves or decisions into a coherent strategy. Rarely, he observed, do policy issues appear in stark black and white, but more usually emerge from shadings of interpretation. Decisions can accumulate into significant revisions of policy even though they began as minor departures.[3]

Some of the President's most important decisions are really nondecisions, or decisions to do nothing. A President's nondecisions may be as exacting as his decisions. John Kennedy, faced with Castro's refusal to permit on-the-spot inspection for the presence of missiles and launching sites in Cuba, made several protests, and then apparently relegated the thorny matter to the limbo of nondecision. But some Presidents specialize in nondecisions; Warren Harding smiled and maneuvered his way out of difficulty until his whole kingdom of neglect tumbled down upon him.

Some of the President's decisions come in response to emergencies, but more are called for automatically at established intervals by a network of fixed deadlines that he does not set and cannot change. He faces the catalysis of the electoral calendar—the next congressional or national election. His State of the Union message, his Economic Report, his budget, which together are a massive compilation of decisions embracing the full sweep of policy, are all rendered up to Congress in January. Each of these documents has an extended subcalendar for its preparation. Budget ceilings are set in April; departments prepare their estimates in the summer; the Office of Management and Budget reviews them in the fall. His fixed schedule heightens the tyranny of events. In Monroe's day, the surge of revolutions in Latin America and the opportunistic stirrings of the imperial European powers lent special force to the President's oncoming State of the Union message. Since it would have been unthinkable for the President not to discuss in its paragraphs relations between the hemispheres, his Union message posed, in actuality, a deadline by which he was forced to formulate his historic doctrine. The Monroe Doctrine was a "declaratory" decision, a common variety, indicative of the President's policy intentions and objectives.[4]

Decisions vary in the risks they hold for the President's prestige and political fortunes and the nation's welfare and safety. In putting forward his Supreme Court packing plan in 1937, Franklin Roosevelt risked the prestige of his smashing electoral victory the year before that had lifted him to the crest of his influence.* In arranging the sale of wheat to the U.S.S.R. in 1963, John Kennedy risked offending sectors of American opinion and probably losing votes. His stand on civil rights appeared to alienate millions of white voters; yet to have refused to take it would have alienated millions of blacks and damaged his country in the eyes of the world. In granting a full pardon to Richard Nixon, Gerald Ford imperiled and sacrificed a substantial measure of the public approval built up during his early presidential tenure.

Since Dwight Eisenhower's second term, presidential risks have acquired a new and forbidding dimension. Eisenhower became the first President to live with the Soviet Union's possession of a substantial nuclear delivery capability. The mutual nuclear capacities of the United States and the U.S.S.R. give the decisions of their chief executives the quality of "irreversibility." Decisions based upon miscalculation cannot be called back nor can actions once taken be revised. Nothing that the erring Chief Executive might do subsequently could compensate for the costs levied upon humankind.

Time is a boon when it is available. "I'd rather be slow and right," drawled Lyndon B. Johnson, "than smart and dead." He was seldom impetuous or careless in considering an important matter, preferring to appraise the big factors—"feelin', smellin', knowin'."[5] After the 1962 Cuban crisis President Kennedy expressed his thankfulness for the length of time—some fourteen days—that the situation permitted him to take to determine the nation's response. "If we had had to act in the first twenty-four hours," Kennedy observed, "I don't think . . . we would have chosen as prudently as we finally did."[6]

## The Environment

The President is driven to make decisions by the vast, dynamic environment in which he works. The environment is laden with situations and events pressing for attention; with ideas and movements; with the interests and ambitions of men and nations; with political friends and foes; with history—the previous decisions that have failed and succeeded. The environment is the first of several elements that comprise the process of decision-making. The President maintains surveillance over the environment for developments on which to act. If he overlooks history or misperceives

---

*In 1935 and 1936 the Supreme Court worked havoc upon Roosevelt's New Deal legislative program by declaring one measure after another unconstitutional. Roosevelt interpreted his imposing reelection victory in 1936 as a popular endorsement of his program and decided to move against the Court. In a message of February 5, 1937, he asked Congress for legislation that would add "younger blood" to the Court. A justice, upon reaching age seventy, under the President's proposal, could resign at full pay. If he did not resign, an additional judge would be appointed. The plan aroused a political furor. Roosevelt was accused of seeking to "pack" the Court, lusting for power, and undermining the sacred principle of separation of powers. Conservative and progressive legislators alike, most of the press, and distinguished lawyers, among others, rallied against the President, who had few defenders. Debate raged in Congress through the spring and summer of 1937. The bill was eventually defeated, not so much by popular opinion as by the Court's turnabout, by which it now proceeded to find New Deal legislation constitutional.

events, the consequences can be costly. Preaching in his 1976 campaign that the tax system was "a disgrace" and making its reform a solemn high priority, Carter's efforts were hobbled by his ignorance of past failures of reform and by his inattention to the intricate task of surmounting them. So unaware was he of the past that he deemed his approach utterly new, a miscalculation that was swiftly exposed when his early efforts were crushed by legislators, the loyal guardsmen of special interests who felt endangered.[7]

The President cannot act without situations, which may develop spontaneously or which he may manage somehow to contrive. But there are limits to his inventions. If fate had wafted Franklin Roosevelt into the presidential chair in 1880, the serenity of that age would have presented only a miniature opportunity for decision-making compared with the broad canvas of trouble on which he could leave his imprint a half-century later.

Situations may develop into events that are more focused and visible. Abraham Lincoln, considering the realities that would make the issuance of his Emancipation Proclamation a plausible act, gave great weight to a victory on the battlefield. Abolitionists and others had long urged Lincoln to deliver his proclamation and criticized his delay. He held back, fearful that border states would join the Confederacy if it were issued. He believed that without a victory the proclamation would be a hollow gesture. Finally, the battle of Antietam came, and though the Union's claim of victory was disputed, Lee had been checked. This was enough for Lincoln, and he hurried off to the quiet of the Soldiers' Home to put the finishing touches on his Emancipation Proclamation.[8] Issued September 22, 1862, the proclamation declared that slaves who were in rebellion on New Year's Day, 1863, would henceforth be free.

Situations and events are not simply physical and material things; they encompass the world of the mind. Ideas, assumptions, motives, and values abound in the President's environment. Many great presidential decisions borrow heavily from the previous formulations of other politicians and associates. Elements of the Monroe Doctrine, for example, were provided some years prior to its appearance by the utterances of Henry Clay and Thomas Jefferson.* Of the incipient Latin American revolts, a key event in the doctrine's development, Jefferson said in 1808, "We consider their interests the same as ours, and the object of both must be to exclude all European influence in this hemisphere." The roots of the great doctrine reached back before Jefferson and Clay to the formative years of the republic and the pronouncements of Washington, particularly his Farewell Address. In an important sense Monroe's decision had been made for him.[9]

The President, of course, can turn anywhere for ideas: to Congress, the universities, friends, his wife, old classmates, anyone. The operative ideas of many a great presidential decision may emerge from the researches and findings of the bureaucracy. The idea of how to pack the Court seems to have come from Roosevelt's Justice Department. The Attorney General,

---

*Monroe proclaimed his doctrine in a message to Congress, December 2, 1823, of which Secretary of State John Quincy Adams was principal draftsman. The message was evoked by the revolt of the Latin American colonies from Spain about 1815, the creation of new republics in Latin America, and the gestures of several European nations toward intervention. Monroe, in effect, threatened war against European powers that attempted to "extend their system to any portion of this hemisphere."

Homer S. Cummings, a lanky, elderly politician, had been given an important secret assignment by Roosevelt. His task was nothing less than to contrive a plan that would thwart the Court's tendency to rule unconstitutional many of the most sacred laws of the New Deal. As he mused over this delicate assignment in his lavish office, pince-nez in hand, Cummings was picking aimlessly through a pile of books one day when he came upon a volume, *Federal Justice*, that had been written by Carl McFarland, a departmental aide. The book, a study of the ills of the lower federal courts, posed a most intriguing solution. Let "worn-out" judges be retired on respectable pensions, the author argued. If after a reasonable interval an eligible federal judge did not retire, let the President add a judge to the court. McFarland's prescriptions for lower federal courts were joyfully taken up by Cummings for the Supreme Court. When the Attorney General spread his handiwork before the President, Roosevelt was enormously pleased. Here in essence was what quickly became the Court-packing plan.

The presidential environment is strewn with assumptions that he and his aides fashion and entertain. Assumptions preclude certain decisions and shape and control others. In a deepening energy crisis, Gerald Ford clung to assumptions that had undergirded his lengthy earlier political career, namely, that individual self-reliance provided better answers to most social problems than the federal government. Ford spurned the urgings of Henry Ford and General Motors for a big gasoline tax to exact greater savings of fuel than voluntary action was achieving. The President drew strength from the public's sharing of his assumptions, citing an opinion poll revealing that "81 percent of the people agree with me. . . . I think I'm on pretty solid ground." Meanwhile members of his cabinet, who increasingly despaired of voluntarism, openly lobbied for governmental controls.[10]

The President beholds his environment through political lenses. He knows that much of what he does faces the hostile scrutiny of the opposition party bent upon dragging him from office at the next election. Unfriendly factions in his own party may manipulate against him. In his 1803 move to purchase Louisiana, Jefferson knew full well that he was supplying the rival Federalist party with invaluable political capital.* The Federalists, who had been shouting for a war of conquest, greeted his decision with the cry that he was bankrupting the Treasury to buy a desert. But in Jefferson's own party the purchase was a huge political success. The Republican factions scrambled madly to claim credit for it. Northern Republicans, sniffing hungrily for a strong candidate to rid them once and for all of the "Virginia succession" to the presidency, aimed to establish one of their own as the hero of the Louisiana conquest, and a lavish campaign was launched to prove that Robert Livingston of New York, who with James Monroe negotiated the purchase, deserved entire credit for its success.[11]

In choosing what to decide, the President acts as a kind of filter between his office and its environment. The state of his political fortunes, his interpretation of them, his miscalculations, and how he hopes the record of his

---

*Jefferson moved to purchase the vast tract known as Louisiana when Napoleon forced a weakened Spain to cede him the entire territory. War with England soon dissolved Napoleon's dream of a vast overseas empire. He suddenly decided to sell the territory to the United States for an estimated fifteen million dollars, and a treaty was signed April 30, 1803. Jefferson thus chose to add territory to the United States by purchase rather than by conquest.

administration will be engraved on the pages of history all may influence his choices. President Johnson's decisions, announced on March 31, 1968, to deescalate the Vietnam War and not to seek another term of office, served almost to quiet the severe attacks upon him from domestic quarters and to stake out an advantageous ground upon which his eventual reputation in history might be established.

## The Alternatives

Having chosen an event or situation as the occasion for a decision, the President and his aides canvass the alternative courses of action. These must be formulated and analyzed, pursuits that Herbert Simon, a leading scholar of management and administration, calls "design activity." Before the alternative courses can be plotted, the raw information amassed from the environment must be studied for meaning, particularly as it foreshadows the future.

Interpretation, at its best, is a frail and inexact enterprise. At the level of the presidency, a seemingly simple act can mean many things. When North Korean troops marched across the thirty-eighth parallel into South Korea in 1950, President Truman and his counselors started with the plausible assumption that the heavy hand of the Soviet Union was behind the venture and faced the question of the Kremlin's motive and purpose. General Omar Bradley, chairman of the Joint Chiefs of Staff, contended that the North Korean attack was a diversionary gambit preparatory to a major Soviet blow, possibly against Iran, and urged that few American troops, therefore, be committed to Korea, since they would be needed elsewhere. George Kennan, a premier authority on Soviet behavior, argued that the communists were engaging in "soft-spot probing" and advised that "situations of strength" be created wherever the Soviet thrust came, even in Korea. Others believed that the Soviets were testing the will of anticommunist nations to resist open aggression, as Hitler did when he reoccupied the Rhineland. Still other counselors advanced a "demonstration" theory stating that the U.S.S.R. expected to make Korea a show of their strength and of allied impotence, with worldwide repercussions. Finally, there was the view that the Soviet Union was promoting a general "Far Eastern strategy."[12] For example, John Foster Dulles, then negotiating the Japanese peace treaty, saw the Korean attack as a Soviet thrust to block American efforts to bring Japan into its alliances.

Once having interpreted the environment, the President and his aides advance to the next hurdle—developing alternative responses. Not infrequently, this step may be dispensed with in the face of what seems to the President a clear, convincing solution. Harry Truman, boarding his plane after violence in Korea had rudely terminated his weekend back home, came quickly and solitarily to a fundamental decision: North Korea's aggression across the thirty-eighth parallel must be countered by force. The communists had launched a challenge that could not be sidestepped: "An outlaw was terrorizing the world community"; to ignore him meant risking "a third world war." At a meeting with his military and diplomatic aides at Blair House that evening for dinner and discussion, Truman apparently did not even consider the possibility of a nonviolent response.[13] An implicit decision that American armed forces must be committed provided the operating premise. From it other necessary decisions and their alternatives would follow; what kind of force, how many men, and within what territorial confines should the Americans fight?

Alternatives may be developed by random steps over a period of time by the President and others commanding his attention. Franklin Roosevelt, vexed by the Supreme Court's mounting tendency to strike down New Deal laws as unconstitutional, developed a variety of alternatives during the exasperating months of rebuff. An earlier forceful Chief Executive, who also suffered from the judiciary, was instructively recalled. Andrew Jackson, for the moment, became Roosevelt's inspiration. When the Court weighed one important case, Roosevelt, anticipating a hostile decision, prepared an address, which borrowed Jackson's famous defiance of the Court, "You have made your law, now enforce it." But the Court's deciding in the government's favor made the address unnecessary. When, subsequently, the justices struck down the New York minimum wage law, boding ill for a great amount of national and state labor legislation, the eminent progressive, Senator George Norris, urged Roosevelt to center his approaching 1936 electoral campaign upon the Court. Of these alternatives, electoral campaigning versus packing, Roosevelt eventually chose the latter.

*Advisers*    Alternatives are manufactured by scores of aides in the executive branch who earn their daily bread by anticipating situations and events well before they occur and preparing possible responses when they do. Some of this preparation is "contingency planning"—preparation for emergencies that might happen—a process applied since the Second World War to the world's most likely trouble spots, especially, in the Eisenhower, Kennedy, and Johnson periods, to Berlin. The planners have built up crowded files of events likely to take place in Berlin and the appropriate responses. Ironically, none of these plans anticipated the wall the East Germans threw up in 1961. Another hazard is the adviser who offers up too many rejected alternatives, too much dissenting advice. To such offenders, Carter, despite his gracious Southern charm, gave the cold shoulder. "He simply stares at you, or ignores you completely for a while," reported one victim. Others have cited Carter's "icy look." Each President has his own preferences and work habits, to which advisers, if they are to survive, must be finely tuned. Observed Kissinger, a practiced survivor, "If Nixon hated anything more than being presented with a plan he had not considered, it was to be shown up in a group as being less tough than his advisers." [14]

For some presidential advisers and assistants, developing alternatives may be preferable to another common process of decision-making, developing a consensus. As national security adviser to Nixon and Ford, Henry Kissinger, in meetings with the Department of Defense leadership, invariably employed those occasions not to formulate recommendations that would give the President a consensus view or a range of disagreeing views, but "to concoct options, every possible option. . . ." This stratagem enabled Kissinger to make his own private recommendation to the President without the Defense Department's competition, and it preserved to maximum degree the President's own freedom to make a decision. [15]

More than any other contemporary President, Eisenhower relied upon subordinates to define situations and present alternative approaches to them. The President's own contribution was largely one of choosing between alternatives in whose formulation he had had little part and with whose substance he may have been unfamiliar. The Eisenhower method placed a premium on "presentations" and "briefings," on charts and one-page summaries. Eisenhower also made heavy use of committees of presidential aides drawn from departments and the White House staff. Such committees selected problems for study, developed alternative solutions, and chose between them, leaving the President the simple task of ratification. Critics of the committee system contend that it rewards the wrong qualities by stressing fluency and "averageness," promoting agreement but discouraging creativity. They contend that Eisenhower was often kept ignorant of alternatives that his subordinates rejected and therefore never laid before him. Eisenhower's defenders point to a considerable body of "split decisions," or alternatives that his subordinates could not decide between themselves and did lay before the President for his choice.

John Kennedy, eschewing the Eisenhower method and vowing to put himself into "the thick of things," expended great quantities of energy and time spreading himself all across the decisional spectrum. The President, he thought, should hover constantly over the quest for alternatives, and if he does not, he is a prisoner of the choices that his aides finally put before him. Kennedy consulted with many advisers both outside the executive branch and inside, at various ranks in the hierarchy, at deskside conferences and over the telephone. Political scientist Hans J. Morgenthau argued that the Kennedy method exposed him to too much advice, steeping him with all shades of opinion, engendering a state of mind that makes timely and forceful decision difficult. He cited the Cuban invasion fiasco of 1961 and the delayed response to the rise of the Berlin wall as case studies of presidential irresolution. Kennedy's reaction when the Russians built the Berlin wall in 1961 was characterized, Morgenthau noted, by a duality. Kennedy responded with a "hard" line in what he said and how he said it. His style was truly Churchillian. But what he did was something else. He acted "flexibly," or, less euphemistically, he did little, and he did it late. His deeds were reminiscent not of Churchill but of Chamberlain. The contradiction, this analysis concluded, confused the American public, the nation's allies, and probably the U.S.S.R.[16]

The gathering and weighing of alternatives may be more than a private act, reflecting the President's own necessities. The act may also bear dimensions in public relations. In 1965, Lyndon Johnson, before deciding to increase the American commitment in the Vietnam war, weighed his alternatives in a fashion evidently intended to refute critics who charged that he was given to impulsiveness in conducting foreign affairs. In preparation for the President's decision, Defense Secretary McNamara made a five-day tour of battle areas and consulted with United States and Vietnamese leaders. Upon McNamara's return, Johnson began a series of conferences with his principal advisers: McNamara, Secretary of State Dean Rusk, Undersecretary George Ball, Presidential Assistant McGeorge Bundy, CIA Chief William Raborn, Joint Chiefs of Staff Chairman Earle G. Wheeler, the newly appointed ambassador to South Vietnam, Henry Cabot Lodge, and other officials. At the end of the second day's meeting, Bill Moyers, the President's assistant, disclosed to the press, "I think it is safe to say that a lot of the deliberation is behind the group now, and the next stage involves what to do about these recommendations and deliberations."

But the discussions still continued for days and were joined by two leading Republicans experienced in foreign affairs, Arthur H. Dean and John J. McCloy. Johnson also consulted former President Eisenhower by telephone. After these discussions, Johnson ordered further special studies on "the additional strength that each military service may need in South Vietnam." These several procedures served to suggest that Johnson's decisions for Vietnam would be methodical and controlled.[17]

## Choice-Making

The climactic stage of decision-making is the President's "choice activity"—selecting a particular course of action from the alternatives available. Of the several steps of decision-making, choice is the one the President is least able to escape. He can delegate the tasks of watching the environment, selecting problems for action, fashioning alternatives, and even making some choices or decisions. Yet he is expected to make the important choices or decisions as the unavoidable price of his incumbency.

Despite their monopoly of responsibility for hard choices, some Presidents excel in bringing others to make them. As revelations of the Teapot Dome corruptions of the previous Harding administration unfolded in his own young presidency, Coolidge resisted counsel, urgently pouring upon him, that he fire his Attorney General, Harry Daugherty. Even when the prestigious progressive leader, Senator William E. Borah of Idaho, proposed the step, Coolidge demurred. "I am here to carry out the Harding policies," he said. "I am here as a Republican President. Daugherty was Harding's friend. He stands high with the Republican organization. I do not see well how I can do it." The importunities from many sides to dump Daugherty continued, but the President would not act.

At last, when a Senate resolution was introduced calling upon the President to dismiss Daugherty, Coolidge summoned Borah to the White House one night for "urgent business." After several minutes of presidential silence, Borah was still puzzled about what the urgent business was when Daugherty came up the grand stairway to Coolidge's study, "his jaw set," according to a White House secretary, "and his eyes like flint." Coolidge tersely introduced his visitors, adding, "Well, don't let my presence embarrass you!" This instruction was superfluous. Borah and Daugherty went at it for an hour of shrill debate. Coolidge sat by, slumped in his chair smoking. In the din of the exchange, Borah exclaimed that it was not for him to tell the Attorney General to resign; it was the President's duty. Coolidge said not a word. When at last the antagonists finished, the little President, standing to hurry his parting guests, quacked, "Senator, I reckon you're right!" Daugherty, "white with rage," according to the secretary, who witnessed the encounter, stomped "angrily down the stairs and out of the White House."[18] He soon resigned. Coolidge had put upon Borah the burden of confronting Daugherty, thus forcing the decision.

The President determines what choices or decisions are possible. His choices are influenced not only by his personal ideals but by his knowledge of what has worked in the past, his estimate of the response of his adversaries, his judgment of what his publics at home and abroad will bear, of whether the bureaucracy will comply, and whether his party will go along.

No one else in American government or society has a sweep of duties, and therefore of decisions, like his.

**Methods**    Each President has his own preferred manner of choice. Eisenhower preferred to be calm and composed. "Boy, there's just one thing I really *know*," he once said, "You *can't* decide things in a *panic*. Any decision you make when you are panicked, you can be sure of only one thing. It will be a bad one."[19]

Franklin Roosevelt's method of making choices was, as Arthur M. Schlesinger, Jr., has described it, "involved and inscrutable." Roosevelt weighed a basket of factors in a typical major decision: political timing, consequences to his personal public fortunes, interest group reactions, partisan advantage, impact on Congress and the public.[20] He permitted situations to develop and crystallize, he let competing forces pull in conflict, and then through some system of "unconscious calculation," as Rexford Tugwell termed it, the decision finally emerged. Roosevelt's method, Tugwell observed, made it seem that "no choosing had taken place" and forestalled discovery of his "governing principle."[21] Decision and policy were not thought out; rather, the President's intuitions seemed to coalesce and initiate a result. That his decisions were sometimes untidy never troubled the President. Clear-cut administrative decisions, he felt, worked only if they reflected clear-cut political realities. If they did not, the decisions would prove hollow and weak. He was devoted to final objectives and flexible means. Roosevelt, like many another President, valued procrastination. Wait long enough for clamoring forces to settle, for the momentum of events to slacken, and the imperatives of today will be gone tomorrow. Time he considered a great corrective, one that spares the President many hard choices. He loved to make minor choices in a dramatic way that shocked and surprised the public. "I'm going to spring a bombshell," he delighted to announce, and then stunned his gaping audience with a novel proposal such as changing the date of Thanksgiving or imposing national daylight-saving time the year around to aid the war effort. "He delights in surprises—clever, cunning and quick," Hugh Johnson observed. "He likes to shock friends as well as enemies with something they never expected."[22]

A difficulty, especially evident early in the Carter administration, was the slow pace of the pre-White House stages of decision-preparation, that left the President inadequate time for his own choice-making. Carter's urban program of 1978, for example, finally reached the Oval Office after interminable delays in the departments, allowing the President a mere twelve hours to study a 178-page "decision memorandum," requiring him to make seventy-five decisions. On the scheduled day of the plan's announcement, Carter told aides that he had serious doubts about some proposals, which he nevertheless approved. "Things are always late, and nobody gets on anybody's back," observed a White House aide. "I don't think that the President should wait on other people's schedules."[23]

Often a mighty inhibiting factor in choice-making is risk-aversion, a phenomenon that is, of course, distributed unevenly among Presidents. Critical in choice-making are factors that decrease risk-aversion, such as the counsel of respected advisers and the occurrence of benign new events. Ideally, the decision-maker, faced with the task of choice under conditions of uncertainty, should choose the alternative that is consistent with his basic judgment and preferences, his strategy.[24]

That much presidential choice-making is a rough approximation of this model is suggested by Nixon's 1970 decision to send American forces into Cambodia. The President consulted with a wide circle of advisers who rallied around two alternatives: to do nothing, and to move American troops into Cambodia to attack North Vietnamese installations there. As chief spokesman for the first alternative, Secretary of State William Rogers argued that the invasion of Cambodia meant widening the war and running the risk of entrapment in an inconclusive outcome that had befallen Johnson. Already, the President had won wide popular support for his policy of gradual withdrawal from Vietnam, and he should not hazard its loss. Further, Rogers argued, the military objectives to be sought in Cambodia could be achieved by South Vietnamese forces alone.

The Pentagon contended that a full assault, with American troops participating, was essential. Military intelligence disclosed that the enemy aimed either to overthrow the Lon Nol government or to open a supply lane to the sea in eastern Cambodia. Either development imperiled South Vietnam and American withdrawal.

After a three hour debate, Nixon withdrew to his hideaway office in the Executive Office Building and on a pad of yellow legal paper jotted down the arguments for and against an invasion, and the tenor of his notations suggests that the survival of the Nol regime was tied, in his thinking, to American success in Vietnam. In reviewing whether there should be some action in Cambodia, Nixon listed only favorable arguments—"Time running out," "Military aid" to Lon Nol could be "only symbolic." A scribble followed that inaction might tempt North Vietnam to set up a puppet regime in Phnom Penh, and, finally, a comment that inaction by both sides would leave an "ambiguous situation" that eventually would favor the communists.

Nixon then recorded the pros and cons of American action in Cambodia and for a South Vietnamese attack alone. He recognized that use of American troops would foment a "deep division" of domestic opinion, might instigate collapse of the Paris peace talks, a communist attack on Phnom Penh, or a major North Vietnamese initiative across the Demilitarized Zone. Just as Nixon was about to approve an attack with American troops, someone, probably Rogers, suggested that the military might be telling the President only what they thought he wanted to hear. Troubled, Nixon dispatched to his Vietnam field commander, General Creighton Abrams, an out-of-channels message requesting "the unvarnished truth." The participation of American troops, Abrams replied, was essential, and Nixon, after more consultations, ordered the attack.[25]

Viewed collectively over time, presidential choices appear wavering and inconsistent. They seldom approximate neat consistent patterns like soldiers on parade. Shifting events, the alchemy of competing pressures, the President's own political sensitivities, bring disarray. Franklin Roosevelt, therefore, almost alternatingly advanced upon and backed away from a progressive line. He began with an isolationist economic policy and shifted to an internationalist trade policy. He turned from cooperation with business to regulation. In reality, he was responding to changing events and situations, to the necessity of winning and holding a broad base of support.

# Making the Decision Known

The President, having made his choice or decision, next makes it known. The means of promulgation are usefully varied. The President can convey his choice by simple statement or artful interference, by silence or gesture, by proclamation signed and sealed. How he communicates may be idiosyncratic. Presidents, for example, are wont to incorporate important decisions about their administrations in carefully prepared inaugural addresses. Not Franklin Pierce; despite the significant policy it had to convey, his inaugural was unwritten and extemporized without a note. Most presidential decisions are not deliberately and systematically promulgated. As Chester Barnard, business executive and a leading authority on decision-making, observes, "most executive decisions produce no direct evidence of themselves and . . . knowledge of them can only be derived from the cumulation of indirect evidence."

In his many decisions concerning the Vietnam war, Richard Nixon habitually announced his choices after, rather than during, a National Security Council meeting. After deliberating privately, he issued instructions in writing or through intermediaries. By doing so, he emphasized that the NSC was an advisory, not a decision-making, body, and he avoided the embarrassment of challenges to his orders.[26]

Presidential decisions, when they become known, produce sensations of pleasure and pain. Some Chief Executives limit as far as possible their own acts of promulgating to the announcements of pleasurable decisions. They leave the dispensing of the hard negative to subordinates. Harry Hopkins in his day securely established himself in the craw of many a defeated decision-seeker as Franklin Roosevelt's abominable no-man. Sherman Adams excelled in the same role for Dwight Eisenhower. Indeed, Adams' eventual departure from the presidential scene was hastened by the large and ever-growing body of the disgruntled created by his capacity to say no. Some decisions, regardless of their effect, can be communicated only by the President. It is inconceivable that President Johnson's decision not to seek re-election, which produced pain for his friends and pleasure for his foes, could have been disclosed by anyone but himself.

A President's own mood and gesture can enhance the force of his decision, just as diffidence can drain a strong decision. Lincoln added immeasurably to the force of the Emancipation Proclamation when he declared, upon signing it, "I never, in my life, felt more certain that I was doing right than I do in signing this paper."[27] Johnson's decision to halt the bombing of North Vietnam was given special force when he coupled it with his disclosure that he would not accept another term of office.

Promulgation involves timing. The decision must be revealed neither too late nor too soon. Not surprisingly, Presidents withhold their decision until the time is ripe. Lincoln had composed and firmly decided upon his Emancipation Proclamation some weeks before he finally issued it. He bided his time, waiting for a Union victory on the battlefield to enhance the historic document's importance and reception. Union victories were not easily come by at this stage in the war, and weeks passed. While he waited, one of his most formidable critics, Horace Greeley, editor of the New York *Tribune*, took him to task in a moving, widely read editorial, "The Prayer of Twenty

Millions." The President's followers, Greeley charged, were "deeply pained by the policy you seem to be pursuing with regard to the slaves of rebels. . . . We think you are strangely and disastrously remiss in the discharge of your official and imperative duty with regard to the emancipating provisions of the new Confiscation Act."[28]

Some Presidents precede a statement of their choices with a subtle ritual. Franklin Roosevelt, fresh from his decision to launch the Court-packing plan, tendered the annual presidential dinner for the judiciary. All the high court justices appeared at the White House except the aged Louis Brandeis, who never ventured out in the evening, and Harlan F. Stone, who was ill. Approximately eighty notables gathered, and those seated at the President's table presented a spectacle tinged with an irony that Roosevelt relished. At his table were all but two of the justices he was about to subjugate, and at the table also were Attorney General Cummings and several other faithful helpers who had prepared the artifacts for the subjugation. When the packing plan would be sprung, the justices would recall, and presumably with not a little awe, the President's droll finesse.[29]

## Consequences

Decisions are applied and implemented, and, like all acts, have consequences. For the President, decisions represent successes and losses, costs and gains. A presidential decision of magnitude may lead to bitterness or it may touch off national exultation and create a mood rich with political promise. When a horseman rode into Washington from New Orleans on January 15, 1804, with the news that Louisiana had been peaceably delivered to the United States three weeks before, the nation rejoiced. Congress gave a great dinner, with the President and the cabinet as the honored guests, to celebrate the gain of a new empire. French representative Louis Pichon, informing his government of the jubilation, well observed that "the acquisition of Louisiana and the peaceful manner of possession have raised Jefferson and his friends to a high point of popularity and regard. His re-election must be considered as assured."[30] In great decisions it is ordinarily not the President's fate to receive the lavish approval that befell Jefferson, but mixed praise and censure.

But most presidential decisions lead only to probable outcomes, rather than to certain consequences. Even under conditions of perfect information, the decision-maker must hazard a guess that a particular choice will lead to particular results.[31] Nixon's 1970 decision to send American troops into Cambodia reveals the possible magnitude of unanticipated consequences. In his television address explaining his decision, Nixon depicted its likely outcome in grandiose terms: the invasion would clear out communist sanctuaries that served as bases for attacks on "both Cambodia and American and South Vietnamese forces in South Vietnam as well." Wiping out these bases would get to the "heart of the trouble," bring the boys home sooner, remind the Russians and Chinese of American determination, and contribute to a just and lasting peace.

The invasion revealed, however, that the sanctuaries had been largely abandoned, yielding only a modest cache of armaments. Meanwhile, at home, an agitated Senate was spurred to new effort to clip the wings of the

President's war-making power. Protests and rioting by college students, which Nixon had anticipated on a modest scale, flamed to high intensity when a sudden unexpected event exploded—the killing of demonstrating students at Kent State University by National Guardsmen.

Decisions have consequences that cannot be immediately, if ever, perceived. A weapons system requiring seven years in passage from drawing board to operations plainly forestalls any prompt revelation of the consequences of the decisions it represents. Consequences may not be perceived because the President is blinded by prejudices and ambitions. Weeks passed in the Court-packing fight before Roosevelt regarded as credible the grim daily reports his lieutenants brought him of voting prospects on Capitol Hill. He was unaccustomed to the possibility of defeat. When his Court fight wallowed inconclusively for weeks in Congress, Thomas Corcoran and Secretary of the Interior Harold Ickes noticed a marked shrinkage in their chief's aggressive leadership. The President, Ickes noted in his diary, "has acted to me like a beaten man." [32]

# Pathologies of Decision-Making: The Case of the Vietnam War

Unfortunately, presidential decision-making is not immune to bad choices and disastrous outcomes. A mark of the strong presidency is the capacity to make gross errors. All contemporary Chief Executives, from Franklin Roosevelt onward, have contributed to some of the more notable failures of presidential decision-making. Roosevelt's fiasco was his unpreparedness for the attack on Pearl Harbor. Truman erred in the invasion of North Korea, which brought Communist China into the Korean War. Lyndon Johnson was caught up in decisions escalating the Vietnam war that ultimately cost him the presidency, and Nixon failed to check overzealous subordinates from committing the criminal folly of Watergate, which ultimately destroyed his presidency.

One of the more involved and extended of these presidential disasters, decision-making in the Vietnam war, has been examined for causal weakness by key participants. From their observations, caveats can be extracted that should serve as warning signs in future presidencies.

What went wrong with the decision-making of the Vietnam war, particularly in the Johnson era, when the war's steepest escalations transpired? For one thing, as the war proceeded, the choices formulated for decision-making were loaded with false options. Memoranda to the President invariably contained three options, two of which were patently unacceptable, since they posed the extremes of humiliating defeat and total war, and the third, "Option B," which always prevailed, encompassed what nearly everyone wanted to do. Option B was a magical preserver of policy consensus and it precluded complaints from presidential counselors that their advice was not heeded. But a consensus-type option such as Option B can bear contradictions potentially debilitating for policy. Thus, at one juncture, the United States moved both to bomb more and to negotiate seriously, though the bombing forestalled significant negotiations.[33]

In presidential councils, tactical arguments rather than fundamental concepts were focused on. Fundamental assumptions were rarely, if ever questioned. Participants argued not in terms of what they thought was right, but what they perceived would be persuasive. One participant, Leslie Gelb, organizer of the written assessment of the war subsequently known as "the Pentagon Papers," felt that the community of presidential counselors lived in a "house without windows." With similar backgrounds in education and public service, they possessed a common view of the world, which in the context of the war was a world of dominoes, where a threat anywhere was a threat everywhere, and any adviser who challenged such assumptions was derided and discounted as "soft-headed."[34] Another constraining force was the judgment of the advisory groups that a member was "losing his effectiveness," a fate to be shunned by remaining silent, going along, or salving one's conscience with resolve to fight another day.[35]

The endless demands for Vietnam decisions brought on the malady of executive fatigue, when tired decision craftsmen from the White House and the State and Defense Departments became increasingly entrapped in their narrowing view of the world and an ever more cliché-ridden discourse. The inertia of bureaucracy, wishful thinking, took over, and there followed a weary surrender to the semantics of the military that concealed the reality of the war. For some advisers, the war's decisions were an upward-spiraling ego investment whose stakes increased with such commitment, making them less prone to question and reject.[36] Finally, the President himself. Had Johnson been more confident in foreign policy—his experience had been almost wholly in domestic politics—he could have raised the hard questions that excessive consensus submerged. Johnson had emerged from the 1964 elections with an overwhelming mandate to deescalate the war, but he failed to impose it on his advisers.

How can the strong presidency and the country be spared from costly bad decisions? Carefully defined roles for each adviser, particularly of powers and functions, will serve as a barrier against group dominance. The establishment of operating procedures and the cultivation of traditions of workmanship that enhance critical inquiry also can help. Old assumptions need to be periodically reevaluated. Most of all, a wary President can cultivate the representation of divergent views among the counselors, competition of ideas, and freedom of argument. An alert President can be his own best insurance against big trouble.

# Rival Models of Decision-Making

Amidst the 1980 Democratic convention, Jimmy Carter approved a document, Presidential Directive 59, containing a new strategy for nuclear war that gave priority to attacking military targets in the Soviet Union rather than to destroying cities and industrial complexes. The new policy contrasted with the policy adopted in the 1960s that relied on the threatened destruction of Soviet cities to deter a major war. The new policy presumably would enhance deterrence by putting the Soviet on notice that if it used nuclear weapons anywhere, the United States could make a precise response on their military installations, rather than exercising merely the older option of a massive strike that no President would willingly order.

The policy drew little attention until Secretary of State Edmund S. Muskie disclosed that he learned about it only when he read newspaper accounts. He declared that a matter with such important foreign policy implications should have been discussed with him before the President acted. Instead, he was bypassed by the President, Secretary of Defense Harold Brown, and national security adviser Zbigniew Brzezinski. Muskie made clear that his complaints were not so much over the policy itself as over being frozen out of the discussions preceding its adoption. Muskie could not determine if the decision-making machinery was at fault or if he was the victim of administration infighting.[37] Only weeks earlier, on taking over as Secretary of State, he told an audience of State Department employees that he was aware that many felt the Secretary's powers had been usurped by the President's national security adviser. "I'm the President's principal adviser on foreign policy," he declared, "Or so he told me."[38]

Accounts of the Muskie episode asserted that the secretary and the entire State Department were deliberately kept in ignorance of the new policy by the national security adviser, Zbigniew Brzezinski. Muskie's predecessor, Cyrus Vance and his aides were included in three perfunctory meetings in the spring of 1979, but not in the bureaucratic processes that mattered. With the 1980 election at hand, Brzezinski was thought to have rushed through the proposal to make Carter look tough as commander-in-chief, thus refuting Ronald Reagan's charges of nuclear weakness induced by Carter's policies. Excluding Muskie and the State Department made it easier to push the new policy through.[39]

## The Unitary Rational Method

Muskie's experience spotlights attention on rival models of decision-making, which with modifications have been operative in contemporary presidential administrations. In one, the President is defined as a unitary, rational decision-maker, exemplified by the National Security Council's functioning under Nixon. Under the unitary, centralized model, the NSC's staff operation distills, analyzes, and develops options, protecting the President against exposure to undigested proposals and *ad hoc* controversy over policy choices. Nixon was attracted to this model by its likely reduction, if not elimination of "bureaucratic politics" in developing the executive branch's foreign policy. Bureaucratic politics—the strivings of departments and agencies and their subunits to influence, and even control, policy and decision—was perceived as threatening to the President's own primacy.

In bureaucratic politics, the departments may keep policy issues from rising to the presidential level, or when they do, they may bear concealed compromises embodying the special interests of the departments and their subunits. Nixon and his national security adviser, Kissinger, moved to enhance presidential control and to weaken the leverage of departmental officials over presidential decision-making. "I refuse to be confronted with a bureaucratic consensus," Nixon stated, "that leaves me no options but acceptance or rejection, and that gives me no way of knowing what alternatives exist."[40]

The highly centralized or unitary system easily overburdens the ultimate decision-making, the President and his principal aide, his national security adviser, with decisions and details. It can lapse into a lumbering pace in crises when time pressures for decision become severe. It is apt to produce analyses and decision-choices reflecting the biases of the President and his close associates, and it fails to develop friendly baronies of strength in the bureaucratic outlands where implementation takes place, if it does at all.

## The Multiple Advocacy Model

A principal alternative model is the multiple advocacy model, elucidated by political scientist Alexander George.[41] Here the President functions as a "magistrate" who listens in a structured setting to various, well-prepared advocates, pressing their case for alternative options. This model encourages competition among advisers seeking to influence the President's decision. If significant disagreement arises, a more critical examination and assessment of the available options ensues than under the highly centralized system.

The task of the Chief Executive in the multiple advocacy model is to harness a diversity of views and functional perspectives in the interest of rational policy-making. By prudent management, the President can foster balanced, structured debate among policy advocates, representing different functional interests identified with the departments and agencies of the executive branch. Competitive, representative, pluralistic, participatory—these are the identifying marks of the multiple advocacy system. But multiple advocacy can deteriorate into quarrelsome, manipulative, self-interested bureaucratic politics dysfunctional to the President's needs and interests, a consideration that prompted Nixon to adopt a more centralized system.

The successful maintenance of a multiple advocacy process, George contends, requires a high order of management attention by the President. The participating departments and agencies must not suffer any major maldistribution of resources like power and influence, competence in dealing with policy issues, relevant information, analytical talent, and bargaining and persuasion skills. Time must be provided for sufficient debate. If there are substantial disparities in resources between the agencies, the Chief Executive, or his national security assistant, acting as "custodian" of the system, must somehow provide redress. As George asserts, the assistant can perform these critical tasks "only if he scrupulously refrains from becoming an advocate himself."

The national security assistants of the Truman and Eisenhower administrations best approximate the custodial role. But since the Kennedy era, with McGeorge Bundy's ascendance to the post, the assistant became a premier policy advocate, as well as a public spokesman for the President's policies. The expansion of the advocacy role peaked in Kissinger's tenure.[42]

## Choosing Between the Models

What comfort, if any, could Secretary Muskie derive from these models in his pain of being left out of a key presidential decision, and hoping that the experience would never be repeated? The danger of repetition would clearly be greater in the unitary model, unless as Secretary of State he enjoyed the same close personal relationship with the President that Kissinger as Secretary of State did with Nixon. By every sign, Muskie was far from that attainment. Under a well-managed multiple advocacy model, Muskie would have far better opportunity to share regularly in the President's decision-making.

Each model is susceptible to malfunction, and several kinds of malfunction that afflicted Muskie could have occurred under either model. Like other Presidents, Carter was more receptive to the multiple advocacy model when he was in doubt over decision and policy; then a President's appetite is whetted to hear the opinions advocated by his departmental advisers. But if the President's mind is made up, he will likely prefer the unitary model. Carter, facing an underdog's struggle for reelection and attacked by his opponent Ronald Reagan for management of the arms competition with the Soviet Union, had by every inference a closed mind on Presidential Directive 59; and the readiest and most assured way to enjoy its political fruits immediately in the 1980 campaign was to bypass Edmund Muskie.

By Muskie's own account, the Carter presidency in its foreign policy-making was well distant from the multiple advocacy model. He complained that inadequate time was given to discussion of critical foreign policy issues by the President and his top advisers. He noted that meetings for that purpose lasted no more than an hour or so, and he was told by a regular participant, before he joined the administration, that they were a charade. Another decision-making mechanism was the regular weekly luncheon meetings of Muskie, Brown, and Brzezinski. The agenda, Muskie noted, often included up to twenty-five items to be discussed and decided upon during an hour or two, and this, he said, was inadequate for serious debate.[43]

Both Carter and Brzezinski conducted themselves in ways repugnant to the multiple advocacy model. As the Presidential Directive was being prepared, Muskie met several times with Brzezinski, but the pending directive was never mentioned. On the day the directive was signed, Muskie had breakfast with Brzezinski, Brown, and President Carter, nor was he told then of the directive. The peculiar vulnerability of any model to the timing of decision-making is suggested in Kissinger's astute assessment of the episode: "Highly delicate, controversial issues that have remained unsettled for three and one-half years (as the Presidential Directive did) should not be resolved by public pronouncements in the middle of an election campaign."[44]

# ★ ★ ★ An Overview ★ ★ ★

The President's method in decision-making has something of the quality of fire. It can serve for good or ill; it can be a virtue or a vice; at one time it can succeed, at another it leads to abysmal failure. There is no available body of absolute directives like the Ten Commandments to assure correct decision-making. "Don't put off unto tomorrow what can be done today," the adage says. But, according to another, "Sufficient unto the day is the evil thereof." A Franklin Roosevelt can long postpone a key decision, and, endowed with a kind of charmed political life, manage to get away with it. William McKinley on the eve of the war with Spain, a peace-minded man eager to avoid conflict, delayed so in his bewilderment at events that war-minded legislators and the yellow press grabbed the initiative and with it the issue of war or peace.

The President does well to consult, but he does ill to consult too much. Truman and the Democratic party paid dearly for his failure to involve Congress substantially in his early Korean decisions. Later, when the Korean War became unpopular, he could not share the resulting political liabilities with a Congress shut out from his original decisions. But consultations also can be too wide and can produce such contradictory counsel and excessive information that decision is delayed and weakened. Decision is a blend of fact, thought, incisiveness, and vigor; to stress one ingredient is to diminish others.

When the occasion requires a decision, the President must communicate his will clearly and not create havoc, as Wilson did in proclaiming, "We are too proud to fight," a well-intentioned moral standard for the nation, which the Allies understandably misinterpreted as an evidence of cooling ardor toward their cause. Yet the President will also need an instinct for ambiguity in his daily grapple with petitioners and their pressures for his favor. For others to know his will too clearly and too soon may bring him political trouble and grief.

There are discernible in the world of the President several principles that seem far more often right than wrong. Above all, the President must keep the initiative in decisions that are his and not permit it to be grabbed by Congress or private groups. But neither should he preempt decisions or participation that in a democracy are rightfully theirs. For decision, as the Vietnam war makes clear, must be a continuous process of winning consent. The President should not decide in anger, or grief, or other high emotion, but only in composure. Presidents by this standard have been remarkably successful. As a lot they have not been hotheads or desk-pounders. The magnitude of the Chief Executive's power and responsibility and his need to maintain to the outside world an image of self-confidence require that he appear to be "in charge," that he speak and act with assurance, hold his subordinates in rein, and comprehend the problems they are struggling with. Decision is more than the creation of policy. It reveals the President as a person.

# Chapter Fifteen

# Crisis

Crisis is a crucible in which a President and his administration are tested as nowhere else. No other condition tries so rigorously the capacity of the President for decision, perceptiveness, physical endurance, self-confidence, and prudence. In crisis, boldness is often the safest course; hesitation encourages the adversary. The elements that shape policy suddenly become fluid, conferring unusual opportunities for creative action. Passivity leads to mounting impotence, to a posture of being forced to react on issues, and in circumstances contrived to produce maximum disadvantage.

Crisis is a cruel master that forces the Chief Executive to rearrange his priorities and recast his plans. If it brings him to wage war, he will do less in social policy, no matter how high his aspirations are for that endeavor, no matter how solemnly he laid his plans before the electorate and how enthusiastically they were approved. At no other time are the stakes so high as in crisis. The consequences of his actions are enormously magnified; he may find new strengths; and his weaknesses may be glaringly exposed. His decisions may determine nothing less than national survival and the preservation of the existing social order. What he does in crisis will be more remembered in history than anything else he does. If he fails, his shortcoming will be recalled, when a thousand successes he may have won in quieter times are long forgotten.

Most great Presidents have been crisis Presidents. Lincoln brought the nation through the holocaust of civil war, Wilson through the First World War, and Franklin Roosevelt through the depression and toward victory in the Second World War. But the brilliant success of Presidents in crisis cannot blind us to the debit side of the balance sheet, to the substantial failures. James Madison, administrator of the War of 1812, suffered defeats and retreats and the ignominy of having the White House burned from under him. Lincoln was preceded by Buchanan's administration, which failed to stay the onrush of civil war.

Contemporary Presidents face crises of a scale unknown to their predecessors. Since the end of the American nuclear monopoly, the presidency has existed in a state of perpetual crisis in its enforced vigil to prevent some incident or issue from escalating into general war. Presidents since the Second World War have chronically been caught up in multiple crises, thanks to the capacity of communist nations to strike on many fronts and domestic society's capacity to churn up big trouble. For John Kennedy, 1962 was a year of crisis. The Soviets placed missiles in Cuba. Civil rights crises exploded in Mississippi and Alabama, and a price rise in steel threatened to smother the administration's foremost economic goals: curbing inflation, bettering the balance of payments, speeding economic growth, and relieving unemployment. Fortunately, Kennedy resolved the missile crisis, the first confrontation between the U.S. and the U.S.S.R. as nuclear powers. Because of the uniqueness and success of Kennedy's approach, it provides guidance, in terms of both what to do and what not to do, for future Presidents should they have the misfortune to face a similar conflict situation.

# John Kennedy
# and the Cuban Missile Crisis

## Beginnings

The Cuban crisis of 1962 began in the whirring camera of an Air Force U-2 reconnaissance plane high over San Cristobal on October 14. Analysis of the developed films the next day struck the Kennedy administration with massive impact. Soviet medium-range missiles, a mobile type used by the Soviet Army, were in place near San Cristobal, one hundred miles west of Havana. Every American city was potentially only a few minutes away from them. The revelation set off fourteen days of diplomatic maneuver and military buildup that brought the United States to the threshold of nuclear war.[1]

The executive branch was not alone in its watch. Republican and Democratic legislators alike followed and exclaimed upon the ominous developments. A frequent Republican critic of Kennedy's Cuban course was Senator Kenneth B. Keating of New York. On September 2 he urged that an Organization of American States mission investigate reports of Cuban missile bases. If the OAS failed to act, the United States should blockade Western Hemispheric waters against vessels carrying armed forces personnel or material.[2] In early September, at the instigation of Democratic Senator Richard B. Russell of Georgia, chairman of the Armed Services Committee, Congress passed a resolution invoking the Monroe Doctrine against foreign intervention in the Western Hemisphere and the 1947 Rio pact for joint Western Hemispheric defense. The United States, the resolution declared, was determined to prevent, by "use of arms" if necessary, any Cuban military buildup threatening American security. The resolution's backers, who hailed from both parties, had a double purpose: to warn Khrushchev and Castro, and to invigorate certain administration policymakers who seemed to them to be taking too detached a view of the Cuban developments.[3]

The administration appeared to accept Khrushchev's characterization of the weapons imported into Cuba as "defensive," although the President stated publicly on September 4 that "were it otherwise the gravest issues would arise." The close surveillance the United States intelligence community was simultaneously maintaining upon Cuba was spurred by reports from Cuban refugees in Florida that surface-to-surface missiles with nuclear warheads capable of reaching American cities were on the island. But Kennedy, having been burnt by inaccurate intelligence that led to the Bay of Pigs fiasco, adopted a "twice-shy" attitude.

The implications of the Soviet move were clear enough. By placing medium-and intermediate-range missiles in Cuba, Russia was narrowing its gap with the United States. Missiles of such range in Cuba would provide the Russians with immediate power without the long wait necessary for equivalent increases in its intercontinental missiles arsenal. A missile fired from Cuba promised far more accuracy than an ICBM from Russia. Cuba-based missiles would reduce the United States' attack-warning time virtually to seconds. The Strategic Air Command would have to be dispersed on a more or less permanent basis.

## The Decision-making Struggle

At 11:45 A.M. on October 16 Kennedy met with a group later known as the Executive Committee (Ex Com) of the National Security Council. The President presided, and his fellow conferees included Vice President Johnson, Secretary of State Dean Rusk, Secretary of Defense Robert McNamara, Secretary of the Treasury, C. Douglas Dillon, Attorney General Robert Kennedy, Undersecretary of State George Ball, Deputy Secretary of Defense Roswell Gilpatric, CIA Deputy Director Marshall Carter (CIA Director John McCone was away from Washington in the crisis's first days), Assistant Secretary of State for Inter-American Affairs Edward Martin, General Maxwell Taylor (chairman of the Joint Chiefs of Staff), and Theodore Sorensen, presidential counsel and principal speech-writer.

The atmosphere of crisis hung thickly over the group as they canvassed the possible responses to the Soviet thrust. If the United States did nothing, it would have to live with communist missiles at its doorstep, its prestige would tumble, and the credibility of its pledges would be destroyed. Latin America might fall into the Soviet basket. If, as a second possibility, the United States bombed or invaded Cuba, its moral position would be tainted, its alliances would be disarrayed, the neutral nations would burst into great cry, and the Russians might make a countermove in Berlin or elsewhere. A third possibility was a blockade, but it too might stir a Soviet response and offend our allies, particularly the maritime powers. On the other hand, a blockade would provide the opportunity both for the United States to prepare and the Soviets to recede.[4] The meeting produced two immediate decisions. One was that air surveillance over Cuba should be intensified and the other that any action the United States took should as nearly as possible coincide with United States' public disclosure of the Russian bases.[5]

The vast departmental machinery began to turn. The Defense Department estimated the kinds of units, numbers of men, and time factors necessary for various military actions. The State Department explored the possibilities of Latin-American and European support, and its most sophisticated analysts of Soviet behavior began mulling over the probable effects of various actions on the Russians. United Nations Ambassador Adlai Stevenson was brought into the discussions.

The President had other commitments in addition to the crisis. The congressional electoral campaign was in full swing, and Kennedy set out for Connecticut to honor long-established speaking dates. The discussions on Cuba were to be kept secret—Khrushchev did not know that Kennedy knew about the offensive missiles, and the secret could best be kept by maintaining a normal presidential schedule. During his absence, the Ex Com met day and night in Undersecretary of State Ball's conference room, or "think tank" as it was dubbed, a windowless chamber furnished with a long table, pumpkin leather chairs, prosaic water decanters, and Dixie cups. The meetings were informal, the participants wandering in and out to keep up simultaneously with their regular duties. Further incoming U-2 reports of new discoveries of medium- and intermediate-range missile sites compounded the situation's urgency. Former Secretary of State Dean Acheson was brought into the meetings.[6]

Upon returning to Washington from the Connecticut campaigning, the President took up a varied schedule of regular business, ceremonial duties, and crisis management. He met often with the Ex Com, brought former Defense Secretary Robert Lovett into the discussions, and deliberately absented himself to encourage his aides to express their views uninhibitedly. Although poised on the knife's edge of incipient decision that could long determine the fate of the nation, the West, and humankind, Kennedy maintained his accustomed composure even in his severest test, a White House meeting with Andrei A. Gromyko. The visit of the Soviet Foreign Minister had been arranged prior to the crisis. In his two hours and fifteen minutes with Kennedy, Gromyko reaffirmed previous assurances that Soviet activity in Cuba was defensive only. Kennedy repeated to Gromyko his belief that the Soviet effort in Cuba was defensive and his warning that any change in this estimate would have grave consequences. The President refrained from confronting Gromyko with the damning truth because the administration had not yet decided what action to take, and the Russians, faced with exposure, might resort to an evasive counterthrust to blunt the eventual decision.

Gromyko dined that evening with Secretary of State Rusk and other officials on the eighth floor of the department. On the floor below, in the "think tank," the planning group continued its crisis discussions. In midevening they piled into a single limousine, sacrificing comfort for security, and journeyed to the White House. In this meeting the President seemed to be moving toward a blockade. Ambassador-at-large Llewellyn Thompson, Jr., stressed the need for the solid legality of any action taken. The Russians, he said, had a feeling for "legality," and well-grounded legal action would impress world opinion. The State and Justice Departments began work on the legal justification for a blockade.

On October 19 Kennedy resumed his political campaigning, partly to quiet press suspicions that great happenings were afoot, with stops at Cleveland, Chicago, and at Springfield to lay flowers on Lincoln's tomb. Before departing, he expressed approval to the Ex Com of the trend of decision toward a blockade. In the continuing Ex Com discussions, advocates of an offensive air attack vigorously pressed their case, but the blockade attracted the dominant support, even with its admitted danger that, in Vice President Johnson's words, "stopping a Russian ship is an act of war." Staff work proceeded on each alternative to preserve the President's choices to the very moment of decision.

The next day a telephone call from Robert Kennedy brought the President back from Chicago to Washington. Time was running out and secrecy was crumbling, said the Attorney General. The White House informed the press that the President was forced to return by a slight infection of the upper respiratory tract, with one degree of fever. In actuality, the President's cold, which was mild, did not require his return, but it was considered necessary to mislead the reporters by some contrivance in the interest of security. Kennedy, arriving at 1:37 P.M., went over a speech Sorensen had prepared upon the assumption that a blockade would be imposed. The final speech emerged after five drafts. The President all but clinched the decision for blockade and directed the relevant operations to proceed, subject only to his final word the next day. The State and Defense Departments drafted a blockade proclamation, the chief of Naval Operations made the plans necessary to enforce it, the State Department laid out an approach to the Organization of American States, Acheson prepared to embark for Paris to confer with De Gaulle and the NATO council, and Alexis Johnson, Deputy Undersecretary of State for Political Affairs, worked up a "master scenario" depicting every necessary preparation prior to the President's speech; briefings, orders to embassies, ship movements, and the like. A military helicopter picked up former President Eisenhower at his Gettysburg farm and flew him to Washington for a briefing by the CIA. Vice President Johnson dropped his election campaigning in Hawaii and flew back to Washington.

The next day, October 21, the scenario was converted into action. Kennedy, after conferring again with numerous key officials, definitely decided upon the blockade. In the afternoon he met with the statutory National Security Council. The State Department drafted forty-three presidential letters to the heads of government of all the alliances and to Willy Brandt, mayor of West Berlin. A Kennedy-to-Khrushchev letter was prepared to accompany a copy of the TV speech announcing the blockade. Instructions were readied for distributing the speech to sixty embassies. On October 22 Lawrence O'Brien, the President's congressional liaison assistant, telephoned twenty congressional leaders of both parties for a meeting with Kennedy. The Soviet ambassador to Washington, Anatoly Dobrynin, was called to the State Department. General Lauris Norstad, the NATO commander, was alerted. In the meeting with congressional leaders, Senator Richard B. Russell, backed by Senator J. William Fulbright, the Foreign Relations Committee chairman, who had opposed the Bay of Pigs attack (an abortive invasion of Cuba in 1961 by forces of Cuban exiles, supported by the United States, to overthrow Fidel Castro) bluntly asserted that a blockade was too slow and therefore involved great risk, but the President was not to be dissuaded.[7] At the State Department, Undersecretary Ball and Intelligence and Research Director Roger Hilsman briefed forty-six allied ambassadors in the State Department's International Conference Room.

At 7 P.M. in a calm but intense and blunt eighteen-minute television report, the President delivered his speech alerting the public for the first time. He blamed not Cuba but the Soviet Union for the crisis, which, he said, had violated its leaders' most solemn assurances that only defensive weapons were going to Cuba. The President said he had ordered a "quarantine"—a word he had substituted for "blockade"—on all offensive weapons for Cuba. Ships carrying them would be turned back. Furthermore, he said, the preparation of the missile sites must cease, and if it did not, "further action" would be taken. He was ordering the surveillance continued, and he called upon Khrushchev to withdraw "all offensive weapons" from Cuba.[8]

While the President was speaking, his vast administrative machinery was in full motion. At the State Department the forty-six allied ambassadors watched the speech on a large screen, Assistant Secretary Martin gave a further private briefing to Latin American ambassadors, Secretary Rusk and Director Hilsman briefed the neutral nations, including Yugoslavia, Undersecretary Ball briefed the diplomatic correspondents, and Defense Secretary McNamara the military correspondents. "Whatever force is required"— even striking—said McNamara, would be employed to enforce the blockade. At the United Nations, Ambassador Adlai Stevenson requested a special meeting of the Security Council.

Thirteen hours after Kennedy's speech came the Soviet's first reaction, a long, rambling, published statement of accusations and warnings of thermonuclear war, plus a letter from Khrushchev to Kennedy. These the administration interpreted as betraying that the Kremlin was caught off guard and playing for time to think out its moves. Developments elsewhere were encouraging despite protest marches in various world capitals. In Paris marchers carried placards reading "Kennedy the Assassin" and "Peace in Cuba," and in London two thousand demonstrators screamed "Long Live Castro" and "Down with Kennedy." British Prime Minister Harold Macmillan telephoned his full support. In a meeting with Dean Acheson, Secretary of State in the Truman administration, West German Chancellor Konrad Adenauer was equally positive. At the United Nations the NATO countries supported a United States resolution calling upon the Soviet Union to withdraw the missiles and dismantle the sites under United Nations verification, after which the United States would end the quarantine. Citing the Rio pact of 1947, Secretary of State Rusk offered the Organization of American States a resolution authorizing the use of force, individually or collectively, to enforce the blockade. The OAS Council adopted the resolution nineteen to zero. The NATO and OAS unanimity surprised both the United States and the Soviet Union and apparently added to the latter's confusion.

There were less gratifying developments, however. U Thant, Acting Secretary General of the United Nations, urged several weeks' suspension of the blockade and arms shipments to Cuba while negotiations were held.

Khrushchev accepted with alacrity, but Kennedy, anticipating the disarming of his powerful diplomatic and military initiative and doubting that they could ever regain momentum if negotiations failed, as they were expected to, turned down Thant's request. "The existing threat," the President replied, "was created by the secret introduction of offensive weapons into Cuba, and the answer lies in the removal of such weapons."[9]

A nearly two-day lapse between the announcement of the blockade and its imposition permitted the Soviets to redirect any ships headed for Cuba. On October 25, twenty hours after the blockade began, the United States Navy made its first interception, stopping a Soviet tanker, the *Bucharest*. It was allowed to proceed without search because the Navy was satisfied it carried only petroleum. Kennedy and his associates agreed that in the interests of establishing the principle of the blockade without humiliating the Russians the first ship to be boarded should not be a Soviet ship but a vessel of a neutral nation.[10] Two days later the Lebanese freighter *Marucia* was stopped, boarded, and searched by a five-man party from the destroyers *Joseph P. Kennedy, Jr.*, and *John R. Pierce*. The *Marucia* was also allowed to proceed after it was ascertained that it carried nothing but peaceful cargo.

## Understanding Khrushchev

On October 26 and 27 Khrushchev dispatched two letters to Kennedy. Embedded in the first, although not explicitly stated, was an offer to withdraw the offensive weapons under United Nations supervision if the United States would lift the blockade and promise not to invade the island. The President heard the transcription of this letter with great relief. Then a second Khrushchev letter came clattering over the wires bearing another catch. The Soviet Union would trade its bases in Cuba for the NATO missile base in Turkey. In a National Broadcasting Company telecast of February 9, 1964, McGeorge Bundy, the President's assistant for national security affairs stated that the Soviet offer also proposed that the United States pull its missiles out of Greece as well. As Kennedy and his aides pondered a reply, incoming intelligence reports disclosed that Soviet technicians were building away furiously at the Cuban sites. It was estimated that the sites would be ready for missile launchings within a mere five days. Kennedy decided to write again to Khrushchev, saying that if he understood the Premier correctly—that the offensive weapons would be removed in return for an end of the blockade and a promise of no American invasion of Cuba—then it was a deal. It could now go "either way," the President remarked grimly.[11]

If it should go the bad way, the United States armed forces were ready. The Tactical Air Command's 19th Air Force had moved into the sprawling base outside of Homestead, Florida. By October 23 nearly one thousand attack-fighter and fighter-bomber aircraft were poised in Florida, with a conventional airborne firepower rivaling that of the Allied forces in England prior to the Normandy invasion in 1944. Army divisions from Fort Bragg, North Carolina; Fort Campbell, Kentucky; Fort Riley, Kansas; and Fort Benning, Georgia, were on full alert. These divisions plus marines at sea, in Florida, and at Guantánamo, formed a one hundred thousand-man force the United States stood ready to hurl into Cuba. Drop-zones in the Cuban interior had been carefully designated for paratroopers of the 82nd and

101st Airborne Divisions. Globemaster transports poured into the Key West naval base with soldiers, sailors, marines, mobile radar units, photographic gear, trucks and jeeps, and weapons of all types. The Association of American Railroads was alerted, and 2,418 flatcars and 299 equipment cars from as far distant as Denver and Minneapolis began rolling to Fort Hood, Texas, to take on Honest John Rockets and rocket-launcher vehicles, Patton tanks, self-propelled howitzers, and other cargo. Bases at Miami, Canaveral, Orlando, and Homestead were mushrooming with fighter and fighter-bomber aircraft.

The United States military preparations indeed were proceeding on a global scale. U.S. Navy ships and submarines in the European Atlantic, Pacific, and Mediterranean were hurrying out to sea. Three Polaris-firing submarines scurried to sea from their berths at Holy Loch, Scotland. The Strategic Air Command was on Defcon 2, or full war footing, from which it needed but one signal to go to Defcon 1, which puts it at war. For the first time in history, SAC's medium-range bomber force of B-47's were ordered to disperse. ICBM firing crews, spread in complexes throughout the United States, were brought to full alert and missiles were raised. The Navy's Fleet Ballistic Missile submarines were on station, carrying 128 Polaris missiles, within range of major Soviet targets. The United States had made full preparations to lay the explosive equivalent of more than thirty billion tons of TNT upon the Soviet Union.

The United States was also maintaining close air surveillance over Cuba. On October 27 Major Rudolf Anderson, Jr., one of two U-2 pilots whose photographs touched off the crisis, was shot down over Cuba.[12] In cryptic comment during a speech at Columbia, South Carolina, on April 25, 1963, six months after the crisis, Attorney General Robert Kennedy said that Major Anderson's death "led the President to notify Mr. Khrushchev that strong and overwhelming retaliatory action would have been taken unless he received immediate notice that the missiles would be withdrawn." United States officials connected with the crisis believe that this presidential message, the text of which was not revealed, coupled with the open movement of American military power were the factors that really brought Khrushchev around to his ultimate decision in the immediate crisis. "What got the message through to Khrushchev was action," one official said. "The message was clear that something was going to happen and happen soon."[13]

October 28 brought Khrushchev's answer, the fifth Premier-President exchange in seven days. Khrushchev said that he had ordered work on the bases stopped and the missiles crated and returned to the Soviet Union. Representatives of the United Nations, he promised, would "verify the dismantling." In return, the President's no-invasion pledge would be trusted. After hurried consultations with his aides, the President issued a statement welcoming Khrushchev's "statesmanlike decision," and the blockade was lifted.[14]

## Aftermath

In the months following the crisis, the United States and the Soviet Union handled the Cuban question with high caution, neither side appearing to contemplate any drastic action so long as the other kept the October "gentlemen's agreement." Senator Keating remained attentive to Cuba, de-claring on the Senate floor on January 31, 1963, that "there is continuing, absolutely confirmed and undeniable evidence that the Soviets are maintain-ing the medium-range sites they had previously constructed in Cuba. . . . Without on-site inspection, it is hard to see how we will ever know for sure the true missile situation in Cuba." In a press interview, Keating said he would be glad to disclose his information, but not his sources, to the Pres-ident.[15] Senator Strom Thurmond, Democrat of South Carolina, made sim-ilar charges. But intelligence estimates one year after the crisis disclosed that the Soviet force in Cuba was down to ten thousand from twenty-two thousand at the peak of the crisis. The remaining personnel were believed to be devoted to training the Cuban armed forces.

In a 1966 interview Premier Castro, asked if he could "state unequivo-cally" that there were no offensive ground-to-air nuclear missiles in Cuba, replied that he had "no objection to declaring that those weapons do not exist in Cuba" and added that "unfortunately, there are none." In the same interview, Castro also remarked, mysteriously and without elaboration, that "one day, perhaps, it will be known that the United States made some other concessions in relation to the October crisis besides those that were made public."[16]

In 1970 Richard Nixon neared the brink of a second confrontation when the Soviet Union began building facilities for nuclear submarines in the Cuban port of Cienfuegos, with a submarine tender and other Soviet vessels standing by. To cope with this ominous situation, Nixon and his aides re-sorted to processes of quiet diplomacy, in which was cited the Kennedy-Khrushchev agreement to keep Soviet nuclear weapons out of the Western Hemisphere. What the U.S.S.R. sought to do in 1970 was the equivalent of what it had failed to do in 1962. With facilities in Cuba, Russian nuclear submarines could operate in the Atlantic and avoid the 8,000-mile round trip back to their Soviet base. This time assertive presidential diplomacy produced an unwritten Soviet pledge not to base missile-carrying nuclear submarines, store nuclear weapons, or install repair and servicing facilities anywhere in the Western Hemisphere. In return, the United States would closely watch, but not obstruct, periodic visits by the Soviet fleet to Cuban and other Western Hemispheric ports for crew shore leave and routine ship maintenance.[17] The incipient crisis dissolved, although how fully the agree-ment is adhered to remains obscure, and crisis can flame anew simply with the embarking of a Soviet tender for Cuban waters.[18]

In 1978, Jimmy Carter commenced photo reconnaissance flights over Cuba to determine whether MIG-23 fighter planes, based in Cuba and flown by Soviet pilots, had been modified to carry nuclear weapons. Such a mod-ification would have violated a United States–Soviet understanding con-cluded after the missile crisis. A year later, the Carter administration disclosed the presence of a Soviet combat brigade in Cuba. Both Cuba and the Soviet contended that the troops were there solely for training purposes and did not violate a 1962 agreement banning the Russians from using the island for any offensive purposes. In later comment, Carter chose to defuse the situation. Kennedy's success established a standard for future Presi-dents to maintain, a task that will become more difficult to accomplish as it becomes more difficult to define.

## The Art of Crisis Management

The Cuban crisis was the first confrontation of its kind since the onset of the age in which the two great nuclear powers possessed the capacity to destroy each other and much of the world. The decisions that Kennedy was called upon to make were therefore the most delicate and the most perilous that any President has ever faced. Not only the welfare of the American public, but the fate of peoples everywhere who had no voice in his selection, of unborn generations, of western civilization itself depended upon his choices.

The stressful decision-making of the Cuban crisis—the pattern of action by which the President mastered the tangled skein of intense events—was a nightmarish experience. The President is often spoken of, to the point of cliché, as a lonely figure. He has never appeared more solitary than in nuclear confrontation. Surrounded though he is by aides and data and counsel, he must decide alone. His choice cannot be delegated. It is a cruel test of self-confidence that has undeniably removed the presidency for all time as a refuge for the faint-hearted.

Kennedy followed several elementary procedures in facing the nuclear showdown. He rightly insisted that before publicly according the Cuban events the status of crisis, he needed "hard intelligence" and could not act simply upon rumor and report. He held to his course despite the revelations and criticisms of legislators of both his own and the opposition party and despite the hostile congressional resolutions. To be careful and responsible, as Kennedy had to be, is neither easy nor popular. Political outcry was perhaps not the worst of the afflictions he had to bear. The atmosphere in which the President acted was charged with danger and uncertainty, with inexorable climax and with scores of opportunities for surprise. For all their knowledge of the Soviet Union, American officials could not predict what the Soviet leader would decide to do—especially since he delighted in surprise as a source of strength in foreign affairs. The Russians took advantage of seasonal flunctuations in our political system, launching their gambit during an election campaign. They expected that the President would be eager to postpone the prickly Cuban issue until after the election, and by that time it would be too late.

In the Cuban crisis the President sought always to leave Khrushchev with an option or choice. Above all, the aim of Kennedy and his advisers was to avoid backing him into a corner, where his only recourse would be military. A military attack of any kind upon Cuba, a communist power, would have posed to the Soviet Union the necessity of either a military response or a humiliating surrender, badly damaging to its prestige around the world. The blockade afforded the advantage of giving Khrushchev a choice. He did not need to have his ships approach the blockade and be stopped and searched but could divert them, as he did. The blockade, therefore, left an acceptable way out for the Soviet Union, a cardinal principle of decision-making in the nuclear confrontation. Equally important, Kennedy carefully preserved the United States' own options; that is, he did not rely wholly upon the blockade but simultaneously speeded the full-scale alert of American forces, a procedure that many felt finally prodded Khrushchev to agree to remove the missiles from Cuba.[19]

Another cardinal principle was evident in the effort of the President and his aides to slow down the escalation of the crisis to permit Khrushchev time to consider his next moves. Deliberation, it was hoped, might produce a more measured and less drastic response than fast-moving exchanges— hence the value of notes and ambassadorial visits and the preferability of a blockade, a relatively gradual procedure compared with the precipitous engagement of an invasion or an air strike.

Kennedy took the fullest precautions to keep the decisions in his own hands, both the initial decision settling upon the blockade and the further critical decisions required to implement it. When a United States Navy reconnaissance plane spotted the *Marucia* headed for Cuba, the information was sped to the President, and it was he who gave the order to board and search it. Other procedures assured that control of the blockade operation remained in his hands. Kennedy was resolved that the issue of peace or war should not turn upon the decision of a local commander.

In making his choices, the President must be mindful of several constituencies but still keep decision in his grasp. He must be willing to act, as Kennedy was, notwithstanding the express disapproval of certain of these constituents. Kennedy accordingly convened members of his legislative constituency, leaders of both parties. Paradoxically, his party's leading legislators in the fields of foreign affairs and national security held that his decision was inadequate for the situation and urged him to do more. The House Republican leader, however, Congressman Halleck, declared, "I'm standing with the President." The dissent of several of his own party leaders did not deter the President. He won the approval of another great constituency: the leaders of the nation's major allies—Macmillan, De Gaulle, and Adenauer—and the member countries of the principal alliances, NATO and the OAS. Kennedy was fortunate enough to win an approval from his foreign constituency extending well beyond his expectations. But it is also clear that he was prepared, as a President in a nuclear confrontation may need to be, to carry forward his decision even without allied endorsement. In choosing his course, the President must weigh and balance factors that no ally can know or perceive, owing to the simple circumstance that only he occupies his presidential place, and only he, therefore, holds the responsibility.

Nuclear crisis is more than an intensive exercise in decision-making. Equally, if not more important, it is an enterprise in communication. The evidence is impressive that a major cause of the crisis was a misreading by Khrushchev and his colleagues of the Kennedy administration's attitude and intentions. In their June 1961 Vienna meeting, Khrushchev reportedly found Kennedy somewhat deferential, which the Soviet leader apparently interpreted as weakness. The disaster of the Bay of Pigs and Kennedy's restrained response to the Berlin wall may well have encouraged a Soviet impression of American softness. The strength of this impression was conveyed in Khrushchev's remark to Robert Frost that the United States was "too liberal to fight."

A nuclear confrontation involves a desperate resort to various communications channels and an intensive scrutiny of the opponent's act and word for clues of his intent and meaning. Kennedy and his counselors were heavily occupied in the dangerous and difficult task of estimating the probable Soviet reaction to possible United States moves. Equally to be anticipated was the effect upon our allies, upon trouble spots around the world, whether Berlin or Turkey, which held American bases that the Soviet Union was discussing, or the Formosa straits, where the Chinese were preparing for belligerent action. Likewise the effect upon Latin America: If the United States responded strongly, would the Latin countries become alarmed? Would they be even more alarmed if we did too little? For Kennedy and his aides, the crisis was a rigorous introspective experience in determining American purposes, in anticipating what our reaction might be to the Soviet reaction, and so on, until each possible course that might be chosen was followed to its ultimate conclusion. From the highly consequential endeavors of the Ex Com, public opinion and the individual citizen were shut out. Robert Kennedy was impressed with the necessity of adhering to this undemocratic scenario, evocative of the handful of kings and emissaries who in olden days decided man's fate. "If our deliberations had been publicized," he wrote, ". . . I believe the course that we ultimately would have taken would have been quite different and filled with far greater risks. The fact that we were able to talk, debate, argue, disagree, and then debate some more was essential in choosing our ultimate course."[20] Paradoxically, the putting aside of external democratic norms enhanced the internal democratic processes of the decision-makers. Kennedy's preference for secrecy was assisted by the successful handling of the missile crisis. But in an earlier episode, the failure of the Bay of Pigs invasion, secrecy also prevailed, for which John Kennedy subsequently voiced regret. To preserve that secrecy, he personally intervened to forestall publication of reports in the press that deliberations on launching the enterprise were proceeding. But after the disaster he ruefully acknowledged that he might have been spared the debacle if public discussion and opinion had accompanied executive deliberations.

Although Kennedy was an action-oriented, strong President, he was not, in any degree, a creature of impulse. The latter type, installed in the contemporary presidency, would be disastrous for the nation and humankind. An activist President triggered by emotion, who neither consulted advisers nor pondered consequences, would be both decisive and wrong-headed. Chief Executives such as Kennedy root their actions in thought and validated evidence. They are decisive and forceful only in response to reason tested by qualified opinion. Here the strong President and the President who abides by democratic norms coincide.

# Hostages in Iran

A less reassuring portraiture of crisis management is provided by the train of events that began with the seizure of the United States embassy in Teheran on November 4, 1979 by some 500 militant Iranians. An estimated 54 Americans who were in the embassy and its compound at the time were held as hostages. The seizure occurred following the exiled Shah of Iran's entry into the United States for medical treatment. The captors vowed not to release the hostages until the Shah was returned to stand trial in Iran. The United States declined to comply with this demand, and the Shah left the United States on December 15, after completion of his treatment and settled temporarily in Panama.

Crisis management embraces the arts of crisis prevention, a priceless skill curiously lacking in the hostage situation. A clear early warning that serious trouble was brewing for the United States occurred in February when armed guerillas attacked the American embassy in Teheran, holding the American ambassador and his staff of about 100 inside for more than two hours until they were freed by forces of Iran's supreme potentate, Ayatollah Ruhollah Khomeini. Two Iranians were killed and two United States marines wounded. Although other nations drastically scaled down the rosters of their embassies, the United States made only modest reductions in succeeding months, retaining a sizable complement of personnel when the hostages were seized. It was readily forseeable that the admission of the Shah to the United States would send the new Iranian rulers and other revolutionaries into quavering rage. In their eyes, the Shah and his henchmen had tortured and murdered thousands of Iranians, including kin of leaders of the Khomeini regime. Rioting and demonstrations against the United States would surely occur, directed at the most evident symbol of its presence in Iran, the United States embassy. No extra security measures were taken at the embassy nor were any known steps to forestall or diminish the crisis initiated by the Carter administration or the State Department. In response to criticism, Carter explained that he had received assurances from both Iran's Prime Minister and Foreign Minister that their government would protect the embassy.[21]

## Management by Prudence

Carter's initial responses to the crisis combined firmness and prudence. He denounced the "inhuman and degrading conditions" imposed on the hostages and warned of "grave consequences" if they were harmed. Simultaneously, he reminded the nation that "our will, our courage, and our maturity" were being tested. Military options, he said, would be considered only after peaceful means had been exhausted.[22] Despite daily, invariably televised demonstrations against the United States in Teheran, Carter remained unprovoked, and he managed with remarkable success to keep the anger of the American people from boiling over and endangering the hostages. Administration officials shook at the prospect of the "political firestorm" that would erupt if the hostages were harmed. Reports that they were "loosely tied" provoked angry remonstrations by political leaders, and the hostage situation, joined to a series of other distasteful events, contributed to a potential major issue of the 1980 presidential election. A State Department official articulated it, "There's a growing feeling out in the country that the United States is taking a beating in the world and the situation in Teheran is feeding on it."[23]

Carter and his aides meanwhile carefully pursued a course seeking a diplomatic solution, and left literally no stone unturned. Candidates campaigning in the presidential primaries declaimed the necessity of developing a "paramilitary plan" to free the hostages, but it generated little enthusiasm in the administration and Congress. Although military efforts to free hostages in past situations were sometimes successful, the military and political contexts differed drastically from the realities of Teheran. Above all, the American embassy was located in the midst of a large and turbulent city, many of whose inhabitants were armed. Surprise, crucial in rescue operations, would be difficult to achieve. A flight of transports bearing rescue teams from the United States or from bases in Britain and West Germany could be readily detected.[24]

Carter's diplomatic efforts included plans for an international panel to "review the dossier of crimes by the U.S. Government in Iran" since the 1953 CIA-supported coup that brought the Shah to power. Simultaneously, an exchange would be sought for the hostages' release.[25] Eventually such a panel journeyed to Iran, took evidence of anti-Shah grievances, but was barred from visiting the hostages. Against threats by the Ayatollah Khomeini to the hostages' safety, Carter repeatedly warned that the consequences would be "extremely grave" if any American were harmed.

For Carter, a major diplomatic forum was the United Nations. Secretary General Kurt Waldheim deemed the crisis "the most serious threat to peace since the Cuban missile crisis." Waldheim, strongly backed by the United States, requested an "urgent meeting" of the UN Security Council to deal with it. But whatever hopes the move generated were instantly crushed when the Ayatollah Khomeini attacked the Security Council meeting as a venture dictated by the United States, with an outcome that "has been predetermined." In a further thrust, the United States successfully requested the Security Council to call for the hostages' release and to dispatch Secretary General Waldheim to Teheran to seek the hostages' release. Despite Waldheim's heroic efforts, this venture also failed.

Hereupon the United States petitioned the International Court of Justice to order Iran to release the hostages. The judges, from 15 countries, were of exceedingly diverse political and religious backgrounds and ruled unanimously that Iran must immediately release the hostages. The Court also forbade the Iranians to put any of them on trial and determined that Iran was liable for reparations. Iran's Prosecutor General declared that the verdict had no meaning because only one side had taken part in the proceedings, and a Foreign Ministry official said Iran refused to participate because "we think the court is not entitled to hear such an issue."

While pursuing these diplomatic avenues, Carter resorted to another, quite different, option and imposed sanctions against Iran of varying severity. He was not lacking in counselors who maintained that in a presidential election year, he must radiate a tough image in foreign affairs. Contemporary presidential elections characteristically find at least one candidate expounding the virtues of "standing up to the Russians" and not letting the United States be "pushed around any more," both long considered politically profitable themes. But any toughness Carter might display would be constrained by the desire and the necessity of avoiding harm to the hostages.

Early in the crisis, a tough-acting Carter suspended purchases of Iranian oil, deported Iranian students living illegally in the United States, and blocked Iranian assets in American banks. These moves were expected to have only weak effect at best. World oil markets, for example, could readily absorb the Iranian oil that would have gone to the United States, and oil companies could acquire oil for American needs from other sources. Each day, said Carter, he would "turn the screws a little tighter" to increase pressure on Iran. His moves were received with warm approbation in Congress and in other leadership quarters. AFL-CIO president George Meany, while often caustic toward Carter, found that in the hostage crisis he was acting "wisely and well." Senator Jacob K. Javits (R-N.Y.), ranking member of the Foreign Relations Committee, said that Carter was doing "everything that can be done" to gain the hostages' release. Even Senator Edward M. Kennedy, Carter's highly critical rival in the 1980 primaries, assured the President of his support.[26]

Not equally forthcoming were the allies, whom Carter asked to demonstrate their support of the United States by not expanding oil imports from Iran. Although West Germany, France, and Italy responded approvingly, Japan, Iran's major oil client, did not. As time dragged on, with the hostages still captive, Carter urged the allies to follow the American lead and ban all exports to Iran except food and medicine, withdraw their ambassadors, and consider breaking diplomatic relations. But the allies, for whom such steps would be far more costly than for the United States, declined to comply. Carter's opponents, sectors of the press, and even some supporters began asserting that his presumably tough moves were more cosmetic than real, at least for the United States.

Despite these rumblings, the hostage crisis was for Carter manna from the political heavens. With the 1980 presidential election only a year away, his standing in public opinion polls had dropped to the depths occupied by Richard Nixon in his worst moments of the Watergate scandal. In the suddenly erupting hostage crisis, Americans, as they generally do in national emergency, rallied around the President. Carter made an extraordinary recovery in the polls, spurred also by the nation's approval of his course of prudence and restraint. The earlier gaffes of his administration now seemed forgotten, his faltering bid for reelection was revived, and Democratic and Republican professionals alike agreed that Carter's handling of the crisis made him look more like a leader, more presidential.[27] But as months passed and the crisis persisted, its seriousness suddenly magnified by the Soviet's invasion of Afghanistan, the public grew restive and Carter's popularity again skidded. By April 1980 it was racing toward its precrisis low, which it attained in June.[28]

## Acting Tough

With his political prospects again heavy with gloom, Carter now abandoned his course of restraint. He raised, not once but repeatedly, the possibility of such military moves as a blockade or mining Iranian harbors if the earlier imposed sanctions failed to achieve the hostages' release. Under stepped-up American pressure, the foreign ministers of the European Economic Community agreed that at a future date, if "decisive progress" had not been made toward the hostages' release, they would reduce diplomatic ties with Iran and ban all exports to Iran except food and medicine. Although the date finally chosen was somewhat later than it preferred, the administration hailed the allies' step, hoping to gain benefits for the President's weakening political fortunes.

The allies had reached their decisions with unconcealed reluctance, due, at this juncture, less to the high costs involved than to growing doubts about the Carter administration's competence in conducting foreign policy

---

### Public Opinion in the Hostage Crisis

---

Do you approve or disapprove of the way Jimmy Carter is handling the crisis in Iran?

|            | April 1980 | Dec. 1979 |
|------------|------------|-----------|
| *Approve*    | 40%        | 77%       |
| *Disapprove* | 49%        | 19%       |
| *Don't know* | 11%        | 4%        |

---

President Carter severed diplomatic relations with Iran, ordered Iranian diplomats out of the U.S., and placed a formal embargo on trade between the two countries. What do you think of these actions?

| | |
|------------------|------|
| *Too tough*        | 4%   |
| *Not tough enough* | 51%  |
| *About right*      | 42%  |
| *Don't know*       | 3%   |

---

---

linked to the hostage crisis. At the 1980 Common Market meetings, the West European foreign ministers acknowledged privately that their public actions were really designed to keep the President from doing something calamitous. "We're not sure, frankly, what Carter intends to do," a foreign minister said. The allies' chosen course was "to go along with his preliminary arrangements for Armageddon and spin them out as long as possible in the hope that something would turn up to ease the situation in the meantime." [29] Above all, the Europeans meant to head off American military action.

In diplomatic circles and in the European press, comment was increasingly disparaging of American policy and its makers. Editorial assessments in the British, French, and German press included such expressions as "incompetent," "Amateur Night," "failure to think things through," "faulty crisis planning," "Washington's Babel of statements." André Fontaine, deputy director of *Le Monde*, wrote, "If there is unanimity in France today, it is on the low esteem in which Jimmy Carter is held." Of the President's foreign policy-making associates, the Europeans often praised Secretary of State Cyrus R. Vance, an advocate of patient negotiation who had declared he would retire at the end of 1980 regardless of the election results. They scorned the President's national security adviser, Zbigniew Brzezinski, perceived as a tireless exponent of hard-line approaches to foreign policy issues. They blamed Carter for not making clear which of his two associates really spoke for the United States.[30]

Amidst these grumblings, a startling and explosive event fulfilled the allies' misgivings. A military effort to rescue the hostages ended in failure almost as it began, leaving behind eight bodies in the flaming wreckage of one helicopter and a C-130 transport, and five other helicopters, one crippled by a hydraulic malfunction. According to White House explanations, President Carter decided on April 11, 1980 to go ahead with the rescue mission and on April 14 ordered it to proceed. On April 25, after extensive preparations and maneuvers, eight RH-53 helicopters on the carrier *Nimitz*, stationed off the Iranian coast, took off for Iran. Their destination was the Dasht-i-Kavit salt desert in eastern Iran near the town of Posht-i-Badan. One helicopter turned back because of mechanical problems, and mechanical failures forced a second to land short of the destination. The helicopter fleet, reduced to six, with no margin for further errors, rendezvoused in the desert with six C-130s, arriving from staging areas in the Middle East. The rescue plan called for the helicopters to refuel and then fly on to "nest" overnight in mountains near Teheran.

While refueling was proceeding, still another helicopter suffered mechanical failure, leaving the rescue mission with only five usable helicopters, one fewer than the minimum the mission's planners had specified as necessary. At this point Defense Secretary Harold Brown and top military commanders decided to terminate the mission and ordered the planes and helicopters to return to their bases. As the transports and helicopters prepared to take off, a helicopter collided with a C-130. Both craft were instantly engulfed in flames, killing eight aboard and injuring four. The rescue team, which had been on the ground for nearly three hours, abandoned the helicopters, and boarded the five remaining C-130s.[31]

## Crisis as Administrative Politics

In the aftermath of surprise, regret, criticism, and renewed commitment, another jarring event quickly followed. Secretary of State Cyrus Vance resigned on the ground, he stated, of his inability to support Carter's decision to attempt to rescue the hostages. The President accepted the resignation as a "correct decision." Surprise and shock welled up in Washington, since the resignation of a cabinet officer is a rarity, and Vance was reputedly a team player who disliked public venting of internal administrative conflicts. Following the Soviet invasion of Afghanistan and the Iranians' endless intransigence, Vance's preference for patient negotiation fell into eclipse, with the President no longer willing to follow what a White House aide called "Vance's soft policy." Vance, who knew of the rescue plans in advance, told the President on April 21, three days before they commenced, that he would quit if the effort went ahead.[32]

In the special policy review structures provided for the Iranian crisis, Vance's competitor, Brzezinski, had thrust himself into a highly advantageous position, both to assert his point of view and to make it prevail. Each morning a small group of senior officials met in the windowless, wood-paneled Situation Room in the basement of the White House to review the hostage situation and its latest manifestations. Brzezinski prepared the agenda, presided over the meeting, and at its close, he or an aide prepared a memorandum for the President, usually three pages long, typed single-spaced. Known as the Special Coordinating Committee of the National Security Council and spoken of as the "crisis management" unit for the hostage situation, the committee characteristically brought together the top membership of the National Security Council, including Vance, various White House aides, and the Secretaries of Treasury and Energy. Carter himself did not usually attend, preferring to meet with smaller groups of senior advisers, without their aides present.[33] In presiding, in setting the agenda, and especially in preparing the summary for the President's information, Brzezinski had unique and potent opportunities, far superior to those of his colleagues, to make his views prevail in the President's decision.

Secretary of State Vance, the principal victim of this imbalance in the structure of advice, also suffered from unfavorable twists and turns of the presidency's bureaucratic, policy-development operations. Sometime before leaving for a long-planned weekend in Florida on April 10, he had been shown the latest Pentagon rescue plan, with the understanding that no subordinate would be told about it. In Vance's absence, the Deputy Secretary of State, Warren M. Christopher, represented the State Department at a meeting of the National Security Council on April 11. President Carter disclosed his inclination to proceed with the rescue mission and solicited opinions from those present. Christopher said nothing since he had not been briefed by Vance. The President stated that he wanted Vance to be heard following his journey to Florida. When he returned Vance was promptly briefed on April 14 by Christopher on the NSC session. On April 15, Vance met with the President and with other advisers and on both occasions stated his opposition to the idea of the rescue mission, a naval blockade, or any other use of force against Iran.

A former Deputy Secretary of Defense and therefore highly knowledgeable about the Pentagon's workings, Vance considered the rescue plan impractical and too risky. Despite the long impasse with Iran, Vance continued to advocate patient diplomatic efforts, supplemented by moderate political and economic sanctions, to achieve a solution. The use of force, accompanying a rescue operation, he feared, would excite the Moslem world, generate unpredictable problems, deflect attention from the Soviet invasion of Afghanistan, offend the allies, and endanger the hostages. According to an aide of Vance, the Secretary's contentions met "a loud silence" from Carter.[34]

## Safeguards That Failed

The collapse of the rescue mission exposes the presidency's large capacity for error in crisis management. Vance's resignation fortified the impression that the rescue mission was poorly considered, a reckless gambit with little chance for success, rather than the reasoned "completely practicable operation" that Carter claimed it was. The hostage crisis and the abortive rescue attempt revealed that the presidency and its decision-making capabilities are highly vulnerable to a President whose political fortunes are disintegrating as he struggles for a second term in office. In desperation, Carter abandoned his course of prudence, crossed to the other side of the policy street and gambled on an improbable quick success. The rescue mission, if it had succeeded, would doubtless have provided him a new lease on public favor for months if not years to come. But as Vance and others readily predicted, the venture failed.

No mechanisms in the presidency worked to save Carter from this folly. The processes of the National Security Council, originally conceived to promote debate among the President's counselors in his presence to assure his exposure to a breadth of views, succumbed to Brzezinski's Special Committee and his tight grip on its proceedings and to Carter's disinclination to attend its meetings or to convoke the full NSC into regular session. These procedural choices speeded the National Security adviser's ascent and the Secretary of State's decline. If salutary foreign policy-making requires continuing dialogue between advisers of differing perspectives, Carter did not encourage or safeguard that process. The spectacle of Vance standing alone among his top advisers in counseling against the rescue operation, implies that the President himself contributed to an atmosphere depressing to the free exchange of views among his counselors. Carter also revealed by the wide swings in his choices of policy that he lacked any world view to regulate his own conduct, which proved merely pliant to the surges and falls of the public opinion polls and the imperatives of his quest for reelection.

Two other potential safeguards against presidential folly were inoperative in the rescue mission's fiasco. The allies were neither consulted nor forewarned, and the opportunity for independent reasoned opinion from that invaluable source was lost. When failure struck the mission, the allies were virtually unanimous in expressions of sympathy and concern, but privately their leaders were troubled by the crisis's possible advance to more ominous stages.

A further safeguard, equally inoperative, was Congress. "They didn't consult anyone up here," said Senator Henry M. Jackson (D.- Washington), a leading advocate of strong defense. Senate Majority Leader Robert C. Byrd, who saw the President on another matter when the rescue attempt began, was furious at not being informed. Several legislators contended that the rescue attempt violated the War Powers Resolution of 1973, which requires prior consultation with Congress. But Senator Alan Cranston, the Democratic Whip, stated that in a postfiasco briefing at the White House of some dozen congressional leaders, not one dissented from "the President's right as Commander-in-Chief to take the action he took." Cranston noted that the Resolution applied to military actions, and that "This was viewed as a rescue mission, not a military action."[35]

The events just reviewed reveal how the presidency can be pushed off the track of prudent policy-making by the overriding personal political necessities of the President. For all of its abundance of cabinets and councils, expert bureaucracies, and talented officials, the executive branch could interpose no effective constraint on the President who apparently concluded that his own political survival required a big policy gamble risking the use of force. Despite the horrendous character of the Cuban missile crisis and its successful resolution, it is important to note that Kennedy was not pressed by anything like the severe political survival test confronting Carter.

A momentous question remains: How can crisis management be conducted rationally, without the use of force, when the President concludes that his political well-being requires actions risking violence?

# ★ ★ ★ The Future Presidency ★ ★ ★

1. The failure of any individual or mechanism to bring the President up short as he weighed the hostage rescue mission, to face questions and doubts, except the solitary Vance, underscores the wisdom of Kennedy's practice of consulting figures outside the circle of public office-holders, a path that led to former Presidents and patriarchs like Dean Acheson and Robert Lovett. A variant of this practice might be a formally established panel of former senior officials in the foreign affairs and national security areas whose wisdom and experience, untempered by temptations of present and future office-holding, might help give the President pause before plunging into error when other constraints fail.

2. The experience just examined invites a reconsideration of the War Powers Resolution of 1973. The Resolution's underlying operating principle is "consultation," but how the President consults Congress is not defined, and Carter easily shunned it in proceeding with the hostage rescue mission. The Resolution might be amended to delineate more closely specific situations in which presidential consultation of Congress should transpire, and included in that catalogue might be a broadened requirement of consultation before the President deploys armed forces to places where their involvement in combat might be reasonably anticipated, as in the rescue effort.

   Consultation would expose the President to questioning and candid opinion from an independent and highly knowledgeable source—Congress. The 1973 Resolution might also be amended to specify who in Congress the President must consult. By leaving this question unanswered, the law's existing provisions imply it is the entire Congress. For the President to consult with 535 legislators is unworkable; only a far smaller group is feasible. Conceivably those consulted might be designated as the foreign relations and armed services committees of the two houses. The President might consult more faithfully if the path of consultation led to some relatively small group with whom he could deal readily and meaningfully.

3. The allied countries and their leaders too might become more closely linked to the President's crisis management activities, a fair objective, since the fate of their people can be determined by his stewardship. The outline of a possible development is suggested by the recent practice of holding an annual economic conference of the President and the heads of government of the larger European allies and Japan. An additional meeting might deal with a military-foreign affairs agenda that might include discussion of developing military trouble-spots, including some just barely visible on the international horizon.

   The President might enhance his perspectives by soliciting the counsel of the allied leaders. The allies' likely preference is for peaceful options, as in the hostage crisis, and that sentiment, voiced by many leaders, might prompt the President to value nonviolent solutions of a crisis more highly.

4. The President might be more apt to pursue a nonviolent course if the Secretary of State were allotted a loftier, more secure place in his counsels. As principal manager of the diplomatic function, the Secretary is the officer of the executive branch whose mission and interest is most identified with maintaining peace as an uppermost priority of crisis management.

How might the Secretary be restored to an estate of influence? His hand could be strengthened if the committee structure of the National Security Council, which now enhances the influence of the national security adviser, were revised to enlarge the role of the Secretary of State. In the NSC's early years, in the Truman and Eisenhower eras, the Secretary of State was the chief developer of the NSC's agenda, a circumstance fostered by his dominance of the NSC's staff and committee processes. Both Truman and Eisenhower closely confined the national security assistant's role and he lacked any semblance of the committee functions the assistant wields today. For the Secretary of State to ascend again, he must be a figure who is solid in the President's confidence, knowledgeable about foreign affairs, and skilled in bureaucratic politics. Kissinger, Acheson, Dulles are serviceable prototypes of the ascendant Secretary of State.

# Chapter Sixteen

# The Presidency Compared

Comparisons, we are often warned, are odious. But comparisons have a special usefulness in the study of political institutions. We can better estimate the value of one political institution if we measure its performance against other institutions. We can better perceive what the American presidency has been and what it might become if we compare it with other relevant institutions of our own and other political societies. The comparisons may illuminate those aspects of the presidency that reflect our deepest traditions and most tightly held values and those aspects, as well, that represent large and clear exceptions to the established ways of our political community. In other political systems may be discovered democracy-enhancing practices that may be adapted to the American system.

The American President invites comparison with the other members of the nation's family of political executives: the state governor and the local chief executive. As with most families, the several executives bear certain resemblances to each other, and any one of them has influenced the development of all. They have imitated and inspired one another and have felt the brunt of common historical forces. The governor and the mayor can rightfully be viewed as presidential-type executives, having the contours and much of the power and function of the national executive.

# The Governor

In shaping the presidency, the Founding Fathers were influenced to a large degree by the New York governorship; weaknesses in other governorships warned them of mistakes to avoid. The state governorship was influenced by experience with the colonial governorship, which was commonly viewed as the agency of monarchic tyranny. Thus, state constitution-makers in the Revolutionary era tended to look askance at the strong executive, and they chose to concentrate power in the state legislatures, which during the colonial crisis acquired a reputation as defenders of the popular interest. But the abuses that state legislatures made of their powers caused the Founding Fathers to resolve to create a presidency of substantial strength.

Although the presidency and the governorship have swelled in influence and power since the eighteenth century, the latter has always been the substantially weaker of the two executive offices. The change was slow-building for the governor. In the early state constitutions, legislative supremacy was firmly established. According to many constitutions, the legislature appointed the governor, and the governor lacked a veto power over legislation. Leadership in public policy reposed with the legislature. Unlike the President, whose power derived from general constitutional provisions permitting generous interpretation and enlargement, the governor had to struggle for the increase of power through the rewriting of state constitutions and by wringing out concessions of power from the legislature. The Jacksonian era caused more governors and their fellow executive officials (including, sometimes, even prison superintendents) to be popularly elected and entrusted more power to their care, but all through the nineteenth century, while Jackson, Lincoln, and Cleveland demonstrated the primacy of the presidency, the legislature endured as the dominant instrument of state policy-making.

It is in the twentieth century that the governor comes into his own, through forces in that era that served to enlarge the President's influence and power. The increase of government's social and economic tasks, especially from the First World War onward, and the ever-broadening base of democratic government profited both the governor and the President. In addition, the governor gained from new constitutions and executive reorganizations that imitated the presidential model. As well, the clear inadequacy of the state legislature in an era of positive government contributed to the governor's growth in function and power. Yet there remains an ambiguity about the role of the states, and therefore of the governor, in public affairs. The states fall somewhere between local government, with its natural responsibility for urban or local problems, and the national government, which most naturally deals with foreign affairs and problems incident to a grand-scale economy. The states lack any comparable natural jurisdictions enjoyed by the other governments.

## The Presidency's Influence

If a typical early governor were compared with a typical contemporary governor, the influence of the presidency upon gubernatorial change would become evident. Most contemporary governors enjoy a four-year term rather than the one- or two-year span of their predecessors. A little more than half the governors can be reelected to the office indefinitely, while in earlier times a one-term limitation was commonplace. Early governors shared the exercise of their veto power with a council, on which legislators might be represented, yet the present-day governor enjoys a veto power over his legislature fully equal to the President's. Indeed four-fifths of the governors enjoy an advantage that the President lacks, except by the questionable exercise of impoundment—an item veto over individual appropriations in general revenue bills. The governor's power to appoint his administrative colleagues, long a source of weakness because these key figures might be popularly elected or chosen by the legislature, has improved to the point where more than half the governors can appoint, with or without the consent of their senates, the heads of the chief departments and the budget and tax officers. A major source of the President's power in the executive branch is his strong appointing power.

In the general layout of his functions and powers, in the relationship of the incumbent's personality to the office, the governor resembles the President, although with important variations springing from differences between the nation and the states and the imprint of historic forces and tradition. Like the presidency, the governorship provides a spacious arena for the play of personality. Just as the presidency has developed under the touch of creative incumbents, the governorship developed strength and resilience in the tenures of Robert M. La Follette in Wisconsin, Hiram Johnson and Earl Warren in California, Charles Evans Hughes and Alfred E. Smith in New York, Gifford Pinchot in Pennsylvania, to mention a few. Some governors, such as Woodrow Wilson of New Jersey and Franklin Roosevelt of New York, displayed skills and indulged in techniques of leadership that they later applied with marked success in the Presidency. In the 1970s, the energy crisis, revenue sharing, and the scaled-down domestic priorities of the Nixon presidency shunted more burdens on the governors. The conservative tendencies of the Ford presidency continued the trend and spurred more innovative policies from the governors. Gasoline rationing was first instituted by Governor Tom McCall of Oregon, who also rallied his state to antigrowth policies by illuminating the dangers of Oregon's unchecked expansion of population and industry. In Pennsylvania, Governor Milton J. Shapp advanced a comprehensive, state-wide plan to regulate and administer health services in seeking to contain "skyrocketing medical costs."[1] Long a source of recruitment for the presidency, the governor after World War II was eclipsed by United States Senators and other national offices. Carter was the first governor to occupy the White House since Franklin Roosevelt.

## Power and Politics

Just as the President tends to be the outstanding political leader in the nation, the governor enjoys the same distinction in the smaller domain of the state. The governor, more than other political personalities in the state, is identified with the "general public good." Whatever he does makes news in the local press. Radio and television can command him a state-wide audience; he travels frequently about the state, makes numerous personal appearances, handles a high volume of correspondence and telephone calls, and receives large quantities of visitors. Many governors keep their doors open to one and all who wish to interview them. Coleman B. Ransone, Jr., in his study of the governorship, concluded that public relations is the most time-consuming role of the state executive.[2] As with the President, much of the governor's success turns upon his skill as a party and legislative leader. His party role most resembles the President's in states that are populous and where a genuine two-party system flourishes. The interparty competition fosters a discipline that the governor can exploit as party leader. In some states, particularly in the South and Middle West, there is a steady one-party dominance that casts the governor in a role as the leader of a party faction or a coalition of factions whose support he manages to attract. In the factional structure, state politics may become highly responsive to the governor's personality. Georgia, therefore, in the era of its colorful Governor Gene "Red Suspenders" Talmadge, was dominated by Talmadge and anti-Talmadge factions, and Louisiana, in the heyday of Huey Long, by Long and anti-Long factions. A governor is less apt than the President to be the acknowledged leader of his party because he may have rivals for the role in one or both of the United States Senators of his state.

The governor, like the President, is heavily judged by his success as legislative leader. Increasingly most of the important policies that the legislature considers come from the governor or the executive departments. As legislative leader, the governor enjoys political means that are fully comparable to the President's. He reports to the legislature on the conditions of the state and recommends legislation. Much turns upon his ability to persuade legislators of both major parties to support his proposals. He has the inducements of patronage and public works construction—nothing can be more eloquent than building a new highway in a legislator's district; he can speak in support of a legislator's candidacy; or he can grant a pardon to one of his constituents. The governor's power is also buttressed by substantial formal authority. He gains leverage from budget-making powers if he has them, which enables him to include or omit the favorite projects of legislators.

Most governors can also gain leverage with the item veto, enabling them to veto particular provisions of a bill rather than the entire bill. Legislators, however, may blunt the effect of the item veto by combining objectionable and unobjectionable items in the same clause. The item veto also invites buckpassing, by which legislators vote appropriations with the expectation that the governor will bear the political blame for disallowing them.[3] In four states—Alabama, Massachusetts, New Jersey, and Virginia—the governor has an "amendatory" veto. He can return a bill without his signature to the house where it originated, with suggestions for change that would make it acceptable to him. The legislature first considers the question of accepting the changes before deciding whether to pass the bill over his veto or return it to him for final consideration. The device has strengthened the governor's hand in shaping legislation. Like the President, the governor can call the legislature into special session, and, unlike the President, he can, in about half the states, specify the matters to be considered, thus increasing executive authority over the legislative agenda.

But even more than the President, the governor faces a formidable legislative power structure. In most state legislatures, the speaker of the house, the presiding officer of the senate, and the chairmen of the leading standing committees, enjoy authority and influence that overshadow the substantial power of their counterparts in Congress. In the states, the rules of seniority, geographical distribution, and party representation are often far less well established than in Congress, thus enhancing the leaders' influence. The leaders, that is, can be more arbitrary in the selecting of committee slates and committee chairmen. Further, the general body of legislators are more dependent upon the personal favor of the legislative leaders and more pressed to win and keep their approval than in the national Congress where these matters are more regularized. The actions of state legislative leaders are, in addition, less covered by official written records and the press. The resulting obscurity increases the power of legislative leaders to manipulate against the governor.

The governor is also an administrative chief whose powers are more qualified than the President's. In nearly four-fifths of the states, he shares administrative power with other elected executives: the secretary of state, the attorney general, the treasurer, the controller, and others who already are or will be his political competitors. A heavy trend in the states toward the creation of independent agencies, authorities, and commissions, endowed with their own fiscal powers, represents incursions into the governor's administrative primacy on a scale well exceeding the President's difficulties with the independent commissions. Frequently the governor lacks power to appoint or remove a department head, and many departments may not be subject to the executive budget and other fiscal controls. Not surprisingly, governors tend to feel that administration should receive no heavy portion of their time and that success in that endeavor contributes little to their reelection.

For the rest, the governorship reflects the presidential system, although on a smaller scale and with milder strength. The governor is commander-in-chief of the state military forces, a capacity of special importance in the Revolutionary era, when not a few governors commanded in the field. The governor may enter into industrial and civil rights disputes, under his duty to assist local officials in maintaining public order. The governor conducts various external relationships that more or less parallel the President's activity in foreign affairs. He is the official organ of communications between his state and other states and with the national government. He certifies election results in his state for national officers; the state's participation in federal-state cooperative programs may turn upon his approval; he may make "good will" visits abroad and compete with other governors for foreign investments in his state.

# The Mayor

Of the several types of local executives, the one most deeply rooted in the American tradition—the mayor—also fits most securely into the presidential pattern. Two other forms of the local executive that first appeared in the twentieth century—the city manager, who is a professional and appointed executive, and the commission, in reality a plural executive—constitute sharp departures from the presidential format and therefore will not concern us here.

Some mayors have become Presidents: Cleveland of Buffalo, Andrew Johnson of Greenville, Tennessee, and Coolidge of Northhampton, Massachusetts. But according to a long-standing axiom, the office of mayor is a political deadend. Political scientist Russell Murphy challenges this contention after studying the careers of several major categories of officeholders. He found that although the record of further officeholding by mayors is modest, it compares favorably with other offices—not significantly better or worse than the advancement rate for governors, Congressmen, and Senators.[4]

For the mayor, the political process is more personalized than for the President and the governor. The mayor's policies have more immediate and tangible impact on his constituents, and his constituents have direct knowledge of his performance. A standard mayoral experience is face to face confrontations with citizens. The supposition that different personality traits and political skills are attracted to the mayoralty than to the governorship and the presidency is encouraged by the difficulty of imagining John Kennedy as mayor of Boston, Richard Nixon as mayor of Los Angeles, or Richard Daly as President.[5]

Like the governor, the mayor has long been engaged in a struggle to convert insubstantial powers into strength. Of the two general types of mayor plans, the older is the "weak mayor," widely prevalent in the nineteenth century and still the predominant plan in middle-size and smaller cities. Under that plan, various executive and administrative officers are either popularly elected or are appointed by the city council or legislature. Budget-making powers and powers of administrative supervision are reserved to the council. Los Angeles and Atlanta are the principal cities employing the "weak mayor" plan.

In the twentieth century the nation's largest cities have been veering sharply to the second type of mayor plan—the "strong mayor"—which bears greater resemblances to the presidential model. In theory, at least, the plan seeks to establish the mayor as the chief executive with the fullest possible control over departments and agencies; it empowers him to prepare a comprehensive executive budget and to propose legislation. He possesses a strong veto power and enjoys broad powers of appointment and removal. Practice is some steps removed from theory. Of the largest cities, only Boston and Cleveland make the mayor the sole elected incumbent of the principal executive offices; in New York, Chicago, and Detroit, the mayor shares budget and administrative powers with other governmental organs that he does not direct or control. In Chicago, for example, a council committee prepares the budget.

## The Big City Mayor

It is useful for students of the presidency to examine the strong, big city mayor type because it illuminates dependence and weakness at the local level of government that could conceivably appear in a later day at the presidential level. The big city mayor is the front-line soldier who deals with major problems of American domestic politics located as they are in the urban sector. The problems of health, education, civil rights, housing, and the others that are prominent on the President's agenda are the daily grist of the big city mayor. The mayor meets close up, and in the most concentrated form, problems from which the President enjoys a greater distance and whose priority he can balance and juggle with his nonurban concerns, especially those in foreign affairs. Despite the resemblances of his formal powers to the President's, the mayor's actual power to deal with the problems is only a fraction of the national executive's substantial capacity to act.

The gap between what the mayor can do and what the President can do is all the more striking since both officers have been buffeted by common historic social forces. Both the President and the mayor are affected by the radical change in the urban environment of late decades. The radical alteration of the composition of its population, the ever-enlarging bureaucratization of government, and the almost infinite appetite for government services are the common lot of mayors and Presidents. Faced with these common pressures, the President, on the whole, has been able to respond— if he chooses to—with greater initiative and force than the mayor. The explanation does not lie wholly in the superiority of federal resources. Especially important are essential differences in the political environments of the mayor and the President.

The mayors of the great cities, as political sociologist Scott Greer has suggested, reign but do not rule.[6] Big city mayors often assume heroic or presidential poses and work hard at constructing images of vigorous creative leadership that are some distance removed from the record of actual achievement. The watchword with big city mayors is caution. They preside over routine, caretaker governments and struggle with urgent and complex problems without the capacity to mount major offensives or launch bold initiatives. Meanwhile the problems and the forces producing them work their havoc. Industry continues its move to the suburbs; the differentiation between the central city and the suburban populations becomes ever sharper; the predominance of city groups who suffer most from economic depression grows apace. The strong mayor must endure several handicaps from his political environment. His governmental jurisdiction, although large, is not large enough. His city is one among a number of governmental divisions of a metropolis, which consists of numerous municipalities, counties, and special districts, each empowered to do certain tasks and to withhold cooperation from other local governments.

Big city government is largely one-party government, or in reality nonpartisan government. The big city mayor tends to be the dominant political personality in the metropolitan area. Yet for all of his prominence, his ability to achieve political results is modest. One-party government frees the mayor from many pressures, but the freedom he enjoys is negative rather than positive. He is free from partisan limitations, but not free to make new and radical departures. With the evaporation of the threat of electoral defeat that the one-party system affords, the party structure loses its discipline, on which the mayor, or any executive, depends to push his program through the legislature. In the one-party arrangement, the central city electorate becomes a captive electorate of the Democratic party, which dominates the big cities. There is no effective alternative party to turn to, and the electorate tends toward passivity. The mayor must cope with factional leaders who have substantial personal and political power, wielded in the legislature and in appointed and elected executive posts.

The big city mayor must also cope with a huge bureaucracy that easily eludes his control. New York City, for example, has a bureaucracy of 350,000. There and elsewhere, the bureaucracy may cling to established ways and resist innovation, which is viewed as a threat to the existing distribution of power and privilege. In the cities, the indulgence in independent agencies and authorities is even greater than in the states, which further bolsters the autonomy of municipal bureaucracies.

Above all, the big city is hobbled by political segregation, by the separation of numbers and wealth, by the concentration of population in the central city and resources in the suburbs, by the separation of need from means. In effect, government is segregated by social class, with the middle class on the one hand, and the lower classes on the other, each having its own local government. Relations between the central city and the suburb are ruled by mutual suspicion, an attitude that can be profitably exaggerated by candidates for office.

The Carter presidency reinforced the heavy clouds hanging over the cities. Preaching a gospel of retrenchment in an era of high inflation, with reduced spending for urban and social programs, Carter was denounced by an aggrieved United States Conference of Mayors who called his fiscal 1980 budget a "disappointment to the cities." The cities reflect regional differences in their perceptions of appropriate presidential policies. Leaders of older Northern cities seek more fiscal aid and funds for public jobs to maintain basic services, while still-growing Western and Southern cities tend toward fiscal conservatism and are preoccupied with paving streets and adding sewer lines. Growing realization that federal aid is no longer expanding adds heat to the squabbling over urban priorities. Particularly mayors of the older great cities felt caught between a frugal President, Carter, and a conservative Congress. Mayor Coleman Young of Detroit posed the unhappy prospect: "As conservative as the President's proposals are, Congress' attitude is even worse."[7]

# Foreign Executives: Selection and Tenure

The strengths and weaknesses of the American Presidency and the possible linkings of Executive power with democratic norms also may be better perceived if we examine the chief executives of other major nations. We may find in the experience of others clues for eliminating flaws from our own system and for keeping up better in the race every nation is running against the forces of change. Possibly, too, we may take some small comfort if we find that weaknesses that afflict the American Chief Executive are also bedeviling other nations.

The 1970s, which brought Watergate and Richard Nixon's resignation, was a period of general instability for the leaderships of major western political systems. In Britain, Edward Heath was deposed by a national election, and the ministry of his successor, Harold Wilson, was tarnished by a land-buying scandal that touched his personal staff.

Ultimately, Wilson resigned. His successor, James Callaghan, after scraping by a series of votes of confidence, was turned out of office by a margin of just one vote, and replaced by the Conservative government of Margaret Thatcher, the first such overthrow since Labor Prime Minister Ramsay MacDonald was defeated in 1924. In France, after the death of President Georges Pompidou, his Gaullist party failed in the national elections to prevail in the selection of his successor. Willy Brandt, seemingly popular and enduring in the West German chancellorship, was suddenly ejected from office when it was revealed that an East German spy occupied a principal position on his staff. In the Middle East, Israel witnessed a shift of leadership, as did Japan in the Far East. Canadian Prime Minister Joe Clark, after a tenure of a mere six months, lost a vote of confidence in the House of Commons largely because of his policy of energy conservation through modest price increases.

Why this sudden general political "decline of the West"? A pervasive factor is the frailty of leaders and their associates, physically and judgmentally. Another is the juggernaut of problems that democratic governments seem incapable of solving or even slowing—unemployment and inflation as well as shortages of food, energy, and other life essentials. Still other forces beset leadership: Enhanced education levels that have fostered rising expectations and a greater willingness to sharply question institutions and to reject leadership; the media's capacity for instant global communication as well as the availability of a limitless canvass more than sufficient to support the journalistic penchant for bad news rather than good news; and the rapidity and severity of change that befalls the individual and with which government constantly demonstrates it cannot cope.[8] The nations yearn for leaders who will achieve, but they seldom appear.

Even when they offer themselves, no major nation can boast a method of selecting its chief executive that assures a choice from among the proverbial "best men available" by means that are assuredly democratic. Because of the enormous stakes, the contest is almost universally a great scramble to which the arts of pressure and maneuver are fully committed. It is an enterprise in which democratic values and procedures are vulnerable. The United States prefers its Presidents from large states and therefore arbitrarily excludes worthy contenders from the small. It requires long primary campaigns, thus loading the dice for the candidate with money, and who is politically unemployed and therefore has unlimited disposable time. The creaky electoral college machinery is a standing invitation to disaster in opening wide the gates of chance that a presidential cnadidate with a minority of popular votes may be elected.

## Choosing the British Prime Minister

In Great Britain the selection of the Prime Minister after a national election follows a well-regulated routine. The voters elect a new House of Commons, and the leader of the majority party is automatically made the new Prime Minister. Following the election, the Queen requests the leader of the winning party to form a government, in effect ratifying the electorate's choice. But the selection of the party leader in the first place, prior to his appearance before the electorate, is largely a matter of intraparty maneuver. The magic key is the building of support among the factions. Harold Wilson bested George Brown in their contest for the Labor leadership in 1963 as a kind of middle-of-the-roader who had least offended the factions whose support was vital. When Labor won the national elections the following year, it was only a formality for the Queen to summon Wilson to form a new government. Wilson's successor as Prime Minister, Edward Heath, outpaced his chief rival in the Conservative party, Reginald Maudling, an achievement that was enormously aided by the previous Conservative Prime Minister, Sir Alec Douglas-Home, who meted out to Heath the choice ministerial appointments, assignments, and other preferences.[9] And party leaders were impressed that in a potentially close election some of Heath's personal qualities might provide the margin of victory—his possession of Wilson's most attractive attributes: humble origins, drive, comprehension of technical economics, and commitment to efficiency and modernization.

But the progression of Margaret Thatcher to the post of Conservative Party Leader, the springboard from which she catapulted into the Prime Ministership in 1979, was rather less orthodox. Traditionally, the party leader is a conciliator of factions and, as seeker of the Prime Ministership, exponent of broad doctrines to capture a majority of voters. Thatcher, however, is an ideologue who both as Party Leader and as Prime Minister means to restore her party's historic conservativism as she perceives it. The party rank and file were dismayed that Heath had taken the Conservative party too far to the left, was insufficiently responsive to their views, and was the engineer of defeats in two successive national elections. Conservatives widely supported Thatcher's contest with Heath's factional heirs to become Party Leader. Like Carter, Mrs. Thatcher was an outsider to the Conservative party's leadership circle, and like Reagan, and perhaps even more so, she expounded right-of-center policies represented as the true heritage of her party.[10]

The American President, once elected, enjoys extraordinary stability of tenure, decidedly greater than the British Prime Minister's and rather less than that of the President of the French Fifth Republic. The sole legitimate means of removing the American President—impeachment—is constructed to operate only in the utmost extremity. Presidents as unpopular as Buchanan and Hoover persisted in office until the next inauguration even though the majority of public opinion was set against them.

For more than a year, until he resigned in the face of certain impeachment, Nixon endured despite widespread public belief that he was guilty of criminal acts and the severe drain that this shadowed status inflicted upon his effectiveness. In Britain, Nixon would have been ejected from office in a matter of weeks by the pressure of his parliamentary party responding to hostile public opinion.

## France and West Germany

France's selection process can be as lengthy as the United States' process, although their governmental structures differ. President Valéry Giscard d'Estaing and Prime Minister Raymond Barre govern through a coalition.

With a presidential election scheduled for 1981, coalition politics was used tactically in Parliament by aspirants for the office more than a year before the election. A principal candidate, Jacques Chirac, head of the Gaullist party, a coalition partner of the Government, repeatedly forced the President and Prime Minister to use an emergency procedure to get important legislation through Parliament. The procedure, under Article 49 of the Constitution, is humiliating and undemocratic, since the Government is forced to declare the legislation a question of confidence. It automatically became law, because the Gaullists were pledged not to bring down the Government and force elections. Why did Chirac resort so often to this convoluted procedure? Because, politicians agreed, he was seeking to discredit Giscard before launching his own bid for the presidency in 1981.[11]

In West Germany, the election of 1980 bore resemblances to many an American presidential election with narrow policy differences between the candidates for Chancellor, incumbent Helmut Schmidt of the Social Democrats and Franz Josef Strauss standard-bearer of the Christian Democrats. Like the British Prime Minister, the Chancellor is not elected by the public directly, but by the Bundestag, the popular branch of the two-house Parliament. Similar to American elections, the 1980 election emphasized personality and tactics. Given the importance of American foreign policy to Germany, both candidates vied to demonstrate their capacity for close ties with President Carter; both visited Carter soon after the electoral campaign began.[12]

## Terminating Tenure: U.S.S.R.

In 1964, Russia experienced another October revolution, this time a palace revolution resulting in Premier Nikita Khrushchev's overthrow. The initial external signs of that event were placid but lethal. First, Khrushchev had not spoken to the cosmonauts after their landing, contrary to custom, which reserves proud national ceremonies to the top leader. As it happened, he could not, since he was flying to Moscow at that joyous moment under heavy escort. In the press, his name was not mentioned, as normally it would be, in an article in *Izvestia* commemorating the twenty-fifth anniversary of the liberation of the Ukraine in the Second World War. Indeed, his name had suddenly vanished everywhere, as though a blue pencil had deleted all references to him from every Soviet newspaper on the first evening of his apprehension. Thus began the plunge of Khruschev, the leader who had presided over the country's fortunes for a decade, into the ignominy of an unperson.[13] Where before his friends of the Central Committee had saved him, they now forsook him. The committee replaced Khrushchev as First Secretary of the party with his own protégé of many years, Leonid Brezhnev, and delivered the crowning blow of disgrace by taking away Khrushchev's seat on the party Presidium. He next was stripped of his governmental position as Premier, and that post was handed to his successor, Alexei Kosygin.[14]

# Succession Compared

When the vice presidency is filled, the American presidency clearly holds the advantage over other chief executives in handling the problem of succession. John Kennedy's assassination, for all its rending tragedy, was also the occasion of a remarkable demonstration of the velocity and assurance with which executive power can be transferred in the American system. Less than two hours after Kennedy's death the presidential oath was administered to Vice President Johnson, with Mrs. Kennedy by his side, herself a brave witness to the continuity of the American system. With Nixon ousted, Ford immediately succeeded him.

## British Succession

Nearly a month before the catastrophe in Texas, a succession occurred in the British Prime Ministership. The procedure of deciding who the new Prime Minister should be took all of eleven days to consummate, with lengthy passages of farce and satire. Through much of this anguished interlude, the effort to find a successor to the ill and hospitalized Prime Minister Harold Macmillan foundered upon the deadlock of two intractable and opposed groups in the Conservative party. To the left were the liberal revisionists, headed by R. A. Butler, Deputy Prime Minister in the Macmillan cabinet and the man who, according to party and public opinion polls, enjoyed the greatest backing. Prime Minister Macmillan reportedly wished above all else to bar Butler's succession. A second major contender was Viscount Hailsham of the Conservative right wing. Several lesser contenders made up the field. Early in his quest for an heir, Macmillan pressed Alec Douglas-Home, the Foreign Secretary, to enter the lists, but Home declined.

Buttonholing and telephoning proceeded intensively. Hailsham's candidacy began to sag with Home's advance, although Butler's held strong. Meanwhile Home, notwithstanding heavy pressure from Macmillan, would not declare his candidacy. Macmillan, bound to his sickbed, dreaded a deadlock that would entitle the monarch to send for Harold Wilson, leader of the opposition Labor Party, who would have then formed a government, dissolved Parliament, and called an election. Macmillan again appealed to Home, who now acquiesced.

Hours before Macmillan resigned and presented Home's name to the Queen, an emergency cabal led by Ian Macleod, cochairman of the Conservative party and leader of the House of Commons, and Enoch Powell, Minister of Health, met with Martin Redmayne, the party's chief whip, who was requested to inform Macmillan that both Hailsham and a third candidate, Reginald Maudling, were prepared to support Butler. Michael Adeane, the Queen's link with the party, was telephoned and told that, irrespective of what Macmillan might say, Butler could now form a government. Butler telephoned Macmillan at King Edward VII's Hospital, but the call was not accepted. Macmillan resigned, presented his written estimate to the Queen, with supplementary oral comment. The Queen sent for the Earl of Home. In the aftermath, critics assailed Home's elevation "on the heap of blackballs cast against his three rivals" and the "tricky maneuver-ings" of Macmillan and Redmayne and called for "modernization" of the selection procedure.[15] More typically, succession in the Prime Ministership is simple and assured. The Parliamentary Party of both the Conservative and Labor parties elect a leader, and he normally is tapped for the Prime Minister post if his party attains a majority.

## Soviet Succession

Soviet Russia, like other dictatorships, has not solved the problem of succession. The transfer of power, for which the Soviet constitution makes no provision, can be the occasion of numbing uncertainty, subterfuge, terror, and violence. One or more of those elements attended the successions to Lenin, Stalin, and Khrushchev. Stalin's death and its aftermath disclose the jagged course of dictatorial succession. The announcement of his demise was withheld for six hours and ten minutes. A statement accompanying the eventual disclosure declared that the "most important task of the party and the government is to insure uninterrupted and correct leadership . . . the greatest unity of leadership and the prevention of any kind of disorder and panic." As historian Bertram D. Wolfe has well observed, admonitions against "disorder and panic" are inconceivable in an American transfer.[16] When power passed from Roosevelt to Truman and from Kennedy to Johnson, there were, needless to say, no comparable warnings from high places.

With Stalin's passing, a reshuffling of state and party positions proceeded. Khrushchev eventually took over the post of First Secretary of the party and consolidated his power to the point where, in an extraordinary address to the Twentieth Party Congress, he denounced the memory of Stalin, depicting him as a tyrant, a sadist, and a glutton for adulation. Among the interpretations placed upon this grotesque performance is one that Khrushchev, in effect, was pledging not to employ his newly won power according to Stalin's example.

But in time, Khrushchev too veered toward the Stalinist prototype of personalized leadership, which with his ill-regarded management of the Cuban missile crisis, plus other policy lapses, produced his overthrow. As before, in the obscure turnings of the succession machinery the identity of his successor emerged slowly. Again an interval of "collective leadership" set in, and then, by deft maneuver, Leonid Brezhnev emerged head and shoulders above such fellow sharers of leadership as Kosygin, Shelepin, and Podgorny. By mid-1965 undeniable external signs attested to Brezhnev's succession. Once the First Secretary of the party, he was now its "Secretary General"; at victory celebrations he monpolized the prime roles; in foreign relations he became the sole authoritative spokesman; and he took over the range of accessory functions that once belonged to Khrushchev.[17] Increasingly his face beamed benignly from posters and his deeds were acclaimed, more than any other figure's, on Soviet television.

With passing time, Brezhnev's colleagues of the Politburo found him less threatening to their security and confidently entrusted him with the traditional vast power of general secretary of the party. As frosting on the cake the national legislature, the Supreme Soviet, elected and reelected him President, or chairman, of its Presidium. His reelection in 1979 occurred in less than thirty-five minutes. The decision was unhampered by his visibly fragile health, making reading and enunciating difficult, and requiring an usher to assist him in ascending and descending the stairs of the podium.[18]

As Brezhnev's health deteriorated at least several rules seemed operative for choosing an eventual successor. The decision-makers, the Politburo, composed of men of advanced years, wish, above all, to avoid any prospect of reviving a "personality cult," threatening to their own security. A younger successor enhances the danger—Stalin succeeded Lenin at the age of 45—while an older successor could not govern very long if he became, like Stalin, giddy with his own importance.

Any Soviet leader aspiring to the succession must muster sufficient credentials as a "hawk" in his disposition toward the United States. Like the plague, he must shun any suspected tendency of "excessive concessions to the West," or build up too many foreign contacts that might cast doubt on his loyalty to the party faith. On the other hand, he must impress his colleagues that he is not hell-bent for confrontation with the United States.[19] In the Politburo, prudence has long reigned as a core value.

# The British Parliamentary System

Many a critic of the presidency gazes admiringly upon the British parliamentary system and proposes to graft upon the American structure some of the better elements of the British. Woodrow Wilson, both as a youthful political scientist and as a practicing President, longed to introduce the British method into American politics. He would greatly have preferred to have been a Prime Minister rather than a President and indeed tried manfully during his incumbency to nudge the office into the ways of the British model. Such legislators as George Pendleton of the nineteenth century and Estes Kefauver of the twentieth doggedly proposed to borrow from British practice to bring executive and legislative effort into purposeful cooperation. A study committee of the American Political Science Association in 1950 emerged with an ingenious plan for adapting the British party system to the circumstances of American parties.[20]

In Canada, where the parliamentary system closely resembles that of the British, the chairman of the House of Commons committee engaged in assessing a key parliamentary institution, the daily question period, asserted: "Looking at the United States, there's a lot of feeling that the whole Watergate thing might not have gone along so far if the members of the President's Cabinet had been required to spend 40 minutes in Congress every day answering questions."[21] Is the British parliamentary system better for the United States than the existing presidential system? The leading attractions of the parliamentary system are unity and coherence of policy. It encourages the executive to tackle the major problems of the day, to propose bold plans and broad programs. When the system is working at its best, the British executive has every assurance that every major thing he asks for will be enacted, not the 40 or 50 percent of the important measures that the American President is likely to secure but 100 percent. The secret weapon of the parliamentary system is tight party discipline.

## The Historic System

When the system is functioning optimally, the Prime Minister's party, be it Conservative or Labor, provides him with a majority of legislators whose obedience, with few exceptions, is granitic, "solid masses of steady votes," Walter Bagehot, Britain's master political essayist, once put it, for policy and program. The party leader, who is ordinarily either the Prime Minister or leader of the opposition, possesses powers that are well-nigh autocratic and against which the American President's party powers are limp and pallid. The Prime Minister has the sole ultimate responsibility for formulating policy and an electoral program. The party secretariat or central office is his personal machine. He appoints the principal officers and thereby controls propaganda, research, and finance. He is vested with lordly power over his party followers in Parliament. An M.P. can ill afford to incur his dread wrath by challenging, criticizing, or publicly differing with his party. No M.P. who has crossed the floor, or aligned himself with the opposition, on a major issue has won reelection since 1945.[22] All this, needless to say, is a far cry from the American President's circumstances. Franklin Roosevelt was the only President to launch a substantial purge upon recalcitrant Democrats, with results so inglorious that no successor has dared repeat the venture.

In the selection of candidates for American national legislative office, state and local organizations and primaries dominate the decisions. The result is a goodly crop of Senators and Congressmen opposed to the President of their own party on principal policy questions. In Britain the local choice of the candidate must win central approval. The Labor party's constitution provides that a candidate's selection "shall not be regarded as completed until the name of the person has been placed before a meeting of the National Executive Committee, and his or her selection has been duly endorsed." The Labor constitution clearly stipulates the conditions of approval: The candidate must conform to "the Constitution, Program, Principles and Policy of the Party" and "act in harmony with the Standing Orders of the Parliamentary Labor Party."[23] Even if a rebel is backed by his own constituency, the Labor party will enter a candidate against him, thus dividing the party's usual vote and making almost certain his defeat.

British party discipline depends not simply on organization and gadgetry. It also reflects the lesser role of pressure groups in national life. The United States, in contrast, is a land where pressure groups flourish and regional differences are vast; their influence is divisive, preventing the tight integration of opinion and leadership in the major parties. Above all, differences between the British and American peoples are an influence, the latter's heterogeneity forcing the parties to be broad and flexible in method. British party methods in the areas of finance, selection of candidates, and platform-development, however, deserve close study for possible borrowings and adaptations to the United States.

## Contemporary Reality

But the experiences of contemporary Prime Ministers expose some of the vulnerabilities of the system. Like presidential elections, British elections have become close elections. In the ten national elections since 1950, only five have produced a majority of thirty seats or more. In 1974, the February election produced no majority and the October election gave Labor a majority of only five seats, which quickly evaporated in by-elections. In 1979, the Labor government of James Callaghan was turned out of office by a margin of merely one vote on a motion of no confidence. The absence of a single Labor member, bedridden after a heart attack, cost Callaghan his tenure. The Labor Government, which lacked a clear majority in the House of Commons, was also torpedoed by eleven Scottish Nationalists, whose support of Callaghan vanished when they became disenchanted with the Prime Minister's lukewarm support of their cause of home rule. When the Scots abandoned Callaghan, the Conservative opposition moved in for the kill.[24]

Even before his fall, Callaghan's experiences as Prime Minister and party leader were more akin to an American President's travail than to the historic British model. Divisions in the ranks of his own Labor party reduced his government to a caretaker, administering existing laws, rather than enacting innovative socialist programs. In 1977, for example, the Prime Minister, committed to direct election of British delegates to the European Parliament and dependent upon the Liberal party for support, was undercut by Labor's left wing long hostile to British membership in the Common Market. Anthony Wedgwood Benn, Minister for Energy, and five other members of the cabinet threatened to resign if the Prime Minister insisted that they vote in favor of direct elections. Callaghan quickly capitulated by permitting cabinet members to vote as they wished on the issue. After that pitiful display of weakness, Callaghan suffered such further prestige-eroding reverses as defeat of seven Government budget proposals in the Commons finance committee; abandonment, under duress, of the Government's attempts to enact limited self-government for Scotland and Wales; and failure to negotiate with the powerful unions antiinflationary pay restraints.[25] Gladstone and Disraeli, the Conservatives' nineteenth-century heroes, must have blinked in wonder.

# The British Prime Minister

Whereas the American President's weakness as party leader earns him unreliable congressional support for his program—once when the House of Representatives overrode his veto, Gerald Ford mustered only seven votes, most of them from lame-duck Republicans[26]—the British Prime Minister, when his system is working at its traditional best, knows the luxury of enduring legislative backing. The President, viewing the British executive, across the Atlantic, must see him as abiding in a political utopia that assures that whatever he asks for, the legislature will provide.

In theory, the President is more powerful than the Prime Minister in legislation. Head of the executive branch, he is the coequal of Congress. He is not responsible to Congress in the sense that the Prime Minister is to Parliament. To become Prime Minister, Margaret Thatcher had to be elected to the House of Commons, where she answers daily for the actions of her government. In British constitutional theory she, her cabinet, and other ministers are a committee of the House of Commons.

In theory the Prime Minister and his government are the servants of the House of Commons, but traditionally they are in fact its masters. The government, not the House, legislates. The government plans and controls the House's time. The introduction of legislation is almost completely the government's monopoly. A rule requiring that all legislation involving expenditure bear the crown's, or in actuality the government's, approval invests the government with a sweeping control, since virtually all legislation of significance requires money. This order of things is supported by an implicit democratic rationalization: parties contest elections on platforms; upon winning a popular, and therefore a legislative, majority a party should command priority for its program in the House.

Normally, the British government is certain that any important bill it introduces will pass without significant change, in good time. Although the cannonade of brilliant oratory and merciless jibes may beat upon its program in House debate, the government ultimately prevails. It knows no evil like the subcommittee bottleneck and the crippling amendment that kills or damages beyond recognition the President's requests. Ordinarily, Parliament can only influence the government's future course. Flaws exposed in legislative debate presumably will not be prolonged or repeated.

In his daily legislative life the Prime Minister sails a smooth sea compared with the American President. Harold Wilson squeaked through the national elections of 1964 with a four-seat margin in the House of Commons. Despite this slim margin, he announced that the bold program promised in his campaign would be fully presented to the House. "Nothing could be worse," Wilson declared, "than failing both at home and abroad because of the parliamentary balance of power." He brought forward his program, and it proceeded with assurance through Parliament, even when, through attrition, his margin fell to one vote. But Wilson still moved ahead, and the country approved and rewarded his effort by returning him to office in 1966 by a landslide.

The Prime Minister, also unlike the President, shares power with fellow executives, the ministers, and particularly those who comprise the cabinet. The Prime Minister, however, enjoys powers his fellow ministers do not have. In constitutional practice all ministerial offices derive from him and depend upon him, since he can make and unmake ministers. The Prime Minister can prompt the dissolution of the entire government simply by resigning, as Edward Heath did in 1974 to force a general election. No minister has such power. The Prime Minister alone can make certain great decisions without cabinet approval. His fellow ministers have small choice but to back him. To repudiate him is to split the party and deliver the government to the enemy.

## The Cabinet

Yet, in choosing his cabinet, the Prime Minister faces ground rules far more restrictive than any confronting the President. The Prime Minister is literally forced to work with certain associates; the President is not. John Kennedy could choose a cabinet in which not a single major legislative figure of his party was represented, and in Richard Nixon's original cabinet there was only one. The President, it is true, must pay heed to some customary limitations in constituting his cabinet: give Interior to a Westerner, and Labor, Agriculture, and perhaps Commerce to appointees acceptable to the clienteles of those departments. But these are generalized frameworks within which the President can select among scores, if not hundreds, of individuals. "It is important," Prime Minister Harold Macmillan has written of cabinet-forming, that "different groups of opinion within the party should be represented." [27] The Prime Minister's choices, on the other hand, are definite and particular. To form a government, the Prime Minister must build upon the support of the principal factions of his party. Factional allegiance requires a *quid pro quo*, a seat for the factional leader in the cabinet. Accordingly, Margaret Thatcher, in constructing her cabinet, maintained a careful balance between right-wingers like herself and moderates. Mindful of her less than overwhelming mandate, with a majority of only 43 seats in the House of Commons, Thatcher exercised extra caution in filling her cabinet. Particularly circumspect was her selection of James Prior as Employment Minister, the one Conservative leader with strong personal ties to the unions whose decisions concerning wage demands and possible reactive strikes can shape the government's fate. [28]

## President-Prime Minister Comparisons

It is a commonplace of Anglo-American comparison to suggest that the British Prime Minister is coming to resemble more and more the American President. Impetus for the observation is provided especially by the growing involvement of the Prime Minister in television activity, projecting, as the President is prone to, the image of the leader in a mass democracy. Increasingly, British elections are contests between rival leaders, and one, the incumbent Prime Minister, easily dominates the news with the bountiful resources of his office. As his power and impact flourish, that of other institutions has diminished, whether the Monarch, the houses of Parliament, or the cabinet. Nonetheless, differences between the President and the Prime Minister remain substantial. For the active, assertive President, for example, the American system provides no substitute. Eisenhower, felled by illness, and Nixon, wounded by Watergate, were not replaced in their enfeeblement by any other locus of effective executive power. But in Britain, when Prime Minister Sir Alec Douglas-Home lapsed into semiretirement by choosing to function modestly and to withdraw from making initiatives and from steering and maneuvering, his ministers solidified working relations with each other, united in common action, and produced a viable government position that they guided through the cabinet and the House of Commons. [29]

Nonetheless, Margaret Thatcher, a fundamentalist conservative ideologue will put severe strains on the system if she holds to her resolve to abandon collectivism, reduce government spending, cut taxes, restore free collective bargaining, and revive private enterprise. Any American President who launched a comparable program would face many of the formidable obstacles confronting Thatcher. British ministers and American department heads typically resist efforts to reduce spending, pressed by client groups and civil servants whose prosperity and careers are furthered by maintaining programs at existing levels, or, even better, by expanding them. In Britain, militant unions are a far more potent force in politics and the economy than American unions, and their reply to challenges to their interests—protest marches, political propaganda, and industrial action—makes Prime Ministers tremble.

If Jimmy Carter has been discredited and hobbled by low ratings in public opinion polls, that fate is even more disastrous for a Prime Minister. She and her parliamentary party watch the polls even more avidly. If slippage occurs, pressures for the Prime Minister to alter policy quickly follow.[30] By-elections are another barometer, which, if they reveal unfavorable trends, can be both distressful to the Prime Minister and her party. Like the American President, the British Prime Minister and her policy positions are exceedingly vulnerable to events. Carter's promise of a balanced budget fell victim to a recession. Thatcher could be endangered by galloping inflation and a recession so deep that hundreds of businesses are driven into bankruptcy. High unemployment, coupled with reduced welfare programs, will foment unrest. Her political well-being will decline if the public becomes disinclined to suffer until the benefits promised by her program of lower taxes and more economic freedom materialize.

# The Parliamentary System Evaluated

The supreme attractiveness of the historic parliamentary system is the ease and assurance with which it produces policy. In its ideal workings, the executive has charge of legislation, guided by public opinion as it is expressed by interest groups, the press, and in the House of Commons. Administration, whether it concern organizational structure, program, finance, or personnel, is the secure province of the executive. The House votes the funds that the cabinet requests. The House lacks constitutional power to vote more money for any purpose than the cabinet asks for, a situation that is the bane of budget-minded Presidents. Thanks to iron party discipline, the cabinet can count not only on a majority but regularly on the same majority. Lyndon Johnson, who knew the luxury of large congressional majorities for his party, never ceased to marvel at Harold Wilson's ability to act decisively in domestic and international affairs with merely a paper-thin legislative margin.[31] Parliament's orientation, like the cabinet's, is national rather than local. The lack of a tradition that the legislator reside in his own district, the common incident of an M.P. elected from a district he has never visited, the party's intolerance of any local deviation from the national policy, give Parliament an orientation as resolutely national as the consciousness of Congress, and particularly the House of Representatives, is local.

### Weaknesses

But the parliamentary system, for all its undeniable excellence as a vehicle of national policy, also carries weakness. It is immediately suspect because of Britain's own decline in power and place in the family of nations, which although a product of many factors, strongly suggests that the parliamentary method smacks excessively of the past and has not adjusted sufficiently to modern change. There is indeed much that is anachronistic in the British parliamentary model, much that once was meaningful but that time and change have reduced to hollow pretense. What was constitutional political fact in that nation in the nineteenth century, as political scientist Don K. Price has put it, has become constitutional fiction in the twentieth. The House of Commons in bygone days did control the government and could, when it chose, dismiss it. Nowadays, however, public opinion rather than the House determines cabinet tenure.[32]

The House of Commons has been reduced to a passivity that even the most resolute critic of Congress would not wish upon it. In its tightly restricted capacity, the House resembles the American electoral college, registering the popular will in choosing a government and then automatically ratifying its program and voting the funds it asks for. The House lacks means of initiating policy; unlike Congress, it has no standing committees to investigate and recommend, deprivations that preclude any legislative capacity to take an independent line and exercise meaningful control. More than three decades ago Prime Minister Stanley Baldwin rightly observed that House members widely felt they had "nothing much to do of a responsible nature."[33]

Nowadays outcries are rising in Britain against Parliament's general ineffectuality. Brian Chapman of Manchester University voiced the wide concern of responsible Britons when he wrote, "We need a state in which Parliament is an effective partner in the process of government, and not simply an ineffectual appendage employed to make noises of approval or discontent." Seeking a rearranged governmental structure enabling Parliament to "play a vital role in the formulation of policy," Chapman looked admiringly upon the American Congress, with its subject matter and joint committees and urged that the House of Lords be reconstituted by regions.[34]

The experience of British Parliaments and Prime Ministers since Chapman voiced his concern discloses a high vulnerability of the Prime Minister to external forces in an era of close elections. Parliament's resulting role, although not as Chapman envisaged it, is significant. The intense divisions between Left and Right in Labor's parliamentary party, and a heavy dependence on minor parties like those for Soctland and Wales, allowed the Callaghan government only a feeble hold on policy and soon led to its overturn.

The Thatcher government functions with a slender majority in the House of Commons, which increases Thatcher's vulnerability to a developing public opinion hostile to her policies of heavy tax increases, of self-reliance for business, however important particular enterprises may be to the national economy, and however much their backs are to the wall. If Thatcher persists as a hell-bent ideologue on policy, rather than being flexible and adjusting, she could well become another one-term Prime Minister like two of her immediate predecessors, Edward Heath and James Callaghan.[35]

Thatcher could adjust her policies as her Conservative predecessor Heath did, in a series of memorable "U-turns," when he relaxed monetary controls and imposed an incomes-policy in the face of bad economic trends, yet the turns availed him little politically. The sad truth is that Britain's severe economic problems allow few alternatives that have reasonable prospects of success, whether proposed by the Prime Minister or by back-bench rebels of her parliamentary party.

## Administration

The administrative features of the parliamentary system are also questionable. The minister, the equivalent of the American departmental Secretary, is primarily a legislative leader and not an administrator. He is chosen not so much for administrative ability as for his command of House support and his skill in defending party policy. He makes his way by shining in debate and by leadership in party affairs. Accordingly, if Henry Kissinger, the gifted Secretary of State, were to live and work as a Briton, chances are less that he would achieve the place and make the contribution permitted him in American public affairs.

Finally, much of the criticism that Britons themselves have levied against their governmental system has fallen upon the civil service. Long and rightly hailed as a model career system for other nations, including the United States, to emulate, the British civil service is handled roughly by its present-day critics. It is viewed as ingrown, uninspired, uncreative, and out of step with the swift pace of Britain's problems. In essence, the administrative class, or policy-making career service, is recruited at a youthful age, when its members complete their university education, after which they pass all their working lives in governmental service. Except for specialized employment, it is difficult to bring into the civil service those midway and beyond in a business, academic, or professional career.[36]

The British ministerial system reinforces the tendency of large bureaucratic organizations to be cautious and safe, and therefore unenterprising. A minister progresses in his political career if the civil service keeps him out of trouble. The civil service reads the handwriting on the wall, which instructs that they will gain more by caution (which avoids trouble) than by initiative (which invites it). Furthermore, the civil servant figures that even if the initiative succeeds, the minister will receive most of the credit. Some Britons looking for reform take their cues from American practice. They propose a generous use of a "brain trust" to be attached to the Prime Minister's and each minister's office, an injection of new blood into the civil service at many levels from the untapped talent of the professions, business, and local government.

Changes have transpired. In 1971 the several personnel classes, including the administrative class, were merged into a single structure, and the interview procedure that is used in recruitment and that facilitates indulgence of class and educational biases was overhauled to enhance its objectivity. A Civil Service College was established for postentry training and a reform study has urged at least a year's experience in banking or industry for the young recruit. Whether these changes are enough to produce variety and vitality remains to be seen. Both Wilson and Heath abandoned traditionally exclusive reliance on the civil service for developing policy and imported several private economists into the government. Heath also recruited a cadre of business executives to enhance civil service management and to effect savings, a high commitment of his Conservative government.[37]

# The Administrative State

All nations have donned increasingly the trappings of the administrative state. Managing the economy, providing welfare services, and maintaining the military force and weaponry have compounded executive tasks, resources, and power in society. In most of the nations of the world, administration has gained in power and autonomy at the expense of the legislature. The United States, however, for all the expansion of its governmental responsibilities displays far less of a shift of power from the legislature to the executive. The American Congress exerts controls over administration that other legislatures do not possess. Its legislation is more detailed, its controls over administrative structure, finance, program, and personnel are far tighter than those exercised by other legislatures of the world.

## Separation of Powers

In Great Britain Parliament practices a relationship with the executive in matters of administration that, were it followed in the United States, would immeasurably strengthen the President's position as administrative chief. Although Britain has a unified political system, with both legislative and executive power concentrated in Parliament, administration is treated altogether differently. Administration is accorded the full benefit of the doctrine of separation of powers. Paradoxically, the United States claims to observe a separation of powers, but Congress freely breaches it in matters of administration. The British, applying separation of powers, leave to executive discretion the employment of the basic means of administration. The organizational structure of departments, which Congress provides for in close detail, Parliament delegates to executive decision. Personnel policy, for which Congress has compiled a thick volume of close legislation, the British leave to the executive. The executive budget, which Congress can deal roughly with when it chooses, remains fully intact in the hands of Parliament. A shattering exception was the floundering Callaghan government, a sizeable portion of whose budget was savagely vetoed by the Commons finance committee in 1977. If even one of these instances of normal legislative self-denial were adopted by Congress, the President's prowess as administrative chief would be vastly strengthened.

But here the claims of the strong presidency clash with the requisites of democracy. In the abuses of executive power that surfaced in the Watergate scandals, the departmental bureaus sometimes provided the most effective resistance to the overweening demands of the White House staff. A potent ingredient of the bureaus' capacity to resist was the actual or potential backing of congressional power centers—committees, leaders, and individual legislators—whose availability stemmed from Congress's traditional involvement all along the broad front of administration.

## The French Presidency

The Fifth French Republic is the ultimate in the democratic administrative state, veering as it does in certain seasons into constitutional dictatorship.[38] As a model of the continuously strong chief executive in a more or less democratic setting, it is too extreme for adaptation to the United States. In the Fourth Republic a well-nigh powerless executive was subordinate to an all-powerful lower legislative house, the Chamber of Deputies. In the Fifth Republic much of the Deputies' power has been transferred to the executive, chiefly to the President and, to a much lesser degree, to the Prime Minister in subordination to the President. The President controls policy-making in foreign affairs and national security, and he can, when he chooses, extend his powers by revising constitutional practice at will and ruling under emergency powers for periods extending well beyond the actual emergency. The Prime Minister and his cabinet wield so many powers not subject to the approval of the Assembly, the lower legislative house of the Fifth Republic, that they can confidently anticipate the enactment of most of their vital policies for the low price of occasional minor changes in program and personnel shifts. Parliament's lawmaking powers are limited to specific subjects set out chiefly by the constitution. The administration, in turn, wields a rule-making power over all matters not specifically reserved to Parliament.

French parliamentary lawmaking is subordinate to administrative necessity. Article XXXVIII of the constitution provides that "for the execution of its program" the executive may ask Parliament for power temporarily to take measures by ordinance that constitutionally are among the subjects reserved to the legislature. The French Senate, which belongs to the administrative tradition of French politics works as an ally of the executive. A Constituional Council tests the constitutionality of laws enacted by Parliament. The Council, too, is an auxiliary of executive dominance, watchful that Parliament remains within the confines of its inferior position. De Gaulle conducted his presidential office as a crisis executive, and under Article XVI, which provides unlimited emergency powers in external and internal crisis, he enjoyed authority that largely subjected the government and its policies to Presidential control. His presidential successor, Georges Pompidou, former premier, professor, and banker, governed with the same sweep of power, but unlike DeGaulle, who disdained administration, Pompidou directly and personally supervised all the business of government except a small domain of social and economic affairs allotted to the Premier. In 1974 incoming President Giscard d'Estaing recruited a cabinet whose strength was more administrative than political. Generally, the Ministers were highly qualified in technical fields, having been drawn substantially from the professions and the civil service, including the key incumbencies for foreign affairs and finance.[39]

Both the French President and the British Prime Minister have personal staffs, but they are far less numerous than the American President's. These staffs, though they play a significant role in policy development, have generally less impact than their American counterparts. Particularly in France, the personal staffs are enlarging their influence on policy. Pompidou's initial Secretary General of the Elysée Palace, a kind of chief of staff, Michel Jobert, was known as the "French Kissinger." Matters in both foreign and domestic affairs filtered through Jobert as they moved toward Pompidou, and the Secretary General, like Kissinger as national security assistant, was entrusted with crucial diplomactic negotiations, including some with Kissinger himself.[40] The parallelism persisted when both moved subsequently to cabinet posts, Kissinger as Secretary of State and Jobert as Foreign Minister.

In France and Britain, the top executive's use of personal staff is regulated by forces that are less prevalent, or even nonexistent, in the United States, with the consequent danger of excesses by the White House staff. While a British Prime Minister looks to his personal staff and the cabinet secretariat for political advice, he is, unlike the American President, constrained by the likely resentment of senior ministers if they suspect that the counsel of nonelected persons—the staff—is preferred to theirs. In both France and Britain, irritation and conflict between the staff on the one hand and the ministers and civil service on the other is diminished by the practice of constituting the staffs heavily, if not entirely, with civil servants. In light of the misdeeds of the White House staff in Watergate, a possible safeguard against future aberrations might be to draw more of the Presidential staff from the departmental civil service and to move more toward the British conception of a loyal staff that will serve succeeding Presidents or Prime Ministers, with the right to return to departmental duty protected.

The United States, an executive-legislative state, faces in its competitor, the Soviet Union, a monolithic administrative state. The Soviet Union is in the hands of party administrators, a political bureaucracy or "new class," as Milovan Djilas, former Yugoslav vice president who fell into disfavor, terms it. The governmental and economic apparatuses are part of the party organism, but each has its separate structure, caste characteristics, and narrower self-interests. The new class members enjoy special privileges and economic preferences derived from their administrative monopoly. Unlike bureaucracies in the noncommunist world, which are subject to political authorities, "the Communists," as Djilas has written, "have neither masters nor owners over them." [41]

The Soviet Union's top leadership is produced by the party administrative system. Stalin was himself the epitome of the party administrator, rising not as a charismatic leader but as one skilled in the ways of the party apparatus, who outdid competitors who excelled as orators or theoreticians. Stalin neither preached nor inspired but made decisions, spoke without ardor or color, and stressed the concrete administrative tasks of industrializing the Soviet Union and collectivizing its agriculture. To retain power, he incorporated a system of relentless terror into the administrative apparatus. [42]

Stalin's successors, Malenkov and Khrushchev, and their successors, Kosygin and Brezhnev, all were party administrators who climbed the career ladder. The ascent to the top is by apolitical means, accomplished without a struggle for votes or an assertion of new ideas for program and policy but dependent rather upon one's usefulness to the incumbent leadership and upon choosing the right protectors. Unlike Khrushchev, an erratic gambler, Brezhnev is a stolid bureaucrat, with acute instincts for self-preservation and a robust flair for eliminating potential rivals. [43] Conservatism is the dominant characteristic of the Soviet new class, which, while enormously capable of maintaining itself, is little capable of creating change and is apprehensive of it as a threat to its position and privilege. Hence the bureaucratic oligarchy is locked in its ideology and fears debate and free opinion as threats to its power. The banishment of novelist Alexander Solzhenitsyn, the penalization of other dissidents, and the greater latitude given the secret police illustrate the problem.

Such a posture chills the hopes of those who look for increasing convergence of the Soviet and American systems, which might diminish the incidence of violence in international affairs, and therefore the American presidency's preoccupation with national security pursuits and their consequent strains on the compatibility of the office's acts with democracy. As yet, the most promising possibilities for convergence center upon Soviet-American approaches to common problems like those of outer space and control of nuclear armaments. Among the more formidable roadblocks are the Soviet's bureaucratic rigidities and political conformities. Although political freedom occasionally sprouts and external developments are eroding traditional Russian isolation, little prospect appears of disturbing the entrenched bureaucratic oligarchy in the near future. For the Soviet and American systems to converge, a drastic change of direction must occur in the path of development of one of them. But healthy political systems change only gradually, and there is little spur to change on a drastic scale, since the Soviet and American systems, each in their own way, are highly successful.[44]

# Decision-making Compared

Lyndon Johnson's commitment to an eighteen-hour workday, Eisenhower's extensive overhaul of his top-level staff machinery, Kennedy's overhaul of Eisenhower's overhaul, Nixon's aberrations, Ford's correctives, and Carter's reorganizations evidence a restless dissatisfaction with the means and processes of decision-making. Is the Soviet leadership similarly troubled? Does internal, top-level executive decision-making differ substantially in method in the monolithic Soviet system from that in the normally pluralistic American system? Is Soviet experience at all relevant and instructive for American needs?

After Khrushchev was overthrown in October 1964, the Soviet Union was governed by a "collective leadership," in which Kosygin as Premier was teamed with Brezhnev, the party's General Secretary. In 1965 Brezhnev added a state post to his party capacity by becoming a member of the Presidium of the Supreme Soviet, or legislature. His election as President of the Presidium in 1977 gave him parallel protocol status with other non-Communist heads of state, and he became head of state as well as head of party. In the 1970s, collective leadership became somewhat tattered by Brezhnev's clear emergence as head of the Soviet political machinery. But his ascendance was constrained by his apparent judgment that he must follow a consensus course, and according to the evidence of Soviet decision-making, Brezhnev's voice, while persuasive, is not necessarily conclusive.

The top policy organ, over which Brezhnev presides, is the Politburo of the party, which since 1977 has comprised fourteen full, voting members, and eight nonvoting or candidate members, who participate to varying degrees in decision-making. Djilas provided insight into the functioning of a top-level communist policy group when he wrote, "In the Communist system, exclusive groups are established around political leaders and forums. All policy-making is reduced to wrangling in these exclusive groups, in which familiarity and cliquishness flower. The highest group is generally the most intimate."[45] The Politburo and the huge party Central Committee are packed with Brezhnev's protégés, enabling him to push through his policies when he chooses, and diminishing the indecision of Soviet policy-making that was characteristic in earlier stages of the Brezhnev-Kosygin take-over.

## The Politburo

But even in the full sun of his power, Brezhnev sometimes falters. The Politburo was divided on whether he should proceed with his summit talks with Nixon after the United States mined North Vietnam's ports. Some Politburo members appear to have favored challenging the American block-ade of North Vietnam, or at least cancelling Nixon's impending visit, to protest the mining of Haiphong harbor. Just before Nixon's arrival, one Politburo member, Pyotr Y. Shelest, long a hard-liner toward the West, was demoted by appointment to a less important post, and, as is customary, the announcement was made without public explanation.[46]

The precise role of Brezhnev in the decision to invade Afghanistan remains a matter of uncertainty and speculation. Aging and infirm, incapable at international conferences of participating in sustained discussion, and sometimes out of public view for several weeks, Brezhnev was reported to have been incapacitated or unavailable at the time of the decision, or outvoted and overruled. Doubts about Brezhnev were fanned by the Politburo's habit of deliberating in absolute secrecy and by not making its decisions public. The view that Brezhnev's grip on the Politburo was weakening is challenged by the elevation, near the time of the Afghan invasion, of his long-time associate Nikolai Tikhonov, from alternate to fourteenth member of the Politburo.[47]

All members and candidate members of the Politburo are either officials or deputies of the Supreme Soviet. Thus the highest policy decisions are made in a relatively small group bearing governmental and party authority. The Politburo appears to meet frequently and to work out many decisions on the spot.[48] The American President does not work with any single group as regularly as the Soviet leadership does. The President distributes his consultations among large groups such as the cabinet, the National Security Council, and *ad hoc* groups thrown together for such critical situations as Cuba in 1962 and Panama in 1964. The President, unlike Soviet leaders, may feel behooved to touch base with figures outside the executive branch, such as legislators, private group leaders, and former Presidents. The Politburo seems to have nothing of the elaborately prepared and negotiated papers that characterized Eisenhower's National Security Council. Yet Soviet departments have access to the Politburo through its members and the Secretariat, the party's principal administrative apparatus, over which Brezhnev presides. Agencies like the Ministry of Foreign Affairs report to the Politburo directly.

In actual decision-making, the American President is rather more apt to employ competing sources of information and advice than the Soviet leadership. Brezhnev has revealed that an inner cabinet of four members—himself, Kosygin, Suslov, and Podgorny—maintain continual discussions of major policy issues. The other members of the Politburo carry responsibilities for overseeing departments and bring to the Politburo information and recommendations from their departments. The Politburo receives regular reports on scientific and military developments, the economy, and foreign policy.

The Soviet administrative system is an elaborate mechanism of control from the top. There are no departmental bureaus with the autonomy of an FBI and an Army Corps of Engineers. In Soviet practice the party, which dominates the government apparatus from top to bottom, leaves nothing undone to assure that the orders of the top command are carried out. The Soviet leader can act with a rigor toward his administrators and ministers that no American President would dare consider even in his fondest dreams. The top leadership must appear infallible despite the treachery of events and human error. If it falters, others must bear the blame.

# The Presidency Abroad

The presidency is America's foremost political export. The Philippines and most of all Latin America have grafted onto their governments elements of the American presidential model. At one time or another all the Latin American countries have adopted the strong presidency. It is instructive to study what they have borrowed, added, or left out in their adaptation of the American prototype because it reveals what they believe to be the strengths and shortcomings of the presidential institution.

The powers of the Latin American President invariably exceed those of the United States Chief Executive.[49] The Latin American President's appointment power is stronger. He can fill most offices on his own authority, referring relatively few for senatorial or congressional approval. He sends messages and appears personally before congress to request action. In Venezuela he can even introduce bills, a power treated somewhat ambiguously in several other constitutions, which assertive presidents have interpreted to their own advantage. He presents the budget in the form of an appropriation bill, enjoys a broad and strong veto power, including an item veto for appropriations, and has a sweeping power to issue decrees and administrative orders. Laws are passed in far more general terms than the American Congress would ever tolerate, affording the President broad discretion. He enjoys extraordinary powers to cope with civil disorder, invasion, or other crisis and to intervene in the provincial governments.

Latin American experience abundantly demonstrates, however, that in spite of all his impressive power the President must dominate the army and build a political party or following of "interests," especially the organized urban workers, if he is to succeed.

Even the best Latin American presidents have indulged in what is termed "exaggerated presidentialism," by which they assume dictatorial powers for brief or substantial periods. Simón Bolívar, for one, was convinced that exceptional executive powers must be readily available to counter the demagogic exploitation of racial-cultural tensions. The spectacle of the presidency transformed into an outright military dictatorship is all too common. Although the United States' transplant has not proved to be the means to good government, it is reassuring that each departure from legitimate government for some variant of dictatorship has been marked by an eventual return to the presidential form.

As is the fate of merchandise, not every potential foreign buyer who has looked at the American presidential system has bought it. Charles de Gaulle, beholding the American presidency in 1964, turned aside clamors in certain domestic quarters that France repattern its own presidency along American lines. De Gaulle would have nothing of it. The American system, he declared in a press conference, was functioning in a limping way, and if it were applied in France he foresaw only "a chronic opposition" between the executive and the legislature that would lead to "general paralysis." Presumably De Gaulle had in mind the breakdowns in presidential-congressional cooperation that provide the American nation with a frequent diet of political futility. The American presidential system, De Gaulle contended, had thrived in the peculiarly favorable environment of the United States:

> it is in a country which because of its technical make-up, its economic riches, its geographical position, never knew invasion, and which for a century has known no revolution; in a country where, moreover, there are only two parties that are divided by nothing essential in any field, national, social, moral, international; in a federal country where the Government assumes only general tasks—defenses, diplomacy, finance—while the 50 states of the union are entrusted with all the rest.[50]

The American presidency was not transferable, at least not to France.

# Epilogue

# The Future of the American Presidency

As this is written, Ronald Reagan is commencing his presidential incumbency. One challenge that awaits him and perhaps his successors is terminating the present interval of the diminished presidency and placing the office on a secure upward course in the ever-working cycle of presidential history.

Like other Presidents since the mid-1970s, when the era of the diminished presidency began, Reagan is handicapped by the fractionalization of power in Congress and the decline of the political parties. Congress has become largely a market place of individual political enterprise. All recent Presidents have been beset by excessive deadlock and defeat in their initiatives in Congress, and Reagan will post a solid milestone if he improves on that record.

Especially troublesome for Reagan and his fight against the demon inflation is the enlistment of Congress's consent to cuts in federal expenditure. Even more formidable are the hosts of awaiting pressure groups that in countless ways depend for their economic well-being on federal largess. These groups, practiced and comfortable in dealing with legislators, are the lobbyists for thousands of state and local officials, for corporate and business groups, and for labor unions. Presidents must reckon with the truth that in a special interest state, government best serves the interests that are organized, not the unorganized majority.

In his initial approaches to Congress, Reagan disclosed that he learned well the lessons of recent presidential debacle and trouble. He appreciates the value of symbolic attentions and shuns the reclusiveness of Carter and others that added obstacles to an already difficult road. Reagan's preinaugural visits to Capitol Hill, his cultivation of bonhomie, his master stroke in announcing in a surprise gesture to Senate Democrats the retention of Mike Mansfield, former Senate Democratic leader, as ambassador to Japan, laid a foundation of bipartisian good will. But an unresolved question asks how much mileage Reagan can gain from courtesies and blandishments when he commences the grim business of budget-cutting, a moment of blood-letting in politics. To the legislator, the fall of the budget axe inflicts wounds on constituents whose support is valued, especially in the next election.

Like other Presidents, Reagan has his own distinct preferences in organizing the White House office both for its role in assisting the workings of the presidency and for the arduous and uncertain venture of asserting influence and direction over the executive branch's tenured bureaucracy. Reagan's White House operation is headed by three key deputies reporting directly to the President. A former aide to President Ford and Vice President Bush, James A. Baker III is chief of the White House staff and superintends assistants handling political, congressional, and intergovernmental liaison, along with speechwriters, the press secretary, and the assistant for communications. A second top deputy, Edwin Meese III, a long-time associate and chief of staff in Reagan's governorship, is counselor to the President with cabinet rank. Meese oversees both the national security and domestic policy staffs, whose roles were defined to be considerably less than in the Carter years. Both Meese and Baker serve as members of the National Security Council. The third principal deputy, Michael K. Deaver, assistant to the President and deputy chief of the White House staff, is also a long-time aide from Reagan's California days. His responsibilities include the President's military office and daily schedule of appointments and trips. Deaver also oversees the office of Nancy Reagan.

Germs of trouble lurk in some of the ambiguities and overlappings in the Baker-Meese operations, and only experience and further honing of Reagan's own work preferences can offer a cure. When Reagan's administrative plan was originally announced, it was not at all clear how Meese's and Baker's activities would mesh. Staff frictions would likely arise if national security and domestic staffs under Meese were required to coordinate with congressional and political aides under Baker. Other trouble might erupt if Meese were to extract policy from the department secretaries and from their competitors on the national security and domestic policy staffs. A continuing melee might disrupt the jurisdictional boundaries of the President's principal deputies. Still another force for disarray would be the likely fluctuations of the personal standing and fortunes of the White House staff and the cabinet secretaries in the President's confidence and esteem.

To reduce the usual yawning chasm between the President and his White House office on the one hand, and the executive branch bureaucracies on the other, Reagan proposed to adapt to his new responsibilities a practice of his governorship. His policy-making machinery will be built around a small six- to ten-member inner cabinet or executive committee, principally of cabinet members. According to its California regimen, the inner cabinet met regularly and deliberated on all major policy decisions. The participating secretaries functioned in a dual capacity—as administrators with specific responsibilities and as sources of advice in across the board policy discussions. Whether this practice is workable on the far larger scale of Washington is problematic, especially in view of the large block of time the secretaries must pass on Capitol Hill testifying before congressional committees. The secretaries must also provide leadership and, to a degree, managerial supervision of the departments, some of them gigantic and complex organizations. Altogether these sundry claims may spread the department head too thin.

For the Reagan transition staff, the task of filling hundreds of subcabinet positions was considered as crucial as recruiting for cabinet appointments. These subcabinet positions will become, as they do in any administration, strategic command posts where it will be largely determined whether Reagan's policies are carried out or distorted or ignored. Reagan's two elected predecessors, Nixon and Carter, made serious initial efforts to keep subcabinet selection under White House control. But the voluminous character of the task eventually overwhelmed the White House labors, and control passed to the departments. Both Nixon and Carter subsequently complained that of the hundreds of appointees who filled the posts, many were memorable for their lack of sensitivity and accountability to their respective Presidents. Resolved to succeed where his predecessors failed, Reagan was aided by a professional executive recruiter and a computer with ten thousand resumes. But even this process may not work rapidly enough for Reagan to avoid a crucial interval of early months—when the policy directions of a new administration are set—with a subcabinet composed largely of carry-overs from the Carter administration.

In his strivings to cope with congress, the special interest groups, and the bureaucracy, Reagan could borrow a leaf from the President he cited most in his speech accepting nomination, Franklin Roosevelt. Roosevelt's addresses rallied the public as a counterforce against Congress and the interest groups, and his statements of purpose and program stirred bureaucratic support. In the presidency's lengthy experience, there have been intervals when leadership has been largely manifested by the pursuit of consensus, at other times in the building of institutions, and in this present era of technologies and expertise, by communications. By conveying vision, momentum, and direction, Reagan and his successors can go far toward reversing the diminished presidency of declining power.

# Notes

## 1 Perspectives on Presidential Power

1 In "Carter Finding Power Limited," *New York Times*, November 11, 1977.
2 *New York Times*, November 11, 1977.
3 In *Congressional Quarterly Weekly Reports*, October 16, 1979, p. 2202.
4 Adam Clymer, "Carter's Vision of America," *New York Times Magazine*, July 27, 1980, p. 19.
5 Edward Cowan, "The Problems Facing Reagan in Trying to Reduce Inflation," *New York Times*, November 6, 1980.
6 In Tom Wicker, "Reagan's Real Test," *New York Times*, November 7, 1980.
7 Clinton Rossiter, *Constitutional Dictatorship* (Princeton: Princeton University Press, 1948).
8 Thomas E. Cronin, *The State of the Presidency* (Boston: Little, Brown, 1980), pp. 76–77.
9 In *New York Times*, January 15, 1960.
10 In *National Journal*, August 7, 1976, p. 993.
11 Cronin, p. 76.
12 James MacGregor Burns, *The Deadlock of Democracy* (Englewood Cliffs, N.J.: Prentice-Hall, 1963).
13 Committee on Political Parties, American Political Science Association, *Toward a More Responsible Two-Party System* (New York: Holt, Rinehart & Winston, 1950).
14 Richard E. Neustadt, *Presidential Power: The Politics of Leadership* (New York: Wiley, 1960).
15 See Peter B. Sperlich, "Bargaining and Overload: An Essay on Presidential Power," in *Perspectives on the Presidency*, ed. Aaron Wildavsky (Boston: Little, Brown, 1975), pp. 406–31.
16 Henry Fairlie, *The Kennedy Promise* (Garden City, N.Y.: Doubleday, 1973).
17 Richard M. Pious, *The American Presidency* (New York: Basic Books, 1979).
18 Pious, pp. 49–50.
19 Clinton Rossiter, *Constitutional Dictatorship*, p. 212.
20 Arthur M. Schlesinger, Jr., *The Imperial Presidency* (Boston: Houghton Mifflin, 1973), pp. viii–ix.
21 In *New York Times*, May 19, 1977.
22 George E. Reedy, *The Twilight of the Presidency* (New York: New American Library, 1971), p. 4.
23 Thomas L. Hughes, "Foreign Policy: Men or Measures?" *The Atlantic Monthly* (October 1974): 53.
24 In Reedy, p. 1.
25 In Schlesinger, pp. 222–23.
26 In *New York Times*, January 22, 1973.
27 See Robert C. Tucker, "Personality and Political Leadership," *Political Science Quarterly* 92 (Fall 1977): 390–93.
28 In Neustadt, pp. 10–12.
29 Woodrow Wilson, *Constitutional Government in the United States* (New York: Columbia University Press, 1911), p. 59.
30 Neustadt, p. 34.
31 In Allan Nevins, *Grover Cleveland: A Study in Courage* (New York: Dodd, Mead, 1932), p. 510.
32 In Nevins, p. 308.
33 William Howard Taft, *Our Chief Magistrate and His Powers* (New York: Columbia University Press, 1915), p. 144.
34 In Philip Shriver Klein, *President James Buchanan* (University Park, Pa.: Pennsylvania State University, 1962), p. 337.
35 James Bryce, *The American Commonwealth*, Vol. 1 (New York: Macmillan, 1907), p. 58.
36 Taft, p. 13.
37 William Henry Harbaugh, *Power and Responsibility: The Life and Times of Theodore Roosevelt* (New York: Farrar, Straus & Giroux, 1961), p. 282.
38 Theodore Roosevelt, *An Autobiography* (New York: Scribner's, 1920), p. 406.

## 2 Beginnings

1 In Charles C. Thach, *The Creation of the Presidency*, Johns Hopkins University Studies in Historical and Po-

litical Science, Ser. 40, No. 4 (Baltimore: Johns Hopkins University Press, 1922), p. 22.

2  Evarts Boutell Greene, *The Provincial Governor in the English Colonies of North America* (New York: Russell & Russell, 1898).

3  Thach, p. 29.

4  In Thach, p. 30.

5  Thach, pp. 34–40.

6  E. Wilder Spaulding, *His Excellency George Clinton* (Port Washington, N.Y.: I. J. Friedman, 1964), pp. 95–138.

7  George Bancroft, *History of the Formation of the Constitution of the United States of America* (New York: Appleton, 1885), pp. 326–28.

8  Carl Van Doren, *The Great Rehearsal* (New York: Viking, 1948), pp. 88–90, 272–73.

9  Van Doren, pp. 91–94.

10  Max Farrand, ed., *The Records of the Federal Convention of 1787*, Vol. 2 (New Haven, Conn.: Yale University Press, 1921), p. 135; Max Farrand, *The Framing of the Constitution of the United States* (New Haven, Conn.: Yale University Press, 1913), p. 129.

11  Farrand, *Framing the Constitution*, p. 77.

12  In Van Doren, pp. 59–60.

13  Van Doren, p. 145.

14  In Farrand, *Records*, Vol. 2, p. 318.

15  In Farrand, *Records*, Vol. 2, pp. 59, 100, 105.

16  Farrand, *Records*, Vol. 2, pp. 335, 537.

17  Farrand, *Framing the Constitution*, p. 166.

18  Farrand, *Records*, Vol. 2, pp. 538–39.

19  Farrand, *Records*, Vol. 2, pp. 318, 427, 535.

20  Farrand, *Records*, Vol. 2, p. 318.

21  Van Doren, pp. 139–42.

22  Van Doren, pp. 292–94.

23  Farrand, *Records*, Vol. 2, p. 568.

24  In Bancroft, p. 208.

25  In Douglas Southall Freeman, *Patriot and President*, Vol. 6 of *George Washington* (New York: Scribner's, 1943), p. 117.

26  In Farrand, *Records*, Vol. 1, p. 140.

27  In Farrand, *Records*, Vol. 1, p. 100.

28  In Farrand, *Records*, Vol. 1, p. 82.

29  Thach, p. 169.

30  Thach, pp. 191–95.

31  In Thach, p. 252.

32  Leonard D. White, *The Federalists: A Study in Administrative History* (New York: Macmillan, 1948), p. 103.

33  J. C. Fitzpatrick, ed., *The Diaries of George Washington*, Vol. 4 (Boston: Houghton Mifflin, 1925), p. 82.

34  Freeman, p. 265.

35  John A. Carroll and Mary W. Ashworth, *First in Peace*, Vol. 7 of *George Washington* (New York: Scribner's, 1957), pp. 353–57.

36  Saul K. Padover, ed., *The Complete Jefferson* (New York: Arno, 1943), pp. 138–39.

37  In Jared Sparks, *The Writings of George Washington*, Vol. 10 (Boston: F. Andrews, 1836), p. 186.

38  Edward S. Corwin, *The President's Control of Foreign Relations* (Princeton: Princeton University Press, 1917), Chapter 1.

39  In Carroll and Ashworth, p. xxiii.

## 3  Selection

1  Paul T. David, Ralph M. Goldman, and Richard C. Bain, *The Politics of National Party Conventions* (Washington, D.C.: Brookings, 1960), p. 311.

2  Theodore H. White, *The Making of the President, 1960* (New York: Atheneum, 1961), p. 50.

3  Richard Reeves, *Convention* (New York: Harcourt Brace Jovanovich, 1977), p. 10.

4  In Arthur S. Link, *Wilson: The Road to the White House* (Princeton: Princeton University Press, 1947), p. 405.

5  In James A. Farley, *Behind the Ballots* (New York: Harcourt Brace Jovanovich, 1938), p. 101.

6  In Farley, p. 89.

7  Margaret Leech, *In the Days of McKinley* (New York: Harper & Row, 1959), pp. 55–57.

8  E. J. Dionne, "Primaries Drawing Increased Turnouts," *New York Times*, March 9, 1980.

9  *Congressional Quarterly Weekly Reports*, July 8, 1972, p. 1650.

10  In Hedrick Smith, "Politicians Debate Change in Primaries," *New York Times*, June 15, 1980.

11  "Primaries '80: The System Worked, Sort Of," *New York Times*, June 8, 1980.

12  In Reeves, pp. 74–75.

13  Malcolm Moos and Stephen Hess, *The Making of Presidential Candidates* (New York, 1960).

14  *New York Times*, May 14 and 28, 1972; *Congressional Quarterly Weekly Reports*, February 19, 1972, p. 231.

15  Jeane Kirkpatrick, "Representation in

the American National Convention: The Case of 1972," *The British Journal of Political Science*, 5 (July 1975): 283.

16 E. J. Dionne, Jr., "Minorities and Women Gain," *New York Times*, August 12, 1980.

17 Richard A. Watson, *The Presidential Contest* (New York: Wiley, 1980), p. 16.

18 Watson, pp. 16–17; *Congressional Quarterly Weekly Reports*, August 4, 1979, p. 1609.

19 Gerald Pomper, "New Roles and New Games in the National Convention," paper presented at the 1977 annual meeting of the American Political Science Association.

20 In Frank Freidel, *Franklin D. Roosevelt: The Triumph* (Boston: Little, Brown, 1956), p. 294.

21 *New York Times*, August 24, 1972.

22 Freidel, *Franklin D. Roosevelt*, pp. 308–09.

23 Link, p. 462.

24 Howell Raines, "Reagan Studying an Opinion Poll on His Potential Running Mate," *New York Times*, July 4, 1980.

25 Howell Raines, "Ford Advisers Reportedly Asked Wide Concessions From Reagan," *New York Times*, July 18, 1980.

26 *New York Times*, August 11, 1968.

27 Jules Witcover, *Marathon: The Pursuit of the Presidency* (New York: Viking, 1977), p. 529.

28 *New York Times*, May 17, 1968.

29 Theodore H. White, *The Making of the President, 1972* (New York: Atheneum, 1973), pp. 49–50.

30 White, *Making of the President, 1972*, pp. 276–77; *Congressional Quarterly Weekly Reports*, August 12, 1972, pp. 1984–85.

31 White, *Making of the President, 1972*, p. 224.

32 Alfred Steinberg, *The Man from Missouri: The Life and Times of Harry S Truman* (New York: Putnam, 1962), pp. 322–24.

33 In Witcover, p. 598; see also Kandy Stroud, *How Jimmy Won* (New York: Morrow, 1977), pp. 373–74.

34 *Congressional Quarterly Weekly Reports*, April 15, 1972.

35 *Congressional Quarterly Weekly Reports*, April 15, 1972.

36 *New York Times*, October 4, 1972.

37 In Thomas E. Patterson and Robert D. McClure, *The Unseeing Eye: The Myth of Television Power in National Elections* (New York: Putnam, 1976), pp. 21–23.

38 Patterson and McClure, pp. 21–23.

39 Harold Mendelsohn and Irving Crespi, *Polls, Television, and the New Politics* (Scranton, Pa.: Chandler, 1970), p. 272.

40 Patterson and McClure, p. 22.

41 Herbert E. Alexander, "Communications and Politics: The Media and the Message," *Law and Contemporary Problems* (Spring 1969): 257–58.

42 Theodore H. White, *The Making of the President, 1964* (New York: Atheneum, 1965), p. 396.

43 In White, *Making of the President, 1972*, p. 429.

44 White, *Making of the President, 1972*, p. 166.

45 David Lee Rosenbloom, *The Election Men: Professional Campaign Managers and American Democracy* (New York: Quadrangle, 1973), pp. 30–58.

46 Herbert E. Alexander, *Financing Politics: Money, Elections and Political Reform* (Washington, D.C.: Congressional Quarterly Press, 1976), p. 28.

47 In *Congressional Quarterly Weekly Reports*, October 6, 1979, p. 2228.

48 *Congressional Quarterly Weekly Reports*, October 6, 1979, p. 2230.

49 Alexander, *Financing Politics*, pp. 30–33.

50 Adam Clymer, "Inflation and a Limit on Contributions Strain Presidential Hopefuls' Budget," *New York Times*, February 4, 1980.

51 Lucius Wilmerding, Jr., *The Electoral College* (New Brunswick, N.J.: Rutgers University Press, 1958), pp. 46–59.

52 Wilmerding, pp. 38–42. The most careful evaluation of the present electoral system and its alternatives is found in Wallace S. Sayre and Judith Parris, *Voting for President* (Washington, D.C.: Brookings, 1970).

53 Wilmerding, p. xi.

54 Wilmerding, p. 89.

55 This discussion draws upon the excellent analysis in Watson, *Presidential Contest*, pp. 91–102.

56 See Jeane Kirkpatrick, *The New Presidential Elite* (New York: Russell Sage Foundation, 1976).

57 V. O. Key, Jr., *The Responsible Electorate* (Cambridge, Mass.: Harvard University Press, 1966), pp. 7–8.

58 Jonathan Bingham, Letter to Editor, *New York Times*, March 15, 1979.

## 4 *Tenure*

1   Joseph E. Kallenbach, "Constitutional Limitations on Reeligibility of National and State Executives," *American Political Science Review* 46 (June 1952): 443

2   In Fred Rodell, *Democracy and the Third Term* (New York: Howell, Soskin, 1940), pp. 13–28.

3   Richard L. Strout, "The Twenty-second Amendment: A Second Look," *New York Times Magazine*, July 28, 1957, p. 5.

4   R. S. Baker, *Woodrow Wilson*, Vol. 6 (Garden City, N.Y.: Doubleday, 1927–39), pp. 438–52.

5   *New York Tribune*, November 5, 1920.

6   Concerning the resignation, see *New York Times*, August 9, 1974.

7   Richard M. Nixon, *RN: The Memoirs of Richard Nixon* (New York: Grosset & Dunlap, 1978), pp. 1056–58.

8   Concerning impeachment, see Raoul Berger, *Impeachment: The Constitutional Problems* (Cambridge, Mass., Harvard University Press, 1973) and Charles L. Black, Jr., *Impeachment: A Handbook* (New Haven, Conn.: Yale University Press, 1974).

9   Gideon Welles, *Diary of Gideon Welles*, Vol. 3 (Boston, 1911), p. 292.

10  Eric McKitrick, *Andrew Johnson and Reconstruction* (Chicago: University of Chicago Press, 1960), p. 318.

11  In McKitrick, p. 309.

12  In John F. Kennedy, *Profiles in Courage* (New York: Harper & Row, 1955), pp. 168–69. For a revisionist view, see M. L. Benedict, *The Impeachment and Trial of Andrew Johnson* (New York: Norton, 1973).

13  David E. Rosenbaum, "A Catalogue of Matters Involving the President," *New York Times*, February 10, 1974.

14  Concerning the articles of impeachment, see *New York Times*, July 22–August 1, 1974. For the House Judiciary Committee's final report, see *New York Times*, August 26, 1974.

15  The text of the Supreme Court's ruling in *Nixon* v. *United States* is in *New York Times*, July 25, 1974.

16  Thanks to legislation and court decisions, anyone can now listen to the Nixon tapes, currently available at the National Archives.

17  New York Times, July 25, 1974.

18  *Congressional Quarterly Weekly Reports*, May 26, 1973, p. 1314.

19  *New York Times*, March 12, 1974.

20  *New York Times*, June 12 and July 25, 1974.

21  Leon Jaworski, *The Right and the Power* (New York: Reader's Digest Press, 1976), p. 57.

22  The text of the President's declination is in *New York Times*, February 27, 1974.

23  *New York Times*, February 26, 1974.

24  The text of the Supreme Court's ruling is in *New York Times*, July 25, 1974.

25  The text of the President's letter is in *New York Times*, June 11, 1974.

26  The texts of the Proclamation of Pardon and accompanying statements by Ford and Nixon are in *New York Times*, September 9, 1974.

27  Jaworski, pp. 237–38.

28  *Congressional Quarterly Almanac, 1979* (Washington, D.C.: Congressional Quarterly, 1980), p. 361.

29  For extended treatment of the President's relationships with legal processes, see Edward S. Corwin, *The President: Office and Powers* (New York: New York University Press, 1957), pp. 119–58.

30  420 U.S. 35 (1974).

31  12 Wheat. 19 (1827).

32  Theodore Roosevelt, *Autobiography* (New York: Scribner's, 1931), pp. 388–89.

33  *Youngstown Sheet and Tube Company* v. *Sawyer*, 343 U.S. 579 (1952).

34  For discussion of the constitutional and legal background of the President's power, see *Note*, "Congress, the President, and the Power to Commit Forces to Combat," *Harvard Law Review*, vol. 81 (June 1968): 1771–1801.

35  For extended treatment of disability and succession problems see John D. Feerick, *From Failing Hands: The Story of Presidential Succession* (New York: Fordham University Press, 1965); Richard Hansen, *The Year We Had No President* (Lincoln, Neb.: University of Nebraska Press, 1962); and Ruth Silva, *Presidential Succession* (Ann Arbor, Mich.: University of Michigan Press, 1951).

36  Robert G. Caldwell, *James A. Garfield: Party Chieftain* (New York: Dodd, Mead, 1931), pp. 350–52; Theodore Clarke Smith, *The Life and Letters of James Abram Garfield*, Vol. 2 (New Haven, Conn.: Yale University Press, 1935), pp. 1194–97.

37  George F. Howe, *Chester A. Arthur:*

*A Quarter-Century of Machine Politics* (New York: Dodd, Mead, 1935), p. 152; David S. Muzzey, *James G. Blaine: A Political Idol of Other Days* (New York: Dodd, Mead, 1934), p. 197.

38  Howe, pp. 150–53.

39  Howe, p. 53.

40  Cary R. Grayson, *Woodrow Wilson: An Intimate Memoir* (New York: Holt, Rinehart & Winston, 1960), p. 99.

41  Joseph Tumulty, *Woodrow Wilson as I Know Him* (Garden City, N.Y.: Doubleday, 1921), pp. 446–48.

42  Grayson, p. 52.

43  In Edith Boling Wilson, *My Memoir* (Indianapolis, Ind.: Bobbs-Merrill, 1939), pp. 289–90.

44  Wilson, p. 290.

45  Tumulty, p. 443.

46  Herbert Hoover, *The Ordeal of Woodrow Wilson* (New York: McGraw-Hill, 1958), p. 275.

47  See Sherman Adams, *First-Hand Report* (New York: Harper & Row, 1961), pp. 181–87; Richard M. Nixon, *Six Crises* (Garden City, N.Y.: Doubleday, 1962), pp. 144–51.

48  In U.S. Senate Subcommittee on Constitutional Amendments, Judiciary Committee, *Hearings*, 88th Congress, 2nd Session (Washington, D.C.: U.S. Government Printing Office, 1964), p. 22.

49  In Clinton Rossiter, *The American Presidency*, rev. ed. (New York: Harcourt Brace Jovanovich, 1960), p. 214.

50  Nixon, *Six Crises*, p. 168.

51  *New York Times*, February 11, 1967.

52  In *New York Herald Tribune*, June 9, 1964.

53  Louis W. Koenig, *The Truman Administration* (New York: New York University Press, 1956), p. 43.

54  *New York Times*, October 13, 1973.

55  Laurin L. Henry, *Presidential Transitions* (Washington, D.C.: Brookings, 1960), pp. 474–76.

56  David T. Stanley, *Changing Administrations* (Washington, D.C.: Brookings, 1965), p. 6; *New York Times*, August 16, 1972.

57  Douglas E. Kneeland, "Triumphant Reagan Starting Transition to the White House," *New York Times*, November 7, 1980.

58  Warren Weaver, Jr., "Law Experts Critical of 25th Amendment," *New York Times*, December 19, 1974.

59  James M. Naughton, "Ford Backs Reappraisal of Presidential Succession," *New York Times*, February 27, 1975.

## 5  Publics

1  The leading general work is Elmer E. Cornwell, Jr., *Presidential Leadership of Public Opinion* (Bloomington, Ind.: University of Indiana Press, 1964).

2  In H. C. F. Bell, *Woodrow Wilson and the People* (Garden City, N.Y.: Doubleday, 1945), p. 113.

3  Theodore H. White, *Breach of Faith: The Fall of Richard Nixon* (New York: Atheneum, 1975), p. 268.

4  "Javits Says President Doubts Public Support," *New York Times*, February 21, 1979.

5  Everett Carll Ladd, Jr., "The Polls: The Question of Confidence," *Public Opinion Quarterly* 40 (Winter 1976–77): 544–55.

6  James MacGregor Burns, *Leadership* (New York: Harper & Row, 1978), pp. 141–254.

7  C. Wright Mills, *The Power Elite* (New York: Oxford University Press, 1956), p. 231.

8  See Joseph Schumpeter, *Capitalism, Socialism, and Democracy* (New York: Harper & Row, 1942), Part IV; and Peter Bachrach, *The Theory of Democratic Elitism* (Boston: Little, Brown, 1967).

9  Anthony Downs, *An Economic Theory of Democracy* (New York: Harper & Row, 1957).

10  Richard E. Neustadt, *Presidential Power: The Politics of Leadership* (New York: Wiley, 1960).

11  Transcript of news conference, *New York Times*, November 14, 1966.

12  Ralph H. Turner and Lewis M. Killian, *Collective Behavior* (Englewood Cliffs, N.J.: Prentice-Hall, 1957), pp. 308–10.

13  Fred Greenstein, "What the President Means to Americans," in *Choosing the President*, ed. James David Barber (Englewood Cliffs, N.J.: Prentice-Hall, 1974), p. 125.

14  Greenstein, p. 126.

15  Everett Ladd, p. 545.

16  In Robert E. DiClerico, *The American President* (Englewood Cliffs, N.J.: Prentice-Hall, 1979), p. 154.

17  Samuel Kernel, Peter Sperlich, and Aaron Wildavsky, "Public Support for Presidents," in *Perspectives on the Presidency*, ed. Aaron Wildavsky (Boston: Little, Brown, 1975), p. 153.

18  Arthur Miller et al., "Presidential Crises and Political Support: The Impact of Watergate on Attitudes toward Institutions," paper presented at the Midwest Political Science Association Convention, Chicago, May 1–3, 1975, pp. 27–28.

19  Francis Rourke et al., *Trust and Confidence in the American System* (Washington, D.C.: Potomac Associates, 1976), p. 22.

20  Everett Ladd, p. 546.

21  For discussion of these studies, see Martha Wolfenstein and Gilbert Kliman, eds., *Children and the Death of a President* (Garden City, N.Y.: Doubleday, 1965), pp. 33–40.

22  Wolfenstein and Kliman, pp. 184–88.

23  Louis Harris, *The Anguish of Change* (New York: Norton, 1974), pp. 231–32.

24  Nadine Brozan, "Between Parent and Child, What Does Watergate Mean?" *New York Times*, November 23, 1973.

25  F. Christopher Arterton, "Watergate Children's Attitudes Toward Political Authority Revisited," *Political Science Quarterly* 90 (Fall 1975): 477–96.

26  *New York Times*, March 24, 1974.

27  For background on concepts, see James T. Tedeschi, ed., *The Social Influence Process* (Chicago: Aldine, 1972), pp. 51–53.

28  Quoted in *New York Times*, October 9, 1974.

29  William S. White, *The Responsibles* (New York: Harper & Row, 1972), pp. 178–79.

30  Eric F. Goldman, *The Tragedy of Lyndon Johnson* (New York: Knopf, 1969), p. 416.

31  James Reston, "Washington: On the Art of Backing into the Future," *New York Times*, March 11, 1970.

32  For discussions of roles, see Luigi Petrullo and Bernard M. Bass, eds., *Leaderships and Interpersonal Behavior* (New York: Holt, Rinehart & Winston, 1961), pp. 17–75; and Erving Goffman, *Encounters: Two Studies in the Sociology of Interaction* (Indianapolis, Ind.: University of Indiana Press, 1961), pp. 85–88.

33  Newton N. Minow, John Bartlow Martin, and Lee M. Mitchell, *Presidential Television* (New York: Basic Books, 1973), pp. 5–6. See also Stewart Alsop, *The Center* (New York: Harper & Row, 1969); and Douglass Cater, *The Fourth Branch of Government* (Boston: Houghton Mifflin, 1959).

34  In Minow et al., p. vii. For comprehensive treatment of the presidency and television, see William C. Spragens, *The Presidency and the Mass Media in the Age of Television* (Washington, D.C.: University Press of America, 1978).

35  Michael J. Robinson, "Television and American Politics," *Public Interest* (Summer 1977), p. 11.

36  Frank Mankiewicz and Joel Swerdlow, *Remote Control: Television and the Manipulation of American Life* (New York: Times Books, 1978), pp. 78–79.

37  Richard A. Watson, *The Presidential Contest* (New York: Wiley, 1980), pp. 98–99.

38  David Broder, "Political Reporters in Presidential Politics," in *Inside the System*, eds. Charles Peters and John Rothchild (New York: Praeger, 1973), p. 29.

39  In George Christian, *The President Steps Down* (New York: Macmillan, 1970), p. 188. Concerning the problem of the credibility gap, see David Wise, *The Politics of Lying* (New York: Random House, 1971); Bruce Ladd, *The Crisis of Credibility* (New York: New American Library, 1968).

40  Robert Sherrill, "Tales of the White House Press Corps," *The Nation* 229 (December 1, 1979): 555–56; see also Thomas Collins, "The President and the Press," *Newsday*, November 15, 1977; and James Reston, "Carter and the Press," *New York Times*, April 12, 1978.

41  Michael B. Grossman and Francis E. Rourke, "The Media and the Presidency: An Exchange Analysis," *Political Science Quarterly* 91 (Fall 1976), pp. 455–70.

42  In Terence Smith, "Rafshoon Plays Down Role in White House," *New York Times*, November 27, 1978.

43  Harry McPherson, *A Political Education* (Boston: Little, Brown, 1972), p. 265.

44  Dom Bonafede, "Powell and the Press: A New Mood in the White House," *National Journal* (June 25, 1980): 980–86.

45  Leo Rosten, *The Washington Correspondents* (New York: Arno, 1974), p. 47.

46  See Cornwell, pp. 189–90.

47  *New York Times*, April 27, 1969.

48  *New York Times*, June 19, 1972.
49  *New York Times*, August 29, 1974.
50  James Reston, "The Uses of the Press," *New York Times*, March 25, 1977.
51  Arthur Krock, "Mr. Kennedy's Management of the News," *Fortune* 67 (March 1963), p. 82.
52  Krock, "Mr. Kennedy's Management," p. 82.
53  George F. Howe, *Chester A. Arthur: A Quarter-Century of Machine Politics* (New York: Dodd, Mead, 1934), p. 173.
54  Bonafede, p. 986.
55  Bonafede, p. 981.
56  Minow et al., pp. 55–56.
57  Les Brown, "Files Show the Nixon White House Tried to Mold Public TV Politically," *New York Times*, February 24, 1979.
58  *New York Times*, November 1, 1973.
59  See James Reston, *The Artillery of the Press* (New York: Harper & Row, 1967), pp. 20–21.
60  In James G. Randall and Richard N. Current, *Lincoln the President: Last Full Measure* (New York: Dodd, Mead, 1955), pp. 42–44.
61  Harold Mendelsohn and Irving Crespi, *Polls, Television, and the New Politics* (Scranton, Pa.: Chandler, 1970), p. 16.
62  Mendelsohn and Crespi, pp. 73–74.
63  Henry Kissinger, *White House Years* (Boston: Little, Brown, 1979), pp. 512–13.
64  "Approval of Carter Drops to 46% in Poll," *New York Times*, April 14, 1978.
65  Robert Reinhold, "Experts Ask Changes to Ease Flow of Information to the Public," *New York Times*, November 20, 1973.

# 6  Party Chief

1  Norman H. Nie et al., *The Changing American Voter* (Cambridge, Mass.: Harvard, 1976), p. 347.
2  Richard L. Rubin, *Party Dynamics: The Democratic Coalition and the Politics of Change* (New York: Oxford, 1976), p. 13.
3  Everett Carll Ladd, Jr. and Charles D. Hadley, *Transformations of the American Party System* (New York: Norton, 1978), pp. 232–34.
4  Ladd and Hadley, pp. 238, 269.
5  Ladd and Hadley, pp.. 259, 293–94.
6  In Clinton Rossiter, *Parties and Politics in America* (Ithaca, N.Y.: Cornell University Press, 1960), p. 15.
7  In James A. Farley, *Behind the Ballots* (New York: Harcourt Brace Jovanovich, 1938), p. 293.
8  Allan Nevins, *Grover Cleveland: A Study in Courage* (New York: Dodd, Mead, 1932), p. 401.
9  In Jules Witcover, *Marathon: The Pursuit of the Presidency, 1972–1976* (New York: Viking, 1977), pp. 517–18.
10  Sherman Adams, *First-Hand Report* (New York: Harper & Row, 1961), p. 167.
11  Adams, p. 167.
12  Hedrick Smith, "The Message of Memphis," *New York Times*, December 11, 1978; David Broder, "Will the Democrats Lose Their Soul?," *Newsday*, December 13, 1978.
13  Cabell Phillips, *The Truman Presidency* (New York: Macmillan, 1966), p. 195.
14  Terence Smith, "Carter Said to Ask for Loyalty Check," *New York Times*, November 7, 1979.
15  Comment, *The New Republic* 181 (December 15, 1979): 5.
16  Editorial, *The Nation* 229 (December 22, 1979): 641.
17  Douglas Kneeland, "Mrs. Byrne a Target of Carter Campaign," *New York Times*, December 9, 1979.
18  Carl R. Fish, *The Civil Service and the Patronage* (Cambridge, Mass: Harvard, 1920), p. 82.
19  Nevins, p. 219.
20  Farley, *Ballots*, p. 267.
21  Martin and Susan Tolchin, *To the Victor* (New York: Random House, 1971), pp. 283–88.
22  Frank J. Sorauf, *Political Parties in the American System* (Boston: Little, Brown, 1964), pp. 82–89.
23  Helmut Norpath, "Explaining Party Cohesion in Congress: The Case of Shared Policy Attitudes," *American Political Science Review* 70 (December 1976): 1156–71.
24  Hugh Bone, *Party Committees and National Politics* (Seattle: University of Washington, 1958), p. 219.
25  *New York Times*, October 1, 1972.
26  In Nathan Schachner, *Thomas Jefferson: A Biography* (New York: Yoseloff, 1951), p. 703.
27  Schachner, p. 704.
28  Schachner, pp. 709, 810.
29  William Cabell Bruce, *John Randolph of Roanoke* (New York: Octagon, 1969), p. 265.

30  Bennett Champ Clark, *John Quincy Adams* (Boston: Little, Brown, 1932), pp. 242–46.

31  Clark, pp. 252–53.

32  Oliver Perry Chitwood, *John Tyler: Champion of the Old South* (New York: Russell, 1964), p. 217.

33  Chitwood, p. 317.

34  Chitwood, p. 317.

35  Chitwood, p. 317.

36  Farley, *Ballots*, p. 231.

37  James A. Farley, *Jim Farley's Story* (Westport, Ct.: Greenwood, 1964), p. 96.

38  Farley, *Story*, pp. 122–33.

39  Farley, *Story*, p. 133.

40  The most extended analysis of presidential abuses is in Arthur Schlesinger, Jr., *The Imperial Presidency* (Boston: Houghton Mifflin, 1973), pp. 409–23.

41  Schlesinger, pp. 598–99.

42  Adams, pp. 25–26.

43  Adams, p. 21.

44  Dwight D. Eisenhower, *Mandate for Change* (Garden City, N.Y.: Doubleday, 1963), p. 431.

45  Robert J. Donovan, *Eisenhower: The Inside Story* (New York: Harper & Row, 1956), p. 56.

46  Adams, p. 166.

47  Adams, p. 287.

48  Theodore H. White, *The Making of the President, 1972* (New York: Atheneum, 1973), pp. 49–50; Philip Shabecoff, "Hard Hats Spurred Nixon Labor Bid," *New York Times*, October 12, 1972.

49  Kevin P. Philips, *The Emerging Republican Majority* (New Rochelle, N.Y.: Arlington House, 1969), pp. 437–40.

50  *Congressional Quarterly Almanac, 1969*, p. 114. Concerning Nixon's Southern strategy, see Leon Panetta and Peter Call, *Bring Us Together* (Philadelphia: Lippincott, 1971); and Reg Murphy and Hal Gullever, *The Southern Strategy* (New York: Scribners, 1971).

51  In White, *Making of the President, 1972*, p. 49.

52  Clayton Fritchey, "Nixon Isn't the GOP's Man Any More," *Newsday*, January 17, 1973.

53  Robert Bendiner, "Election 'Bible' Reexamined," *New York Times*, November 9, 1970.

54  Robert Kelley, "America's 6th Major Voter Shift," *New York Times*, November 11, 1980.

55  Kandy Stroud, *How Jimmy Won* (New York: Morrow, 1977), pp. 16–17.

56  Witcover, pp. 521–22.

57  *Congressional Quarterly Almanac, 1978* (Washington, D.C.: Congressional Quarterly, 1979), p. 11.

58  Haynes Johnson, *In the Absence of Power* (New York: Viking, 1980), pp. 158–60.

59  *Congressional Quarterly Almanac, 1978*, p. 11.

60  Dom Bonafede, "A New Look for White House Lobbyists," *National Journal* 11 (January 13, 1979): 55.

61  *Congressional Quarterly Almanac, 1978*, p. 10.

62  *Congressional Quarterly Weekly Reports*, January 27, 1979, p. 107.

63  Ladd and Hadley, p. 278.

64  Richard E. Neustadt, "The Presidency after Watergate," *New York Times Magazine*, October 13, 1973.

65  Nie, p. 352.

66  *New York Times*, October 25, 1973; Newton N. Minow, John Bartlow Martin, and Lee M. Mitchell, *Presidential Television* (New York: Basic Books, 1973), pp. 126–58.

# 7  Legislative Leader

1  *New York Times*, October 10, 14, and 19, 1974.

2  Dwight D. Eisenhower, *Mandate for Change* (Garden City, N.Y.: Doubleday, 1963), p. 502.

3  Eisenhower, pp. 194–95.

4  *Congressional Quarterly Weekly Reports*, August 12, 1972, pp. 2002–004.

5  *Congressional Quarterly Almanac, 1965*, vol. 21 (Washington, D.C., 1966), p. 67.

6  In Ralph K. Huitt, "Democratic Party Leadership in the Senate," *American Political Science Review* 55 (June 1961): 353.

7  In Charles Mohr, "Carter and Congress," *New York Times*, December 9, 1977.

8  Stephen J. Wayne, *The Legislative Presidency* (New York: Harper & Row, 1978), pp. 21–22.

9  See Jack Van Der Slik, *American Legislative Processes* (New York: Crowell, 1977), pp. 104–22.

10  For thoughtful elaboration, see Louis Fisher, *Presidency and Congress* (New York: Free Press, 1972), pp. 122–27; and for critiques of Nixon's impound-

ments, see *New York Times*, June 8, 1972 and February 12, 1973.

11  See *New York Times*, March 5, 13, and July 23, 1973. The leading work on executive privilege is Raoul Berger, *Executive Privilege: A Constitutional Myth* (Cambridge, Mass.: Harvard, 1974). A valuable collection of materials is in U.S. Senate Subcommittee on Separation of Powers, Committee on the Judiciary, *Executive Privilege: The Withholding of Information by the Executive* (Washington, D.C.: U.S. Government Printing Office, 1971).

12  For excerpts from the court's opinion, see *New York Times*, October 13, 1973.

13  In *Congressional Quarterly Almanac, 1970*, pp. 89, 154–56.

14  *Congressional Quarterly Almanac, 1974* (Washington, D.C.: Congressional Quarterly, 1975), p. 153.

15  *Congressional Quarterly Almanac, 1974*, pp. 145–52.

16  Randall B. Ripley, "Carter and Congress," in Steven A. Shull and Lance T. LeLoup, *The Presidency: Studies in Policy Making* (Brunswick, Ohio: King's Court, 1979), pp. 71–72.

17  Public Law 94-412, National Emergencies Act, 94th Congress, September 14, 1976; *Congressional Quarterly Almanac, 1976*, pp. 521–22.

18  Ripley, p. 81.

19  David E. Rosenbaum, "Carter's Program Will Face a More Assertive Congress," *New York Times*, November 28, 1976.

20  *Congressional Quarterly Almanac, 1978*, pp. 6–7. Michel's quotation is from Steven V. Roberts, "G.O.P. Faces Reality in Running Congress," *New York Times*, November 16, 1980. Concerning Dole and Thurmond, see Steven V. Roberts, "G.O.P. Chiefs Dissent on Aims Reagan Supports," *New York Times*, November 7, 1980.

21  *Congressional Quarterly Almanac, 1975*, p. 28; Ripley, pp. 72–73.

22  *Congressional Quarterly Weekly Reports*, November 24, 1979, pp. 2631–47.

23  See Richard E. Neustadt, "Presidency and Legislation: Planning the President's Program," *American Political Review* 49 (December 1955): 980.

24  Robert Donovan, *Eisenhower: The Inside Story* (New York: Harper & Row, 1956), p. 83.

25  *Congressional Quarterly Weekly Reports*, January 15, 1972, pp. 74–75.

26  *Congressional Quarterly Almanac, 1973*, p. 946.

27  *Congressional Quarterly Almanac, 1978*, p. 34C.

28  Sherman Adams, *First-Hand Report* (New York: Harper & Row, 1961), pp. 25–26.

29  Huitt, p. 353.

30  Wayne, pp. 8–19.

31  George C. Edwards III, *Presidential Influence in Congress* (San Francisco: Freeman, 1980), p. 97; Walter Dean Burnham, "Insulation and Responsiveness in Congressional Elections," *Political Science Quarterly* 90 (Fall 1975), pp. 412–13.

32  Edwards, *Presidential Influence in Congress*, pp. 191, 202.

33  Lyndon B. Johnson, *The Vantage Point* (New York: Holt, Rinehart & Winston, 1971), pp. 326–27.

34  Louis W. Koenig, *The Truman Administration* (New York: New York University Press, 1956), pp. 240–46.

35  Arthur S. Link, *Wilson: The New Freedom* (Princeton, N.J.: Princeton University Press, 1956), pp. 146–49.

36  Link, p. 151; Arthur W. Macmahon, "Woodrow Wilson as Legislative Leader and Administrator," *American Political Science Review* 50 (September 1956): 656.

37  In Tom Wicker, "The Johnson Way with Congress," *New York Times Magazine*, March 8, 1964, p. 103.

38  See Marshall E. Dimock, "Wilson the Domestic Reformer," *Virginia Quarterly Review* 32 (Autumn 1956): 549–50.

39  Helen Fuller, *Year of Trial: Kennedy's Crucial Decisions* (New York: Harcourt Brace Jovanovich, 1962), pp. 255–57.

40  Marjorie Hunter, "President Seeks Congress Accord," *New York Times*, August 13, 1974.

41  Fuller, p. 97.

42  Neustadt, p. 980.

43  Koenig, pp. 148–76.

44  Martin Tolchin, "Congressional Priorities Proposed by Congress," *New York Times*, January 15, 1978.

45  Link, pp. 146–57.

46  Macmahon, pp. 651–56.

47  *New York Times*, July 12, 1965.

48  In James MacGregor Burns, "The One Test for the Presidency," *New York Times Magazine*, May 1, 1960, p. 102.

49  Eisenhower, p. 286.
50  Adams, pp. 25–27.
51  Adams, p. 9.
52  *New York Times,* March 23, 1966.
53  News conference, *New York Times,* November 14, 1966.
54  Macmahon, pp. 652–56.
55  See Edward S. Corwin, *The President: Office and Powers,* 4th ed. (New York: New York University Press, 1957), pp. 250–52.
56  Philip S. Klein, *President James Buchanan* (University Park, Pa.: Pennsylvania State University Press, 1962), pp. 396–97.
57  This discussion draws upon *Congressional Quarterly Almanac, 1978,* pp. 3–7.
58  Jim Toedtman, "Unsettled Congress Forces Concessions," *Newsday,* January 10, 1979.

## 8  *Administrative Chief*

1  Richard Rose, "The President: A Chief But Not an Executive," *Presidential Studies Quarterly* 7 (Winter 1977): 5.
2  William D. Carey, "Presidential Staffing in the Sixties and Seventies," *Public Administration Review* 29 (September–October 1969): 450–52. See also Norman C. Thomas, "Presidential Advice and Information," *Law and Contemporary Problems* 35 (Summer 1970): 540–72; and Alex B. Lacy, "The White House Staff Bureaucracy," *Trans-Action* 6 (January 1969): 50.
3  Lecture, "Training for the Presidency," delivered at New York University, May 2, 1957. For a cogent discussion of the President's relations with the departments, see Thomas Cronin, "Everybody Believes in Democracy Until He Gets to the White House," *Law and Contemporary Problems* 35 (Summer 1970): 573–625.
4  Cronin, p. 365.
5  In Richard P. Nathan, "The Administrative Presidency," *The Public Interest* (Summer 1976): 40–44.
6  Cronin, pp. 364–66.
7  Cronin, pp. 366–67.
8  Joel D. Aberbach and Bert A. Rockman, "Clashing Beliefs Within the Executive Branch: The Nixon Administration Bureaucracy," *American Political Science Review* 70 (June 1976): 467–68.
9  Robert Sullivan, "The Role of the Presidency in Shaping Lower Level Policy-Making Processes," *Polity* 3 (Winter 1970): 201–21.
10  Richard Nathan, *The Plot That Failed* (New York: Wiley, 1976), pp. 37–54.
11  Richard F. Fenno, Jr., *The President's Cabinet* (Cambridge, Mass.: Harvard, 1959), p. 5.
12  Hugh Heclo, *A Government of Strangers* (Washington, D.C.: Brookings, 1977).
13  Nelson W. Polsby, "Presidential Cabinet Making: Lessons for the Political System," *Political Science Quarterly* 93 (Spring 1978): 15–25.
14  Keith Clark and Laurence Legere, *The President and the Management of National Security* (New York: Praeger, 1969), pp. 37–54.
15  *New York Times,* November 29, 1969.
16  Steven R. Weisman, "McIntyre Gains as Carter Aide," *New York Times,* January 28, 1980. For an informed and cogent account of the Office of Management and Budget, see Larry Berman, *The Office of Management and Budget and the Presidency* (Princeton: Princeton University Press, 1979).
17  John H. Kessel, *The Domestic Presidency* (North Scituate, Mass.: Duxbury, 1975).
18  Clyde H. Farnsworth, "Eizenstat Is Helping to Fill a Vacuum," *New York Times,* December 3, 1978; Dom Bonafede, "New Habits for a New Year," *National Journal* 11 (January 6, 1979): 24.
19  White, p. 83. For extended discussions of recent Vice Presidents, see Donald Young, *American Roulette* (New York: Holt, Rinehart & Winston, 1974); Leonard Baker, *The Eclipse of Lyndon Johnson* (New York: Macmillan, 1966); concerning Hubert Humphrey, see Allan B. Ryskind, *Hubert* (New Rochelle: Arlington House, 1968), and Hubert H. Humphrey, *The Education of a Public Man* (Garden City, N.Y.: Doubleday, 1976), pp. 313–423; concerning Spiro Agnew, see Theodore Lippman, *Spiro Agnew's America* (New York: Norton, 1972), and Richard M. Cohen and Jules Witcover, *A Heartbeat Away* (New York: Viking, 1974). The case for abolishing the Vice Presidency is found in Arthur M. Schlesinger, Jr., "Is the Vice Presidency Necessary?" *Atlantic* 234 (May 1974): 37–44.
20  In Louis Koenig, *The Invisible Pres-*

idency (New York: Holt, Rinehart & Winston, 1960), p. 308.

21 New York Times, December 21, 1940.
22 Rexford G. Tugwell, The Democratic Roosevelt (Garden City, N.Y.: Doubleday, 1957), p. 14.
23 Dwight D. Eisenhower, Mandate for Change (Garden City, N.Y.: Doubleday, 1963), p. 87.
24 Eisenhower, p. 135.
25 Sherman Adams, First-Hand Report (New York: Harper & Row, 1961), p. 51; Koenig, p. 338.
26 Ezra Taft Benson, Cross Fire: The Eight Years with Eisenhower (Garden City, N.Y.: Doubleday, 1962), pp. 386–89.
27 James Reston, "Washington: A 'Small' Staff in an Open Administration," New York Times, June 17, 1970; New York Times, May 10, 1970. For a critique of the Nixon staff, see Richard Whalen, Catch the Falling Flag (Boston: Houghton Mifflin, 1972).
28 R. W. Apple Jr., "Haldeman the Fierce, Haldeman the Faithful, Haldeman the Fallen," New York Times Magazine, May 6, 1973; Mary McCarthy, The Mask of State: Watergate Portraits (New York: Harcourt Brace Jovanovich, 1974), pp. 108–15.
29 In J. Anthony Lukas, "The Story So Far," New York Times Magazine, June 22, 1973, p. 13; McCarthy, pp. 108–09.
30 John Pierson, "Right-Hand Man," Wall Street Journal, January 22, 1970. For an insider's account, see Jeb Stuart Magruder, An American Life: One Man's Road to Watergate (New York: Atheneum, 1974).
31 William V. Shannon, "The Sad Young Men," New York Times, July 25, 1973.
32 New York Times, June 22, 1970. For extended treatment of the Nixon staff's misdeeds, see Bob Woodward and Carl Bernstein, All the President's Men (New York: Simon & Schuster, 1974).
33 New York Times, July 8, 1973.
34 New York Times, July 28, 1970.
35 New York Times, March 26, 1971.
36 Joseph A. Califano, "The Nixon Plan Makes Sense," New York Times, January 29, 1971; New York Times, March 26, 1971.
37 James L. Sundquist, "Jimmy Carter as Public Administrator: An Appraisal at Mid-Term," Public Administration Review 39 (January-February, 1979): 3–9.

38 Stephen Hess, Organizing the Presidency (Washington, D.C.: Brookings, 1976).
39 Timothy R. Clark, "The Power Vacuum Outside the Oval Office," National Journal 11 (February 24, 1979): 296–97.
40 In Clark, pp. 298–99.
41 Sundquist, p. 6.
42 Charles Mohr, "Carter Advisers Ask Revision and 30% Cut in White House Staff," New York Times July 7, 1977.
43 Sundquist, pp. 4–5.
44 John R. Dempsey, "Carter Reorganization: A Midterm Appraisal," Public Administration Review 39 (January-February 1979), pp. 75–76.
45 Terence Smith, "President Summons Aides to Camp David for a Broad Review," New York Times, July 7, 1979.
46 George Reedy, The Twilight of the Presidency (New York: NAL-World, 1970).
47 William Safire, Before the Fall (Garden City, N.Y.: Doubleday, 1975), p. 350.
48 Charles Hardin, Presidential Power and Accountability (Chicago: University of Chicago Press, 1974), p. 41.
49 In Lewis J. Paper, The Promise and the Performance (New York: Crown, 1975), p. 119.
50 Henry Kissinger, White House Years (Boston: Little, Brown, 1979), pp. 245–46.
51 In Stephen J. Wayne, The Legislative Presidency (New York: Harper & Row, 1978), p. 54.

## 9 Chief Diplomat

1 In Clinton Rossiter, The American Presidency, rev. ed. (New York: Harcourt Brace Jovanovich, 1960), p. 10.
2 Rossiter, p. 10.
3 Edward S. Corwin, The President: Office and Powers, 4th ed. (New York: New York University Press, 1957), p. 180.
4 New York Times, July 24, 1973.
5 New York Times, July 24, 1973.
6 See Louis W. Koenig, The Invisible Presidency (New York: Holt, Rinehart & Winston, 1960), p. 14.
7 Adam Clymer, "Senate Votes to Give up Canal," New York Times, April 19, 1978.
8 New York Times, October 19, 1972. On Congress's power, see Jacob K. Javits, "The Congressional Presence

in Foreign Relations," *Foreign Relations* 48 (January 1970): 232; Jacob K. Javits, *Who Makes War: The President Versus Congress* (New York: Morrow, 1973); and Louis Fisher, *President and Congress* (New York: Free Press, 1972), pp. 225–28.

9  Leslie H. Gelb, "A Domestic Challenge to Executive Agreements," *New York Times*, September 17, 1975.

10 Sherman Adams, *First-Hand Report* (New York: Harper & Row, 1961), pp. 93–94.

11 For the text of the President's statement, see *New York Times*, December 16, 1978, p. 8.

12 For extended discussion see *Congressional Quarterly Guide to American Government* (Washington, D.C., Autumn 1966), pp. 4–5.

13 In James Grafton Rogers, *World Policing and the Constitution* (Boston, 1945), p. 36.

14 Dwight D. Eisenhower, *Mandate for Change* (Garden City, N.Y.: Doubleday, 1963), pp. 129–30.

15 Eisenhower, p. 271.

16 David Halberstam, *The Best and the Brightest* (New York: Random House, 1972), p. 419.

17 *New York Times*, May 9, 1972.

18 Jacob K. Javits, "The Balance in the War Powers Bill," *New York Times*, February 14, 1972.

19 In *New York Times*, November 8, 1973.

20 *New York Times*, May 15, 1975; see also Michael F. Kelley, "The Constitutional Implications of the Mayaguez Incident," *Hastings Constitutional Law Quarterly* 3 (Winter 1976): 301.

21 David Binder, "Angola Reported Getting $50 Million in U.S. Arms," *New York Times*, December 12, 1975.

22 Bernard Gwertzman, "Carter Cites Limits on Policy in Angola," *New York Times*, May 24, 1978.

23 Graham Hovey, "U.S. Will Send Zaire $13 Million Package," *New York Times*, April 13, 1977.

24 Terrence Smith, "President to Oppose Any Further Limits on Right to Give Aid," *New York Times*, May 26, 1978.

25 Thomas Franck and Edward Weisband, "Lapdogs No More," *New York Times*, November 28, 1976; Martin Tolchin, "Congress Broadens Its Influence on Foreign Policy," *New York Times*, December 24, 1979.

26 In Tolchin, *New York Times*, December 24, 1979.

27 In Eleanor Lansing Dulles, *John Foster Dulles: The Last Year* (New York: Harcourt Brace Jovanovich, 1963).

28 Adams, *First-Hand Report*, pp. 89–90.

29 In Commission on Organization of the Executive Branch of the Government, *Task Force Report on Foreign Affairs* (Washington, D.C.: U.S. Government Printing Office, 1949), p. 83.

30 Commission on Organization, p. 266.

31 Harry S Truman, *Year of Decisions*, Vol. 1 of *Memoirs* (Garden City, N.Y.: Doubleday, 1955), pp. 22–23.

32 For studies of Kissinger, see David Landau, *Kissinger: The Uses of Power* (Boston: Houghton Mifflin, 1972), and Stephen R. Graubard, *Kissinger: Portrait of a Mind* (New York, 1973).

33 Landau, p. 92; Richard M. Nixon, "Asia after Viet Nam," *Foreign Affairs* 46 (October 1967): 111.

34 Subcommittee on Separation of Powers, Senate Judiciary Committee, "Executive Privilege: The Withholding of Information by the Executive" (Washington, D.C., 1971), p. 270.

35 *New York Times*, March 3, 1971.

36 Joseph Kraft, "Secretary Henry," *New York Times Magazine*, October 28, 1973, p. 82.

37 David Broder, "A Time of Testing for Brzezinski," *Newsday*, November 7, 1977.

38 Dom Bonafede, "Who's On First in the Foreign Policy Game?," *National Journal*, February 17, 1979, p. 271.

39 Richard Burt, "Brzezinski Seeking Stronger Influence," *New York Times*, November 5, 1979.

40 Frederick C. Thayer, "Presidential Policy Processes and 'New Administration': A Search for Revised Paradigms," *Public Administration Review* 31 (September-October 1971): 555–56.

41 Edward A. Kolodziej, "The National Security Council: Innovations and Implications," *Public Administration Review* 29 (November-December 1969): 578–81.

42 Charles W. Yost, "The Instruments of American Foreign Policy," *Foreign Affairs*, 50 (October 1971): 64; the Reagan quotation is from "An Interview with Ronald Reagan," *Time*, November 17, 1980, p. 37.

43   John Robinson Beal, *John Foster Dulles* (New York, 1957), p. 279.

44   Lyndon Baines Johnson, *The Vantage Point: Perspectives on the Presidency, 1963–1969* (New York: Holt, Rinehart & Winston, 1971).

45   Chester L. Cooper, "The CIA and Decision-Making," *Foreign Affairs* 50 (January 1972): 223–36. For comprehensive treatment of the CIA, see Victor Marchetti and John D. Marks, *The CIA and the Cult of Intelligence* (New York, 1974).

46   For details concerning the CIA and Chile, see *New York Times*, September 8 and 23, 1974.

47   *New York Times*, October 23, 1974.

48   Hedrick Smith, "CIA Director Given Wide Budget Power," *New York Times*, August 4, 1977; Nicholas M. Horrock, "The Carter Solution is to Try Centralizing," *New York Times*, August 7, 1977.

49   Richard Burt, "President is Seeking to Ease C.I.A. Curb," *New York Times*, January 11, 1980.

50   In *New York Times*, May 21, 1961.

51   In I. M. Destler, *Presidents, Bureaucrats, and Foreign Policy* (Princeton: Princeton University Press, 1972), pp. 87–88.

52   In *New York Times*, October 8, 1972.

53   *New York Times*, November 17, 1970. Concerning Nixon's foreign policy generally, see Robert Osgood, ed., *Retreat from Empire* (Baltimore: Johns Hopkins, 1973).

54   *New York Times*, January 7, 1972.

55   *New York Times*, August 4, 1971.

56   Jonathan Kandell, "Carter Warns Chief of French Socialists," *New York Times*, January 7, 1978.

57   Max Frankel, "Behind the Cold Print," *New York Times*, February 29, 1972; *Newsweek*, "First Steps of a Long March," March 6, 1972, pp. 14–23; the Reagan quotation is from "An Interview with Ronald Reagan," *Time*, November 17, 1980, p. 36.

58   Terrence Smith, "President and Teng Confer Four Hours," *New York Times*, January 30, 1979.

59   *New York Times*, May 8, 1972.

60   In *New York Times*, July 26, 1972.

61   John Vinocur, "It's Both Style and Substance That Divide Bonn and U.S.," *New York Times*, March 2, 1980.

62   John Vinocur, "Schmidt's Personal Victory," *New York Times*, March 10, 1980.

63   In Jonathan Daniels, *The Man of Independence* (Philadelphia: Lippincott, 1950), p. 285.

64   Edward Schumacher, "For Carter, a Shift in View on Russians," *New York Times*, January 24, 1980.

65   Terrence Smith, "The World Has Changed and So Has Jimmy Carter," *New York Times*, January 20, 1980.

66   Henry Kissinger, *White House Years* (Boston: Little, Brown, 1979), p. 1422.

67   Kissinger, p. 963.

68   William Borders, "Carter Criticized in London Study," *New York Times*, May 16, 1979.

69   Craig R. Whitney, "In Moscow, Uncertainty on U.S. Policy," *New York Times*, October 12, 1979.

70   Thomas L. Hughes, "Carter and the Management of Contradictions," in Steven A. Shull and Lance T. Le Loup, *The Presidency: Studies in Policy Making* (Brunswick, O.: King's Court Communications, 1979), pp. 255–69.

71   *New York Times*, September 21, 1963.

72   *New York Times*, November 6, 1974.

## 10   Commander-in-Chief

1    Adam Yarmolinsky, *The Military Establishment* (New York: Harper & Row, 1971), pp. 381–91. McNamara's budget and systems analysis innovations are examined in Leonard Merewitz and Stephen Sosnick, *The Budget's New Clothes* (Chicago: University of Chicago, 1971).

2    David Halberstam, *The Best and the Brightest* (New York: Random House, 1972), p. 405; Yarmolinsky, *Military Establishment*, p. 91.

3    Neil Sheehan, "Influence of Joint Chiefs Is Reported Rising," *New York Times*, June 30, 1969.

4    Elmo R. Zumwalt, Jr., *On Watch* (New York: Quadrangle, 1976), p. 290.

5    Bernard Weinraub, "Joint Chiefs Losing Sway Under Carter," *New York Times*, July 6, 1978.

6    Drew Middleton, "Shaping Policy: A Military Role," *New York Times*, November 1, 1977.

7    Henry Kissinger, *White House Years* (Boston: Little, Brown, 1979), p. 217.

8    Morton H. Halperin, "The President and the Military," *Foreign Affairs* 50 (January 1972): 310–12.

9    In Harry S Truman, *Years of Trial*

and Hope, vol. 2 of Memoirs (Garden City, N.Y.: Doubleday, 1956), p. 354.

10 Truman, pp. 365–83.

11 Truman, pp. 384–85.

12 Truman, p. 445; Richard H. Rovere and Arthur M. Schlesinger, Jr., The General and the President (New York: Macmillan, 1951), p. 169.

13 Truman, p. 356; Walter Millis, Arms and the State (New York: Kraus, 1958), pp. 319–20.

14 Edward S. Corwin, The President: Office and Powers, rev. ed. (New York: New York University Press, 1957), pp. 229–32; J. G. Randall, The President: Midstream (New York: Dodd, Mead, 1952), pp. 152–53.

15 New York Times, March 9, 1962.

16 In Randall, pp. 132–34.

17 Randall, p. 186.

18 New York Times, July 26, 1973 and April 16, 1974.

19 New York Times, June 14, 1972.

20 New York Times, March 7 and 13, 1979.

21 For the C.I.A. report, see New York Times, January 27, 1980; Secretary Brown's comment is in Bernard Weinraub, "Pentagon Chiefs Warn of Soviet Progress in Weapons," New York Times, January 26, 1979.

22 Drew Middleton, "Pentagon, Despite Budget Increase, Sees Decade to Match Soviet Gains," New York Times, January 7, 1980.

23 Graham Hovey, "Vance Asking O.A.S. to Aid in Nicaragua," New York Times, June 21, 1979.

24 Graham Hovey, "U.S. Planning $49.8 Million Aid to Beleaguered Salvador Regime," New York Times, February 12, 1980.

25 New York Times, December 6, 1962.

26 New York Times, January 12, 1972.

27 New York Times, November 30, 1973.

28 C. L. Sulzberger, "Three for the Seesaw," New York Times, May 24, 1972, and "The Non-Allied Alliance," New York Times, June 2, 1972.

29 In Drew Middleton, "NATO Views Carter Policies with Unease," New York Times, May 9, 1978.

30 James Reston, "The Allies' Doubting Assent," New York Times, January 18, 1980; Drew Middleton, "NATO," New York Times, May 9, 1978; Drew Middleton, "Allied Attitudes on Gulf War Troubling U.S.," New York Times, February 17, 1980.

31 Dwight D. Eisenhower, Mandate for Change (Garden City, N.Y.: Doubleday, 1963), p. 181.

32 New York Times, October 27, 1973.

33 See Peter Wyden, "The Chances of Accidental War," Saturday Evening Post (June 3, 1961), p. 58.

34 New York Times, July 6, 1962.

35 New York Times, December 10, 1966.

36 In New York Times, July 22, 1973.

37 New York Times, May 27, 1972.

38 John W. Finney, "Soviet Arms Data Raise Suspicions," New York Times, November 6, 1974.

39 New York Times, January 25, 1977.

40 In Richard Burt, "Setback on Arms Treaty Signals New Era of Uncertainty," New York Times, January 4, 1980.

41 For the treaty's provisions, see New York Times, May 10, 1979.

42 Charles Mohr, "Arms Pact Outlook Called Dim Anyway," New York Times, January 4, 1980.

43 In John W. Finney, "Pentagon Backs Production of B-1," New York Times, December 3, 1976.

44 Bernard Weinraub, "Defense Chief Sees A Saving of Billions By Dropping the B-1," New York Times, July 2, 1977.

45 In Bernard Weinraub, "Without the B-1, A Lot of Responsibility Rests with the Cruise," New York Times, June 26, 1977.

46 In Drew Middleton, "A Controversy on 3 Weapons," New York Times, December 14, 1977.

47 "Air Force Planning Strategic Weapon," New York Times, February 23, 1979.

48 Bernard Weinraub, "Study for Carter Asks Bigger Role for Joint Chiefs," New York Times, July 13, 1978.

49 Halperin, "The President and the Military," pp. 319–22.

50 Halperin, pp. 323–24.

51 Drew Middleton, "World Military Situation Confronting Carter," New York Times, January 4, 1977.

52 Thomas S. Gates, "Reviewing National Security Policy Before Approving SALT," New York Times, December 29, 1979.

## 11  The Economy

1 New York Times, August 19, 1974.

2 Frances Perkins, The Roosevelt I Knew (New York: Viking, 1946), p. 330.

3  Arthur M. Schlesinger, Jr., *The Coming of the New Deal*, vol. 2 of *The Age of Roosevelt* (Boston: Houghton Mifflin, 1959), p. 567.

4  In Schlesinger, pp. 425, 431.

5  C. Wright Mills, *The Power Elite* (New York: Oxford, 1956).

6  Irving Louis Horowitz, *The Foundations of Political Sociology* (New York: Harper & Row, 1972).

7  William Safire, "Think," *New York Times*, January 16, 1976.

8  Tom Wicker, "Carter's Spending Games," *New York Times*.

9  In *New York Times*, March 20, 1972.

10  Leonard Silk, "Inflation Fight: How Costly," *New York Times*, August 15, 1979; "New Strategy to Fight Inflation," *Congressional Quarterly Weekly Reports*, March 15, 1980, pp. 707–09.

11  In *New York Times*, March 24, 1971.

12  For Carter's budget message, see *Congressional Quarterly Weekly Reports*, February 2, 1980, pp. 239–45.

13  In Edward Cowan, "President Opposes Compromise Budget," *New York Times*, May 28, 1980.

14  See *Congressional Quarterly Weekly Reports*, January 19, 1980, pp. 117–18.

15  Martin Tolchin, "Leaders in Congress Split with Carter on Revising Budget," *New York Times*, May 29, 1980.

16  In Clyde H. Farnsworth, "Recession Foreseen by Congress Agency," *New York Times*, December 12, 1978.

17  Leonard Silk, "The Recession and U.S. Policy," *New York Times*, May 21, 1980.

18  Adam Clymer, "On Oil, Carter Credibility Is Still Not High," *New York Times*, April 15, 1979.

19  Steve Lohr, "Duncan Memo Asks Cut in Solar Energy Funds," *New York Times*, May 24, 1980.

20  Philip Shabecoff, "President to Vow Strong Support to Protect Nation's Environment," *New York Times*, May 23, 1977.

21  Philip Shabecoff, "President Pledges Energy Crisis Won't Alter Environment Goals," *New York Times*, August 3, 1979.

22  Philip Shabecoff, "Some in E.P.A. Assail White House Moves," *New York Times*, February 22, 1979.

23  Steven Rattner, "White House Aides Seek to Raise Efficiency of Regulatory Boards," *New York Times*, March 12, 1979.

24  Martin Tolchin, "Chrysler Loan Guarantee Plan," *New York Times*, August 10, 1979. See also "Chrysler Loan Guarantees OKd," *Congressional Quarterly Weekly Reports*, May 17, 1980, p. 1311.

25  In "Chrysler Aid Cleared," *Congressional Quarterly Weekly Reports*, June 28, 1980, p. 1781.

26  Edward Cowan, "Auto Aid Study and 'Industrial Policy,'" *New York Times*, May 20, 1980.

27  "Carter Eases Pay Guidelines," *Congressional Quarterly Weekly Reports*, March 22, 1980. See also Steven Rattner, "Zig-Zag Policies: Carter's Record in Economics," *New York Times*, March 23, 1980.

28  Edward S. Flash, *Economic Advice and Presidential Leadership* (New York: Columbia, 1965); Steven R. Weisman, "Politics Put the Frosting on Carter's Plain Cake," *New York Times*, August 31, 1980; and Clyde H. Farnsworth, "Economic Plan, Bruised Egos," *New York Times*, September 1, 1980.

29  Sir John Hicks, *Causality and Economics* (New York: Basic Books, 1979), p. 102; Leonard Silk, "Flawed Data Not Uncommon," *New York Times*, November 2, 1979.

30  In Matthew Josephson, *Sidney Hillman: Statesman of American Labor* (Garden City, N.Y.: Doubleday, 1952), p. 431.

31  Josephson, p. 404.

32  In Saul Alinsky, *John L. Lewis: An Unauthorized Biography* (New York: Putnam, 1949), p. 165.

33  Josephson, p. 474.

34  Alinsky, p. 189.

35  *New York Times*, September 7, 1970; A. H. Raskin, "George Meany's Way Isn't the President's," *New York Times Magazine*, January 23, 1972, p. 10ff.

36  Raskin, p. 33; *New York Times*, November 25, 1971.

37  *New York Times*, September 1 and 12, 1974.

38  Edward Cowan, "Carter and Unions Announce Accords on Inflation Curbs," *New York Times*, September 29, 1979.

39  Philip Shabecoff, "Labor Officials Cite Concessions in Wage Accord," *New York Times*, October 3, 1979; and "Unions Are Advised to Seek Big Raises," *New York Times*, May 7,

1980. Concerning labor's 1980 vote, see Philip Shabecoff, "Voter Shifts and Conservatives' Gains Worry Labor," *New York Times*, November 9, 1980.

40  Alinsky, p. 162.

41  Josephson, p. 447

42  *Congressional Quarterly Almanac, 1971*, vol. 27 (Washington, D.C., 1972), p. 804.

43  James Tracy Crown, "Organized Labor in American Politics: A Look Ahead," *Proceedings of the Fourteenth Annual New York University Conference on Labor* (New York, 1961), p. 261.

44  In *New York Times*, November 24, 1971.

45  Josephson, p. 618.

46  Crown, p. 265.

47  Josephson, p. 399.

48  John M. Blum, *The Republican Roosevelt* (Cambridge, Mass: Harvard, 1961), p. 59.

49  In A. H. Raskin, "Organized Labor: Awaiting the Crash," *New York Times*, September 2, 1974.

50  In Philip Shabecoff, "Carter Was Not All That Eager to Get Involved," *New York Times*, February 26, 1978.

51  Haynes Johnson and Nick Kotz, "Hard Times in the House of Labor," *Newsday*, April 18, 1972.

52  Edward Cowan, "Auto Aid Study and 'Industrial Policy,'" *New York Times*, May 20, 1980.

## 12  Social Justice

1  William D. Carey, "Presidential Staffing in the Sixties and Seventies," *Public Administration Review* 29 (September-October 1969): 450–51.

2  Concerning Nixon's welfare proposals, see Daniel P. Moynihan, *The Politics of a Guaranteed Income* (New York: Random House, 1973).

3  *New York Times*, August 23, 1974.

4  *New York Times*, October 10, 1974.

5  *New York Times*, August 23 and October 30, 1974.

6  *New York Times*, August 14, 1974.

7  *Congressional Quarterly Weekly Report*, January 27, 1979, p. 107.

8  In Hedrick Smith, "Budget-Cutting Drive is Reshaping Democratic Party," *New York Times*, March 25, 1980.

9  Martin Tolchin, "Carter Aide Finds Limit to Party Aims," *New York Times*, January 5, 1979.

10  Lester C. Thurow, "Unkind Cuts," *New York Times*, March 9, 1979.

11  Ben A. Franklin, "Curbs on Strip Mining Put Off," *New York Times*, January 7, 1979.

12  Charles Mohr, "Environmentalists Fear Cost Cutting," *New York Times*, June 12, 1978.

13  *Congressional Quarterly Almanac, 1977* (Washington, D.C.: Congressional Quarterly, 1978), pp. 472–75.

14  *Congressional Quarterly Almanac, 1979*, pp. 508–09.

15  *Congressional Quarterly Almanac, 1979*, pp. 536–38; Philip Shabecoff, "President Outlines His Plan on Health," *New York Times*, July 30, 1978.

16  *Congressional Quarterly Almanac, 1979*, p. 512; Martin Tolchin, "Carter Asks Action on Hospital Costs," *New York Times*, March 7, 1979.

17  *Congressional Quarterly Almanac, 1978*, pp. 314–15.

18  In Louis W. Koenig, *The Invisible Presidency* (New York: Holt Rinehart & Winston, 1960), p. 215.

19  John M. Blum, *The Republican Roosevelt* (Cambridge, Mass.: Harvard, 1961), p. 60.

20  In Rexford G. Tugwell, *The Democratic Roosevelt* (Garden City, N.Y.: Doubleday, 1957), p. 153.

21  Tugwell, p. 54.

22  Tugwell, pp. 153, 215.

23  In Blum, p. 107.

24  In Tugwell, p. 151.

25  Tugwell, p. 231. Concerning the impact of coalitions on domestic programs, see James L. Sunquist, *Politics and Policy* (Washington, D.C.: Brookings, 1968).

26  George E. Mowry, *The Era of Theodore Roosevelt, 1900–1912* (New York: Harper & Row, 1958), p. xii.

27  Henry F. Pringle, *Theodore Roosevelt* (New York: Harbrace, 1956), p. 427.

28  *Congressional Quarterly Almanac, 1971*, p. 714; *New York Times*, January 2, April 16 and June 6, 1970.

29  *Congressional Quarterly Weekly Reports*, June 3, 1972, pp. 1271–72; *New York Times*, July 21, 1973.

30  In Arthur M. Schlesinger, Jr., *The Politics of Upheaval*, vol. 3 of *The Age of Roosevelt* (Boston: Houghton Mifflin, 1960), p. 29.

31  Arthur M. Schlesinger, Jr., *The Coming of the New Deal*, vol. 2 of *The Age*

*of Roosevelt* (Boston: Houghton Mifflin, 1959), p. 322.

32  *Congressional Quarterly Almanac, 1978*, p. 600.

33  *Congressional Quarterly Almanac, 1970*, p. 1030; *New York Times*, January 14, 1971.

34  *Congressional Quarterly Almanac, 1971*, pp. 521–22.

35  In Leonard Silk, "Missing: Energy Policy," *New York Times*, November 13, 1974.

36  See Edwin E. Witte, *The Development of the Social Security Act* (Madison, Wis.: University of Wisconsin, 1962).

37  Witte, p. 45.

38  Koenig, p. 260.

39  Koenig, p. 260.

40  Frances Perkins, *The Roosevelt I Knew* (New York: Viking, 1946), p. 197.

41  In *New York Times* January 29, 1973.

42  *New York Times*, February 20, 1969 and February 17, 1973.

43  *New York Times*, March 4, 1971.

44  In Hedrick Smith, "Budget-Cutting Drive Is Reshaping Democratic Party," *New York Times*, March 25, 1980.

45  *Congressional Quarterly Almanac, 1978*, p. 602; *Congressional Quarterly Almanac, 1979*, p. 509.

46  A. O. Sulzberger, Jr., "Black Caucus Says Budget Plan For 1981 Is 'Disaster' for the Poor," *New York Times*, February 6, 1980.

47  *Congressional Quarterly Almanac, 1979*, p. 603.

48  *Congressional Quarterly Almanac, 1979*, pp. 606–07.

49  Martin Tolchin, "Corporate Use of Political Action Panels Growing," *New York Times*, April 19, 1978.

50  *Congressional Quarterly Almanac, 1979*, pp. 343–45.

51  John Herbers, "Special Interests Gaining Power," *New York Times*, November 14, 1978.

52  Philip Shabecoff, "Federal Rules' Impact on Inflation Found to be Slight," *New York Times*, January 20, 1979.

53  Robert Reinhold, "Public-Service Jobs Program Upheld in New Study," *New York Times*, March 18, 1979.

54  In Philip Shabecoff, "Environment Vow Made By President," *New York Times*, February 28, 1979.

55  In Schlesinger, *Politics of Upheaval*, p. 428.

56  In *New York Times*, June 12, 1963.

57  *New York Times*, September 24, 1969, September 19, 1972, and January 17, 1973.

58  *New York Times*, May 26, 1972.

59  *New York Times*, October 16, 1974.

60  *New York Times*, October 11, 1974.

61  *New York Times*, September 13, 1974.

62  *New York Times*, August 13, 1974.

63  *New York Times*, November 12, 1974.

64  *New York Times*, November 7, 1974.

65  Nathaniel Sheppard, Jr., "Jordan Charges Congress Is Callous Toward Minorities," *New York Times*, August 7, 1978.

66  Marjorie Hunter, "Fair-Housing Bill Sought by Carter Voted by House," *New York Times*, June 13, 1980.

67  Roger Wilkins, "New Legal Effort to End Job Discrimination," *New York Times*, January 9, 1978.

68  Robert Lindsey, "Study Finds Gap Between Races Narrowing," *New York Times*, May 8, 1978.

69  Steven V. Roberts, "Black Progress and Poverty Are Underlined by Statistics," *New York Times*, February 28, 1978.

70  Roberts, February 28, 1978.

71  Jon Nordheimer, "1978 Race Relations," *New York Times*, February 27, 1978.

72  See William Julius Wilson, *The Declining Significance of Race* (Chicago: University of Chicago Press, 1978); and his "Poor Black's Future," *New York Times*, February 28, 1978.

73  *Congressional Quarterly Almanac, 1979*, p. 525.

74  *Congressional Quarterly Almanac, 1979*, p. 480.

75  David Vidal, "Hispanics Seek Bigger Role at White House," *New York Times*, July 31, 1979; and "Carter and Close Aides Meet With Hispanic Leaders," *New York Times*, August 11, 1979. For discussion of Hispanics in present-day politics, see David Broder, *Changing of the Guard* (New York: Simon and Schuster, 1980), pp. 279–301.

76  Mary Gray Peck, *Carrie Chapman Catt* (New York: Octagon, 1944), pp. 338–39; Wilson is quoted in *New York Times*, August 27, 1920.

77  "Miss Costanza Resigns as Assistant to Carter," *New York Times*, August 2, 1978.

78  Terence Smith, "Carter in Angry Exchange, Ousts Bella Abzug," *New York Times*, January 13, 1979.

79  Michael D. Reagan, "Toward Im-

proving Presidential Level Policy Planning," *Public Administration Review* 23 (March-April 1963): 177–86; William D. Carey, "Presidential Staffing," pp. 456–58.

## 13  Political Personality

1  For extended studies of presidential and related personalities see Alexander L. George and Juliette L. George, *Woodrow Wilson and Colonel House: A Personality Study* (New York: John Day, 1956); Erwin C. Hargrove, *Presidential Leadership: Personality and Political Style* (New York: Macmillan, 1966); Arnold Rogow, *James Forrestal* (New York: Macmillan, 1964).
2  In Hargrove, pp. 12–13.
3  George and George, passim.
4  Fred I. Greenstein and Michael Lerner, *A Source Book for the Study of Personality and Politics* (Chicago: Markham, 1971), pp. 434–35.
5  Greenstein and Lerner, pp. 68–70.
6  Gordon W. Allport, *Personality: A Psychological Interpretation* (New Haven: Yale, 1955), p. 229. See also his *The Nature of Personality: Selected Papers* (Cambridge, Mass.: Harvard, 1950).
7  Paul M. Sniderman, *Personality and Democratic Politics* (Berkeley, Calif.: University of California Press, 1975), p. 222.
8  Sniderman, pp. 189–201.
9  Kandy Stroud, *How Jimmy Won* (New York: Morrow, 1977), pp. 149–51.
10  James Fallows, "The Passionless Presidency," *Atlantic Monthly* (May 1979): 42.
11  Erwin C. Hargrove, "Presidential Personality and Revisionist Views of the Presidency," *American Journal of Political Science* 17 (November 1973): 826–27.
12  Address to Congress, August 12, 1974; see transcript in *New York Times*, August 13, 1974.
13  William B. Hesseltine, *Ulysses S. Grant, Politician* (New York: Ungar, 1935), p. 392.
14  Robert W. Winston, *Andrew Johnson: Plebian and Patriot* (New York: Holt Rinehart & Winston, 1928), p. 373.
15  In Marquis Childs, *Eisenhower: Captive Hero* (New York: Harcourt Brace Jovanovich, 1958), p. 245.
16  Childs, p. 247.

17  Emmet John Hughes, *The Ordeal of Power* (New York: Atheneum, 1963), pp. 268–69.
18  Hargrove, "Presidential Personality," p. 822.
19  News Conference, August 28, 1974; see transcript in *New York Times*, August 29, 1974.
20  Address to Congress, August 12, 1974; see transcript in *New York Times*, August 13, 1974.
21  Winston, p. 342
22  In *New York Times*, September 20, 1968.
23  In *New York Times*, November 10, 1972.
24  Tom Wicker, "What Kind of Moral Fiber?" *New York Times*, November 17, 1972.
25  Charles P. Henderson, Jr., "Mr. Nixon's Theology," *New York Times*, July 3, 1972.
26  Doris Kearns, *Lyndon Johnson and the American Dream* (New York: Harper & Row, 1976), pp. x, 156.
27  Philip S. Klein, *President James Buchanan* (University Park, Pa.: Pennsylvania State University Press, 1962), p. 331.
28  Arthur M. Schlesinger, Jr., *The Coming of the New Deal*, vol. 2 of *The Age of Roosevelt* (Boston: Houghton-Mifflin, 1959), p. 585. Concerning Truman, see Merle Miller, *Lyndon: An Oral Biography* (New York: Putnam, 1980), p. 541.
29  Fallows, p. 42.
30  See Karen Horney, *Neurosis and Human Growth* (New York: Norton, 1950).
31  See Horney.
32  In Betty Glad, *Jimmy Carter In Search of the Great White House* (New York: Norton, 1980), p. 496.
33  Glad, p. 499.
34  Haynes Johnson, *In the Absence of Power; Governing America* (New York: Viking, 1980), p. 290.
35  Johnson, pp. 248, 295–96.
36  Adam Clymer, "Carter's Vision of America," *New York Times Magazine*, July 27, 1980, pp. 16–18.
37  James MacGregor Burns, "The Four Kennedys of the First Year," *New York Times Magazine*, January 14, 1962, p. 72.
38  Alfred Steinberg, *The Man From Missouri* (New York: Putnam, 1962), p. 250.
39  Harold D. Laswell, *Power and Per-*

*sonality* (New York: Viking, 1948), p. 203.

40  Allan Nevins, *Grover Cleveland: A Study in Courage* (New York: Dodd, Mead, 1932), p. 206.

41  Comment, *The New Republic* 181 (December 15, 1979): 5–6; Editorial, *The Nation* 229 (December 22, 1979): 641.

42  Klein, p. 285.

43  Schlesinger, p. 575.

44  In Max Frankel, "Why the Gap Between L. B. J. and the Nation," *New York Times Magazine*, January 7, 1968, p. 37.

45  John S. Bassett, *The Life of Andrew Jackson* (New York: Macmillan, 1925), p. 702.

46  Hesseltine, pp. 315–16.

47  Frankel, p. 37.

48  Steinberg, p. 256.

49  T. W. Adorno et al., *The Authoritarian Personality* (New York: Norton, 1950).

50  Harold D. Lasswell, *Power and Personality* (New York: Viking, 1948), pp. 162–63.

51  Alan C. Elms, *Personality in Politics* (New York: Harcourt Brace Jovanovich, 1976), p. 15.

52  Kearns, p. 314.

53  For elaboration, see Fred I. Greenstein, *Personality and Politics* (New York: Norton, 1975), pp. 108–10.

54  Paul M. Sniderman, *Personality and Democratic Politics* (Berkeley, Calif.: University of California Press, 1975), 189.

55  Lasswell, pp. 108–10.

56  Bruce Mazlish, *In Search of Nixon: A Psychological Inquiry* (New York: Basic Books, 1972), pp. 142–43.

57  Mazlish, p. 132.

58  Mazlish, pp. 153–54.

59  James David Barber, *The Presidential Character: Predicting Performance in the White House* (Englewood Cliffs, N.J.: Prentice-Hall, 1972), pp. 362–63.

60  Alexander George, "Assessing Presidential Character," *World Politics* 26 (1974): 234–82.

61  Henry Fairlie, *The Kennedy Promise: The Politics of Expectation* (Garden City, N.Y.: Doubleday, 1973), p. 107.

62  Childs, p. 4.

63  Winston, pp. 329–30.

64  Barber, pp. 157–73.

65  Barber, p. 163.

66  Barber, p. 156.

67  Vincent DeSantis, "Eisenhower Revisionism," *Review of Politics* 38 (April 1976), pp. 195–200.

68  Arthur Larson, *Eisenhower, The President Nobody Knows* (New York: Scribner, 1968), p. 14.

69  Richard M. Nixon, *Six Crises* (Garden City, N.Y.: Doubleday, 1962), p. 161.

70  Fred I. Greenstein, "Eisenhower as an Activist President," *Political Science Quarterly* 94 (Winter 1979–80): 577.

71  Greenstein, "Eisenhower as Activist," p. 584.

72  Greenstein, "Eisenhower as Activist," p. 588.

73  Douglas Kinnard, "Eisenhower and the Defense Budget," *Journal of Politics* 39 (August 1977): 596–623; Douglas Kinnard, *President Eisenhower and Strategic Management: A Study in Defense Politics* (Lexington, Ky.: University of Kentucky Press, 1977); Arnold Kanter, *Defense Politics: A Budgetary Perspective* (Chicago, Ill.: University of Chicago Press, 1979).

## 14  *Decision-Making*

1  Interview, televised December 17, 1962.

2  Hedrick Smith, "Problems of a Problem Solver," *New York Times Magazine*, January 8, 1978, p. 30.

3  Henry Kissinger, *White House Years* (Boston: Little, Brown, 1979), p. 415.

4  See John Spanier, *Games Nations Play* (New York: Praeger, 1972), p. 36.

5  In Eric F. Goldman, *The Tragedy of Lyndon Johnson* (New York: Knopf, 1969), p. 23.

6  Interview, televised December 17, 1962.

7  "Ex-Speech Writer Views Carter," *New York Times*, April 23, 1979.

8  John Hope Franklin, *The Emancipation Proclamation* (Garden City, N.Y.: Doubleday, 1963), p. 26.

9  William Cresson, *James Monroe*, (Chapel Hill, N.C.: University of North Carolina Press, 1946), pp. 449–50.

10  Joseph Alsop and Turner Catledge, *The 168 Days* (Garden City, N.Y.: Doubleday, 1938), pp. 33–35. J. F. ter Horst, *Gerald Ford and the Future of the Presidency* (New York: Third Press, 1974), p. 58; James Reston, "Nice-Guy Leadership," *New York Times*, December 4, 1974.

11  Cresson, *James Monroe*, pp. 185–86.
12  Albert L. Warner, "How the Korea Decision Was Made," *Harper's Magazine* (June 1951), p. 99; Richard C. Snyder and Glenn D. Paige, "The United States Decision to Resist Aggression in Korea," *Administrative Science Quarterly*, 3 (December 1958): 348. The most comprehensive study is Glenn Paige, ed., *1950: Truman's Decision—The United States Enters the Korean War* (New York: Chelsea House, 1970).
13  Harry S Truman, *Years of Trial and Hope*, vol. 2 of *Memoirs* (Garden City, N.Y.: Doubleday, 1956), pp. 185–86.
14  Kissinger, p. 491.
15  Elmo R. Zumwalt, Jr., *On Watch* (New York: Quadrangle, 1976), p. 295.
16  Hans J. Morgenthau, "The Trouble with Kennedy," *Commentary* (January 1962), p. 51.
17  *Newsweek*, August 2, 1965, p. 15.
18  William Allen White, *Puritan in Babylon* (New York: Peter Smith, 1938), pp. 267–69.
19  In Sherman Adams, *First-Hand Report* (New York, Harper & Row 1961), p. 252.
20  Arthur M. Schlesinger, Jr., *The Coming of the New Deal*, vol. 2 of *The Age of Roosevelt* (Boston: Houghton Mifflin, 1959), pp. 528–31.
21  Rexford G. Tugwell, *The Democratic Roosevelt* (Garden City, N.Y.: Doubleday, 1957), p. 546.
22  In Schlesinger, p. 531.
23  In Timothy R. Clark, "The Power Vacuum Outside the Oval Office," *National Journal* 11 (February 24, 1979): 296–97; Martin Tolchin, "Carter Is Said to Seek Centralizing of Policy-Making in White House," *New York Times*, April 15, 1978.
24  Howard Raiffa, *Decision Analysis* (Reading, Mass.: Addison-Wesley, 1968), pp. 128–29.
25  "Reconstruction of Cambodia Decision," *New York Times*, June 30, 1970.
26  Kissinger, p. 491.
27  In Franklin, p. 95.
28  In Franklin, p. 26.
29  Alsop and Catledge, p. 63.
30  In Cresson, p. 445.
31  James T. Tedeschi, ed., *The Social Influence Process* (Chicago: Aldine-Atherton, 1972), pp. 352–53.
32  Harold L. Ickes, *The Inside Struggle*, Vol. 2 of *The Secret Diary of Harold Ickes* (New York: Simon & Schuster, 1954), p. 339.
33  L. Gelb, *Life*, September 17, 1971, p. 34.
34  Gelb, pp. 35–36.
35  James C. Thomson, Jr., "How Could Vietnam Happen?" *The Atlantic Monthly* (April 1968), p. 47.
36  Thompson, Jr., pp. 49–52; Irving L. Janis, *Victims of Groupthink* (Boston: Houghton Mifflin, 1972); Irving L. Janis, "Groupthink in Washington," *New York Times*, May 28, 1973.
37  Bernard Gwertzman, "Muskie Wasn't Told of New War Policy," *New York Times*, August 10, 1980.
38  In Bernard Gwertzman, "Muskie Outlines Plan to Promote An Active Policy," *New York Times*, May 10, 1980.
39  Anthony Lewis, "The Brzezinski Puzzle," *New York Times*, August 8, 1980.
40  Richard Nixon, *U.S. Foreign Policy for the 1970's: A New Strategy for Peace, A Report to Congress* (Washington, D.C.: Government Printing Office, 1970), p. 22. Kissinger criticizes bureaucratic politics in decision-making in "Domestic Structure and Foreign Policy," *Daedalus* 95 (Spring 1966): 503–29.
41  Alexander L. George, "The Case for Multiple Advocacy in Making Foreign Policy," *American Political Science Review* 66 (September 1972): 751–85.
42  George, pp. 782–83.
43  Gwertzman, "Muskie Wasn't Told," August 10, 1980.
44  Lewis, "Brzezinski Puzzle," August 18, 1980.

## 15  Crisis

1  Elie Abel, *The Missile Crisis* (Philadelphia: Lippincott, 1966) p. 16. For discussions of the crisis see Henry M. Pachter, *Collision Course: The Cuban Missile Crisis and Coexistence* (New York: Praeger, 1963); Abel, *Missile Crisis;* James Daniel and John Hubbell, *Strike in the West: The Complete Story of the Cuban Missile Crisis* (New York: Holt, Rinehart & Winston, 1963); Arthur M. Schlesinger, Jr., *A Thousand Days: John F. Kennedy in the White House* (Boston: Houghton Mifflin, 1965); Theodore C. Soren-

sen, *Kennedy* (New York: Harper & Row, 1965); David L. Larson, *The "Cuban Crisis" of 1962: Selected Documents and Chronology* (Boston: Houghton Mifflin, 1963); Robert F. Kennedy, *Thirteen Days: A Memoir of the Cuban Missile Crisis* (New York: Norton, 1969). For conceptual models applicable to the missile crisis, see Graham T. Allison, *Essence of Decision: Explaining the Cuban Missile Crisis* (Boston: Little, Brown, 1971).

2   Kenneth Keating, *Cuba Chronology, 1962* (Washington, D.C., 1962), mimeographed.

3   Daniel and Hubbell, p. 88.

4   Robert F. Kennedy, p. 111.

5   Daniel and Hubbell, pp. 64–67.

6   For a detailed chronology of the crisis see "The Cuban Crisis: Fourteen Days That Shook the World," *New York Times,* reprint, November 3, 1962 (includes texts appearing in the *Times,* October 23-November 3, 1962).

7   Daniel and Hubbell, pp. 92–93.

8   *New York Times,* October 22, 1962.

9   In *New York Times,* October 25, 1962.

10   Abel, p. 168.

11   *New York Times,* October 27, 1962.

12   Daniel and Hubbell, pp. 95–125.

13   In *New York Times,* April 26, 1963.

14   *New York Times,* October 28, 1962; Daniel and Hubbell, pp. 150–53.

15   Kenneth Keating, news release, January 31, 1963, mimeographed.

16   In *New York Times,* November 12, 1966.

17   *New York Times,* November 15, 1970.

18   For distinctions between the 1962 and 1970 situations, see George G. Quester, "Missiles in Cuba, 1970," *Foreign Affairs* 49 (April 1971): 493–506. Negotiations with the Soviet are reviewed in Henry Kissinger, *White House Years* (Boston: Little, Brown, 1979), pp. 649–52.

19   See comment by Theodore Sorensen, *NBC White Paper,* Feb. 9, 1964.

20   Robert F. Kennedy, p. 111.

21   Terence Smith, "Test of Will Is Seen," *New York Times,* November 29, 1979.

22   Smith, November 29, 1979.

23   In Richard Burt, "U.S. Quandry in Iran Crisis," *New York Times,* November 9, 1979.

24   Drew Middleton, "In Iran Crisis Few Choices," *New York Times,* December 11, 1979.

25   Bernard Gwertzman, "U.S. Sends

Teheran Plan to End Crisis and Free Hostages," *New York Times,* December 9, 1979.

26   Steven R. Weisman, "Carter Orders Halt to Buying Iran's Oil," *New York Times,* November 13, 1979.

27   Hedrick Smith, "Carter's Second Chance: Political Benefits in Iranian Crisis," *New York Times,* December 5, 1979.

28   "Carter and Nixon Score Low in Popularity Polls," *New York Times,* August 12, 1979.

29   In Flora Lewis, "Allies' Decision to Follow U.S. Lead," *New York Times,* April 23, 1980; R. W. Apple, Jr., "Allies' Unspoken Fear," *New York Times,* April 24, 1980.

30   Flora Lewis, April 23, 1980.

31   Bernard Gwertzman, "Carter Vows to Pursue Hostages' Release," *New York Times,* April 26, 1980.

32   Bernard Gwertzman, "Vance Quits, 'Heart Heavy'," *New York Times,* April 29, 1980.

33   Steven R. Weisman, "White House Panel Keeps Close Watch on Iran Crisis," *New York Times,* November 25, 1979.

34   Gwertzman, "Vance Quits," April 29, 1980.

35   Martin Tolchin, "Some in Congress Criticize Mission Because of Lack of Consultation," *New York Times,* April 26, 1980.

## 16 The Presidency Compared

1   *New York Times,* April 27 and May 7, 1973.

2   Coleman B. Ransone, Jr., *The Office of Governor in the United States* (University, Ala.: University of Alabama, 1956), pp. 116–17.

3   Joseph E. Kallenbach, *The American Chief Executive: The Presidency and the Governorship* (New York: Harper & Row, 1966), pp. 364–65.

4   Marilyn Gittel, "Metropolitan Mayor: Dead End," *Public Administration Review* 23 (March 1963): 21; Russell D. Murphy, "Whither the Mayors? A Note on Mayoral Careers," *Journal of Politics* 42 (February 1980): 289.

5   Murphy, p. 288.

6   See Scott Greer, *Governing the Metropolis* (New York: Wiley, 1962).

7   In John A. Hamilton, "Mayors on the

March," *New York Times*, June 26, 1973, and *New York Times*, February 22, 1973.

8  Robert Reinhold, "Nation's Mayors Disagree Over Cuts In Urban Funds," *New York Times*, January 26, 1979.

9  See James Reston, "The Crisis of Democracy," *New York Times*, March 3, 1974; Theodore C. Achilles, letter to the editor, *New York Times*, May 24, 1974.

10  Richard Eder, "Tory Leadership is Won Decisively by Mrs. Thatcher," *New York Times*, February 12, 1975. See also Anthony King, ed., *The British Prime Minister* (New York: Macmillan, 1969), pp. 56–57.

11  Paul Lewis, "France's Coalition Wins a Vote but Faces New Strains," *New York Times*, December 29, 1979. For discussion of the French presidency, see Richard Rose and Ezra N. Suleiman, eds., *Presidents and Prime Ministers* (Washington, D.C.: American Enterprise Institute, 1980), pp. 94–138.

12  John Vinocur, "Bonn, Expecting Clash of Ideas in Campaign, Gets a Clink," *New York Times*, April 14, 1980. Analysis of the German Chancellorship is found in Rose and Suleiman, *Presidents and Prime Ministers*, pp. 139–70.

13  Michel Tatu, *Power in the Kremlin from Khrushchev to Kosygin* (New York: Viking, 1969), p. 413.

14  *New York Times*, October 16, 1964.

15  *London Times*, October 22, 1963.

16  Bertram D. Wolfe, *Khrushchev and Stalin's Ghost* (New York: Praeger, 1957), pp. 22–25.

17  Tatu, *Power in the Kremlin*, pp. 511–25.

18  Craig R. Whitney, "Tired-Looking Brezhnev Named to Another Term by Legislature," *New York Times*, April 19, 1979.

19  Michel Tatu, "Transferring Power in the Kremlin," *New York Times*, February 17, 1975.

20  American Political Science Association, Committee on Political Parties, *Toward a More Responsible Party System* (New York, 1950).

21  *New York Times*, December 22, 1973.

22  R. T. McKenzie, *British Political Parties* (New York: Praeger, 1963), pp. 297–99.

23  In Samuel H. Beer et al., *Patterns of Government: The Major Political Sys-*
tems of Europe, rev. ed. (New York: Random House, 1962), pp. 183–84.

24  William Borders, "Labor Government Is Ousted in Britain by Vote in Commons," *New York Times*, March 29, 1979.

25  R. W. Apple, Jr., "British Labor—A Government in Disarray," *New York Times*, June 18, 1977.

26  *New York Times*, November 21, 1974.

27  Harold Macmillan, *Riding the Storm 1956–1959* (New York: Harper & Row, 1971), p. 191.

28  R. W. Apple, Jr., "Margaret Thatcher Names Her Cabinet," *New York Times*, May 6, 1979.

29  Richard E. Neustadt, "White House and Whitehall," in King, p. 140.

30  R. W. Apple, Jr., "Mrs. Thatcher's Uphill Task," *New York Times*, May 7, 1979.

31  Harold Wilson, *A Personal Record: the Labour Government 1964–1970* (London: Weidenfeld and Nicolson, 1971), p. 47.

32  Don K. Price, "The Parliamentary and Presidential Systems," *Public Administration Review* 3 (Winter 1941): 360.

33  Price, p. 322.

34  *London Times*, October 22, 1963.

35  R. W. Apple, Jr., "Is Maggie Thatcher Just Making Things Worse?," *New York Times Magazine*, December 16, 1979.

36  Apple, December 16, 1979.

37  Gwendolen M. Carter and John H. Herz, *Major Foreign Governments*, 6th ed. (New York: Harcourt Brace Jovanovich, 1972), pp. 175–80.

38  See Roy C. Macridis and Bernard E. Brown, *The De Gaulle Republic* (Homewood, Ill.: Dorsey, 1960). For an analysis of democracy and administration, see Emmette Redford, *Democracy in the Administrative State* (New York: Macmillan, 1969).

39  *New York Times*, May 29, 1974.

40  C. L. Sulzberger, " 'Kissinger' and Kissinger," *New York Times*, June 24, 1973.

41  Milovan Djilas, *The New Class* (New York: Harcourt Brace Jovanovich, 1957), pp. 44–47.

42  Boris Souvarine, *Stalin* (New York: Longmans, 1939), pp. 407–09.

43  David K. Shipler, "Brezhnev Leadership: Bureaucracy Ascendant," *New York Times*, June 5, 1977.

44  Milovan Djilas, "The 'New Class'—Faceless, Fearful," *New York Times,* January 7, 1971; Zbigniew Brzezinski and Samuel Huntington, *Political Power: USA/USSR* (New York: Penguin, 1977), p. 436.

45  Djilas, "The 'New Class'," p. 82.

46  Bernard Gwertzman, "Brezhnev's Future Priorities," *New York Times,* April 12, 1971, and *New York Times,* June 16, 1972.

47  Craig R. Whitney, "Diplomats in Moscow Speculating Soviet Misjudged West's Reaction," *New York Times,* January 11, 1980.

48  U.S. Senate Subcommittee on National Policy Machinery, Committee on Government Operations, *National Policy Machinery in the Soviet Union,* 86th Congress, 2nd Session (Washington, D.C., 1960), pp. 36–42.

49  See Charles O. Porter and Robert J. Alexander, *The Struggle for Democracy in Latin America* (New York: Macmillan, 1961).

50  In *New York Times,* February 1, 1964.

# Presidents of the United States

| | PARTY | TERM |
|---|---|---|
| 1. George Washington (1732–99) | Federalist | 1789–1797 |
| 2. John Adams (1735–1826) | Federalist | 1797–1801 |
| 3. Thomas Jefferson (1743–1826) | Democratic-Republican | 1801–1809 |
| 4. James Madison (1751–1836) | Democratic-Republican | 1809–1817 |
| 5. James Monroe (1758–1831) | Democratic-Republican | 1817–1825 |
| 6. John Quincy Adams (1767–1848) | Democratic-Republican | 1825–1829 |
| 7. Andrew Jackson (1767–1845) | Democratic | 1829–1837 |
| 8. Martin Van Buren (1782–1862) | Democratic | 1837–1841 |
| 9. William Henry Harrison (1773–1841) | Whig | 1841 |
| 10. John Tyler (1790–1862) | Whig | 1841–1845 |
| 11. James K. Polk (1795–1849) | Democratic | 1845–1849 |
| 12. Zachary Taylor (1784–1850) | Whig | 1849–1850 |
| 13. Millard Fillmore (1800–74) | Whig | 1850–1853 |
| 14. Franklin Pierce (1804–69) | Democratic | 1853–1857 |
| 15. James Buchanan (1791–1868) | Democratic | 1857–1861 |
| 16. Abraham Lincoln (1809–65) | Republican | 1861–1865 |
| 17. Andrew Johnson (1808–75) | Union | 1865–1869 |
| 18. Ulysses S. Grant (1822–85) | Republican | 1869–1877 |
| 19. Rutherford B. Hayes (1822–93) | Republican | 1877–1881 |
| 20. James A. Garfield (1831–81) | Republican | 1881 |
| 21. Chester A. Arthur (1830–86) | Republican | 1881–1885 |
| 22. Grover Cleveland (1837–1908) | Democratic | 1885–1889 |
| 23. Benjamin Harrison (1833–1901) | Republican | 1889–1893 |
| 24. Grover Cleveland (1837–1908) | Democratic | 1893–1897 |
| 25. William McKinley (1843–1901) | Republican | 1897–1901 |
| 26. Theodore Roosevelt (1858–1919) | Republican | 1901–1909 |
| 27. William Howard Taft (1857–1930) | Republican | 1909–1913 |
| 28. Woodrow Wilson (1856–1924) | Democratic | 1913–1921 |
| 29. Warren G. Harding (1865–1923) | Republican | 1921–1923 |
| 30. Calvin Coolidge (1872–1933) | Republican | 1923–1929 |
| 31. Herbert Hoover (1874–1964) | Republican | 1929–1933 |
| 32. Franklin Delano Roosevelt (1882–1945) | Democratic | 1933–1945 |
| 33. Harry S Truman (1884–1972) | Democratic | 1945–1953 |
| 34. Dwight D. Eisenhower (1890–1969) | Republican | 1953–1961 |
| 35. John F. Kennedy (1917–1963) | Democratic | 1961–1963 |
| 36. Lyndon B. Johnson (1908–1973) | Democratic | 1963–1969 |
| 37. Richard M. Nixon (b. 1913) | Republican | 1969–1974 |
| 38. Gerald R. Ford (b. 1913) | Republican | 1974–1977 |
| 39. Jimmy Carter (b. 1924) | Democratic | 1977–1981 |
| 40. Ronald W. Reagan (b. 1911) | Republican | 1981– |

# Constitutional Provisions
# Relating to the Presidency

SECTION 3

6. The Senate shall have the sole power to try all impeachments. When sitting for that purpose, they shall be on oath or affirmation. When the President of the United States is tried, the Chief Justice shall preside; and no person shall be convicted without the concurrence of two-thirds of the members present.

7. Judgment in cases of impeachment shall not extend further than to removal from office, and disqualification to hold and enjoy any office of honor, trust, or profit under the United States; but the party convicted shall, nevertheless, be liable and subject to indictment, trial, judgment, and punishment, according to law.

SECTION 7

2. Every bill which shall have passed the House of Representatives and the Senate shall, before it becomes a law, be presented to the President of the United States; if he approve he shall sign it, but if not he shall return it, with his objections, to that house in which it shall have originated, who shall enter the objections at large on their journal and proceed to reconsider it. If after such reconsideration two-thirds of that house shall agree to pass the bill, it shall be sent, together with the objections, to the other house, by which it shall likewise be reconsidered, and if approved by two-thirds of that house it shall become a law. But in all such cases the votes of both houses shall be determined by yeas and nays, and the names of the persons voting for and against the bill shall be entered on the journal of each house respectively. If any bill shall not be returned by the President within ten days (Sundays excepted) after it shall have been presented to him, the same shall be a law, in like manner as if he had signed it unless the Congress by their adjournment prevent its return, in which case it shall not be a law.

3. Every order, resolution, or vote to which the concurrence of the Senate and House of Representatives may be necessary (except on a question of adjournment) shall be presented to the President of the United States; and before the same shall take effect, shall be approved by him, or being disapproved by him, shall be repassed by two-thirds of the Senate and House of Representatives, according to the rules and limitations prescribed in the case of a bill.

ARTICLE II

SECTION 1

1. The executive power shall be vested in a President of the United States of America. He shall hold his office during the term of four years, and, together with the Vice President, chosen for the same term, be elected as follows:

2. Each state shall appoint, in such manner as the legislature thereof may direct, a number of electors, equal to the whole number of Senators and Representatives to which the State may be entitled in the Congress; but no Senator or Representative, or person holding an office of trust or profit under the United States, shall be appointed an elector.

3.* The electors shall meet in their respective states and vote by ballot for two persons, of whom one at least shall not be an inhabitant of the same state with themselves. And they shall make a list of all the persons voted for, and of the number of votes for each; which list they shall sign and certify, and transmit sealed to the seat of the government of the United States, directed to the President of the Senate. The President of the Senate shall, in the presence of the Senate and House of Representatives, open all the certificates, and the votes shall then be counted. The person having the greatest number of votes shall be the President, if such a number be a majority of the whole number of electors appointed; and if there be more than one who have such majority, and have an equal number of votes, then the House of Representatives shall immediately choose by ballot one of them for President; and if no person have a majority, then from the five highest on the list the said House shall in like manner choose the President. But in choosing the President the votes shall be taken by states, the representation from each state having one vote; a quorum for this purpose shall consist of a member or members from two-thirds of the states, and a majority of all the states shall be necessary to a choice. In every case, after the choice of the President, the person having the greatest number of votes of the electors shall be the Vice President. But if there should remain two or more who have equal votes, the Senate shall choose from them by ballot the Vice President.

4. The Congress may determine the time of choosing the electors and the day on which they shall give their votes, which day shall be the same throughout the United States.

5. No person except a natural born citizen, or a citizen of the United States at the time of the adoption of this Constitution, shall be eligible to the office of President; neither shall any person be eligible to that office who shall not have attained to the age of thirty-five years, and been fourteen years a resident within the United States.

6. †In case of the removal of the President from office, or of his death, resignation, or inability to discharge the powers and duties of the said office, the same shall devolve on the Vice President, and the Congress may by law provide for the case of removal, death, resignation, or inability, both of the President and Vice President, declaring what officer shall then act as President, and such officer shall act accordingly until the disability be removed or a President shall be elected.

7. The President shall, at stated times, receive for his services a compensation, which shall neither be increased nor diminished during the period for which he shall have been elected, and he shall not receive within that period any other emolument from the United States or any of them.

8. Before he enter on the execution of his office he shall take the following oath or affirmation:

> I do solemnly swear (or affirm) that I will faithfully execute the office of President of the United States, and will to the best of my ability preserve, protect, and defend the Constitution of the United States.

SECTION 2

1. The President shall be Commander-in-Chief of the Army and Navy of the United States, and of the militia of the several states when called into the actual

---

*This paragraph was superseded by the Twelfth Amendment.

†This paragraph was modified by the Twenty-fifth Amendment.

service of the United States; he may require the opinion, in writing, of the principal officer in each of the executive departments, upon any subject relating to the duties of their respective offices, and he shall have power to grant reprieves and pardons for offenses against the United States, except of impeachment.

2. He shall have power, by and with the advice and consent of the Senate, to make treaties, provided two-thirds of the Senators present concur; and he shall nominate, and, by and with the advice and consent of the Senate, shall appoint ambassadors, other public ministers and consuls, judges of the Supreme Court, and all other officers of the United States, whose appointments are not herein otherwise provided for, and which shall be established by law; but the Congress may by law vest the appointment of such inferior officers, as they think proper, in the President alone, in the courts of law, or in the heads of departments.

3. The President shall have power to fill up all vacancies that may happen during the recess of the Senate, by granting commissions which shall expire at the end of their next session.

SECTION 3

He shall from time to time give to the Congress information of the state of the union, and recommend to their consideration such measures as he shall judge necessary and expedient; he may, on extraordinary occasions, convene both houses, or either of them, and in case of disagreement between them with respect to the time of adjournment, he may adjourn them to such time as he shall think proper; he shall receive ambassadors and other public ministers; he shall take care that the laws be faithfully executed, and shall commission all the officers of the United States.

SECTION 4

The President, Vice President, and all civil officers of the United States shall be removed from office on impeachment for and conviction of treason, bribery, or other high crimes and misdemeanors.

AMENDMENT XII

The electors shall meet in their respective states and vote by ballot for President and Vice President, one of whom, at least, shall not be an inhabitant of the same state with themselves; they shall name in their ballots the person voted for as President, and in distinct ballots the person voted for as Vice President, and they shall make distinct lists of all persons voted for as President and of all persons voted for as Vice President, and of the number of votes for each; which lists they shall sign and certify, and transmit sealed to the seat of the government of the United States, directed to the President of the Senate. The President of the Senate shall, in the presence of the Senate and House of Representatives, open all the certificates and the votes shall then be counted. The person having the greatest number of votes for President shall be the President, if such number be a majority of the whole number of electors appointed; and if no person have such majority, then from the persons having the highest numbers not exceeding three on the list of those voted for as President, the House of Representatives shall choose immediately, by ballot, the President. But in choosing the President the votes shall be taken by states, the representation from each state having one vote; a quorum for this purpose shall consist of a member or members from two-thirds of the states, and a majority of all states shall be necessary to a choice. And if the House of Representatives shall not choose a President whenever the right of choice shall devolve upon them, before the fourth day of March next following, then the Vice President shall act as President, as in the case of the death or other constitutional disability of the President.

The person having the greatest number of votes as Vice President shall be the Vice President, if such number be a majority of the whole number of electors appointed; and if no person have a majority, then from the two highest numbers on the list the Senate shall choose the Vice President; a quorum for the purpose shall consist of two-thirds of the whole number of Senators, and a majority of the whole number shall be necessary to a choice. But no person constitutionally ineligible to the office of President shall be eligible to that of Vice President of the United States.

## AMENDMENT XX

SECTION 1

The terms of the President and Vice President shall end at noon on the 20th day of January, and the terms of Senators and Representatives at noon on the 3rd day of January, of the years in which such terms would have ended if this article had not been ratified; and the terms of their successors shall then begin.

SECTION 2

The Congress shall assemble at least once in every year, and such meeting shall begin at noon on the 3rd day of January, unless they shall by law appoint a different day.

SECTION 3

If, at the time fixed for the beginning of the term of the President, the President elect shall have died, the Vice President elect shall become President. If a President shall not have been chosen before the time fixed for the beginning of his term, or if the President elect shall have failed to qualify, then the Vice President elect shall act as President until a President shall have qualified; and the Congress may by law provide for the case wherein neither a President elect nor a Vice President elect shall have qualified, declaring who shall then act as President, or the manner in which one who is to act shall be selected, and such person shall act accordingly until a President or Vice President shall have qualified.

SECTION 4

The Congress may by law provide for the case of the death of any of the persons from whom the House of Representatives may choose a President whenever the right of choice shall have devolved upon them, and for the case of death of any of the persons from whom the Senate may choose a Vice President whenever the right of choice shall have devolved upon them.

## AMENDMENT XXII

No person shall be elected to the office of the President more than twice, and no person who has held the office of President, or acted as President, for more than two years of a term to which some other person was elected President shall be elected to the office of the President more than once. But this article shall not apply to any person holding the office of President when this article was proposed by the Congress, and shall not prevent any person who may be holding the office of President, or acting as President, during the term within which this article becomes operative from holding the office of President or acting as President during the remainder of such term.

## AMENDMENT XXV

### SECTION 1
In case of the removal of the President from office or of his death or resignation, the Vice President shall become President.

### SECTION 2
Whenever there is a vacancy in the office of the Vice President, the President shall nominate a Vice President who shall take office upon confirmation by a majority vote of both Houses of Congress.

### SECTION 3
Whenever the President transmits to the President pro tempore of the Senate and the Speaker of the House of Representatives his written declaration that he is unable to discharge the powers and duties of his office, and until he transmits to them a written declaration to the contrary, such powers and duties shall be discharged by the Vice President as Acting President.

### SECTION 4
Whenever the Vice President and a majority of either the principal officers of the executive department or of such other body as Congress may by law provide, transmit to the President pro tempore of the Senate and the Speaker of the House of Representatives their written declaration that the President is unable to discharge the powers and duties of his office, the Vice President shall immediately assume the powers and duties of the office as Acting President.

Thereafter, when the President transmits to the President pro tempore of the Senate and the Speaker of the House of Representatives his written declaration that no inability exists, he shall resume the powers and duties of his office unless the Vice President and a majority of either the principal officers of the executive department or of such other body as Congress may by law provide, transmit within four days to the President pro tempore of the Senate and the Speaker of the House of Representatives their written declaration that the President is unable to discharge the powers and duties of his office. Thereupon Congress shall decide the issue, assembling within forty-eight hours for that purpose if not in session. If the Congress, within twenty-one days after receipt of the latter written declaration, or, if Congress is not in session, within twenty-one days after Congress is required to assemble, determines by two-thirds vote of both Houses that the President is unable to discharge the powers and duties of his office, the Vice President shall continue to discharge the same as Acting President; otherwise, the President shall resume the powers and duties of his office.

# Sources

## General Works on the American Presidency

Bailey, Thomas A. *Presidential Greatness*. New York: Appleton-Century-Crofts, 1966.

Barber, James David. *The Presidential Character*. Englewood Cliffs, N.J.: Prentice-Hall, 1977.

Brownlow, Louis. *The President and the Presidency*. Chicago: University of Chicago, 1949.

Burns, James MacGregor. *Presidential Government*. Boston: Houghton Mifflin, 1965.

Califano, Joseph. *A Presidential Nation*. New York: Norton, 1975.

Corwin, Edward S. *The President: Office and Powers*. New York: New York University Press, 1957.

_____, and Koenig, Louis W. *The Presidency Today*. New York: New York University Press, 1956.

Cotter, Cornelius, and Smith, J. M. *Powers of the President During National Crises*. Washington, D.C.: Public Affairs Press, 1961.

Cronin, Thomas E. *The State of the Presidency*. Boston: Little, Brown, 1980.

DiClerico, Robert E. *The American President*. Englewood Cliffs, N.J.: Prentice-Hall, 1979.

Finer, Herman. *The Presidency: Crisis and Regeneration*. Chicago: University of Chicago Press, 1960.

Goldsmith, William M. *The Growth of Presidential Power: A Documented History*. New York: Chelsea House, 1974.

Greenstein, Fred, et al. *Evolution of the Modern Presidency: A Bibliographical Survey*. Washington, D.C.: American Enterprise Institute, 1977.

Hardin, Charles M. *Presidential Power and Accountability*. Chicago: University of Chicago Press, 1974.

Hargrove, Erwin C. *The Power of the Modern Presidency*. New York: Knopf, 1974.

_____.*Presidential Leadership: Personality and Political Style*. New York: Macmillan, 1966.

Herring, E. Pendleton. *Presidential Leadership*. New York: Holt, Rinehart & Winston, 1940.

Hoxie, R. Gordon. *The Presidency of the 1970's*. New York: Center for the Study of the Presidency, 1973.

Hughes, Emmet John. *The Living Presidency*. New York: Coward, McCann & Geoghegan, 1973.

Hyman, Sidney. *The American President*. New York: Harper & Row, 1954.

James, Dorothy. *The Contemporary Presidency*. New York: Pegasus, 1974.

Kallenbach, Joseph. *The American Chief Executive*. New York: Harper & Row, 1966.

Lammers, William W. *Presidential Politics: Patterns and Prospects*. New York: Harper & Row, 1976.

Laski, Harold J. *The American Presidency*. New York: Harper & Row, 1940.

Loss, Richard, ed. *Presidential Power and the Constitution, Essays by Edward S. Corwin*. Ithaca, N.Y.: Cornell, 1976.

McConnell, Grant. *The Modern Presidency*. New York: St. Martin's, 1967.

Mullen, William F. *Presidential Power and Politics*. New York: St. Martin's, 1976.

Neustadt, Richard E. *Presidential Power*. New York: Wiley, 1980.

Orban, Edmond. *La Présidence Moderne Aux États-Unis*. Montreal: University of Quebec Press, 1974.

Pious, Richard M. *The American Presidency*. New York: Basic Books, 1979.

Reedy, George. *The Presidency in Flux*. New York: Columbia, 1973.

_____.*The Twilight of the Presidency*. New York: World, 1970.

Rossiter, Clinton. *The American Presidency*. New York: Harcourt Brace Jovanovich, 1960.

Schlesinger, Arthur M., Jr. *The Imperial Presidency*. Boston: Houghton Mifflin, 1973.

Sorensen, Theodore C. *Watchman in the Night: Presidential Accountability and Watergate*. Cambridge, Mass.: M.I.T. Press, 1975.

Strum, Philippa. *Presidential Power and American Democracy*. Pacific Palisades, Cal.: Goodyear, 1979.

Sundquist, James L. *Politics and Policy: The Eisenhower, Kennedy, and Johnson Years.* Washington, D.C.: Brookings, 1968.

Taft, William H. *Our Chief Magistrate and His Powers.* New York: Columbia, 1916.

Tugwell, Rexford G. *The Enlargement of the Presidency.* Garden City, N.Y.: Doubleday, 1960.

U.S. National Archives, *Public Papers of the Presidents of the United States.* Washington, D.C.: Government Printing Office, 1957 and after.

Vinyard, Dale. *The Presidency.* New York: Scribner's, 1971.

Young, James S. *The Washington Community 1800–1820.* New York: Columbia, 1966.

## Specialized Works

Abraham, Henry. *Justices and Presidents: A Political History of Appointments to the Supreme Court.* New York: Oxford, 1974.

Anderson, Patrick. *The President's Men.* Garden City, N.Y.: Doubleday, 1968.

Barber, James David, ed. *Choosing the President.* Englewood Cliffs, N.J.: Prentice-Hall, 1974.

_____. *The Pulse of Politics.* New York: Norton, 1980.

_____. *Race for the Presidency: The Media and the Nominating Process.* Englewood Cliffs, N.J.: Prentice-Hall, 1978.

Berger, Raoul. *Executive Privilege: A Constitutional Myth.* Cambridge, Mass.: Harvard, 1974.

_____. *Impeachment: The Constitutional Problems.* Cambridge, Mass.: Harvard, 1973.

Binkley, Wilfred. *President and Congress.* New York: Knopf, 1974.

Bishop, George F., et al. *The Presidential Debates: Media, Electoral and Policy Perspectives.* New York: Harper & Row, 1978.

Black, Charles L., Jr. *Impeachment: A Handbook.* New Haven, Conn.: Yale, 1974.

Brams, Steven. *The Presidential Election Game.* New Haven, Conn.: Yale, 1978.

Brant, Irving. *Impeachment.* New York: Knopf, 1972.

Brown, Stuart Gerry. *The Presidency on Trial: Robert Kennedy's 1968 Campaign and Afterwards.* Honolulu: University of Hawaii, 1972.

Ceaser, James W. *Presidential Selection: Theory and Development.* Princeton, N.J.: Princeton University Press, 1979.

Chamberlain, Lawrence H. *The President, Congress, and Legislation.* New York: Columbia, 1946.

Commission on Organization of the Executive Branch of the Government (Hoover Commission). *Reports.* Washington, D.C.: Government Printing Office, 1949 and 1953.

Committee on Government Operations, Senate Subcommittee on National Policy Machinery. *Reports.* Washington, D.C.: Government Printing Office, 1959 and after.

Congressional Quarterly. *Presidential Elections Since 1789.* Washington, D.C.: Congressional Quarterly Press, 1975.

Cornwell, Elmer E., Jr. *Presidential Leadership of Public Opinion.* Bloomington, Ind.: Indiana University, 1965.

Cronin, Thomas E., and Greenberg, Sandford D. *The Presidential Advisory System.* New York: Harper & Row, 1969.

David, Paul, et al. *Presidential Nominating Politics.* Washington, D.C.: Brookings, 1954.

Davis, James. *Presidential Primaries.* New York: Crowell, 1967.

Destler, I. M. *Presidents, Bureaucrats, and Foreign Policy.* Princeton, N.J.: Princeton University Press, 1972.

Dunn, Delmer D. *Financing Presidential Campaigns.* Washington, D.C.: Brookings, 1972.

Edwards, George C. *Presidential Influence in Congress.* San Francisco: Freeman, 1980.

Feerick, John D. *From Failing Hands: The Story of Presidential Succession.* New York: Fordham, 1965.

Fenno, Richard F. *The President's Cabinet.* Cambridge, Mass.: Harvard, 1959.

Fisher, Louis. *President and Congress.* New York: Free Press, 1972.

_____. *Presidential Spending Power.* Princeton, N.J.: Princeton University Press, 1975.

Flash, Edward S. *Economic Advice and Presidential Leadership.* New York: Columbia, 1965.

George, Alexander. *Presidential Decision-Making in Foreign Policy.* Boulder, Col.: Westview Press, 1979.

Grabner, Doris. *Public Opinion, The President and Foreign Policy.* New York: Holt, Rinehart & Winston, 1968.

Graff, Henry. *The Tuesday Cabinet*. Englewood Cliffs, N.J.: Prentice-Hall, 1970.

Grossman, Michael B., and Kumar, Martha J. *Portraying the President: White House Press Operations and the News Media*. Baltimore: Johns Hopkins, 1980.

Henry, Laurin L. *Presidential Transitions*. Washington, D.C.: Brookings, 1960.

Hess, Stephen. *Organizing the Presidency*. Washington, D.C.: Brookings, 1976.

_____. *The Presidential Campaign: The Leadership Selection Process After Watergate*. Washington, D.C.: Brookings, 1978.

Hobbs, Edward H. *Behind the President: A Study of Executive Office Agencies*. Washington, D.C.: Public Affairs Press, 1954.

Holtzman, Abraham. *Legislative Liaison: Executive Leadership in Congress*. Chicago: Rand McNally, 1970.

Hoxie, R. Gordon. *Command Decision and the Presidency*. New York: Reader's Digest Press, 1977.

_____, ed. *The White House: Organization and Operations*. New York: Center for the Study of the Presidency, 1971.

Humbert, W. H. *The Pardoning Power of the President*. Washington, D.C.: Public Affairs Press, 1941.

Jackson, Henry M., ed. *The National Security Council*. New York: Praeger, 1965.

Javits, Jacob. *Who Makes War?* New York: Morrow, 1973.

Johnson, Richard. *Managing the White House*. New York: Harper & Row, 1974.

Keech, William, and Matthews, Donald. *The Party's Choice*. Washington, D.C.: Brookings, 1976.

Kessel, John. *The Domestic Presidency*. N. Scituate, Mass.: Duxbury Press, 1975.

_____. *Presidential Campaign Strategies and Citizen Response*. Homewood, Ill.: Dorsey, 1980.

Kirkpatrick, Jeane. *The New Presidential Elite*. New York: Russell Sage Foundation, 1976.

Koenig, Louis W. *The Invisible Presidency*. New York: Holt, Rinehart & Winston, 1960.

Labovitz, John R. *Presidential Impeachment*. New Haven, Conn.: Yale, 1978.

Longaker, Richard. *The Presidency and Individual Liberties*. Ithaca, N.Y.: Cornell, 1961.

Longley, Lawrence D., and Braun, Alan G. *The Politics of Electoral College Reform*. New Haven, Conn.: Yale, 1972.

McClure, Wallace M. *International Executive Agreements*. New York: Columbia, 1941.

McConnell, Grant. *Steel and the Presidency*. New York: Norton, 1963.

McGinniss, Joe. *The Selling of the President 1968*. New York: Trident Press, 1969.

Mansfield, Harvey C., Sr., ed. *Congress Against the President*. New York: Harper & Row, 1975.

Matthews, Donald R., ed. *Perspectives on Presidential Selection*. Washington, D.C.: Brookings, 1973.

Minow, Newton, et al. *Presidential Television*. New York: Basic Books, 1973.

Moos, Malcolm. *Politics, Presidents, and Coattails*. Baltimore: Johns Hopkins, 1950.

Morgan, Ruth. *The President and Civil Rights*. New York: St. Martin's, 1970.

Mueller, John. *War, Presidents, and Public Opinion*. New York: Wiley, 1973.

Nash, Bradley D. *Staffing the Presidency*. Washington, D.C.: Public Affairs Press, 1952.

Nathan, Richard. *The Plot That Failed: Nixon's Administrative Presidency*. New York: Wiley, 1975.

Novak, Michael. *Choosing Our King*. New York: Macmillan, 1974.

Page, Benjamin I. *Choices and Echoes in Presidential Elections*. Chicago: University of Chicago Press, 1978.

Parris, Judith H. *The Convention Problem*. Washington, D.C.: Brookings, 1972.

Pollard, J. E. *The Presidents and the Press*. Washington, D.C.: Public Affairs Press, 1964.

Polsby, Nelson W. *Congress and the Presidency*. Englewood Cliffs, N.J.: Prentice-Hall, 1971.

_____, and Wildavsky, Aaron. *Presidential Elections*. New York: Scribner's, 1980.

Pomper, Gerald. *Nominating the President*. Evanston, Ill.: Northwestern University Press, 1963.

_____. *The Election of 1976*. New York: McKay, 1977.

President's Committee on Administrative Management (Brownlow Committee). *Report with Special Studies*. Washington, D.C.: Government Printing Office, 1937.

Ranney, Austin. *Participation in American Presidential Nominations, 1976*. Washington, D.C.: American Enterprise Institute, 1976.

Rose, Richard. *Managing Presidential Objectives*. New York: Free Press, 1976.

Roseboom, Eugene H. *A History of Presidential Elections*. New York: Macmillan, 1964.

Rossiter, Clinton, with Longaker, Richard P. *The Supreme Court and the Commander-in-Chief.* Ithaca, N.Y.: Cornell, 1976.

Sayre, Wallace S., and Parris, Judith H. *Voting for President: The Electoral College and the American Political System.* Washington, D.C.: Brookings, 1970.

Schlesinger, Arthur M., Jr., and de Grazia, Alfred. *Congress and the Presidency.* Washington, D.C.: American Enterprise Institute, 1967.

_____, and Israel, Fred, eds. *History of American Presidential Elections 1789–1968.* New York: Chelsea House, 1971.

Schubert, Glendon. *The Presidency in the Courts.* Minneapolis: University of Minnesota Press, 1957.

Scigliano, Robert. *The Supreme Court and the Presidency.* New York: Free Press, 1971.

Sickels, Robert J. *Presidential Transactions.* Englewood Cliffs, N.J.: Prentice-Hall, 1974.

Silverman, Corinne. *The President's Economic Advisers.* University, Ala.: University of Alabama Press, 1959.

Sullivan, Dennis, et al. *Explorations in Convention Decision Making.* San Francisco: Freeman, 1974.

Thomas, Norman C., and Baade, Hans W., eds. *The Institutionalized Presidency.* Dobbs Ferry, N.Y.: Oceana, 1972.

Tolchin, Martin, and Tolchin, Susan. *To the Victor: Political Patronage from the Clubhouse to the White House.* New York: Random House, 1971.

Tugwell, Rexford G. *How They Became President.* New York: Simon & Schuster, 1965.

Warren, Sidney. *The President as World Leader.* New York: Lippincott, 1964.

Watson, Richard. *The Presidential Contest.* New York: Wiley, 1979.

Wayne, Stephen J. *The Legislative Presidency.* New York: Harper & Row, 1978.

_____. *The Road to the White House.* New York: St. Martin's, 1980.

White, Theodore. *The Making of the President, 1960.* New York: Atheneum, 1961. See further volumes for 1964, 1968, and 1972.

Williams, Irving G. *The Rise of the Vice-Presidency.* Washington, D.C.: Public Affairs Press, 1956.

Wilmerding, Lucius, Jr. *The Electoral College.* New Brunswick, N.J.: Rutgers, 1958.

Witcover, Jules. *Marathon: The Pursuit of the Presidency, 1972–1976.* New York: Viking, 1977.

Young, Donald. *American Roulette: The History and Dilemma of the Vice Presidency.* New York: Holt, Rinehart & Winston, 1965.

## Biographies, Papers, Memoirs, and Studies of Presidents

### Pre-twentieth Century Presidents

Adams, Charles Francis, ed. *Memoirs of John Quincy Adams.* Philadelphia: Lippincott, 1875.

Bemis, Samuel Flagg. *John Quincy Adams and the Union.* New York: Knopf, 1956.

Barnard, Harry. *Rutherford B. Hayes and His America.* Indianapolis: Bobbs-Merrill, 1954.

Brant, Irving. *Madison the President.* Indianapolis: Bobbs-Merrill, 1970.

Cresson, William P. *James Monroe.* Chapel Hill, N.C.: University of North Carolina, 1946.

Curtis, James C. *The Fox at Bay: Martin Van Buren and the Presidency, 1837–1841.* Lexington, Ky.: University of Kentucky Press, 1970.

Dangerfield, George. *The Era of Good Feelings.* New York: Knopf, 1962.

Davison, Kenneth E. *The Presidency of Rutherford B. Hayes.* Westport, Conn.: Greenwood, 1972.

Flexner, James Thomas. *George Washington and the New Nation* (1783–1793), and *George Washington: Anguish and Farewell* (1793–1799), Vols. III and IV. Boston: Little, Brown, 1969–1972.

Freeman, Douglas Southall. *George Washington: A Biography,* 7 Vols. New York: Scribner's, 1948–1957. Vol. VI is *Patriot and President* (1954).

Hesseltine, William B. *Ulysses S. Grant, Politician.* New York: Ungar, 1935.

Howe, George Frederick. *Chester A. Arthur: A Quarter-Century of Machine Politics.* New York: Ungar, 1957.

James, Marquis. *Andrew Jackson: Portrait of a President.* Indianapolis: Bobbs-Merrill, 1937.

Johnstone, Robert M., Jr. *Jefferson and the Presidency.* Ithaca, N.Y.: Cornell, 1978.

Ketcham, Ralph. *James Madison: A Biography.* New York: Macmillan, 1971.

Klein, Philip Shriver. *President James Buchanan, A Biography*. University Park, Pa.: Pennsylvania State University, 1962.

Leech, Margaret. *In the Days of McKinley*. New York: Harper & Row, 1959.

McKitrick, Eric L. *Andrew Johnson and Reconstruction*. Chicago: University of Chicago Press, 1960.

Malone, Dumas. *Jefferson and His Time*, 5 Vols. Boston: Little, Brown, 1948–1974. Volume V is *Jefferson the President, 1805–1809* (1974).

Merrill, Horace S. *Bourbon Leader: Grover Cleveland and the Democratic Party*. Boston: Little, Brown, 1957.

Morgan, H. Wayne. *William McKinley and His America*. Syracuse, N.Y.: Syracuse University Press, 1963.

Nevins, Allan. *Grover Cleveland, A Study in Courage*. New York: Dodd, Mead, 1932.

————. *Hamilton Fish: The Inner History of the Grant Administration*. New York: Dodd, Mead, 1936.

Nichols, Roy F. *The Disruption of American Democracy*. New York: Macmillan, 1948.

————. *Franklin Pierce, Young Hickory of the Granite Hills*. Philadelphia: University of Pennsylvania Press, 1958.

Peterson, Merrill D. *Thomas Jefferson and the New Nation*. New York: Oxford, 1970.

Quaife, Milo M., ed. *The Diary of James K. Polk*. Chicago: A. C. McClurg, 1910.

Randall, James G. *Constitutional Problems under Lincoln*. New York: Appleton-Century-Crofts, 1926.

————. *Lincoln the President*, 2 Vols. New York: Dodd, Mead, 1945 and 1955.

Rayback, Robert J. *Millard Fillmore: Biography of a President*. Aurora, N.Y.: Stewart, 1962.

Reeves, Thomas C. *Gentleman Boss: Chester Allen Arthur*. New York: Knopf, 1975.

Remini, Robert V. *Martin Van Buren and the Making of the Democratic Party*. New York: Columbia University Press, 1959.

Schlesinger, Arthur M., Jr. *The Age of Jackson*. Boston: Little, Brown, 1945.

Seager, Robert. *And Tyler Too*. New York: McGraw-Hill, 1963.

Sellers, Charles Grier. *James K. Polk, Jacksonian, 1795–1843* and *James K. Polk, Continentalist, 1843–1846*. Princeton, N.J.: Princeton University Press, 1957–1966.

Sievers, Harry J. *Benjamin Harrison, Hoosier President, 1888–1901*. Indianapolis: Bobbs-Merrill, 1968.

Smith, Page. *John Adams*. Garden City, N.Y.: Doubleday, 1962.

## Twentieth Century Presidents

Adams, Sherman. *First-Hand Report: The Story of the Eisenhower Administration*. New York: Harper & Row, 1961.

Anderson, Donald F. *William Howard Taft: A Conservative's Conception of the Presidency*. Ithaca, N.Y.: Cornell, 1973.

Bailey, Thomas A. *Woodrow Wilson and the Great Betrayal*. New York: Macmillan, 1945.

————. *Woodrow Wilson and the Lost Peace*. New York: Macmillan, 1944.

Blum, John Morton. *The Republican Roosevelt*. Cambridge, Mass.: Harvard, 1954.

————. *Woodrow Wilson and the Politics of Morality*. Boston: Little, Brown, 1956.

Burner, David. *Herbert Hoover: A Public Life*. New York: Knopf, 1978.

Burns, James MacGregor. *Roosevelt: The Lion and the Fox*. New York: Harcourt Brace Jovanovich, 1956; and *Roosevelt: The Soldier of Freedom*. New York: Harcourt Brace Jovanovich, 1970.

Donovan, Robert J. *Conflict and Crisis: The Presidency of Harry S Truman, 1945–1948*. New York: Norton, 1977.

————. *Eisenhower: The Inside Story*. New York: Harper & Row, 1956.

Downes, Randolph C. *The Rise of Warren Gamaliel Harding, 1865–1920*. Columbus, Ohio: Ohio State University, 1970.

Eisenhower, Dwight D. *The White House Years, 1953–1961*, 2 Vols. Garden City, N.Y.: Doubleday, 1963–1965.

Fairlie, Henry. *The Kennedy Promise*. Garden City, N.Y.: Doubleday, 1973.

Ford, Gerald R. *A Time to Heal: The Autobiography of Gerald R. Ford*. New York: Harper & Row, 1979.

Freidel, Frank. *Franklin D. Roosevelt*, 4 Vols. Boston: Little, Brown, 1952–1973.

Gatewood, Willard B., Jr. *Theodore Roosevelt and the Art of Controversy*. Baton Rouge, La.: University of Louisiana, 1970.

George, Alexander, and George, Juliette L. *Woodrow Wilson and Colonel House: A Personality Study*. New York: John Day, 1956.

Glad, Betty. *Jimmy Carter: In Search of the Great White House*. New York: Norton, 1980.

Goldman, Eric. *The Tragedy of Lyndon Johnson*. New York: Knopf, 1969.

Gosnell, Harold. *Harry Truman: A Political Biography*. Westport, Conn.: Greenwood, 1980.

Haldeman, H. R. *The Ends of Power*. New York: New York Times Books, 1978.

Harbaugh, William Henry. *The Life and Times of Theodore Roosevelt*. New York: Farrar, Straus & Giroux, 1963.

Hoover, Herbert. *The Memoirs of Herbert Hoover*. New York: Macmillan, 1951–1952.

Hughes, Emmet John. *The Ordeal of Power*. New York: Atheneum, 1963.

Johnson, Lady Bird. *A White House Diary*. New York: Holt, Rinehart & Winston, 1970.

Johnson, Lyndon B. *The Vantage Point: Perspectives of the Presidency 1963–1969*. New York: Holt, Rinehart & Winston, 1971.

Kearns, Doris. *Lyndon Johnson and the American Dream*. New York: Harper & Row, 1976.

Latham, Earl. *J. F. Kennedy and Presidential Power*. Lexington, Mass.: D. C. Heath, 1972.

Leuchtenburg, William E. *Franklin D. Roosevelt and the New Deal, 1932–1940*. New York: Harper & Row, 1963.

Link, Arthur S. *Woodrow Wilson*, 5 Vols. Princeton, N.J.: Princeton University Press, 1947–1955.

Lyon, Peter. *Eisenhower: Portrait of a Hero*. Boston: Little, Brown, 1974.

McCoy, Donald R. *Calvin Coolidge: The Quiet President*. New York: Macmillan, 1967.

Mazlish, Bruce. *In Search of Nixon: A Psychohistorical Inquiry*. New York: Basic Books, 1973.

Miller, Merle. *Lyndon: An Oral Biography*. New York: Putnam, 1980.

Mowery, George F. *The Era of Theodore Roosevelt, 1900–1912*. New York: Harper & Row, 1958.

Murray, Robert. *The Harding Era: Warren G. Harding and His Administration*. Minneapolis: University of Minnesota, 1969.

Nixon, Richard M. *RN: The Memoirs of Richard Nixon*. New York: Grosset & Dunlap, 1978.

O'Brien, Lawrence. *No Final Victories: From John F. Kennedy to Watergate*. Garden City, N.Y.: Doubleday, 1974.

Parmet, Herbert S. *Eisenhower and the American Crusades*. New York: Macmillan, 1972.

Phillips, Cabell. *The Truman Presidency*. New York: Macmillan, 1966.

Romasco, Albert U. *The Poverty of Abundance: Hoover, the Nation, the Depression*. New York: Oxford, 1965.

Rudoni, Dorothy. *Harry S Truman: A Study in Presidential Perspective*. Ann Arbor, Mich.: University of Michigan, 1969.

Safire, William. *Before the Fall: An Inside View of the Pre-Watergate White House*. Garden City, N.Y.: Doubleday, 1974.

Schlesinger, Arthur M., Jr. *The Age of Roosevelt*, 3 Vols. Boston: Houghton Mifflin, 1957–1960.

————. *A Thousand Days: John F. Kennedy in the White House*. Boston: Houghton Mifflin, 1965.

Sorensen, Theodore C. *Kennedy*. New York: Harper & Row, 1965.

Truman, Harry S. *Memoirs*, 2 Vols. Garden City, N.Y.: Doubleday, 1955 and 1956.

Tugwell, Rexford G. *The Democratic Roosevelt*. Garden City, N.Y.: Doubleday, 1957.

Warren, Harris G. *Herbert Hoover and the Great Depression*. New York: Oxford, 1959.

# Chief Executives of Other Countries

## General

Rose, Richard, and Suleiman, Ezra N., eds. *Presidents and Prime Ministers*. Washington, D.C.: American Enterprise Institute, 1980.

## Great Britain

Alexander, Andrew, and Watkins, Alan. *The Making of the Prime Minister 1970*. London: Macdonald, 1970.

Beer, Samuel H. *British Politics in the Collectivist Age.* New York: Knopf, 1965.
Carter, Byrum E. *The Office of Prime Minister.* Princeton, N.J.: Princeton, 1956.
Eden, Anthony (Earl of Avon). *Memoirs,* 2 Vols. Boston: Houghton Mifflin, 1960 and 1965.
Jennings, Sir Ivor. *The Queen's Government.* London: Pelican, 1967.
King, Anthony, ed. *The British Prime Minister.* London: Macmillan, 1969.
Mackintosh, John P. *The British Cabinet,* 2nd ed. London: Methuen, 1968.
_____. *The Government and Politics of Britain,* 3rd ed. London: Hutchinson, 1974.
Macmillan, Harold. *Memoirs,* 4 Vols. New York: Harper & Row, 1966–71.
Walker, Patrick Gordon. *The Cabinet.* London: Fontana, 1972.
Wilson, Harold. *A Personal Record: The Labour Government, 1964–1970.* London: Weidenfeld and Nicolson, 1971.

## France

Anderson, Malcolm. *Government in France: An Introduction to the Executive Power.* London: Pergamon, 1970.
Aron, Robert. *An Explanation of de Gaulle.* New York: Harper & Row, 1966.
Colliard, Jean Claude. *Les Républicains Indépendants: Valérie Giscard d'Estaing.* Paris: Gallimard, 1971.
Grégoire, Roger. *The French Civil Service.* Brussels: International Institute Administrative Services, 1965.
Mauriac, François. *De Gaulle.* Garden City, N.Y.: Doubleday, 1966.
Suleiman, Ezra N. *Politics, Power, and Bureaucracy in France.* Princeton, N.J.: Princeton, 1974.
Viansson-Ponte. *The King and His Court (Les Gaullistes).* Boston: Houghton Mifflin, 1965.

## The Soviet Union

Crankshaw, Edward. *Khrushchev Remembers.* Boston: Little, Brown, 1970.
Deutscher, Isaac. *Stalin: A Political Biography.* New York: Oxford, 1967.
Djilas, Milovan. *The New Class.* New York: Harcourt Brace Jovanovich, 1957.
Juviler, Peter H., and Morton, Henry W. *Soviet Policy Making.* New York: Praeger, 1967.
Rush, Myron. *Political Succession in the USSR.* New York: Columbia, 1968.
Schapiro, Leonard. *The Communist Party of the Soviet Union.* New York: Random House, 1971.
Strong, John W., ed. *The Soviet Union under Brezhnev and Kosygin.* New York: Van Nostrand, 1971.
Tatu, Michel. *Power in the Kremlin, from Khrushchev to Kosygin.* New York: Viking, 1969.

## *The American Governor and Mayor*

Banfield, Edward C., and Wilson, James Q. *City Politics.* Cambridge, Mass.: Harvard, 1963.
Greer, Scott. *Governing the Metropolis.* New York: Wiley, 1962.
Jacob, Herbert, and Vines, Kenneth N., eds. *Politics in the American States.* Boston: Little, Brown, 1976.
Jewell, Malcolm E. *The State Legislature.* New York: Random House, 1962.
Kammerer, Gladys, et al. *The Urban Political Community.* Boston: Houghton Mifflin, 1963.
Key, V. O., Jr. *American State Politics.* New York: Knopf, 1956.
Lockard, Duane. *The Politics of State and Local Government.* New York: Macmillan, 1969.
Ransone, Coleman B., Jr. *The Office of Governor in the United States.* University, Ala.: Alabama, 1956.
Sayre, Wallace S., and Kaufman, Herbert. *Governing New York City.* New York: Russell Sage Foundation, 1960.

# Index

A 1
B 2
C 3
D 4
E 5
F 6
G 7
H 8
I 9
J 0